FRENCH AIR SERVICE WAR CHRONOLOGY
1914-1918

FRENCH AIR SERVICE WAR CHRONOLOGY 1914-1918

DAY-TO-DAY CLAIMS AND LOSSES BY FRENCH FIGHTER, BOMBER AND TWO-SEAT PILOTS ON THE WESTERN FRONT

Frank W. Bailey and Christophe Cony

GRUB STREET · LONDON

Published by Grub Street
10 Chivalry Road, London SW11 1HT

British Library Cataloguing in Publication Data
Bailey, Frank W.
  The French air service war chronology, 1914-1918:
  day-to-day claims and losses by French fighter, bomber and
  two-seat pilots on the Western Front
  1. France. Armee de l'air – History 2. World War, 1914-1918 –
  Casualties – France 3. World War, 1914-1918 – Aerial
  operations, French
  I. Title II. Cony, Christophe
  940.4'6744

ISBN 1 902304 34 9

Typeset by Pearl Graphics, Hemel Hempstead

Printed and bound in Great Britain by
Biddles Ltd, Guildford and King's Lynn

CONTENTS

Introduction

The information in this book was extracted from the daily reports (Compte-Rendus) of the various armées, groupes d'armées and the Résumés des Opérations Aériennes of the General Headquarters, plus extracts from citations shown in the Journal Officiel for the Légion d'Honneur, Médaille Militaire and citations promulgated de l'Ordre de l'Armée.

The Résumés des Opérations Aériennes starting in 1917 gave a monthly list of confirmed victories, and GQG published Casualty Lists throughout the war. The records of aerial activities (Compte-Rendus) from the following listed organizations were consulted in compiling the information presented in this book.

G.A.N. Groupe d'Armées du Nord
G.A.C. Groupe d'Armées du Centre
G.A.E. Groupe d'Armées de l'Est
G.A.R. Groupe d'Armées de Réserve
G.A.F. Groupe d'Armées des Flandres
Ière Armée, II° Armée, III° Armée, IV° Armée, V° Armée, VI° Armée, VII° Armée, VIII° Armée, IX° Armée and X° Armée.

These casualty listings cannot be considered definitive because of many missing dates concerning casualties; also in one record one date may be given and another record might show another. Therefore, we used the date that was given in the escadrille personnel listings as we believe them to be more accurate. Also in many cases citations mentioned that an airman was wounded or killed, but did not give the date, nor did the individual appear in the regular casualty lists. Also in many cases in French reports it will be stated that an enemy aircraft crashed in the French lines and the occupants were killed, but the German casualty listings do not mention any losses for that date or place making it very difficult to determine the facts. Note that also these victories and casualties are from operations on the Western Front only.

The reader will probably find some differences in material presented in this book than shown in previous books regarding probable victims. This is due to new material being made available.

Where multiple-seater crews are mentioned in victories or casualties the pilot is always listed first. Also, given names are used only in the casualty listings, and not in the victory listings. In a few cases the initial of the given name is used in the victory list where there are two or more pilots with the same last name, i.e., Victor (V) Regnier and Emile (E) Regnier. Note too that early records were not kept as accurately as those later, once the administration had got going.

For reasons of limited space certain aircraft designations are indicated as Albatros D3 for Albatros DIII, Fokker D 7 for Fokker DVII, etc.

Acknowledgments: We wish to thank the Service Historique de l'Armée de l'Air (S.H.A.A.) and the Service Historique de l'Armée de Terre (S.H.A.T.) for providing us with material over many years, as well as the Association pour la Recherche de Documentation sur l'Histoire de l'Aéronautique Navale, (A.R.D.H.A.N.), and in alphabetical order, Daniel Brunet, A.E. Clausen, Jr., Dr. James Davilla, Richard Duiven, Paul Joly (+), Peter Kilduff, Bernard Klaeylé, Philippe Lagnier, Russell Manning (+), Lucien Morareau, Mike O'Neal, Iver Penttinen (+), O.A. Sater (+) Jean-Claude Soumille, Alan Tolle, who provided many of the aircraft serial numbers, and George H. Williams. A special thanks to Mr Norman Franks for his guidance and encouragement which greatly enhanced this project. (+ deceased)

French Equivalent Military Ranks

American Army		*French Army*	
Colonel	Col	Colonel	Col
Lieutenant-Colonel	Lt/Col	Lieutenant-Colonel	Lt/Col
Major	Maj	Chef de Bataillon (Infantry)	Cdt
		Chef d'Escadron (Art/Cav)	Cdt
Captain	Capt	Capitaine	Capt
1st Lieutenant	1/Lt	Lieutenant	Lt
2nd Lieutenant	2/Lt	Sous-lieutenant	S/Lt
Officer Candidate		Aspirant	Asp
Chief Warrant Officer	CWO	Adjudant-Chef	Adj-Chef
Warrant Officer	WO	Adjudant	Adj
Sergeant-Major	SgtMaj	Maréchal-des-Logis-Chef (Art/Cav)	MdL-Chef
First Sergeant	1/Sgt	Sergent-Major	SgtMaj
Quartermaster-Sergeant	Sgt	Maréchal-des-Logis-Fourrier	MdL
Sergeant	Sgt	Maréchal-des-Logis (Art-Cav)	MdL
Sergeant	Sgt	Sergent	Sgt
Quartermaster-Sergeant	Sgt	Sergent-Fourrier	Sgt
Corporal	Cpl	Brigadier (Cavalry/Artillery)	Brig
Corporal	Cpl	Caporal	Cpl
Quartermaster-Corporal	Cpl	Caporal-Fourrier	Cpl
Private 1st Class	PFC	Soldat de 1ère Classe	Sol
Private	Pvt	Soldat de 2ème Classe	Sol

American Naval Ranks		*French Naval Ranks*	
Captain	Capt	Capitaine de Vaisseau	CV
Commander	Cdr	Capitaine de Frégate	CF
Lieutenant Commander	Lcdr	Capitaine de Corvette	CC
Lieutenant	Lt	Lieutenant de Vaisseau	LV
Lieutenant Junior Grade	Ltjg	Enseigne de Vaisseau de 1ère Classe	EV1
Ensign	Ens	Enseigne de Vaisseau de 2ème Classe	EV2
Plebe		Aspirant de Marine	Asp
Chief Warrant Officer	CWO	Maître Principal	MP
Warrant Officer	WO	Premier Maître	PM
Chief Petty Officer	CPO	Maître	M
1st Class Petty Officer	PO1	Second Maître	SM
2nd Class Petty Officer	PO2	Second-Maître	SM
3rd Class Petty Officer	PO3	Quartier-Maître	QM
Seaman 1st Class	S1c	Matelot	Mat
Seaman 2nd Class	S2c	Matelot	Mat

Notations and Abbreviations

X	Destroyed/détruit
XF	Down in Flames/Abattu en Feu
FTL	Forced to Land (German Lines)/Contraint à 'atterrissage (lignes allemands) or survived a crash inside French Lines
POW	Prisoner of War
P	Probable over German lines)/Au-dessus de lignes allemands
2	Two-seater

KIA	Killed in Action/Tué au combat
MIA	Missing in Action/Disparu en mission
WIA	Wounded in Action/Blessé au combat
KIAcc	Killed in an Accident/Tué sur accident
Injured	Injured in an Accident/Blessé sur accident
DOW	Died of wounds-injuries/Mourir

P	Pilot/Pilote
O	Observer/Observateur

B	Bombardier/Bombardier
Ph	Photographer/Photographe
M	Mechanic/Mécanicien
G	Gunner/Mitrailleur
CAM	Naval Aviation Center/Centre Aviation Maritime
CIACB	Centre d'Instruction d'Avions de Combat et de Bombardement
CRP	Paris Defense Group/Camp Retranche de Paris
CRP	Centre de Rassemblement des Pilotes
DAN	Detachement d'Armée de Nord
DCA	Defense against aircraft/Defense Contra Avions (Anti-aircraft fire)
DMA	Direction du Matériel Aéronautique
EM	État-Major (Staff)
GDE	Groupe de Divisions d'Entraînement
LTA	Air Ship – Lighter than Air
RGé	Réserve Générale de l'Aviation
STAé	Service Technique Aéronautique

French and German Abbreviations

Bl	Blériot
BM	Bréguet-Michelin
BR	Bréguet
C	Caudron
CAM	Centre d'Aviation Maritime (Dunkerque, etc)
CEP	Caproni
Cie d'Aérostiers	Balloon Company
D	Aircraft type, Deperdussin
F	Farman
FAbt	Fliegerabteilung
FEA	Flieger Ersatz Abteilung
FFA	Feld-Flieges Abteilung
GB	Groupe de Bombardement
HF	Henri Farman
Let	Letord
LTA	Lighter Than Air
MF	Maurice Farman
MS	Morane-Saulnier
N	Nieuport
PS	Paul Schmitt
REP	Aircraft type: Robert-Esnault-Pelterie
Sal	Salinson
SM	Salmson-Moineau
Sop	Sopwith
Spa	Spad
V	Voisin
VB	Aircraft type Voisin, Escadrille designation VB

Victories
Only confirmed victories were credited; unconfirmed being noted as probables and not included in a pilot, or observer's score. Shared victories gave all participants a credit. In these lists a running score of confirmed kills are given on the far right.

Escadrilles
Whilst a designation normally indicated equipment, eg, Sop = Sopwith, F = Farman, etc, other types were used. Where other types are known which are different from the apparent designation, they'll be noted in the remarks column.

American Expeditionary Force
In the spring of 1918, the arrival of the US AEF, which flew under the control of the French, meant that their combats and casualties were listed with their French compatriots, and are therefore shown in the lists.

French Combat Log 1914

---

2 – 3 August – No Claims – No Casualties

---

4 August – No Claims
Casualties:

???	MF 2 85			III° Armée

---

5 August – No Claims
Casualties: None

---

6 August – No Claims
Casualties:

Capt Tiersonnier	Bl 3	P	WIA	Flak

---

7 – 12 August – No Claims – No Casualties

---

13 August – No Claims
Casualties:

Sgt André Bridou &	Br 17	P	KIAcc
Sol Vinel	Br 17	B	KIAcc

---

14 August

Infantry fire	D4	2 seater	POW	Norroy-Vaudières	0700	–

Casualties: None

---

15 August

Infantry fire	a. ???	Taube 2	POW	Florenville	1800	–
Infantry fire	b. ???	Albatros B	POW	Pagny-sur-Moselle	0500	–

a.   Both officers WIAs.
b.   Probably Ltn Ehrhardt & Ltn von Liessin, FlAbt 6, POWs N of Pagny.
Casualties:

Soldat Victor Garaix &	???	P	KIA	Paul Schmitt
Lt Albert de Taizleux	???	O	KIA	

NOTE: Garaix was a well known aviator who had set several altitude records before the war.

---

16 – 17 August – No Claims – No Casualties

---

18 August

Infantry fire	???	Taube	FTL	Hastières	a.m.	–
Infantry fire	???	Aviatik B	X	Stenay		–

Casualties: None

---

19 August

Infantry fire	a. ???	2 seater	X	Dinant	–

a.   Pilot, Ltn Herbert Giesche, KIA, observer POW, FFA 1.
Casualties: None

---

20 – 21 August – No Claims – No Casualties

---

22 August

Ground fire	a. ???	Zeppelin	X	Celle-Badonviller
Ground fire	b. ???	2 seater	X	Sedan

a.   Zeppelin N° 8, was severely hit by ground fire but made it back across the lines into Germany. However, four officers must have jumped and were taken prisoner.
b.   FFA 22, Ltn Erich Janson KIA & Obltn von Stietenkron WIA/POW, but escaped a short time later.
Casualties: None

---

23 August – No Claims –No Casualties

---

24 August – No claims

Casualties:

??? Dupuy-de-Lôme	LTA		KIA	Killed by French DCA at Reims, who thought his dirigible was a German Zeppelin.

25 August – No Claims

Infantry fire	a. ???	2 seater	XF	Quesnoy	–

a.   Crew KIAs.
Casualties: None

26 August

Infantry fire	a. ???	2 seater	X	Cambrai	–

a.   Pilot WIA/POW, observer POW.
Casualties:

MdL Octave Benoit	HF 19	P	KIA	

27 August – No Claims
Casualties:

Lt Louis Mendès	???	P	KIA	Fighting on ground on his airfield which was attacked by advancing German troops.
Adj Gaston Guidon &	Bl 18		WIA	
Cpl Durand	Bl 18		WIA	
Lt Dalaplane &	MS 26	P	KIAcc	
Lt Barbier	MS 26	O	KIAcc	Villacoublay

28 – 31 August – No Claims – No Casualties
No Known date, an Albatros B was captured and sent to Lyon on 29 August, and a Taube captured and sent to Tours on 2 September.

1 September

???	???	2 seater	X	Sommepy	–

Casualties:

Lt Gaston Grandry	MS 23	P	KIA	II° Armée
Sgt Georges Cohen &		P	KIA	
Lt Ragot		O	KIA	Meaux
Sgt Plaisson &		P	KIA	
Sol Vallier		G	KIA	III° Armée
Capt Delavaux		O	KIA	Verdun
Sol Garaix &		P	MIA	
Sol de Saizieux		O	MIA	
Lt Adrien Gautier &		P	WIA	
Sgt Finck		O	WIA	
Sol Bagnol &		P	KIAcc	
Sol Langeron		G	KIAcc	
MdL Bartoud		P	KIAcc	
Lt de Neuville		O	KIAcc	

2 September

Infantry fire & Sgt Védrines a. 0750	CRP –	Taube	X	Suippe	

a.   First French victory claim of WWI, but it was not confirmed. Védrines was flying his monoplane Blériot "la Vache". EA was able to regain its own lines before crashing.
Casualties: None

3 September

Infantry fire	a. ???	EA	X	Ostende	–

a.   Crew of two officers POWs.
Casualties: None

4 September – No Claims
Casualties:

Lt Nicolas Faurite	Bl C2	P	MIA	V° Armée
Lt Charles Mendes	HF 1	P	KIAcc	V° Armée
Lt Jean Devainne &	D 6	P	KIAcc	
Lt Jacques Baneat	D 6	O	KIAcc	V° Armée

5 September

Infantry fire	a. ???	Taube	POW	Ft de Chelles	0500	–

a.   One officer killed during combat on the ground.

Casualties:

Lt Roger Trétare	Blc 3	P	KIAcc	Epinal, Ière Armée	

6 September – No Claims

Casualties:

Sol Cribeillet &	D 4	P	MIA	
Sol Cossnier	D 4	G	MIA	V° Armée

7 – 8 September – No Claims – No Casualties

9 September

Infantry fire	a. ???	2 seater	XF	Châlons	–

a.   Pilot, Ltn Hänichen, KIA, observer WIA/POW.

Casualties: None

10 – 11 September – No Claims – No Casualties

12 September

Dragon Regiment	a. ???	2 seater	X	Montigny	–
???	b. ???	2 seater	X	Piney	–

a.   Crew KIAs.

b.   Crew, Hptm & Obltn, KIAs.

Casualties: None

13 – 17 September – No Claims – No Casualties

18 September – No Claims

Casualties:

Capt Chopier &	P	KIAcc	
Sol Clout	G	KIAcc	V° Armée

19 – 22 September – No Claims – No Casualties

23 September – No Claims

Casualties:

Sgt Vidal	O	Killed	II° Armée
Bernard Howard, RFC &	P	MIA	
Sol Freville	G	MIA	VI° Armée
S/Lt Louis Noël &	P	KIAcc	
MdL Emery	G	KIAcc	Ière Corps

24 – 30 September – No Claims – No Casualties

Date Unknown:

An Aviatik B captured and sent to Meudon, on 1 October.
Aviatik B 219 captured and sent to Lyon on 15 September.

Casualties:

Sgt Lucien Finck	WIA

1 – 4 October – No Claims – No Casualties

5 October

Sgt Frantz &	V 24					1
Sol Quénault	a. V 24	Aviatik B	X	Jonchery-sur-Vesle	1005	1

a.   Sgt Wilhelm Schlichting & Obltn Fritz von Zangen, FlAbt 18, KIAs, aircraft N? B 114/14. This was the first air to air victory recorded during the war.

Casualties: None

6 October

???	DCA	Taube	X	Romilly-sur-Seine	1500	–

7 October

Sgt Gaubert		MF				1
Capt Blaise	a.	MF	2 seater	X	Metz-Verdun	1

a.   Uffz Willi Finger, WIA/DOW 8 December & observer WIA.

Casualties: None

---

8 October – No Claims – No Casualties

---

9 October

Verdun		DCA	Taube	POW	Verdun	–
Verdun	a.	DCA	Taube	X	Verdun	–
Artillery		???	Taube	X	Fuyes	–

a.   Both officer occupants were KIAs, one was probably Uffz Willi Finger, KIA at Ste Menehould.

Casualties: None

---

10 – 11 October – No Claims – No Casualties

---

12 October

Five aircraft	a.	???	2 seater	X	Saint Omer	–

a.   Crew, pilot KIA, observer WIA/POW. Possibly Gefr Johann Okenfels, KIA & Lftsch Adolf Bünte, WIA, at Pannes.

Casualties:

Lt Maurice Schlumberger	MS 31	P	WIA

---

13 October

Infantry fire	???	2 seater	X	Ressaincourt	–

Casualties:

Lt Maurice Happe &	MS 26	P	FTL Biervliet, Holland.
Lt de Cartier (Belgian Army)		O	Interned both escaped and returned to France on 20 October.

---

14 October – No Claims

Casualties:

Lt Marcel Baudot	P	Killed
Sol Lefalive	G	Killed

---

15 – 16 October – No Claims – No Casualties

---

17 October

Dunkerque	a.	DCA	2 seater	POW	Furnes-Nieuport	–

a.   One occupant KIA and one POW.

Casualties: None

---

18 October

???	DCA	Taube	X	Mailly	–

Casualties: None

---

19 October – No Claims – No Casualties

---

20 – 21 October – No Claims – No Casualties

---

22 October – No Claims

Casualties:

S/Lt Reymond &	Bl 9	O	KIA	Had motor trouble and forced to land
Adj Alfred Clamadieu	Bl 9	P	KIA	between the lines, killed by infantry fire.

NOTE: Reymond was a Senator and the head of the Comité National pour l'Aviation Militaire.

---

23 October – No Claims – No Casualties

---

24 October

Cpl Emile Stribick &	HF 28				1
Sol David	HF 28	Taube	XF	E Amiens	1

Casualties: None

25 October

Infantry fire	???	Taube	X	Gravelines	–
Infantry fire	???	Taube	X	Méharicourt	–
Infantry fire	???	Aviatik	X	Méharicourt	–
French pilot	???	2 seater	X	Epernay	–

Casualties: None

26 October – No Claims – No Casualties

27 October – No Claims
Casualties:

MdL Fremont &		P	MIA
Lt Belisson		P	MIA

28 & 29 October – No Claims – No Casualties

30 October – No Claims
Casualties:

Sgt Geoffroy		?	Killed

31 October – No Claims – No Casualties

October, date unknown:

Adj Mezergues &					1
???	V 21	Balloon	XF		1

1 November

Navigation error	a. ???	2 seater	POW	Arques	–

a.   Crew killed during an escape attempt.
Casualties: None

2 November

Sgt Gilbert &	MS 23				1
Capt de Vergnette	MS 23	Taube	X	German Lines	1
Four aircraft	???	Taube	P	Blankenberghe	–

Casualties: None

3 November

Lt Vogoyeau &	MF 8				1
Lt Juvigny	MF 8	Aviatik	X	Souain	1
???	DCA	EA	X	Souain	–
???	DCA	EA	X	Souain	–

Casualties: None

4 November

Infantry	a.	Taube	X	Saint Charles	–

a.   Occupants KIAs.
Casualties: None

5 November

???	a. ???	Taube	X	Reims	–

a.   Crashed in the German Front lines, two occupants KIAs.
Casualties:

Adj Rondeau &	V 21	P	KIA	Flak
Sol Vernier	V 21	G	KIA	Flak, IV° Armée
Lt Victor Radisson	MS 26	P	WIA	Poperinghe, DOW 6 November.
Capt Rémy &	RGAé	P	KIAcc	
Capt Faure	RGAé	O	KIAcc	

6 November

Infantry fire	???	EA	X	Arras	–

Casualties: None

7 – 8 November – No Claims – No Casualties

9 November

Infantry fire	a. ???	2 seater	X	Sapignal	–

a.   Crew KIAs.
Casualties: None

---

10 – 17 November – No Claims – No Casualties

---

18 November

Sgt Gilbert &	MS 23				2
Sol Bayle	a. MS 23	LVG	POW	Reims	1
???	DCA	2 EA	X	Armentières	–

a.   LVG B 451/14, two officers POWs, aircraft sent to St. Cyr on 21 November. Fuel tank hit during combat, losing petrol and disoriented, landed in French territory.
Casualties: None

---

19 November

Navigation error	a. ???	Aviatik	POW	Reims	–

a.   Crew two officers.
Casualties: None

---

20 November – No Claims – No Casualties

---

21 November

French DCA &					
RFC aircraft	a.	Aviatik	X	Soissons	1000 –

a.   Two officers and one mechanic KIAs.
Casualties: None

---

22 November

Soissons &	DCA				
RFC pilot	a. ???	Taube	X	Soissons	–
S/Lt Mahieu &	b. V 24				1
Maître Ouvrier Mauduit	V 24	EA	X		1
„	V 24	EA	FTL		–
„	V 24	EA	FTL		–
???	MS ??	2 seater	POW	Clairmarais Forest	–

a.   Crew of three all KIAs.
b.   Gefr Theodor Salwiczek, KIA, observer.
Casualties:

???	35° Cie Aérostiers XF		By a shell burst, no casualties.

---

23 – 26 November – No Claims – No Casualties

---

27 November

???	a. DCA	3 seater	X	S Ypres	–

a.   Crew, one KIA, two POWs.
Casualties: None

---

28 – 29 November – No Claims – No Casualties

---

30 November – No Claims
Casualties:

Lt Paul Heysch	???	P	Killed

---

1 December – No Claims – No Casualties

---

2 December – No Claims
Casualties:

Sol Marc Pourpe &	MS 23	P	KIAcc
Lt Vauglin	MS 23	O	KIAcc	Verdun, Bad weather

---

3 – 4 December – No Claims – No Casualties

5 December

???	a. DCA	Bomber	X	Chaumont-sous-Oise	0830	–

a.   Crew KIAs.
Casualties: None

6 December – No Claims
Casualties:

Lt Germain	???	P	KIAcc

7 – 10 December – No Claims – No Casualties

11 December – No Claims
Casualties:

S/Lt Jean Peretti	MS 31	P	WIA	Flak

12 – 14 December – No Claims – No Casualties

15 December – No Claims
Casualties:

Sgt Pierre Aubry	RGAé	P	KIAcc
Sol Granel	???		Killed
Sol Montmain	???		Killed

16 December – No Claims – No Casualties

17 December

Sgt Gilbert &	MS 23					3
Sol Bayle	a. MS 23	EA	X	Albert-Bapaume		2

a.   Possibly Ltn Hans von Bojanowski, (O), FlAbt 32, WIA Cambrai, DOW 1 Jan 1915. Aircraft said to be a prototype LVG E VI, with first synchronized machine-gun.
Casualties: None

18 December

???	???	EA	FTL		–

Casualties: None

19 December – No Claims – No Casualties

20 December

Sgt Gamaury, &	???				1
???	DCA	Taube	XF	Pontoise	–
MdL de Neufville &	VB 2				–
Cdt de Goys	GB 1	Aviatik	FTL		–
Lt Mouchard &	VB 1				–
Cpl Maillard	VB 1	Aviatik	FTL		–
???	a. ???	Balloon	P		

a.   Destroyed with fléchettes (darts) and bombs.
Casualties:

Adj Joseph Vuarin &	VB 3	P	OK
Sol Michard	VB 3	M	WIA
Matelot Piegniez	VB 102	O	WIA Ground fire.

21 December

???	???		EA	FTL	–

Casualties: None

22 December

???	???	EA	FTL	–
???	a. ???	Balloon	X	–

a.   By fléchettes and bombs.
Casualties: None

23 – 26 December – No Claims – No Casualties

27 December

???   a.   ???   Balloon   P   –

a.   By bombs.

Casualties: None

28 – 31 December – No Claims – No Casualties

French Combat Log 1915

---

1 – 3 January – No Claims – No Casualties

---

4 January

| ??? | DCA | 2 seater | POW | Vatinsénil | – |

Casualties: None

---

5 – 9 January – No Claims – No Casualties

---

10 January

Sgt Gilbert &		MS 23	Albatros BI			4
Lt de Puechredon	a.	MS 23	N° 26/14	POW	Villers-Bocage/Raineville	1
Sgt Pégoud &		2° Gp d'Av				–
Sol Le Rendu		2° Gp d'Av	Balloon	P		–

a.   Probably Ltn Franz Keller, WIA/POW & Hptm Otto Karl Ferdinand Vogel von Falkenstein, KIA, FlAbt 23, near Amiens.

Casualties: None

---

11 – 13 January – No Claims – No Casualties

---

14 January – No Claims

Casualties:

| Sgt Jean Montmain | MS 26 | P | KIAcc | Roossbrude |

---

15 January – No Claims – No Casualties

---

16 January – No Claims – No Casualties

---

17 January – No Claims – No Casualties

---

18 January

Adj Pégoud		2° Gp d'Av EA		FTL		
Navigation error	a.	???	2 seater	POW	Bihonne	–
Navigation error	b.	???	Taube	POW	St Mard-le-Mont	1600 –

a.   Probably OfStv Paul Müller & Hptm Wolfgang Schmidt, FlAbt 25, POWs.
b.   Fw Niensteldt & Obltn Wenkler, POWs.

Casualties: None

---

19 January – No Claims – No Casualties

---

20 January

Capt Happe &		MF 29				–
Sgt Leleu	a.	MF 29	Balloon	P	Remingen	–
Mechanical trouble	b.		Taube	POW		–
Mechanical trouble	b.		Aviatik	POW		–

a.   Attacked with fléchettes & bombs.
b.   Sent to Chaville-Vélizy on 20 January.

Casualties: None

---

21 January – No Claims – No Casualties

---

22 January

| French & RFC combined | ??? | Bomber | X | Bry-sur-Somme | – |

Casualties: None

---

23 – 25 January – No Claims – No Casualties

---

26 January

| Nieuport | DCA | EA | X | Nieuport-Ypres | – |

Casualties:

| ??? | ??? | | P | Interned |

27 January – No Claims
Casualties:

Sgt Le Lohe	???		WIA

28 January

??? &	VB 2				–
Lt de La Morlais	VB 2	Aviatik	FTL		–

Casualties: None

29 January

Navigation error	a. ???	Albatros	POW	E Gerbeviller	–
???	DCA	Aviatik	POW	Zuydcote	–

a. One officer and one NCO POWs.

Casualties: None

30 January

Navigation error	???	EA	POW		–
Navigation error	???	EA	POW		–

Casualties: None

31 January – No Claims – No Casualties

Late January or early February:

Sgt Gamaury &	???				2
???	???	EA	X	Somme-Suippes	–

1 February – No Claims – No Casualties

2 February

???	???	EA	FTL	Mulhouse	–

Casualties: None

3 February – No Claims
Casualties:

Capt André d'Humières &	MF 35	P	Interned. Forced to land in Holland
Capt Armand Coutisson	MF 35	O	because of motor trouble flying
			Voison LB (IV Ca.2), both escaped 29 March 1916.

4 February

Lt de Beauchamp,	MS 23				1
Lt Moision &	MS 23				1
???	a. DCA	Aviatik C	POW	Beaumont	–

a. Ltn Ferdinand von Hidessen WIA/POW & Lt Fritz Müller, WIA/DOW 7 February 1915. Briest Abt "O".

Casualties: None

5 February

Adj Pégoud &	2° Gp d'Av					1
Sol Lerendu	MF 37	Taube	X	S Grand Pré	1000	1
Adj Pégoud &	2° Gp d'Av					2
Sol Lerendu	MF 37	Aviatik C	X	NE Montfaucon	to	2
Adj Pégoud &	2° Gp d'Av					3
Sol Lerendu	MF 37	Aviatik C	X	E Montfaucon	1145	3
Artillery	???	Balloon	X	NE Sommepy		–

Casualties: None

6 & 7 February – No Claims – No Casualties

8 February

???	DCA	EA	XF	German lines	–

Casualties:

S/Lt Armand Pinsard &	MS 23	P	POW	Pinsard escaped in March 1916 and
S/Lt Amaudrio de	MS 23	O	POW	returned to active duty.
Chaffaud				II? Armée

9 February						
???	DCA	EA	X	Dunkerque	1100	–
Casualties: None						

10 February – No Claims – No Casualties

11 February					
???	???	Balloon	X	Cagny	–
???	DCA	EA	X	Verdun	–
Casualties: None					

12 – 25 February – No Claims – No Casualties
16 February: The French attack in the Eastern part of the Champagne, in the area East of Reims, near Souain, commenced.

26 February					
???	a. DCA	2 seater	POW	Noeux	–
a. Two officer POWs.					
Casualties:					
S/Lt Maurice Gabriel &	MF 19	P	Killed		
S/Lt Belloudeau	MF 19	O	Killed		

27 February					
???	DCA	2 seater	POW	Bacarrat	–
Casualties: None					

28 February – No Claims					
Casualties:					
Lt René Mouchard &	CO VB 1	P	KIA		
Sgt Emile Maillard	VB 1	O	KIA	Near Lépine	

1 March – No Claims – No Casualties

2 March					
???	REP ??	Aviatik	XF	Lanevin	–
Casualties:					
Cpl Louis Mouthier &	MS 23	P	POW	Engine failure, Péronne	
Lt de Teuchet	MS 23	O	POW	II? Armée	

3 March – No Claims – No Casualties

4 March					
Verdun Sector	a. DCA	Aviatik	POW	Verdun	–
a. Probably Ltn Theldeck & Uffz ???, FEA Metz, POWs.					
Casualties: None					

5 March – No Claims				
Casualties:				
Sgt René Naud de Fontermann	MF 33	P	KIAcc	
Lt Ernest Coutisson &	MF 35	P	Interned in Holland.	
Lt André d'Humières	MF 35	O	Interned, both escaped 29 Mar 1916.	

6 – 16 March – No Claims – No Casualties

17 March – No Claims			
Casualties:			
Sgt Lumière	VB 106	P	Killed

18 – 19 March – No Claims – No Casualties

18 March – The French attack east of Reims was terminated.

20 March

Nancy	DCA	Taube	X	German lines		–
Casualties:						
???				Caudron G.3 N° 216, III° Armée.		

21 March

Sgt Salze &	MF 14					1
S/Lt Moreau	MF 14	Aviatik C	X	Turckheim		1
??? a.	???	Balloon	P	Champagne		–
a. By fléchettes, 500 dropped.						
Casualties:						
Cpl Ulysse Guinard &	???	P		Injured Landing accident.		
MdL-Chef Jean Luciani	???	O		Injured		

22 March

Altkirch	VB ???	EA	X	Helfranzkirch	1830	–
Altkirch	VB ???	EA	X	Helfranzkirch		–
Altkirch	VB ???	EA	X	Helfranzkirch		–
Casualties:						
Sgt Augustin Flandrin &	VB 107	P	POW			
MdL Bursignier	VB 107	O	POW			

23 March

Nancy	DCA	Taube	X	Malzéville	0815	–
Casualties: None						

24 March – No Claims – No Casualties

25 March – No Claims

Casualties:				
Lt Feugère	???	O	Injured	

26 March – No Claims

Casualties:				
Capt Chaulin	GB 3	O	WIA	

27 March

Sgt Jensen &	MS 31					–
MdL Morel	MS 31	EA	FTL	Bois de Hingry		–
??? a.	DCA	2 seater	POW	Vého-Manonviller		–
a. OfStv Fritze & Ltn von Saft, POWs.						
Casualties: None						

28 – 30 March – No Claims – No Casualties

31 March

Sgt Bonette &	C 47			
???	C 47	2 EA	FTL	
Casualties:				
Sgt de Bernis	MS 48	P	KIAcc	
S/Lt de La Barre	MS 48	O	KIAcc	

1 April

S/Lt Garros	MS 26	Albatros B	POW	Westkapelle		1
Sgt Navarre & a.	MS 12					1
Lt Robert b.	MS 12	Aviatik	POW	Merrval	0625	1
a. Gefr August Spacholz & Ltn Walter Grosskopt, FlAbt 40, KIAs Oudecappelle.						
b. Ltn Engelhorn & Obltn Wittenberg.						
Casualties:						
Capt René Marlin &	MF 7	P	KIAcc			
Lt Joseph Mingal	MF 7	O	KIAcc			

2 April

Adj Pelletier Doisy &	MS 12					1
Lt Chambe a.	MS 12	Albatros C	POW	Vaudemange	0600	1

Adj Pégoud &	2° Gp d'Av				4
???	???	Taube	POW	Somme-Bionne	–

a.   Possibly Uffz Otto von Keussler & Obltn Brobuggle, POWs.
Casualties: None

---

3 April – No Claims – No Casualties

---

4 April – No Claims
Casualties:

Sol Jean Burel &	HF 13	P	MIA		
Cpl Brebis	HF 13	O	MIA	III° Armée	

---

5 April – No Claims
Casualties:

Sol Tixier &	GB 3	P	Injured
Cpl Nicolas	GB 3	O	Injured

---

6 April – No Claims
Casualties:

Sol Pierre Hennion	C 42	P	Injured
Sgt Georges Madon &	MF 30	P	Interned
Cpl Chatelain	MF 30	O	Interned

---

7 April – No Claims – No Casualties

---

8 April

S/Lt Garros	MS 26	EA	P		–

Casualties: None

---

9 April – No Claims – No Casualties

---

10 April – No Claims
Casualties

LV Dutertre	CAM	?	Injured	Dunkerque

---

11 April – No Claims – No Casualties

---

12 April

Infantry fire,	???				–
Sgt Navarre &	MS 12				–
Sol Gérard	MS 12	Aviatik	P		–

Casualties: None

---

13 April

Sgt Navarre &	MS 12				2
Sol Gérard	MS 12	Aviatik	POW	Ste Menehould	1
???	???	2 seater	POW	Lunéville	–
???	a. ???	LVG B	POW	Viel-Arcy	–

a.   LVG B 521/15.
Casualties:

Lt Villiet	GB 1	O	WIA

---

14 April – No Claims – No Casualties

---

15 April

S/Lt Garros	a. MS 26	Aviatik	X	Ypres-Armentières	2
MdL Chatain &	MS 48				1
Lt Achard	MS 48	Albatros C	X		1
???	DCA	EA	X	N Ypres	–

a.   Probably Btsmt Ernst Reuber, KIA. FA11.
Casualties:

Sgt François de Marmier	VB 105	P	WIA	Flak

---

16 April

Adj Poggi &	VB 103				–
MdL Chastaing	VB 103	Aviatik	FTL	Chérisy	–

Adj Dubius &	VB 1				–
Sol Couratin	VB 1	Aviatik	FTL	Nomeny-Delme	–
???	VB	Aviatik	FTL	Metz	–

Casualties: None

---

17 April – No Claims
Casualties:

QM Sauzay &	* CAM	P	POW	Voisin III L, shot down by	
EV Nozal	* CAM	O	POW	flak near Zeebrugge.	

* Dunkerque.

---

18 April

S/Lt Garros	MS 26	Albatros	X	Cortemarck	1000	3
Adj Hecfeuille &	VB 103					–
MdL Besson	VB 103	Aviatik	FTL	Metz		–

Casualties:

S/Lt Roland Garros	MS 26	P	POW	Inglemunster, Belgium, escaped 18 February 1918.
Cpl Feucher &	V 24	P	KIAcc	
Lt Gramier	V 24	O	KIAcc	

---

19 April – No Claims
Casualties:

Lt Jean Amoudruz	MF 35	O	WIA	Flak	
LV Fournié &	* CAM	P	Injured	Voisin III L, at St Pol.	
QM Robert	* CAM	O	Injured		

---

20 April

Adj Bunau-Varilla &	VB 103		
Sol Bouvier	VB 103	EA	FTL

Casualties:

Lt Gaston Fournier	GB 2	P	WIA

---

21 April – No Claims
Casualties:

Cpl Robert Simoni	C 46	P	KIAcc

---

22 April – No Claims
Casualties:

Sol Lanier	C 43	P	Injured

23-25 April – No Claims – No Casualties
24 April – Battle of the Woëvre ended.

---

26 April – No Claims
Casualties:

EV1 Renot	* CAM	?	WIA	Voisin III L, over Ostende.

* Dunkerque.

---

27 April – No Claims – No Casualties

---

28 April

Adj Pégoud &		MS 48				5
Sol Lerendu		MS 48	Aviatik	X	Guebwiller-Thann	4
Sgt Ortoli &		MF 8				1
S/Lt Menj	a.	MF 8	Rumpler C	X	Miraumont-Beaumont	1
Sgt Mesguich &		MS 12				1
S/Lt Ferru	b.	MS 12	Albatros	X		1
Lt Mahieu &		MF 63				2
Lt Dunoyer		MF 63	2 seater	X	NE Hisinger	1
Sgt Navarre		MS 12	Aviatik	P	St Thierry-Brémont	–
Lt de Bernis &	CO	MS 12				1
S/Lt Jacottet		MS 12	Albatros BI	POW	Muiazon	c.

a. Aircraft was on the ground and completely destroyed by French artillery.
b. Ltn von Lederur, FlAbt 13, POW, French V° Armée Prisoner Interrogation Report states he was shot down by MS 12.
c. Albatros BI N° 133/15, POWs.

Casualties:

Sgt Caron &	VB 109	P	KIA		
Sol Crouzier	VB 109	G	KIA		
Cdt Joseph Avon &	GB 2	P	MIA		
Sol Furgeront	GB 2	G	MIA		
Sol Marie Magneval	V 24	P	WIA		

29 April – No Claims – No Casualties

30 April – No Claims
Casualties:

Adj Jaquenan &		P	OK	
Sol Paul Vasseur		O	WIA	
Sgt Beulanger	MF 35	O	WIA	
Capt Jean Dessirier &	MF 2	P	KIAcc	
Sol Jules Grégoire	MF 2	G	KIAcc	

Date unknown in April:

MdL Salmet &	???			–
S/Lt Hertz	???	EA	FTL	–

1 May – No Claims – No Casualties

2 May

Sgt Frantz &	V 24				2
Mat Fralin	V 24	Aviatik	X		1

Casualties:

Cpl Gustave Mosnier &	MS 48	P	POW	Forced to land because of motor
S/Lt Léopold Louis	MS 48	O	POW	trouble.
Sol Victor Gariax	F 13	P	MIA	III° Armée
Lt Albert Barthelemy de Sa...	F 13	P	MIA	III° Armée
Capt Georges Delaveau	EM	O	KIA	III° Armée

3 & 4 May – No Claims – No Casualties

5 May – No Claims
Casualties:

Sgt Naud	MF 33	P	KIAcc	MF N° 384, III° Armée.

6 – 9 May – No Claims – No Casualties
9 May – The French Battle of Souchez commenced in the area of Vimy Ridge.

10 May

Sgt René David &	MF 2				1
???	MF 2	Aviatik C	XF	Meuse-Argonne	1

Casualties: None

11 May – No Claims
Casualties:

Capt Guy des Hautschamps & CO	MS 31	P	KIAcc	Nieuport X
Capt Edmond Mathieu	MS 31	O	Injured	

12 May – No Claims – No Casualties

13 May – No Claims
Casualties:

Lt Lucas	???	O	KIA	

14 May – No Claims
Casualties:

Adj Georges Bordeux &	GB 3	P	POW	
Sol Bussac	GB 3	G	POW	
Sol Debergues	GB 3	P	Injured	

15 May – No Claims – No Casualties

16 May

Artillery	???	Balloon	X	E Vimy	–
Casualties:					
Sgt Lucien Jailler	MS 15	P	WIA		

17 – 19 May – No Claims – No Casualties

20 May

Sgt Frantz &	V 24				2
Matelot Fralin	V 24	Aviatik	X		1
???	DCA	EA	X		–
Casualties:					
Cpl Paul Thoreau &	MF 54	P	KIA		
Lt Blancpain	MF 54	O	KIA	X° Armée	

21 May – No Claims – No Casualties

22 May – No Claims

Casualties:				
Lt Jean d'Hautefort	C 34	P	Injured	

23 – 24 May – No Claims – No Casualties

25 May – No Claims

Casualties:				
Capt Albert Moris	MF 8	P	MIA	X° Armée
S/Lt Robert Damberville &	MS 15	P	KIAcc	
Sol Edmond Perret	MS 15	G	Injured	

26 May

Sgt Mesguich &	MS 12				2
S/Lt Jacotte a.	MS12	Albatros B	X	Braisne	2

a.   Probably Ltn Gerhard Nette & Obltn von Bülow-Bussow, FlAbt 12, KIAs, at Braisne.

Casualties:				
Cpl Maxime de Verrier &	GB 3	P	MIA	
Sol Lattard	GB 3	G	MIA	
Capt Pierre Chevrier &	MS 31	P	Injured	
Sol Pierre Roger	MS 31	G	WIA/DOW	
Lt Jacques Martin	MF 41	P	WIA-Flak	
Sgt René Mesguich	MS 12	P	WIA	

27 May – No Claims

Casualties:				
Adj Etienne Bunau-Varilla &	GB 1	P	POW	Engine failure, E of Neustadt.
Cdt Louis de Goys de				
Mezeyrac CO	GB 1	O	POW	
Capt Jules Aubry CO	C 43	P	KIAcc	

28 May – No Claims – No Casualties

29 May

???	DCA	Aviatik	XF	Thiescourt	–
Casualties: None					

30 – 31 May – No Claims – No Casualties

May – Dates unknown

Sgt Gamaury	???	EA	X		3
Casualties:					
Sol Badre	GB 3	G	Injured		
Sgt Mennerat	MF 36	P	Injured		

1 June – No Claims – No Casualties

2 June – No Claims
Casualties:

Sol Timachoff &	RGAé	P	KIAcc		
Sol Zwiback	RGAé	G	KIAcc		
Sol Cherblanc	RGAé	G	Injured		

3 June – No Claims
Casualties:

Sgt Roger Jupin &	RGAé	P	Injured	
Sol Albert Arrault	RGAé	M	Injured	

4 June – No Claims
Casualties:

S/Lt Pierre Pardieu	MS 31	O	WIA	

5 June

Brig Lenoir &		C 18				1
Lt Rivier		C 18	Aviatik C	X	Sivry-la-Perche	1
Capt Quillien &	CO	MS 37				2
Lt d'Anchauld	a.	MS 37	Aviatik C	X	Béthelainvillers	1

a.　Probably Ltn Fritz Rössler, FlAbt 34, KIA.
Casualties: None

6 June – No Claims
Casualties:

Capt Delgorgue	V 24	P	KIAcc	

7 June

Sgt Gilbert	a.	MS 49	Aviatik	X	St Amarin	5

a.　First French pilot to obtain five victories.
Casualties:

Cpl Chapius &	GB 3	P	MIA	
Lt Codet	GB 3	O	MIA	
Sol Maurice Counort &	RGAé	P	Injured	
S/Lt de Jaeglière	RGAé	O	Injured	
PO Lallemant	C 28	P	Injured	

8 June – No Claims
Casualties:

Sol Fanton	GB 3	G	KIAcc	

9 – 10 June – No Claims – No Casualties

11 June

Sgt Gilbert	a.	N 49	Aviatik C	P		–

a.　Possibly Vfw Rudolf Weingärtner, WIA & Ltn Joachim Frhr von Maltzahn, FlAbt 48b, KIA, Mühlhausen.
Casualties: None

12 June

Sgt Chaput &	C 28				1
???	C 28	Fokker E	X	Esnes	?

Casualties: None

13 June – No Claims
Casualties:

Capt Roux	VB 106	P	WIA	

14 June – No Claims – No Casualties

Between 1 and 14 June:

Adj Hostein &	C 6				1
Cpl de La Motte Ango de Flers					
	C 6	2 seater	FTL		1

Casualties:

Capt Auguste Le Reverend &	P	WIA	
???	O	WIA	

Sgt Henri Thouroude (dit de Losques)	VB 110	B	WIA		

15 June

Brig Lenoir	C 18				2
Lt Rivier	C 18	Balloon	XF		2
Mechanical trouble a.		Taube	POW	Noroy-sur-Ourcq 1230	–

a. Two officers POWs.

Casualties:

Adj Jean Sismanoglou &	MF 44	P	KIA		
S/Lt Eugène Virolet	MF 44	O	KIA		
Adj Antonin Argogues &	GB 1	P	MIA		
Lt Georges Boques	GB 1	O	MIA	VB 101	
Adj Mullen &	GB 1	P	MIA	VB 101	
Sgt Deshuillier	GB 1	O	MIA		
Cpl R Zevaco	MF 13	P	WIA	Flak	
Sol Marsac	C 51	P	Injured		

16 June – No Claims

Casualties:

Lt Jacques Sabattier de Vignolle				
	MF 36	O	WIA	Flak

17 June

Sgt Gilbert	a. MS 49	Aviatik C	X	NE St Amarin Wood	6

a. Probably Vfw Hugo Grabnitz & Ltn Karl Schwartzkopf, FlAbt 48, KIAs N Thann.

Casualties: None

18 June

MdL Sayaret &	V 24				1
???	V 24	EA	X		1

Casualties:

Cpl Tisserenc	C 43	P	WIA	
Cpl Jean Loste	C 56	P	Injured	

19 June – No Claims

Casualties:

Sgt Emile Devienne &	MS 15	P	OK	
Sol Lucien Dinaux	MS 15	M	KIA	
Cpl René Garbet	C 13	P	KIA	III° Armée

20 June – No Claims

Casualties:

Capt Auguste Le Révérend		P	WIA	

21 June – No Claims – No Casualties

22 June – No Claims

Casualties:

Cpl Ferdinand Servies &	MF 32	P	MIA	Shot down by FA 8
Lt Hippolyte Gatel	MF 32	O	MIA	X° Armée
???	???			Caudron G.3 N° 300, III? Armée.

23 June – No Claims

Casualties:

Sgt Paulli Krause	CRP	P	Injured	

24 – 25 June – No Claims – No Casualties

26 June – No Claims

Casualties:

S/Lt Aurélien Richard &	MF 14	P	KIA	
Lt Marcel Chardin	MF 14	O	KIA	VII° Armée
S/Lt Jules Mahieu &	GB 3	P	WIA	
Sol Mauger	GB 3	G	WIA	

27 June – No Claims
Casualties:

Sgt Eugène Gilbert	MS 49	P		Forced to land in Switzerland and Interned, VII° Armée. Escaped June 1916; KIAcc 17 May 1918.	

---

28 June – No Claims – No Casualties

---

29 June

Capt Quillien	MS 37	EA	P	–

Casualties: None

---

30 June – No Claims – No Casualties
The Battle of Souchez ended.
Dates during June unknown.

Adj Hostein &	C 6			–
???	C 6	EA	FTL	–

Casualties:

Lt Georges de La Rochefordière	MS 38	O	KIA
Capt Auguste Le Reverend		P	WIA
Sgt Thouroude (dit de Losques)	VB 110	B	WIA

On unknown dates during May and June 1915, Sgt Pulpe and his observer were credited with two enemy aircraft destroyed near Verdun.

---

1 July – No Claims
Casualties:

Capt Paul du Peuty &	MS 48	P	WIA	Probably by Ltn Kurt Wintgens,
Lt Louis de Boutiny	MS 48	O	WIA	FlAbt 6.
Sgt Jean Bailleux &	C 34	P	KIAcc	
Sol Dupouy	C 34	G	KIAcc	

---

2 July – No Claims – No Casualties

---

3 July

Capt Brocard	CO a. MS 3	Albatros C	X	Dreslincourt	1725	1

a.   Probably from FlAbt 2.
Casualties: None

---

4 July – No Claims
Casualties:

Lt Maurice Tetu &	MS 15	P	MIA	Probably by Ltn Oswald Boelcke
Lt Georges de La Rochefoucauld	MS 15			of FAbt 62.
Sgt André Baras	V 21	P	WIA	
Lt Paul Tourtel	MS 3	O	Injured	

---

5 July – No Claims
Casualties:

Brig Ballaigue	GB 1	P	Injured

---

6 – 7 July – No Claims – No Casualties

---

8 July

Lt Robert de Beauchamp	N 37	Aviatik	FTL	Vouziers

Casualties:

Lt Albert Auger	C 11	P	WIA	Flak

---

9 July – No Claims
Casualties:

Sgt Jean Chaput	C 28	P	WIA

---

10 July – No Claims – No Casualties

11 July

Adj Pégoud	a. MS 49	Aviatik C	XF	Altkirch	0815	6

a.   Probably Uffz Walter Hoffmann, KIA & Ltn Heinrich Calberla, WIA FlAbt 48b, Mühlhausen.
Casualties: None

12 July – No Claims
Casualties:

S/Lt Paul Courrière	MS 49	P	KIAcc	Fontaine

13 July

Cannon Aircraft	???	Albatros	FTL	Libercourt	–

Casualties: None

14 – 18 July – No Claims – No Casualties

19 July

Cpl Guynemer &	MS 3					1
Sol Guerder	a. MS 3	Aviatik B	X	Septmont	1415	1

a.   Probably Ltn Werner Johannes & Uffz August Ströbel WIA/DOW 27 July 1915, FlAbt 26, near Reims.
Casualties:

Adj-Chef Gaston Verdié &	C 56	P	OK	
MdL Saint Genis	C 56	O	KIA	
S/Lt Gustave Poinsard &	MF 8	P	WIA	
Lt Pierre Hervet	MF 8	O	WIA	
Sgt Georges Magnier	MF 8	P	WIA	Flak
Cpl Casimir Bonnet-Labranche	VB 114	P	WIA	
Sol Charles Guerder	MS 3	M	WIA	

20 July

Sgt Desmoulins &	VB 102				–
Sgt Thevenard	VB 102	Aviatik	FTL	Conflans-en-Jarny	–

Casualties:

Sgt Fenech &	MF 29	P	OK	Departed 17h26 on MF XI N° 742,
Sol Péaulte	MF 29	B	KIA	combat with two Aviatik Cs after
				bombing of Münster railway station.
Sgt André Bobba	MS 23	P	WIA	Flak
Capt Philippe Féquant CO	VB 101	O	WIA	Flak
Sgt Emile Desmoulins &	VB 102	P	WIA	
Sgt Paul Thevenard	VB 102	O	WIA	

21 July – No Claims – No Casualties

22 July

Cpl Comès &	VB 101				1
Cpl Chevalier	VB 101	Aviatik	XF	Pont-à-Mousson	1
???	GB	Aviatik	FTL		–
???	GB	Aviatik	FTL		–

Casualties:

Adj Henri Moutach	MS 26	P	WIA	Flak

23 July – No Claims – No Casualties

24 July

Mechanical problems		2 seater	POW	Bétancourt	–

Casualties: None

25 – 29 July – No Claims – No Casualties

30 July

Adj Moutach &	MS 26				1
Sol Murat	MS 26	Seaplane	X	W Nieuport	1
??? &	MS 48				–
Lt du Plan	MS 48	EA	FTL		–

Casualties:

Sgt Maxime Cochet &	MF 29	P	POW	MF XI N? 746, FTL in German lines.
Sol Bizay	MF 29	G	POW	Flak
Mat François Le Gland	EP Avord	P	Injured	DOW 2 August 1915.

31 July

Lt Achard &	MS 48				−
Brig de Layens	MS 48	EA	FTL	Dombach	−
Adj Nungesser,	VB 106				1
Sol Pochon &	VB 106				1
Nancy	DCA	Albatros C	X	Nancy	−

Casualties:

MdL Mellinger &	VB 103	P	MIA	Voisin N° V475, FTL near
Cpl Jean Vialatoux	VB 103	B	MIA	Bublengen.
S/Lt Perrin	MF 8	P	Injured	
S/Lt Perbosc	C 9	O	WIA	

1 August – No Claims

Casualties:

Sgt Paul Féraud	19° Cie d'Aérostiers		XF	Destroyed by German
		O	WIA	artillery, S Ban de Sept.

2 August – No Claims

Casualties:

MdL F N L Simon	28° Cie d'Aérostiers			Balloon broke loose during
		O	KIA	a storm, drifted into German territory
				where obs was killed.

3 August – No Claims – No Casualties

4 August – No Claims

Casualties:

QM Amédée Navarre &	*	CAM	P	POW	Shot down in North Sea, 15 miles NE
QM Bourdais	*	CAM	O	POW	Dunkerque on FBA 100 HP, codé 3.
*	Dunkerque.				

5 August

S/Lt Burgun &	MF 50				−
???	MF 50	Aviatik	FTL		−

Casualties:

Sgt Paul Dechoz	C 43	G	WIA

6 – 8 August – No Claims – No Casualties

9 August – No Claims

Casualties:

MdL Louis Pasco &	VB 112	P	KIA	One of these three was
Sgt Philippe Toureille	VB 112	B	KIA	claimed by Ltn Kurt
Cpl Emile Charamelet &	GB 4	P	POW	Wintgens (4), FFA 48, and
Sol Renaudeau d'Arc	GB 4	B	POW	another by Ltn Pherdron &
S/Lt Edouard Lemoine &	VB 110	P	KIA	Ltn von Sprunner, unit not known.
Sgt Henri Thouroude				
(dit de Losques)	VB 110	O	WIA	
Sgt Paul Martin &	GB 4	P	Interned	Grances, Switzerland, at 10h50.
Cpl Charles Pary	GB 4	B	Interned	Combat (VB 111)

10 August – No Claims

Casualties:

Sol Uzeward	C 9	M	Injured

11 August – No Claims

Casualties:

MdL Emile Ortstein	MF 55	P	WIA	Flak

12 August – No Claims

Casualties:

Lt François Barberet &	MF 14	P		KIAcc
Sol Adolphe Julien	MF 14	G		KIAcc
Sgt François Drouhet &	C 17	P		OK
Lt Pierre Guillemin	C 17	O	WIA	DOW 18 August 1915

13 August – No Claims – No Casualties

14 August – No Claims
Casualties:

Lt Louis Dubuis	GB 3	P	Injured	
Sol Jaffro		M	Injured	

15 August – No Claims – No Casualties

16 August – No Claims
Casualties:

Sgt Georges Brun	MS 49	P	KIAcc

17 August

Cpl Fabert &	MF 8				–
Sgt Laurenceau	MF 8	2 seater	FTL		–
Casualties:					
Adj Marcel Nigoud	RGAé	P	KIAcc		

18 August – No Claims – No Casualties

19 August – No Claims
Casualties:

S/Lt Guy de Lubersac	· C 11	O	WIA	Flak

20 August

Cpl Fabert &	MF 8				–
Sgt de Ram	MF 8	EA	FTL		–
Casualties:					
Sol Eugène Laraud	C 47	P	Injured		

21 August – No Claims – No Casualties

22 August – No Claims
Casualties:

Cpl Paul Chevron	RGAé	P	KIAcc

23 August – No Claims
Casualties:

Sgt Louis Bonnetète &	C 42	P	OK
Lt André Félix	C 42	O	KIA
S/Lt Jean Cabanes &	MF 22	O	KIA
Cpl Pierre Meunier	MF 22	P	WIA

24 August – No Claims
Casualties:

Sgt Eugène Bertin	MS 38	P	WIA	Flak
Sgt Léon Pauly	MS 38	P	WIA	Flak

25 August – No Claims
Casualties:

MdL Gabriel Thomas &	GB 2	P	MIA	
Sol André Delille	GB 2	B	MIA	
Cpl René Courtet de l'Isle &	VB 111	P	MIA	
S/Lt François Jean	VB 111	O	MIA	
S/Lt Jean Chortard &	GB 2 P		Injured	In landing accident.
Lt André Fernet	GB 2		,,	,,

26 August

Lt de Dampierre &	V 21				–
S/Lt Hérischer	V 21	EA	FTL		–
Capt Vuillemin &	C 11				–
S/Lt de Lubersac	C 11	Albatros C	FTL	Vigneulles	–
Casualties: None					

27 August – No Claims – No Casualties

28 August

Capt Brocard	CO a. MS 3	EA	XF	N Senlis, VI° Armée	2
Mechanical problems	b.	Aviatik	POW	Breuil-le-Sec	–

a.   Probably Ltn Heinrich Diederich & Ltn Kurt Bailer, FlAbt 33, KIAs at Fleurines, about 10 km N of Senlis, aircraft C.311/15.
b.   Aircraft B.II 558/15.
Casualties: None

29 – 30 August – No Claims – No Casualties

31 August – No Claims
Casualties:

S/Lt Adolphe Pégoud	MS 49	P	KIA	II° Armée, probably by Uffz Kandulski
Lt Jean Michon	RGAé	P	KIAcc	& Obltn Pilitz, near Belfort.

August Date unknown:
Casualties:

Capt Rémy	CO V 29	P	KIAcc

1 September

Capt Verdon &	VB 113				1
QM Fralin	VB 113	EA	X		2
Adj Védrines	a. MS 3	LVG C.I	POW	Moreuil	–

a.   Although this aircraft, #280/15, was captured and tested it was never credited to Védrines.
Casualties:

Sgt Claude Couturier &	MF 2	P	KIA	MF N? 603. Combat
Lt Louis Moisan	MF 2	O	KIA	III° Armée

2 September – No Claims – No Casualties

3 September

S/Lt Feierstein	N 37	EA	FTL	–

Casualties: None

4 September – No Claims
Casualties:

Lt Jean Devienne &	C 6	P	KIA	
Lt Jacques Baneat	C 6	O	KIA	
Sgt Gustave Laffon &	MF 36	P	WIA	Flak
Lt Jacques Sabattier de Vignolle	MF 36	O	WIA	Flak

5 September – No Claims
Casualties:

Cpl Constantin Constantinou &	C 56	P	OK
Asp Ernest Jean	C 56	O	WIA

6 September

Infantry	a. ???	Albatros B	POW	Calais	–

a.   NCO pilot & officer observer POWs, aircraft N° 220/.
Casualties:

Capt Paul Bousquet &	VB 105	P	KIA	Shot down by FA 6 on Saarbrucken
Lt Prosper Jamaux	VB 105	O	KIA	raid.
Sgt Charles Niox &	VB 102	P	OK	
Capt Albert Féquant	VB 102	O	KIA	

7 September

Sgt Teulon &	MF 63				1
Cpl Demeuldre	MF 63	Scout	X	Bois de Forges	1
Sgt H. Mahieu &	MF 63				–
S/Lt Heintz	MF 63	EA	FTL		–

Casualties:

Capt Jean Sallier &	MF 8	P	KIA	By FA 53

Lt Le Gall	MF 8	O	KIA		

---

8 September – No Claims – No Casualties

---

9 September

Lt Bonneau &	N 48				–
S/Lt Grandelain	N 48	Fokker	FTL	Avricourt	–
Capt Vuillemin &	C 11				–
???	C 11	Albatros C	P	Vigneulles	–
Casualties:					
Lt Georges Perrin-Pelletier	MF 22	P	WIA		

---

10 September

Mechanical problems		Aviatik	POW	Hangest-en-Santerre	–
Casualties:					
Capt Walter Watt *	MF 44	P	WIA	Flak	
Capt René Turin CO	N 15	P	WIA		
* Australian.					

---

11 September – No Claims – No Casualties

---

12 September

Capt Vuillemin &	C 11				1
Lt Dumas	C 11	EA	X	Vigneulles	1
Capt Vuillemin &	C 11				–
Lt Dumas	C 11	EA	FTL	Vigneulles	–
Casualties:					
Lt Jean Lamasse	MF 25	P	KIA		
Lt Pierre Saulnier d'Anchauld	MF 37	O	KIA	III° Armée	
Lt Lamarque Peyrecave	C 51	P	WIA	Flak	
Cpl Peter-Usse	RGAé	P	KIAcc		

---

13 September – No Claims
Casualties:

Sgt Charles Niox &	VB 102	P	KIA	During raid on Trier.
Asp Gaston de la Guerande	VB 102	O	KIA	N Briey, MF N° 678, III° Armée.

---

14 September – No Claims
Casualties:

Sgt Longueteau &	MF 29	P	KIAcc	Belfort, accidental explosion of a
Cpl Doux	MF 29	?	Injured/DOW	bomb on the ground.

---

15 September

Sgt Brou &	MF 62				–
Capt Simeon	MF 62	Aviatik	FTL		–
Sgt Brou &	MF 62				–
Capt Simeon	MF 62	Aviatik	FTL		–
Casualties: None					

---

16 September – No Claims
Casualties:

Lt Jules Carré	???	O	KIAcc	

---

17 September – No Claims – No Casualties

---

18 September

Artillery	???	Balloon	X	E Chatillon	–
Sgt Robillot &	V 21	EA			–
S/Lt Zuber	V 21	EA	FTL		–
Casualties: None					

---

19 September

Adj Varcin &	MF 5				–
Lt Pierrey	MF 5	EA	FTL		–

Capt Vuillemin &	C 11					–
Lt Dumas a.	C 11	Albatros	FTL	St Mihiel		–

a.   Destroyed by French artillery.

Casualties:

Lt Jacques Halbronn	MF 19	O	WIA	Flak	

---

20 September

Sgt Mangeot	N 38	Balloon	XF			1

Casualties:

Lt Jacquemont	MF 20	O	KIA	Flak	

---

21 September – No Claims – No Casualties

---

22 September

Sgt Simon &	N 26				1400	–
S/Lt Maria	N 26	EA	FTL	N Furnes	1600	–
S/Lt Bourhis	N 31	2 seater	X			1
??? &	N 37					1
Adj Caffarel	N 37	EA	X			1

Casualties:

Sgt Michel Doré &	VB 114	P	MIA		
Sol Eugéne Volot	VB 114	G	DOW	By Fokker FA 53.	
Capt Louis Mathieu & CO	N 31	P	KIA	Nieuport X	
Capt Gabriel Petit-Jean	N 31	O	KIA	Shot down in flames.	
Lt René de Peyrecave de Lamarque					
	C 61	P	WIA		
Lt Simon de Maud'Huy	MF 36	P	KIAcc		

---

23 September – No Claims

Casualties:

Adj Noël Paolacci &	N 37	P	POW		
Sol Pierre	N 37	G	MIA	III° Armée	
Sgt Casimir Poznanski	N 37	P	MIA	III° Armée	
Sgt Georges Mangeot	N 38	P	POW		
Cpl James J Bach	N 38	P	POW		
Lt Albert Coué &	C 56	P	WIA	Fokker combat	
Lt Louis Escolle	C 56	O	OK		

---

24 September – No Claims

Casualties:

S/Lt Lucien Bordas &	GB 1	P	OK	Shot down & FTL E Pont-à-Mousson.	
Asp Renaud	GB 1	O	OK	Their aircraft destroyed by enemy Artillery.	

---

25 September – No Claims

The French reopened the attack in the area of Vimy Ridge, as well as commencing another attack in the Champagne in the area east of Reims.

Casualties:

Sgt Henri Pigot &	MF 29	P	KIA	Departed 05h40 on MF XI #742, FTL	
Sol Marcel Vermet	MF 29	B	KIA	near Triberg, by Uffz Böhn (3), FFA 9b?	
S/Lt Paul Mouilières &	MF 16	P	MIA		
MdL Paul Samarcelli	MF 16	O	MIA		
Lt Charles Devin &	MF 29	P	POW	Departed 05h40 on MF XI #750	
Sol Clément Vérité	MF 29	G	POW	FTL in German lines.	

---

26 September – No Claims

Casualties

Cpl Pierre Melon &	C 61	P	WIA		
Sol Maigniaux	C 61	G	WIA		
S/Lt Antoine Laplace	N 57	O	WIA	Flak	
EV1 Jean Bouye	MF 8	O	WIA		
Cpl François Guerner	C 47	P	WIA		
Adj Emmanuel Travers	C 27	O	WIA		
Lt Georges Perrin-Pelletier &	C 27	P	Injured		
Lt Henri Chabardes	C 27	O	Injured		

27 September – No Claims
Casualties:
???				MS N° 366, III° Armée.

28 September – No Claims
Casualties:
Cpl Henri Mayoussier &	MF 36	P	POW	Flak
Lt Milat	MF 36	O	POW	
S/Lt Paul Weiller	V 21	O	WIA	

29 September – No Claims
Casualties:
Lt Philippe Champetier de Ribes	C 46	O	WIA

30 September
Cpl Raux &	C 47				–
Lt Choupaut	C 47	EA	P		–
Lt Lecour Grandmaison &	C 47				
Lt Romazzoti	C 47	Aviatik C	FTL		–
??? &	N 15				–
Lt Montassin	N 15	2 seater	FTL		–
Casualties:					
Adj Paul Schneider &	N 15	P	OK		
S/Lt Gaston de Ronseray	N 15	O	KIA		
MdL Georges Maguet	VB 108	O	WIA	Flak	

September date unknown:
Casualties:
Sol Charles Quette	C 64	G	WIA

1 October
MdL Duflos &	*				1
QM Jean Le Port	*	EA	X		1

a.   Flying an aircraft armed with a cannon, 10° Section d'Avions Canons.
Casualties:
Lt Alexandre Radot &	CRP	P	POW	Flak S of Laon.
S/Lt Iglesis	CRP	O	POW	

2 October
Sgt Comés &	*				2
Mat Jousselin	*	Balloon	XF	Champagne	1

*   10° Section d'Avions Canons.
Casualties:
Lt Hubert de Geffrier	VB 107	O	WIA	
Lt Cohen	**		KIA	Rethel

**   In a dirigible, shot down by Flak rest of the crew was taken prisoner.

3 October – No Claims
Casualties:
Adj Jean Bourhis	N 31	P	WIA	Flak

4 October
Artillery	a. ???	Balloon	X	French lines	–

a.   Two officers taken prisoner.
Casualties: None

5 October – No Claims – No Casualties

6 October – No Claims
Casualties:
Adj Emile Boland &	MF5	P	KIAcc
S/Lt Bernard de Montbrond	MF5	O	KIAcc

7 October

Artillery	???	Balloon	X	Champagne	–

Casualties: None

8 October

Lt Ruby &	MF 20				1
???	MF 20	EA	X		?

Casualties:

Lt André Stromeyer &	N 68	P	Injured
Sol Michel	N 68	G	KIAcc
Cpl Paul Jacquillard &	VB 102	P	KIAcc
MdL Levillian	VB 102	B	KIAcc

9 October – No Claims

Casualties:

Brig Decasso	RGAé	P	Injured		
MdL Georges Schmitt	20° Cie d'Aérostiers	XF	Somme-Suippes	09h40
		O	WIA		

10 October

S/Lt Bourhis	a. N 31	Aviatik C	X	Puvenelle Forest	2
Sgt Coupet &	MF 25				–
Sgt Delcamp	MF 25	Fokker	FTL		–
MdL Lenoir	N 23	EA	P		–

a.   Gefr Kurt Kröner & Ltn Guido Wolff, FlAbt 70, KIAs Pont-à-Mousson, Ière Armée Report.

Casualties:

Sgt Henri Mahieu &	MF 63	P	KIA	Hattonchâtel, possibly by
S/Lt Henri Merillon	MF 63	O	KIA	Ltn Robert Greim, FFA 3 (1).
Cpl René Bret	C 61	P	WIA	
Lt Daniel Fevre	MF 50	O	WIA	
MdL Antonin Fedière	C 11	P	KIAcc	
MdL Paul Bourillon &	VB 114	P	Killed	A bomb exploded while being loaded.
MdL Etienne Le Moine des Mares	VB 114	O	Killed	,,
Sgt Bernard Denizot	VB 114	P	Injured	,,

11 October – No Claims

Casualties:

Sgt Henri Thamin &	C 61	P	KIA	Possibly by Ltn Otto
Sol Lasserre	C 61	G	KIA	Parschau, KG1, (1)
Adj Camille Clery &	RGAé	P	KIAcc	
S/Lt Foucade	RGAé	O	KIAcc	
Sgt Michel Acquart	RGAé	P	Injured	

12 October – No Claims

Casualties:

Lt du Beauviez &	VB 112	P	POW	By FA 25 in combat.
Sol Bremond	VB 112	B	POW	
S/Lt Abel d'Astanières	MF 2	P	KIA	MF N° 784, III° Armée,
S/Lt Henry	MF 2	O	KIA	Downed by a Fokker.
S/Lt Christian Patrimonio	C 54	O	WIA	

13 October – No Claims – No Casualties

14 October

Artillery	???	Balloon	X	S Monthois	–
Artillery	???	EA	X	N Bucy-le-Long	–

Casualties:

Lt Christiani	V 24	O		WIA-Flak
Lt Paul Girard	C 64	O		WIA
MdL Emile Roze	34° Cie d'Aérostiers,	XF	Jonchery, the second balloon
		O	KIA	flamed by an EA and the first observer killed.

15 October

Capt Roeckel &	CO a.	F 7				1
???		F 7	Aviatik	X	Tahure	1
Cpl Bouderie &		C 61				1
Sol Alloncle		C 61	EA	X		1
Sgt Carrier		C 65	EA	FTL	Château-Salins	–

a.   Probably Vfw Oswald Frischbier & Ltn Gustav Kaspereit, FlAbt 53, KIAs Butte de Tahure.

Casualties:

Sgt Maurice Colombe	N 23	P	WIA

16 October

Sgt Carrier &	C 65				–
Lt Skadowski	C 65	EA	FTL		–

Casualties:

Cpl Gaston Vibert &	VC 110	P	MIA	St. Souplet, Boelke (5)
Sgt Robert Cadet	VC 110	B	MIA	
S/Lt Jean de la Rochefoucauld	N 49	O	WIA	
Sgt Hourlier	VB 113	P	KIAcc	
Sgt Léon Comès *		P	KIAcc	

*   10° Section d'Avions Canons.

17 October – No Claims – No Casualties

18 October – No Claims

Casualties:

Cpl Henri Contré	MF 60	P	Injured	
QM Louis Kergosein &		P	KIAcc	Voisin III LAS N° 903, codé 23.
Mat Maurice Doualle		M	KIAcc	

19 – 22 October – No Claims – No Casualties

23 October

Adj Guingand ?	N 37			–
Lt Caffarel	N 37	EA	FTL	–

Casualties:

Lt Raymond Caffarel	N 37	O	WIA	III° Armée

24 – 25 October – No Claims – No Casualties

26 October

Sgt Navarre	a. N 12	LVG CII	POW	Jaulgonne	3

a.   Possibly Uffz Otto Gerold, KIA, & Ltn Paul Buchholz (O), FlAbt 33, WIA/POW, Moorseele, aircraft N° 523/15.

Casualties: None

27 October

??? & *				–
QM Franzouski *		EA	X	1

*   10° Section d'Avions Canons.

Casualties:

S/Lt Robert Maurin	RGAé	P	Injured

28 October – No Claims – No Casualties

29 October – No Claims

Casualties:

Sgt Gustave Gobeau &	C 4	P	KIAcc
Sol Dubreuil	C 4	M	Injured

30 October – No Claims

The attack in the area of Vimy Ridge was terminated.

Casualties:

Lt Alfred Dullin &	MF 8	P	KIA	In combat
Lt Leclerc	MF 8	O	KIA	
Cpl Dieudonne	C 42	G	WIA	

Lt Mathieu Tenant de La Tour	RGAé	P	Injured		

---

31 October – No Claims – No Casualties

October dates unknown:					
Between 10 & 14 October		2 seater	POW	Wilvik, N Courtrai	–
Mechanical problems		EA	POW	Inze-Thiel	–
Casualties:					
Lt Pierre de Langle de Cary	N 38	O	Injured		

---

1 November

S/Lt Le Coq de Kerland	N 68	Aviatik C	X	Forêt de Gremesey	1

Casualties: None

---

2 – 3 November – No Claims – No Casualties

---

4 November – No Claims
Casualties:

Cpl Emile Moreau &	RGAé	P	KIAcc
Sgt Godard	RGAé	G	KIAcc
Sgt Henri Despres &	C 43	P	Injured
Sgt Serf	C 43	G	Injured

---

5 November – No Claims
Casualties:

Sol Saboureau	VB 106	G	Injured

---

6 – 8 November – No Claims – No Casualties
8 November the French attack east of Reims ended.

---

9 November

Lt Bonneau &	N 48				–
S/Lt Gandelin	N 48	Fokker	FTL	Avricourt	–

Casualties: None

---

10 – 11 November – No Claims – No Casualties

---

12 November

Lt de Langle de Carry	N 23	EA	P		–
S/Lt Raymond	N 3	EA	P	Ornes	1400 –
Casualties:					
Sgt Jean Carrier	C 65	P	KIAcc	Drowned in water crash.	

---

13 November – No Claims – No Casualties

---

14 November

Adj Faure &	N 26				1
Lt Dumamès	N 26	Fokker	X	Coucklaere	1

Casualties: None

---

15 November – No Claims
Casualties:

Lt Jacques Bignon	MF 1	O	WIA	Flak

---

16 November – No Claims – No Casualties

---

17 November – No Claims
Casualties:

Adj André Massue	???	P	WIA
Sgt Joseph Ronserail	C 30	P	Injured

---

18 November – No Claims – No Casualties

19 November – No Claims
Casualties:

Lt Henri Le Cour Grandmaison	RGAé	P	Injured		

20 November – No Claims – No Casualties

21 November – No Claims
Casualties:

Lt Raymond Caffarel	N 37	O	KIA	
Cpl Marcel Risler &	RGAé	P	KIAcc	
Sol Florisson	RGAé	G	KIAcc	

22 November

Sgt Fabert &	MF 8				1
Lt Dardayrol	MF 8	Aviatik	X	Adreuil	1
MdL Desbruères &	C 28				1
Lt Gambier	C 28	Aviatik	XF		1
Adj Faure &	N 26				–
Lt Dumêmes	N 26	LVG	P	Ghistelles	–
Adj Faure &	N 26				–
Lt Dumêmes	N 26	EA	FTL	Belgium	–
Lt de Beauchamp &	N 37				–
Adj de Guingand	N 37	Aviatik	FTL		–
Lt de Beauchamp &	N 37				–
Adj de Guingand	N 37	Aviatik	FTL		–
Sgt Coupet &	MF 25				–
Sol Lucien Coupet	MF 25	Aviatik	FTL		–

Casualties:

Capt Maurice Schlumberger &	N 23	P	KIA	Forced to land in German Lines near Aure, after combat, Spad S.A.1 #10, killed on the ground.
Capt Montezuma	N 23	O	KIA	
Sgt Marcel Teulon &	MF 63	P	OK	
Sgt Gaston Rivier	MF 63	O	KIA	
Sgt Coupet &	MF 25	P	OK	
Sol Léon Coupet	MF 25	G	WIA	III° Armée.

23 November

Cpl Gindner &	MF 16				1
???	MF 16	EA	X		1

Casualties: None

24 – 25 November – No Claims – No Casualties

26 November

???	DCA	2 seater	X	E Berry-au-Bac	–
???	???	2 seater	POW	Jaulgonne	–

Casualties: None

27 November – No Claims – No Casualties

28 November

Sgt Simon &		N 26				2
S/Lt Lt Maria	a.	N 26	2 seater	X	NW Middlekerke	2
Adj Nungesser	b.	C 65	Albatros C	X	Nomeny	2
Adj de Guingand		N 37	Albatros	FTL	Habsheim	–
Adj Faure &		N 26				–
Lt Dumêmes		N 26	LVG	FTL	German Lines	–
???		MF 29	Aviatik C	FTL	Habsheim	–

a. Probably Ltn Oskar Rössline, BAO, KIA Middlekerke.
b. Probably Vfw August Blank & Ltn Wilhelm von Kalckreuth, BAM, KIAs Nomeny-Mailly.

Casualties:

Sgt Charles Mengelle-Touya	MF 1	P	WIA	
Lt Schroeder	MF 33	O	Injured	

29 November – No Claims – No Casualties

30 November

???	???	EA	FTL	Artois		–

Casualties:

Cpl Marcel Gindner &	MF 16	P	POW	Escaped 8 Dec 1915.
S/Lt Villiers	MF 16	O	POW	Combat NE Arras

1 December – No Claims – No Casualties

2 December – No Claims

Casualties:

Sgt Tiesserenc &	C 43	P	MIA
Capt Aveline	C 43	O	MIA

3 – 4 December – No Claims – No Casualties

5 December

Sgt Guynemer	N 3	Aviatik C	X	Bois de Carré	1020	2

Casualties:

Sgt Victor Chauliaguet	C 27	P	WIA

6 – 7 December – No Claims – No Casualties

8 December

Sgt Guynemer	a. N 3	LVG C	X	Beauvraignes	1035	3

a.   Probably Vfw Kurt Biesendahl & Ltn Hans Reitter, FlAbt 27, KIAs Beauvraignes-Roye.

Casualties:

Cpl René Receveur &	C 4	P	MIA
S/Lt Mesrine	C 4	O	MIA

9 December – No Claims – No Casualties

10 December – No Claims

Casualties:

MdL M D Delamotte	44? Cie d'Aérostiers		X	Hangest-en-Santerre
		O	KIA	(Somme).

11 December – No Claims – No Casualties

12 December – No Claims

Casualties:

S/Lt Jules Troncy	C 4	P	Injured

13 December – No Claims

Casualties:

Sgt de Guibert	C 10	P	Injured	
QM Aristide Copit	* CAM	P	Injured	DOW 23 December 1915.
				FBA 100 HP Codé 15.

*   Centre d'Aviation Maritime de Dunkerque.

14 December

Sgt Guynemer,	N 3					4
Sgt Bucquet (P) &	N 3					1
Lt Pandevan (O)	N 3	Fokker A	X	SE Noyon, Couracy	1415	1
??? &	MF 29					1
MdL Grelat	MF 29	Aviatik	X			1

Casualties:

Lt Jean Dutreuil & CO	MF 29	P	KIA	Flak, MF XI N? 1090, over the
Sol Fréjus Boudet	MF 29	G	KIA	Forêt de Hart.
MdL François Marcot &	C 61	P	KIA	Caudron G.4, combat with 5 Aviatik
Sol Philippe Alloncle	C 61	G	KIA	& 2 Fokker E, between Mülheim &
				Neuenberg.
S/Lt Pierre Bery	MF 36	O	WIA	

Sgt Guillaume Prevost de St Cry &	VB 109	P	WIA		
Sol Henri Gendarme	VB 109	G	WIA		

15 December

???	DCA	EA	FTL	St Mihiel	–

Casualties: None

16 December – No Claims – No Casualties

17 December

French Navy		Seaplane	POW	Nieuport

Casualties: None

18 December – No Claims – No Casualties

19 December – No Claims

Casualties:

Sgt André Simon &	N 26	P	WIA	Shot down while flying
S/Lt Joseph Maria	N 26	O	WIA	Nieuport X N° 403.

20 December

MdL de Layens	N 48	Aviatik	FTL	German Lines	1
MdL Julien de Courcelles &	C 65				–
???	C 65	EA	FTL		–
Sgt Combret &	C 18				–
???	C 18	Fokker	FTL		–

Casualties:

Cdt Louis Guillabert	IV? Armée	P	Injured

21 December – No Claims

Casualties:

Lt Michaud	MF 58	O	KIA

22 December

Casualties:

Lt Jean Goursat	MF 45	P	KIAcc

23 – 27 December – No Claims – No Casualties

28 December – No Claims

Casualties:

S/Lt Amédée Froger	???	P	Injured

29 December – No Claims

Casualties:

MdL Edouard de Layens	N 48	P	KIAcc	Ponnier M.1
S/Lt Emile Goubet	???	P	KIAcc	
S/Lt de Kerangue	RGAé	P	Injured	

30 December – No Claims

Casualties:

Sgt Jean Argouet &	C 27	P	KIAcc
Lt Resch	C 27	O	KIAcc

31 December – No Claims

Casualties:

Sgt Poulain	C 28	P	WIA

December dates unknown					
??? &	AM				1
EV1 Higrel	CAM	EA	X		1

French Combat Log 1916

1 – 4 January – No Claims – No Casualties

---

5 January – No Claims
Casualties:

Lt Jacques Landron &	MF 7	P	KIA	
Capt Roger Courtois de Maleville	MF 7	O	KIA	

---

6 – 8 January – No Claims – No Losses

---

9 January – No Claims
Casualties:

Adj Maurice Faure &	N 26	P	WIA	Nieuport X N° 403,
Lt Daniel Dumêmes	N 26	O	WIA	Near Ostende

---

10 January

Cpl Padieu &				
Mat Falher	a. 36 CA	Fokker E	X	SE Dixmuide
Sgt Treille de Grandseigne &				
Mat Baron	* 36 CA	Fokker E	X	Forêt d'Houthulst

a.　This crew shot down the aircraft that had shot down de Grandseigne and Baron.
*　Section d'Avions Canon du 36° Corps d'Armée.
Casualties:

Sgt Parent &	36 CA	P	POW	Possibly by Ltn Wilhelm
Sol Bonnier	36 CA	O	POW	Frankl, KekV, (2).

---

11 – 12 January – No Claims – No Casualties

---

13 January – No Claims
Casualties

S/Lt Allain de Kerangue	RGAé	P	KIAcc	

---

14 January – No Claims
Casualties:

Sol Georges Piquet	CRP	M	Injured in crash-landing.

---

15 January – No Claims
Casualties:

S/Lt Paul Billard	RGAé	P	KIAcc

---

16 January – No Claims
Casualties:

S/Lt Berger	MF 16		O	Injured

---

17 January

Sgt Guillamont &	MF 1				1
Capt de Miribel	MF 1	LVG	X	German Lines	1
Lt Robert &	N 26				–
Lt Dumêmes	N 26	LVG	P	Hooglur	1035 –

Casualties:

Cpl Henri Follot &	VB 105	P	POW	Voisin #1096, probably by
MdL Hennequet	VB 105	O	POW	Ltn Walter Höhndorf, FlAbt12, (1).
S/Lt Georges Momet	N 26	O	WIA	10h15 over Roulers
				DOW 21 January 1916.

---

18 January

Motor trouble	a.	2 seater	POW	Flin	–

a.　Both officer occupants taken prisoner.
Casualties:

Sgt Paul Chevalier &	VB 101	P	MIA	
Sgt Corroenne	VB 101	B		Voisin

19 January – No Claims
Casualties:

Sgt Jules Laroche	MF 16	P	KIAcc		
Lt René Itier	CEP 115	P	Injured		
Adj Charles Nungesser	CEP 115	P	Injured		
Sol Noël	CEP 115	G	Injured		

20 – 21 January – No Claims – No Casualties

22 January – No Claims – No Casualties

23 January

Sgt Barnay	N 37	EA	X		1210	1
MdL Poreaux &	???					1
???	???	Fokker	X			1

Casualties:

S/Lt René Morgand	MF 5	O	WIA	
Sgt Eugène Euryale &	C 42	P	Injured	
Cpl Dieudonne	C 42	G	Injured	
Cpl Marien Roche &	VB 102	P	POW	Motor hit by flak and FTL
Capt Jean Legrand	VB 102	O	POW	SE of Metz.

24 January

Capt Gonnet-Thomas	CO	N 65	EA	P	–

Casualties:

Sgt Colcombe &	N 67	P	MIA
S/Lt Joseph Michel	N 67	O	MIA
MdL Smaragd Jullien de Courcelles	N 65	P	WIA
Sol Maeght	N 23	G	Injured
Lt Charles Labouchère	C 47	P	Injured

25 January

Capt François &	N 57				1
S/Lt Tenant de la Tour	N 57	Balloon	XF	Adinfer	1

Casualties: None

26 January – No Claims – No Casualties

27 January – No Claims
Casualties:

S/Lt Paul Chausse	RGAé	P	KIAcc
Lt Georges Courtois	MF 20	P	Injured
Lt Richelieu	MF 20	O	Injured

28 January – No Claims
Casualties:

MdL Jean de Fontaine &	C 17	P	MIA	
Sol Tors	C 17	G	MIA	
LV Emile Janvier	* CAM	P	KIAcc	FBA 100hp, N° 95
MdL Marcel Berode &	MF 55	P	Injured	
Sol Charpentier	MF 55	G	Injured	

* St Raphaël.

29 January

Asp Gayral &	C 18			–
Sol Lefortier	C 18	EA	P	–

Casualties:

Asp Georges Gayral &	C 18	P	OK	
Sol Lefortier	C 18	G	WIA	DOW

30 – 31 January – No Claims – No Casualties

Date unknown in January 1916

Sgt O'Doul &	???					–
Lt Vernin	???	EA	FTL			–

1 February – No Claims
Casualties:

Sgt Joseph Hiriat &	C 28	P	MIA	Caudron, possibly by Ltn		
Sol Jean	C 28	G	MIA	Josef Jacobs, FlAbt 11, unconfirmed.		

2 February – No Claims
Casualties:

Cpl Jacquin &	VB 108	P	POW	Voisin, possibly by either		
Sol Segaud	VB 108	G	KIA	Obltn Ernst von Althaus (2) or Obltn		
				Rudolf Berthold (1), both of FlAbt 23.		
S/Lt Emile Ader	N 57	P	Injured	DOW 3 February 1916.		

3 February

Sgt Guynemer	a.	N 3	LVG C	X	Roye	1110	5
Sgt Guynemer		N 3	LVG C	X	Carrépuis, E Roye	1140	6
Sgt Guynemer		N 3	LVG C	P	Roye	1150	–

a. Probably Ltn Heinrich Zwenger (O), FlAbt 27, KIA at Roye.
Casualties:

Sgt Victor Grivotte &	N 3	P	KIA	One of these crews downed by		
Lt Grassel	N 3	O	KIA	Von Althaus (3).		
Cpl Marcel Voyer &	VB 107	P	MIA			
Sol Capdeville	VB 107	G	MIA			

4 February

Adj Metairie	N 49	Aviatik	X	W Lutterbach	1000	1

Casualties: None

5 February

Sgt Guynemer	a.	N 3	LVG C	XF	Herbecourt	1130	7
???		???	Balloon	XF	S Péronne		–
S/Lt Malavaille		N 69	EA	P			–

a.   Possibly Ltn Rudi Lumblatt (O), FlAbt 9, KIA Moreuil.
Casualties:

S/Lt Maxime Guilloteau	Buc	P	KIAcc			
Capt Eugène Verdon &	VB 113	P	Injured			
QM Fralin	VB 113	G	Injured	During a test flight.		

6 February

MdL Rabatel &	VC 111					1
QM Le Caignec	VC 111	Balloon	XF	Eterpigny		1
??? &	MF 63					–
Cpl Demeuldre	MF 63	Albatros	P			–
Sgt Guynemer &	N 3					–
S/Lt de La Fressange	N 3	LVG C	P			–

Casualties:

Capt Besnier	N 37	O	KIA			
Adj Jacques Loviconi &	MF 63	P	OK			
S/Lt Jean Dagnaux	MF 63	O	WIA			
Adj André Delorme &	C 56	P	OK			
Sol Jobelin	C 56	G	WIA	Flak		
EV Georges Le Diabat	EM 1A	P	KIAcc	Ambérieu		
Adj Charles Nungesser	N 65	P	Injured			

7 February – No Claims
Casualties:

Adj Paul Mère &	C 34	P	KIAcc			
Sol Fleutot	C 34	G	KIAcc			

8 February – No Claims
Casualties:

Cpl Lucièn Chambray	C 56	P	Injured			

9 February – No Claims
Casualties:

MdL Charles Ouvrard &	MF 35	P	MIA			
Sol Bruneteau	MF 35	G	MIA			

10 February

S/Lt Deullin &	MF 62					–
Capt Colcombe	MF 62	EA	FTL			–

Casualties:

Lt Jacques Bignon	AL 205	O	WIA
Sgt Marcel Goffin &	C 56	P	KIAcc
Sgt Ponche	C 56	G	KIAcc

11 – 12 February – No Claims – No Casualties

13 February

???	DCA	EA	XF	E Givenchy	2200	–

Casualties:

Sgt Leclerc	C 9	P	Injured

14 – 19 February – No Claims – No Casualties

20 February – No Claims
Casualties:

S/Lt Jean de Landrain	MF 71	P	WIA
Lt Amédée Reverchon &	MF 19	P	Injured
Sol Polland	MF 19	G	Injured
Cpl Jean Duhaton &	VB 114	P	Injured
MdL Morin-Pons	VB 114	G	Injured

21 February
Battle of Verdun commences.

Capt Thenault &	CO	C 42					1
Lt Humann		C 42					1
Sgt Federoff &		C 42					1
S/Lt Gauthier		C 42					1
Adj Duran &		C 42					1
???		C 42					1
Unknown crew		C 42	Albatros C	X	N Forêt de Parroy		1
Adj Ortoli		N 31	EA	X	Vigneulles		2
Cpl Léon Givon &		C 34					1
Brig Delon &		C 61					1
Cpl Happe &		MF 29					1
Sol Breton		MF 29	Fokker	X	Tagsdorf, E Altkirch		1
??	a.	DCA	Aviatik	XF	Epinal		–
17° Section d'auto-canons de 75							
Capt Dupont	b.	DCA	Zeppelin	XF	Brabant-le-Roi	2040	–
Capt Quillien	CO c.	N 37	LVG C	POW	Givry-en-Argonne		3
Capt Quillien	CO	N 37	EA	FTL	”		–
Capt Quillien	CO	N 37	EA	FTL	”		–
Capt Auger		N 31	2EA	FTL	La Chaussée		–
Adj Navarre		N 67	2 seater	P	Ft de Badonvillers		–

a.   Probably Uffz Artur Reuschling & Hptm Ernst Erdmann, FlAbt 65, KIAs Epinal.
b.   Zeppelin LZ 77, CO Hptm Alfred Horn and crew KIAs over Brabant-le-Roi.
c.   Both occupants taken prisoner.

Casualties:

Cpl Astorgis	MF 29	G	WIA
Lt Marcel Bonnevay	N 38	P	Injured
Lt René de Peyrecave	C 61	P	Injured
Brig Emile Delon	C 61	G	WIA
Cpl Maurice de la Perche &	VB 106	P	Injured
Sgt Laurent	VB 106	G	Injured
Cpl Tribouillard	GDE	P	Injured

22 February – No Claims
Casualties:

Name		Unit		Result	Notes	
S/Lt Michel Laguerre		N 37	P	KIA		
Cpl Georges de Geuser		N 37	P	OK		
Cpl Emile Laurent		N 37	G	Injured	Nieuport XII N° 688.	
???		59° Cie d'Aérostiers			Cable cut by artillery fire, broke	
			O	OK	loose and came down near Souilly.	

23 February – No Claims
Casualties:

Name		Unit		Result		
Cpl Blanc		GDE	P	Injured		

24 February

Name		Unit	Type	Result		
Sgt Coache &		C 11				–
Lt Angot		C 11	EA	FTL		–

Casualties:

Name		Unit		Result		
Lt René Vandelle		C 13	P	WIA		
S/Lt André Boyer		N 23	P	Injured		

25 February – No Claims
Casualties:

Name		Unit		Result	Notes	
Sgt Robert Gorlacher &		VB 101	P	MIA	Night raid on Chambly Stn.	
Adj Hugo Laux		VB 101	O	POW		

26 February

Name		Unit	Type	Result	Location	Score
Adj Navarre	a.	N 67	2 seater	X	Dieue	4
Adj Navarre	b.	N 67	2 seater	POW	Maheulles	5
??? &		MF 71				1
Lt Pierrey		MF 71	Albatros	X	German lines	1
??? &		C 11				–
Capt Vuillemin		C 11	Aviatik C	P	Les Eparges	–

a.   Probably Ltn Georg Heine & Ltn Alfons von Zeddelmann, KG1/KSt4, KIAs Dieue-sur-Meuse.
b.   Probably Obltn Heinrich Kempf (O), KG1/KSt4, POW Dieue-sur-Meuse.

Casualties:

Name		Unit		Result	Notes	
Capt Tony Audrain & CO		BM 117	P	POW	Attack on Metz	
Capt Louis Linyer		BM 117	O	POW		
Lt Jean de Landrain		F 71	P	WIA		
Lt de Fernand Cosnac &		BM 118	P	KIAcc		
MdL Chatelard		BM 118	G	KIAcc		

27 February – No Claims
Casualties:

Name		Unit		Result		
Sgt Pradeau		C 10	P	Injured		

28 February

Name		Unit	Type	Result		
Cpl Charpentier &		N 68				–
Lt Vernin		N 68	Fokker	P		–

Casualties:

Name		Unit		Result		
Sgt René Driholle		BM 119	P	Injured		

29 February

Name		Unit	Type	Result	Location	Score
Adj Trepp &		C 27				1
???		C 27	EA	X	La Bassée	?

Casualties:

Name		Unit		Result	Notes	
Cpl Charles Jourdain &		GDE	P	POW	Possibly by Ltn Kurt Haber	
S/Lt Chiaroni		GDE	O	POW	FlAbt 6, (1).	
Adj André Delorme &		C 56	P	OK		
Capt Dourif		C 56	O	WIA		
Sgt Joseph Pingray		VB 112	P	KIAcc		

Unknown date in February 1916

Name		Unit	Type	Result		
Sgt Le Roy		N 65	EA	P		–

1 March

Name		Unit				
Sgt Fonck &		C 47				–

Adj Jaunaut		C 47	Fokker E	P			–
Casualties:							
MdL Descamps		VB 105	P	Injured			
MdL Jean d'Audeville &		MF 71	P	Injured			
Lt de La Houssaye		MF 71	O	Injured			

2 March

S/Lt Navarre	a.	N 67	Albatros C	POW	Fleury-Douaumont	1130	6
???		DCA	EA	XF	Suippes		–

a.   Occupants WIA/POWs.

Casualties:

Lt Faga	MF 8	O	WIA
Sgt Georges Treca	C 53	P	WIA

3 March – No Claims – No Casualties

4 March – No Claims

Casualties:

S/Lt Lecam	C 53	O	KIA
Lt Vittu de Keraoul	C 13	O	WIA

5 March – No Claims

Casualties:

Brig Charles Sprenz &	GDE	P	Injured
S/Lt Baudoin	GDE	O	Injured

6 March

S/Lt Guynemer &		N 3				–
S/Lt de La Fressange		N 3	LVG C	P		–
Adj Navarre		N 67	EA	P		–

Casualties:

Lt Poussin		C 27	O	KIA
S/Lt Laffont		C 27	O	KIA
Capt René Roeckel	CO	MF 7	P	WIA
Sgt Marius Essers &		C 66	P	Injured
Sol Comte		C 66	G	Injured

7 March

Adj R David &	MF 2				2
Cpl Eymery	MF 2	EA	POW		1
VII° Armée	DCA	2 seater	POW	Avocourt	–

Casualties:

Sgt Clément &	VB 108	P	KIAcc
Cpl Lecomte	VB 108	O	KIAcc

8 March

S/Lt Varcin &	MF 5				1
Asp Fayet	MF 5	Fokker E	X	Beauvallon	1
Lt Malavialle	N 69	LVG C	X	Etain	1
Adj Jailler	N 15	LVG C	X	Spincourt	1
Adj Dufaur de Gavardie	N 12	EA	X	Warmerville	1
Sgt Chainat	N 3	EA	P		–
MdL Vaillet &	C 53				–
Lt Dubois de La Sablonière					–
Asp P Navarre	N 69	EA	FTL	Verdun	–
???	C 53	Scout	FTL	German lines	–

Casualties:

Lt Charles Dutertre &	GBM	P	POW	By FA 71
Sol René Demont	GBM	G	KIA	
Sgt Castel &	C 18	P	MIA	Combat, FA 211
S/Lt O'Quin	C 18	O	MIA	II° Armée
Sgt Charles Maillet	C 11	P	KIA	
Lt André Roussel	C 11	O	KIA	II° Armée
S/Lt Charles Picard	C 11	O	KIA	II° Armée
Sol Pierre Beauvais	MF 35	O	KIA	II° Armée
Sgt Maurice Collet	MF 35		WIA	II° Armée

Asp Pierre Navarre	N 69	P	WIA	II° Armée, Verdun		
S/Lt Louis Pandevan	N 3	O	WIA	Possibly by Obltn Hans Berr, KekA, (1).		
Lt Maurice Barthe &	C 11	P	OK			
Capt Robert du Bois de Beauchesne	C 11	O	WIA	II° Armée		
Lt Jean Merlou	GDE	P	KIAcc			
Sgt Jules Lejeaille	GDE	P	KIAcc			
Brig Vincent Dubufe	GDE	P	KIAcc			
MdL Raymond Richard	N 3	P	KIAcc			
& Sol Etienne Pillon	N 3	G	KIAcc			
MdL Robert Hennion	RGAé	P	KIAcc			
Capt de la Morlais	MF 40	P	Injured			
Cpl François Carayon	MF 29	P	Injured			

9 March

Brig Barioz &	MF 8					1
S/Lt Wiedemann	MF 8	Fokker	X	German lines		1
Casualties:						
Sgt Collet	MF 35	G	WIA			

10 March – No Claims

Casualties:						
S/Lt Eugène Delerue &	C 9	P	KIA	Flak		
S/Lt Perbosc	C 9	O	KIA			

11 March

Sgt Chainat	N 3	EA	X	Douaumont	0900	1
S/Lt Peretti	N 67	Fokker	XF	Douaumont	1025	1
Casualties:						
Lt Henri Pacaud	C 28	O	WIΛ			
Adj Joseph Kerneis &	MF 35	P	KIAcc			
Asp André Huré	MF 35	O	KIAcc			
Lt André Stromeyer &	Avord	P	KIAcc			
Cpl Giriend	Avord	O	KIAcc			

12 March

S/Lt Guynemer	a.	N 3	LVG C	X	Thiescourt	1100	8
Sgt de Rochefort &		N 26					1
Capt Perrin	b.	N 26	LVG C	X	W Keyem	0900	1
S/Lt de Jumilhac &		N 37					1
Sol Picoche		N 37	EA	X	German lines		1
Adj E Stribick &		MF 19					2
Lt Mutel		MF 19	2 seater	X	N Recicourt		1
S/Lt Laffon &		MF 36					1
Lt Walckenaer		MF 36	EA	X	German lines		1
Cpl Lagrande &		C 61					1
Asp Marchais		C 61	Fokker	X	German lines		1

a.   Possibly Uffz Friedrich Ackermann & Ltn Friedrich Marquardt, FlAbt 61, KIAs Thiescourt.
b.   Probably VzFlugMstr Fritz Stiefvatter, KIA, & Steuermann Jost, WIA, MFA I, Pervyse.

Casualties:

EVA Gabriel Ecomarol &		CAM	P	MIA	North Sea, FBA 100hp
QM Jules Quicray	*	CAM	O	MIA	N° 123, Code B.1
Capt Henri d'Aragon		MF 63	P	KIA	
Adj Auguste Metairie		N 49	P	WIA	By Ltn Otto Parschau, KG 1, (3).
S/Lt Henri Louis &		N 69	P	WIA	
Lt Alexandre d'Orsetti		N 69	O	WIA	II° Armée
Sgt François Deperi &		C 47	P	WIA	
Lt Gaudillot		C 47	O	OK	
MdL Jean Cellière		MF 63	P	WIA	
Adj-Chef Georges Loviconi		MF 63	P	WIA	
Cpl Jacques Gout &		MF 8	P	KIAcc	
S/Lt Blandin		MF 8	O	KIAcc	
Cpl Perthuy &		MF 8	P	KIAcc	
S/Lt Lasbarrières		MF 8	O	KIAcc	
S/Lt Brulard		N 37	P	Injured	
S/Lt Pierre de Jumilhac		N 37	P	Injured	

Sol Flamarels	VB 107	G	Injured		

* CAM Boulogne.

13 March

Capt Auger	CO a.	N 31	LVG C	X	Cumières	1
Sgt Hott &		MF 228				1
S/Lt Naudeau	b.	MF 228	Scout	X	Chattancourt	1

a. Possibly Ltn Wilhelm Otto, KG2, KIA Douaumont, about 15 km SE Cumières.
b. Possibly Ltn Ludwig Kielin & Obltn Franz Frhr von Linden, FlAbt 25, KIAs Verdun, about 15 km SE Chattancourt.

Casualties:

Sgt Georges Guynemer	N 3	P	WIA	Nieuport XI N° 836
Capt Jacques du Plan de Sieyes de Veynes	N 65	O	WIA	
Sgt Alphonse Vitry &	BM 118	P	WIA	
Brig Augereau	BM 118	O	WIA	
Cpl Marcel Gelle &	MF 16	P	Injured	
Lt de Saint-Laurent	MF 16	O	KIAcc	
Sgt Adrien Delille	GDE	P	Injured	
MdL René Delbos	GDE	P	Injured	
Sol Lodier	GDE	G	Injured	
Lt de Boisgelin	GDE	O	Injured	
Sgt Armand Viguier	VB 107	P	Injured	

14 March

S/Lt Jensen	N 31	EA	X	Montfaucon	1
Sgt Fedoroff &	C 42				2
Sol Lanero	C 42	EA	X	Cernay	1
Cpl de Gaillard de la Valdene &	MF 123	Aviatik	X	Cernay, E Lure	1
Sol Breton					1
Lt Dubois de Gennes	N 57	Albatros	FTL		–
Patrol	MF 20	EA	FTL	German lines	–
Patrol	N 31	2EA	P		–
Cdt de Tricornot de Rose *		EA	P	Verdun	–
Sgt Gervais &	C 66				–
Capt Faye	GB 2	EA	P		–

* CO Groupement de Verdun.

Casualties:

Sgt Gaston Delpech &	C 6	P	MIA	By FA(A)203
S/Lt Georges Thevenin	C 6	O	MIA	
Cdt Alphonse Roisin &	GB 1	P	POW	Flak
Sol Pierre Gousset	GB 1	G	KIA	
S/Lt Jean Bourhis	N 31	P	WIA	DOW 21 March 1916
Adj Jean Raulet	C 17	P	WIA	
Capt Léon Bruyère	VB 106	O	WIA	
Lt Raymond Oblin	C 4	O	Injured	

15 March

Adj Réservat	N 65	EA	P		–
MdL Decazes de Glucksbierg &					–
S/Lt Lefebvre	C 28	EA	FTL		–

Casualties:

MdL Jacques Decazes de Glucksbierg &	C 28	P	MIA	Fokker combat
S/Lt François Lefebvre	C 28	O	MIA	
Lt Léon Remy	MF 35		WIA	

16 March – No Claims

Casualties:

QM Frédéric Dejean	* CAM	P	Injured	St Pol-sur-Mer, Morane G N° 497, code 5, DOW 18 March 1916.
Lt Gabriel Martin	???	P	KIAcc	
S/Lt Jean Levassor d'Yerville 68° Cie d'Aérostiers				Cable cut by enemy air attack, observer made first parachute jump of the war by a French balloonist. He jumped to avoid being taken prisoner in the loose balloon.

* CAM Dunkerque.

17 March

Sgt Pulpe &		N 23				1
Sgt Lenoir		N 23	Fokker E	X	Dun-sur-Meuse	3
Capt Thonel d'Orgeix		N 48	LVG	FTL		–
Adj Duran &		C 42				–
???		C 42	2 seater	FTL	German lines	–

Casualties:

Sgt Marcel Garet &	N 23	P	WIA		
Lt Jean Rimbaud	N 23	O	WIA		
Sgt Henri Labeille	C 64	P	KIAcc		
Lt André Fouillard &	C 27	P	KIAcc		
S/Lt Henri Virrion	C 27	O	KIAcc		
Sol Guitard	C 64	G	Injured		

18 March

Lt Floch &	CO	MF 29				1
Sol Rode	a.	MF 29	EA	X	Habsheim	1
Cpl Rins &		MF 29				1
Sgt Dubar	a.	MF 29	Fokker E	X	Habsheim	1
Sgt Chaput		N 31	LVG C	XF	Les Eparges	2
Adj Navarre	b.	N 67	2 seater	X	Vigneville	7
S/Lt Marinkovitch &						1
S/Lt Perrault	c.	GB 4	AEG	X	Habsheim	1
Cpl de Gaillard de La Valdene &						2
Sgt Robillot		MF 123	Fokker	X	Habsheim	1
Cpl de Gaillard de La Valdene &						3
Sgt Robillot		MF 123	Fokker	X	Habsheim	2

a.   Intentionally crashed into their opponents during combat.
b.   Possibly Obltn Heinrich von Blanc & Obltn Rudolf Gramich, KG 1, KIAs Verdun.
c.   Probably OfStv Fritz Hopfgarten, Ltn Walter Kurth, & Vfw Max Wallat, FlAbt 48, KIAs.

Casualties:

Lt Robert Floch &	CO	MF 29	P	KIA	MF XI, collided with their opponent.
Sol Paul Rode		MF 29	B	KIA	
S/Lt Roger Loumiet &		MF 29	P	MIA	In flames.
Sgt Joseph Vaysset		MF 29	B	MIA	
Cpl Henri Rins &		MF 29	P	KIA	Collided with Flg Ludwig
Sgt Robert Dubar		MF 123	B	KIA	Fischer, who was also KIA.
MdL Edouard Leroy &		MF 29	P	KIA	Farman, probably by Vfw
Capt Victor Emile Bacon		MF 29	O	KIA	Ernst Udet, KekH, (1).
Lt Léon Mouraud &		MF 123	P	WIA	DOW 8 April 1916.
Sol Goeury		MF 123	G	WIA	
Sol Steinbach		C 42	G	WIA	
Adj Asa Robillot &		GB 4	P	WIA	
Lt Patriarche		GB 4	O	WIA	
Adj Revoil		C 51	P	WIA	
MdL Poindrelle		MF 59	O	Injured	

19 March

Lt Deullin		N 3	EA	X		2
??? &		C 28				1
S/Lt Delasalle &		C 28				1
Lt Doumer		C 64				1
Sol Warnotte		C 64	LVG C	X	Pont-Faverger	1
Capt Brocard	CO	N 3	Scout	P		–
Lt Doumer &		C 64				–
Sol Warnotte		C 64	LVG C	FTL		–

Casualties:

Sgt Pierre Galiment &		MF 19	P	KIA	Probably by Obltn Oswald
Lt Jacques Libman		MF 19	O	KIA	Boelcke, FlAbt 62, (12).
S/Lt Alfred Auger &		MF 20	P	OK	
Lt René Pilard		MF 20	O	KIA	
Capt Félix Brocard	CO	N 3	P	WIA	
Lt Martin &		AL 212	P	KIAcc	
S/Lt Laporterie		AL 212	O	KIAcc	
S/Lt de Loiray		N 48	O	KIAcc	
Adj Louis Cormier		GDE	P	Injured	

20 March

Adj Pulpe	N 23	EA	X	N Maucourt		3
Casualties:						
MdL Edouard Rousseau	N 67	P	WIA			

21 March

Sgt Fedoroff &	C 42					3
Sol Larus	C 42	2 seater	XF	W Douaumont		1
Casualties:						
Lt Jean Antonioli &	VB 109	P	KIA	Boelcke (13)		
Capt Félix Le Croart	VB 109	O	KIA			
Cpl Marcel Bornet &	VC 111	P	KIA	Flak		
Mat François Le Maout	VC 111	G	KIA	Flak		

22 March – No Claims

Casualties:					
S/Lt Henri Balasse	Avord	P	KIAcc		
Sgt Armand Legube	66° Cie d'Aérostiers			Possibly attacked by Ltn Josef	
		O	Injured	Jacobs, Fokker Staffel West.	

23 March – No Claims – No Casualties

24 March – No Claims

Casualties:				
Capt Joseph Jolain	Bourget	P	KIAcc	

25 March – No Claims

Casualties:				
MdL René Saint-Didier &	MF 35	P	KIA	II° Armée
Asp Robert Bel	MF 35	O	Injured	II° Armée
Adj Léon Acher	N 57	P	WIA	II° Armée
S/Lt Albert Deullin	N 3	P	WIA	II° Armée

26 March

Sgt Chainat	N 3	2 seater	XF	N Douaumont	0820	2
Casualties:						
Sgt Eugène Thomelin	GDE	P	Injured			

27 – 28 March – No Claims – No Casualties

29 March

13° Section d'auto canons		EA	X		
Casualties:					
MdL René Delamarre	GDE	P	KIAcc		
Sol Abran	GDE	G	KIAcc		
Sgt Josset &	VB 107	P	Injured		
Sol Coutat	VB 107	G	KIAcc		
Cpl Marcel Blondin	GDE	P	Injured		
Cpl Bertholon	GDE	P	Injured		

30 March

Capt Vuillemin &		C 11					2
Lt Moulines		C 11	Fokker E	X	Marchéville		1
Adj Becquet &		N 63					1
Sgt des Allimes		N 63					1
Adj Trepp &		C 27					2
Sol Fabre		C 27	EA	XF	SE Azannes		1
Sgt Fedoroff		C 42	EA				4
Sol Lanero		C 42	EA	X	Moranville		2
???		DCA					–
Lt Doumer &		C 64					
2 Sol Warnotte	a.	C 64	Fokker E	X	St Marie-à-Py		2
???		DCA	2 seater	X	W Nouvion		–
S/Lt Mesguich		N 12	EA	X	German lines		3

Sgt Barault		N 57	EA	P	Charny		–
Adj J Dumas &		C 51					–
Lt Copin		C 51	Fokker	FTL			–

a.   Probably Gefr Cësar Becker, KIA St Souplet, about 5 km SW St Marie-à-Py.

Casualties:

Asp Raybaud	C 51	O	KIA	
S/Lt Henri Mesmacre &	C 51	P	OK	
Asp Georges Gounon	C 51	O	WIA	
Lt Remy	MF 35	O	WIA	
Capt Pierre Moitessier	C 61	P	Injured	
Sgt Henri Bardel	C 46	P	Injured	
Cpl Lemaitre	GDE	P	Injured	
Sgt Joseph Ronserail	C 34	P	Injured	

---

31 March

Lt Deullin		N 3	Fokker E	X	Beaumont-Consenvoye	3
Sgt Ingold,		N 23				1
Sgt de Ram &		N 23				3
Adj Pulpe	a.	N 23	2 seater	X	Ornes	3
Adj Pulpe		N 23	EA	X	Consenvoye	4
S/Lt Boillot		N 49	Aviatik C	X	La Chapelle	1
MdL Prevost &		MF 2				1
???		MF 2	EA	XF	German lines	?
???		DCA	EA	XF	N Tahure	–
Sgt Fedoroff &		C 42				
Sgt Bonnetète		C 42	2 EA	P		–
Lt Dubois de Gennes		N 57	Fokker	P		–
Capt Vuillemin &		C 11				–
???		C 11	Fokker E	FTL		–

a.   Possibly Vfw Hans Haza-Radlitz & Ltn Erich Bardenwerper, KG 2, KIAs at Douaumont, about 10 km S Ornes.

Casualties:

S/Lt Louis Beaujard	N 57	P	KIA	
Sgt Jacques Quellenec &	N 12	P	KIA	
Lt Jean Mourier	N 12	O	KIA	Flak
Sgt Marie Renault	MF 41	P	KIA	
Lt Henri Garriau	MF 41	O	KIA	
??? &	N 23	P	KIA	
Lt Dardayrol	N 23	O	KIA	Ornes
Lt Maurice de	GDE	P	Injured	
St Jean-Lantillac				

---

1 April

Sgt Jailler	a.	N 15	LVG C	X	Etain-Spincourt		2
Lt Schneider	a.	N 15	Aviatik	FTL	Etain		–
Sgt de Rochefort &		N 26					
Capt Perin	b.	N 26	LVG	FTL	E Nieuport	1025	–
S/Lt J Navarre		N 67	EA	P			–
Patrol		N 23	EA	FTL			–

a.   Possibly Ltn Karl Christian Graf von Ahlefeld (O), KG 2, KIA Douaumont, about 15 km W Etain.
b.   Possibly Ltn Georg Wollenburg, KIA Dixmuiden.

Casualties:

Adj Achille Degon &	MF 62	P	KIA	
S/Lt Madelin	C 43	O	KIA	
Sgt Louis Paoli &	MF 54	P	KIA	Probably by Obltn Rudolf
Lt Alfred Braut	MF 54	O	KIA	Berthold, KeKV (4).
MdL Lucien Prevost	MF 2	P	KIA	III° Armée
Adj René Pelissier	C 53	P	WIA	
Lt Marie Barbot	MF 54	O	Injured	

---

2 April

S/Lt Lis		N 15	Aviatik	X	Dannevoux	1
Capt Auger	CO	N 31	Aviatik	X	Creue	2
Adj Nungeser		N 65	Balloon	XF	Septsarges	3
???		N 23	EA	FTL	Near Verdun	–
???		???	EA	P	Near Verdun	–

Casualties:

Lt Albert Deullin	N 3	P	WIA

Cpl André Godefroy &	N 37	P	WIA	III° Armée	
MdL Jean Courtel	N 37	O	OK	Nieuport XII N° 791	
S/Lt de Raimond &	C 17	P	WIA		
Lt de Boerepos	C 17	O	WIA		

3 April

Adj Nungesser	a.	N 65	LVG C	X	Hauts-Fourneaux	4
S/Lt Navarre		N 67	EA	X	Bois de Cumières	8
Adj Duran &		C 42				2
???		C 42	EA	X	S Moranville	?
Adj Dorme &		C 94/CRP				1
Sol Huillet		C 94/CRP	LVG C	X	Carlepont	1
Capt Auger		N 31	Fokker E	FTL	St Maurice	–
Adj Nungesser		N 65	EA	P		–
Capt Gonnet-Thomas		N 65	EA	P		–
Lt Lesort		N 65	EA	P		–

a.   Possibly Ltn Hans Keithe (O) FlAbt (A) 211, KIA, Chassonge Ferme.

Casualties:

Capt Louis Quillien	CO	N 37	P	KIA	
Sgt Victor Fedoroff		C 42	P	WIA	
S/Lt André Baras		C 21	P	WIA	
MdL Maurice Zobel		MF 123	P	Injured	
Sol Delecourt		MF 123	G	Injured	

4 April

Adj Jailler	N 15	LVG C	X	Bois de Tilly	3
Adj Nungesser	N 65	2 motor	X	Hauts-Fourneaux	5
MdL Cowdin	N 65	LVG	X		1

Casualties: None

5 April – No Claims

Casualties:

Sgt Alexandre Coste &	GDE	P	Injured	
Sol Depont	GDE	G	Injured	

6 – 7 April – No Claims – No Casualties

8 April – No Claims

Casualties:

Cpl Lanero	C 42	G	WIA	
Lt Marc Malcor &	VB 101	P	KIAcc	
Sgt-Maj Georges Ancelin	VB 101	O	KIAcc	

9 April

S/Lt Lis	N 15	EA	X		2
Capt de Beauchamp &	N 23				2
Lt de Lage	N 23				1
??? &	C 42				1
Sol Steinbach	C 42	Fokker	X	Esnes	1
???	DCA	EA	X	Woëvre	–
Patrol	N 37	EA	FTL		–

Casualties:

Sgt Gaston Guidicelli &	C 27	P	KIA	Possibly by Obltn Franz Walz (1)
Lt Gaston Marchand	C 27	O	KIA	& Ltn Gerlich (1) KSt 2.
Sgt René Scampucci &	VB 108	P	KIAcc	
Sol Charles Jayme	VB 108	G	KIAcc	
Lt Alexander Dumas	GDE	P	KIAcc	
Adj William Harrison	MF 5	P	Injured	
Cpl Gouin	C 51	P	Injured	
Cpl René Altmayer	C 17	P	Injured	
MdL Georges Bouisson &	AL 221	P	Injured	
Cpl Nadal	AL 221	G	Injured	

10 April

Sgt Douchy &	N 38			
S/Lt Roedère	N 38	Fokker	FTL	Courmelois	–

Ran out of petrol	a. ???	Fokker	POW	Châlons-sur-Marne		–

a.   Uffz Roessler, FlAbt 22, POW, flying Fokker EIII N 196/16 which was captured intact according to prisoner interrogation.

Casualties

S/Lt Marcel Tiberghein	N 68	P	MIA	Probably by Ltn Walter Höhndorf, KekV (3).	
Sgt Jean Odoul &	N 68	P	WIA		
Capt Jean Dubois de la Villerabel	N 68	O	KIA		

11 April

S/Lt Laporte &	MF 45				1
S/Lt Oppermann	a. MF 45	Aviatik	X	Badonvillers	1

a.   Possibly Uffz Erich Kracht & Ltn Gustav Heinzelmann, FlAbt 103b, KIAs, at Badonvillers-Montigny.

Casualties:

Cpl André Bobba	N 57	P	MIA

12 – 14 April – No Claims – No Casualties

15 April – No Claims

Casualties:

Capt Georges CO			
Lecompte-Boinet &	MF 8	P	KIAcc
S/L Lehodey	MF 8	O	Injured

16 April – No Claims

Casualties:

Capt Alfred Auger CO	N 31	P	Injured
Lt Hirsch	C 46	O	Injured

17 – 20 April – No Claims – No Casualties

21 April – No Claims

Casualties:

S/Lt Lucien Hudellet	N 67	P	WIA

22 April – No Claims

Casualties:

MdL Charles Violette &	RGAé	P	KIAcc
Sol Brision	RGAé	G	KIAcc

23 April

S/Lt Tenant de La Tour	N 3	EA	X	Bois de Septsarges	2

Casualties:

Lt Emile Lacouture &	MF 62	P	KIAcc
S/Lt Julien Jaulin	MF 62	O	KIAcc

24 April

S/Lt J Navarre &	N 67				9
French artillery	???	LVG C	X	Vauquois	–
S/Lt J Navarre	N 67	3 Fokker E	P		–

Casualties:

MdL Georges Charreau	GDE	P	Injured
MdL Arthur Multin	GDE	P	Injured
S/Lt Henriot	GDE	O	Injured
MdL Brun	GDE	P	Injured
Cpl Boucher &	RGAé	P	Injured
Adj Carric	RGAé	O	Injured
MdL Guy de la Brosse &	MF 72	P	Injured
Lt Champetier de Ribes	MF 72	O	Injured

25 April

S/Lt Robert	N 57	Fokker	X	Hattonchâtel	1
S/Lt Nungesser	a. N 65	LVG C	X	N Verdun	6
S/Lt de Neufville	N 65	EA	X	Bois de Forges	1
S/Lt Nungesser	N 65	LVG C	FTL	Cuisy	–
Became lost	b. ???	Aviatik	POW	Rosières	–

a. Probably Vfw Helmuth Peters & Ltn Walter Kaehler, KG 5, KIAs, Verdun.
b. Ltn Paul-Friedrich Klüter & Ltn Otto von Rottenburg, POWs, Rosières.

Casualties:

Ens Jean Vassenot	Navy	P	KIA		
S/Lt Mathieu Tenant de La Tour	N 57	P	WIA		
S/Lt Ménard	C 46	O	WIA		
Adj Pierre Pauthe &	C 30	P	WIA		
S/Lt Robert L'huillier	C 30	O	WIA		
Lt Pierre Courtois-Suffit	MF 63	O	Injured	Landing accident.	

26 April

S/Lt Nungesser	N 65	LVG C	XF	Forêt de Spincourt	7
Lt Brun &	C 66				1
Sgt Laguesse	a. C 66	Fokker	POW	Hoéville	1
???	DCA	EA	XF	Bagatelle-Pavillon	–
???	DCA	EA	X	Fort de Vaux	–
Lt de Chivre	N 69	EA	FTL		–
Lt Dumas &	C 11				–
???	C 11	Fokker	FTL		–

a. Possibly Obltn Friedrich Gatterbauer, KIA, & Ltn Ludwig Haugg, WIA, FlAbt 6b, Lunéville. Gatterbauer DOW 28 April 1916.

Casualties:

Capt Maurice Mandinaud &	CO MF 36	P		Flying Maurice Farman type 37 N° 1186, shot down by a Zeppelin in Holland	
S/Lt Pierre Deramond	MF 36	O	FTL	where they were Interned, both escaped 12 September 1916.	
Lt Dellon	C 6	O	WIA		
MdL Jean Casale	N 23	P	WIA		
S/Lt Robert	C 27	P	Injured		
S/Lt Garret-Flandy	C 27	O	Injured		

27 April

Adj Dufaur de Gavardie &	N 12				2
Sol Carré	N 12	LVG	X		1
Sgt de Ridder &	C 42				1
Sol Steinbach	C 42	EA	X	Fromezey	1
??? &	N 62				?
Lt J Billon du Plan	N 62	EA	X	German lines	1
Sgt de Coucy &	C 43				1
???	C 43	Fokker	X	German lines	?
Lt Deullin &	N 3				–
Adj Houssemand	N 3	Aviatik C	P	Bethincourt	–

Casualties:

MdL Maurice Deitz	N 23	P	KIA	
MdL Louis Duchaussoy &	MF 59	P	OK	
Asp Félix Prat	MF 59	O	WIA	
Sgt Jean de Ridder &	C 42	P	OK	
Sol Yvan Steinbach &	C 42	G	WIA	
Lt Fabre	MF 35	P	WIA	

28 April

MdL Viallet &	C 53					
S/Lt Dumas	C 53	Fokker E	X	Bois de Caures		1
Sgt de Marolles &	N 67					1
Brig Vitalis	N 67	Fokker E	X	Froides	1555	1
Sgt Trelluyer &	MF 33					1
Lt Grange	MF 33	2 seater	X	French lines		1
Sgt Lagrande &	C 61					–
???	C 61	EA	FTL			–

Casualties:

S/Lt Jean Peretti	N 3	P	KIA	Verdun
S/Lt Philippe Léo	MF 7	P	KIA	Flak
S/Lt Lucien Sartori	MF 7	O	KIA	Flak
S/Lt Paul Fabre	C 53	P	WIA	
S/Lt Paul Bernard	MF 59	O	WIA	
QM Jacques Daniel	Navy	M	KIAcc	
Sgt Poulain	MF 72	P	Injured	

29 April

Lt Gastin		N 49	Bomber	P		–
Casualties:						
Asp Pierre Perdriat		C 11	O	WIA		
MdL Jean Charrier &		MF 16	P	WIA		
S/Lt Karl Favre		MF 16	O	OK		
MdL-Chef Edouard Merceron		GDE	P	KIAcc		

30 April

S/Lt de Guibert	a.	N 3	Fokker	X	Carrepuis	1030	1
S/Lt de Guibert	a.	N 3	Fokker	X	Roye	1035	1
Lt Deullin	b.	N 3	Fokker E	X	S Douaumont	1100	4
Sgt de Rochefort		N 26	2 seater	X	Middlekerke		2
Sgt Chaput		N 31	Fokker	X	Les Eparges	1745	3
??? &		C 53					–
Lt Dumas		C 53	EA	X			2
MdL Flachaire	c.	N 67	Aviatik CI	POW	Vienne-le-Château		1
Lt de Chivre		N 69	LVG	XF	S Verdun		1
???		DCA	EA	X	S Verdun		–
Sgt Massot		N 67	Bomber	P			–

a.   Possibly Ltn Otto Schmedes, FlAbt 32, KIA Combles, in the vicinity of these claims.
b.   Possibly Ltn Ernst Müller & Hptm Rainer-Eugen von Beck, KG 5, KIAs Verdun, about 10 km SSW Douaumont.
c.   N 817/15, two officers POWs.

Casualties:					
Cpl Antoine Chassin &		N 3	P	KIA	Probably by Ltn Röhr, KekE (1).
Adj Paul Hatin		N 3	O	KIA	
LV Jean Vasserot &	*	CAM	P	KIAcc	
QM René Caraman	*	CAM	M	KIAcc	Voisin VM 24.
Lt Gambier		V 212	?	Injured	
MdL Paul Suisse		N 37	P	Injured	DOW 1 May 1916.
* Dunkerque.*					

Date unknown in April 1916:

Lt Lecomte &	CO	C 42				1
Sol Maniquet		C 42	Fokker	POW		1
Casualties:						
S/Lt Clément Varnet		MF 29	P	KIA		

1 May

Sgt Buis &		C 27				1
Adj Travers		C 27	EA	X	N Douaumont	1
S/Lt Auger &		MF 20				1
Lt Richelieu		MF 20	EA	X		1
Casualties:						
S/Lt Jean Cournot		MF 1	O	WIA		
Lt Armand Richelieu		MF 20	O	WIA	DOW	
Sol Joseph Lansade		N 38	G	WIA		
Sgt Edmond Roume		CRP	P	KIAcc		
Adj Abdon Adam		N 48	P	Injured		

2 May

Lt de Chivre	a.	N 69	EA	X	N Douaumont	2
Lt Dumas &		C 11				2
???		C 11	Aviatik C	X	German lines	?

a.   Probably Gefr Walter Oswald & Ltn Karl Schunk, FlAbt 209 (A), KIAs at Douaumont.

Casualties:				
Cpl Bourley		N 15	P	KIA
Capt Louis Gonnet-Thomas	CO	N 65	P	KIAcc

3 May

Sgt Delaruelle		N 49	EA	FTL
Casualties:				
Lt Hubert Jahard &		GDE	P	KIAcc
Sol Petex		GDE	G	KIAcc

4 May

Sgt Coudouret	N 57	LVG C	X	Hermeville	1
Sgt Pons &	MF 221				1
S/Lt Guérin	MF 221	Fokker	X	Champneuville	1
Lt Heurtaux	N 3	EA	P		–
Lt Jaille	N 49	Ea	P		–

Casualties:

Adj Comier &	VB 104	P	MIA		
Sol Thery	VB 104	G	MIA		
Sgt Marcel Delaruelle	N 49	P	WIA		

5 May – No Claims

Casualties:

Lt André Landre	C 18	O	KIA	
Capt Honoré Baillardel				
de Lareinty-Tholozan CO	N 73	P	KIAcc	
Lt Charles Orine	MF 32		Injured	
Sgt Raymond Leleu &	MF 2	P	Injured	
Sol Las	MF 2	G	Injured	
Adj Albert Foubert	58 Cie d'Aérostiers			All these balloons broke loose during
		O	Injured	violent wind storms and drifted
				towards the German lines.
S/Lt José Garcia-Calderon				
(Peruvian)	30° Cie d'Aérostiers			
		O	Killed	Braban on the Meuse.
Sgt-Maj Monneron	43° Cie d'Aérostiers			
		O	MIA	
MdL André &	24° Cie d'vAérostiers			
MdL J L Salats		O	Killed	Mézières (Somme)
Cpl Debregeas	63° Cie d'Aérostiers			
		O	Injured	
Sgt Dubrulle	26° Cie d'Aérostiers			
		O	Injured	
MdL Saint-Etienne	72° Cie d'Aérostiers			
		O	Injured	
Adj Amiot &	38° Cie d'Aérostiers		OK	
Adj G Contentin		O	Killed	Somme-Suippes
MdL Jean Celle	21° Cie d'Aérostiers			This balloon came down inside
		O	POW	the German lines and was destroyed
				by Artillery and machine gun fire.
S/Lt Jean Bassetti	51° Cie d'Aérostiers			His basket detached from
		O	Killed	the balloon and dropped over
				1,000 metres at Dannemarie.
Lt Teillhard	23° Cie d'Aérostiers			
		O	OK	
Lt de Champeaux &	56° Cie d'Aérostiers			Came down inside German lines.
Asp Girard		O	POWs	
Sgt Georges Spiess	53° Cie d'Aérostiers			At Bras, on the Meuse.
		O	Killed	

6 May – No Claims – No Casualties

7 May

Sgt Chainat	N 3	LVG C	P	Ornes	–
S/Lt Boillot	N 65	Albatros	FTL	S Azannes	–

Casualties: None

8 May – No Claims

Casualties:

S/Lt Augustin Laporte &	MF 45	P	KIAcc
Lt Henri Obellaine	MF 45	O	KIAcc

9 May – No Claims

Casualties:

Sgt Revoil &	MF 70	P	KIAcc		
S/Lt Frantz	MF 70	O	KIAcc		

10 May

Sgt Mengelle &	MF 1				1
Lt Bazin	MF 1	Fokker	X		1
Capt de Marancour & CO	N 69				–
Patrol	N 69	Fokker E	FTL	Maucourt	–

Casualties:

Lt Paul Rouch	MF 33	O	Injured	In landing accident.	

11 May – No Claims

Casualties:

Cdt de Tricornot de Rose	V° Armée	P	KIAcc	
S/Lt Soulle	GDE	O	KIAcc	

12 May

Cdt du Peuty,	N 69				1
Lt de Chivre &	N 69				3
Lt Pelletier Doisy	N 12	Fokker	X	Vaux	2

Casualties:

MdL Jean Bozon-Veduraz	C 11	P	Injured	
MdL Auguste Hulin	C 30	P	POW	Josef Jakobs Fokkerstafel West (1).

13 May – No Claims

Casualties:

Lt L.A.N. Lucas	N 49	P	WIA

14 – 15 May – No Claims – No Casualties

16 May

Cpl Hentsch	a.	N 15	EA	X	N Vic-sur-Aisne	1
Cpl Grés &		C 64				–
Sol Vitecocq		C 64	EA	FTL		–

a. Possibly Ltn Alfons Huber & Ltn Karl Scheffer, FlAbt 11, KIAs, Blérancourt.

Casualties:

Sgt Adrien Mion &	C 27	P	OK	
Capt Alfred Ponroy	C 27	O	WIA	
S/Lt Crosnier	AL 211	O	WIA	
S/Lt Gabriel Foucault &	N 3	P	KIAcc	
Sol Paul Soreau	N 3	G	KIAcc	

17 May

Lt Pelletier Doisy		N 12	Fokker E	X	Bezonvaux	3
Cpl Funck-Bretano &		N 73				1
Cpl Sabatier		N 73	Aviatik C	X	Chatas	1
???	a.	???	2 seater	X	Ste Menehould	–
Lt Richard		N 3	EA	P		–
Lt J de Boutiny		N 23	Fokker	FTL	Mangiennes	1
Lt Bastien		N 57	Fokker	FTL		–

a. Crew POWs.

Casualties:

MdL Frédéric Waddington	VC 116	P	MIA
Sol Joseph Carbucia	VC 116	G	MIA
Sol de Gombert	C	G	Injured

18 May

Sgt Ronserail &	C 34				1
Sol Montels	C 34	EA	XF	NW Mühlhausen	1
Cpl Rockwell	N 124	LVG	XF	Thann	1
S/Lt J Navarre	N 67	EA	P	Bolante	–

Casualties:

MdL Hubert Cagninacci &	C 56	P	KIA	Probably by Obltn Oswald
S/Lt Louis Vivien	C 56	O	KIA	Boelcke, FlAbt 62 (16).
MdL Georges Suchet	MF 70	P	Injured	

19 May

Sgt Barnay	a.	N 37	Rumpler CI	POW	NE Isettes	2
S/Lt Nungesser	b.	N 65	LVG C	X	Bois des Forges	8
S/Lt Navarre	c.	N 67	Aviatik C	POW	Chattancourt	0600 10
Adj Acher		N 57	EA	X	Ville-devant-Chaumont	1

a. Rumpler CI 439/15, POWs.
b. Possibly Uffz Friedrich Nottebohm, FL Truppe, KIA Pierreville Wald.
c. First French pilot to attain ten victories.

Casualties:

S/Lt Georges Boillot	CO	N 65	P	KIA
S/Lt Jean Mélion		C 6	O	KIA
S/Lt Raymond Viraut &		MF 63	P	MIA
S/Lt Henri Dufort		MF 63	O	MIA
Brig Leguet		GDE	P	Injured

20 May

???	DCA	EA	X	Verdun	–
Adj Ribière &	MF 32				–
Lt Oudin	MF 32	Fokker	P		–
Cpl Hentsch	N 15	LVG	X	German lines	2
Cpl Martenot de Cordoux	C 28				1
& Sol de Martin	a. C 28	Fokker	FTL	Nr Forêt de Bézange	1
S/Lt de Toulouse &	C 47				–
???	C 47	EA	FTL		–

a. Destroyed by French artillery.

Casualties:

Lt Gilles de Chivre	N 69	P	KIA	
S/Lt Jean de Subervie	N 69	P	KIA	
S/Lt Bernard de Curel	MF 72	P	KIA	Avocourt, possibly by Obltn Oswald Boelcke, FlAbt 62, unconfirmed.
MdL Léon Beauchamps &	N 68	P	POW	Probably by Ltn Kurt Wintgens,
S/Lt Debacker	N 68	O	KIA	FlAbt 6 (4).
Soldat Guilianc	MF 123	M	Killed	Killed during an enemy
Soldat Latre	MF 123	M	Killed	bombardment of the MF 123 airfield.
Soldat Bouteillier	MF 123	M	Killed	
Adj Léon Acher	N 57	P	WIA	
Adj Roger Ribière &	MF 32	P	OK	
Lt Henri Oudin	MF 32	O	WIA	III° Armée
Asp Pierre Perdriat	C 11	O	WIA	Flak
Cpl André Martenot de Cordoux &	C 28	P	WIA	
Sol Maurice Martin	C 28	G	OK	

21 May

Sgt Chainat		N 3	2 seater	X	Chilly	0435 3
Lt Dumas		N 57	Aviatik	X	Les Éparges	2
S/Lt Navarre		N 67	2 seater	X	Avocourt	11
S/Lt Raty	a.	N 95/CRP	2 seater	X	Fontenoy	1

a. KIAs.

Casualties:

Cpl Gaston Mireau &	AL 209	P	KIA	
Lt Althusser	AL 209	O	KIA	III° Armée.
Sgt Noël	C 47	P	KIA	Flak, Bois de Loges.
Brig Vincent &	C 42	P	KIA	Wintgens (5)
S/Lt René Gauthier	C 42	O	KIA	
Adj Henri Brion	N 65	P	WIA	Possibly by Hptm Oswald Boelcke
Sgt Georges Kirsch	N 65	P	WIA	FlAbt 62, (17 & 18).
Sgt Pierre Alexandre	C 4	P	Injured	
MdL Maxime Gaullier	C 11	P	Injured	
Sgt Oliver Schneider &	C 43	P	POW	
S/Lt Danne	C 43	O	KIA	

22 May

Capt Robert de Beauchamp	CO	N 23	Balloon	XF	Verdun	3
Sgt de Rochefort &		N 26				3
Capt Perrin		N 26	LVG C	X	Wizzele	1145 2

Lt Gastin	a.	N 49	Aviatik	X	Sentheim	1
S/Lt Chaput		N 57	Balloon	XF	Verdun	4
Lt Dubois de Gennes		N 57	Balloon	XF	Verdun	1
Capt Féquant	CO	N 65	LVG	X	Beaumont	2
Adj Réservat		N 65	Balloon	XF	Verdun	1
S/Lt Nungesser		N 65	Balloon	XF	Verdun	9
Adj Le Roy	b.	N 65	Aviatik	X	Flabas	1
Lt Weiss &		F 71				1
Cpl du Bois d'Aische		F 71	Albatros	X	Varninay	1
Cpl Funck-Bretano		N 73	Aviatik	X	Linge	2
Adj Guiguet	c.	N 95/CRP	Balloon	XF	Sivry	1
Sgt B Hall		N 124	Aviatik C	X	Malancourt	1
Sgt Schneider &		C 43				1
S/Lt Danne		C 43	EA	X		1
S/Lt Guynemer		N 3	2 seater	P	Noyon	–

a.   Probably Gefr George Schöpf & Ltn Ludwig Frhr von Türcke, FlAbt (A) 206, KIAs,Gewenheim.
b.   Probably Ltn Georg Meineke, KIA, Flabas.
c.   Possibly Obltn Friedrich von Zanthier, BO, FLA 12, KIA, Sivry.

Casualties:

Adj Henri Réservat	N 65	P	POW	Nieuport XVI N° 959.
Lt Julien Pranville	MF 71	O	WIA	
Lt Jacques Caffet &	MF 52	P	WIA	
Lt Georges Lombard	MF 52	O	OK	
Cpl Dubuffe	RGAé	P	Injured	
S/Lt Henri Guérin	MF 221	O	Injured	Landing accident.

23 May – No Claims
Casualties:

Lt Robbe	MF 221	P	Injured

24 May

S/Lt Thaw	N 124	Fokker E	X	N Vaux	1
Adj Tarascon	N 3	EA	P		–
Patrol	N 124	2 EA	FTL	Etain	–

Casualties:

Lt Jean Robert	N 57	P	MIA	II° Armée
Lt Jean Roux &	MF 8	P	MIA	By Baldamus FA20(2).
S/Lt Masson	MF 8	O	MIA	
Lt Charles Dupuy	N 48	P	WIA	Lunéville
S/Lt William Thaw	N 124	P	WIA	II° Armée
Cpl Kiffin Rockwell	N 124	P	WIA	II° Armée
CPL Victor Chapman	N 124	P	WIA	
S/Lt Petit	MF 5	P	Injured	

25 May – No Claims
Casualties:

MdL Stephane Vernay &	MF 14	P	KIAcc
Lt Olivier	MF 14	O	KIAcc

26 May – No Claims – No Casualties

27 May – No Claims
Casualties

Sgt Jacques Desurmont	MF 36	P	KIAcc
MdL Félicien Borie	CRP	P	KIAcc

28 May

Adj Lebeau		N 12	EA	X	Sainterne	1
Sgt Rodde &		MF 55				1
Lt Bos		MF 55	Fokker E	X	Bourgogne-Fresnes	1
S/Lt Delorme &		C 56				1
Lt Barthe		C 56	Fokker	XF	German lines	1
???	a.	DCA	EA	X	N Avocourt	–
???		DCA	EA	X	Forges	–

a.   Possibly Hptm Georg Arntzen, WIA/DOW 2 June 1916 & Obltn Kurt von der Osten, WIA/DOW 2 June 1918, KG4/KSt 21, KIAs Morthomme, near Verdun.

Casualties:

MdL Rose	GDE	P	KIAcc
QM Jacques Daniels	Navy	P	KIAcc

29 May

Adj Lenoir &	N 23				–
Sgt Casale	N 23	EA	FTL	Brieulles	–

Casualties: None

---

30 – 31 May – No Claims – No Casualties

Dates unknown during May 1916:

Adj Jullien de Courcelles	N 65	EA	X		1
Adj Jullien de Courcelles	N 65	EA	P		–

Sgt Adrien Mion, C 27, was cited on 27 May 1916, for having forced two enemy aircraft to land during 14 aerial combats, but could be prior to May 1916.

Casualties:

Sgt Georges Spiess	53° Cie d'Aérostiers XF		
		O	KIA

---

1 June

Adj Touvet,		N 31				1
Adj Duchenois &		MF 44				1
Sol Balthazar	a.	MF 44	LVG C	POW	S Bernécourt-Royauneix	1
Lt Lafay &		C 53				1
Lt Perrault &		C 53				1
Sgt Marquisan &		C 53				1
Lt Crepin		C 53	Fokker	X	Bouconville	1
S/Lt Pelletier Doisy		N 69	EA	FTL	Etain	–
Lt Perrault		???	EA	FTL		–

a.   LVG C.II N° 2160/15, probably Uffz Arnold Walter and Ltn Schulze-Dellwig, KG 1, POWs, flying a LVG & FTL at Bernecourt near Royauneix, Ière Armée Prisoner Interrogation Report.

Casualties:

S/Lt André Fernet &	C 42	P	MIA	Caudron N 2474, probably
Lt Brien	C 42	O	MIA	by Ltn Walter Hühndorf, KeKV, (4).
S/Lt Marcel Merlant	N 67	O	WIA	
MdL Félix de Saint Martin &	MF 203	P	WIA	
S/Lt Robert Viaria de Lesegno	MF 203	O	OK	

---

2 June – No Claims

Casualties:

Sgt Guy Dussumier-Latour				Possibly by Ltn Walter
&	C 4	P	MIA	Höhndorf (4) KeKV, West
S/Lt Henri Thévenin	C 4	O	MIA	of Möchingen.
Sol Edmond Gloux	N 31	G	KIA	
Cpl Jules Chabaud &	C 51	P	KIAcc	
S/Lt Marcel Langevin	C 51	O	KIAcc	
S/Lt Aristide Quennehen	???	P	KIAcc	
MdL Adrien Delhummeau	N 23	P	Injured	
MdL Bertrand	MF 35	P	Injured	

---

3 June – No Claims

Casualties:

Sgt Gustave Lafosse	C 6	P	WIA	
Capt Boussion	C 46	O	Injured	
Lt Poincon de Villeramond		Buc	P	KIAcc	Collided with another a/c.

---

4 June

Adj Ortoli	a.	N 31	LVG C	X	Sanzey/Mesnil-les-Toul	3
Patrol		N 69	EA	FTL	Bois des Forges	–

a.   Probably Uffz Egger & Ltn Fieser, FlAbt 71, KG1, POWs, Ière Armée Prisoner Interrogation Report.

Casualties:

Cpl Georges Dubois &	MF 228	P	WIA
S/Lt Alexandre	MF 228	O	KIA
Sgt Georges Kirsch	N 65	P	WIA
Capt Paul Cottrets	RGAé	P	KIAcc

Adj Smaragd Jullien de Courcelles	N 65	P	Injured			

5 June – No Claims
Casualties:

S/Lt Richard	C 6	O	WIA/DOW			

6 – 7 June – No Claims – No Casualties

8 June

Sgt Leblond &	C 89					–
???	C 89	Fokker	FTL			–

Casualties: None

9 June

S/Lt Lis	N 15	EA	X			3
Patrol	N 65	EA	FTL	Dieppe		–

Casualties:

QM Henri Mercier &	* CAM	P	POW	Donnet-Denhaut 150 HP code 5,		
QM Le Prévost	* CAM	O	POW	between Ostende & Zeebrugge.		

10 June – No Claims
Casualties:

MdL Jean Cosse &	MF 29	P	KIAcc	Collision.		
Cpl Paul Chanteclair	MF 29	G	KIAcc	Collision.		
Lt Williams	(RFC)	P	KIAcc	Collision.		
Sol Beaucourt	MF 29	G	KIAcc	Collision.		
Adj Edmond Baldit &	MF 72	P	Injured			
Lt André Locquin	MF 72	O	Injured	Crashed while landing.		

11 June – No Claims
Casualties:

Cpl Rodolphe Filaines	MF 44	P	KIAcc			
Sol Chaux	MF 44	G	Injured			

12 – 13 June– No Claims – No Casualties

14 June – No Claims
Casualties:

S/Lt Honoré de Bonald	N 69	P	WIA			

15 June

S/Lt Roty	CRP	EA	X	Fontenoy		1

Casualties: None

16 June

Sgt Chainat	N 3	EA	P			–

Casualties:

Sgt André Chainat	N 3	P	WIA			
Brig Jules Briffaut	MF 206	O	WIA			
Lt Fernand Herran	MF 58	P	KIAcc			
Lt Philippe Rey	N 49	P	Injured			
Sgt Robert Balland	C 21	P	Injured			

17 June

Adj Sayaret	N 57	2 seater	X	Malancourt		2
S/Lt Navarre &	N 67					12
S/Lt Pelletier Doisy	N 69	2 seater	X	Samogneux	0600	4
Sgt Vigouroux &	N 68					1
S/Lt Burgue	N 68	Fokker	X	E Bezanges		1
Adj Lenoir	N 23	LVG C	XF	Septsarges		4
S/Lt Chaput	N 57	EA	FTL	Fresnes		–
Cpl Chapman	N 124	EA	FTL	Béthincourt		–

Casualties:

Lt Raymond Brunel &	MF 70	P	KIA	Farman, probably by Ltn Kurt
S/Lt Pierre Hermand	MF 70	O	KIA	Wintgens, FlAbt 6, (6).
MdL Pierre Noël &	C 47	P	WIA/DOW	III° Armée.
S/Lt Henri Guizol	C 47	O	KIA	Shot down by Flak.
S/Lt Jean Navarre	N 67	P	WIA	One of these two probably by Ltn
Sgt Victor Chapman	N 124	P	WIA	Walter Höhndorf, KeKV, (5).
Cpl J.B. Dessarce	BM 118	P	KIAcc	
Sgt Leroux	MF 5	G	KIAcc	
Lt Marcel Falouet	C 43	P	KIAcc	
Lt Marcel Pamart	C 43	P	KIAcc	
Lt Jean Derode	N 67	P	Injured	
Sgt Joseph Borde &	N 68	P	Injured	
Sol Blaine	N 68	G	Injured	

18 June

S/Lt Delorme &	C 56				2
Sol Jobelin	C 56	Fokker	X	Amifontaine	1
S/Lt Chaput	N 57	EA	P		–

Casualties:

Sol Charles Jobelin	C 56	G	KIA	
Cpl Clyde Balsley	N 124	P	WIA	
Sgt Charles Mengelle-Touya	MF 1	P	KIAcc	
Sgt Ange Rusterucci	MF 204	P	KIAcc	
S/Lt Olivier	MF 204	O	KIAcc	
Lt Gabet	C 46	O	Injured	

19 June

S/Lt Chaput	N 57	EA	X	Varvinay	5

Casualties:

Mat Joseph Carbuccia	* CAM	M	MIA	North Sea
Sgt Paul Houillon	MF 55	P	WIA	
* Dunkerque.				

20 June – No Claims

Casualties:

S/Lt Menneret &	BM 119	P	MIA	
S/Lt Zirnheld	BM 119	O	MIA	Bréguet-Michelin N° 145
MdL Pierre d'Hespel &	BM 118	P	MIA	
Sol Perrin	BM 118	G	MIA	Bréguet-Michelin N° 140
S/Lt Anselme Marchal	???	P	POW	Departed Nancy at 21h00 to drop leaflets on Berlin, had motor trouble and FTL at Chalm (Poland) at 08h30 on 21 June, escaped 18 February 1918.
Capt Pierre de Lajudie	MF 63	P	KIA	Bombardment of airfield.
Sgt Lucien Arnaud	VII° Armée		P	Injured

21 June

S/Lt Chaput	a.	N 57	2 seater	XF	NE St Mihiel	6
S/Lt Chaput	b.	N 57	Rumpler C	X	Ft de Génicourt	7

a. Possibly Ltn Erich Deliser, KIA, & Sgt Alois Hosp, FlAbt 3b, WIA/DOW 22 June 1916, S of Verdun.
b. Possibly Obltn Hans Bailer & Hptm Günther von Detten, KG4/KSt22, KIAs, Génicourt.

Casualties:

Lt Jean Chabuel &	MF 22	P	WIA	Flak
Lt René Bouisseau	MF 22	O	KIA	Flak, II° Armée
Lt Maurice Barthe	C 11	P	WIA	
MdL Jean Bernajuzan	C 89	P	WIA	
MdL Philippe Grellou	GDE	P	KIAcc	
Sgt Pierre Villemin	BM 119	P	Injured	
Sgt André Condeau &	BM 118	P	Injured	
MdL Léonce Mariani	BM 118	B	Injured	
Sgt Léon Flameng	MF 25	P	Injured	
Lt Poirot	C 104	O	Injured	DOW 7 July 1916.

22 June

S/Lt Guynemer &		N 3					9
Sgt Chainat	a.	N 3	LVG C	XF	Vrély	1000	4

Adj Lenoir		N 23	EA	X	Douaumont-Etain	2000	5
S/Lt Nungesser	b.	N 65	Aviatik C	X	Lamorville		10
S/Lt Nungesser	b.	N 65	Aviatik C	X	Lamorville		11
???		DCA	EA	X	Einville		–
Capt Happe &	CO	GB 4					1
Cpl Pautrat		GB 4	Fokker	X	Mulheim		1
Adj Laplace &		N 65					–
Capt Féquant	CO	N 65	EA	FTL			–

a.　　Probably Ltn Erwin Bredow & Ltn Peter Tülff von Tscheppe und Weidenbach, FlAbt 42, KIAs near Parroy.
b.　　One possibly OfStv Fritz Müller & Ltn Walter von der Ohe, FlAbt 59, KIAs Lihons, in the vicinity of Lamorville.

Casualties:

Cpl Léon Petit &	N 37	P	MIA	Nieuport XII, N° 1221, probably
Lt Edmond Enos	N 37	O	MIA	by Ltn Ernst Hess, FSC, (2).
Sgt René Seitz &	C 66	P	POW	
S/Lt Léopold Mirabail	C 66	O	POW	Caudron N° 1337.
Cpl Pierre Fournet &	C 66	P	POW	
Capt Louis Faye	GB 2	O	POW	Caudron N° 2470.
MdL Jacques Bousquet &	C 66	P	KIA	
Cpl de Maualeon	C 66	B	KIA	Caudron N° 2184.
Sgt Marc Auzanneau &	MF 29	P	MIA	Farman F 43, possibly by
Sol Schmidt	MF 29	B	MIA	Ltn Kurt Haber, FlAbt 6, (3).
Lt Marcel Brice-Bretocq	MF 29		WIA	
S/Lt Edouard Goldschmidt &	C 34	P	WIA	
S/Lt Grandperrin	C 34	O	WIA	FTL in French lines.
QM Frédéric Lemoine	PilSch	P	KIAcc	St Raphaël.
Sgt Coulonge	GDE	P	Injured	
Cpl André Duhart	GDE	P	Injured	
S/Lt Fabert	GDE	P	Injured	
S/Lt Charles Nungesser	N 65	P	Injured	

23 June

Adj Semelin &	MF 58				1
S/Lt Gallon	MF 58	Fokker	X	Blamont (see Casualties).	1
Adj Bucquet	N 3	EA	P		–

Casualties:

Adj Jacques Semelin &	MF 58	P	MIA	Collided with enemy aircraft
S/Lt Théophile Gallon	MF 58	O	MIA	Possibly Gefr Hermann Keller, FlAbt 32.
MdL Martin	MF 29	P	MIA	Solo reconnaissance.
Sgt Victor Chapman	N 124	P	KIA	Nieuport XVI N° 1334, possibly by Ltn Kurt Wintgens, FlAbt 6, (7).
Mat Alex Merienne	GDE	G	KIAcc	Flying school at Avord.
Lt Maurice Nogues	VB 107	P	Injured	
Sgt Dieudonne Bart &	C 202	P	Injured	
Sol Maitre	C 202	G	Injured	
Sgt Casenove	GDE	P	Injured	
MdL Roger Poumet	GDE	P	Injured	

24 June – No Claims

Casualties:

S/Lt Louis Duplessis	C 11	P	Injured
MdL Benjamin de Tascher	C 30	P	Injured
Sgt Jean Cherel	C 30	P	Injured

25 June

S/Lt Havet	N 77	EA	X	German lines	1

Casualties:

Cpl Ernest Bresch &	C 9	P	KIA	Caudron N° 1202, probably by Ltn
S/Lt Joseph Ransom	C 9	O	KIA	Walter Höhndorf, KeKV, (7).
Sgt Théophile Funck-Bretano	N 73	P	KIA	
Asp Capgras	GDE	O	Injured	
Capt Simian	MF 55	O	Injured	

26 June

S/Lt Deullin	N 3	Balloon	XF	Péronne	0900	3
Adj Jailler	N 15	Balloon	XF	Appilly	0833	4

Sgt Hentsch	N 15	Balloon	XF	St Aubin	0854	3
Adj de Guibert	N 62	Balloon	XF			3
Adj de Guibert	N 62	EA	FTL			–

Casualties:

Lt Marcel Brice-Bretocq	MF 29	P	WIA			
Cpl Cayre	MF 29	G	WIA			
S/Lt Georges Negre	GDE	P	Injured			
Sol Brech &	??	P	KIA			
S/Lt Ranson	??	O	KIA			

---

27 June – No Claims – No Casualties

---

28 June – No Claims
Casualties:

S/Lt Georges Tourdes &	MF 55	P	KIA	Flak
Lt Robert Saint-Martin	MF 55	O	KIA	Flak
Cpl Henri Jacque	C 47	P	KIAcc	III° Armée.

---

29 June – No Claims – No Casualties

---

30 June

| S/Lt de La Brunetière | N 68 | Fokker | X | Forêt de Bezange | 1 |

Casualties:

Lt François Mouronval	N 62	P	MIA	Nieuport XI N° 1159.
Sgt Pierre Lamielle &	MF 7	P	MIA	Flak
Lt Amédée Pluven	MF 7	O	MIA	Flak
S/Lt Gaëtan de la Brunetière	N 68	P	WIA	
Cpl Jean Duminy	C 106	P	KIAcc	
MdL Jean Bigeard	GDE	P	Injured	
Cpl Marcel Broussard	C 4	P	Injured	

---

1 July

The Battle of the Somme starts in the area between Bapaume and Chaulnes.

Lt Senart &		N 12					1
Sgt Dufaur de Gavardie		N 12	Fokker	X	Anizy		3
Sgt Casale		N 23	Balloon	XF	Rt Bank of Meuse		1
MdL Macquart de Terline		N 38	Aviatik	POW	Amagne-Lucquy		1
Lt Dubois de Gennes		N 57	Balloon	XF	Rt Bank of Meuse, by FA 209		2
Sgt Bloch		N 62	Balloon	XF	,,		1
Sgt Bloch		N 62	Balloon	XF	,,		2
Lt Bonneau		N 65	Balloon	XF			2
MdL Macquart de Terline		N 38	Fokker	P			–
MdL F Raty		N 38	Aviatik	P			–
Adj Dorme	a.	N 3	2 fuselage	FTL	Péronne-Ham	1420	–

a.   Possibly Ltn Georg Kullmann (O), FlAbt (A) 225, KIA Matigny, between Ham and Péronne.

Casualties:

Sgt Joseph Halmans &	F 20	P	KIA	
Lt Albert Pauchon	F 20	O	KIA	II° Armée
MdL Henri de Kylspotter &	C 207	P	KIA	
Lt Sains	C 207	O	OK	Frise
Lt André Dubois de Gennes	N 57	P	POW	Nieuport N° 1182
S/Lt Guilleron	C 106	O	MIA	Wintgens KG1(6)
Sgt Eugène Lesire &	C 106	P	MIA	
Sol Coat	C 106	G	MIA	Caudron N° 2235.
Adj Joseph Guiguet	N 3	P	WIA	
MdL Maurice Tartaux	C 47	P	WIA	
S/Lt Paul Gama	C 47	O	WIA	
Sgt René Pillot	C 43	P	WIA	
Sgt Dumont	Parc 101	M	KIA	Artillery barrage.

---

2 July

Sgt Chainat		N 3	2 fuselage	X	Péronne	1045	5
Sgt Chainat		N 3	Balloon	XF	Brie	1630	6
Sgt Garet	a.	N 23	Fokker	X	Vaux – collision.		1
Lt Dumas		N 57	Fokker	P			–

MdL Boniface &	C 6					–
Lt Dellon	C 6	Scout	P	German lines		–
MdL de Bonnefoy	N 65	EA	X	Samogneux		1

a.   Probably Ltn Werner Neuhaus (P), FlAbt (A) 203, KIA Damloup-Verdun, about 2 km E Vaux.

Casualties:

Sgt Marcel Garet	N 23	P	KIA	Collided with EA, probably Ltn Werner Neuhaus, FlAbt (A) 203.	
MdL André Seigneurie	N 103	P	MIA	Probably by Obltn Ernst Frhr von Althaus, KeKV (7).	
Sgt Lucien Laroque &	C 64	P	WIA		
Sol Charles Quette	C 64	O	OK		
Sgt Chauleur	???	P	KIAcc		
Lt Pierre Pardieu &	C 56	P	Injured		
Sgt Piron	C 56	G	Injured		
MdL André Mendel &	MF 63	P	OK		
S/Lt Jacques de Coye de Castelet	MF 63	O	Injured		
Sgt Clément Voltz	27° Cie d'Aérostiers		XF	II° Armée (see 15 July 1916)	
		O	WIA		

3 July

Capt de Sieyes	CO	N 26	Balloon	XF	1400	1
Sgt Bloch		N 62	Balloon	XF	N Frise	3
Adj Dorme		N 3	LVG C	P		–
Adj Dorme		N 3	Fokker	P		–

Casualties:

Capt Jacques de Sieyes de Veynes	CO	N 26	P	POW	Departed at 13h35, Nieuport XI N° 1135.
Sgt Charles Hardoin &		C 30	P	KIA	
Sgt L.M. Schwander		C 30	G	WIA	Caudron, Juvincourt
S/Lt François Ciccoli &		C 11	P	WIA/POW	Caudron, possibly by Ltn
Lt Eugène Angot		C 11	O	WIA/POW	Richard (1), Kek E. Angot escaped in August 1918.
Sgt Marcel Bloch		N 62	P	WIA	During balloon attack.
Sol Loison		GDE	G	KIAcc	
Sol Dufresne		N 3	G	Injured	
MdL Maurice Tartaux		C 47	P	Injured	DOW 14 July 1916.

4 July – No Claims – No Casualties

5 July – No Claims
Casualties:

Cpl Martin Pelhat	N 26	P	POW	Nieuport

6 July

Sgt Macquart de Terline	N 38	LVG C	X	Mezières	2
Sgt Roger &	C 64				1
Sgt Ramponi	C 64	Fokker	X	Leffincourt	1

Casualties:

S/Lt Jean Raty	N 38	P	WIA/POW	Nieuport XI N° 1324, by Ltn Kurt Student, AOK 3, (1).
Cpl Riess &	C 206	P	MIA	
S/Lt Gilleron	C 206	O	MIA	
Lt Louis Arbitre	C 51	O	WIA	
MdL Joseph Cabirol &	F 52	P	OK	
MdL Christian	F 52	O	WIA	
Sol Prince	BM 117	G	Injured	
Adj Clément Engerer	C 6	P	Injured	
MdL Charles Kaciterlin	BM 119	P	Injured	

7 July – No Claims
Casualties:

Sgt Daniel Fusier &	F 35	P	Injured	
S/Lt Robert Grohin	F 35	O	Injured	

8 July – No Claims
Casualties:

Lt Jean Riché	C 74	O	WIA			
Sgt Léon Malbec	BM 117	P	KIAcc			
Adj François Battesti &	C 10	P	Injured			
S/Lt Clément	C 10	O	Injured			
S/Lt Emile Deviterne	N 38	O	WIA			

9 July

Adj Dorme	N 3	LVG C	X	Péronne	0910	1
S/Lt de La Tour	N 3	EA	X	Péronne	2005	3
Lt Heurtaux	N 3	LVG C	X	Bertincourt	0900	1
Cpl J Sauvage	N 65	EA	X	Amiens		1
???	???	Fokker	X	Mariakerke		–
Adj Dorme	N 3	LVG C	P			–
Adj Lemaire	N 3	EA	P			–

Casualties:

S/Lt André Baras	C 21	P	WIA	
Sgt Marcel Joannes	F 211	P	Injured	
Adj M Mallet	55° Cie d'Aérostiers,	XF		Probably by Ltn Otto Parschau, FlAbt 32
		O	KIA	(8), or Ltn Hans Müller, KekA, (2).

10 July

Sgt Tsu	N 37	EA	X	German lines	1
Lt Deullin	N 3	EA	P		–

Casualties:

Lt Henri Blanchon &	C 51	P	KIA	
S/Lt Plasse	C 51	O	KIA	
Adj Georges Cattaert &	VC 110	P	OK	
MdL Le Gall	VC 110	G	WIA	Flak
Lt Joseph Desjardins	???	O	WIA	
Cpl Jeon Millet	F 25	P	Injured	
Brig Jean Labadie	C 28	P	Injured	
MdL Nicolas Marfaing	C 202	P	Injured	
Cpl Auguste Pouchelle	N 26	P	OK	Shot down in flames inside French lines, but he was not harmed.
???	85° Cie d'Aérostiers			Attacked, not flamed, Soissons area.
		O	OK	

11 July

Sgt Chainat	N 3	EA	XF	Combles		7
Lt Deullin	N 3	LVG C	X	Saint Christ	2010	5
Lt de Sevin	N 12	EA	X	Monthenault		1
Lt Bastien	N 57	Balloon	XF	S Etain		1
S/Lt Guynemer	N 3	LVG	P	Péronne		–
Lt Lemaire	N 3	EA	P			–
Adj Dorme	N 3	EA	P			–

Casualties:

Sgt Emile Bouderie	N 38	P	MIA	Nieuport N° 1355.
MdL Emile Esnault &	F 44	P	MIA	Flak
S/Lt Albert Laprouche	F 44	O	MIA	Flak
MdL Amaury de Saint-Pol	C 64	P	KIA	
Sol Gabriel Farigoul	C 64	G	KIA	Caudron N° 1392
Capt Henri Horment CO	N 62	P	WIA	
Cpl Robert Sabatier	N 23	P	WIA	Nieuport
MdL Robard &	F 63	P	Injured	
Asp Daine	F 63	O	Injured	
S/Lt Xavier de La Rochebrochard	C 6	O		

12 July

Sgt de Rochefort	N 26	LVG C	X	Combles	0830	4
Sgt Barra &	N 26					–
Sgt de Rochefort	N 26	LVG C	P	E Maurepas		–

Casualties:

S/Lt Aubril	F 205	O	WIA

Sgt Marcel Gilbert &		F 8	P	KIAcc			
Sol Nivart		F 8	G	KIAcc			
Sgt Amans		GDE	G	Injured			
Sol Frugier		GDE	G	Injured			
Sgt Hamond		GDE	G	Injured			

13 July – No Claims
Casualties:

| MdL Pelletier | GDE | P | MIA | Voisin |
| Sgt Alfred Mantels | Juvisy | P | KIAcc | |

14 July – No Claims
Casualties:

Sgt Gaultier	GDE	P	KIAcc	
Sgt Joanny Burtin &	F 41	P	Injured	
Sol Lemarie	F 41	G	Injured	

15 July

Lt de La Tour		N 3	EA	X	W Combles	0900	4
Sgt de Rochefort	a.	N 26	Aviatik	X	E Péronne	1845	5
Lt Lachmann		N 57	Balloon	XF	Verdun		1
Adj Tarascon	b.	N 62	Aviatik C	X	Amiens		1
MdL Sanglier	a.	N 62	LVG	X	NE Péronne	1125	1
Capt Lecour-Grandmaison,		C 46					1
Lt Campion &		C 46					1
Sol Vitalis		C 46	LVG C	X	Forêt de Bry		2
Adj Dorme		N 3	EA	P			–
Adj Bucquet		N 3	EA	P			–
Sgt Chainat		N 3	EA	P			

a.   One possibly Ltn Wilhelm Hadloff, (O), KG 4, KIA, Péronne.
b.   Possibly Ltn Walter Sieber & Obltn Jakob von Hartsen, FlAbt 23, KIAs Mons-en-Chaussée, in the Amiens Sector.

Casualties:

MdL Georges Nautre	N 62	P	KIA	Possibly by Ltn Walter Höhndorf (8) KekVaux.
Cpl André Pichard &	C 106	P	MIA	Caudron N° 2149, probably by
Sgt Pierre Tabateau	C 106	G	MIA	Obltn Franz Walz, KSt 2, (5).
Lt Georges Lehmann &	MF 123	P	MIA	
Lt Perrault	MF 123	O	MIA	Farman N° 1898.
Sgt Pierre Lacombe &	VI° Armée	P	KIAcc	
Sol Desmit	VI° Armée	G	KIAcc	
Sgt Clément Voltz	27° Cie d'Aérostiers		XF	Vadelaincourt (see 2 July 1916).
		O	WIA	Died several days later.

16 July

| Lt Heurtaux | a. | N 3 | LVG C | XF | Barleux | 1000 | 2 |
| S/Lt Guynemer | a. | N 3 | LVG C | X | Barleux | 1002 | 10 |

a.   Possibly Ltn Franz Sigwart & Obltn Ludwig König, FlAbt 8, KIAs at Misery, about 10 km S Barleux.

Casualties:

Sgt Théophile Ingold (Swiss National)	N 23	P	WIA	DOW 19 July 1916.
???	73° Cie d'Aérostiers			Attacked by a LVG, not flamed.
		O	OK	

17 July – No Claims
Casualties:

| ??? | 23° Cie d'Aérostiers | | | Attacked by a Fokker, not flamed. |
| | | O | OK | |

18 July – No Claims
Casualties:

| Sgt Augustin Wavrin | V 107 | P | WIA | |
| Cpl Rusch | GDE | P | Injured | |

19 July

Cpl J Sauvage	a.	N 65	EA	X	E Péronne		2
Lt Privat		N 65	EA	X	S Péronne		1
Sgt Dupré		N 102	EA	X	Gremilly		1

???		b. DCA	2 seater	X	Braine	–

a. Possibly Uffz Karl Steinhorst & Obltn Walter Theel, FlAbt 13, KIAs, Templeuve (Templeux), E of Péronne.
b. POWs.

Casualties:

Lt Lucien Rousselet &	F 207	P	MIA	Probably by Ltn Walter Höhndorf	
S/Lt André Frémont	F 207	O	MIA	KekV (9)	
Sgt Pardieu &	VC 116	P	KIAcc		
Sol Mary	VC 116	G	KIAcc		
Asp Jacques Laneyrie	C 6	P	Injured		
Sgt de Coucy	C 43	P	Injured		
MdL Schal	C 43	G	Injured		
Lt Henri Mesmacre	C 51	P	Injured		
Lt Leduc	C 10	O	Injured		
S/Lt Joseph Maura	88° Cie d'Aérostiers			Cable severed by artillery fire, observer	
		O	OK	jumped to avoid being taken prisoner.	

20 July – No Claims

Casualties:

Lt Raymond Bonneau	N 65	P	POW	Nieuport XVI N° 1333, departed 11h50.
Adj Albert Court	C 34	P	KIAcc	
Sol René Peault	MF 29	M	KIA	
Lt Henri Dagonet	N 37	P	WIA	DOW 22 July 1916.
MdL Joseph de Bailleul &	F 16	P	Injured	
S/Lt Emile Goilbault	F 16	O	Injured	
MdL Georges Robart	F 63	P	Injured	

21 July

MdL Bonnefort &		F 20				1
Lt Laperotte		F 20	EA	XF	Eix	1
Lt Beraud-Villars &		MF 44				1
Lt Le Barbu		MF 44	LVG	X	Forges	1
Adj Tarascon		N 62	LVG	X	Nesle	2
S/Lt Nungesser	a.	N 124	Aviatik	X	Seuzey	12
MdL Sanglier	b.	N 62	EA	P	Liancourt-Fosse	–
Lt Heurtaux		N 3	Fokker	P		–

a. Possibly Obltn Otto Parschau, FlAbt 32, KIA Grevillers.
b. Ltn Werner Schramm (P) KG 1, KIA Combles, Amiens Sector.

Casualties:

Capt Marcel Dubois & CO	F 16	P	MIA	
S/Lt Georges Gounon	F 16	O	MIA	
S/Lt Pierre Limet	???	O	KIA	
Lt Henri Dagonet	N 37	P	WIA/DOW	One of these two probably by Ltn
Lt Albert Deullin	N 3	P	WIA	Kurt Haber, FlAbt 6, (4).
Sol Nicolas Comte	C 106	G	Injured	
Sgt Roger Reygal	C 43	P	Injured	
Capt Georges Benoist	???	P	Injured	

22 July

Adj Vial &		MF 29				1
Cpl Nepveu	a.	MF 29	EA	X	Mülhouse	1
Adj Canivet &		MF 29				2
Adj Gr'lat	a.	MF 29	Scout	X	Mülhouse	2
Lt Tourtel &		MF 123				1
Sol Laage	a.	MF 123	Fokker	XF	Mülhouse	1
Cpl Tanner &		GB 4				1
Cpl Viaris de Lesegno	a.	GB 4	Fokker	X	Mülhouse	1

a. Vfw Kurt Schörf, FlAbt (A) 216w, KIA Ensisheim, near Mülhouse.

Casualties:

MdL René Weisse &	F 123	P	MIA	Maurice Farman N° 1899, probably
Sol Aviez	F 123	B	MIA	by Vfw Stober, (1).
Adj Colin &	F 29	P	MIA	Nieuport XII N° 1282, possibly by
Sol Pauly	F 29	G	MIA	Ltn Walter, Hühndorf, KekV, (10).
Sgt Louis Happe &	F 29	P	WIA	
Sgt Emile Barlatier	F 29	B	KIA	
S/Lt Marius Michon &	F 35	P	KIA	
S/Lt Darliguie	F 35	O	KIA	Infantry fire.

23 July

S/Lt Chaput	a.	N 57	Aviatik C	X	Fresnes-en-Woëvre	0745	8
Adj B Hall		N 124	Fokker E	X	Ft de Vaux	1500	2

a.   Possibly Ltn Walter Bräutigam (O), KampfSt 33, KIA Tavannes (Fresnes).

Casualties:

Cpl Robert Sangy &	C 17	P	Injured
Adj-Chef Pierre Darnaud	C 17	O	KIAcc

24 July – No Claims

Casualties:

S/Lt Limet	F 41	O	KIA	Ground fire.
Cpl René Blanc &	C 6	P	KIA	Caudron N° 2236, probably by Ltn
S/Lt Bayard	C 6	O	KIA	Hartmut Baldamus, AOK3 (4).
S/Lt Jean Chaput	N 57	P	WIA	
MdL Gontran Dezert	N 31	P	WIA	
Cpl Aleide Harfaux	GDE	P	Injured	

25 July

Sgt Douchy		N 38	2 seater	X		1
??? &		C 43				1
Adj Borzecki	a.	C 43	EA	X	Combles	1

a.   Possibly Uffz Georg Röder & Ltn Friedrich Zilling, KSt 11, KIAs, near Bapaume, about 10 km N of Combles.

Casualties:

Cpl Henri Alavoine	???	P	KIAcc
Capt Benjamin Lefort &	CEP 115	P	OK
Cpl Denis Auda	CEP 115	G	Injured
Lt Joseph Azire	GDE	P	Injured
MdL Emile Mary	V 116	P	Injured
Sol Pinel	V 114	G	Injured
Capt Etienne Gailhac	F 41	P	Injured

26 July

Lt de Sevin	N 12	Fokker	FTL	Oulches	–
Lt de Sevin	N 12	Fokker	FTL	Oulches	–

Casualties:

MdL André Waldmann &	C 39	P	MIA	Caudron N° 1527, probably by Ltn
S/Lt Félix Giacomelli	C 39	O	MIA	Werner Lehmann, (1).

27 July

MdL Macquart de Terline	a.	N 38	Rumpler C	X	Collided with enemy plane over Minaucourt.	3
S/Lt Loste,		C 46				1
S/Lt Barbou &		C 46				1
Sol Martin	b.	C 46	2 motor	X	St Christ	1
MdL de Bonnefoy	c.	N 65	EA	X	Brie	2
Lt de Laage de Meux		N 124	Aviatik	X	Ornes-Bezonvaux	2
MdL de Bonnefoy		N 65	EA	FTL		–
Sgt Dufresne &		F 14				–
Capt de Marolles		F 14	Scout	X	Vosges	–
S/Lt Guynemer		N 3	3 motor	P	Combles	–
Adj Dorme		N 3	EA	P		–
Adj Dorme		N 3	EA	P		–
Lt Heurtaux		N 3	EA	P		–
Lt de La Tour		N 3	EA	P		–

a.   Probably Uffz Erich Finck and Obltn Günther Freytag, FlAbt 17, KIAs near Massiges.
b.   Possibly Gefr Georg Scholz and Ltn Hans Seulen, FeldFlgTrp, KIAs at Estrées, about 10 km NE of St Christ.
c.   Probably Gefr Heinrich Gerischer & Ltn Hans Schmidmann, KG4, KIAs at Brie.

Casualties:

MdL Jean Macquart de Terline	N 38	P	KIA	IV° Armée, intentionally collided with EA, probably Uffz Erich Finke & Obltn Günther Freytag FlAbt 17.
Adj Joseph Guiguet	N3	P	WIA	
MdL Gontran Dezeret	N 31	P	WIA	
Cdt Louis Morisson	V° Armée	P	Injured	
MdL Fruchement	C 207	P	Injured	

28 July

Adj Dorme	a. N 3	2 motor	XF	Chaulnes-Roye	1915	2
S/Lt Guynemer	b. N 3	LVG C	X	Gandau-Barleux	1645	11
Lt Matton,	N 57					1
Lt Lachmann &	N 57					2
MdL Flachaire	c. N 67	Albatros CIII	POW	Souilly		2
Sgt Daguzan	N 15	Aviatik C	P	Hallu	1015	–
MdL Seillière &	F 2					–
Cpl Eymery	F 2	EA	P			–
Sgt Rockwell	N 124	EA	FTL			–
Capt Duseigneur	N 57	2 seater	FTL			–

a. Two fuselage & two motors.
b. Probably Vfw Wilhelm Kroker, KIA Grandau.
c. Officer pilot WIA, observer OK, POWs.

Casualties:

Cpl Fontaine &	C 47	P	Injured	
Sol Genin	C 47	G	Injured	
Cpl Jean Lescuyer &	VB 101	P	KIAcc	
Adj Paul Thévenard	VB 101	B	KIAcc	III° Armée

29 July

Sgt de Geuser &	N 37				1
Sgt Garrigou	N 37	Aviatik	X	German lines, Somme	1
Adj Pélissier &	C 202				1
S/Lt Homo	a. C 202	Fokker E	X	St Christ	1
Sgt Bajac	N 48	Aviatik C	P		–
Cpl J Sauvage	N 65	EA	P		–
MdL Seillière &	F 2				–
Cpl Eymery	F 2	Fokker	P	Argonne	–

a. Probably Ltn Phillipe Cherdron (O), FlAbt 102, KIA at Misery, about 5 km WSW of St Christ.

Casualties:

MdL Albert Divry &	F 2	P	KIA	Possibly by Ltn Hartmut Baldamus,
S/Lt Henri Santrot	F 2	O	KIA	AOK3 (5).
S/Lt Boissan &	F 29	P	MIA	Farman N° 2118.
Brig Vermillet	F 29	B	MIA	FTL near Cernay, POWs??
Lt Marcel de Flers	???	P	WIA	
Cpl Morel &	C 66	P	OK	FTL during combat at 08h40,
Cpl Osmond	C 66	G	OK	near Nancy.

30 July

Adj Lenoir &	N 23				6
Lt Brindejonc des Moulinais	N 23	Fokker E	X	Souilly-Etain	1
Sgt Lufbery	a. N 124	2 seater	X	W Etain	1
??? &	C 66				?
S/Lt Hegay	C 66	EA	X	German lines	1
Lt de La Tour	N 3	EA	P		–
Adj Bucquet	N 3	EA	P	Cléry	–
Lt Raymond	N 3	EA	P		–
Capt Duseigneur	N 57	2 seater	FTL	Etain	–
Sgt Epitalon	N 15	LVG	FTL	Chaulnes	–

a. Possibly Obltn Oskar Illing & Obltn Hermann Kraft, KG6/KSt33, KIAs Vaux, about 10 km W Etain.

Casualties:

Cpl Paul Pierrard &	V 223	P	MIA	Flak, Farman 3?02.
S/Lt Théo Schmoukee	V 223	O	MIA	Flak, N Bois de Mortmare.
Sgt Girard-Varet	C 10	P	WIA	
Lt Jacques Caffert	F 52	P	WIA	
Lt Weiss &	F 60	P	Injured	
S/Lt Maurice Petit	F 60	O	KIAcc	
Cpl Hyacinthe Sartorio	39° Cie d'Aérostiers			
		O	WIA	

31 July

Sgt Lufbery	N 124	2 seater	X	Fort Vaux	2

Casualties:

S/Lt André Delorme	C 56	P	WIA	Flak
Adj Constantin Oru	C 64	P	WIA	
Lt Henri Mesmacre	C 51	P	WIA	

Sgt Louis Gérard-Varet		C 10	P	WIA		
Lt Antonin de Dore		GDE	P	Injured		

July dates unknown:

MdL de Bonnefoy		N 65	EA	P		–

1 August

Sgt Chainat		N 3	EA	X	German lines	8
Sgt Hentsch &		N 15				4
Sgt Daguzan		N 15	Aviatik	XF	Marchélepot	2
Cpl Pendaries		N 69	EA	XF	German lines, Somme	1
S/Lt Guynemer		N 3	EA	P	Biaches	–
Lt Heurtaux		N 3	EA	FTL		–
Lt Heurtaux		N 3	EA	FTL		–
Sgt Chainat		N 3	EA	FTL		–
Adj Tarascon	a.	N 62	Aviatik	FTL	Roye	–
S/Lt de Bonald		N 69	EA	FTL		–
Groupement de Cachy			8 EA	FTL		–

a.   Possibly Uffz Johann Hoscheck and Ltn Otto Bitzer, Schusta 21, KIAs at Morchain, about 15 km NNE of Roye.

Casualties:

Cpl Marcel Broussard &	C 4	P	MIA	II° Armée, Caudron N 2059, probably
Brig Fouche	C 4	G	MIA	by Obltn Kurt Student, AOK3, (2).
Lt Achille Bernard	N 112	P	WIA	

2 August

Sgt Chainat	N 3	LVG	X	Marchélepot	1010	9
Sgt Chainat &	N 3					10
Lt Heurtaux	N 3	LVG	X	Vermandouillers	1020	3
Sgt Pillon	N 102	EA	X	Chauny	1430	1
Lt d'Erceville	N 23	EA	FTL	Chaumont		–
Sgt Garrigou	N 37	EA	FTL	Mons-en-Chaussée		–

Casualties:

S/Lt Pulpe		P	WIA		
S/Lt André Brun	C 202	O	WIA		
Lt Jean Mongin	C 106	P	WIA		
Sgt Gauthier	C 106	G	WIA		
Cpl Pierre Jammy &	F 71	P	KIAcc		
Cpl Joseph Cartier	F 71	G	Injured		
Sol André Séguin	43° Cie d'Aérostiers		XF	(18h30)	
		O	WIA		

3 August

Adj Dorme	a.	N 3	LVG C	X	Maurepas	1425	3
S/Lt Guynemer &		N 3				12
Lt Heurtaux		N 3	EA	X	Barleux	0945	4
Patrol		N 26	EA	X	Guillemont		–
Sgt de Bonnefoy		N 65	EA	XF	Maurepas		3
Lt d'Harcourt		N 103	EA	X			1
MdL Sollier &		C 105					1
Adj Peignat		C 105	Fokker	X	Dannevoux		1
Sgt Chainat		N 3	EA	P			–
S/Lt Raymond		N 3	EA	P			–
Lt Heurtaux		N 3	EA	P		1245	–
Lt de La Tour		N 3	EA	P			–
MdL de Linière		N 103	EA	FTL			–

a.   Probably Uffz Fritz Levique & Ltn Walter Bollow, Kampf St 2, KIAs Montauban.

Casualties:

Sgt Jean Maffert	N 103	P	MIA	VI° Armée, Nieuport N 833, probably
				by Vfw Hans Müller, Kek3 (2)
MdL Debrod	N 103	P	MIA	
Sgt André Chainat	N 3	P	Injured	

4 August

Adj Lenoir	a.	N 23	EA	X	Moranville	7
Adj Sayaret &		N 57				3
Sgt Lufbery	b.	N 124	2 seater	X	Avocourt	3

Artillery	???	Balloon	X	Ennemain	–
Sgt Barra	N 26	2 seater	FTL		–
MdL Sanglier	N 62	EA	FTL		–

a.   Possibly Vzfw Wilhelm Kreye and Ltn Wilhelm Grossmann, KG6/Kasta 34, KIAs near Moranville.
b.   Probably Uffz Peter Engel & Ltn Otto Maiwald, FlAbt 34, KIAs Avocourt.

Casualties:

Lt Jean Heintz	N 65	P	MIA	VI° Armée
Sgt Roger Daguzan	N 15	P	MIA	
Adj Henri Théry &	F 7	P	OK	
S/Lt de Mijolla	F 7	O	WIA	Flak
Sgt Joseph Davrichewy	GDE	P	Injured	
Sgt Camille Jousse	F 25	B	Injured	

5 August

Sgt Barra	N 26	Balloon	P	–

Casualties:

Cpl Georges Halier &		V 114	P	KIA	
Asp Arthur Barat		V 114	O	KIA	
EV1 Jules Delaunay &	*	CAM	P	KIA	FBA 150 HP N° 306, codé D.1
QM Piena Amossé	*	CAM	M	KIA	probably by FlgObMt Franz Meyer (3)
					& Ltn Bönisch (5), SFS 1.
Adj Robert de Bonnefoy		N 65	P	WIA	Flak, balloon attack, VI° Armée.
Cpl André Veillon		GDE	P	Injured	
S/Lt René Michas &		C 207	P	Injured	
S/Lt André Sayn		C 207	O	OK	
Adj Charles Decorby		CEP 115	P	OK	
Cpl Besnard		CEP 115	G	Injured	

*   Dunkerque.

6 August

Sgt de Rochefort		N 26	Balloon	XF	NE Nesles		6
Adj Fonck &		C 47					1
S/Lt Thiberge	a.	C 47	Rumpler	POW	Villeneuve-les-Vertus	1030	1
MdL Viallet	b.	N 67	Aviatik	X	Avocourt	0900	2
MdL Viallet		N 67	Aviatik	X	Vauquois	0910	3
MdL Darblay		N 69	2 seater	X	Omiecourt		1
S/Lt Malleterre		N 69	Balloon	XF	Somme		1
S/Lt Guynemer		N 3	EA	P	Amiens Sector		–
Adj Dorme		N 3	LVG C	P	N Nesles	1410	–
S/Lt Guynemer		N 3	EA	FTL	Amiens Sector		–
S/Lt Guynemer		N 3	EA	FTL	Amiens Sector		–
S/Lt Chevillon		N 15	LVG	FTL	Roiglise-Margny		–

a.   Rumpler CI N 4593/15 was only slightly damaged, III Armée Sector, probably Obltn Adam Brey and Ltn Hermann von Raumer, KG6/KSt 33, POWs.
b.   Probably Uffz Peter Engel & Ltn Otto Maiwald, FlAbt 34, KIAs Avocourt.

Casualties:

S/Lt Jean Verdie &	C 56	P	MIA	Caudron N° 1467, probably by Ltn
Lt Escolle	C 56	O	MIA	Hermann Pfeiffer, AOK3, (1)

7 August

S/Lt de La Tour		N 3	Balloon	XF	Manancourt	1815	5
Lt C Dumas	a.	N 57	LVG	X	Hannonville		3
Adj Teulon &		???					–
Lt de Castelet		???	Aviatik	FTL	Etain		–

a.   Probably Uffz Martin Wiener & Ltn Josef Nonn, FlAbt 19, KIAs Hannonville.

Casualties:

MdL Maurice Martin	C 21	P	KIA	
Lt Paul Weiller	C 21	O	WIA	
Sgt Etienne Jagerschmidt	MF 205	P	WIA	
Lt Henri Le Sueur	F 221	O	WIA	II° Armée, ground fire.
Sgt-Maj Eugène Commeau	F 216	P	KIA	
& S/Lt René Daude	F 216	O	KIA	II° Armée

8 August

S/Lt Burguin	a.	N 38	Fokker	XF	German lines	1
Adj Adam	b.	N 48	Aviatik	XF	Lunéville	1
Sgt Lufbery	c.	N 124	Aviatik	XF	S Douaumont	4
Lt Deullin		N 3	EA	P		–

Lt de Fels &	N 38				–
S/Lt Deviterne	N 38	Scout	P		–
Sgt de Rochefort	N 26	EA	FTL		–
MdL Carlier &	C 51				–
S/Lt Chifflet	C 51	EA	FTL	German lines	–

a.   Probably Ltn Benno Berneis, AOK 3, KIA St Souplet.
b.   Forced to land in German lines, destroyed by French artillery fire.
c.   Possibly Uffz Georg Gering & Ltn Max Sedlmair, KG6/KSt36, KIAs near Douaumont.

Casualties:

Lt Hubert de Fels &	N 38	P	OK	Probably by Obltn Kurt Student
S/Lt Emile Deviterne	N 38	O	WIA	AOK3, Nieuport two-seater FTL (3).
S/Lt Casier	F 210	O	Injured	
Lt Collard	F 7		Injured	
???	73° Cie d'Aérostiers			Attacked, not flamed.
		O	OK	

9 August

Adj Tarascon		N 62	Aviatik	XF	Rethonvillers-Herly	3
Capt Féquant	CO	N 65	EA	P	Morchain	–
MdL Sanglier		N 62	EA	FTL	Mesnil-St Nicaise	–
Adj Lenoir &		N 23				–
Sgt Casale		N 23	EA	FTL	N Beaumont	–
Cpl Calmon &		???				–
Cpl Prou with		???				–
Two British planes		???	EA	FTL	Combles	–

Casualties:

MdL Herman Hentsch &		N 15	P	POW	
Sgt Verret		N 15	O	POW	Nieuport N° 1179.
Sgt Raymond Boudou &	*	N 48	P	POW/WIA	Nieuport N° 1520, shot down over
Lt de Rolland de Blomac		N 48	O	POW/WIA	Blamont.
Adj Paul Tarascon		N 62	P	WIA	
Adj Maxime Lenoir		N 23	P	WIA	Flak, II° Armée
Lt Louis Contamin &		C 13	P	WIA	Flak
S/Lt Boilève		C 13	O	OK	II° Armée
Cpl Etienne Boussenot du Clos &		F 35	P	KIAcc	
Lt de Bellefond		F 35	O	Injured	VI° Armée
Adj Léon Streicher &		C 61	P	Injured	
S/Lt Despres		C 61	O	Injured	

*   Sgt Boudou escaped captivity in February 1918, returned to Spa 48.

10 August – No Claims – No Casualties

11 August – No Claims
Casualties:

Adj Pierre Violet &	F 55	P	OK	
S/Lt Mailloux	F 55	O	WIA	Flak, II° Armée
Cpl Dennis Dowd	Buc	P	KIAcc	

12 August

Adj Lenoir &	N 23				8
Lt Lachmann	N 57	EA	X	Gincrey	3
Lt Privat	N 65	EA	P	Ablaincourt-Fresnes	–

Casualties:

S/Lt Jean de La Brosse	F 208	O	WIA	
Adj Henri Despréz &	C 43	P	WIA	
Lt François Bouchonnet	C 43	O	OK	
Sgt Louis Veran &	RGAé	P	Injured	
Sol Delordre	RGAé	G	Injured	
Cpl Ange Mandoline	C 202	M	Injured	

13 August – No Claims
Casualties:

Cpl Paul Pavelka	N 124	P	Injured	

14 – 15 August – No Claims – No Casualties

16 August

Lt Heurtaux		N 3	EA	P		–

Casualties: None

---

17 August

S/Lt Guynemer		N 3	Albatros C	X	Grancourt	1005	13
Lt Heurtaux	a.	N 3	Aviatik C	X	Barleux	1815	5
S/Lt Guynemer		N 3	Albatros C	P	N Combles		–

a.   Possibly Uffz Johannes Schröter & Ltn Paul Wagner, FlAbt 108.

Casualties:

Sgt Octave Lafay &	F 123	P	KIAcc	
Sol Dez	F 123	G	KIAcc	

---

18 August

S/Lt Guynemer	a.	N 3	Rumpler	X	Bouchavesnes	1500	14

a.   Probably Ltn Walter Strauss & Ltn Karl Ramfeld, FlAbt 26, KIAs Cléry, about 6 km S of Bouchavesnes.

Casualties:

Sgt Robert Denain	F 5	P	WIA	II° Armée, ground fire.
Cpl Alberto Bucciali	F 55	P	WIA	Flak, II° Armée
MdL Auguste Pouchelle	N 26	P	WIA	
Cpl Najean &	GDE	P	KIAcc	
Lt Laumain	GDE	O	KIAcc	
S/Lt Marcel Brindejonc des Moulinais	N 23	P	KIA	Verdun

---

19 August – No Claims

Casualties:

Sgt Joseph Gros	N 67	P	WIA	
Adj Pierre Besnier	N 62	P	KIAcc	
MdL Jean d'Audeville	GDE	P	Injured	

---

20 August

S/Lt Guynemer		N 3	LVG	P	Bois Madame	1630	–
S/Lt Guynemer		N 3	LVG	P	Somme	1930	–
Adj Dorme		N 3	LVG	P	Manancourt	1825	–
Adj Dorme		N 3	EA	P			–
Sgt Tsu		N 37	Albatros	P	Moislains	1645	–

Casualties:

SM Charles Perron	*	CAM	P	KIA	FBA 150 HP,N 316. codé D.6, by
SM Guesne	*	CAM	O	POW	Marine-Artillerie-Batterie "Beseler" Ostende.

*   Dunkerque.

---

21 August

S/Lt de La Tour		N 3	EA	X	Flaucourt	0930	6
Lt Lis		N 15	Albatros C	X	SE Nesles	0815	4
Lt L Billon du Plan	a.	N 65	EA	X	Berny-en-Santerre		1
S/Lt Barbier,		C 46					1
S/Lt Labussière &		C 46					1
Sol Mondème		C 46	Aviatik C	X	Athies		1
S/Lt Raymond		N 3	EA	P			–

a.   Possibly Obltn Friedrich Hirschfeld (O), FlAbt (A) 205, KIA Horgny, about 3 km NNE Berny-en-Santerre.

Casualties:

S/Lt Henri Bonin	MF 1	O	WIA	Ground fire
MdL Eugène Letrémy	F 5	P	WIA	Flak, II° Armée
Adj Auguste Vinnera &	RGAé	P	Injured	
Sol Groulade	RGAé	G	Injured	

---

22 August

Adj Dorme	a.	N 3	LVG C	X	NE Moislains	1835	5
Lt Barbier,		C 46					1
Lt Labusserie &		C 46					1
Sol Mondème		C 46	EA	X	Athies		1
Adj d' Aux,		C 46					1
Lt de Montcarbier &		C 46					1
Sgt Steuer		C 46	EA	X	German lines		1

S/Lt Nungesser		N 65	EA	P	Aizécourt	1820	–
Adj Dorme		N 3	LVG C	P	Sailly-Sallisel	1835	–
Adj Lemaire	b.	N 3	LVG C	P	Combles-Rancourt	1840	–
Lt de Rochefort	b.	N 26	LVG C	P	Combles-Athies	1720	–
Adj Borde		N 65	EA	P			–
Lt Pinsard	b.	N 26	LVG C	FTL	Combles-Rancourt	1815	–

a.   Possibly Gefr Heinrich Bock, KIA Barastre.
b.   Probably Ltn Hans Becken, KIA about 5 km S of Combles.

Casualties:

Sgt Marcel Poisot &	C 43	P	KIA		
S/Lt René Guillet					
de La Brosse	C 43	O	KIA		
Sgt Pierre Steuer	C 46	G	WIA	DOW 25 Aug 1916.	
MdL Gabriel Dormet &	C 4	P	WIA	Ground fire-DOW 23 August 1916.	
Lt Soubeyean	C 4	O	Injured	Crash landing.	
EV1 Théodore Philippe	PilSch	O	KIAcc	St Raphaël	

23 August

Adj Dorme	N 3	LVG C	X	S Marchélepot	1055	6
Lt Burguin	N 38	Fokker	X			2
Sgt Douchy &	N 38					2
Adj Revol-Tissot	N 38	Albatros	X	N Epoye		1
Adj de Bonnefoy	N 65	LVG	X	Marchélepot	1030	4
???	DCA	Balloon	X	Bezonvaux		–
S/ Lt Raymond	N 3	LVG C	P	Marchélepot	1055	–
Lt de La Tour	N 3	EA	P	Pertain	1025	–
Capt Féquant CO	N 65	EA	P	Haplincourt	0725	–
Capt J de Boutiny	N 49	EA	FTL	Ensisheim		–

Casualties:

MdL Charles Cancalon &	F 59	P	WIA
Lt Edouard Le Mounier	C 61	P	WIA
Lt de Vernilliat	C 61	O	WIA
S/Lt Pierre Janet	C 28	O	WIA

24 August

Lt Deullin	N 3	EA	XF	Marchélepot	1900	6
MdL Soulier	N 26	Balloon	XF	N Bois de Vaux	1930	1
Adj Gros	N 48	EA	X	German lines		1
Cpl Leau &	C 66					1
???	C 66	EA	X	Forêt de Cremecy	1420	?
MdL de Linière	N 103	Rumpler	X	E Péronne	1120	1
Adj de Guibert	N 62	EA	P	NE Péronne	1630	–
Sgt Lemaire	N 3	EA	P	Maurepas-Combles	1640	–
Sgt Lemaire	N 3	EA	P			–
Sgt Etienne Tsu	N 37	EA	FTL			–
Asp Antoni &	C 6					–
Sol Schwartz	C 6	Fokker	FTL	German lines		–

Casualties:

Adj André Gros	N 48	P	KIA	Nieuport N 1472, probably by Obltn Rudolf Berthold, KekV, (6). 18h30 at Roisel
Cpl Henri Dangueuger	N 37	P	KIA	Nieuport N 1552, probably by Obltn Rudolf Berthold, KekV, unconfirmed.
Sgt André Jouanny &	C 64	P	POW	Caudron N 1309, probably by Ltn Hermann Pfeiffer, AOK3, (2).
Asp Florentin	C 64	O	POW	
Brig Joseph Gaubert &	F 203	P	MIA	
Lt Paulon	F 203	O	MIA	VI° Armée
Sgt Serge Lecornu &	C 53	P	KIA	Flak
S/Lt Jules Zuckmeyer	C 53	O	KIA	Flak, VI° Armée
Sgt Etienne Laliat &	F 216	P	WIA	II° Armée, FTL near Verdun
S/Lt Bernard Poulain	F 216	O	WIA	DOW 24 August 1916.
Lt Pierre Barbey	N 103	P	WIA	
Adj Robert de Bonnefoy	N 65	P	WIA	VI Armée
Sgt Marcel Joannes &	F 211	P	WIA	VI° Armée
S/Lt Eugène Martinot	F 211	O	OK	
Sgt Birac &	VC 110	O	Injured	
Sol Gillard	VC 110	G	KIAcc	

Sgt Roux	C 53	P	Injured			
???	83° Cie d'Aérostiers			Attacked, not flamed Verdun Sector.		
		O	OK			

25 August

S/Lt de La Tour	N 3	EA	X	Pertain-Hallu	0830	7
Adj Dorme	N 3	LVG C	X	Mesnil-St Nicaise	0945	7
Adj Dufaur de Gavardie &	N 12					4
Sol Carré	N 12	Balloon	XF	Passy		2
Lt Beissac &	N 38					1
Lt Mahieux	N 38	Fokker	X	N Châlons		1
Adj Sayaret &	N 57					4
Cpl Triboulet	N 57	EA	XF	Mogeville		1
Lt Dumas	N 57	EA	X	Fossieux		4
S/Lt Nungesser	N 65	LVG C	X	Roye-Nurlu	1150	13
Adj Prince	N 124	2 seater	X	Bois d'Hingry	0842	1
???	DCA	Fokker	X	Craonne		–
Adj Prince	N 124	EA	FTL	N Forêt de Spincourt		–
Sgt Chainat	N 3	EA	P	S Combles	1020	–
Lt Deullin	N 3	EA	P	Le Transloy	1025	–
Lt Deullin	N 3	EA	P	Mesnil-en-Arrouaise		–
Sgt Soulier	N 26	Balloon	P	Mesnil-St Nicaise		–
S/Lt de Rochefort	N 26	EA	P	St Pierre-Vaast	1630	–
Sgt Sendral	N 26	EA	P	E Bouchavesnes	1605	–
Lt E Billon du Plan	N 65	EA	P	Ablaincourt-Berny	1120	–
Casualties:						
Sgt Gabriel Buellet &	F 224	P	KIA	II° Armée		
Asp Pierre Guis	F 224	O	KIA	Down in flames near Eix.		
Lt Charles Dumas	N 57	P	POW	Nieuport N° 1573.		
MdL Steuer	C 46	G	WIA/DOW			

26 August – No Claims
Casualties:

| Sgt Armand Mars & | C 53 | P | MIA | Possibly by Vfw Hans Müller, | | |
| S/Lt Humbert | C 53 | O | MIA | Jasta 5, (5). | | |

27 August – No Claims
Casualties:

Sol Barthélémy	C 13	M	WIA			
Sol Racine	C 13	M	WIA	DOW 28 August 1916.		
Sol Dechoz	C 13	M	WIA			

These three were wounded during an artillery barrage on their airfield.

28 August

Adj B Hall	N 124	EA	X	NE Douaumont	1900	3
S/Lt Thirouin	???	EA	X	French lines		1
Lt Pinsard	N 26	LVG C	P	Fourchette	0735	–
Casualties:						
S/Lt Jean Krebs	F 52	O	KIAcc			

29 August

Adj Sayaret &	N 57					5
MdL Clarinval	N 57	EA	X	Fresnes-en-Woëvre		1
MdL Sanglier	N 62	EA	P			–
MdL Sanglier	N 62	EA	P			–
Casualties:						
Cpl Auguste Louis &	C 34	P	KIA	Caudron N° 1325,		
Sol Auguste Guillard	C 34	G	KIA	XF, Schweighausen		
Capt Pierrey	F 71	O	WIA			
MdL Charles Lamelle	F 60	P	WIA			
Adj Gilbert Catteau &	F 63	P	KIAcc			
S/Lt Andre Labrie	F 63	O	KIAcc	II° Armée		
Cpl Lauque	F 210	P	Injured			
Sgt Carretier	C 18	P	Injured			
Lt Dautriche	C 18	O	Injured			
Cpl René Gustin	46° Cie d'Aérostiers		Injured	These balloons were hit by lightning and ignited.		

Sol Charles Domanget		46° Cie d'Aérostiers		KIAcc	Domanget & Gustin were ground	
S/Lt Pierre Caro		46° Cie d'Aérostiers			crew members and victims	
			O	OK	lightning strike.	
Adj Eugène Hoppe &		24° Cie d'Aérostiers				
Sgt Breuil			O	Injured		
Sgt Jacques Ledeuil		75° Cie d'Aérostiers		XF		
			O	OK		

30 August – No Claims
Casualties:

Sgt Pierre Garretier	C 18	P	WIA		

31 August

Adj Dorme	a.	N 3	LVG C	X	Manicourt	1750	8
Lt de Fels		N 38	Aviatik	X	N Somme-Py		2
Adj Tarascon		N 62	Albatros	X	Pargny	0820	4
Cpl J Sauvage		N 65	EA	X	Bois de Devise	1050	3
???	b.	DCA	Rumpler	POW	NE Somme-Suippes		–
S/Lt Raymond		N 3	EA	P	Manancourt	1745	–
S/Lt Raymond		N 3	EA	P	Sailly-Sallisel	1050	–
Lt Pinsard		N 26	EA	FTL	SE Bois de Raucourt		–
S/Lt Prudhommeaux		N 37	EA	FTL	Chaulnes	1000	–
Motor trouble	c.	???	2 seater	POW	Ricquebourg		–

a.   Possibly Uffz Kurt Richter, WIA, Nesle, about 3 km E of Manicourt, DOW 11 September 1918.
b.   Probably Vfw Strattus & Ltn Berger, FlAbt 17, POWs, shot down by Flak in this sector.
c.   Both occupants taken prisoner.
Casualties:

Sgt Charles Flory	C 10	P	WIA	Flak	

1 September

???	DCA	EA	X	Rt Bank Oise River	–
???	DCA	EA	X	Rt Bank Oise River	–
???	DCA	EA	X	Douaumont	–

Casualties:

MdL Georges Duc	GDE	P	POW	Nieuport XII N° 1276.	
Cpl Firmin Civiletti &	C 43	P	MIA	Flak	
S/Lt Emile Chery	C 43	O	MIA	Flak, Caudron G4	
Adj Charles Baudrin	VB 109	P	KIAcc	Morane 2 motor	
Sol Joseph Mange	26° Cie d'Aérostiers				
		O	WIA		

2 September

Adj Casale		N 23	EA	X	Dieppe, NE Verdun	2
Lt Malavialle		N 69	EA	X	Nesles	2
Lt de La Tour		N 3	EA	P	Haplincourt	1930	–
S/Lt Prudhommeaux		N 37	EA	P	Sept-Fours	1340	–
Adj Tarascon		N 62	EA	P	Misery	1745	–
S/Lt Raymond	a.	N 3	EA	P	Combles	1700	–

a.   Possibly Ltn Wilhelm von der Ohe, FlAbt 42, KIA Les Beoufs, about 6 km N of Combles.
Casualties:

S/Lt Marcel Burguin	N 38	P	KIA	Nieuport XVII, S Aubérive	
Sgt Henri Clarinval	N 57	P	KIA	II° Armée, Nieuport XXI N° 1640, at Douaumont.	
Capt Gabriel Berthin &	C 64	P	MIA	Caudron G4 N° 1574,	
Sgt Ramponi	C 64	G	MIA	probably by Ltn Hermann Pfeiffer AOK3, (3).	
Adj Pierre Besnier	N 62	P	KIAcc	Nieuport XVII	
Cpl Marcel Gobert &	F 33	P	KIAcc		
Sol Lavigne	F 33	G	KIAcc	Caudron R4	
Sgt Albert Gaygal	F 228	P	Injured	Farman 56	

3 September

S/Lt Prudhommeaux	a.	N 37	EA	X	E Brie	1210	2
Lt E Billon du Plan		N 65	EA	P	E Péronne	1235	–
Sgt Desot		N 62	EA	FTL			–

a.   Probably Uffz Walter Hofmann & Ltn Hans Ehlers, FlAbt (A) 231, KIAs at Brie.

Casualties:

Sgt Edouard Rousseau &	N 67	P	MIA	VI° Armée		
Lt Paul Richard	N 67	O	MIA	Nieuport XIIbis N° 146.		
Cpl Barthes &	C 47	P	MIA			
S/Lt Claudel	C 47	O	MIA	Caudron G4 N° 1475.		
Sgt Fresche &	C 104	P	MIA	II° Armée,		
S/Lt Durand	C 104	O	MIA	Caudron G4 N° 1457.		
Lt Yves Garnier du Plessix &	C 106	P	WIA			
S/Lt Pierre Albertini	C 106	O	WIA	Caudron G4		
MdL Furhel	GDE	P	Injured	Caudron G4		
???	69° Cie d'Aérostiers		XF	Flamed by an artillery barrage.		
		O	OK			

4 September

S/Lt Guynemer	a.	N 3	Rumpler C	X	Ablaincourt	1825	15
MdL Babault &		MF 32					1
Lt Boudreau		MF 32	EA	X	Chaulnes		1

a.   Possibly Ltn Otto Fresenius & Ltn Hans Steiner, KG7/KSt37, KIAs Lihons, about 4 km SW of Ablainsourt.
Casualties: None

5 September – No Claims – No Casualties

6 September

S/Lt Prudhommeux	N 37	EA	XF	Gueudecourt	3
Capt Lecour Grandmaison,	C 46				2
S/Lt Arthur &	C 46				1
MdL Vitalis	C 46	Fokker	X	Brie	3
Lt de La Tour	N 3	EA	P		–
???	???	2 EA	P	Somme	–
Adj Tarascon	N 62	EA	FTL		–
Lt d'Astier de la Vigerie	N 65	EA	FTL		–

Casualties:

Capt Paul Turin	CO	N 15	P	KIA	Nieuport XVI, Vermandovilllers, 16h00.
Sgt Jean Dalesme		C 28	P	WIA	Caudron G4
Cpl Paul Goffi &		C 11	P	WIA	Caudron G4
S/Lt Charles Luguet		C 11	O	OK	
Cpl Philippe Dubrac		C 74	P	KIAcc	Caudron G4
Lt Raymond Lis		N 15	P	Injured	Nieuport XVII, crash-landed at Chilly after hit by infantry fire.
Sol Léon Reulle		???	?	Injured	

7 September

Lt Deullin		N 3	EA	X	Bouchavesnes	0900	7
MdL Hudellet		N 38	DFW C	X			1
Adj Dorme		N 3	Albatros	P	Epenancourt	0955	–
Adj Dorme		N 3	LVG	P	Herly	1600	–
Adj Bucquet		N 3	2 seater	P	Rancourt		–
Lt Pinsard	a.	N 23	EA	FTL	Pertain		–
Sgt Chainat		N 3	Scout	FTL	Berny-en-Santerre		–

a.   Destroyed by British artillery.
Casualties:

Sgt Guy Grosourdy de Saint Pierre	N 38	P	KIA	Nieuport XI, possibly by Ltn Hans von Keudell, Jasta 1, (2).
Sgt Bordes	N 73	P	MIA	VI° Armée, Nieuport XVIIbis, possibly by Ltn Wilhelm Frankl, Jasta 4 (10).
Sgt André Chainat	N3	P	WIA	VI° Armée, Spad VII,
MdL Fernand Boon	N31	P	KIAcc	Nieuport XVII

8 September

Lt Loste,	C 46				2
Lt Barbou &	C 46				2
Sol Martin &	C 46				2
Sgt Combret,	C 46				1
Brig Rousseaux &	C 46				1
Brig Cadot	C 46	EA	X	German lines	1

Casualties:

S/Lt Roger Prudhommeux	N 37	P	MIA	VI° Armée, Nieuport XVII.

Cpl Lucien Faure	BM 117	M	KIA			
S/Lt Lucien Duchenois &	F 44	P	Injured			
Cpl Henri Thibault	F 44	G	KIAcc	Farman 56, II° Armée		

9 September

Adj Dorme	N 3	LVG C	X	SW Beaulencourt	1530	9
Lt V Régnier &	N 112					1
Adj Prince	N 124	Fokker	X	Dieppe		2
Adj Rockwell	N 124	2 seater	X	Vauquois	0950	2
Adj Dorme	N 3	Rumpler C	P	Brie	1600	–
S/Lt Guynemer	N 3	EA	P	NE Péronne	1425	–
S/Lt Guynemer	N 3	LVG C	P	SE la Maisonnette	1830	–
Adj Bucquet	N 3	EA	P	E Bapaume	1755	–
Adj Galvin &	F 52					–
???	F 52	Scout	FTL			–
Casualties:						
Brig Jules Acquaviva &	F 216	P	KIAcc			
Sol Paterno	F 216	M	KIAcc	Farman 40 T56, II° Armée		
Cpl Charles Dubar &	F 29	P	KIAcc	Test flight.		
Sol Bertrand	F 29	G	KIAcc	Farman 40		

10 September – No Claims
Casualties:

MdL August Troude &	C 104	P	MIA	Flak, II° Armée, N Thiaumont		
Cpl Marcel Flauraud	C 104	G	MIA	Flak, Caudron G4 N° 2614.		
Lt Jean de Landrain	F 71	P	WIA	Flak, Farman 40 T42		
Cpl Henri Roy	N 12	M	Injured			
S/Lt Cyprin Raymond	CEP 115	P	Injured			

11 September

MdL Steuer	N 103	Rumpler	X	E Rancourt	0900	1
Casualties:						
Cpl André Veillon	GDE	P	KIAcc	Nieuport "Bebe"		
Sgt Oscar Nuez &	F 215	P	KIAcc			
S/Lt Charles Tabourot	F 215	O	Injured	Farman 42		

12 September

Sgt Sendral	N 26	Albatros	XF	Aizecourt	1915	1
Sgt Tsu	N 37	EA	X	Moislains		2
Groupement de Cachy	???	4 EA	P	N Péronne		–
Casualties:						
Capt Bernard Ayral CO	F 208	P	KIA	Flak, Farman 42		
Sgt Laurent Desperi	F 208	P	KIA	Flak, VI° Armée		
Adj André Maguet &	VB 108	P	WIA	Flak, DOW, Night bombing mission		
Brig Henry	VB 108	B	WIA	Flak, Voisin T3		
QM Marceau Lemaire	PilSch	P	KIAcc	La Varennes St Hilaire		
Sgt Benoit Varenne	C 46	P	Injured	Caudron R4		
Sgt Machaux	C 39	P	Injured	Caudron G4		

13 September – No Claims
Casualties:

???	73° Cie d'Aérostiers			Attacked, not flamed.		

14 September

Adj Lenoir	N 23	EA	X	N Douaumont		9
S/Lt de Rochefort	N 26	LVG C	X	Mont St Quentin	1155	7
S/Lt Nungesser	N 65	Albatros	X	E Falvy	0706	14
Lt Heurtaux a.	N 3	EA	P	W Bois de Vaux	0845	–
???	DCA	Fokker	X	Lusse		–
Adj Tarascon	N 62	EA	P	Cizaucourt	0750	–
S/Lt Nungesser	N 65	EA	FTL			–
MdL Sanglier b.	N 62	EA	P	Rancourt		–

a.   In collaboration with British aircraft.
b.   Possibly Ltn Fritz Gerstle (P), FlAbt 5b, KIA Rancourt.

Casualties:

MdL Marcel Babin &	F 24	P	KIA	Flak		
S/Lt Fernand Bonzom	F 24	O	KIA	Flak, Farman F42		

MdL Louis de Neel &	C 202	P	OK			
S/Lt Jean Monpetit	C 202	O	KIA	Caudron G4		
Sgt Lucien Gillet	GDE	P	KIAcc	Farman 43		
Cpl Maurice de Baudoin &	C 64	P	Injured			
Sgt Roger Maire	C 64	G	KIAcc	Caudron G4		

15 September

S/Lt Guynemer	a.	N 3	Rumpler	X	St Cren	1125	16
Lt Heurtaux		N 3	Scout	X	St Pierre-Vaast	1515	6
Adj Dorme		N 3	Rumpler	X	Brie-Ennemain	1720	10
Lt d'Astier de la Vigerie		N 65	EA	X	E Estrées	1819	1
Lt Privat		N 65	EA	P	Barleux	1800	–
Patrol		N 3	EA	P	Belloy		–
Sgt Destot		N 62	EA	FTL			–

a.   Uffz Josef Obermaier & Obltn Hans Sommer, FlAbt 8b, KIAs at Mons-en-Chaussée, immediate vicinity of St Cren.

Casualties:

S/Lt Hugues de Rochefort	N 26	P	POW	WIA/DOW 23 September 1916, by AA fire near Péronne. Nieuport XVIIbis N° 1581.	
Sgt Léonard Martin	F 24	P	WIA		
Sgt Charles Desmesières	C 21	P	OK		
S/Lt Porion	C 21	O	WIA	Caudron G4	
Cpl Ragneau	RGAé	G	Injured	Caudron G4	

16 September

Lt Gigodot &		N 103					1
Sgt Steuer	a.	N 103	EA	X	Chaulnes-Biaches	1835	2
Groupement de Cachy		???	EA	X	Belloy-en-Santerre		–
Sgt Destot		N 62	EA	FTL			–

a.   Probably Uffz Hans Böcker WIA/DOW 17 September 1916 & Ltn Hans Rübsmen KIA, KG 4, at Barleux, about 7 km S of Biaches.

Casualties:

S/Lt Jean Porian	C 21	O	WIA	
Lt Dumêmes	GDE	O	Injured	Nieuport XII
Sgt Octave Guiol &	PilSch	P	KIAcc	
Sgt Gallet	PilSch	S	KIAcc	
QM Yves Roland	PilSch	P	KIAcc	St Raphaël
Cpl Maurice Letourneur,	CEP 115	P	KIAcc	CEP T4
Cpl Girard &	CEP 115	P	Injured	CEP T4
Sol Fournat	CEP 115	M	Injured	
S/Lt Pierre Maitre	MF 1	P	Injured	
Capt Edward Thibault de Chanvalon	MF 1	O	Injured	Farman 42

17 September

Lt Heurtaux	a.	N 3	Roland D	X	Brie	0945	7
Adj Tarascon		N 62	LVG C	X	Deniécourt	0930	5
Lt Malavialle		N 69	EA	X	Misery		3
MdL Sanglier		N 62	EA	P	N Le Forest	0945	–
Adj Tarascon		N 62	LVG C	P	Deniécourt		–
Adj Dorme		N 3	LVG C	FTL	Moislains	0940	–
Sgt M Paris		N 73	EA	FTL			–

a.   Possibly Uffz George Eggers & Ltn Josef Klein, Ks.S.II, KIAs Péronne, about 10 km N Brie.

Casualties:

Cpl Georges Marcowitz	N 37	P	MIA	Nieuport XVII
Sgt Georges de Geuser	N 37	P	MIA	Nieuport XVII
Lt Henri Graff	C 43	O	WIA	Caudron G4
Adj Simon	RGAé	P	KIAcc	Verdrine

18 – 19 September – No Claims – No Casualties

20 September

Lt E Billon du Plan	N 65	EA	P	Moislains	1050	–

Casualties:

Cpl Pierre Desthuillers	F 44	P	OK	II° Armée
Lt Pierre Le Delchault de Mouredon	MF 44	O	Injured	Hit by flak and made a crash-landing. Farman 40 T42.

21 September

Capt Roeckel &	CO	F 7					
???		F 7	EA	X	Combles-Morval	0900	2

Casualties:

MdL Valentin Bourdet	N 112	P	MIA	Nieuport XVII N° 3315
S/Lt Eric Joly de				Nieuport XXI N° 1712
Bammeville	N 26	P	POW	WIA/DOW, 22 Sept; Balloon attack.

22 September

Lt Deullin		N 3	EA	X	S Doingt	0900	8
Adj Dorme	a.	N 3	LVG C	X	Guyencourt	0920	11
Adj Lenoir &		N 23					10
Adj Casale		N 23	EA	X	N Douaumont		3
Sgt de la Motte de la							
Motte Rouge &		C 43					1
Lt Salanson		C 43					1
Sgt Guertiau &		C 43					1
Sgt Dechoz		C 43	EA	X			1
Adj Tarascon		N 62	EA	X	SW Horgny	1410	6
MdL Sanglier		N 62	EA	X	Misery	0930	2
Cpl Massot		N 67	Scout	X	SW Rocquigny	1505	1
Capt de Marancour	b.	N 69	EA	X	Chaulnes		1
Adj Bucquet	c.	N 3	EA	P	S Riencourt	0925	–
MdL Sanglier		N 62	EA	P	Hynecourt-le-Petit	0940	–
Sgt J Sauvage		N 65	EA	P	E Brie	1045	–
S/Lt Le Sort		N 65	EA	FTL	St Cren	1500	–
Adj Bucquet	d.	N 3	EA	FTL	Rocquigny		–
Lt Heurtaux		N 3	EA	FTL	S Péronne	1810	–

a.   Possibly Uffz Karl Köhn, KIA, & Flg Albert Reicht, WIA/DOW 27 September 1916, Bertincourt.
b.   Possibly Obltn Franz Freye (P), KG 7, KIA, Chaulnes.
c.   Probably Ltn Winand Grafe, Jasta 2, KIA E Bapaume, about 3 km W Reincourt.
d.   Possibly Ltn Eberhard Fügner, Jasta 4, WIA SE Bapaume.

Casualties:

Lt Joseph Masquelier	N 37	P	MIA	Nieuport XVIIbis N° 3315.
Sgt Jean Canitrot	C 28	P	KIA	
S/Lt Louis Lecomte	C 28	O	KIA	Caudron G4
S/Lt Hector Varcin	N 37	P	WIA	Nieuport XVII
S/Lt Simonet	C 34	O	WIA	Caudron G4
Brig Bernard Schwartz	C 74	P	WIA	Flak, Caudron G4
Sgt Robert Chasle	F 210	P	KIAcc	Farman 37
Cpl Jacques Danziger	F 123	B	Injured	Farman 40
Sol Durin	RGAé	G	Injured	Farman 40

23 September

S/Lt Guynemer	a.	N 3	Fokker	XF	Erches	1120	17
S/Lt Guynemer	b.	N 3	Fokker	X	Roye	1123	18
Adj Jailler		N 15	EA	X	Morchain	0900	5
Cpl Grillot		N 48	Aviatik	X	Bois de Cheppy		1
Sgt Koch &		C 56					1
Adj Fouert		C 56	Scout	X	German lines		1
Cpl J Sauvage		N 65	EA	X	S Misery	1005	4
Sgt Flachaire		N 67	EA	XF	Bois de Vaux	0940	3
Capt de Marancour		N 69	EA	XF	Chaulnes		2
Capt de Marancour	c.	N 69	EA	XF	Andechy		3
MdL Darblay		N 69	EA	X	Licourt		2
S/Lt Mathis		N 69	EA	X	Parvillers		1
Sgt Baudson &		F 71					1
Lt Danery		F 71	Fokker	X	E St Mihiel		1
S/Lt V Régnier		N 112	EA	X	SE Léchelle	1830	2
Adj P de Marmier		N 112	EA	X	Poivre		1
Lt de Saint Fern &		C 212					1
Lt de Pommereau	d.	C 212	Fokker	XF	N Châlons		1
Capt Gignoux &	CO	F 20					1
Lt La Laperotte		F 20	Fokker	X	German lines		2
S/Lt Guynemer		N 3	EA	P			–
Adj Dorme		N 3	EA	P			–

Sgt Rapin &	C 66					–
Cpl Merveille	C 66	2 seater	P			–
Lt Le Mounier &	C 61					–
Lt Petyst de Morcourt	C 61	EA	P			–
Capt Ménard	N 26	EA	FTL	Rocquigny	0800	–
Sgt M Paris	N 73	EA	FTL	SE Léchelle	1530	–
MdL Lamy	C 46	EA	FTL	Aizecourt-Templeu		–
??? &	C 66					–
S/Lt Celerier	C 66	EA	FTL			–
Lt Daney	F 71	Fokker	FTL			–

a. Probably Ltn Fritz Neumann & Ltn Walter Blume, KG7/KSt39, KIA Erches.
b. Probably Ltn Ernst Raffauf (O), FlAbt 61, KIA Lignières-Roye.
c. Possibly Ltn Günther Dörrien & Ltn Walter Gericke, FlAbt 61, KIAs W Verpilières, about 10 km SE of Andechy.
d. Possibly Ltn Werner Lehmann, Jasta 9, (2v), KIA in combat with Caudrons at Sommepy.

Casualties:

Sgt Kiffin Rockwell	N 124	P	KIA	Nieuport XVII	
MdL Lecour Grandmaison	N 75	P	MIA	Nieuport XXI N° 1706	
MdL Louis Rosenlecker	N 26	P	POW	Nieuport XVIIbis	
Adj René David	N 49	P	KIA	Nieuport	
Capt Max Munch & CO	C 61	P	KIA		
S/Lt Charles de Merlis	C 61	O	KIA	Caudron G4	
Sgt Rapin &	C 66	P	WIA		
Cpl Merveille	C 66	G	KIA	Caudron G4, Bezange	
Sgt Léopold Dupont,	C 46	P	WIA		
Capt Maurice Gay &	C 46	O	KIA		
Brig Pierre Gaudin de Villaine	C 46	G	WIA	Caudron R4	
Sgt Fernand Guyou	N 15	P	WIA	Nieuport XVI	
Lt François d'Astier de La Vigerie	N 65	P	WIA	Nieuport XVII	
Sgt Camille Nageotte	F 20	P	WIA	Farman 42	
MdL Chutard &	GDE	P	KIAcc		
S/Lt Yribaren	GDE	O	KIAcc	VLAS 3	
Adj Robert Brazillier &	F 218	P	KIAcc		
Sgt Pelissier	F 218	G	KIAcc	Farman 40 T43	
Lt Guillaume Busson	N 48	P	OK	After combat FTL N Chattancourt, a/c destroyed by enemy artillery fire. Attacked by a Fokker, not flamed.	
???	73° Cie d'Aérostiers				
		O	OK		

24 September

Lt de Moulignon	N 3	EA	P	N Misery	1140	–
MdL Allez	N 65	EA	P	Aizécourt-Nurlu	1530	–
Sgt Massot	N 67	EA	P	E Péronne	1810	–
Lt E Billon du Plan	N 65	EA	FTL	Moislains	1455	–

Casualties:

Sgt André Steuer	a. N 103	P	MIA	Both pilots flying	
Sgt François Roman	a. N 103	P	MIA	Nieuport XVIIs, one of them probably claimed by Obltn Rudolf Berthold, Jasta 4, unconf.	
Cpl André Dumart &	F 204	P	MIA		
S/Lt Henri Desnos	F 204	O	MIA	Farman 130hp T1914	
Capt Lecomte & CO	C 42	P	MIA		
Cpl Maniquet	C 42	G	MIA	Caudron G4	
Lt Georges Vouaux &	CEP 115	P	MIA	CEP T4	
Sgt Joseph Reydellet	CEP 115	P	MIA		
S/Lt Louis Fromont	C 43	O	WIA	Caudron G4	
Sol Le Pallec	VC 116	G	Injured	VLC 150R	
Sgt Roger Thuau	N 62	P	Injured	Nieuport XVIIbis	
???	85° Cie d'Aérostiers			Attacked, not flamed.	
		O	OK		

a. These two collided in mid-air at 11h00 over Morval, while attacking an enemy aircraft.

25 September

Lt Heurtaux	a. N 3	Fokker	X	Villers-Carbonnel	1000	8
Adj Dorme	b. N 3	LVG	X	Nurlu-Liéramont	1715	12
S/Lt Raymond	N 3	EA	X	Bois de Vaux	1715	1
Adj Lenoir	N 23	3 seater	X	Fromezey		11
MdL Viallet	N 67	EA	XF	Ablancourt-Briost	1015	4

Sgt Aristide Jan		N 37	EA	X	W Brie	1405	1
MdL Viallet		N 67	EA	P	S Péronne	0930	–
S/Lt Raymond &		N 3					
Adj Dorme		N 3	EA	P	Manancourt	1645	–
Sgt Jan		N 37	EA	FTL	NW Nurlu	1350	–
Sgt Tsu		N 37	EA	FTL	Berthincourt	1350	–
Sgt Jan		N 37	EA	FTL	St Pierre Haut	1430	–
Sgt Garrigou		N 37	EA	P	Mesnil-Bruntel	1430	–

a.   Probably Ltn Kurt Wintgens, Jasta 1, (19v), KIA Villers-Carbonnel.
b.   Possibly Gefr Paul Tewes, WIA, & Ltn Martin Hoffmann (O), FlAbt (A) 237, KIA Combles, about 12 km west of Nurlu.

Casualties:

Adj Maxime Lenoir	N 23	P		WIA	Nieuport XVII
Lt Louis Genevois &	C 4	P		WIA	II° Armée, Caudron G4, probably
Sgt Emile Cabella	C 4	G		WIA	by Vfw Schürz, FeldFlgAbt 19.
Lt Maurice Blanchy	F 1	O		WIA	Farman 42
MdL Charles Albanal &	F 24	P		OK	
Lt Ducourtion	F 24	O		WIA	Farman 42
Cpl Paul Degraves	C 21	G		WIA	
Asp Parent de Chatelet &	F 209	P		KIAcc	
Sol Vergnol	F 209	G		KIAcc	Farman 40 T42 N° 2341
Adj Labonellie	RGAé	P		KIAcc	Farman 43
S/Lt Richard	F 36	P		KIAcc	Farman 43
MdL Yves Harzo &	GDE	P		Injured	
S/Lt Mairesse	GDE	O		Injured	Farman 43
Lt Jean Fonquernie	C 17	O		Injured	Caudron G4
Adj Félicien Combaz	C 21	P		Injured	Caudron G4

26 September

Sgt Delmas &		C 64					1
Sgt Maunoury		C 64					1
MdL de Dreux-Brèze &		MF 40					1
Lt Collet		MF 40	Fokker	X	Grateuil		1
S/Lt Nungesser	a.	N 65	2 seater	X	Le Transloy	0745	15
S/Lt Nungesser		N 65	Balloon	XF	Neuville	0805	16
S/Lt Nungesser	b.	N 65	Albatros C	X	Rocquigny	1045	17
Sgt Tsu		N 37	Balloon	P	N Nurlu	1540	–
S/Lt Nungesser		N 65	2 seater	P	Spincourt-Lechelle	0715	–
Sgt Jan		N 37	EA	FTL	Le Transloy	0905	–

a.   Possibly Ltn Richard Holler (O), FlAbt 6, KIA Bouchavesnes, about 8 km S of Le Transloy.
b.   Possibly Ltn Max Pawlowski (O), FlAbt (A) 222, KIA La Faux-Ferme.

Casualties:

L/Cdr d'Amecourt &	F 211	P	KIA	
S/Lt Georges Martinot	F 211	O	KIA	Farman 46
Lt Maurice Munier	C 6	P	MIA	Caudron G4 N° 2208,
Lt André Dellon	C 6	O	MIA	by Ltn Wilhelm Frankl, Jasta 4, (13).
Adj André Delcamp	F 25	P	KIA	Flak, II° Armée, Farman 56, 150 hp,
S/Lt Jean Belloc	F 25	O	KIA	Flak, down in flames over Verdun.
S/Lt Vermoral	F 41	O	WIA	Farman 42
S/Lt Louis Darligne	F 35	O	KIAcc	
QM Pierre Dieu	Navy	G	Injured	
???	24° Cie d'Aérostiers			Attacked, not flamed.
		O	OK	Moreuil Sector.

27 September

Sgt Tsu	N 37	Balloon	P	Bus	1515	–
Sgt Garrigou	N 37	Balloon	P	Equancourt	1520	–

Casualties:

Adj Clément Engerer	GDE	P	KIAcc	Farman 80hp
MdL Alfred Bazot	N 103	P	Injured	DOW 1 October 1916, Nieuport XXI landing accident.

28 September

Sgt Madon	N 38	Fokker	X	Pomacle	1
Sgt M Paris	N 73	EA	FTL		–
Lt Beissac	N 38	EA	FTL		–
Lt Lavidalie	CRP	EA	FTL		–
Lt Lavidalie	CRP	EA	FTL		–

Casualties:

Lt Jean-Pierre Lavidalie	CRP	P	Injured		
Cpl Pleuchot	GDE	P	Injured	Farman 80hp	

29 September – No Claims – No Casualties

30 September

Adj Dorme	N 3	Roland	P	Bertincourt	1015	–
Adj Bruneau	N 26	EA	P	Rancourt	1245	–
Sgt Calmon	N 37	EA	P	Misery-Licourt	1415	–
Cpl Raux &	C 47					–
Lt Choupaut	C 47	EA	P			–
Sgt Massot	a. N 67	EA	P	Léchelle	1245	–
Sgt Cacheux	N 73	EA	P	Rancourt	1245	–

a.   Possibly Ltn Ernst Diener, Jasta 2, KIA Bapaume, about 12 km NE of Léchelle.

Casualties:

Sgt Robert du Maroussem &	C 47	P	WIA	
Sgt Constant Lethon	C 47	G	WIA	Caudron G4
Sgt Canitrot	C 28	P	KIAcc	Caudron G4
Brig Delorme	GDE	P	KIAcc	Farman 42
Lt Lavidalie &	N 62	P	Injured	
Lt de la Motte-Rouge	N 62	O	Injured	Nieuport XIIbis

Unknown dates in September 1916:

MdL de Lageneste &	C 33				–
Sol Gatbois	C 33	EA	P		–

1 October

Lt Weiller &	C 21					1
???	C 21	EA	X			?
Adj Bloch	Spa 62	Balloon	XF	Longuavesnes	1500	4
Adj Dorme	N 3	EA	P	Villers-Carbonnel	1655	–
S/Lt Raymond	N 3	EA	P	Villers-Carbonnel	1655	–
Adj de Bonnefoy	N 65	EA	P	Puzeaux	0900	–
Adj de Bonnefoy	a. N 65	EA	P	Rancourt	1110	–
Adj de Bonnefoy	N 65	EA	P	Bois de Vaux	1410	–
Lt E Billon du Plan	N 65	EA	P	Chaulnes-Roye		–

a.   Possibly Ltn Ernst Reuter, FlAbt 2, KIA, Rancourt.

Casualties:

Sgt Fernand Garrigou	N 37	P	WIA		16h45
MdL Alphonse Vitry &	BM 118	P	KIAcc		
Mat Jean Peyrisson	BM 118	M	KIAcc	Bréguet-Michelin 4	
Sgt Ernest Duramel	C 228	P	Injured		

2 October

Cpl Hudellet	N 38	EA	X	Condé-sur-Autry		2
Adj Bloch	N 62	Balloon	XF	E Bapaume	1500	5
Sgt J Sauvage	N 65	EA	X	S Le Transloy	0920	5
Patrol	N 76	Fokker	P	N Brimont		–

Casualties: None

3 October – No Claims
Casualties:

MdL Maurice Joly &	F 2	P	KIA	
Lt Jean Delalandre	F 2	O	KIA	Farman 42

4 October

Adj Borde	N 65	Fokker	P	Bois de Pierre Vaast	–

Casualties: None

5 October – No Claims – No Casualties

6 October

Adj Violet-Marty	N 57	Fokker	X	Woëvre		1
Lt P Sauvage	a. N 112	EA	X	S Péronne	0800	1

a.   Probably Flg Georg Asen, FLAbt 7b, KIA Mons-en-Chausée, about 8 km SE of Péronne.

Casualties:

S/Lt Jean Lemarie	???	O	WIA			
MdL Georges Robart &	F 63	P	OK			
Sol Marcel Clément	F 63	G	KIA	Farman 43		
Adj Jaunaut	C 46	P	WIA	Flak		
SM Jean Mousset	PilSch	P	KIAcc	St Raphaël, FBA 100 HP #45.		

7 October – No Claims

Casualties:

Cdt Maurice Challe &	F 24	P	MIA	Nieuport XIIbis, probably by	
S/Lt Henri Mewius	F 24	O	MIA	Hptm Boelcke, Jasta 2, (31).	
Brig Bernadet	GDE	P	Injured	V3 (LAR)	

8 October – No Claims – No Casualties

9 October

S/Lt Guynemer	N 3	EA	P	Villers-Carbonnel	1700	–

Casualties:

Lt Paul Laffont	C 74	P	Injured	Caudron G4

10 October

Adj Dorme	N 3	Aviatik	XF	Nurlu-Bertincourt	1540	13
S/Lt Caissac,	C 46					1
Adj Mazeron &	C 46					1
Sol Tévenin	C 46	EA	X			1
Lt Campion,	C 46					2
Adj Jaunaut &	C 46					1
Sol Moutet	C 46	EA	X			1
Sgt Huffer &	N 62					1
Sgt Borzecki	N 62	EA	X	Doingt		2
Adj Prince a.	N 124	Fokker	X	Altkirch	1200	3
S/Lt Guynemer	N 3	2 seater	P	Villers-Carbonnel		–
Lt Heurtaux	N 3	EA	P	N Somme		–
S/Lt Rougevin	N 67	EA	P			–
Lt Derode	N 67	EA	P			–
S/Lt de Bruce	N 69	EA	FTL	Falvy		–

a.   Possibly Uffz Julius Heck, Kest 5, KIA, Freiberg.

Casualties:

Sgt Roger Thuau &	N 62	P	MIA	Nieuport XIV, probably by Ltn	
Lt Jean Billon du Plan	N 62	O	MIA	Wilhelm Frankl, Jasta 4, (14).	
MdL Henri					
Vincent-Darasse &	F 201	P	KIA	Flak	
Lt Alexis Bouzereau CO	F 201	O	KIA	Flak, Farman 40	
Sgt Léopold Delaquerrière	F 36	P	KIAcc		
& Sol Baboin	F 36	M	KIAcc	Farman 42	
Capt Maurice Bernard	Pau	P	KIAcc		
Sol Henri Carol	B		Injured		

11 October – No Claims

Casualties:

Lt André Bastien	N 57	P	Injured	Nieuport XVII
Sgt Georges Thomas &	N 68	P	Injured	
Sol Tarinot	N 68	M	Injured	Nieuport XIIbis

12 October

Sgt Despert &	F 29					1
MdL Buisson	F 29	Fokker	X	Oberndorf		1
Brig de Gaillard de						3
La Valdene &	F 123					
Cpl Pichon	F 123	EA	X	Oberndorf		1
Adj Prince	N 124	Fokker EIII	X	Oberndorf		4
Adj Lufbery	N 124	Roland CII	X	Oberndorf		5
Adj Masson	N 124	Fokker	X	Oberndorf		1
???	???	EA	X	Oberndorf		–

Casualties:

MdL Léon Mottay &	BM 120	P	WIA/POW	
Sol Marchand	BM 120	B	KIA	Bréguet-Michelin IV N° 436.

MdL Lucien Barlet &	BM 120	P	MIA			
Sol Luneau	BM 120	B	MIA	Bréguet-Michelin IV		
Cpl Noël Bouet &	BM 120	P	POW			
Sol Delcroix	BM 120	B	POW	Bréguet-Michelin IV		
Cpl Robert de Montais &	BM 120	P	KIA			
Sol André Haas	BM 120	B	KIA	Bréguet IV		
				Two of these probably downed by Ltn Ernst Udet (2) and Ltn Pfälzer (1), Jasta 15.		
Adj Henri Baron &	F 123	P	KIA	Farman 40, probably by		
Sgt André Guerineau	F 123	B	KIA	Ltn Otto Kissenberth,		
S/Lt Armand Georges &	F 123	P	KIA	Kek Einsisheim, (1 & 2).		
Sgt Ernest Jouan	F 123	B	KIA	Farman 42		
Sgt Ganthes,	R 210	P	OK	V° Armée, Lavannes, FTL		
S/Lt Buvry &	R 210	O	WIA	during combat, Letord.		
Sol Albrecht	R 210	G	WIA			
Adj Norman Prince	N 124	P	Injured	DOW 16 October 1916, Nieuport XVII.		
Cpl Henri Tondu	F 123	P	Injured	Farman 42, hit by flak & FTL in the Vosges.		

13 October – No Claims
Casualties:

Lt André Patry	F 205	P	KIA	Flak, Farman 60		
Lt Constant Perrodin	C 27	O	KIA	Flak, Farman 60		

14 October

Adj Fonck &	C 47					–
Capt Bosc	C 47	2 seater	P	Somme Sector		–
Casualties:						
Lt Victor Goupil &	F 52	P	KIAcc			
Lt Jean Godillot	F 52	O	Injured	Farman 42		
Sgt Marin Million &	C 47	P	Injured			
Lt Albert Lelloche	C 47	O	OK	Caudron G4		

15 October

MdL Sanglier	N 62	EA	X	Bouchavesnes		3
???	DCA	EA	XF	Lassigny		–
Adj Bordes	N 65	EA	P	Moislains	1635	–
Lt E Billon du Plan	N 65	EA	P	Bouchavesnes	1645	–
Lt E Billon du Plan	N 65	EA	P	Allaines	1650	–
Casualties:						
MdL Jean Bigeard &	C 207	P	KIAcc			
S/Lt Léon	C 207	O	Injured	Caudron G4		

16 October

Adj Dorme	N 3	Fokker	X	N Péronne	1635	14
Sgt Major,	F 16					1
Cpl Laffon &	F 16					1
Sol Legrende	F 16	EA	XF	Roye-Lassigny		1
Sgt Soulier	N 26	EA	X	Manancourt	0750	2
Capt Ménard	a. N 26	EA	X	Beaulencourt	1439	1
Adj Bucquet	N 3	EA	P	Hynecourt	0925	–
Adj Borde	N 65	EA	P	Moislains		–
Cpl Goux	N 67	EA	P	Bois de Vaux	0900	–
Lt Derode	N 67	EA	P			–
Sgt Soulier	N 26	EA	FTL	E Allaines		–

a.   Possibly Uffz Max Reichel & Ltn Kurt Hottop, FlAbt 57, KIAs between Grévillers and Cambrai, about 7 km NW Beaulencourt.
Casualties:

Capt René Dreyfus	R 203	O	WIA			
Sgt Marcel David	C 18	P	WIA	Flak, Caudron G4		
S/Lt Auguste Azaïs	49° Cie d'Aérostiers			Cable broke by artillery fire,		
		O	OK	observer jumped to avoid being a POW.		

17 October

Lt Heurtaux	a. N 3	Albatros	XF	Rocquigny	1055	9
Sgt Sendral	N 26	Rumpler	X	Aizecourt-le-Haut	0905	2

Sgt Sendral		N 26	EA	P	E Bouchavesnes	1610	–
Lt Gigodot		N 103	EA	P	Ablaincourt	0855	–
Sgt Larroucau &		Sop 107					–
???		Sop 107	EA	P			–

a.   Probably Ltn Walter Palm & Ltn Emil Dabelow (O), KG 3, KIAs Rocquigny.

Casualties:

Lt Pierre Labaurie &		C 207	P	MIA			
Lt Jacques Chaney		C 207	O	MIA	Caudron G4		

---

18 October – No Claims
Casualties:

Adj André Melin			P	WIA			
Cpl Georges Hennequin &		GDE	P	Injured			
Sol Marquin		GDE	M	Injured	Farman 130hp		

---

19 October – No Claims – No Casualties

---

20 October

Lt Heurtaux	a.	N 3	2 seater	X	Bouchavesnes	0740	10
Capt Roeckel &	CO	F 7					3
???		F 7	EA	XF	Moislains		?
Capt Roeckel &	CO	F 7					4
???		F 7	EA	XF	Moislains		?
S/Lt Baras &		C 21					1
???		C 21	EA	X			1
Capt Lecour-Grandmaison,		C 46					3
MdL Vitalis &		C 46					4
S/Lt Labussière &		C 46					2
Cpl Rivière,		C 46					1
S/Lt Barbier &		C 46					2
Sgt Girod		C 46	LVG C	X			1
Sgt Blanc &		C 47					1
???		C 47	EA	X	German lines		1
Sgt Flachaire	b.	N 67	EA	X	Rancourt	0840	4
Sgt M Paris		N 73	EA	X	Bois de St Pierre-Waast		1
Lt Heurtaux		N 3	EA	FTL	Moislains	1020	–

a.   Probably Ltn Erwin Zass & Ltn Rolf Blessing, KG5/KSt 28, KIAs, Bouchavesnes.
b.   Possibly Flg Paul Greitschat POW & Ltn Gottfried Thiemann KIA, KG1/Kasta1, Rocquigny, about 10 km N Rancourt.

Casualties:

MdL Edmond Lods &		N 69	P	MIA	Morane XXI, probably by		
S/Lt Genay		C 27	O	MIA	Vfw C Kress, Jasta 6, (3).		
Adj Robert Bruneau		N 73	P	WIA	Nieuport XI		
MdL Jacques Beney &		C 17	P	WIA	DOW 21 October 1916		
Lt Naudeau		C 17	O	KIA	Caudron G4		
MdL Sutter		21° Cie d'Aérostiers			Cable cut by artillery, he		
			O	OK	jumped to avoid being taken prisoner.		

---

21 October

Adj Dorme	a.	N 3	Roland D	X	Barleux	1521	15
Sgt Villars &		N 23					1
Sgt Sabatier		N 23	Balloon	XF	N Verdun		1
MdL Flachaire	a.	N 67	EA	X	Barleux	1510	5
Sgt Dupre		N 102	EA	X			2
???		DCA	EA	X	French lines		–
Lt Deullin		N 3	EA	P	Villers-Carbonnel	1450	8
Sgt Soulier		N 26	EA	P	Sailly-Sallisel	1500	–
MdL Flachaire		N 67	EA	FTL	S Bussu	1500	–
Lt Heruet		N 103	EA	P	Villers-au-Flos	1420	
Sgt Massot		N 67	EA	P	E Eterpigny	1505	

a.   Possibly Ltn Hans Petersson, Jasta 3, KIA Péronne, about 7 km NNE of Barleux.

Casualties:

MdL André Bonnafont		F 20	P	KIA			
Sgt Charles Couget &		C 28	P	KIA	Caudron G4, possibly by		
Sol François Poisard		C 28	M	WIA	Ltn Otto Bernert, Jasta 4,(4).		
Sgt Robert Destot		N 62	P	WIA	During a night combat.		
Lt Frodolliet &		C 64	P	Injured			
Sol Charles Quette		C 64	M	Injured	Caudron G4		

22 October

Adj Violet-Marty	N 57	EA	X			2
Sgt Viallet	N 67	EA	X	Metz-en-Couture	1425	5
MdL Flachaire	N 67	EA	X	Metz-en-Couture	1600	6
Adj Coudouret	N 102	EA	X			2
Lt Heurtaux	N 3	EA	P	Barleux	1015	–
Adj Bucquet	N 3	EA	P	Balâtre	1255	–
Sgt Bergot	N 73	EA	P	Brie	1210	–
Sgt Hébert	N 62	EA	FTL	German lines		–
Sgt Hébert	N 62	EA	FTL	German lines		–

Casualties:

Brig Claudius Decorme	N 38	P	MIA	Nieuport XI, probably by Ltn A Frey, Jasta 9, (1).	
MdL Jean Aubijoux	N 76	P	MIA, POW?	Morane XXI, departed 06h00, became lost..	
Adj Pierre Delacroix &	F 204	P	MIA		
Lt René Vidus	F 41	O	MIA	Farman 42	
MdL Pic	VB 114	B	Injured	Voisin B 150hp	

23 October

Lt Languedoc	N 12	EA	X	Ornes		1
Lt Gastin	N 49	Aviatik	X	Cernay	1100	2
Lt Doumer	N 76	EA	X	N Azannes		3
Lt Doumer	N 76	EA	X	N Romange		4
EV1 de Salins &	* CAM					1
Sgt Médeville	* CAM	Seaplane	X	Ostende		1
Sgt Agostini &	C 105					–
???	C 105	EA	P			–

Casualties:

Adj Maxime Lenoir	N 23	P	MIA	Spad VII	
MdL Louis Paga	N 76	P	MIA	Nieuport XVI	
S/Lt Charles Aimard	N 76	P	MIA	Nieuport XVII	
Capt Georges Gassier	C 105	P	MIA	Caudron G4	
Cpl Camille Sennegond	C 56	P	MIA	Caudron G4	
Sgt Médeville	O		MIA	Seaplane	
Lt José Maria	N 77	P	POW	Nieuport XVII N° 1831, FTL motor trouble, after combat with FlAbt 65.	
EV1 Robert Guyot d'Asnière de Salins &	* CAM	P	POW	FTL, FBA 150 HP N° 332, codé	
Sgt Médeville	* CAM	O	POW	D.11. Probably by Ltn.z.S. Niemeyer, SFSII, (2).	
Sol Cochet	C 42	M	WIA	Caudron G4	
Asp Lejeune	???	P	KIAcc	Mid-air collision	
Adj Magnier &	F 25	P	Injured		
Adj Bigot	F 25	G	Injured	Farman 42	

* Dunkerque.

24 October – No Claims
Casualties:

MdL André Bonnafont &	F 20	P	WIA		
Lt Charles Mouget	F 20	O	WIA	Farman 43	
S/Lt Pierre Frelezeau	???	P	KIAcc		

25 October

Adj Dufaur de Gavardie	N 12	Balloon	XF		5
Auto-Canons	DCA	EA	X	Vauquois	–
Adj Barbaza	N 77	2 seater	FTL	SW Etain	–

Casualties: None

26 October – No Claims
Casualties:

Adj Charles Guilhaumon &	F 33	P	MIA	Farman 60, probably by Ltn	
Lt Paul Rouch	F 33	O	MIA	Roland Nauck Jasta 6, (1).	
Lt Jean Lemarie	F 205	O	WIA	Farman 60	
Sgt Roger &	C 64	P	Injured		
Sol Auguste Chaverebière de Sal	C 64	M	Injured	Caudron G4	

27 October

MdL Sanglier	N 62	EA	P			–

Casualties:

Lt Albert Dupont &	C 104	P	MIA		
Lt Choisy	C 104	O	MIA	Caudron G4	
Lt Marcel Brice-Bretocq & CO	F 29	P	KIAcc		
Sol Nahe	F 29	B	KIAcc	Farman 40	

---

28 October – No Claims

Casualties:

Cpl Jacques de Sars &	C 207	P	MIA	Caudron G4. probably by Ltn	
S/Lt Louis Resseguier	C 207	O	MIA	Friedrich Mallinckrodt, Jasta 6, (1).	
Lt de Bains	N 68	O	Injured	Nieuport XIIbis	

---

29 October

Adj Sicot	EA	X		1

Casualties: None

---

30 October – No Claims – No Casualties

---

31 October

Adj Sanglier	N 62	EA	X	Rocquigny		4
S/Lt Ledeuil	N 103	EA	X	Le Transloy	1640	1
S/Lt Lafargue	N 112	EA	X	Rocquigny		1
Capt Thenault	N 124	EA	P	Villers-Carbonnel	1545	–

Casualties:

EV1C Emile Hariat	Navy	P	KIAcc	Bomb explosion
Lt Antoine Reynaud	Navy	P	KIAcc	Bomb explosion
Sol Théodore Hulet	F 211	M	Injured	

---

1 November

Lt Pinsard	N 26	EA	X	Lechele	1525	2
S/Lt Loste,	C 46					3
Capt de Peytes de Montcabrier &						2
Sol Martin	C 46	EA	X	Metz-en-Couture		3
S/Lt Loste,	C 46					4
Capt de Peytes de Montcabrier &						3
Sol Martin	C 46	EA	XF	Mont St Quentin		4
Lt Gastin	N 49	EA	X	Altkirch		3
Adj Sayaret	N 57	EA	X	Mogeville		6
Adj Tarascon	N 62	LVG C	X	Moislains		7
Lt de Bonald &	N 69					1
Cpl Boy	N 69	EA	X	E Ablaincourt		1
Sgt Madon	N 38	EA	FTL	Fromezey		–

Casualties:

Cpl Ravel	N 103	P	MIA	Nieuport XXI, probably by a Kasta 25 crew, departed at 13h50.
Adj Aristide Jan	N 37	P	WIA	Flak
Sol Louis Martin	C 46	G	WIA	Flak, Caudron R4
Sgt Marius Pivard	C 224	P	Injured	Caudron G4
Brig Emmanuel du Lac	N 62	P	Injured	
Lt Dambon	N 62	O	Injured	Sopwith
???	74° Cie d'Aérostiers			Attacked, not flamed.
		O	OK	

---

2 November

Lt Campion,	C 46				3
S/Lt Arrault &	C 46				1
Brig Lamy	C 46	EA	X	Allaines	1
???	DCA	EA	X	Forêt de Nonnenbruch	–
Sgt Destut	???	EA	P	St Pierre-Waast	–
Capt Colcomb CO	N 38	EA	P	Allaines	–

Casualties:

Sgt Hippolyte Dolo &	C 34	P	Injured	
Sgt Bouttier	C 34	M	Injured	Caudron G4

3 November

Lt Heurtaux	a.	N 3	Aviatik C	XF	Rocquigny	1400	11
Capt Guilloux &	CO	F 24					1
S/Lt Coustau		F 24	Scout	XF			1
Sgt J Sauvage	b.	N 65	EA	XF	Mesnil-en-Arrouaize	1207	6
Sgt Viallet		N 67	EA	XF	Mesnil-Bruntel	1230	6
S/Lt Guynemer		N 3	Aviatik C	P	Bertincourt	1350	–
S/Lt Tsu		N 37	EA	P	Bois de la Ville	1550	–
Sgt Baron		N 103	EA	FTL	NW Mesnil-Bruntel	1300	–

a.　Probably Uffz Ernst Honold & Ltn Max Steiner, FlAbt 42, KIAs Rocquigny.
b.　Probably Ltn Spindler, WIA, & Ltn Alexander Kullmann (O) FlAbt 2, KIA Sailly, about 5 km SE Mesnil-en-Arrouaize.

Casualties:

Adj Maurice Saillard &	F 24	P	MIA	Farman 40, probably by Rittm
S/Lt Charles Trehout	F 24	O	MIA	Josef Wulff, Jasta 6,(2).
Sgt René Levarlet &	C 220	P	WIA	II° Armée
Capt Pierre Gardet	C 220	O	WIA	Caudron G4
Lt Philippe	C 61	O	WIA	Flak, Caudron G4
MdL de Garagnol &	F 215	P	KIAcc	
Asp Bloy	F 215	O	Injured	Farman 40

4 November

Lt P Sauvage &	N 112				1550	2
Adj de Bonnefoy	N 65	EA	XF	La Ferme de l'Hôpital		5

Casualties:

Sgt-Maj Albert Tessier	GDE	P	Injured	Caudron G4
MdL Delreux	GDE	P	Injured	Maurice-Farman 130hp

5 November

Cpl Boy	N 63	EA	P	–

Casualties:

MdL Raymond Enjolras	GDE	P	Injured	Nieuport XI

6 November

Adj Thery &	F 7					1
Lt Trimbach	F 7	EA	X	French lines		1
Adj Hall	N 103	EA	P	Buire	1530	–

Casualties:

Cpl Jacques Boy &	N 69	P	KIA	Type "P"
Lt Pierre Delaine	N 69	O	KIA	Morane-Saulnier XXI
S/Lt Dupont	F 33	O	WIA	Farman 42
Lt Florian Henry	F 221	O	WIA	

7 November

MdL Sardier &		N 77				1
S/Lt Georgeot	a.	N 77	Scout	X	Vieville-en-Haye	1
Lt Boulanger &		???				1
Lt de Mentière		???	EA	X	Vilcey-sur-Trey	1

a.　Ltn Solter, unit unknown.

Casualties:

S/Lt Henri Paillard	N 49	P	KIA	Nieuport XI, Thann
Adj Raoul Monrouzeau &	N 77	P	MIA	
Sgt Koestner	N 77	G	MIA	Nieuport XIIbis N° 1864
Lt Henry	F 221	O	WIA	Farman 40
Lt Georges Homolle	N 75	P	Injured	Nieuport XXI
MdL ??? &	F 20	P	Injured	
S/Lt René Meric	F 20	O	Injured	Farman 40

8 November

Sgt Baron	N 103	EA	P	Ligny-Beaulencourt	1600	–

Casualties:

Adj Lucien Charbonnier	F 204	P	MIA	
S/Lt Pierre Sonet	F 204	O	MIA	Farman 42 N° 2434
Cpl Bournet	GDE	P	Injured	Caudron G4

9 November

Adj Dufaur de Gavarde	a.	N 12	Aviatik C	X	S Verdun	6
Sgt Madon &		N 38				2

S/Lt Mosnier		N 38	Fokker D	X	Sommepy		1
S/Lt Ledeuil	b.	N 103	EA	X	NE Manancourt	1140	2
???		DCA	Rumpler C	POW	St Hilaire-le-Grand		–
Adj Bertrand		N 57	EA	FTL			
Lt Deullin		N 3	EA	P	Villers-Carbonnel	1005	–
Lt Deullin	c.	N 3	EA	P	Sailly-Sallisel	1040	–
Lt Deullin		N 3	EA	P	Bouchavesnes	1045	–
Sgt J Sauvage	d.	N 65	Aviatik	P	Fonches	1557	–
Adj B Hall	c.	N 103	EA	P	Sailly-Sallisel	1130	–
Adj Lufbery		M 124	EA	P	Ablaincourt	0945	–
Sgt Pavelka		N 124	EA	P	Aizecourt	0950	–
??? &		C 27					
Lt Hanus		C 27	EA	P			–

a.   Aircraft N 1667/16, possibly OfStv Paul Baumann & Ltn Karl Reichard, KG6/Kasta36, KIAs Verdun.
b.   Possibly Ltn Kral Staemm & Ltn Albert Eder, FlAbt 13, KIAs Beaulencourt, about 12 km NE of Manancourt.
c.   Possibly Ltn Rudolf Satter (O), FlAbt (A) 295b, KIA between Combles and Driencourt, Sailly-Sallisel about 4 km NE of Combles.
d.   Possibly Vfw Christian Kress, Jasta 6, KIA Nesle, about 6 km ESE Fonches.

Casualties:

Lt Jules Leleu,	F 208	P	MIA	Caudron R4 #1636/839
S/Lt Léon Guedon &	F 208	O	MIA	probably by Rittm Josef Wulff
Sgt Desprats	F 208	G	MIA	Jasta 6, (3).
Lt Hubert de Fels	N 38	P	KIA	Nieuport XVII
Cpl Léon Millot	N 103	P	KIA	Nieuport XVII, VI° Armée, near Sailly-Sallisel, departed 15h45, possibly by Ltn Helmut Baldamus, Jasta 9, (6).
Brig François Comte &	F 205	P	WIA	
Lt Borel	F 205	O	WIA	Farman 43
S/Lt Jean Renoir	C 64	P	Injured	Caudron G4

10 November

S/Lt Guynemer	a.	N 3	Aviatik	X	S Nesle	1215	19
S/Lt Guynemer	b.	N 3	Albatros C	X	Morcourt	1225	20
Lt Deullin		N 3	EA	X	Mont St Quentin	1340	9
MdL Soulier		N 26	Aviatik C	X	E Péronne	1015	3
Capt Lecour-Grandmaison		C 46					4
MdL Vitalis &		C 46					5
Cpl Rousseaux		C 46	Roland	X	E Barleux		2
Adj Covin,		F 52					1
S/Lt Vuillaume &		F 52					1
Sol Michel		F 52	Scout	XF			1
S/Lt Lecoq de Kerland		N 68	Scout	X	Forêt de Gremessey		1
Adj Bourdet		N 112	2 seater	X			1
Cpl Taffe		N 112	EA	X	St Pierre-Vaast		1
Sgt Sabattier &		N 23					–
Sgt Baron		N 103	EA	P	St Pierre-Vaast	0750	–
Lt Matton		N 48	EA	P			–
Sgt Lannes		N 73	EA	P		0945	–
Sgt Lutzius		N 103	EA	P	St Pierre-Vaast	0750	–
Adj Lufbery	c.	N 124	EA	P	Haplincourt	1228	–
Sgt Prou		N ??	EA	P	Athies	1015	–
S/Lt Lecoq de Kerland		N 68	Aviatik C	P	Forêt de Gremessey		–
S/Lt Mosnier		N 38	EA	FTL			–
MdL Bertrand	d.	N 57	EA	FTL	German lines, II° Armée		–

a.   Probably Vfw Christian Kress (4v), Jasta 6, KIA Nesle.
b.   Possibly Ltn Karl Staemm & Ltn Albert Eder, FlAbt 13, KIAs, Beaulencourt.
c.   Possibly Ltn Max Hülse & Uffz Karl Münster, KG5/KSt30, KIAs Sailly-Saillisel, about 10 km SSW of Haplincourt.
d.   Possibly Uffz Christian Bemsel & Ltn Ernst Müller, KG6, KampfSt 36, KIAs Verdun.

Casualties:

Lt de Roger Saint Pern &	C 212	P	KIA	Caudron G4, probably by
Lt de Pommereau	C 212	O	KIA	Vfw Hermann Pfeiffer, Jasta 9, (6).
Lt Henri Beissac	N 38	P	WIA	Spad VII
Adj Jules Covin	F 52	P	WIA	Caudron R4
Sgt Bouilard	C 104	G	WIA	Flak, Caudron G4
Sgt Marcel Bourdarie	N 103	P	Injured	DOW 25 December 1916 Nieuport XVII, VI° Armée, departed 06h30.

11 November

Lt Heurtaux	a.	N 3	Albatros C	XF	Sailly-Saillisel	0900	12

a.   Probably Ltn Max Hülse & Uffz Karl Münster, KG5/KampfSt 30, KIAs at Les Boeufs, about 5 km ENE of Sailly-Saillisel.

Casualties:

Sgt Denis Epitalon	N 15	P	WIA	Flak		
Cpl Paul Matanovitch	N 15	P	WIA	Possibly by Ltn Hermann Kunz, Jasta 7, (2).		
Lt Lamontagne	V 114	O	Injured	Voisin B		
Cpl Marcel Gaudron	C 220	P	Injured	Caudron G4		

12 November

Cpl R Sabatier	N 73	EA	X			2
Adj Violet-Marty	N 57	2 seater	P			–
Lt de Langle de Cary	N 23	EA	P			–

Casualties: None

13 November

S/Lt Guynemer	N 3	EA	P	Hallu	–

Casualties:

Brig Marcel Murel &	F 71		P	Injured	
S/Lt Jeannin	F 71		O	Injured	Farman 43

14 November

Lt de Maison Rouge	a. N 124	EA	P	N Combles	1445	–

a.   Possibly Ltn Max Dieterle & Ltn Hans Gürtler, FlAbt 8, KIAs, Les Boeufs, about 6 km N of Combles.

Casualties: None

15 November

Adj Jeronnez	a. N 26	Aviatik C	X	E Chaulnes	1215	1
Lt Derode	N 67	EA	X	Marchélepot		1
???	b. DCA	EA	POW	S Attichy		–

a.   Probably Vfw Hermann Michel & Obltn Heinrich Bauer, FlAbt 7, KIAs Chaulnes.
b.   Rumpler C.I 1850/15, POWs.

Casualties:

Asp Pierre Navarre	GDE	P	KIAcc	Morane-Saulnier 80 hp	

16 November

Lt Heurtaux	a. N 3	Fokker	X	E Le Pressoire	0930	13
S/Lt Guynemer	N 3	Fokker	X	Pertain-Omiécourt	1340	21
Adj Dorme	N 3	Rumpler C	XF	E Marchélepot	1515	16
Sgt Sabattier	N 23	EA	X			2
S/Lt Loste,	C 46					5
MdL Vitalis &	C 46					6
Cpl Rousseaux	C 46	Albatros	X	Brie		3
???	b. DCA	Rumpler C	POW	Roye-en-Matz		–
S/Lt Blanchard &	C 11					1
???	C 11	EA	X			?
Cdt Féquant CO	GC 13	EA	P	Hallu	1010	–
Sgt J Sauvage	N 65	EA	P	Aumencourt	1115	–
Sgt Sendral	N 26	EA	P	Barleux	1145	–
Sgt Bardel	N 103	EA	P	Moislains	1045	–

a.   Probably Ltn Ernst Wever, Jasta 6, KIA Pressoire Wald.
b.   LVG C.II 850/16, possibly OfStv Phillip Jung & Obltn Herman von Gillhausen, FlAbt 34, POWs.

Casualties:

Sgt Roger Girard &	C 66	P	KIA	Caudron G4, probably by	
Adj Robert Laguesse	C 66	G	KIA	Vfw Fritz Loerzer, Jasta 6 (1). E Ablaincourt, 08h30.	
MdL Georges Morel &	C 66	P	WIA		
Cpl Elie Osmond	C 66	G	WIA	Caudron G4, 09h50.	
S/Lt Pierre Gaudillot	C 47	O	WIA	Caudron G4	
Cpl Chapelle &	F 123	P	Injured		
Cpl Marcel Nepveu	F 123	B	Injured	Farman 42	

17 November

Sgt Madon	a. N 38	Fokker	X	Marvaux	3
S/Lt de Turenne	N 48	Albatros	X	II° Armée	1
Adj Tarascon	b. N 62	Aviatik	X	Manancourt	8
Adj Bergot	N 73	EA	X	German lines	1
S/Lt Havet	c. N 77	EA	X	Vieville-en-Haye	2

MdL Brioude &	F 32					1
S/Lt Desquibes	F 32	EA	X	Hallu		1
Adj Bucquet	d. N 3	2 seater	PF	Liancourt-Fosse	1040	–
Adj Dorme	e. N 3	LVG	P	Manancourt	1525	–

a. Possibly Ltn Wilhelm Schoulat, Jasta 9, KIA Monthois, Jasta 9 at Leffincourt, in the N 38 operating area.
b. Possibly Ltn Walter Andreae & Ltn Hans Renschenberg, KG5, KIAs Ytres, about 8 km N of Manancourt.
c. Possibly Ltn Anton Mayer & Ltn Hans Lenhartz, FlAbt 70, KIAs near Jaulny, AOK "C" Sector.
d. Possibly Ltn Karl Germaer & Obltn Roland Müller, FlAbt (A) 266, KIAs Liancourt.
e. Possibly Vfw Arno Zimmermann, KIA & Obltn Oskar Kriegbaum, WIA, FlAbt 256 (A), KIA Etricourt, about 1 km NE of Manoncourt.

Casualties:

Sgt Georges Sendral	N 26	P	WIA	Nieuport XVII	
Sol Henri Chedeville	N 26	M	WIA	Nieuport XVII	
Sol Maurice Grenez	N 3	M	WIA	Aerial bombardment	
Brig Joseph Auvray	???	P	Injured	DOW same day	
Cpl Marchand &	F 72	P	Injured		
Sol Lucien Drigny	F 72	O	Injured	Bréguet-Michelin	
Sol Brunerie	C 9	M	Injured	Caudron G4	

18 November – No Claims
Casualties:

Sgt Plouvy &	N 38	P	MIA	
S/Lt François Roederer	N 38	O	KIA	Nieuport XIIbis N° 1746

19 November – No Claims
Casualties:

Capt Bataille &	F 221	P	KIAcc	
Lt Max Laffont	F 221	O	Injured	Farman 60, II° Armée
MdL de La Chapelle &	C 220	P	Injured	
Lt B Lafont	C 220	O	Injured	Caudron G4, II° Armée
S/Lt Buchy	F 216	O	Injured	Farman 42

20 November – No Claims
Casualties:

Adj Paul de Marmier	N 112	P	KIAcc	Nieuport XVII
Lt Henri Janet &	F 215	P	KIAcc	}Collided
Sgt Maurice Padovani	F 215	G	KIAcc	Farman 42
Sgt Léon Gouvernet &	V 107	P	Injured	
Sgt Pauly	V 107	B	Injured	Voisin

21 November – No Claims
Casualties:

Adj Aristide Jan	N 37	P	Injured	Nieuport XVIIbis, crash-landed returning from a night mission.
S/Lt Henri Ruyant &	C 9	P	Injured	
Cpl Fayard	C 9	G	Injured	Caudron G4

22 November

S/Lt Guynemer	N 3	Halberstadt	X	E St Christ	1445	22
S/Lt Guynemer	N 3	Halberstadt	X	Falvy	1555	23
S/Lt Guynemer	N 3	EA	P	St Christ	1555	–
Adj Violet-Marty	N 57	2 seater	P			–

Casualties:

Sgt Jean de Gromard	???	P	KIAcc	

23 November

Lt Deullin	a. N 3	EA	XF	S Bois de Vaux	1550	10
S/Lt Caissac,	C 46					2
S/Lt Labussière &	C 46					3
Cpl Tenivin	C 46	EA	X			2
S/Lt Barbier,	C 46					2
Adj Mazeron &	C 46					2
Brig Rousseaux	C 46	Aviatik	X			4
Lt L'Huillier	N 62	EA	X	Bus		1
Sgt Hébert &	N 62					1
Adj Borzecki	N 62	EA	X	Ytres		3
Capt E Billon du Plan	N 65	EA	X	Hyencourt	1145	4

S/Lt Nungesser	N 65	LVG C	X	S Falvy	1430	18
MdL Viallet	N 67	2 seater	X	Nurlu-Moislains	0750	7
MdL Flachaire	b. N 67	EA	X	Manancourt	1035	7
MdL Bergot	N 73	EA	X	Fins	0935	2
S/Lt Ledeuil	N 103	EA	X	NE Marchélepot	1435	3
???	DCA	EA	X	N Berry-au-Bac		–
S/Lt Nungesser	N 65	EA	P	Licourt	1315	–
Sgt J Sauvage	N 65	EA	P	Béthencourt	1555	–

a.   Probably Hptm Hans Linke & Ltn Wilhelm Steinbrenner, KG5/Kasta25, KIAs Vaux Wald.
b.   Probably Vfw Friedrich Schwaim & Obltn Johann Köhn, FlAbt (A) 221, KIA Etricourt, immediate vicinity of Manancourt.
Casualties:

S/Lt Roger Arrault	C 46	O	WIA	Flak, Caudron R4
Cpl Achille Rousseaux	C 46	G	WIA	Flak, Caudron R4
S/Lt Duran	C 30	O	WIA	Flak, Caudron G4
Sgt Marcel Jaubert	N 26	P	WIA	N of the Somme, 12h15.
Sol Pilate	RGAé	M	Injured	Morane-Saulnier

24 November

Adj Casale	N 23	Balloon	XF		4
S/Lt Mosnier &	N 38				2
Lt Roederer	N 38	EA	X		1
Adj Casale	N 23	Balloon	P		–
Adj Martinenq	C 222				–
Sol Valarcher	C 222	EA	FTL		–

Casualties:

S/Lt François Roederer	N 38	O	KIA	
S/Lt Henri Roget	F 8	P	Injured	
???	25° Cie d'Aérostiers			
		O	OK	Hit by artillery fire at 1,200 meters height.

25 November – No Claims
Battle of the Somme is concluded.
Casualties:

MdL Quentin de Gromard	RGAé	P	KIAcc	Farman 48

26 November

S/Lt Delorme	N 38	Roland C	X	German lines	3
Adj B Hall	N 103	EA	X		3
S/Lt V Régnier	N 112	EA	X	Manancourt	3

Casualties: None

27 November – No Claims – No Casualties

28 November – No Claims
Casualties:

S/Lt Noël Mosnier	N 38	P	MIA	Nieuport XVII

29 November – No Claims
Casualties:

Capt Jules de Boutiny	N 49	P	Injured	Spad VII
S/Lt Gal Ladevèze	V 109	O	Injured	Voisin

30 November – No Claims – No Casualties
Unknown date in November 1916.

MdL Armand Pousson &	MF 33	P	WIA
Lt André Schroeder	MF 33	O	WIA

1 December

Sgt Madon &	N 38				–
S/Lt Delorme	N 38	2 seater	FTL	W Tahure	–

Casualties:

Adj Emil Merit	GDE	P	KIAcc	Nieuport XI

2 December

S/Lt Delorme	N 38	EA	FTL	Vaudesincourt	–

MdL Poreaux	N 31	Aviatik	P	Fresnes-en-Woëvre		–

Casualties:

Adj Martial Lachat &	F 50	P	KIA	Farman 43, probably by Lt		
S/Lt Marcel Louvet	F 50	O	KIA	Hermann Pfeiffer, Jasta 9,(8).		
				Forêt de Hesse.		
Sgt Lanier &	C 53	P	MIA	Caudron G4, probably by Ltn		
Lt Coutand	C 53	O	MIA	Hartmut Baldamus, Jasta 9, (8).		
Lt André Cuvillier &	C 53	P	MIA	Caudron G4, probably by Ltn		
Cpl Ringuet	C 53	G	MIA	Hartmut Baldamus, Jasta 9, (9).		
Adj Georges Poreaux	N 31	P	WIA	Nieuport XVII		
S/Lt Gustave Laffon	N 31	P	Injured	DOW, Nieuport XVII		

---

3 December – No Claims – No Casualties

---

4 December

Adj Dorme	a.	N 3	Fokker E	X	Mons-en-Chaussée	1425	17
S/Lt Nungesser	b.	N 65	LVG C	X	W Nurlu	1235	19
S/Lt Nungesser		N 65	Halb	XF	Bois de Vallulart	1305	20
MdL Viallet		N 67	Fokker	X	E Beugny	1445	8
Lt Heurtaux		N 3	Aviatik	P	Rocquigny	1045	–
Adj Dorme		N 3	Aviatik	P	E Chaulnes	1350	–
Adj Lufbery		N 124	EA	P	E Chaulnes	1445	–

a.   Possibly OfStv Karl Ehrenthaller, Jasta 1, KIA Proville.
b.   Possibly Ltn Rosenbachs & Obltn Hans Schilling (8v)(O), FlAbt 22, KIA Flesquières.

Casualties:

Sgt Jonas Jouck	F 215	P	WIA	Farman 60
Lt Lucien Gailledrat	F 211	O	WIA	Flak, Farman 42

---

5 December – No Claims
Casualties:

Cpl Migeon	GDE	P	Injured	Caudron G4

---

6 – 9 December – No Claims – No Casualties

---

10 December

Adj Casale		N 23	EA	XF	Brabant-sur-Meuse	4
Sgt Madon &		N 38				4
Adj Barbaza		N 77	LVG C	XF	N Bois d'Autry	1
Sgt J Sauvage		N 38	Rumpler C	XF	S Monthois	7
Adj Fileux		N 48				1
MdL de Larminat &		N 48				1
Adj Belin	a.	N 57	Aviatik	X	N Douaumont-Hermeville	1
???	a.	C 224	EA	FTL	N Douaumont	–

a.   Possibly Uffz Rudolf Vanoli (P) FlAbt 203 (A), KIA Douaumont.

Casualties:

Capt Félix Goudard &	C 224	P	MIA	
Lt Barthe	C 224	O	MIA	Caudron G4
Sol Pottier	41° Cie Aérostiers			
		O	WIA	Artillery fire.

---

11 December

Capt Ménard	N 26	EA	P	N Bois de Vaux	0845	–

Casualties:

Capt Henri Faillant	N 102	P	WIA	Flak, Nieuport XI
S/Lt Alexandre Gomberg *	CAM	P	KIAcc	St Pol-sur-Mer, Nieuport XVII

*   Dunkerque N° 1784 codé 4.

---

12 December – No Claims – No Casualties

---

13 December

Artillery	???	Balloon	X	Bouvancourt	–

Casualties:

Brig Fernand Vernaudon	GDE	P	Injured	Farman 42
Asp Georges Gayral &	RGAé	P	Injured	
Sol Marie	RGAé	M	Injured	Caudron R4

14 December – No Claims
Casualties:

Lt Jean des Vallières	N 12	P		POW	Nieuport XVII N° 1834, probably by Vfw Arno Schramm, Jasta 7, (2).	

15 December

Adj Guiguet	N 3	2 seater	X	Barleux-Belloy	0925	2
Lt Matton	N 48	Albatros C	X	S Bois des Caures		2
Lt Lachmann	M 57	Balloon	P	Bois de Consenvoye	0935	–

Casualties:

Adj François Brun	N 31	P	POW	Nieuport XVII
Sgt Marcel Gelle &	F 5	P	KIA	
S/Lt Fernand Gailly	F 5	O	KIA	Farman 40
Sgt Joseph Audit	F 8	P	WIA	Farman 42, ground fire
MdL Christian Schlumberger	F 5	P	WIA	Farman 42, ground fire
S/Lt Léon Boilève de La Combaudière	C 13	O	WIA	Caudron G4
Sgt Jacques Soumagniat	C 104	P	WIA	Caudron G4
S/Lt Jean Dupuich &	C 220	P	OK	
Asp Ernest Courson	C 220	O	WIA	Caudron G4, ground fire
Adj-Chef Gaston Guidon	RGAé	P	KIAcc	Sopwith
Cpl Maxime Boutet &	F 58	P	Injured	
Sol Aigle	F 58	M	Injured	Farman F42

16 December – No Claims – No Casualties
The French Offensive at Verdun, which commenced on 1 September 1916, ended this date.

17 December

Adj Lebeau	N 12	EA	X	Herbebois	2
Adj Violet-Marty	N 57	EA	XF	Ornes	3

Casualties:

Capt Louis Robert de Beauchamp	N 23	P	KIA	Spad VII, probaby by Ltn Edouard Dostler & Ltn Hans Boes, FlAbt (A) 252, Douaumont.
MdL Emile du Lac	???	P	WIA	
Sgt Raymond Choisnet	C 74	P	Injured	Caudron G4

18 December
The Battle of Verdun ends.

S/Lt Viallet	N 67	Halb DX			9
MdL Hauss &	N 57				–
MdL Bertrand	N 57	EA	P		–

Casualties:

MdL Léon Enard	N 38	P	KIAcc	Nieuport XI

19 December – No Claims
Casualties:

Sgt Philippe Chaubaud	Avord	P	KIAcc	

20 December

Adj Guiguet	a. N 3	2 seater	X	N Marchélepot	1450	3
Adj Jailler	N 15	EA	X	Villers-Carbonnel	1510	6
MdL Boulant	b. N 15	EA	X	Boursier	1245	1
Sgt Gendronneau,	C 46					1
Sgt Lamy &	C 46					2
Cpl Joussen	C 46	Scout	XF	S Cléry		1
S/Lt Nungesser	c. N 65	EA	X	S Rouy-le-Grand	1120	21
MdL Lemelle	N 73	EA	X	SE Devise	0910	1
Adj Bucquet	N 3	EA	P	Lihons	1320	–
Adj Bucquet	N 3	EA	P	Chaulnes	1415	–
Sgt Baron	N 3	EA	P	Rancourt	1525	–
S/Lt Nungesser	N 65	Scout	P	Bouchavesnes	1520	–
MdL Viallet	N 67	EA	P	St Christ	1315	–
S/Lt V Regnier	N 112	EA	P	Manancourt		–

Lt de Maison Rouge	N 124	EA	P	Mont St Quentin	1335	–
???	???	EA	FTL	Warcq		–
???	???	EA	FTL	Samogneux		–

a.   Probably Vfw Karl Bücher & Ltn Erich Sauerbray, KG 4, KIAs at Licourt, about 5 km SE Marchélepot.
b.   Boulant collided with his victim in this area.
c.   Possibly Ltn Kurt Haber (5v), Jasta 3, KIA Péronne-Omiécourt.

Casualties:

Lt Raymond Lis	N 15	P	KIA	Spad VII, Malmaison, departed 14h45.
MdL Charles Boulant	N 15	P	KIA	Nieuport XVII, see b.
Adj René Dorme	N 3	P	WIA	Nieuport XVII N° 1720.
Cpl Jean Eon	C 104	P	WIA	
MdL Henri Naudin	N 38	P	Injured	Nieuport XVII

21 December

S/Lt Delorme	N 38	Halb D	X	N Orfeuil	4

Casualties: None

22 December – No Claims
Casualties:

Cpl Constant Dubled &	GDE	P	KIAcc	
S/Lt Berlan	GDE	O	KIAcc	Voisin type, LASIII
S/Lt Eugène de la Gorgue de Rosnay	PilSch	P	Injured	DOW 4 January 1917
Adj Pierre Galgani &	C 9	P	Injured	
S/Lt Le Meulais	C 9	O	Injured	Caudron G4

23 December – No Claims
Casualties:

MdL Henri Darblay	N 69	P	KIAcc	Nieuport 110hp
QM Alfred Salmon	PilSch	P	KIAcc	Pau

24 December

Lt Heurtaux	N 3	EA	X	Chaulnes-Omiécourt	1130	14
S/Lt Raymond	N 3	EA	X	Ornes	1400	2
???	???	EA	X	Nonnannruck		–
???	???	EA	XF	Bois Remautel	1530	–
Adj Nugue &	F 54					1
S/Lt Mary	F 54	EA	X	German lines		1
Lt Heurtaux	N 3	EA	P	Liancourt	1120	–
MdL Soulier	N 26	LVG C	P	NE Cernay-en-Dormois		–
Adj de Bonnefoy	N 38	EA	P	St Clément-à-Arnes		–
Capt Doumer	N 76	Rumpler	P			–

Casualties:

MdL Allart &	F 22	P	MIA	Departed 14h30, Farman 43
Sol Poussin	F 22	M	MIA	N° 1871, combat with FAA 211 over Mons.
Brig Marcel Murel &	F 71	P	POW	
S/Lt Gavrel	F 71	O	POW	Farman 42
MdL Jean Hourcade &	C 34	P	KIA	Caudron G4, probably by
S/Lt Lombart	C 34	O	KIA	Ltn Ernst Udet, Jasta 15, (3).
S/Lt Leth Jensen	N 76	P	WIA	Combat with FlAbt A 211, NW Barleux.
Lt Gabriel Clouzeau	C 122	P	WIA-Flak	Caudron G4

25 December – No Claims – No Casualties

26 December

Lt Heurtaux	a.	N 3	Aviatik	X	N Bois de Vaux	0940	15
S/Lt Guynemer		N 3	Halberstadt	X	E Misery	0945	24
Lt Heurtaux		N 3	Scout	P	Misery	0945	–
MdL Allez		N 65	EA	P	Mont St Quentin	1030	–

a.   Probably Vfw Friedrich Rau & Ltn Karl Steinmetz, FlAbt 6, KIAs, Vaux Wald.
Casualties: None

27 December

S/Lt Guynemer	N 3	Albatros	X	S la Mousonnette	1145	25
Lt de La Tour	N 3	Halb D	X	Bois de Catelet	1152	8

Lt Heurtaux		N 3	Rumpler C	X	Bois de Mangues	1155	16
Sgt J Sauvage		N 38	Albatros	X	Montonvillers		8
Adj Bergot	a.	N 38	EA	XF	St Etienne-à-Arnes		3
Lt Loste,		C 46					6
Lt Barbou &		C 46					5
Sol Martin	b.	C 46	EA	X	Barleux	1210	5
S/Lt Barbier,		C 46					3
Sgt Girod &		C 46					1
Sol Mondème		C 46	EA				1
MdL Hauss &		N 57					1
Adj Belin		N 57	Scout	X	W Etain		2
Adj Violet-Marty		N 57	Fokker	X			4
Adj Violet-Marty		N 57	Aviatik C	X			5
Lt Privat		N 65	EA	X	Equancourt-Fins	1535	4
Lt Derode		N 67	EA	X	Licourt-Morchain	1320	2
S/Lt Gigodot	c.	N 103	EA	X	Omiécourt-Fonchette	1445	2
Adj Lufbery		N 124	EA	X	SE Chaulnes	1500	6
Adj Trepp		N 12	EA	FTL	Forêt de Spincourt		–

a.   Possibly Ltn Herbert Hotzel & Ltn Paul Becker, FlAbt 17, KIAs Aubérive, about 15 km S St Etienne-à-Arnes.
b. Possibly Vfw Ernst Dörner & Ltn August Gültig, KG 4, KIAs Barleux.
c. Probably Ltn Albert Holl & Ltn Erich Jungmann, FlAbt (A) 287b, KIAs at Fonchette.

Casualties:

Adj Pierre Violet-Marty	N 57	P	KIA	Nieuport XVII, XF Ornes
Sgt Daniel Fusier &	F 5	P	MIA	Farman 42, probably by Ltn
Lt Jacques Thamin	F 5	O	MIA	Johannes Kintzelmann, Jasta 7, (1).
MdL Louis de Mailly-Nesle				
d'Orange	N 12	P	WIA	Nieuport XVII
Sol Meriot	BM 121	M	Injured	
Sgt Philippe Vallée &	V 116	P	Injured	
Sol Elipot	V 116	M	KIAcc	Voisin P
???	94° Cie d'Aérostiers			Attacked by three EA, not
		O	OK	flamed, Châlons Sector.

28 December – No Claims
Casualties:

MdL Couret	F 59	O	WIA	Flak, Farman 56
Cpl Edouard Lepère &	F 29	P	Injured	
Sol Tallet	F 29	B	Injured	Farman 42
Cpl Fernand Planchet &	F 29	P	Injured	
MdL Gougeat	F 29	B	Injured	Farman 42

29 December – No Claims
Casualties:

Sgt Robert Destot	N 62	P	Injured	Nieuport 80hp

30 – 31 December -No Claims – No Casualties

French Combat Log 1917

1 January – No claims
Casualties:

Lt Yves Le Coz &	C 64	P	MIA	Caudron G4, probably by		
S/Lt Grillière	C 64	O	MIA	Flakzug 1, 3.Armee.		
Sol Lameunière	C 64	G	WIA	Caudron G4		

2 January – No Claims
Casualties:

MdL Léon Flameng	GDE	P	KIAcc	Sopwith

3 – 4 January – No Claims – No Casualties

5 January

S/Lt Delorme	N 38	Rumpler C	X	Auves		5
Lt Hervet	N 103	EA	X	Falvy	1525	1
Adj Guiguet	N 3	EA	P	Roye	1300	–
Adj Lemelle	N 73	EA	P	Nurlu	1130	–
Lt Ledeuil	N 103	EA	P	NE Manancourt	1600	–

Casualties:

Brig Gustave Dinoir &	C 6	P	MIA	Caudron G4, probably by Ltn
S/Lt Philippe	C 6	O	MIA	Alfred Mohr, Jasta 3, (4).
Lt Gaston Loup	N 65	P	MIA	Nieuport XVII N° 1476, probably by
				ground fire, SE Chaulnes. Left 15h10.
Lt Jomin	V 107	O	Injured	Voisin B
Lt Henri de Joyet	F 218	P	Injured	Farman 61

6 January – No Claims
Casualties:

Adj Jean Rouquette	N 395/CRP	P	KIAcc	Le Bourget

7 January

Lt Guynemer	N 3	Albatros C	P	Chaulnes-Ablaincourt	1530	–
S/Lt Tsu	N 37	EA	P	Croix Mouligneaux	0905	–

Casualties:

Sgt Johannes Sauvage	N 65	P	KIA	Spad VII N° 145, AA Fire, 15h20,
				E Maisonette, probably by Flakzug
				155, 2.Armee.

8 January

Sgt Johnson	N 124	EA	P	Villers-Carbonnel	1445 –

Casualties: None

9 January – No Claims – No Casualties

10 January – No Claims
Casualties:

Lt Pierre Juvigny	F 45	P	KIAcc	Farman 80 hp
MdL de Dreux-Brèze	F 45	P	Injured	,,

11 January – No Claims – No Casualties

12 January – No Claims
Casualties:

S/Lt Henri Brègi	* CAM	P	KIAcc	FBA 150hp, N° 333.
*	Toulon.				

13 January – No Claims – No Casualties

14 January

Motor trouble	a. ???	LVG C	POW	Pont-à-Mousson	–
a.	POWs.				

Casualties:

S/Lt André Delorme	N 38	P	KIAcc	Nieuport XVII

15 January

Adj Ortoli	N 31	EA	P		–

Casualties:

Sgt Pierre de Fages de la Tour	GDE	P	KIAcc	Nieuport 80 hp

16 January – No Claims – No Casualties

17 January – No Claims

Casualties:

MdL-Chef Léon Paulin	PilSch	P	KIAcc	Mid-air collision.

18 January – No Claims

Casualties:

Adj Dupré	N 102	P	Injured	Crashed on training flight.

19 January – No Claims – No Casualties

20 January – No Claims

Casualties:

Sgt Georges Bessan	Pau	P	KIAcc	
Cpl André Bertrand	N 67	P	Injured	
Sol Georges Ryon	N 67	M	Injured	Nieuport XIIbis

21 January – No Claims – No Casualties

22 January

Adj Douchy	a.	N 38	Albatros C	X	Navarin		3
Adj Benoit	b.	N 57	EA	X	Amel, II° Armée		1
???		DCA	EA	X	Amy		–
???		DCA	EA	X	N Louvremont	am	–
Motor trouble		???	Fokker	POW	Fismes	am	–
S/Lt Lecoq de Kerrland		N 68	EA	P		am	–
S/Lt Hugues		N 77	EA	FTL	Vittonville		–
Adj Duhem &		F 223					–
Adj Chevalier		F 223	EA	P	Bois de Frières		–

a.   Probably Gefr Adam Köhler & Ltn Heinrich Lauter, FlAbt (A) 251, KIAs at Souain, about 5 km S of Navarin.
b.   Possibly Ltn Pertz, Jasta 23, KIA Chambley, AOK "C" Sector.

Casualties:

Sgt Marius Pivard &	C 224	P	WIA	Caudron G4, probably by Obltn
Cpl Mulot	C 224	G	WIA	Edouard Dostler, Jasta 13, (2).

23 January

Lt Guynemer	a.	N 3	Rumpler C	XF	Maurepas	1130	26
Lt Guynemer	b.	N 3	2 seater	X	Chaulnes	1045	27
S/Lt Languedoc		N 12	EA	X	Samogneux		2
MdL Hauss		N 57	EA	XF	S Spincourt		2
Lt de Guibert		N 62	EA	X	Fresnes		3
Capt Doumer &	CO	N 76					5
MdL Bazinet		N 76	EA	X	N Craonne, V° Armée		1
Lt Pinsard	CO	N 78	2 seater	X	Ft de la Pompelle		2
Motor trouble	c.	???	2 seater	POW	St André de l'Eure	1200	–
Adj Ortoli		N 31	EA	FTL	Cunel		–
???	d.	???	AEG C.IV	POW	Lunéville		–

a.   Probably Ltn Bernhard Roeder & Ltn Otto von Schanzenbach, FlAbt (A) 216w KIAs, Maurepas.
b.   Probably Hptm Martin Korner (O), FlAbt (A) 269, KIA Chaulnes.
c.   Two officers POWs.
d.   AEG C IV N° 1103/16.

Casualties:

MdL François de Levis Mire-Poix	N 102	P	POW	Nieuport XVI #828, FTL, motor problems.
Sgt Pierre Lyaudet &	C 56	P	MIA	Caudron G4 #2712, probably by Ltn
S/Lt Colle	C 56	O	MIA	Hartmut Baldamus, Jasta 9, (10).

S/Lt Jean Barbier		C 46	P	KIA	Caudron R4		
Sgt Jean Delmas &		C 64	P	KIA	Caudron G4, a/c flown back		
Sol Léonide Hurey		C 64	G	WIA	and landed by gunner.		
S/Lt Louis de Barthes de Montfort		N 57	P	WIA	Nieuport XVII		
S/Lt Joseph Le Conte		C 224	O	WIA	Caudron G4		
Adj Gimmig		R 213	O	WIA	Caudron G4		
Sgt Charles Destoppelière		GDE	P	KIAcc	Nieuport XVI		
Sgt Petit		F 71	P	Injured	Farman 43		

24 January

Lt Heurtaux		N 3	EA	X	Rocquigny	1130-1145	17
Lt Guynemer	a.	N 3	Rumpler C	X	Goyencourt	1140	28
Lt Guynemer	b.	N 3	Rumpler C	X	Lignières	1150	29
Lt Heurtaux	c.	N 3	EA	X	Parvillers	1425	18
MdL Hauss &		N 57					3
MdL Bertrand		N 57	Scout	X	Maucourt		1
Adj Lufbery		N 124	Aviatik C	X	Chaulnes-Péronne	1005	7
Lt de Laage de Meux		N 124	EA	P	SE Chaulnes	1005	–
Lt Guynemer		N 3	Scout	P	?telfay	1145	–
Lt Orloff		N 3	EA	P	Fresnoy-les-Roye	1145	–

a.   Probably Ltn Kurt Just (O), FlAbt A 234, KIA, Roye.
b.   Probably Gefr Heinrich Bauer & Gefr Anton Haschert, KIAs.
c.   Probably Gefr Franz Budny & Sgt Gottfried Kort, SchSta 13, KIAs Le Quesnoy, immediate vicinity of Parvillers.

Casualties:

Sgt Julien du Rudowski	C 10	P	KIAcc	Caudron G4, test flight.
Sgt Mathieu	GDE	P	Injured	Caudron G4
Lt Alain Jegou du Laz	GDE	P	Injured	Nieuport XVII

25 January

Lt Heurtaux		N 3	EA	X	E Puzeaux	1030	19
Lt Gastin	a.	N 49	EA	XF	NW Altkirch	1600	4
Sgt Givon,		R 214					1
Sgt Lachat &		R 214					1
Sol Mermet		R 214	LVG C	X	S St Etienne-à-Arnes		1
MdL Herbelin &		N 102					1
Lt Laurens		N 102	Aviatik C	X	Noyon		1
Patrol		???	EA	X	E Chaulnes	1005	–
Adj Chainat		N 3	EA	P	Varlencourt	1140	–
Capt Auger		N 3	EA	P	Ham	1430	–
Cpl Papeil		N 3	EA	FTL	Nesles	0940	–
Asp Defourneaux		N 78	EA	FTL	German lines		–
Lt Pinsard &	CO	N 78					–
Patrol		N 78	EA	P	Porquiercourt		–

a.   Probably Vfw Arthur Pfau & Ltn Friedrich Henning, FlAbt 282 (A), KIAs Gomersdorf, about 8 km W Altkirch.

Casualties:

Brig Roger Lafon	GDE	P	Injured	Caudron G4
Sgt Charles Regien	C 51	P	Injured	,,
MdL Tambouze	C 122	P	Injured	,,

26 January

Lt Guynemer	a.	N 3	Albatros C	POW	Monchy	1215	30
S/Lt Loste,		C 46					7
Lt Barbou &		C 46					4
Sol Martin		C 46	Aviatik C	X	N Bapaume		6
MdL Hauss		N 57	2 seater	XF	N Gincrey		4
Adj Belin		N 57	EA	X	Montfaucon		3
Lt Lafon,		R 213					1
Sgt Marault &		R 213					1
Sol Courtois		R 213	EA	XF	Trosly-Breuil		1
Adj Covin,		R 213					2
Adj Gimmig &		R 213					1
Sol Massier		R 213	EA	X	Carlepont	1520	1
???		DCA	EA	X	W Barleux		–

a.   Probably from FlAbt A 266, POWs.

Casualties:

| MdL François Bey | ??? | P | KIAcc | |
| Cpl Simon Mazourock | GDE | P | Injured | Caudron G4 |

27 January

???	DCA	EA	X	Moulainville		–

Casualties:

Lt Cossard	C 104	O	Injured	Caudron G4, landing accident.	

28 January

Lt Gastin &	N 49					5
Lt Jaille	N 49	Albatros C	POW	Soppe, VII° Armée	1500	1
???	DCA	EA	X	Dannemaire		–

Casualties:

Cpl Jean Dart &	C 207	P	Injured	
Sol Blanc	C 207	G	Injured	Caudron G4

29 January

S/Lt Languedoc	N 12	Aviatik	X	Etaing d'Eptainville	3
Adj Combret,	C 46				2
Lt Artur &	C 46				1
Cpl Cadot	C 46	EA	X	NE Chaulnes	1
Cpl Damenez,	C 46				1
Cpl Rivière &	C 46				1
MdL Roblin	C 46	EA	X	NE Bois de Hallu	1
MdL Hauss &	N 57				5
Adj Belin	a. N 57	DFW C	XF	Avocourt-Bois de Hesse	4
S/Lt Maliet	N 112	EA	X	German lines	1

a.   Probably Uffz Hermann Fischer & Ltn Günther Laue, FlAbt 249 (A), KIAs Fôret de Hesse, about 2 km S Avocourt.

Casualties:

Lt Blanc,	???	P	MIA	V° Armée
MdL ??? &	???	O	MIA	
Sol Charreard	???	G	MIA	
Adj Jean de Plagino	R 214	P	KIAcc	(1)
Sol François Beaujon &	R 214	G	KIAcc	
Sol Maurice Bouron	R 214	G	KIAcc	Caudron R4
MdL Jules Perrin, &	C 56	P	KIAcc	
Lt Georges Dupire	C 56	O	KIAcc	Caudron G4
Cpl Ferrie &	GDE	P	KIAcc	
Sgt Vernet	GDE	O	KIAcc	Farman 42
Sgt Yvon Le Troadec	N 81	P	KIAcc	Nieuport XVII

(1)   These two aircraft collided in mid-air over the Ferme d'Alger.

30 January – No Claims

Casualties:

Adj Jean Rigall	C 219	P	WIA	Caudron G4

31 January

Adj Madon	a. N 38	Albatros C	X	N Suippes	5

a.   Probably Ltn Walter Stephan & Ltn Wilhelm Hölscher, FlAbt (A) 251, KIAs, St Hilaire-le-Grand, about 8 km NW of Suippes.

Casualties:

MdL Albert Libeyre &	VB 107	P	MIA	
Sgt Lasserre	VB 107	B	MIA	Voisin B t.III

Date of S/Lt Havet's, N 77, 3rd victory during January 1917, unknown.

1 February – No Claims – No Casualties

2 February

Lt Pinsard	CO N 78	EA	P		–

Casualties:

Lt Jean de Landrain &	F 71	P		Farman t.40, probably by Ltn
S/Lt Berger	F 71	O	MIA	Hartmut Baldamus, Jasta 9, (11).
EV2 Jean de Gail	PilSch	P	KIAcc	Chartres

3 February

S/Lt Languedoc	N 12	EA	X	S Bois de Forges	4
42° Section d'Auto-Canons		Aviatik	X	Ouiches, V Armée	–

Casualties:

Cpl René Faivre-Pierret &	C 222	P	KIA	Caudron G4, probably by Ltn Adolf		
S/Lt Malzac	C 222	O	KIA	Kuen, Jasta 14, (1).		
S/Lt Pierre Desthuilliers &	F 44	P	OK			
S/Lt Robin	F 44	O	WIA	Farman t.42		
S/Lt Pierre Gourdon	F 201	O	WIA	Farman t.42, infantry fire		

4 February

Lt Heurtaux	N 3	EA	P	Emberménil	1530	–

Casualties:

S/Lt Marcel Legrende	C 47	P	Injured	Caudron G4, landing accident.	

5 February

Adj Villars	N 23	EA	P	S Les Eparges		–
Capt d'Harcourt	N 103	EA	P	Chambrey	1345	–
Capt d'Harcourt	N 103	EA	FTL	Moyenvic	1325	–

Casualties:

Sgt Bernard Dufresne &	F 14	P	WIA	Farman t.42	
Asp Holstein	F 14	O	OK	Infantry fire.	
S/Lt Emile Thiry	N 62	O	Injured		

6 February

Lt Heurtaux	N 3	EA	X	Bois de Faulx	1325	20
Adj Casale	N 23	EA	X	Warville		5
Adj Madon	N 38	Rumpler C	X	Butte du Mesnil		6
Lt Heurtaux	N 3	EA	P	Custines	1135	–
Lt Heurtaux	N 3	EA	P	Sivry	1145	–
Lt Heurtaux	N 3	EA	P	Bois de Faulx	1205	–

Casualties – None

7 February

Sgt Huffer	N 62	EA	X	Cerny-les-Bucy		2
Lt Guynemer	N 3	EA	P	Fôret de Bezanges	1120	–

Casualties:

Adj Pierre Dufaur de Gavardie	N 12	P	WIA	Nieuport XVII	
Cpl Georges Dumas &	Pau	P	KIAcc		
Sol Labense	Pau	G	KIAcc		
Sgt Dary	RGAé	P	Injured	Spad VII	
Cpl Brunet	N 504	P	Injured	Nieuport XIbis	

8 February

Lt Guynemer &		N 3					31
Adj Chainat	a.	N 3	Gotha GIII	POW	Bouconville	1115	11
Sgt Bonnet &		N 76					1
Brig Laraud		N 76	EA	X	NE Soissons	1200	1
???		DCA	EA	X	Regniéville-en-Haye		–

a.   Kagohl 2, all three occupants became POWs.

Casualties:

Cpl Louis Danchaud	F 19	G	KIAcc	F.t.42, landing accident.	

9 February

Capt Auger		N 3	Albatros D	XF	Rogéville	1530	3
Adj Bucquet	a.	N 3	EA	P	S Thiaucourt	1130	–
S/Lt Lecoq de Kerland		N 68	EA	P			–
Capt Doumer &		N 76					–
Sgt Bonnet		N 76	EA	FTL	German lines, V° Armée		–

a.   Possibly OffStv Richard Krone, KIA at Pont-à-Mousson, about 15 km SE of Thiaucourt.

Casualties:

Lt Jean Moreau	F 14	P	WIA	Nieuport XVIIbis	
Cpl Louis Musy &	BM 120	P	KIAcc		
Sol Langlet	BM 120	B	KIAcc	Bréguet-Michelin IV	
???	72° Cie Aérostiers		XF	18h15, by bombs dropped from an	
		O	OK	aircraft.	

10 February

Lt Deullin	a.	N 3	2 seater	XF	N Champenoux	1340	11

Sgt Herbert &		N 62				2
S/Lt Borzecki		N 62	EA	X	Etouvelles	4
S/Lt V Regnier		N 112	EA	X	SE Chaulnes	0845 4
Sgt Bazin,		R 210				1
Lt Blanc &		R 210				1
Sgt Lentrain	b.	R 210	Fokker	XF	Cerny-les-Reims	1
Sgt Dumée,		R 209				1
MdL Houssais &		R 209				1
Capt Dreyfus		R 209	EA	XF		1
Lt Guynemer		N 3	2 seater	P	NE Nomeny	1115 –
Capt Ménard	CO	N 26	2 seater	P	Embermeuil	1425 –
Lt Pinsard	c.	N 78	EA	P	Juniville	–
Sgt Maitrot		N 91	EA	P		–

a.   Probably Uffz Hermann Heilte & Ltn Otto Michaelles, FlAbt (A) 257, KIAs, Champenoux.
b.   Probably Vfw Heinrich Tuczek, Jasta 9, KIA at Berru, about 4 km SW of Cerny-les-Reims.
c.   Possibly Obltn Walter Zietlow, Jasta 9, KIA between Hauviné and Leffincourt, Juniville about 10 km from each location.

Casualties:

S/Lt Marius Lautiron &		F 25	P	MIA	Farman t.40, probably by
Cpl Fugerot		F 25	B	MIA	Heimatschutz
Sgt Jean Bourgois &		BM 117	P	KIA	
MdL Jules Le Boulho		BM 117	B	KIA	Bréguet-Michelin IV
QM Joseph Salpin &	*	CAM	P	POW	FBA 150HP N° 412, codé D.1, shot
QM René Deram	*	CAM	O	POW	down in combat and captured by a
					U-Boat. Deram escaped in May 1918.
Lt Paul Weiller		C 219	P	WIA	
Sgt René Bazin,		R 210	P	WIA	V° Armée
Lt Marcel Blanc &		R 210	O	WIA	
Sgt Evremond Lentrain		R 210	G	OK	Caudron R4
Brig Jacquet,		R 214	P	OK	
Cpl Prieur &		R 214	G	WIA	
S/Lt Pierre Henry		R 214	O	WIA	Caudron R4
MdL Paul		C 104	P	Injured	Caudron G4

*   Dunkerque.

11 February

???	DCA	EA	X	Verdun Sector	–
S/Lt Lecoq de Kerland	N 68	EA	P		–

Casualties:

Adj Max Belin	N 57	P	MIA	Nieuport 110 hp, possibly by
				Ltn Sieh & OfStv Brocke, FlAbt (A) 207.
Brig Lambert	N 506	P	POW	Nieuport XVIIbis N° 2405, probably
				by OfStv Hüttner, Jasta 14, (1).
Lt Brun &	C 212	P		Injured
S/Lt Rey	C 212	O	OK	Caudron G4
Cpl Huet	F 216	G	Injured	Farman 170 hp

12 February – No Claims
Casualties:

Adj Martiniau	GDE	P	Injured	Salmson-Moineau 5.t.I
Sgt Alberto Bucciali	GDE	P	Injured	Salmson-Moineau 5.t.I

13 February – No Claims
Casualties:

S/Lt Etienne Collin	N 78	P	MIA	Nieuport XVII, probably by
				Infantry fire, 3.Armee.

14 February

S/Lt Hugues	a.	N 77	EA	XF	N Custines	1
Lt Ledeuil	a.	N 103	EA	XF	Custines-Morey	1035 4
???		DCA	EA	X	Beaumont	1
Adj Bucquet		N 3	EA	P	Domèvre-Blamont	1000 –

a.   Possibly Ltn Rolshoven & Ltn Sievert, FlAbt 39, KIAs, Millery (Malleloy) about 3 km N of Custines, Armee-Abteilung "C".

Casualties:

Adj Auguste Prisset &	F 221	P	KIA	Farman t.42, probably by Vfw
Lt Damien	F 221	O	KIA	Friedrich Manschott, Jasta 7, (6).
Sgt Auguste Marseille	???	?	WIA	
Lt Henri Comère &	GDE	P	Inj	
Lt Grossin	GDE	O	KIAcc	Caudron G4

| Adj Jean-Marie Durand | 83° Cie d'Aérostiers | | XF | Probably by Ltn Lothar Rehm, Jasta | |
| | | O | WIA | 23, (1). | |

15 February

Adj Douchy		N 38	EA	X	E Grateuil		4
Adj Madon	a.	N 38	Albatros C	XF	N Ripont		7
Brig Laraud		N 76	EA	X	German lines	1530	2
Lt Pinsard		N 78	EA	X	Juniville		3
S/Lt Girier,		R 210					–
S/Lt Buvry &		R 210					–
Sgt Lentrain		R 210	EA	FTL	V° Armée	1515	–

a. Probably Uffz Hans Gross & Vfw Emil Stiller, KIAs, Ripont.
Casualties:

Sgt François Raty	N 38	P	KIA	Nieuport XVII, probably by Ltn	
				Hartmut Baldamus, Jasta 9, (12).	
MdL Marcel Hauss	N 57	P	KIA	Nieuport 110 hp, in flames during	
				combat with a two-seater, probably by	
				Ltn Filbig & Uffz Müller, FlAbt 46.	
Adj Georges Driot &	VB 114	P	POW	Voisin CU 150hp, probably	
Sgt Flint	VB 114	G	POW	by "A" Flak.	
Sgt Albert Valiton &	VB 107	P	Injured		
Cpl Marseille	VB 107	G	Injured	Voisin t.VIII	
S/Lt Rodier	GDE	O	Injured	Caudron G4	

16 February

Lt Cabaud	N 31	EA	XF	Tahure	1
Capt Matton	N 48	Balloon	XF	Marvaux	3
Lt de Larminat	N 48	EA	P	Main de Massiges	–

Casualties:

Brig Girard	N 31	P	MIA	Nieuport XVII #2183, probably by Ltn	
				Hartmut Baldamus, Jasta 9, unconfirmed.	
Capt Alfred Auger	N 3	P	WIA	Spad VII, over Lunéville.	
S/Lt François Bouscatie	N 82	P	WIA	Nieuport XVII	
???	90° Cie d'Aérostiers		XF	V° Armée-Pont Faverger.	
???	78° Cie d'Aérostiers			Attacked but not flamed in the	
				Souilly Sector.	

17 February – No Claims
Casualties:

| Sgt Pétrus Lumière | F 123 | P | KIAcc | Sopwith |

18 – 19 February – No Claims – No Casualties

20 February

| ??? | DCA | EA | X | S Cernay | – |

Casualties:

MdL Pierre de Cazenove				Forced to crash-land near Aspach	
de Pradines	N 81		OK	after a combat, probably by Ltn	
				Ernst Udet, Jasta 15, (4).	

21 – 22 February – No Claims – No Casualties

23 February

| S/Lt de Larminat | N 48 | EA | P | | – |

Casualties:

Cpl Emile Delignières &	BM 121	P	KIAcc		
Sol Gaigner	BM 121	M	KIAcc	BM IV	
MdL Roger de Larivière &	GDE	P	KIAcc		
S/Lt Long	GDE	O	KIAcc	Farman t.42	

24 February – No Claims
Casualties:

| MdL Rigaud | Pau | P | KIAcc | |

25 February
The German withdrawal to the Hindenburg Line, between Soissons and Arras, starts.

Brig Fournier &	N 62					1
S/Lt Borzecki	N 62	EA	X	S Pinon	1045	5
Adj Drouhet &	N 76					1
Brig Giovetti	N 76	EA	X	Mersy, V° Armée		1
Lt Pinsard	N 78	EA	X	Grateuil-Manre	1455	4
Cpl Plaisir	N 81	Albatros D	X	SE Altkirch	1000	1

Casualties:

Cpl Rivière	N 81	P	MIA	VII° Armée, Nieuport XVII N° 2409, probably by Ltn Friedrich Weitz, Jasta 26,(2).
Capt André Couder &	V° Armée	P	KIA	Caudron G4, aircraft landed
Lt Robert Graffin	V° Armée	O	OK	safely by observer.
Sgt André Boillot	N 77	P	WIA	Flak, Nieuport XVII
Adj Jean Etcheberry	N 48	P	Injured	Spad VII
Cpl Marius Eme &	PS 125	P	Injured	
Brig Sedlacek	PS 125	G	KIAcc	PS.t.VI
Adj Jean Peuch &	F 40	P	OK	Shot down at Loupmont, probably by
S/Lt Saintot	F 40	O	OK	Ltn Johann Janzen, Jasta 23, (1).
???	78° Cie d'Aérostiers			Attacked by a two-seater but not
???	83° Cie d'Aérostiers			flamed, Souilly Sector.

26 February – No Claims
Casualties:

Capt Edouard Duseigneur	GC 11	P	Injured	Spad VII
Cpl François Simeon &	GDE	P	Injured	
MdL Quentin	GDE	G	Injured	Farman 130 hp

27 February – No Claims
Casualties:

Adj Durand	RGAé	P	Injured	Caudron G4

28 February

S/Lt Vernin &	N 75					1
Cpl Charpentier	N 75	EA				1

Casualties:

Sgt Bernard Schwartz	GDE	P	Injured	Nieuport XI
Cpl Jean Vidal	F 130	P	Injured	Farman t.42

1 March

Adj Laplasse	N 461/CRP	EA	FTL		–
Adj Laplasse	N 461/CRP	EA	FTL		–

Casualties:

Sgt Henri Munier &	C 50	P	Injured	Caudron G6
Sol Goulon	C 50	M	Injured	Landing accident.
Cpl Alphonse Jozereau &	GDE	P	Injured	
Cpl Quentin	GDE	B	Injured	Farman t.42

2 March – No Claims
Casualties:

Adj Caulier &	F 25	P	MIA	DOW 3 March 1917
Adj Planche	F 25	B	MIA	Farman t.60, probably by Vfw Friedrich Manschott, Jasta 7, (8).
Cpl Vidal	F 130	B	KIAcc	Farman t.42
S/Lt Joseph Rouillé &	CEP 115	P	KIAcc	
Sgt Groult	CEP 115	G	Injured	CEP t.4
MdL Georges Groud	CEP 115	P	Injured	CEP t.4
SM Jean Billon &	* CAM	P	Injured	Voisin LAP III N° 1777, codé 22.
QM Georges Tocaven	* CAM	O	Injured	DOW
* Dunkerque.				

3 March – No Claims
Casualties:

S/Lt Auguste Ledeuil	N 103	P	MIA	Spad VII, possibly by Vfw Friedrich Altemaier, Jasta 24, (1).
MdL Joly	C 47	P	Injured	Caudron G4
Lt Richard Robert	N 73	P	Injured	Spad VII

4 March

Sgt Nogues &	N 12					1
S/Lt de Sevin	N 12	EA	X	Autrecourt-Verdun		2
Adj Trepp &	N 12					2
Adj Lebeau	N 12	EA	X	Fôret de Spincourt		3
Adj Casale	N 23	EA	X	Dieppe		7
Capt Ménard &	CO	N 26				2
Adj Jeronnez	N 26					1
Sgt Lancrey &	F 205				1050	1
S/Lt Médeville	F 205	2 seater	X	Juvricourt-Arracourt		1
Sgt de Pracomtal	N 508/F1	Albatros	X	Nampcel		1
Sgt Triboulet	N 57	EA	FTL	Montfaucon		1

Casualties:

Sgt Achille Plaisir	N 81	P	WIA	VII° Armée, Nieuport XVII
S/Lt Royer &	C 220	P	WIA	Caudron G.4, FTL after combat
S/Lt Bonnet	C 220	O	OK	over Belleville, probably by
				Vfw Friedrich Manschott, Jasta 7, (9).
MdL de la Chapelle	C 220	P	OK	Shot down by AA fire.
S/Lt Georges Guyot	C 220	O	WIA	Flak, Caudron G4
MdL Georges Robart,	F 63	P	KIAcc	Crashed during takeoff
Sgt Raveneau &	F 63	G	KIAcc	and burned.
MdL-Chef Barberot	F 63	G	Injured	Salmson-Moineau #41.
S/Lt Seyllier	F 44	O	Injured	Farman t.60, landing.
MdL Moulard	58° Cie d'Aérostiers			Attacked, not flamed in the Souilly
		O	WIA	Sector.
???	38° Cie d'Aérostiers			Attacked, not flamed in the Souilly
				Sector.

5 March

Ground Fire	VII° Armée EA		X	Burnhaupt-les-Bains	1700 –

a.   Possibly Ltn Otto Sandler, (P), FlAbt 289 (A), KIA, Oberburnhaupt.

Casualties:

Sgt Maurice Patricot	RGAé	P	Injured	Nieuport XVII

6 March

Adj Ortoli	N 31	EA	X	Nogent l'Abbesse	4
Adj Casale	N 23	EA	X	Dieppe	6
Lt Pinsard	N 78	Rumpler C	X	N Laval	5
Sgt Pillon	N 82	EA	X	Feldbach-Altkirch	2
Capt Auger,	N 3				–
Lt Raymond &	N 3				–
S/Lt Dorme	N 3	2 seater	P	NE Fôret de Parroy	1435 –
MdL Daubail	N 49	Scout	P		–

Casualties:

MdL Pierre Daubail	N 49	P	WIA	Nieuport XVII, VII° Armée
Lt Onokitu Isobe	N 57	P	Injured	Nieuport XXIII, crashed on takeoff.

7 March – No Claims

Casualties:

S/Lt Pauffin de St Morel	C 122	O	KIAcc	

8 March – No Claims – No Casualties

9 March

???	DCA	EA	X	St Mihiel Sector	–

Casualties:

Adj René Gibaud &	C 10	P	MIA-Flak	III° Armée
S/Lt Auguste Le Mevel	C 10	O	MIA-Flak	Caudron G4
Lt Théodore de Baral				
d'Arène,	F 45	P	KIA	
S/Lt Bacon &	F 45	O	KIA	
Sol Gaillot	F 45	G	KIA	Salmson-Moineau
Lt Noël de Rivoire de				Spad VII, probably by Ltn Jäger &
La Batie	N 37	P	WIA	Flg Schrickel, FlAbt (A) 249.
Cpl Jean Charvat	N 505	P	Injured	Nieuport XIbis, crashed during takeoff.

Sol Félix Sarry	C 56	M	Injured		
S/Lt Billardon	40° Cie d'Aérostiers	XF		Probably by Ltn Werner Albert,	
	O		OK	Jasta 31 (1).	
S/Lt Maurice Guillotin	48° Cie d'Aérostiers	XF		Probably by Vfw Friedrich	
	O		Injured	Manschott, Jasta 7, (11).	
???	78° Cie d'Aérostiers			Attacked, not flamed in	
???	58° Cie d'Aérostiers			the Souilly Sector.	

10 March – No Claims
Casualties:

Capt Maurice Mandinaud	N 81	P	KIA	VII° Armée, Spad VII, probably by	
				Obltn Bruno Loerzer, Jasta 26, (4).	
Lt Raguet	74° Cie d'Aérostiers	XF		VII° Armée, probably by Ltn	
				Robert Dycke, Jasta 16, (1).	

11 March

Sgt Fisch &	N 23				1
S/Lt de Ram	N 23	Scout	X	N Varennes	3
78° Cie d'Aérostiers	a. DCA	EA	FTL	German lines	–
Casualties:					
Lt André Maus	N 49	P	KIA	VII° Armée, Nieuport XVII N 2341,	
				over Bernweiler, probably by Ltn	
				Friedrich Weitz, Jasta 26 (3).	
Adj Auguste Robin &	F 54	P	MIA	Sopwith, probably by Ltn Alfred	
Lt Marie Barbot	F 54	O	MIA	Niederhoff, Jasta 20, (1). III° Armée.	
Capt Paul Rochard &	F 71	P	MIA	Farman t.40, probably by Ltn	
S/Lt Henri Litaud	C 219	O	MIA	Hartmut Baldamus, Jasta 9, (13).	
Brig Max Dubourg &	F 5	P	WIA	DOW	
Lt Berthault	F 71	O	OK	Farman t.60	
Sgt Léon Gouvernet	VB 107	P	KIAcc	Nieuport XVII	
Cpl Lucien Patte,	R 209	P	Injured		
Asp Louis Rozain &	R 209	O	KIAcc	III° Armée	
MdL Tirefort	R 209	G	Injured	Caudron R4.t.19	
S/Lt Boulanger	F 36	O	Injured	Farman t.42	
Lt R.G. Partridge	VB 101	P	Injured	Sopwith t.7	
Sgt François Deperi &	RGAé	P	Injured		
Sol Mallard	RGAé	M	Injured	Caudron G4	
S/Lt Mathieu	48° Cie d'Aérostiers			Attacked, not flamed in Souilly	
	O		OK	Sector.	
???	78° Cie d'Aérostiers			Attacked, not flamed in Souilly	
	O		OK	Sector – See above (a).	

12 March – No Claims
Casualties:

Cpl Paul Perthy	MF 8	P	KIA	

13 March – No Claims
Casualties

Sgt Pierre Guichon	VB 107	P	Injured	DOW 16 March 1917
Cpl Louis Franchisseur	GDE	P	KIAcc	Nieuport XII

14 March – No Claims
Casualties:

Capt de Poligny	N 15	O	WIA	Nieuport XIVbis

15 March

S/Lt Languedoc	N 12	EA	P	Souilly	–
Sgt Bajac	N 48	2 seater	P		–
Casualties:					
MdL François Cathelin &	VB 107	P	KIAcc		
Lt Georges Emin	VB 107	O	KIAcc	Voisin P.t.II	
Sgt René Lejour &	VB 108	P	Injured	DOW 16 March 1917	
Cpl Jean Richard	VB 108	B	KIAcc	Farman t.40	

16 March

Capt Guynemer	a.	N 3	Albatros C	XF	Serres	0908	32
Capt Guynemer	b.	N 3	Roland DII	POW	N Hoéville	0926	33
Lt Raymond		N 3	EA	XF	Courbessaux-Bois de St Hilaire	0928	2
Capt Guynemer	c.	N 3	Albatros C	XF	Regnéville	1430	34
Adj Douchy		N 38	2 seater	X	Bouconville-Rouvroy		5
Capt Matton		N 48	EA	X	N Chavonne	1430	4
Sgt Triboulet	d.	N 57	Scout	X	Damloup	1045	2
Lt Deullin	e.	N 73	Albatros	XF	Einville-en-Haye	0931	12
Sgt Boyau	f.	N 77	Aviatik C	X	S Thiaucourt		1
S/Lt Leps	g.	N 81	2 seater	X	Burnhaupt	1500	1
S/Lt Leps &		N 81					2
Sgt Maillan		N 81	Albatros C	X	Bernweiler	1455	1
MdL Herbelin		N 102	EA	X	Noyon		2
???	h.	DCA	Zeppelin	XF	Compiègne	0527	–
???		DCA	EA	X	Manheulles		–
???		DCA	EA	X	Corbeny		–
Cpl Lesse &		R 210					–
Lt Debect		R 210	EA	P	V° Armée		–
Capt Auger &		N 3					–
S/Lt Dorme		N 3	2 seater	P	Hoéville	0900	–
??? &		N 76					–
S/Lt Henriot		N 76	EA	FTL			–

a. Probably Uffz August Reichenbach & Obltn Wilfried Buchdrucker, FlAbt 12, KIAs Serres.
b. Ltn Lothar von Hausen, Jasta 32, WIA/POW/DOW 15 July 1917, N Höville..
c. Probably Vfw Friedrich Manschott (12v), Jasta 7, KIA Ft Vaux, about 2 km SW of Damloup.
d. Probably Obltn Heinrich Schwander, CO Jasta 32, KIA N Lunéville over Athienville, about 10 km N Valhey, Albatros D3 N 2111/16.
e. Probably Flg Josef Freundorfer & Flg Franz May, KIAs.
f. Probably Uffz Karl Kolrop & Ltn Feodor Kellner, FlAbt 279 (A), KIAs Remenauville, AOK "C" Sector.
g. Possibly Ltn Johann Ganguin, FlAbt 14, KIA Nieder-Burnhaupt.
h. Zeppelin L39, CO Kptltn Robert Koch and crew KIAs.

Casualties:

Adj Emile Golfier &	C 66	P	KIA	Flak
MdL Marcel Farats	C 66	G	KIA	Flak, SOP
S/Lt Raymond Havet	N 77	P	KIA	Nieuport XVII N 2277, probably downed by Vzfw Schlegel & Ltn Metzger of FlAbt 39.
Sgt Louis Pivette	Sop 29	P	MIA	Salmson-Moineau N 5143, possibly by Ltn Hugo Kämmel, Jasta 23, (1).
MdL Maurice Babault &	F 32	P	KIA	III° Armée, by Flak, XF
Lt Paul Boudreaux	F 32	O	WIA	Farman t.40 #2504.
Cpl Paul Lesec	R 210	P	WIA	
Lt Debect	R 210	O	WIA	Caudron R4, V° Armée
Adj Emile Gaulard &	C 51	P	KIAcc	Landing accident.
Lt Copin	C 51	O	Injured	Caudron G4
Sgt Georges Maillan	N 81	P	OK	VII° Armée, Shot down and FTL by one of the EA claimed by himself and S/Lt Leps.
MdL G Bes	78° Cie d'Aérostiers		XF	Balloons were claimed by
		O	KIA	Vfw Friedrich Manschott, Jasta 7,
MdL Berger	58° Cie d'Aérostiers		XF	(12) & Obltn Fritz von Bronsart und
		O	OK	Schellendorf, Jasta 7 (1).
Adj André Bry	36° Cie d'Aérostiers		XF	Probably by Ltn Wilhelm
		O	Injured	Allmenröder, Jasta 29, (1).
???	83° Cie d'Aérostiers			Attacked, not flamed in Souilly Sector.

17 March

Capt Guynemer &		N 3					35
Capt Shigeno	a.	N 26	2 seater	XF	E Atilloncourt	1330	2
Adj Fonck,		C 47					2
S/Lt Marcaggi &		C 47					1
S/Lt Huffer		N 62	EA	XF	N Cerny-en-Laonnois		3
Capt Doumer &		N 76					6
MdL Bazinet	b.	N 76	2 seater	XF	Corbeny	1230	2
Brig Bretillon		N 79	Albatros	X			1
Brig Gerbault		N 79	Albatros	X	E Roye		1

Adj Van Ingelandt	N 510	Albatros	P		–
S/Lt de Turenne	N 48	2 seater	FTL	Filain	–

a.   Probably Uffz Karl Maurer & Ltn Eduard Marcard, FlAbt 12, KIAs.
b.   Probably Ltn Phillipp Lamade & Ltn Eduard Siegel, FlAbt 201, KIAs, Berry-su-Bac, about 8 km SE of Corbeny.

Casualties:

Sgt Maurice Raux &	C 47	P	KIA	Caudron G4, probably by Vfw Karl
Sgt Constant Lethon	C 47	G	WIA	Möwe, Jasta 29, (1).
Brig Pierre Lautier	N 502	P	KIA	DOW VII° Armée, Nieuport XVII, probably by Ltn Hartmut Baldamus, Jasta 9, (14).
Adj Camille Nagoette &	F 20	P	KIA	III° Armée, XF, W Roye.
S/Lt Oscar Bernard	F 20	O	WIA	Farman t.60, probably by Ltn Friedrich Mallinckrodt, Jasta 20 (3). III° Armée.
Sgt Pilleron	R 212	G	WIA	Flak, Caudron G4
Capt Joseph Coutisson	N 12	P	WIA	Nieuport XXIII.
Cpl Charles Morlay	N 112	P	WIA	Nieuport XVII, probably by Uffz Karl Käppeler & Lt Willi Häussler, FlAbt (A) 252.
Sgt Georges Burlaton &	BM 120	P	Injured	VIII° Armée. BM IV.
Cpl Lugon	BM 120	B	Injured	DOW
???	59° Cie d'Aérostiers			Attacked, not flamed in
		O	OK	Tantonville Sector.

18 March

Adj Madon	a.	N 38	2 seater	X	NE Massignes	8
Cpl Hofmann		N 80	Aviatik C	X	S Poucy	1
Lt Echard	CO b.	N 82	2 seater	XF	Altkirch	1000 1
34 Section	c.	DCA	2 seater	X	Virginy	–
???	d.	DCA	EA	X	W Brimont	–

a.   Possibly Ltn Johannes Ohlrau & Obltn Alfred Weser, FlAbt(A) 252w, WIAs NE Massignes.
b.   Probably Gefr Otto Lorenz & Ltn Johann Mohr, Schsta 23b, KIAs Aspach, about 4 km N Altkirch.
c.   Possibly Ltn Friedrich Heinemann & Ltn Karl Birch-Hirschfeld, KG2/Kasta9, KIAs, between Ville-sur-Tourbe & Virginy.
d.   Probably Vfw Ernst Rittmeister & Ltn Heinrich Sauer, FlAbt 262, KIAs, Roucy-Guyencourt, W of Brimont.

Casualties:

Cpl Jean Hofmann	N 80	P	KIA	Nieuport XVII, collided (Czech) with an enemy aircraft, possibly Vzfw Rittmeister & Ltn Sauer of FlAbt(A) 262, who were killed over Guyencourt.
Cpl Jacques Gout	MF 8	P	WIA	
S/Lt Emile Maurel	F 203	O	Injured	
Cpl St Laurent	BM 118	G	Injured	BM IV

19 March

MdL Herbelin	N 102	EA	XF	Guiscard	3
MdL Stugocki &	F 19				1
S/Lt Hericher	F 19	EA	POW	Noyon	1

Casualties:

Sgt James McConnell (American)	N 124	P	KIA	Nieuport XVII N° 2055, probably by Ltn Heinrich Kämmerer Jasta 20, (1).
Lt Max Ducimetière &	C 34	P	MIA	
Lt Conetoux	C 34	O	MIA	Caudron G4 N° 2217.
Cpl Edmond Genet (American)	N 124	P	WIA	Nieuport XVII N° 1962
Sgt Jean Laussedat,	CEP 115	P	KIAcc	
Sgt René Destrez &	CEP 115	O	Injured	
Cpl Fauvre	CEP 115	G	Injured	CEP t.4
Adj Georges de Pimodan	C 11	P	Injured	Caudron G4

20 March – 21 March – No Claims – No Casualties

22 March

Lt Mendigal,	C 11				–
S/Lt Blanchard &	C 11				–
Cpl Deschamps	C 11	Roland D	FTL	VIII° Armée	–
???	a. ???	Albatros D	POW	Vezelize, II° Armée	–

a.   Probably Vfw Georg Hentze, Jasta 34, POW, Pagny-Metz, AOK "C" Sector.

Casualties:

Lt Jean Mendigal	C 11	P	WIA	VIII° Armée	
S/Lt Blanchard	C 11	P	WIA	VIII° Armée	
???	87° Cie d'Aérostiers			Attacked, not flamed, Verdun Sector.	

23 March

Adj Ortoli	N 31	Albatros	X	Aumenancourt	5
???	DCA	Albatros CVII	X	Dieulouard	–

Casualties:

Cpl Marie-Jean Doat	N 79	P	MIA	Nieuport XVII N° 2283, probably by Ltn Georg Weiner, Jasta 20, (1).	
MdL Renard &	F 50	P	KIAcc	Crashed on takeoff.	
Lt Sourges	F 50	O	KIAcc	Farman t.60	
Brig Georges Chaney &	BM 119	P	KIAcc		
S/Lt François Rullier	BM 119	O	Injured	BM IV	
MdL Augustin Tuzet &	BM 118	P	Injured		
MdL Gaston Perreux	BM 118	B	Injured	BM IV	
S/Lt Martin	58° Cie d'Aérostiers			Attacked, not flamed, Verdun Sector.	

24 March

Adj Ortoli	a. N 31	EA	XF	N Reims, V° Armée	6
Adj Delrieu &	N 83				1
Brig Barancy	N 83	EA	X	Bois Soulains, V° Armée	1
???	DCA	Rumpler C	POW	Grandes Loges	–
Motor trouble	b. - - -	Seaplane	POW	au Lorge d'Etyretat	–
Adj Sayaret	N 76	2 seater	P	V° Armée	–

a.   Ltn von Flotten & Hptm von Deval, KG 2, POWs.
b.   Both occupants POWs.

Casualties:

Cpl Jean Peinaud &	F 7	P	MIA	Farman t.61, N° 4100, probably by	
Lt Marcel Vernes	F 7	O	MIA	Obltn Rudolf Berthold, Jasta 14, (9).	
Brig Jean Marquisan &	C 18	P	KIA	Caudron G4, probably by Ltn Hans	
Sgt Jacques Delacharte	C 18	O	KIA	Adam, Jasta 34, (1).	
MdL Paul Resel	N 83	P	WIA	Nieuport XVII, V° Armée	
Cpl Pierre Huet	C 28	P	WIA	Caudron G4, III° Armée, at Dury, probably by Jasta 34.	
Adj Charles Larrouil &	F 20	P	Injured	III° Armée.	
Sol Billy	F 20	O	KIAcc	Farman t.60	
QM Antoine Prévost &	* CAM	P	KIAcc	North Sea, FBA 150 HP N° 413,	
Mat Le Tynevez	* CAM	O	WIA	codé D.4.	
Mat Jules Basile	PilSch	M	KIAcc	Dunkerque.	

*   Dunkerque.

25 March

Cpl Brémond &	C 28				1
S/Lt Cottais	a. C 28	Rumpler C	POW	III° Armée	1
Sgt Lemonon	N 31	EA	X	V° Armée	1
Adj Ortoli	N 31	2 seater	POW	Brimont, V° Armée	7
Adj Ortoli	N 31	EA	X	Freslon, V° Armée	8
S/Lt Baudoin-Roland	N 80	EA	X	Telon	1
Sgt Cauron,	R 210				1
Lt Jansen &	R 210				1
Cpl Grude &	R 210	EA			1
Sgt Menant,	R 210				1
S/Lt Moreau &	R 210				1
Cpl Albrecht	R 210	EA	X	Aubigny, V° Armée	1
Adj Austruy	N 31	EA	P		–

a.   Probably Vfw Gall & Ltn Heinrich, FlAbt 38, POWs.

Casualties:

Capt Louis Faucher	N 12	P	KIA	Nieuport XXIII	
Cpl Joseph Trincot	N 57	P	MIA	Nieuport XXIII N° 3418, probably by Vfw Paul Aue, Jasta 10, (4).	
Adj Charles Cacheux	N 80	P	KIA	Nieuport XVII	
S/Lt Georges Moreau	R 210	O	WIA	Caudron R.4, V° Armée	
Sgt Henri Lémonon	N 31	P	Injured	Spad VII, V° Armée	

26 March – No Claims
Casualties:

Cpl Gustave Huot	C 28	P	WIA	
Lt Robert Jung	Pau	P	KIAcc	

27 March – No Claims
Casualties:

Cpl Marcel Herbert &	F 20	P	Injured	III° Armée
Lt Georges Vercherin	F 20	O	WIA	Farman t.60

28 March

Adj Casale &	N 23					7
Adj Bertal	N 23	EA	X	Dieppe-Ronvaux	1030	1
Adj Villars	N 23	EA	X	Cumières	1055	2
Capt Matton	a. N 48	2 seater	X	S Nauroy, V° Armée	1115	5
Lt de Bonald	N 69	EA	X			2
Capt Doumer	N 76	EA	X	Bermericourt	1040	7
Cpl L de Marmier	N 112	EA	P			–
Cpl Becque	N 85	EA	P	Mouzeville		–

a.   Probably Gefr Bernhard Palm & Ltn Walter Schmidt, FlAbt (A) 203, KIAs, Nauroy.

Casualties:

S/Lt Corsanini	F 206	O	WIA	Flak, Farman t.40, V° Armée, possibly by Flakzug 65.
Cpl Raoul Lestoclet &	VB 108	P	Injured	DOW 29 March 1917
S/Lt Testart	VB 108	O	Injured	Voisin P
Lt Kahn	GDE	O	Injured	Farman t.42
Cpl Leroux &	C 34	P	Injured	Crashed on takeoff.
MdL Nicolas	C 34	O	KIAcc	Caudron G4
Lt Straëhlé	58° Cie d'Aérostiers	XF		Vfw Ulbrich, Jasta 7 (2)
		O	OK	& Ltn Erich Löwenhardt,
MdL Collin	38° Cie d'Aérostiers	XF		Jasta 10 (1) each credited
		O	OK	with a balloon.

29 March – No Claims – No Casualties

30 March – No Claims
Casualties:

MdL Jacques Garrigues	Pau	G	KIAcc	

31 March

S/Lt Dorme	N 3	AEG C	X	NE Fismes	1100	18

Casualties:

MdL Henri Verdier	???	P	WIA	

1 April

Sgt Goux	N 67	2 seater	X		1

Casualties – None

2 April

Ground fire	???	Albatros D3	POW	N° 2107/16 FTL/POW near Rambervillers, at 15h30 Vzfw Rudolf Nebel, Jasta 35. –

Casualties:

Adj Georges Bertal	N 23	P	POW	Nieuport XVII N° 2243, forced to land in enemy territory, cause unknown.
Lt Simonet	C 54	O	WIA	VII° Armée, Caudron G4, ground fire.

3 April – No Claims
Casualties:

Cpl Claude Bernard	N 67	P	WIA	Spad VII
S/Lt Jeannin	C 34		Injured	Crashed during test flight.

4 April

| ??? | | DCA | EA | X | Vosges Sector | | – |

Casualties: None

5 April

German withdrawal to the Hindenburg Line is completed.

S/Lt Chaput		N 57	EA	X			9
S/Lt Chaput		N 57	EA	X			10
S/Lt Leps		N 81	EA	P	Mulhouse		–

Casualties:

Asp d'Hericourt &		C 39	P	KIA	Caudron, V° Armée, probably by
Sgt Mathieu		C 39	O	KIA	Ltn Albert Dossenbach, Jasta 36 (10).
QM Ernest Vienne &	*	CAM	P	MIA	North Sea, Voisin LAP VII
Mat Emile de Houck	*	CAM	M	MIA	N° 1785 code 22.
Cpl Jacques Hérubel		N 78	P	WIA	DOW, IV° Armée, Spad VII.
Cpl Alfred Guyot		N 81	P	WIA	VII° Armée, Spad VII, probably by Ltn Hans Auer, Jasta 26, (1).
Sgt Louis-Gérard Varet		C 10	P	OK	
???		C 10	O	WIA	
Adj Rome &		C 56	P	Injured	
S/Lt Soulier		C 56	O	OK	Crash landing.

* Centre d'Aviation Maritime at St Pol.

6 April

S/Lt Bucquet	a.	N 3	EA	XF	Forges-Hourges	1910	1
Adj Jéronnez		N 26	Balloon	XF	Veslun	1805	2
Lt Mistarlet		N 31	Balloon	XF	Lavannes	1800	1
Adj Douchy		N 38	Balloon	XF	Hauvine		6
S/Lt Tarascon		N 62	Albatros	XF	Marchélepot		9
Brig Le Roy de Boiseaumarie		N 78	Balloon	XF	Ardeuil		1
S/Lt V Régnier		N 112	Balloon	XF	Epoye		5
Cpl Montagne		N 112	EA	X			1
Lt Lorillard		N 48	Balloon	P			–

a. Possibly a Rumpler C.I from Schutzstaffel 7.

Casualties:

MdL Adolphe Clérisse		N 62	P	MIA	Sopwith N° 22
S/Lt Pierre Desbordes,		F 35	P	MIA	Caudron R4 N° 1559, probably by
Lt Jacques Borgoltz &		F 35	O	MIA	Obltn Rudolf Berthold, Jasta 14,
Sol Alexandre Lebleu		F 35	G	MIA	(10).
Lt Auguste Lorillard		N 48	P	MIA	Spad VII N° 164
Lt Jean Mistarlet		N 31	P	POW	Spad VII N° 224, probably by Ltn Heinrich Bongartz, Jasta 36, (1).
Sgt Emile Sommier &		C 224	P	KIA	V° Armée
S/Lt Robert Jouvenot		C 224	O	KIA	Caudron G4
Sgt Georges Gauron,		R 210	P	WIA	V° Armée
S/Lt André Cazier &		R 210	O	KIA	
Sol Max Brasseur		R 210	G	KIA	Caudron R4
Lt Louis Berquet		C 220		WIA	Caudron G4
Sgt Marcel Valence &		F 211	P	WIA	Farman 61
Lt Marcel Beaufils		F 211	O	WIA	
Capt Paul Grimault &	CO	F 208		WIA	
S/Lt Charles Feltin		F 208		WIA	Farman 60
Sgt Pierre Lafaille &		C 227	P	WIA	
S/Lt Charles Vrolyk		C 227	O	KIA	Caudron G4
Sgt Antonin Giraud		N 86	P	KIAcc	Villacoublay
MdL Pierre Savy		???	P	KIAcc	
Cpl Jacques Arnoult		C 56	P	KIAcc	
S/Lt Charles Corsanini		F 206	O	Injured	
???		21° Cie d'Aérostiers		XF	Probably by Ltn Josef Jacobs,
			O	OK	Jasta 22, unconfirmed.
???		52° Cie d'Aérostiers			Attacked, not flamed, Châlons Sector.

7 April – No Claims

Casualties:

| Lt Richard Fanning (Belgian) | | C 74 | O | KIA | |

8 April

Cpl Damenez,		C 46					1
Cpl Rivière &		C 46					1
MdL Théron		C 46	EA	X	Orgeval	1530	1
Lt Bloch,		C 46					1
Sgt Joussen &		C 46					2
Sgt Boyé		C 46	EA	X	Aguilcourt	1615	1
Brig Brunet,		R 214					1
Sgt R Levy &		R 214			V° Armée		1
Sgt Girard		R 214	EA	X	N Berry-au-Bac		1
Lt de Laage de Meux	a.	N 124	Scout	X	N St Quentin	1330	3
Lt de Laage de Meux	b.	N 124	2 seater	X	N Moy	1350	4
Sgt Fournier,		R 209					1
Lt Charpiot &		R 209					1
Sgt P Garros		R 209	EA	X			1
Sgt Gendronneau,		C 46					–
Lt Wilmes &		C 46					–
Adj de Cuypers		C 46	EA	FTL	Orainville	1600	–
Lt Gigodot		N 3	EA	P	Comicy-Berry-au-Bac	1850	–
Lt J Guérin		C 105	Aviatik C	P			–
Adj Lufbery		N 124	EA	FTL			–

a.   Probably Ltn Roland Nauck, Jasta 6, KIA, St Quentin, Albatros D3 2234/16 (G.21).
b.   Possibly Flg Albert Glindkamp, KIA St Quentin, about 10 km NNW Moy.

Casualties:

MdL Célestin Théron	C 46	G	KIA	Caudron R 4
Sgt Marcel Gendronneau	C 46	P	OK	Caudron R4, probably by Obltn Erich
S/Lt René Wilmes	C 46	O	KIA	Hahn, Jasta 19, (2).
Adj Pierre de Cuypers	C 46	G	WIA	
Sgt Léon Joussen	C 46	G	WIA	
Adj André Taixières &	F 19	P	WIA	III° Armée
S/Lt Marc Gervais de Lafond	F 19	O	KIA	Farman F.42
Sgt Jean Charles,	R 209	P	OK	
Lt René Lete &	R 209	O	OK	
Sol Georges Piquot	R 209	G	WIA/DOW	Caudron R4
Sgt René Fournier,	R 209	P	OK	
Lt Paul Charpiot &	R 209	O	WIA	
Sgt Paul Garros	R 209	G	OK	Caudron R4
Lt Gustave Comby	R 209	O	WIA	,,
Sgt Henri Munier	C 30	P	WIA	Caudron G4
S/Lt Villemy	C 202	O	KIA	,,
Cpl Alfred Debrie	C 212	P	WIA	,,
Adj Hervé de Saint Pierre	C 219	P	WIA	,,
Lt Martin	F 201	O	WIA	Farman 40
S/Lt Guillard &	F 218	P	Injured	Farman F.61
Sol Gaston Jouannet	F 218	M	Injured	
Adj André Duhamel	41° Cie d'Aérostiers		XF	Probably by Ltn Heinrich
		O	Injured	Gontermann, Jasta 5, (8).
Adj Fournas	75° Cie d'Aérostiers			Attacked, not flamed Chauny Sector.

9 April

S/Lt Tarascon	N 62	LVG C	P	Pinon	–

Casualties:

Lt Albert Schuester	???	P	KIA	
Capt Ratel	???	P	WIA	
S/Lt Henri Pressac &	F 72	P	Injured	
Lt Alexandre Pierson	F 72	O	KIAcc	
Sgt Pierre Prieur	51° Cie d'Aérostiers		XF	
		O	OK	

10 April

Sgt Douchy &	N 38				–
S/Lt Roederer	N 38	Fokker	FTL	Courmelois	–

Casualties:

Brig Chautard	N 31	P	POW	Nieuport XVII N° 1930, forced to land in enemy lines at Aleucourt, cause unknown.
S/Lt Louis Lefrançois	F 41	O	WIA	Salmson-Moineau

Adj Desvignes,	F 41	P	Injured	V° Armée		
Lt Adolphe Forgues &	F 41	O	Injured			
Sol Fedide	F 41	G	Injured	Salmson-Moineau		

11 April

Adj Jéronnez	a.	N 26	EA	X	Cerny-en-Laonnois	1050	3
Lt Pinsard	b.	N 78	Albatros D	X	SE St Souplet		6
Sgt M Paris		N 73	EA	P	Sissonne	1110	–

a.   Probably Ltn Heinrich Karbe, Jasta 22, WIA over Cerny-en-Laonnois.
b.   Probably Vfw Karl Möwe, Jasta 29, KIA near St. Souplet.

Casualties:

MdL Blaise Préher	N 68	P	POW	VIII° Armée, Nieuport XVII N° 1955 probably by Ltn Gebhardt Salzwedel, Jasta 24, (1).
Adj Albert Barioz	N 73	P	MIA	Spad VII N° 370, departed 05h30, possibly by Obltn Rudolf Berthold, Jasta 14, (11).
Mat Eugène Jullien &	* CAM	P	MIA	
EV1 Charles Prieur	* CAM	O	MIA	FBA 150hp N° 376
Sgt Perseyger &	F 215	P	KIA	N Berry-au-Bac, Farman 61 N° 4170,
Asp Nardon	F 215	O	KIA	probably by Ltn Albert Dossenbach, Jasta 36, (11).
Sgt Marcel Paris	N 73	P	WIA	Spad VII, probably by a Jasta 14 pilot.
Lt Jean Grabes	F 71	O	WIA	Farman 61, ground fire.
Sgt Bodin,	R 214	P	WIA	V° Armée
S/Lt Jean Grignon &	R 214	O	WIA	
Sol Dermirgian	R 214	G	WIA	Caudron R4
Lt Clerc	C 42	O	WIA	Caudron G4
???	F 41			Salmson-Moineau FTL near Berry-au-Bac, reason unknown.
??? &	N 62	P	OK	Nieuport 2 seater, FTL between the
Lt Lemaignen	N 62	O	OK	lines, hit by infantry fire.

*   St Raphaël.

12 April

MdL Nogues	N 12	EA	X	Bois de Chevel	2
Sgt Baudson,	N 15				3
MdL Diesbach &	N 15				1
Adj Jailler	N 15	Scout	X	Rethel	7
Lt Pinsard	N 78	Albatros	X	S Epoye	7
S/Lt Dorme	N 3	EA	P	Loivre	1002 –
S/Lt J de Sevin	N 12	EA	P		–
QM Malvoisin	* CAM	Albatros C	P	Middlekerque	–

*   Dunkerque.

Casualties:

MdL Benjamin de Tascher	N 26	P	POW	Spad VII N° 184, left 05h30 forced to land at Attigny cause unknown, later escaped and rejoined N 26.
Adj-Chef Georges Chemet	N 112	P	POW	Spad VII N° 1200, probably by Ltn Hartmut Baldamus, Jasta 9, (17).
Cpl Marcel Carré	N 112	P	POW	IV Armée, Nieuport XVII N° 2779, forced to land at Leffincourt, cause unknown.
MdL Richard &	N 38	P	MIA	Nieuport XII, probably by Uffz
Lt Jean Hallier	N 38	O	MIA	Eduard Horn, Jasta 21, (1).
Lt de Montfort,	SM 106	P	POW	Salmson-Moineau N° 71, probably by
Sol Portolieu &	SM 106	G	MIA	Obltn Erich Hahn, Jasta 19, (3).
Brig Robillard	SM 106	G	POW	
Brig Brunet,	R 214	P	MIA	V° Armée, Caudron G4, probably by
S/Lt Hembrat &	R 214	O	MIA	Flakzug 54
Sgt Levy	R 214	G	MIA	
??? &	C 10	P	OK	
Lt Léon Thirion	C 10	O	KIA	
Lt Michel Guimberteau	C 222	O	WIA	Caudron G4
Lt Vitout &	C 202	P	KIAcc	V° Armée
???	C 202	M	KIAcc	Landing accident.

Lt Henry de Sauvan d'Aramon &	F 54	P	Injured	DOW		
S/Lt Charles Jallade	F 54	O	KIAcc	Landing accident.		
QM Eugène Jullien &	Navy	P	KIAcc			
EV1 Prieur	Navy	O	KIAcc			
Lt Henri Denis &	C 224	P	Injured	V° Armée		
Lt Raymond Langlais	C 224	O	Injured	Landing accident.		

13 April

Adj Paulli-Krause &	F 2			V° Armée		1
S/Lt Clave	F 2	EA	X	Guignicourt		1
MdL Gros &	F 41			V° Armée		1
S/Lt de Dreux	F 41	Scout	X	Mont Sapignuel		1
Adj Lufbery,	N 124	2 seater	X	NW St Quentin	1730	8
Adj Bertrand	N 57					2
Capt Guynemer	N 3	Albatros C	P	Bétheny	1500	–
MdL Soulier	N 26	EA	P	Cerny-en-Laonnois	1030	–
Capt de Marancour	GC 14	EA	P			–
MdL Fourcade,	R 213					–
Lt Malaguti &	R 213					–
Sol Gailland	R 213	EA	P			–
Lt H de Sevin de Quincy	N 314	EA	FTL			–

Casualties:

S/Lt Paul Féquant,	F 72	P	KIA	V° Armée, Châlons-sur-Vesle	
Lt André Locquin &	F 72	O	KIA	Salmson-Moineau, probably by Ltn	
Sol Maurice Hutreau	F 72	G	KIA	Heinrich Bongartz, Jasta 36, (2).	
MdL Marcel Nogues	N 12	P	POW	Spad VII N° 1057, later escaped and rejoined N° 12. Probably the victim of Ltn Albert Dossenbach, Jasta 36, (12).	
EV1 Robert de la Tullaye	R 210	O	WIA	V° Armée	
Sgt Evremend Lentrain	R 210	G	KIA	Letord	
Adj Niels Paulli-Krause &	F 2	P	OK	V° Armée	
S/Lt Henri Clave	F 2	O	WIA	Sopwith 2	
MdL Louis Gros &	F 41	P	OK	V° Armée	
S/Lt de Dreux	F 41	O	WIA	Farman 40	
Lt Maurice Baudart	F 71	O	WIA		
MdL Pierre Fourcade,	R 217	P	OK		
Lt Pierre Malaguti &	R 217	O	WIA		
Sol Jules Gailland	R 217	G	WIA		
Lt Charles Weiss	F ???	P	Injured		
MdL Colonna de Giovellina	55° Cie d'Aérostiers		XF	Probably by Ltn Heinrich	
		O	OK	Gontermann, Jasta 5, (9).	
Lt Cante	89° Cie d'Aérostiers		XF	VIII° Armée, Probably by Obltn	
		O	OK	Eduard Dostler Jasta 34, unconfirmed.	

14 April

Capt Guynemer	a. N 3	Albatros	XF	La Neuvillette	1030	36
S/Lt Languedoc	N 12	EA	X	Bois de Noyelle	0600	5
Lt Thiriez	N 15	EA	XF	Corbeny		1
Cpl Simon	b. N 37	EA	X	St Marie-à-Py		1
S/Lt Mauduit,	F 41					1
Lt Tartes &	F 41			V° Armée		1
Brig Kissel	F 41	Scout	X	SW Condé	1315	1
Capt Lecour Grandmaison,	C 46					5
Adj Vitalis &	C 46					7
MdL Rousseaux	c. C 46	Scout	XF	S Craonne	1210	5
MdL Harpedanne de Belleville	d. N 49	EA	X	Elbach	1100	1
Lt Pinsard	N 78	2 seater	X	W Sommepy		8
Cpl Benedictus,	R 214					1
S/Lt Muller &	R 214			V° Armée		1
Sol Bessières	R 214	EA	XF	Mont Sapignal	1030	1
Adj Daladier	F 14	2 seater	X	Ste Marie-aux-Mines		1
MdL Vieljeux	F 14	2 seater	X	Bonhomme		1
Adj Hamel	F 14	Balloon	XF	Saulxures		1
Adj Grelat &	GB 4					3
Lt Canivet	e. GB 4	EA	X	VII° Armée, Breisach		3

71° Cie d'Aérostiers	f. - - -	Albatros D3	XF	VIII° Armée	–
???	DCA	2 EA	X		–
Capt Matton	N 48	2 seater	P		–
Adj Vial	g. N 315	EA	P	VII° Armée, Fôret de Rothleiblen.	–

a.   Probably Uffz Karl Abelmann & Ltn Heinrich Schönberg, FlAbt 254 (A), KIAs near Reims about 4 km SE La Neuvillette.
b.   Ltn Hartmut Baldamus (18v) Jasta 9, collided with Cpl Simon over St Marie-à-Py.
c.   Probably Ltn Otto Weigel, Jasta 14, KIA Craonnelle, at 12h45, about 3 km south of Craonne.
d.   Probably Ltn Friedrich Grünzweig, Jasta 16, KIA Near Elbach.
e.   Possibly Uffz Simon Stebel, & Vfw Ludwig Demmel, Schusta 26b, KIAs Neu-Breisach.
f.   Uffz Hermann Jopp, Jasta 37, KIA during a balloon attack at Mont Toulon, by the balloon observer, Henri Peltier.
g.   Possibly Obltn Herbert Theurich, Jasta 35, KIA near Neubreiasach, Albatros D3 2097/16.

Casualties:

Cpl Simon	N 37	P	MIA	Nieuport XVII N° 2539, collided with Ltn Helmuth Baldamus, Jasta 9, (18).
QM Charles Proux &	* CAM	P	WIA/POW	Later escaped, FBA 150 hp N° 323,
Mat Prudhomme	* CAM	O	POW	codé D.8.
QM Charles Huebert &	* CAM	P	POW	FBA 150hp, N° 411, codé D.7.
EV1 Lecoq	* CAM	O	POW	These two aircraft were claimed by Flgom Burgstaller (1) & Vzflgmstr Müller (1),SFS II. Escaped in Jan 1918.
S/Lt Antoine Arnoux de Maison-Rouge &	N 15	P	WIA	DOW 29 May 1917.
S/Lt Robert Levi	N 15	O	WIA	Sopwith 2, S Pontavert.
Sgt André Giraudon &	C 105	P	KIAcc	V° Armée
S/Lt Dupuy	C 105	O	KIAcc	Crash-landing.
Capt Joseph Magne & CO	C 13	P	Injured	
Lt Oddos	C 13	O	KIAcc	
MdL Edouard Jousse	C 10	P	Injured	Caudron G.4
S/Lt Guillotin	48° Cie d'Aérostiers	XF		Probably by Ltn Fritz Pütter,
	O	OK		Jasta 9 (1).
S/Lt M A Sapin	57° Cie d'Aérostiers	XF		Probably by Ltn Hans Adam, Jasta 24
	O	Injured		DOW 17 Apr 1917(2).
???	87° Cie d'Aérostiers			Attacked, not flamed, Nancy Sector

*   Dunkerque.

---

15 April

Lt Deullin	N 73	EA	XF	Festieux	1040	13
Capt Guynemer	N 3	EA	P	Berry-au-Bac	1015	–
Capt Guynemer	N 3	EA	P	Berry-au-Bac	1050	–
Adj Guiguet	N 3	EA	P	Montchâlons	1010	–
Adj Jeronnez	N 26	EA	P	Chamouille	1010	–
Lt de Larminat	N 48	EA	P			–
Capt Lamy	N 65	EA	P	Laffaux	1515	–
Lt Deullin	N 73	EA	P	Festieux		–

Casualties:

Cpl Emile Quaissard	N 102	P	MIA	Spad VII N° 1056, probably by Ltn Werner Albert, Jasta 31, (3).
Adj Jacques Sirieys	N 519	P	MIA	Nieuport XXIII N° 2537, probably by Ltn Dotzel, Jasta 19, (1).
Lt Paul Bergeron	N 15	P	POW	Spad VII N° 1059, probably by Uffz Max Zachmann, Jasta 21, (1).
Adj Denis Epitalon	N 15	P	POW	Spad VII N° 1234, probably Ltn Alfred Dossenbach, Jasta 36, (14).
Sgt Nicolas Buisson	N 15	P	POW	Spad VII N° 373, probably by Vfw Hans Mitzkeit, Jasta 36, (2).
Sgt Achille Papeil	N 3	P	POW	Spad VII N° 117, departed 05h20, by Vfw Julius Buckler, Jasta 17 (4).
S/Lt Robert Senechal	N 83	P	WIA	Nieuport XXIII, probably by Ltn Albert Dossenbach, Jasta 36, (13)
MdL Alphonse Wang	F 71	P	WIA	Salmson-Moineau-Flak
Cpl Max Gouman	???	P	KIAcc	

---

16 April
The ill-fated Second Battle of the Aisne (Nivelle Offensive) between Reims and Soissons.

S/Lt Languedoc	N 12	EA	X	E Cauroy	0600	6
Brig Thomassin	a. N 26	EA	X	NW Guignicourt	1430	1
Cpl Cordonnier	N 57	Balloon	XF	S Bois des Grands Usages	1520	1
Brig Rigault	b. N 73	EA	XF	N Cormicy	1025	1

Brig Rigault	N 73	Balloon	XF	Bruyères	1510	2
MdL Balme &	C 222			V° Ármée		1
Lt de Niort	c. F 72	EA	X	Hermonville	1030	1
21° Cie d'Aérostiers	d. ???	Scout	X			–
Capt Auger	N 3	EA	P	Juvincourt	1445	–
S/Lt Dorme	N 3	2 seater	P	St Etienne-sur-Suippes	1505	–
SgtTriboulet	N57	EA	P			–
??? &	F 72					–
S/Lt Tignolet	F 72	Scout	P			–
Sgt Lutzius	N 103	EA	P	N Corbeny	1540	–
??? &	C 212					–
Asp Bellay	C 212	2 seater	FTL			–

a. Probably OfStv Kern, POW, & Ltn Walter Utermann, FlAbt 228, KIA Juvincourt, collided with Brigadier Thomassin.
b. Possibly Vfw Rieger, Jasta 17, WIA Pontavert, about 8 km NW Cormicy.
c. Possibly Uffz Walter Köppen & Ltn Heinrich Wecke, FlAbt 248 (A), KIAs Villers-Franqueux, about 2 km SE Hermonville.
d. Possibly Ltn Hans-Olaf Esser, Jasta 15, KIA Winterberg-Laon, collided with the balloon he was attacking in the Soissons Sector.

Casualties:

S/Lt Paul de Larminat	N 48	P	MIA	Spad VII N° 1178, during a strafing mission.
Cpl Canivet-Lagrange	N 75	P	MIA	Nieuport XXIII N° 2827.
Lt Morcau	N 75	P	KIA	Nieuport XXIII, collided with a balloon at Villers-en-Pryaère.
Cpl Edmond Genet	N 124	P	KIA	Nieuport XVII N° 1962, AA fire, probably by KFlak 47.
Sgt François Pissavi &	C 228	P	KIA	V° Armée, Sapignal
S/Lt Bekkers	C 228	O	KIA	Caudron G4, N° 3113.
S/Lt Houmens	C 47		MIA	,,
Lt Caudillot	C 47	O	WIA	,,
Lt Pierre Petit	C 39	O	WIA	Caudron G4, V° Armée
Asp Humbert	C 104	O	WIA	Caudron G4, V° Armée
Lt Clavier	F 41	O	KIA	Farman 40, V° Armée
S/Lt Desmyttère	F 226	O	WIA	Farman 40, V° Armée
Lt Marcel Leloup	F 8	O	WIA	,,
S/Lt Adolphe Cote	F 206	O	WIA	,,
Lt Touard-Riolle	F 201	O	WIA	,,
Lt Crosnier	SM 106	O	WIA	Samson-Moineau
Lt Goisbsault	F 16	O	WIA	Sopwith 2
Brig Edmond Thomassin	N 26	P	WIA	Nieuport XXIV, see above.
MdL Robert Dagonet	N 83	P	WIA	Nieuport XXIII, during a balloon attack, possibly. by KFlak 47.
S/Lt Weith &	F 72	P	KIAcc	Crashed during takeoff.
S/Lt Petit	F 72	O	KIAcc	V° Armée
??? &	C 212	P	OK	FTL between lines by infantry fire.
Asp Bellay	C 212	O	OK	
Adj Feraud & Lt Stoehle	21° Cie d'Aérostiers			Attacked by EA which collided
		O	OK	with it killing the pilot.

17 April

Sgt Joussen	C 46	EA	X			2

Casualties:

Sgt Léonard Joussen	C 46	G	WIA	
Adj Firmin Gealageas	F 54	P	WIA	Farman 42
S/Lt Gustave Audrain	??° Cie d'Aérostiers		XF	
		O	OK	

18 April – No Claims

Casualties:

S/Lt du Pasquier	N 78	P	KIA	IV° Armée, Spad VII N° 301, possibly by M Flak 54.

19 April

S/Lt Dorme	a. N 3	Scout	X	W Orainville	1451	19
S/Lt Tarascon	N 62	LVG C	X	E Trucy		10
???	b. ???	EA	X	W Moronvillers		–
???	???	EA	X	SE Fresnes		–
Capt Auger	N 3	EA	P	Orainville	1450	–
Sgt Garrigou	N 37	EA	FTL			–

a.   Possibly Ltn Paul Hermann, Jasta 31, KIA, Bois Malval.
b.   Possibly Uffz Friedrich Schneider (G), Schsta 28, KIA Prosnes, about 6 km SSW Moronvillers.

Casualties:

Capt Daniel Fevre & CO	C 228	P	KIA	Morane Parasol, probably by Ltn
Lt Prince Charles de				Willi Daugs, Jasta 36, (1).
Broglie-Revel	C 228	O	KIA	
S/Lt Alfred Reynaud &	F 205	P	KIA	Probably by Ltn Adolf Frey
S/Lt Henri Marche	F 205	O	KIA	Jasta 9, (2).
Lt Hervé Conneau	N 69	P	WIA	Spad VII, V° Armée, probably by Ltn
				Werner Marwitz, Jasta 9, (1).
Sgt Henri Caillou	N 81	P	KIAcc	
???	65° Cie d'Aérostiers			Attacked, not flamed, Châlons Sector.

20 April – No Claims

Casualties:

QM Jean Godey,	CAM	P	MIA	
Mat Marius Vidal &	CAM	G	MIA	Off Toulon
Mat Joseph Silvy *	CAM	G	MIA	Donnet-Denhaut 150 hp #45
Adj Maurice Bondaire &	F 1	P	KIA	Farman 42, possibly by Ltn Schürz,
Lt Maurice Blanchy	F 1	O	WIA/DOW	Jasta 13, (1).
Lt Jean Verdié	N 73	P	WIA	
Lt Le Barbu	F 44	O	WIA	
QM Gaudet,	Navy	P	KIAcc	
Matelot Silvy &	Navy	G	KIAcc	
Matelot Morel	Navy	G	KIAcc	
???	87° Cie d'Aérostiers		XF	
		O	OK	

*   CAM Toulon.

21 April

S/Lt Languedoc	a.	N 12	Albatros D3	POW	Somme-Suippes	7
Lt Pinsard		N 78	EA	X	Nauroy	9
Lt Pinsard	b.	N 78	Albatros	X	Nauroy-Moronvillers	10
Asp Defourneaux		N 78	EA	X	Somme-Suippes	1
Asp Defourneaux		N 78	EA	P	Somme-Suippes	–

a.   Possibly Ltn Friedrich-Wilhelm Wichard, Jasta 24, POW at 18h30 at Nauroy, flying Albatros D3 2096/16 "Vera".
b.   Probably Ltn Günther von der Hyde, Jasta 9, KIA Nauroy at 20h00.

Casualties:

Cpl Ferret	N 90	P	Injured	Nieuport XXIVbis
				Crashed on landing.

22 April

S/Lt Dorme		N 3	2 seater	X	Beaurieux	1835	20
Capt Auger	a.	N 3	2 Seater	XF	Lierval	1910	4
Sgt Pendaries		N 69	EA	X			2
2Lt Deullin	b.	N 73	EA	X	W Craonne	1730	14
Adj Bergot		N 73	EA	P	Amenaucourt	1710	–
???		C 46	EA	P	Berry-au-Bac	1715	–
Patrol (4 pilots)		GC 12	EA	FTL	NE Fôret de St Gobain	1030	–

a.   Possibly Uffz Gustav Richter & Ltn Erich Bersu, FlAbt 212, KIAs Chevregny, about 5 km SW Lierval.
b.   Possibly Flg Albert Karzmarek & Uffz Karl Schulz, Schsta 10, KIAs, Oulcherwald, about 8 km W of Craonne.

Casualties:

MdL Leclerc &	C 42	P	POW	Caudron G4 N° 1810, probably by
Lt Mercier	C 42	O	POW	Ltn Gerlt, Jasta 19, (1).
MdL Colonna de	55° Cie d'Aérostiers		XF	Probably by Ltn Kurt Schneider,
Giovellina		O	OK	Jasta 5 (7).

23 April

Sgt Reyjal,		F 7					1
Lt Climens &		F 7					1
Brig Leclair		F 7	Scout	X			1
MdL Morizot &		N 23					1
Lt Gouin	a.	N 23	EA	X	Bois d'Avocourt		2
Sgt Goux		N 67	EA	X			2
Adj Pillon	b.	N 82	LVG C	X	French lines	3	
S/Lt Juguin		N 84	Rumpler C	X	NW Itancourt	1815	1
Capt Derode	c.	N 102	2 seater	X	Prosnes		3

Adj Guertiau &		C 43				Epine de Chevregny		2
???		C 43	EA	X		Epine de Chevregny		–
Adj Guillaumot		N 3	EA	P		Jouy	0550	–
S/Lt Dorme		N 3	Albatros C	P		Brimont	0715	–
S/Lt Dorme		N 3	AEG C	P		Witry-les-Reims	0740	–
S/Lt Dorme		N 3	Roland	P		Fôret de Samoussy	1638	–
S/Lt Dorme	d.	N 3	Roland	P		Festieux	1640	–
MdL Soulier		N 26	EA	P		Armenancourt	1515	–
Sgt Naegely		N 15	3 seater	FTL		N Bertricourt		–

a. Probably Vfw Arno Schramm, Jasta 7, KIA Montfaucon, about 10 km N of Avocourt.
b. N° 5155.
c. Possibly Vfw Heinrich Mertens, OK, & Ltn Friedrich Feldmann, WIA-DOW, 26 April 1917, FlAbt (A) 252w, over Festieux.
d. Possibly Gefr Hugo Siebel, KIA Festieux.

Casualties:

Sgt Ronald Hoskier &	N 124	P	KIA	Morane Parasol N° 1112, probably
Sol Jean Dressey	N 124	G	KIA	Ltn Willi Schunke, Jasta 20, (1).
Sgt Eugène Godet &	C ???	P	Killed	
MdL Paul Luche	C ???	O	Killed	
MdL Louis Morizot &	N 23	P	OK	
Lt Jacques Gouin	N 23	O	WIA	DOW, Sopwith 2
S/Lt Pierre de Launay	C 207	O	WIA	
Lt Jean Viennot	F ???	O	WIA	DOW
Sol Le Guino	F 8	G	WIA	DOW 11 May 1917, Caudron G4
MdL Bousquet	N 78	P	KIAcc	Crashed on take-off.
Lt Weiss &	F 60	P	Injured	
S/Lt Gradel	F 60	O	Injured	Crashed on take-off.
???	36° Cie d'Aérostiers			Hit by two bombs dropped by a Rumpler, not flamed, no casualties, Soissons Sector.

24 April

Adj Madon	a.	N 38	Albatros C	X		Cornilette		9
MdL Henriot	b.	N 65	Scout	X		Forêt de Pinon	1720	1
S/Lt Battesti		N 73	EA	X		Ste Croix	0600	1
Adj Baudoin-Roland		N 80	2 seater	XF		l'Ange Gardien	1700	2
Adj Pillon	c.	N 82	Albatros D	X		Dannemarie		4
Cpl Lejeune &		N 83						1
Capt de Marancour	d.	GC 14	2 seater	X		Courson	1640	4
Adj Lufbery		N 124	Aviatik C	X		E Cerisy	1725	9
???		???	EA	X		W Bois d l'Enclume		–
S/Lt Dorme		N 3	Roland D	P		Brimont	0950	–
S/Lt Dorme		N 3	2 seater	P		Vauxcelles	1558	–
S/Lt Bucquet		N 3	EA	FTL		Chivy-les-Etouvelles	1840	–
Adj Fétu		N 26	EA	P		Loivre-Courcy	1010	–
Adj Madon		N 38	2 seater	P		Courson		–
Capt Lecour-Grandmaison		C 46						–
Adj Vitalis &		C 46						–
Sgt Rousseau		C 46	EA	P		Guignicourt	1805	–
Lt Barbier		C 46						–
MdL Roblin &		C 46						–
Sol Mondème		C 46	EA	P		Chevregny	1010	–
Sgt Triboulet		N 57	EA	P				–

a. Possibly Ltn Friedrich Krawolitzki & Vfw Otto Hartung, FlAbt (A) 252w, KIAs Nauroy.
b. Probably Ltn Walter Rudatis & Ltn Karl Jaeger, FlAbt (A) 253, KIA Allemant, about 6 km S Pinon.
c. Probably Vfw Rudolf Rath (1v), Jasta 35, flying Albatros D3 2120/16, KIA Hagenbach, 07h20, corpse identified by the French.
d. Probably Ltn Werner Hecht & Ltn Hugo Schneider, FlAbt 222 (A), KIAs Coucy-le-Château, about 6 km NE Courson.

Casualties:

Sgt Xavier Boiteux-Levret				IV° Armée, Nieuport XXIII N° 2937,
	N 81	P	KIA	probably by OfStv Paul Felsmann Jasta 24, (2).
Cpl René Ménard	N 85	P	Injured	Nieuport XXIII, crash-landing.
Sgt Marcel Carton	F ???	P	Injured	

25 April – No Claims

Casualties:

Adj Georges Langel	N 80	P	POW
Lt Charles Berthault	F 71	O	WIA
MdL Joseph Vittet	N 38	P	KIAcc

Sgt Simon Giacobbi		30° Cie A'Aérostiers					
			O	Killed	At Ventelay.		

26 April

Sgt Sautet &		C 43					1
MdL d'Heudières		C 43	Scout	X	German lines		1
Sgt Gendronneau,		C 46					2
Asp Bruel &		C 46					1
Cpl Cadot		C 46	EA	X	N Ft Brimont	1720	3
Lt de Turenne,		N 48					2
Cpl Montrion &		N 48					1
Cpl Conan		N 48	Albatros C	X	La Ville-aux-Bois	0615	1
Sgt Bajac &		N 48					1
Cpl Roques		N 48	Albatros C	X	Loivre	1740	1
Lt Luc-Pupat	CO	N 79	EA	X	Itancourt-St Quentin		1
Sgt Johnson		N 124	Albatros C	X	E St Quentin	1800	1
Lt Thaw &		N 124					2
Sgt Haviland		N 124	Albatros C	X	Juvincourt	1830	1
EV1 Guierre	*	CAM	2 seater	X	Staden	1730	1
???		???	EA	X	Gratreuil		–
EV1 Guierre	*	CAM	2 seater	P	Staden	1730	–
S/Lt Baudoin-Roland	a.	N 80	Scout	P	Réservoir-Trucy	1000	–

a.   Probably Obltn Max Reinhold, Jasta 15, KIA Lierval, about 3 km NE Trucy.
*   Dunkerque.

Casualties:

Capt René Doumer	CO	N 76	P	KIA	Spad VII N° 1447, 16h00, N Brimont, probably by Obltn Erich Hahn, CO Jasta 19, (4).		
Cpl Marcel Egret		N 78	P	MIA	IV° Armée, Spad VII, probably by Ltn Werner Albert, Jasta 31, (4).		
EV1 Morand de Jouffrey &		CAM	P	POW	FBA 150HP N° 424, codé D.1		
Mat Bois	*	CAM	O	POW	Forced to land.		
Lt Burville		C 56	P	WIA	Caudron G4, Flak.		
Cpl David Raimskop &		???	P	KIAcc			
Sgt Sabatier		???	O	KIAcc			
Sgt S C Saudet		36° d'Cie Aérostiers		XF	Probably by Vfw Julius Buckler,		
			O	KIA	Jasta 17 (6).		

*   Dunkerque.

27 April

Cpl Sigaud,		F 71					1
S/Lt Guye &		F 71					1
Sol Lehemade		F 71	EA	X			1
Sgt Breton &		F 59					1
Sgt Barthes	a.	F 59	2 seater	X	N Réservoir d'Ailette		1
Brig Sigaut,		F 71					1
Sol Lahemade &		F 71					1
S/Lt Guye		F 71	EA	X	German lines		1
???	b.	???	EA	X	Gerardmer		–
???		???	EA	X	S Beine		–
Capt Auger		N 3	EA	FTL	Bétheniville	0900	–
Sgt Naegely	c.	N 15	3 seater	FTL	Eppes-Coucy		–
Adj Pillon		N 82	EA	P	Altkirch		–
Lt Sacksteder		N 85	EA	P	N Moronvillers		–

a.   Pilot KIA, observer, POW.
b.   Probably Ltn Herbert Zimmermann & Ltn Ernst Naumann, FlAbt 14, KIAs Gerardmer.
c.   Possibly Ltn Friedrich Vonschott, Jasta 14, WIA over Montchâlons, about 8 km S of Eppes-Coucy.

Casualties:

Sgt Pierre Bouchon &		F 19	P	OK	
Lt Guatave Fabre		F 19	O	WIA	Farman 42

28 April

Capt de Bernis	CO	N 12	Albatros	X			2
Adj Guillaumot		N 3	EA	P	Ecouffaux	0550	–
Adj Caullier &		C 11					–
S/Lt Robinne		C 11	Scout	P			–

Casualties:

Lt Pomepui,	C 39		KIAcc	V° Armée		
Sgt Durand &	C 39		KIAcc			
MdL Lageneste	C 39		KIAcc	Morane Triplane		
Cpl Jean Argaud &	F 215	P	KIAcc			
Capt Schwebelin	F 215	O	KIAcc	X° Armée, Sopwith		
Adj Henri Bricout &	F 25	P	Injured			
S/Lt Robert Antoine	F 25	O	Injured	Crashed on landing.		
Cpl André Bigot	C 104	P	Injured	X° Armée, Caudron G4		

29 April

S/Lt Dorme	N 3	Albatros C	X	Fleuricourt	1343	21
S/Lt Lebeau	N 12	Scout	X	Orainville	1745	4
Cpl Honorat &	F 25					1
Lt Bizard	a. F 25	Balloon	XF			1
S/Lt Baudoin-Roland	N 80	2 seater	POW	Moulins	0545	3
Lt Béraud-Villars	b. N 102	EA	XF	NE Nauroy		2
???	???	EA	X	Aguilcourt		–
S/Lt Dorme	N 3	Scout	P	Aguilcourt	1025	–
S/Lt de Francq	N 62	EA	P			–
Sgt L de Marmier	N 112	EA	P			–

a.   Destroyed on the night of 28/29 April in its hangar.
b.   Probably Ltn Ludwig Dornheim, Jasta 29, KIA Beine, immediate vicinity of Nauroy.

Casualties:

Lt Jules Campion,	C 46	P	KIA	Letord N° 90, probably by
MdL Marcel Lamy &	C 46	G	KIA	Ltn Walter Böning, Jasta 19,
Cpl Bosquié	C 46	G	KIA	(2). Departed 16h40.
Adj Durand &	VB 114	P	POW	Forced to land, cause unknown,
Lt Lalaune	VB 114	O	POW	Voisin 8 N° 1746.
Sgt Henri Leroy	N 12	P	WIA	Spad VII N° 1177??
Cpl Luizet	C 9	P	WIA	VIII° Armée.
Asp Aubry	C 9	O	OK	Caudron G4
S/Lt de Bussy	C 222	O	WIA	Caudron G4
MdL Gabriel Ravet &	C 122	P	WIA	X° Armée
Sol Marcel Cassonnet	C 122	G	WIA	Morane-Saulnier Parasol
Capt Emile Billon du Plan	N 65	P	KIAcc	X° Armée
Cpl Michel Lescuyer,	F 58	P	WIA	VIII° Armée
Lt Louis Glaenzer &	F 58	O	WIA	
Sol Bertrand	F 58	G	KIA	Crashed on landing.
S/Lt Raymond Hugues	F 216	O	WIA	
MdL Jean Minvielle &	CEP 115	P	KIAcc	
Lt Jean Boisdefire	CEP 115	O	KIAcc	
Capt Christiani &	F 216	P	Injured	
S/Lt Hugues	F 216	O	Injured	Landing accident.
Adj Gaston Guérin	87° Cie d'Aérostiers		XF	Possibly by Ltn Richard Ernert,
		O	KIA	Jasta 34 (1).
???	76° Cie d'Aérostiers			Attacked, not flamed, Soissons Sector.

30 April

Lt Jailler	N 15	EA	X	Laon	0940	8
Lt Bailly	CO a. N 81	EA	XF	N Moronvillers		1
MdL Diesbach	N 15	EA	P	Berry-au-Bac		–
Capt Shigeno	N 26	EA	P	Juvincourt-Prouvais	1707	–
Adj Peronneau	b. N 81	EA	P	IV° Armée		–
S/Lt Mallet	N 112	EA	P			–

a.   Probably a Jasta 9 pilot, Ltn Adolf Frey and Ltn Werner Marwitz both KIAs near Nauroy, about 5 km west of Moronvillers.
b.   Possibly Ltn Karl Beckmann & Ltn Ernst Poetsch, KG 2, KIAs between Aussonce and Reims, IV° Armée Sector.

Casualties:

Cpl Leroy	N 38	P	MIA	IV° Armée, Nieuport XVII, probably by Ltn Otto von Breiten-Landenberg, Jasta 9, (1).
Sgt Briode &	F 32	P	WIA	Probably by Vfw Werner Waegner,
S/Lt Emmanuel Picquet	F 32	O	KIA	Jasta 21, (2).
Sgt Henri Baudson	N 15	P	WIA	Spad VII
Capt Laurent Hugel & CO	F 212	P	KIAcc	
S/Lt Jean Dubrulle	F 212	O	KIAcc	
Cpl Jacques Moureaux	C 222	P	KIAcc	V° Armée

Cpl Pierre Brouillard		N 78	P	Injured	IV° Armée	
Cpl Enrique Martinez &		F 19	P	Injured	Crashed on take-off.	
S/Lt Maurice Malesset		F 19	O	KIAcc	III° Armée	
???		59° Cie d'Aérostiers	XF		V° Armée	
			O	OK		
???		62° Cie d'Aérostiers	XF		V° Armée	
			O	OK		
???		91° Cie d'Aérostiers	XF		V° Armée	
			O	OK		
S/Lt Jean Ray		19° Cie d'Aérostiers	XF		V° Armée, at Pévy, near	
			O	KIA	Fort Brimont.	
???		77° Cie d'Aérostiers			V° Armée, attacked at 13h00, hauled down, not flamed.	
???		80° Cie d'Aérostiers				

NOTE: All of these balloons were claimed by Jasta 19 pilots; Ltn Walter Böning (2), Obltn Erich Hahn (5 & 6), and Vzfw Arthur Rahn (1 & 2), and Ltn Rudolf Matthaei, Jasta 21, (3).

1 May

Lt Echard	CO	N 82	EA	X	VII° Armée		2
Capt d'Astier de la Vigerie	CO	N 88	EA	X	VII° Armée	1015	2
S/Lt Nungesser		V 116	Albatros D3	X	Slype		22
S/Lt Nungesser	a.	V 116	Albatros D3	X	Poperinghe		23
S/Lt Desquibes &		F 32					2
???		F 32	EA	X			?
MdL Billette &		R 217	EA				1
Sgt Poiroton		R 217	EA	X			1
Sgt Mougeot		N 62	EA	P			–
Lt L Séjourne		N 65	EA	P			–
Lt Pinsard	b.	N 78	EA	P	IV° Armée		–

a.   Probably Ltn Alexander Kutscher, Jasta 28, KIA Poperinghe.
b.   Possibly Flg Julius Laugel, KIA Château-Porcien, IV° Armée Sector.

Casualties:

Lt Boniface de Castallane &	VB 101	P	MIA	Voisin LAP N° 1931, probably by
Sgt Blanchard	VB 101	B	MIA	K Flak 97.
Sgt Georges Segond	N 88	P	KIA	VII° Armée, Nieuport XXIII N° 2675, by Ltn Heinrich Kroll, Jasta 9, (1).
Adj Matheron	Sop 111	G	WIA	Flak, Sopwith
Sgt Mancon,	VB 107	P	WIA	
S/Lt Eric de Waubert de Genlis &	VB 107	O	WIA	
Sgt Lavelaine de Maubeuge	VB 107	G	WIA	Voisin
MdL Georges Erb	C 18	P	KIAcc	Caudron G4, crash landing.
Capt Armand de Carbonnier,	SM 106	P	KIAcc	
S/Lt Bourdet &	SM 106	O	KIAcc	
Sol Feigner	SM 106	G	Injured	Salmson-Moineau
Capt Paul Genain &	DCA	P	Injured	V° Armée
Capt Ory	DCA	O	Injured	Nieuport
S/Lt Alessandri	F 58	O	Injured	Farman 60
Lt Léon Cremière	49° Cie d'Aérostiers	XF		Chassemy, Aisne Sector.
		O	KIA	
	42° Cie d'Aérostiers	XF		Aisne Sector
		O	OK	
EV1 Georges M Regnard	31° Cie d'Aérostiers			Attacked, not flamed, at
		O	KIA	Longueval, Aisne Sector
	20° Cie d'Aérostiers			Attacked, not flamed.
		O	OK	Soissons Sector

NOTE: Five balloons were claimed by Jasta 1 pilots, Vfw Paul Bona (5), Vfw Walter Dittrich (2), Obltn Hans Kummetz (4), OfStv Wilhelm Cymera (4) and Ltn Zilcher (1).

2 May

Capt Guynemer	a.	N 3	Albatros	X	Courtecon-Ailles	1935	37
S/Lt Marty	b.	N 77	Scout	XF	La Garde		1
MdL Famin &		N 83					1
Cpl Robert		N 83	2 seater	XF	N Fresnes	0640	1
Adj Ganthes,		R 210					1

Cpl Albrecht &		R 210				1
S/Lt Buvry		R 210	EA	X	German lines	1
Lt Floret &		C 225				1
Lt Homo		C 225	EA	XF		2
Lt Floret &		C 225				2
Lt Homo		C 225	EA	XF		3
Lt Achard	c.	N 510	EA	POW	Taon-les-Vosges	2
???		???	EA	X	N Fismes	–
S/Lt Dorme		N 3	Albatros C	P	Montchâlons	0905	–
Adj Madon		N 38	EA	P	IV° Armée	–
Adj Madon		N 38	EA	P	IV° Armée	–
Adj-Chef Bergot		N 73	EA	P	Berrieux-Aizelles	1505	–
Lt Pinsard		N 78	EA	P	IV° Armée	–
Sgt Haegelen		N 103	Albatros D	P	N Neufchâtel	0805	–
Capt Guynemer		N 3	2 seater	P	Réservoir	1915	–
Capt Auger		N 3	EA	P	Réservoir	1840	–
???		???	EA	P	Binarville	–
???		???	EA	P	Pont-Faverger	–
???		???	EA	P	St Souplet	–
???		???	EA	P	Montchâlons	–
???		???	EA	P	Meurieux	–
???		???	EA	P	Grandelain	–
???		???	EA	P	Berry-au-Bac	–
???		???	EA	P	Laval	–
???		???	EA	P	Varicourt-Pegnicourt	–
???		???	EA	P	Coucy	–
Lt Verdier-Fauvety		N 65	2 seater	FTL		–
S/Lt Nungesser		V 116	EA	FTL		–

a.   Probably Uffz Felix Schilf & Flg Felix Bockenmühl, SchSta 10, KIAs Ailles.
b.   Possibly Vfw Piez, Kest 3, Kofl "A" Sector.
c.   Possibly Vfw Seifert & Uffz Wilhelm Niess, SchuSta 7, POWs.

Casualties:

Cpl Paul Oudard	N 85	P	POW	Spad VII N° 1075.
Cpl Fabien Voisin	N 80	P	POW	Nieuport XVII N° 2309, departed at 12h30.
Sgt Charles Ganthes,	R 210	P	OK	V° Armée, forced to land during
S/Lt Roger Buvry &	R 210	O	WIA	combat, Lavannes,
Sol Antoine Albrecht	R 210	G	WIA	Letord. Possibly by Lt Heinrich Bongartz, Jasta 36, (4).
MdL Jean Dalesme &	C 28	P	KIAcc	Crashed on take-off.
S/Lt Bernard Audollent	C 28	O	KIAcc	Caudron G6
Cpl Saucier &	C 64	P	KIAcc	V° Armée
S/Lt de La Brosse	C 64	O	KIAcc	Caudron G6
Sgt Henri Lerousseau	VB 108	P	KIAcc	Nieuport 80 hp
Lt Jean de Boisdeffre &	???	P	KIAcc	
MdL Minvielle	???	O	KIAcc	
Cpl Roger	F 1	P	Injured	Crash landing.
Cpl James Doolittle	GDE	P	Injured	Nieuport XVII
S/Lt Pierre Claret	F 201	P	Injured	DOW 3 May 1917, Sopwith
Sgt Maurice Verien &	VB 101	P	Injured	
MdL Quoniam	VB 101	G	Injured	
Sgt André	VB 101	B	Injured	Voisin type, LAP VIII
Sgt Georges Quinton	???	P	Injured	
Adj Chevallier	F 58	P	Injured	Farman 60
Sgt Audubert	VB 109	B	Injured	
Sgt Haves	VB 109	B	Injured	
MdL Arnoud	66° Cie d'Aérostiers			Attacked, not flamed, probably by
		O	OK	Ltn Werner Zech, Jasta 1 (1).

3 May

Adj Barny de Romanet		N 37	Scout	X	Craonne	1
Capt Bernon &		N 67				1
Adj Toulze		N 67	2 seater	X	St Quentin	0705	1
Sgt Pendaries		N 69	Rumpler C	X	Aumenancourt-le-Petit	3
Adj Morel &		N 76			V° Armée	1
MdL Laraud		N 76	EA	X	NE Neufchâtel	3
Lt Echard &	CO	N 82				3
Brig de Boigne		N 82	2 seater	POW	Moosch	1

Sgt Castelli		N 102	EA	XF	IV° Armée		1
S/Lt Nungesser		V 116	Rumpler C	X	Nieuport-Marvaux		24
???	a.	???	EA	X	S Beine		–
???		???	EA	X	S Pont-Faverger		–
S/Lt Dorme		N 3	EA	P	Courteçon	0912	–
Capt Heurtaux	CO	N 3	EA	P	Neufchâtel-Pronseux	0953	–
Capt Guynemer		N 3	Albatros	P	Ft de la Malmaison	1120	–
Capt Heurtaux	CO	N 3	Albatros C	P	Aguilcourt-Sapigneulles	1953	–
Lt Barbier,		C 46					–
Adj Roblin &		C 46					–
Sol Mondeme		C 46	EA	P	Bérmericourt	0710	–
S/Lt Chaput		N 57	EA	P	Aguilcourt	1950	–
???		???	2 seater	P	St Quentin		–
Adj-Chef Fonck		N 103	2 seater	P	Berry-au-Bac		–
???		???	Scout	P	Berry-au-Bac		–

a.   Probably Uffz Albert Schötzau & Flg Kurt Stendel, KIAs Beine.

Casualties:

Capt Robert Massenet Royer de Marancour,	CO	GC 14	P	WIA	
MdL Louis de Diesbach de Belleroche		N 15	P	WIA	Spad VII
Sgt André Jarnach		N 78	P	WIA	IV° Armée, Spad VII
S/Lt Vervitch		???	P	KIAcc	Test flight

4 May

Capt Heurtaux	CO a.	N 3	Albatros C	POW	NE Beaurieux	0715	21
S/Lt Dorme	b.	N 3	3 seater	X	Amifontaine	1405	22
Capt Guynemer	c.	N 3	Albatros C	X	Courtecon-Braye	1508	38
Adj Madon		N 38	EA	X	Nogent l'Abbesse		10
Adj Douchy		N 38	EA	X	IV° Armée		7
Lt de Bonald	d.	N 69	Scout	X	Guignicourt		3
???		DCA	EA	X	Servon-Binarville		–
???	d.	???	EA	X	Witry-les-Reims		–
Lt Raymond		N 3	EA	P	Juvincourt-Amifontaine	1850	–
Sgt de Guingand		N 48	Albatros	P	Juvincourt	1850	–
Lt de Guibert		N 73	EA	P	Chivry-les-Etouvelles	1400	–
Lt Vernin		N 75	Halb C	P	Berry-au-Bac		–
Cpl Schmitter		N 103	EA	P	Bourgogne-Brimont	0910	–
Adj Major,		R 213					–
S/Lt Berthelin &		R 213					–
Cpl Lafon		R 213	EA	P			–
Lt Verdier-Fauvety		N 65	2 seater	P	Bertincourt		–
Sgt Lepercq &		F 208					–
S/Lt R Lévy		F 208	Scout	P			–
???		???	EA	FTL	Dunkirk		–
Lt Franc		N 79	2 seater	FTL			–

a.   Possibly Ltn von der Linde & Ltn Wolters, FlAbt 254 (A), WIA/POWs.
b.   Probably Ltn Kurt Leidreiter & Ltn Kurt Böttcher, FlAbt (A) 210, KIA, Flesquières, about 5 km N Amifontaine.
c.   Probably Flg Johann Weidmann & Vfw Walter Lagerhauser, SchSta 25, KIAs Courtecon.
d.   Probably Vfw Hans Brinkmann and Vfw Eduard Horn, Jasta 21, KIAs between Berru and Witry-les-Reims.

Casualties:

Mat Le Creuer	*	CAM	P	KIA	HD.2 N° 226, Code D 30, at Nieuport.
Sgt Emile Bonnomet &		F 55	P	KIA	Farman 60, probably by Ltn Josef
Lt Gilles		F 55	O	KIA	Veltjens, Jasta 14, (4).
Cpl Raoul Narisi &		Sop 123	P	KIA	Sopwith N° 5146, possibly by Vfw
S/Lt Oddos		Sop 123	O	KIA	Hugo Stöber, Jasta 16, (3).
Sgt Pierre Devaulx		N 26	P	WIA	Spad VII, FTL, X° Armée Juvincourt, possibly by Ltn Franz Brandt, Jasta 19, (1).
Lt Jean Beraud-Villars		N 102	P	WIA	Spad VII
Cpl Robert		F 221	P	WIA	Flak, Farman 61, probably by K Flak 37.
S/Lt Marcel Blanchard		C 11	P	WIA	Caudron G4
Adj André Major,		R 213	P	WIA	
S/Lt André Berthelin &		R 213	O	WIA	
Cpl Paul Lafon		R 213	G	WIA	Caudron R4
MdL Pierre Groja		GDE	P	KIAcc	Nieuport X
Asp Masson		GDE	P	Injured	Caudron G4
MdL Frédéric Tache		C 225	P	Injured	,,

S/Lt Odinot		F 201	O	Injured	Morane Parasol	
Sgt Peltier &		F 14	P	Injured		
Sol Colon		F 14	M	Injured	AR	
S/Lt René Rollet		N 12	P	OK	Shot down in flames between trenches, but returned unharmed, X° Armée.	

*   Dunkerque.

---

5 May

Adj Guiguet		N 3	2 seater	X	Guignicourt	1915	4
MdL Delannoy		N 80	2 seater	X	NE Juvincourt	0545	1
Lt Echard	CO	N 82	EA	X			4
Adj Baillou		N 86	2 seater	X	La Neuville		1
Adj-Chef Fonck		N 103	Fokker D	XF	Berry-au-Bac-E St Croix	0730	3
???		???	EA	X	Montchâlons		–
Capt Laurent &		N 80					–
Sgt Durand		N 80	EA	P	Colligis	0630	–
S/Lt Leps		N 81	Scout	P	Pont-Faverger		–
Sgt Laulhe &		N 86					–
Adj Sanglier		N 3	2 seater	P	Bray-en-Laonnois	0510	–
???		???	EA	P	Soissons		

Casualties:

Sgt Eugène Victorin &	C 225	P	MIA	Morane Parasol, probably by Ltn
Lt de Mornac	C 225	O	MIA	Paul Bona, Jasta 1, (6).
Adj Marcel Borne &	F 7	P	WIA	Sopwith, forced to land in flames
S/Lt Anthelme Martin				during combat, probably by Ltn
de Gibergues	F 7	O	KIA	Walter Böning, Jasta 19, zlg.
Capt Alfred Heurtaux CO	N 3	P	WIA	Spad VII, X° Armée, possibly by Ltn Werner Zech, Jasta 1,(2), Nieuport.
Adj Thery	F 7	P	WIA	
Adj Froment &	F 7	P	OK	
Lt Chavanne	F 7	O	WIA	Infantry fire.
S/Lt Etienne Gervais &	R 217	P	KIAcc	Crashed on take-off.
Lt Marie Caillebotte	R 217	O	KIAcc	Caudron G6
Lt André Herissant	N 517	P	KIAcc	Spad VII, crash-landed.
Adj Robert Schildge	???	P	KIAcc	
S/Lt Font-Reaulx	F 32	O	Injured	Farman, crash-landing.
S/Lt Bernard Toscano	F 45	P	Injured	Salmson-Moineau
	20° Cie d'Aérostiers			Attacked, not flamed.
	24° Cie d'Aérostiers			Attacked, not flamed. Soissons Sector.
	31° Cie d'Aérostiers			Attacked, not flamed.
	39° Cie d'Aérostiers			Attacked, not flamed.
	72° Cie d'Aérostiers			Attacked, not flamed.

NOTE: Jasta 14 received credit for two balloons destroyed in this sector.

---

6 May

Capt Pinsard	a.	N 78	EA	X	N Vaudesincourt		11
Capt Pinsard		N 78	EA	X	S Beine		12
Adj Garrigou		N 37	EA	P	IV° Armée		–
Cpl Callinet		N 86	EA	P	Ployart	0640	–
Adj-Chef Fonck		N 103	EA	P	E Neufchâtel	1430	–
???		???	EA	P	Bétheniville		–
???		???	EA	P	Saillevois		–
???		???	EA	P	Chemezy		–
???		???	EA	P	Urcel		–

a.   Probably Ltn Friedrich Oeken & Ltn Hans Weichert, FlAbt 17, KIAs Moronvillers, about 6 km NW Vaudesincourt.

Casualties:

Lt Gaëtan de La Brunetière	N 69	P	WIA	Spad VII, possibly by Vfw Julius Buckler, Jasta 17, Spad FTL at Pontavert.
Brig Maurice Engelhard	C 224	P	KIAcc	Morane Parasol
Cpl Rousselot &	C 42	P	Injured	DOW 9 May 1917
Sol Bacquenois	C 42	M	Injured	Caudron G4
Capt Guy de Lavergne CO	C 6	P	Injured	Letord

---

7 May

Sgt Roland,		N 31					1
Sgt Blanc &		N 31					
Cpl Chapelle	a.	N 31	2 seater	XF	E Courcy	0950	1

Lt Tenant de La Tour CO	N 26	EA	X	N Brimont	0955	9
Adj Guiguet	N 3	EA	P	E Ailette	1045	–
MdL Sauclière	N 79	2 seater	P			–
???	???	EA	P	Bruyères	1440	–
???	???	EA	P	Presles	1455	–
???	???	EA	P	Berru-Caurel		–
???	???	2 EA	P	Pont-Faverger		–
???	???	EA	P	La Fère		–

a.   Possibly Ltn Wilhelm Höding & Ltn Alfred Küffner, FlAbt 286 (A), KIAs Courcy.

Casualties:

Adj Voilleau	N 75	P	MIA	Spad VII, probably by Ltn Heinrich Kroll, Jasta 9, (2), Spad, NE Pontavert.
S/Lt Georges Mesplède	F 16	O	KIA	AR, ground fire
Asp Jean Dubois de Gennes	N 57	P	WIA	X° Armée, Spad VII, possibly by Ltn Werner Zech, Jasta 1, (3), FTL Bouvancourt.
MdL Ferrand,	F 223	P	KIAcc	V° Armée
S/Lt Berthier &	F 223	O	KIAcc	
MdL Borel	F 223	G	KIAcc	Salmson-Moineau
S/Lt Laurenceau	SM 106	P	Injured	Sopwith

8 May

The Nivelle Offensive ends after disastrous results for the French.

MdL Giraud &	N 86				1
Cpl Damidaux	N 86	2 seater	X	Chevreux	1

Casualties:

Lt Léon Cremière	49° Cie d'Aérostiers			Shot while descending in
		O	KIA	his parachute.

9 May

Adj Jailler	a.	N 15	EA	XF	Bruyères	1815	9
S/Lt Nungesser		V 116	DFW C	XF			25
Sgt Duvaut,		R 209					1
Lt Lete &		R 209					1
MdL Tabariès		R 209	Scout	XF	Fôret de Coucy		1
Lt Tenant de La Tour	a.	N 26	EA	P	Bruyères	1820	–
Adj Madon		N 38	EA	P	IV° Armée		–
Sgt Petit-Delchet		N 69	EA	P	Ste Croix	1645	–
???		???	EA	P	Nogent l'Abbesse		–
???		???	EA	P	Fôret de Coucy		–

a.   Probably OfStv Wilhelm Cymera or OfStv Karl Stiller, Jasta 1, KIAs near Chamouille, Bruyères about 8 km NNW of Chamouille.

Casualties:

S/Lt Paul Antoni	C 6	P	WIA	Caudron G6, ground fire.
Sgt Louis Martin &	BM 119	P	KIAcc	Crashed returning from a
Sgt Robert Fauconnier	BM 119	G	KIAcc	bombing mission.

10 May

S/Lt Dorme		N 3	Albatros C	XF	Chivy-les-Etouvelles	1007	23
Adj Casale &		N 23					8
Sgt Legendre		N 23	LVG C	X	Charmontois	1030	1
Sgt Douchy		N 38	EA	X			7
Adj Lemelle		N 73	EA	X	Montchâlons-Bièvre	1310	2
Sgt Ducastel		N 85	EA	X	German lines		1
Sgt Laulhe		N 86	2 seater	X	Guignicourt	1030	2
???		???	EA	X	Verdun		–
???	a.	???	EA	X	NE Aubérive		–
???		???	EA	X	Bièvres-Montchâlons		–
???		???	EA	X	Thourout		–
Adj Guiguet		N 3	EA	P	Guignicourt	1120	–
Adj Pillon		N 82	EA	P	Mülhouse	0800	–
???		???	EA	P	Dieuze		–
???		???	EA	P	NE Vailly		–

a.   Probably Ltn Werner Albert (4v), CO Jasta 31, KIA Vaudessincourt, about 2 km N of Auberive.

Casualties:

Adj Célestin Sanglier	N 3	P	MIA	Spad VII, probably bt Ltn Heinrich Gontermann, Jasta 15, (18), departed 10h40.

Capt Didier Lecour Grandmaison,	CO	C 46	P	KIA	Letord, probably by Ltn Heinrich		
Cpl Joseph Crozet &		C 46	G	KIA	Gontermann, Jasta 15, (19).		
Sgt Alfred Boyé		C 46	G	WIA			
Cpl Maurice Rochat		N 89	P	KIAcc	Nieuport XXIII		
Lt Paul Reverchon		GDE	P	Injured	Nieuport XVII		
MdL Edouard Durand-Dassier		RGAé	P	Injured	Nieuport XIVbis		
S/Lt Jean Drouot		C 6	P	Injured	,,		
Adj Henri Chastin		RGAé	P	Injured	Sopwith		

11 May

Capt Vuillemin,					(1)		3
Lt de Lubersac &		C 11					?
Sgt Descamps		C 11	EA	X	Sapigneule		1
Capt Auger,		N 3					5
S/Lt de Sevin &		N 12					3
Sgt Waddington		N 12	2 seater	X	Vailly	1125	1
Sgt Bouzac		N 12	2 seater	XF	Bazancourt	1715	1
Patrol	a.	N 15	2 seater	X	Craonne	0745	–
Lt Chevillon &		N 15					1
Sgt Naegely		N 15	EA	X			1
Sgt Guillemin &		F 32					1
???		F 32	EA	X	Champagne Sector		1
S/Lt Pelletier Doisy		N 69	Scout	X	Amifontaine	1515	5
Lt Deullin	CO	N 73	Albatros	XF	Loivre	1430	15
Capt d'Astier de La Vigerie	CO	N 88	2 seater	POW	VII° Armée, Soppe	0820	3
Adj-Chef Fonck		N 103	Rumpler C	X	Aguilcourt	1850	4
???		???	EA	X	Loivre		–
???		???	EA	X	Grands Usages		–
???		???	EA	X	Brimont		–
???		???	EA	X	Provieaux		–
S/Lt Bucquet		N 3	EA	P	Bazancourt	0725	–
Adj Guiguet		N 3	EA	P	Guignicourt-Juvincourt	1240	–
Capt Auger &		N 3					–
S/Lt Dorme		N 3	EA	P	Warméréville	1045	–
Adj Baillou		N 75	EA	P	La Neuville	1045	–
Sgt Barthes		N 93	EA	FTL	Luxieul-Remiremont	0930	–
Adj Caël		N 102	EA	P	IV° Armée		–
???		???	EA	P	NE Beine		–

(1)   CO Secteur Aéronautique 2° Corps d'Armée.
a.   Possibly Vfw Heinrich Breidenbach & Ltn Adalbert Rossbach, FlAbt 237 (A), KIAs St Croix, about 4 km N Craonne.

Casualties:

Sgt Henri Reymond	N 81	P	KIA	IV° Armée, Spad VII	
Sgt Louis Sauvet	N 81	P	KIA	Nieuport, collided in mid-air during combat.	
Sgt Maurive Vincent	???	P	KIAcc		
Adj Claude Modelin &	F 54	P	KIAcc		
S/Lt Maurice Mary	F 54	O	KIAcc	Farman 42	
Cpl Charles Eveno	N 84	P	KIAcc	Crashed during take-off.	
Sgt Georges Desmazures	Sop 29	P	KIAcc	Sopwith	
Adj-Chef Louis Manchette &	F 55	P	KIAcc		
Cpl de Scoraille	F 55	G	Injured	Sopwith	
Sol Sauvage	N 26	M	Injured	Spad VII	
Cpl André Lecuit-Monroy	GDE	P	Injured	Farman 42	
Sgt Dorne	C 21	P	Injured	Caudron G4	
Sol Frète	R 209	M	Injured	Caudron R4	
MdL René Kauffmann	N 87	P	Injured	VIII° Armée, Nieuport XXIII, collided with a Sopwith 2 seater of N° 90, crew not harmed.	
???	64° Cie d'Aérostiers		X	Both destroyed by enemy	
???	68° Cie d'Aérostiers		X	artillery fire, Soissons	
		O	OK	Sector.	

12 May

Cpl Garaud	N 38	Scout	X	IV° Armée	1

S/Lt Chaput		N 57	Scout	X	Brimont, V° Armée	1930	11
S/Lt Nungesser		V 116	EA	X	Savy		26
S/Lt Nungesser		V 116	EA	X			27
Adj Cattaert &		VC 110					1
MdL Emerich		VC 110	Scout	X	Mont-Haut	1540	1
???		???	Scout	X	Forêt de Ste Genevieve		–
???		???	EA	X	Gratreuil		–
Adj Douchy		N 38	EA	P	IV° Armée		–
Sgt de Marmier		N 112	EA	P	IV° Armée		–
???		???	EA	P	Semide		–
???		???	EA	P	E St Souplet		–
Patrol		N 83	EA	P	Colligis	0920	–
Patrol		N 103	EA	P	Corbeny	1855	–

Casualties:

Adj-Chef Joussaud	N 75	P	MIA	Nieuport XXIVbis N° 3674, by Vfw Julius Buckler, Jasta 17, (7), Hurtebise-Juvincourt, X° Armée.
MdL André Jean	???	P	KIAcc	
Brig Pierre Mirat &	R 217	P	KIAcc	Crash landing.
S/Lt Paul Brassaud	R 217	O	Injured	Caudron G6

13 May

Adj Madon	a.	N 38	Albatros C	X	N Côte 304		11
Adj-Chef Fonck		N 103	2 seater	XF	Nogent l'Abbesse	1830	5
???		???	EA	X	Ferme Medeah		–
Patrol		???	2 EA	X	Vaudesincourt		–
Patrol		N 86	Scout	P	NE Juvincourt	1000	–
Patrol		GC 12	EA	P	Puisieux	1830	–

a.   Possibly Gefr Max Kintof & Vfw Wilhelm Karcher, KIAs St Souplet.

Casualties:

Adj Fernand Garrigou	N 37	P	MIA	Spad VII N° 1377, probably by Ltn Kurt Wolff, Jasta 29, (30).
S/Lt Charton	C 227	O	KIA	Flak, Caudron G4
Sgt-Maj Eugène Vexenat	R 214	P	WIA	DOW 14 May 1917
Lt Auguste Dhers	R 214	O	WIA	Flak, Caudron G4

14 May

MdL Soulier		N 26	2 seater	X	La Neuville	1955	4
Capt Derode		N 102	2 seater	X	IV° Armée		4
???	a.	???	EA	X	Ste Marie-à-Py		–
Lt Deullin		N 73	EA	P	N Réservoir	1930	–
S/Lt Rabatel		N 3	EA	P	Nonampteuil	1930	–
???		???	EA	P	Laon		–

a.   Probably Vfw Reinhold Nietzsch & Ltn Ulrich Eggerst, FlAbt 270 (A), KIAs at Ste Marie.

Casualties:

Cpl Jean Hiribarne,	F 71	P	MIA	Salmson-Moineau N° 134, probably by Ltn Hermann Pfeiffer, Jasta 9, (11).
S/Lt Hippolyte Mercier &	F 71	O	MIA	
Sol François Rafflin	F 71	G	MIA	
Cpl Roger Legras	N 112	P	POW	IV° Armée, Nieuport XXIII N° 2920, became lost and landed in enemy territory.
S/Lt Cytère	C 18	O	Injured	Caudron G4
Lt Louis Arbitre	GDE	P	Injured	Caudron G4

15 May

Lt Pollet	a.	N 102	Scout	X	Suippe, IV° Armée		1
???		???	EA	X	N Armentières		–
SM Vigneau	*	CAM	Scout	X	Forêt d'Houthulst		1
???		???	EA	P	Foucoucourt		–
???		???	EA	P	S Maurecourt		–

*   Dunkerque.
a.   Ltn Karl Pockrantz (2), Jasta 29, KIA – collided in mid-air.

Casualties:

Lt René Pollet	N 102	P	MIA	Spad VII N° 1199, collided with an enemy aircraft, Ltn Karl Pockrantz, Jasta 29.

QM Antoine						
Chauvignat &	*	CAM	P	POW	FBA 150HP N° 409, codé D.5	
Mat Philibert	*	CAM	O	POW	North Sea, Sandettié.	
QM Boucand &	*	CAM	P	POW	FBA 150HP N° 422, codé D.12.	
EV1 François Carle	*	CAM	O	POW	Sandettié. These two brought down	
					by FlgMstr Huthmacher & Maukisch	
					an And LtnzS Röver & FlgMstr	
					Elsässer, SEE 1.	
SM Bernard Vigneau	*	CAM	P	MIA	Sandettié, Sopwith 130hp, N° SH1,	
					code D.21, by ObltnzS Friedrich	
					Christiansen (1) & VzFlgMstr	
					Menkish (1), SEE 1.	

*   Dunkerque.

---

16 May – No Claims
Casualties:

Cpl Henri Corbel	C 28	P	Injured	Caudron G4	

---

17 May – No Claims
Casualties:

S/Lt Henri Bastide	F 208	P	KIAcc	AR	

---

18 May

Cpl Montrion &	N 48			V° Armée		2
Brig Conan	N 48	Albatros D	X	N Juvincourt	0720	1
Sgt Miguel	N 85	EA	P	IV° Armée		–
Adj-Chef Fonck	N 103	EA	P			–
???	???	EA	P	Epoye-Beine		–
Casualties:						
Sgt Gilbert Triboulet	N 57	P	WIA	Spad VII		
Sol Gabuti	C 6	M	Injured	Caudron G4		
MdL Casson	C ??	P	Injured	„		

---

19 May

Sgt Jean Dedieu	N 26	EA	P	Berrieux-Aubigny	0820	–
Casualties:						
Lt Fichot	89° Cie d'Aérostiers			Attacked, not flamed,		
		O	OK	Nancy Sector.		

---

20 May

Adj Madon	a. N 38	2 seater	POW	SE Sept-Saulx		12
Lt de Fonds Lamothe	C 64					1
Sgt Berthollet &	C 64			V° Armée		1
MdL Laraud	N 76	EA	X	Brimont	1400	4
Adj Pendairies	N 69	2 seater	POW	Berry-au-Bac		4
Lt Pinsard	a. N 78	EA	X			13
S/Lt Hugues	N 81	EA	X	IV° Armée-German lines		2
Lt Hay de Slade	N 86	DFW C	X	Condé-sur-Suippe	1115	1
Adj C Martin	N ???	EA	X	E Pont-Faverger		–
???	DCA	EA	X	Corbeny		–
Adj Bourvet	N 82	EA	P	IV° Armée		–
???	???	EA	P	E Reims		–
S/Lt Ruyant &	C 9					–
Lt Chareyre	C 9	Scout	P	VIII° Armée		–

a.   Possibly Uffz Fölsche & Ltn Heuer, FlAbt 261 Lb, WIA/POWs, or Vfw Guido Kolb, FlAbt 9, POW in this sector.
Casualties:

Lt André Darnaud	Sop 123	P	WIA	Flak, Sopwith 2 seater	
MdL-Chef Jean Isnard	N 82	P	POW/WIA	VII° Armée, Spad VII N° 1325,	
				probably by Ltn Franz Anslinger,	
				Jasta 35, (2).	

---

21 May

Sgt Rodde	MF 32	EA	X			2
???	???	EA	X	N Epoye		–
Cpl Montrion &	N 48					–
Cpl Conan	N 48	Balloon	P	Prouvais		–

Adj Caël	N 102	EA	P	IV° Armée	–
???	???	EA	P	St Gobain	–

Casualties:

Cpl Jean Moineau	N 12	P	KIAcc	V° Armée, Spad VII	
Sgt Tailhard	GDE	P	KIAcc	Spad VII	
Cpl Emile Pacot &	GDE	P	KIAcc		
S/Lt Cristi	GDE	O	KIAcc	Farman 42	
Sgt Sihol	F 60	M	KIAcc	Farman	
Sgt Maurice Guillaux	???	P	KIAcc		
Sgt de Saint Albin	C 229	P	Injured	Caudron G6	
Sgt Charles Debas	69° Cie d'Aérostiers		XF	Soissons Sector	
		O	WIA		
???	59° Cie d'Aérostiers		XF	V° Armée,Châlons-Sector	
		O	OK		
???	77° Cie d'Aérostiers		XF	V° Armée	
		O	OK		
???	53° Cie d'Aérostiers			V° Armée, attacked, not flamed.	
		O	OK		
S/Lt Fichot	89° Cie d'Aérostiers			Attacked, not flamed.	
		O	OK	Nancy Sector.	

NOTE: Jasta 36 pilots claimed six balloons destroyed this date.

22 May

S/Lt Dezarrois	N 26	EA	P	Ailles	1840	–

Casualties:

S/Lt Roger Jupin	N 23	P	WIA	Morane Parasol, possibly by Flg Abel (1) & Ltn Fehser (1), FlAbt 44.	

23 May

Sgt Demeuldre &	F 63					2
Sgt Le Marec	F 63	Scout	X	E Itancourt		1
Sgt Le Mée	a. N 91	Roland D	X	Forêt de Parroy		1
Lt Hervet	N 103	EA	X	Bouconville	1830	2
Sgt Barès	N 26	EA	P	N Craonne	1010	–
Capt Matton &	N 48					–
Sgt de Guingand	N 48	Albatros	P			–
Adj Herisson &	N 75					–
Patrol	b. N 75	Scout	P	NE Bouconville	1040	–
Adj Baillou &	N 86					–
Lt Thiriez	N 86	EA	P	Corbeny	1740	–
Adj Baillou	N 86	EA	P	Grandelain	1825	–
???	???	2 seater	P	Craonne		–
???	???	EA	P	E Vendeuil		–

a. Probably Uffz Tolischuss, Kest 3, shot down and taken prisoner after a balloon attack. Le Mée shot down the German pilot who had attacked the 54° Cie Aérostiers balloon.
b. Possibly Gefr Anton Niemczik, WIA/POW/DOW Festieux, about 6 km N of Bouconville.

Casualties:

Cpl Jean Conan	N 48	P	KIA	Spad VII N° 1318	
S/Lt Plantat	C 56	O	WIA	Caudron G6	
Adj Joseph Guiguet	N 3	P	WIA	Flak	
Lt Alfred de Laage				Crashed while taking-off.	
de Meux	N 124	P	KIAcc	Spad VII N° 1515	
Sgt Gabriel Le Mée	N 91	P	KIAcc	Crashed on landing.	
S/Lt Alfred Besnier &	F 215	P	KIAcc		
Sol Philippe	F 215	M	KIAcc	AR	
Sgt Charbonnel	R 209	P	Injured	Crashed on take-off.	
S/Lt Nébinger &	54° Cie d'Aérostiers			Attacked, not flamed probably by	
Cpl Pourrat		O	OK	Uffz Tolischuss, Jasta 83, unconfirmed, Nancy Sector.	

24 May

Lt Marie Humann	N 49	EA	X	Bannholtz		1
Adj Daladier &	N 92					2
MdL M Robert	N 92	2 seater	X	Schweigshausen		1
Capt Auger	N 3	EA	P	Fresnes-les-Reims	0830	–
S/Lt Dorme	N 3	EA	P	Aizelles	1021	–
Adj Madon	N 38	EA	P	IV° Armée		–

Patrol		N 83	2 seater	P	Aumenancourt	1450	–
Lt de La Tour	CO	N 26	Albatros D	P			–
???		???	EA	P	Condé-les-Autry		–

Casualties:

Lt Pierre Rigoulet		N 92	P	KIA	Nieuport, probably by Ltn Walter Kirchbach, Jasta 35, (1).	
Sgt Ferret		N 90	P	KIA	Nieuport XXIVbis, probably by Obltn Edouard Dostler, Jasta 34, (7).	
Lt Jean Robert		???	P	KIA		
Cpl André Rondot		N 92	P	POW	Nieuport XXIII	
Lt Marie Humann		N 49	P	WIA	VII° Armée, Spad VII, probably by Ltn Franz Anslinger, Jasta 35, (2).	
Adj Maurice Finat		F 20	P	WIA	Farman 41, infantry fire.	
Capt Etienne Gailhac		???	P	KIAcc		
Sgt Joseph Barrère &		C 228	P	KIAcc	Crashed on takeoff at Rosnay.	
Lt Jean Greau		C 228	O	Injured	DOW 25 May 1917. Caudron G.6.	
Adj Thierry &		F 16	P	Injured	AR, crashed on takeoff.	
Cdt Pio (Italian)		F 16	O	Injured	X° Armée	
S/Lt Vieran		50° Cie d'Aérostiers				
			O	WIA	Flak	
Adj Canard		59° Cie d'Aérostiers				
			O	WIA	Flak	

25 May

Capt Guynemer	a.	N 3	LVG C	XF	NW Corbeny	0830	39
Capt Guynemer		N 3	2 seater	XF	Juvincourt	0831	40
S/Lt Rabatel		N 3	2 seater	X	Berrieux	0915	2
Capt Guynemer		N 3	DFW C	X	Courlandon	1215	41
Capt Guynemer	b.	N 3	2 seater	XF	W Guignicourt	1830	42
Adj Jailler		N 15	EA	X			10
Cpl G Guérin		N 15	EA	X			1
Adj Fauvet		N 38	EA	X	IV° Armée		1
Sgt Ambroise-Thomas		N 48	Scout	XF	E Reims	1600	1
Adj Desmond		N 94	EA	X	IV° Armée		1
???	c.	DCA	EA	X	Dontrien		1
QM Le Garrec	*	CAM	Gotha G	X	Nieuport-Bains, at Night		1
Lt Garnier du Plessix &		C 227					1
S/Lt Huguenin	d.	C 227	Scout	XF			?
???		???	EA	X	SW Cerny-en-Laonnois		–
???		???	EA	X	St Martin l'Heureux		–
???		???	EA	X	Vaudesincourt		–
???		???	EA	X	S Nogent l'Abbesse		–
???		???	EA	X	Craonne-Chevreux		–
S/Lt Dorme		N 3	Albatros C	P	Epoye-Berru	0810	–
Capt Auger		N 3	EA	P	Berrieux	0830	–
Sgt Baudry		N 68	EA	P			–
???		???	2 EA	P	Pont-Faverger		–
???		???	EA	P	Clerkem		–
???		???	EA	P	Cuisy		–
???		???	EA	P	Mont Blond		–
???		???	EA	P	Prucy		–
???		???	EA	P	Grandelain		–

* Dunkerque, possibly an aircraft from KG3/KSt13.
a. Possibly Ltn Georg Feldmann & Ltn Georg Oehler, FlAbt 257 (A), KIAs Corbeny.
b. Probably Ltn Werner Gaedicke (O), FlAbt 254 (A), KIA between Guignicourt and Conde.
c. Probably Ltn Alfons Paulus, Jasta 21, KIA Dontrien.
d. It is possible that is two different claims, as citation for Garnier du Plessix states a confirmed and for Huguenin states a probable. If this is so Huguenin's pilot and Garnier du Plessix' observer are unknown.

Casualties:

S/Lt René Dorme		N 3	P	KIA	Spad VII, probably by Ltn Heinrich Kroll, Jasta 9, (3), X° Armée, departed 18h40.	
Sgt Henri Gross		N 94	P	MIA	IV° Armée, Nieuport XVII, probably by Ltn Rudolf Matthaei, Jasta 21, (2).	
Adj Adolphe Baranovitch (Russian)		F 70	P	WIA	VIII° Armée	
Sgt Georges Quinton &		VB 109	P	KIAcc	Their bombs exploded in a	
Sgt Léon Barnichon		VB 109	B	KIAcc	crash-landing.	

Sgt Victor Nicaud	F 44	P	Injured	Crash-landing.		
MdL Pierre Gracionette &	F 5	P	OK	Crash-landing.		
Lt Vallois	F 5	O	Injured	Farman		
Adj Durand &	F 7	P	Injured	Landing accident.		
Lt de Maigret	F 7	O	Injured	Farman		
Cpl Théodore Rochet &	F 25	P	Injured	Crash-landed in trees.		
Sol Menguy	F 25	G	Injured	Farman 60		
Lt Graff	C 43	O	Injured	Caudron G4		
???	89° Cie d'Aérostiers			Attacked, not flamed,		
		O	OK	Nancy Sector.		

26 May

Capt Guynemer	N 3	Albatros C	X	W Condé-sur-Suippe	1000	43
MdL Camus	N 31	EA	X	N Aguilcourt, V° Armée		1
MdL De Cazenove de Pradines	N 81	Scout	X	Reims		1
MdL Soulier	N 26	EA	P	Prouvais-Amifontaine	1210	–
MdL Soulier	N 26	EA	P	N Ursel	1712	–
Adj Madon	N 38	EA	P			–
S/Lt L Milliat a.	N 80	EA	P	Neuville-Chermizy		–
???	???	EA	P	E Lavannes		–
???	???	EA	P	Ferme de Vignes		–

a.   Possibly Ltn Eberhard Haenisch, Jasta 15, KIA between Laon and Chermizy.

Casualties:

S/Lt André Cabaud	N 37	P	KIA	IV° Armée, Spad VII N° 294 probably by Ltn Otto Kissenberth, Jasta 16 (4).	
Cpl Moquet	PS 128	P	MIA	Paul Schmitt N° 4335, probably by	
MdL Giraud	PS 128	G	MIA	Flakzug 53 & K Flak 29.	
SM Pierre Malvosin	* CAM	P	POW	HD.2	
EV1 Robert Battet &	* CAM	P	POW		
QM Millancourt	* CAM	O	POW	FBA 150hp N° 462 codé D8.	
EV1 Paul Ardouin &	* CAM	P	POW		
EV1 Yves Gourguen	* CAM	O	WIA/POW	FBA 150hp N° 472 codé D.7.	
QM François Amiot &	* CAM	P	POW		
EV1 Paul Teste (1)	* CAM	O	POW	FBA 150hp N° 417 codé D.10.	
QM François Cartigny &	* CAM	P	MIA		
Mat Joseph Farenc	* CAM	O	KIA	FBA 150hp N° 418 codé D.11.	
Sgt Tertrun	42° Cie d'Aérostiers	XF		Artillery fire	
		O	Injured		

*   Centre d'Aviation Maritime Dunkerque, these aircraft were brought down by pilots of SFS II; Ltn Strang (1 & 2), Vzflgmstr Müller (2), and Flgomt Burgstaller (2).

(1)   Escaped 10 January 1918, then became the CO of the Aviation Maritime d'Escadre on 1 October 1918.

27 May

S/Lt Languedoc	N 12	2 seater	X	Brimont-Bourgogne	1015	8
Sgt Waddington	N 12	EA	X	Moronvillers	1745	1
MdL Soulier	N 26	DFW C	X	Réservoir-Filain	1835	5
Capt Ménard & CO	GC 15					3
Capt Menj	N 37	EA	X			2
Adj Bajac	N 48	2 seater	X	NW Nauroy	0915	2
Capt Matton	N 48	2 seater	POW	S Moronvillers		6
Sgt Caël	N 102	EA	POW	W Prosner		1
Sgt Haegelen	N 103	2 seater	X	Moronvillers-Nauroy	0910	1
Lt Guichard, CO	R 213					1
Lt Pierrot &	R 213					1
Sgt Briséard	R 213	EA	X	W Mont Haut		–
Capt Guynemer	N 3	2 seater	P	E Aubérive	0905	–
Patrol (2-3 seaters)	C 46	EA	P	Brimont Bourgogne		–
Sgt Caillaux	N 48	EA	P	Nauroy		–
???	???	2 EA	P	Uriel		–
???	???	EA	P	Chivry		–

Casualties:

S/Lt Charrette	C 56	O	Injured	Caudron G4	
MdL Henri Rossez &	VB 114	P	Injured		
Sol Bichaton	VB 114	B	Injured	Voisin P	
Asp Marcel Bouley	42° Cie d'Aérostiers	XF		Probably by Vfw Albert Haussmann,	
		O	Injured	Jasta 23 (4).	

Sgt Icard	64° Cie d'Aérostiers			Attacked, not flamed,		
		O	OK	Soissons Sector.		

28 May

Adj Fauvet	N 38					2
Adj Dramard	N 38					1
Lt Pinsard	N 78					14
S/Lt P Sauvage	N 112	2 seater	X	French lines		3
Adj Fauvet &	N 38					3
Lt Pinsard	N 78	EA	X			15
S/Lt Tarascon	N 62	LVG C	X	Pinon		11
Sgt Durand &	N 80					1
Sgt Haegelen	N 103	2 seater	POW	Chenay-Reims	1045	2
???	???	EA	X	Longva		–
???	???	EA	X	Harazee		–
MdL Soulier	N 26	Scout	P	Pont-Faverger	0810	–
MdL Soulier	N 26	2 seater	P	Pont-Faverger	0825	–
Lt Deullin	N 73	2 seater	P	Neufchâtel	0845	–
Lt de Guibert	N 73	2 seater	P	Neufchâtel	0850	–
S/Lt Vernin &	N 75					–
Adj Herisson	N 75	2 seater	P	SE Corbeny	0510	–
S/Lt Vernin	N 75	EA	P	W Guignicourt	0625	–
Lt Decazes &	N 88					–
Cpl Plessis	N 88	EA	P	Massevaux		–
???	R 214	EA	P	Soissons		–
???	???	EA	P	Laffaux		–
???	???	EA	P	Chevrigny		–
???	???	EA	P	Réservoir d'Ailette		–
???	???	EA	P	Panne-Dunkirk		–
???	???	EA	P	Ostende		–

Casualties:

Sgt Jean Sanchez Toledo Abreau	???	P	KIAcc		
Sgt Marcel Haegelen	N 103	P	Injured	Spad VII, crash-landing.	
Adj Monnot des Angles	54° Cie d'Aérostiers			Wind broke this balloon loose and it	
		O	Injured	was drifting towards German lines, observer jumped to avoid capture.	

29 May

S/Lt de Bruce	a. N 75	Scout	XF	Montchâlons	2000	3
S/Lt Hay de Slade	N 86	2 seater	XF	W Amifontaine	1925	2
Adj Fauvet	N 38	2 seater	X	Amifontaine		4

a.   Probably OfStv Willy Glinkermann, Jasta 15, KIA Orgeval, about 3 km SW Montchâlons.

Casualties:

Cpl Lucien Perrot	N 3	P	WIA/POW	Spad VII N° 265, probably by Vfw Hans Bowski, Jasta 14, (1), departed 18h25.
Adj Adrien Fauvet	N 38	P	WIA	Spad VII
Sgt Louis Peyret-Roque &	C 53	P	Injured	Crashed on landing.
S/Lt Gilg	C 53	O	KIAcc	Caudron G4
???	46° Cie d'Aérostiers			Both attacked, not flamed,
???	51° Cie d'Aérostiers			Châlons Sector.
		O	OK	

30 May

Adj Trepp	N 12	EA	X	E Reims, V° Armée	1610	3
Adj Guertiau,	C 43					3
Lt Fromont,	C 43					2
Sgt Sautet &	C 43					2
MdL Ledesvé d'Heudières	C 43	EA	XF	Bois de l'Echelle		2
Adj Guertiau,	C 43					–
Lt Fromont,	C 43					–
Sgt Sautet &	C 43					–
MdL Ledesvé d'Heudières	C 43	EA	P	Bois de l'Echelle		–

Casualties:

S/Lt Pierre Huguenin &	C 227	O	WIA/DOW	Caudron R4, probably by
Sol Bricourt	C 227	G	WIA	K Flak 12 (Obltn Fritsch).

Name		Unit	Type	Result	Location	Time	Score
MdL Guerin		GDE	P	Injured	Caudron G4		
Asp Cochain		F 221	O	Injured	Crashed on take-off. ???		
???		59° Cie d'Aérostiers		XF	V° Armée, probably by OfStv Grigo,		
			O	OK	Jasta 29 (3).		
???		63° Cie d'Aérostiers			V° Armée, attacked not flamed.		
			O	OK			

31 May

Name		Unit	Type	Result	Location	Time	Score
Lt Pinsard		N 78	EA	X	French lines		15
S/Lt Tarascon		N 62	EA	P			–
Casualties:							
MdL Auguste Pouchelle		N 26	P	WIA	X° Armée, Spad VII, 19h20,		
Lt Pierre Seyer		N 69	O	WIA	Flak, X° Armée, Spad XI		
MdL Michelet &		F 16	P	KIAcc			
Asp Drouette		F 16	O	KIAcc	X° Armée, Farman 4		

1 June

Name		Unit	Type	Result	Location	Time	Score
Cpl ???		N 83	2 seater	X	Réservoir-Ostel	1415	–
Sgt Gilet &		N 86					1
Adj Baillou		N 86	2 seater	X	Aguilcourt	1235	2
S/Lt Bucquet		N 3	EA	P	Monampteuil-Réservoir	1050	–
S/Lt Languedoc &		Spa 12			V° Armée		–
S/Lt Lebeau		Spa 12	EA	P	SE Brimont	1045	–
S/Lt de Rohan		N 65	Scout	P	Pancy		–
???		DCA	EA	P	Guignicourt		–
???		DCA	EA	P	Pinon		–
Casualties:							
Sgt Charles Durand		N 75	P	WIA/DOW	X° Armée, Spad VII, probably by		
					Ltn Josef Veltjens, Jasta 14 (3).		
Sgt Lief N. Barclay		N 82	P	KIAcc	Nieuport		
Sol Beauvallet		F 70	M	KIAcc	Farman 70		
MdL Marcel Bourdonneau &		F 16	P	KIAcc			
S/Lt Lazeuch		F 16	O	KIAcc	X° Armée, Sopwith		
S/Lt Letort		C 47	O	Injured	VIII° Armée, Caudron G6		
Adj Adrien Mathivet &		C 229	P	Injured	V° Armée		
Asp Coignard		C 229	O	KIAcc	Caudron G4		
Sgt Gabriel Ferrier &		C 13	P	Injured			
S/Lt Boilève		C 13	O	Injured	Caudron G4		

2 June

Name		Unit	Type	Result	Location	Time	Score
Sgt Chapelle &		N 31			V° Armée		2
Sgt Blanc		N 31					2
???	a.	DCA	LVG C	POW	Nanteuil-le-Fosse		–
???		DCA	2 seater	X	Lierval		–
MdL Giraud &		N 86					–
Cpl Damidaux		N 86	2 seater	P	Chevreux	1745	–
???		???	EA	P	Berrieux		–
a. Possibly from FlAbt 257.							
Casualties:							
Lt Saumande		F 22	O	WIA	Farman		
Sol Beauvais		GDE	M	KIAcc			
Lt Michel		F 41	O	Injured	Farman 41		

3 June

Name		Unit	Type	Result	Location	Time	Score
Cpl G Guérin		N 15	EA	X	NE Nonampteuil	0905	2
Brig Fontaine &		F 71					1
Cpl du Bois d'Aische		F 71	EA	XF	N Laffaux		2
Sgt Boyau &		N 77					2
MdL Sardier		N 77	Balloon	XF	Geline	0955	2
MdL Sauclière		N 79	2 seater	X	German lines		1
Sgt Chapelle,		N 31					3
MdL Soulier &		N 26					6
Lt de Bonald		N 69	DFW C	X	N Muizon	1855	4
???	a.	DCA	2 seater	X	Forêt de Coucy		–
QM Malvosin	*	CAM	Bomber	X	Dunkerque		1
Capt Guynemer	b.	N 3	Albatros C	P	Craonne	1030	–

Sgt Baudry &		N 68				–
Sgt Gaudermen		N 68	EA	P	Servon	–
Brig Fontaine &		F 71				–
Cpl du Bois d'Aische		F 71	EA	P		–
Sgt Dron		N 73	EA	P	Brimont	0820 –
???	c.	???	2 seater	X	near Toul	–

* Dunkerque.
a. POWs.
b. Possibly Vfw Friedrich Beisecker & Flg Pirmin Bücklein, SchSta 26b, KIAs at Craonelle, about 5 km SE of Craonne.
c. Albatros CX N 9233/16, Ltn Werner & Lt Kittel, FlAbt 46, POWs, AOK "C" Sector.

Casualties:

QM Jean Baudoin	*	CAM	P	MIA	Near Toulon, FBA 150hp N° 333.
Capt Jacques Caffet & CO		F 52	P	KIA	V° Armée, Sopwith flown by observer
Lt Jean Godillot		F 52	O	WIA	regained lines & landed.
Adj Pierre Pendaries		N 69	P	WIA	Spad VII, X° Armée
S/Lt Ducommun		C 220	O	WIA	Caudron G6
Sgt Paul Gignoux		VB 101	P	WIA	Voisin B
Lt Henri Richard		???	O	WIA	DOW
Capt Charles Labouchère		35 CA	P	KIAcc	Caudron G6, III° Armée
Sgt Louis Marsac &		C 4	P	KIAcc	
S/Lt Humdenstock		C 4	O	KIAcc	Caudron G6
Adj Gaillard &		C 4	P	OK	
Lt Elouard		C 4	O	Injured	DOW 7 June 1917
Brig Lucien Bel		RGA'	P	Injured	AR

* Toulon.

4 June

Capt Auger		N 3	2 seater	X	Grandelain	2005	6
Adj Jailler	a.	N 15	EA	X	E Filain	2000	11
MdL Paris	b.	N 65	Roland D	XF	SE Malmaison	0420	1
Lt Deullin	CO	N 73	2 seater	X	Fismes-Bovelle	0940	16
S/Lt Baudoin-Roland	c.	N 80	EA	X	Presles-Bruyères	0830	4
???		???	EA	POW	Gommaine		–
Capt Guynemer		N 3	2 seater	P	Craonne	1030	–
???		DCA	EA	X	Soissons		–
???		???	EA	X	Bevelle		–
???		???	EA	X	N Jouy		–
???		???	EA	X	Chevregny		–
???		???	EA	X	N Cervon		–
???		???	EA	P	Amifontaine		–
???		???	EA	P	Pontfaverger		–
???		???	EA	P	Forêt de Vauclère		–

a. Probably Vfw Wilhelm Eichenauer, Jasta 15, KIA Filain.
b. Possibly Ltn Paul Jänicke, Jasta 22, shot down at Vregny, about 12 km S of Malmaison.
c. Possibly Ltn Erich Hagedorn & Ltn Friedrich Swoboda, FlAbt 234 (A), KIAs Veslud-Laon, about 5 km East of Bruyères.

Casualties:

Brig Pierre Benedictus	R 213	P	WIA	Flak, Caudron R4
Sgt Frédéric Pautrat	Sop 123	G	WIA	Sopwith
S/Lt Barbier	C 9	O	Injured	Caudron G4
Lt Charles Gabreilli &	R 209	P	Injured	III° Armée
Sgt Garros	R 209	G	Injured	Caudron R4

5 June

Capt Guynemer	a.	N 3	Albatros C	X	Loivre	1715	44
Capt Guynemer	b.	N 3	DFW C	X	Fôret de Berru	1730	45
Adj Sayaret &		N 76			V° Armée		7
Lt Cauboue		N 76	2 seater	X	Bermericourt	1855	1
Sgt Boyau		N 77	Balloon	XF	Moussey	1055	3
Lt Pinsard &		N 78					16
S/Lt Hugues		N 81	EA	X			3
V° Armée		???	EA	X	Bois Claquedent	1625	–
???	c.	???	EA	X	Trigny	1715	–
???		???	EA	X	Oivre		–
III° Armée		???	Albatros C	X	W St Quentin		–
Adj Baillou &		N 86					3
Sgt Laulhe		N 86	2 seater	X	Ville-aux-Bois	1625	3
???		???	EA	P	Nogent l'Abbesse		–
???		???	EA	P	Pontavert		–

a. Possibly Ltn Erich Hagedorn & Ltn Friedrich Swoboda, FlAbt 234 (A), KIAs, Veslud-Laon.
b. Probably Ltn Rudolf Lehmann & Ltn Hans Philler, FlAbt 267 (A), KIAs Berru.
c. Probably Vfw Fritz Schröder & Ltn Ernst Scherb, FlAbt 248 (A), KIAs Villers-Farnqueux, about 7 km NE of Trigny.

Casualties:

MdL Jacquet	F 35	P	KIA	Airfield Bombardment		
Adj Félix Durand	N 80	P	WIA	Spad VII, 14h05, combat with two 2 seaters Juvincourt, probably by Uffz Unger (1) & Ltn Schmitt (1), FlAbt (A) 248.		
Cpl Henri Damville	C 227	P	WIA	Flak, Caudron G4		
Sol Florin	F 218	M	Injured	Morane Parasol		
Sol Barrault	F 218	M	Injured	,,		
Brig Hubert Marcieu &	F 201	P	Injured	DOW 18 June 1917		
S/Lt Gourdon	F 201	O	Injured	DOW 7 June 1917 Farman 40, crash-landing.		

6 June

Cpl Le Boucher &		N 65				1
Med-Aux Camplan	a.	N 65	EA	X	Laffaux	1130	1
Sgt Lefevre &		C 4				1
Lt Mignon		C 4	EA	X	Filian		1
Patrol		GC 14	Scout	P	Veslud	1015	–

a. Probably Vfw Paul Bona (6v), Jasta 1, KIA Allemant, about 3 km NE of Laffaux.

Casualties: None

7 June

MdL Fontaine	N 26	EA	P	Berry-au-Bac	1035	–
Adj Fétu	N 26	EA	P	Lavergny	1035	–
S/Lt Tarascon	N 62	LVG C	P	E Fôret de Villers-Cotterêts		
Adj Caël &	N 102					–
Adj Bonnecarre	N 102	EA	P	IV° Armée		–
???	???	EA	P	Montchâlons	1910	–
???	???	EA	P	Sommepy		–

Casualties:

Sgt-Maj Robert de Baillencourt	N 15	P	POW	Nieuport XXIVbis N° 3775 Forced to land S of Malmaison, after a combat.	
Cpl Paul Riche	F 71	P	WIA	Flak, IV° Armée, Salmson-Moineau.	
Adj Henri Bourgain	N 49	P	KIAcc	Spad VII, crashed during take-off.	
Sgt Trappe	GDE	P	Injured	VLAR	
MdL Maurice Montaugeand &	GDE	P	Injured		
Capt d'Avitaya	GDE	O	Injured	Farman 43	
Cpl André Sola	GDE	P	Injured	Caudron G4	
Adj Henri Bremond	N 85	P	Injured		

8 June

Lt Decazes	N 88	EA	XF	German lines	1
Sgt Janny	C 226	Balloon	XF	Ghistelles	1

Casualties:

S/Lt Paquein	GDE	O	KIAcc	Caudron G4
MdL Tache	GDE	?	Injured	Caudron G4
S/Lt Domino	F 50	O	Injured	Landing accident.

9 June – No Claims

Casualties:

Lt Acide Hellon &	* CAM	P	KIAcc	Donnet-Denhaut 150 hp,
QM Jean-Louis Salaun	* CAM	G	KIAcc	N° 461
Adj Jean Gaudray	???	P	KIAcc	
Lt Gouvy	SM 106	O	Injured	Landing accident.

*   Brest.

10 June

Sgt Castan	N 68	EA	FTL		–

Casualties:

Sgt Marius Pivard &	GDE	P	Injured	
S/Lt Pulh	GDE	O	KIAcc	Letord

| Sgt Fernand Despas & | F 14 | P | Injured | VII° Armée | | |
| S/Lt Thomas | F 14 | O | Injured | AR | | |

11 June

| Adj Fétu | N 26 | Scout | X | Laon | | 1 |

Casualties:

SM Marcel Drouet	* CAM	P	KIAcc	FBA 150hp code CH.4.		
Sgt Raymond Eude	N 85	P	KIAcc	Crashed on take-off.		
Adj Havre	F 8	?	Injured			
Adj Havez	45° Cie d'Aérostiers					
		O	Injured			

*   Cherbourg.

12 June

Sgt Hanote &	N 15					1
Adj Jailler	N 15	2 seater	POW	W Jouy	1015	12
Capt Glaize	N 80	2 seater	X	Aguilcourt	0810	1
Adj Lufbery	N 124	2 seater	X	Aguilcourt	0820	10
Adj-Chef Fonck	a. N 103	Albatros	X	Cauroy-Cormicy	0900	6
Sgt Castan	N 68	EA	P	VIII° Armée	1200	–
Adj Daladier	N 92	EA	P	Pont-Faverger		–
Adj-Chef Fonck	N 103	Albatros D	P	N Cormicy	0900	–
???	???	EA	P	Delme		–
???	DCA	2 seater	POWs	Lorraine Sector		

a.   Probably Hptm Eberhard von Seel, CO Jasta 17, KIA Montigny.

Casualties:

Brig Paul de Marcieu	F 201	P	KIAcc	Farman 130 hp		
QM Jean-Louis Salaun	Navy	P	KIAcc			
Lt Armand Pinsard	N 78	P	Injured	Spad VII		
Asp Jean Fraissinet	N 57	P	Injured	Spad VII		
S/Lt Enslen	F 32	O	Injured	Farman, crash-landing.		

13 June

| ??? | DCA | DFW C.V | POW | Baccarat | | – |

Casualties:

| Sgt Marchand | RGAé | P | Injured | AR | | |

14 June

S/Lt Pelletier d'Oisy,	N 69					–
S/Lt de Bonald &	N 69					–
S/Lt Beaudoin	N 86	LVG C	FTL	NE Hurtebise	1725	–

Casualties:

Lt Honoré de Bonald	N 69	P	WIA	Spad VII, X° Armée		
Sgt Aimé Lagarde	F 7	P	KIAcc	Paul-Schmitt		
Sgt Robert &	C 34	P	KIAcc	Crashed during take-off.		
S/Lt Simonet	C 34	O	Injured	Sopwith		
Cpl Georges Creuse	N 15	P	Injured	Nieuport XXIVbis, crash-landing.		
S/Lt Marcel Barrier	N 69	O	Injured	Morane XXI, crash-landing.		

15 June

Cpl G Guérin	a. N 15	Scout	X	Anizy-le-Château	1945	3
Adj Douchy	N 38	EA	P	IV° Armée		–
???	???	EA	P	Pont-Faverger		–

a.   Possibly Gefr Paul Laukandt, Jasta 13, KIA Faucoucourt, about 3 km N Anizy-le-Château.

Casualties:

Sgt Pierre Rey	N 80	P	KIA	Nieuport XXIVbis, probably by Vfw Hans Bowski, Jasta 14, (2).		
MdL Alexandre Miot &	F 215	P	KIA	V° Armée, Farman, possibly by Ltn Günther Schuster, Jasta 17, (2).		
S/Lt Georges Labellie	F 215	O	KIA			
Sgt Joannès Lyonnet &	C 47	P	OK			
S/Lt Paul Marcaggi	C 47	O	WIA	Flak, Caudron G4		
Cpl Eduard Monnard	N 77	P	KIAcc	Nieuport XXIII, taking-off		
EV2 André Marie	* CAM	P	KIAcc	St Raphaël		
Cpl Bonze	N 96	G	Injured	Nieuport XXIVbis		
Brig Georges Dubus &	C 122	P	Injured	Landing accident.		
S/Lt Boulanger	C 122	O	KIAcc	Caudron G4		

Cpl Lincoln Chatkoff		C 11	P	Injured	Crashed on take-off.	
Capt Alexis Van Nieuwenhuysen	CO	C 39	O	Injured	Caudron G4	
S/Lt Heiligeinstein		C 229	O	Injured	Caudron G3	

* St Raphaël.

---

16 June

S/Lt de Rochechouart de Mortemart		N 23	EA	X	St Mihiel		1
Sgt Soumagniat &		N 92				1
Sgt M Robert		N 92	EA	X	Mittlach	2
MdL Chuillot,		F 14				1
S/Lt Desmaroux,		F 14				1
Sgt Latapie,		F 14				1
Adj Vieljeux &		N 93				2
Sgt Deloupy		N 93				1
20° Cie d'Aérostiers	a.		Albatros C	POW	Brouville	–
S/Lt Lejeune		N 83	2 seater	P	Etouvelles	1105 –

a.   Probably Uffz Glaessner & Obltn Gercke, POWs.

Casualties:

Lt Antoine Laplace		N 23	P	KIA	Spad VII, probably by Uffz Rösler, SchSt 10, (2).	
Sgt Joannis Lyonnet &		C 47	P	OK		
Lt Marcagni		C 47	O	WIA	Flak	
MdL Pargeux &		C 225	P	Injured	Crashed while landing.	
Lt Bouche		C 225	O	Injured	Caudron G4	
MdL Roger Gufflet		R 209	G	Injured	Caudron R4, crash-landing.	
MdL Souchet &		RGAé	P	Injured		
Sol Daubercies		RGAé	M	Injured	AR	
Sol Guslet		R 209	O	Injured		
???		20° Cie d'Aérostiers			Attacked, not flamed, Nancy Sector; attacking two-seater shot down.	
???		63° Cie d'Aérostiers			Both attacked, not flamed,	
???		82° Cie d'Aérostiers			Châlons Sector.	
			O	OK		

---

17 June

Cpl Brière		N 3	EA	X	German lines		1
Med-Aux Camplan	a.	N 65	2 seater	XF	N Bruyères	0935 2
MdL Delannoy		N 80	2 seater	X	Guignicourt	2
???		DCA	EA	X	Bouconville	–
Lt Tenant de La Tour	CO	N 3	EA	P	Guignicourt	0640 –
S/Lt Rabatel		N 3	EA	P	Vailly	1035 –
Capt Auger		N 3	EA	P	Chamouille	1152 –
Adj Villars		N 23	2 seater	P		–
Lt Privat,		N 65				–
Cpl Le Boucher &		N 65				–
Med-Aux Camplan		N 65	2 seater	P	Fôret de Pinon	0850 –
Cdt Voisin		(1)	EA	P		–

(1)   Commandant de la Service Aéronautique de la II° Armée.
a.   Possibly Uffz Hans Seidel & Uffz Kurt Knoll, Schsta 14, KIAs Laon, about 4 km N Bruyères.

Casualties:

Sgt Edme Renoult		Sop 123	P	KIAcc	
Lt Jaensen		C 219	O	Injured	Sopwith

---

18 June – No Claims

Casualties:

Sgt Welling Nielsen		F 221	P	Injured	AR, landing accident.
Adj Fernand Moulard		58° Cie d'Aérostiers		XF	Probably by Ltn Ludwig Hanstein
			O	OK	Jasta 16, (4).

---

19 June

Sgt Lefevre &		C 4					1
Lt Mignon		C 4	EA	X	Hericourt	1
Lt de Sevin,		N 12				4
S/Lt Ortoli &		N 31				9
S/Lt Chaput	a.	N 57	EA		X Reims, V° Armée	0720 12

S/Lt Ortoli	N 31	2 seater	X	Bouy, V° Armée	0725	10
MdL Delannoy	N 80	2 seater	X	SE Juvincourt	0645	3
???	b. DCA	EA	X	Craonne	–
Cpl Plessis	N 88	EA	P	Héricourt-Montbéliard	–

a.   Possibly Ltn Friedrich Krämer (O), FlAbt 245 (A), KIA Reims.
b.   Probably Gefr Paul Geller, KIA Craonne, about 5 km NE Ville-aux-Bois.

Casualties:

MdL Fernand Roger	N 97	P	KIA	Nieuport XXIII, probably Ltn Karl Odebrett, Jasta 16, (2).
MdL Pierre Fourcade &	R 217	P	OK	IV° Armée
S/Lt Joseph Bastit	R 217	O	KIA	Sopwith
Sgt Maurice Hanote	N 15	P	WIA	Spad VII
Cpl Clément Moutonnier &	C 34	P	WIA	Flak, VII° Armée
Lt Houdailier	C 34	O	OK	Forced landing.
Sgt Alexandre Coquard &	F 59	P	WIA	VII° Armée
Lt Weist	F 59	O	KIA	AR
MdL Piget	GDE	P	KIAcc	Caudron G4
Cpl Jean Ronchetti	GDE	P	KIAcc	,,
Mat Marcel Poirier	GDE	M	KIAcc	Caudron G4, Ermenonville
Cpl Maurice Brugère	N 88	P	Injured	Crash-landing at Kurth.
MdL Raymond Rodel &	C 27	P	Injured	Crashed during take-off.
S/Lt Hadrot	C 27	O	Injured	Caudron G4
Sgt Fernand Jupeau &	F 40	P	Injured	Crash-landed after combat.
S/Lt Philippe Soule	F 40	O	Injured	Farman 60
Adj Charles Pierrot	38° Cie d'Aérostiers	XF		Probably by Ltn Otto Kissenberth
		O	OK	Jasta 16 (5).

20 June – No Claims
Casualties:

| ??? | 61° Cie d'Aérostiers | | | Attacked, not flamed, Châlons |
| | | O | OK | Sector. |

21 June

| S/Lt Desmaroux & | ??? | | | | 1 |
| Artillerie Divisionnaire | ??? | EA | X | | – |

Casualties:

| Sgt Pierre Castan | N 68 | P | KIA | Nieuport XXIII N° 2783. |
| MdL Pierre Martin | ALVF | P | WIA | |

22 June – No Claims
Casualties:

| Sgt Joseph Goux | N 67 | P | Injured | Spad VII, III° Armée |

23 June

| Capt Matton | N 48 | 2 seater | XF | Aguilcourt | 0915 | 7 |
| Capt Lamy | N 65 | 2 seater | X | N Chavignon | 0430 | 1 |

Casualties:

Lt André Tredicini de Saint Severen	N 79	P	WIA	Spad VII, III° Armée DOW 25 June 1917, probably by a Jasta 1 pilot.
Sol Henri Gigot	F 32	G	WIA	Caudron R4
Sgt Vincent Scalingi	N 73	P	Injured	Spad VII, landing accident
Adj Félécien Combaz &	N 102	P	OK	Hit pylon & crash-landed.
Sol Machebeuf	N 102	M	Injured	Letord
MdL Cusset	GDE	P	Injured	AR

24 June

S/Lt Ortoli	N 31	2 seater	XF	Bouy, V° Armée		11
Sgt Boyau	N 77	Scout	X	Nancy-Goin	0945	5
S/Lt d'Hautefeuille,	N 77					1
Sgt Boillot &	N 77					1
Sgt Boyau	N 77	Balloon	XF	Nancy-Goin		4
MdL Montalègre &	N 80					1
S/Lt L Milliat	N 80	2 seater	X	Hurtebise	0815	1
Adj Rojon &	V 114					1
???	a. V 114	EA	X	Jonchery		1

Adj de Montfort &	C 9					–
S/Lt Peyrachon	C 9	Scout	P	Nancy Sector		–
MdL Lemelle	N 73	EA	P	N Chavignon	0915	–
Sgt Lutzius	N 103	EA	P		2045	–
???	???	EA	P	Chivres		–
???	???	EA	P	Laniscourt		–
???	???	EA	P	Pinon		–
???	???	EA	P	Filain		–

a.   Possibly Gefr Franz Breidenbach & Ltn Ernst Madinger, FlAbt 270 (A), KIAs Souain, about 5 km NE Jonchery.

Casualties:

Cpl Raymond Hegy	N 67	P	POW	Nieuport XVII,N° 2523, probably by Ltn Hans Dannenberg, Jasta 13, (2).	
S/Lt Charles Boudoux d'Hautefeuille	N 77	P	WIA	Spad VII	
Lt Jean Beraud-Villars	N 85	P	WIA	Flak, Spad VII	
Adj Auguste Galvin	N 49	P	KIAcc	Crashed during take-off.	
Adj Jacques de Montfort	C 9	P	Injured	Crashed while landing.	
S/Lt Marius Peyrachon	C 9	O	Injured	Caudron G4	
Cpl du Bois d'Aische	F 71	G	Injured	Sopwith, landing accident.	
Brig Claude Didier	GDE	P	Injured	Sopwith	
S/Lt Patanchon	V 114	O	Injured	Voisin P	
???	90° Cie d'Aérostiers		XF	V° Armée, Châlons Sector	
		O	OK		
???	65° Cie d'Aérostiers		XF		
		O	OK		
???	49° Cie d'Aérostiers			Attacked, not flamed.	
		O	OK	Soissons Sector.	
Sgt Zevaco	80° Cie d'Aérostiers			Attacked, not flamed.	
		O	OK	Nancy Sector.	

NOTE: Balloons were claimed Ltn Heinrich Gontermann (22), Jasta 15 & Ltn Müller (1), Jasta 9, in the Châlons Sector.

25 June

Adj Guertiau &	C 43					4
S/Lt Velte	C 43	Albatros	X	E Grateuil		1
Cpl Bouyer	a. N 49	LVG C	X	Friesen		1
???	???	EA	P	Laon		–
???	???	EA	P	Fontaine-en-Dormois		–

a.   Possibly Gefr Elias KIA & his observer, POW, FlAbt A 244.

Casualties:

Sgt Michel	N 84	P	MIA	Spad VII N° 128, probably by OfStv Karl Lang, Jasta 1, (1).	
Capt François Coli	N 62	P	Injured	Crashed during take-off.	
MdL Veber	GDE	P	Injured	Farman 42	
Sgt Jules Thirion	C 228	P	Injured		
Sol Ferlat	C 228	M	KIAcc	Caudron G4	
Cpl Girault	31° Cie d'Aérostiers		XF	Flamed by artillery fire.	
		O	OK	Soissons Sector.	

26 June

Sgt Renauld &	N 48			V Armée		1
Sgt de Guingand	N 48	Albatros D	X	Berry-au-Bac	2015	1
S/Lt Nungesser	V 116	EA	X	Fôret d'Houthulst		28
S/Lt Nungesser	V 116	EA	X	„		29
Sgt Tassou	N 73	EA	P	Bourgogne	1310	–

Casualties:

Cpl James N. Hall	N 124	P	WIA	Spad VII N° 1386, FTL S of Courtecon, probably by Vfw Karl Schattauer (1), Jasta 23.	
Sgt Dupuy	GDE	M	Injured	Caudron G4	
Sgt Alphonse Gouge	F 215	P	Injured	Farman	
Sgt Gouje	C 222	P	Injured	Morane Parasol XXI N° 1100 Crashed during take-off.	

27 June

S/Lt Leps	a. N 81	Scout	X	N Prosnes	3
Sgt Breton	b. N 93	2 seater	X	Epinal	2

Lt Achard,	N 97					3
MdL Mignot &	N 97					1
Cpl Stenger	N 97	EA	X	Sommedieu		1
MdL Millot	Sop 111	Albatros	X	SE Moronvillers		1
Lt Jéronnez	N 26	EA	P	Moulins	0740	–
Cpl Berthier	N 85	EA	P	Malmaison		–
Sgt Laulhe	N 86	2 seater	P	Ferme Colombo		–

a.　Possibly Vfw Moritz Förster, Jasta 32, KIA St Hilaire-le-Petit, about 12 km NE of Prosnes.
b.　Possibly Ltn Hans Rathmann (O), FlAbt 32, KIA Epinal.

Casualties:

Lt René Grappe	69° Cie d'Aérostiers			Attacked not flamed.
	O	WIA		
Sgt Leclerc	51° Cie d'Aérostiers			Probably by Ltn Heinrich
	O	WIA		Gontermann, Jasta 15 (22).

---

28 June

Capt Auger	a. N 3	2 seater	X	W Pontavert	1700	7
Adj Trepp	N 12	EA	X	Corbeny, V° Armée	1650	4
S/Lt Harpedanne de						
Belleville &	N 49					2
Sgt Arnoux	N 49	EA	XF	Hirsingen		1
S/Lt Marty	b. N 77	2 seater	X	Thiaucourt		2
Cpl Humber	N 83	2 seater	X	Chevregny	1643	1
Sgt Montrion	N 48	EA	P	N Brimont	1920	–

a.　Possibly Vfw Grabow & Ltn Maximilian von Cossel, KG2/KSt8, WIA/POWs, at Pontavert.
b.　Possibly Ltn Georg Imhoff & Ltn Hermann Kuhrs, FlAbt 39, Albatros CVII 2247/16, KIAs, Flirey, AOK "C" Sector.

Casualties:

Adj Martin Trepp	N 12	P	WIA	V° Armée
Sgt-Maj Grabow &	???	P	WIA	
Lt Cassel	???	O	WIA	X° Armée
S/Lt Guy Picard d'Estelan &	C 42	P	KIAcc	
Lt Louis Sillan	C 42	O	KIAcc	Sopwith

---

29 June

Sgt Breton	N 93	EA	X	2

Casualties:

MdL Georges Le Gentil &	C 30	P	KIAcc	Crashed on landing.
S/Lt Calvet	C 30	O	KIAcc	Caudron G6
MdL Barbe	GDE	P	Injured	Caudron G4
Sol Guillie	N 37	M	Injured	Spad VII
S/Lt Henri Hay de Slade	N 86	P	Injured	Spad VII
Cpl François Cariffa	GDE	P	Injured	Voisin P
Sgt Marty	Sop 108	G	Injured	Sopwith

---

30 June – No Claims – No Casualties

---

1 July – No Claims – No Casualties

---

2 July – No Claims
Casualties:

Adj Georges Madon	N 38	P	WIA	Spad VII
Capt J.B. Laurens	GB 2	P	Injured	Sopwith
Adj Bernard	F 221	P	Injured	Sopwith
MdL Jean de Botmiliau	R 209	P	Injured	Sopwith

---

3 July

S/Lt Marty &	N 77					3
Cpl d'Estainville	a. N 87	2 seater	POW	Fôret de Parroy	0900	1
Adj Vigneron,	V 116					1
S/Lt Bussière,	V 116					1
Sgt Lallay &	V 116					1
Capt Lafay	CO V 116	Seaplane	X	Nieuport		1
???	???	EA	X	Lanfroicourt		–
S/Lt Battesti	N 73	EA	P	Pontavert	0800	–
Sgt Bordes &	N 90					–
Sgt Ambrogi	N 90	EA	P	Nonsard		–

a.　Probably Ltn Tolksdorf & Ltn Peters, FlAbt 12, WIA-POWs.

Casualties:

Cpl Ignacio de La Torre	N 77	P	MIA	Nieuport XXIV, probably by Ltn Paul Billik, Jasta 12, (4).		
MdL René Bois	N 95	P	WIA			
Cpl Vassal	N 37	P	KIAcc	Spad		
Lt Barbier	GDE	P	KIAcc	Letord		
Lt Stoffel	GDE	O	KIAcc	Letord		
Adj Louis Pellegry &	GDE	P	Injured	Farman 60		
Lt Fichot	GDE	?	Injured			
S/Lt Dreyfus &	89° Cie d'Aérostiers			The balloon developed a tear during		
S/Lt Fichot		O	Injured	ascension causing it to fall.		

4 July

Lt Bardon,	C 4					1
S/Lt Avril &	C 4					1
Sgt Heroguez	C 4	EA	X			1
S/Lt Battesti	N 73	EA	X	Berry-au-Bac	1600	2
MdL Laurent &	N 92					1
Adj Daladier	N 92	2 seater	X	Aspach		3
Ground fire	???	EA	X	NW Moronvillers		–

Casualties:

Brig Pierre Benedictus	R ???	P	WIA			
SM Albert Bareste	PilSch	P	KIAcc	Hourtin, FBA 100hp N° 254.		
MdL Marin Guyon,	VB 114	P	Injured			
MdL Jean Pic &	VB 114	G	Injured			
S/Lt Daligaut	VB 114	O	Injured	Voisin P		

5 July – No Claims

Casualties:

Sol Blandin	N 69	M	WIA	Bombardment of airfield, X° Armée.		
Adj René Caval	GDE	P	Injured	Farman 42		

6 July

Capt Guynemer	N 3	DFW C	XF	Brimont-Bourgogne	1800	46
Capt Matton &	N 48					8
Lt de Turenne	a. N 48	Albatros DV	X	St Thierry	1035	3
Capt Matton &	N 48					9
Lt de Turenne	N 48	Albatros DV	X	La Neuvilette	1037	4
Capt Derode	N 102	EA	X	Langemarck		5
Capt Guynemer	b. N 3	Albatros	P	Craonne	1645	–
MdL Miot	N 87	2 seater	P	Laon		–
Sgt Baron	c. N 103	EA	P	Brimont	1030	–

a.   Vfw Manfred Stimmel, Jasta 32.
b.   Possibly Ltn Martin Richter, Ltn Josef Heissler & Uffz Wilhelm Bloch, KIAs Corbeny, about 3 km NE Craonne.
c.   Possibly Ltn Martin Hieber, FlAbt 278 (A), KIA E Fort Brimont.

Casualties:

MdL Ulrich de Touchet	F 60	P	KIA	Flak		
S/Lt Saintot	F 60	O	KIA	Flak, AR		
Sgt Georges Silberstein	N 3	P	KIAcc	Spad VII N° 1416, Chery-Chartreux.		
MdL Charles Hervé	GDE	P	KIAcc	Nieuport XXI		
Sgt Robert Balland &	SM 106	P	KIAcc			
Sgt Petit Sapin	SM 106	G	KIAcc	Sopwith		
Capt Georges Matton	N 48	P	Injured	Spad		
Lt Paul Reverchon	GDE	P	Injured	Nieuport XXI		
S/Lt Robert d'Estaintot	BM 118	P	Injured	DOW 9 July 1917		
Cpl Paul Languille &	BM 121	P	Injured			
Cpl Buisson	BM 121	G	Injured			
MdL Jean Jonnard &	C 10	P	Injured			
Lt Charloty	C 10	O	Injured	Caudron G4		
Cpl Henri Galos	GDE	P	Injured	Caudron R4		

7 July

Capt Guynemer	a. N 3	Albatros D	X	Villers-Franqueux	1110	47
Capt Guynemer	N 3	DFW C	X	Moussy-sur-Aisne	1230	48
MdL Pannetier &	C 42					1
S/Lt Etève	C 42	EA	X	German lines		1

Sgt Bouyer	N 49	EA	X	Suarce-Réchezy	2
Ground fire	???	EA	XF	Cerny	–
S/Lt Leps	N 81	EA	P		–
Sgt Dhôme &	N 81				–
Adj Berslin	N 81	EA	P		–
S/Lt Sauvage,	N 112				–
Adj Bourdet &	N 112				–
Sgt Taffe	N 112	EA	P		–
Ground fire	???	EA	P	Forges-Montfaucon	–

a.   Probably Ltn Reinhold Oertelt, Jasta 19, KIA near Cauroy, about 2 km N of Villers-Franqueux.

Casualties:

Adj Antoine Paillard	Sop 111	P	Interned	Sopwith 1B.1 N° 115, FTL at Meylum, Holland, with motor trouble. Escaped 4 November 1917.
S/Lt Lucien Coupet &	* F 25	P	POW	Farman, probably by Flak-Gruppe,
Adj Léon Coupet	* F 25	G	POW	Trier.
S/Lt Jules Jeannin	C 34	P	KIAcc	Sopwith

*   Brothers.

8 July – No Claims
Casualties:

| Sgt Charles Bonnard | F 35 | G | WIA | Caudron R4, during combat with a two-seater. |

9 July – No Claims
Casualties:

EV1 François Michel	* CAM	P	MIA	Spad XIII code 9, North Sea.
MdL Georges Guillée &	GDE	P	KIAcc	
S/Lt d'Albens	GDE	O	KIAcc	Farman 60
Sol Cauchy	C 53	M	KIAcc	Caudron R4

*

10 July – No Claims
Casualties:

MdL Charles Gauthier &	N 31	P	POW	Morane Parasol N° 937, probably by
Sol Abel Denis	N 31	M	POW	Vfw Georg Strasser of Jasta 17,(4).
MdL Pierre Romano	RGAé	P	KIAcc	Nieuport
MdL Jean Desbans	F 60	P	Injured	AR
MdL Léon Thabault	F 60	P	Injured	
Sgt Felix Pataud	GDE	P	Injured	Caudron G4

11 July – No Claims
Groupes de Combat 11 and 12 departed for the Flanders Sector to participate in the upcoming Third Battle of Ypres.
Casualties:

Brig Roberrini	VC 116	G	WIA	Voisin P
Cpl Maurice Vandenberghe &	Sop 123	P	KIAcc	
Adj Jules Veiber	Sop 123	G	KIAcc	Sopwith
MdL Chavalier	RGAé	P	Injured	AR

12 July

Lt Chevillon	N 15	Scout	X	Forêt de Vauclère	1920	2
MdL Naudin &	C 224					1
S/Lt Jean-Marie	C 224	EA	X	Craonne	1750	1
Sgt Poncet &	C 4					–
S/Lt Avril	C 4	Scout	P			–
Adj de Romanet	N 37	EA	P			–
Adj Herbelin	N 81	EA	P			–
???	???	EA	P	Vaucresson		–
???	???	EA	P	Clerkem		–

Casualties:

Lt Marcel Lambert	F 44	O	KIA	AR, XF, Verdun.
S/Lt Antoine de Saint Genest &	F 8	P	KIA	AR, probably by Ltn Ludwig Hanstein.
S/Lt Georges Libkind	F 8	O	KIA	Jasta 16, (7), XF Soissons.

Sgt Pierre Poncet &		C 4	P		KIA	Caudron G4, probably by Ltn Adolf
S/Lt Abel Avril		C 4	O		KIA	Kuen, Jasta 14, (2). XF Cerny.
Lt Charles Beaupierre		???	P		KIA	
Adj Gustave Naudin		C 224	P		WIA	Flak, Caudron G6
QM Pierre Marchand		PilSch	P		KIAcc	Hourtin, FBA 100hp.
S/Lt Ciroux		C 53	O		Injured	Caudron G4
Adj de Dreux-Brèze		VB 101	P		Injured	VLAP
???		61° Cie d'Aérostiers				Attacked, not flamed, Nancy Sector.

13 July

MdL Tachard &		F 60					1
S/Lt Pellet		F 60		EA	X	German lines	1
Adj Bourdet &		N 112					2
Lt Vernin		N 75		LVG C	X	W Maizery	2
S/Lt Boudoux							
d'Hautefeuille &		N 77					2
Adj Boyau	a.	N 77		LVG C	X	Coin-sur-Celles	6
Adj Variot		N 94		Albatros	X	Mont-Haut	1
Adj Colombier &		F 70					–
MdL Hegay		F 70		EA	P		–
Patrol		N 76		EA	P	Trucy-Lierval	1945	–
???		???		EA	P	Pomerieux	–
???		???		EA	P	Laon	–
Adj Duret		???		EA	P	III Armée	–

a.   Possibly Uffz Rühl, OK, & Ltn Seifert, WIA, FlAbt A 276.

Casualties:

Lt Henri Catta &	F 70	P		KIA	AR, possibly by Obltn Edouard von
Lt Louis Bouzac	F 70	O		KIA	Schleich, Jasta 21, (6).
Sgt Edmond Combet	F 205	P		KIA	During Bombardment
Adj Léon Battard	N 102	P		WIA	Nieuport XXIV
Adj René Colombier &	F 70	P		WIA	
MdL Jules Hegay	F 70	G		WIA	Letord
Cpl Gaston Lamarche	N 79	P		KIAcc	Spad
Sgt Gill Manieux &	F 33	P		KIAcc	
S/Lt Cazes	F 33	O		KIAcc	Farman 40
S/Lt de Waubert	VB 107	O		KIAcc	Sopwith
QM Honoré Marchand	Navy	P		KIAcc	
LV Henri Barbier	* CAM	P		KIAcc	St Pol-sur-Mer, Sopwith Triplane
					N° 5385 codé 12.
S/Lt Marc Wolf &	F 71	P		Injured	AR
Lt Baudert	F 71	O		Injured	DOW 17 July 1917
Lt Ancely	41° Cie d'Aérostiers		XF		Probably by Uffz Paul Bäumer,
		O		Injured	Jasta 5, (2).
???	81° Cie d'Aérostiers				Attacked, not flamed, Soissons Sector.

*   Dunkerque.

14 July

Lt Perret,		F 35					1
Lt Daum &		F 35					1
Mdl Thomas		F 35		Scout	X	German lines	1
Sgt M Robert &		N 92					3
MdL Lonet		N 92		EA	XF	Oberdorf	1
???		???		EA	X	Nomeny	–
???		???		EA	P	Château-Salins	–

Casualties:

MdL Octave Lapize	N 90	P		KIA	Nieuport XXIII, codé 4
Lt Louis Palies	N 90	P		WIA	Nieuport XXIVbis
Cpl Edouard Baudoin	???	P		KIAcc	
MdL Picquet	21° Cie d'Aérostiers				Caught in a tornado and ripped
		O		Injured	apart, Soissons Sector.

15 July – No Claims
Casualties:

Asp Gaston Sirven	N 96	P		POW	Nieuport XXIVbis N° 3773,
					apparently became lost and landed
					in enemy territory.

| Sgt René Boniface | | C 6 | P | Injured | Caudron G4 | | |
| ??? | | 45° Cie d'Aérostiers | XF | | Probably by Uffz Paul Bäumer, Jasta 5 (3). | | |

16 July

S/Lt Rabatel		N 3	EA	P	Forêt d'Houthulst	1615	–
MdL Paris		N 65	DFW C	P	Corbeny	1302	–
Adj Lagnel	a.	N 80	Balloon	P			–
Adj-Chef Fonck		N 103	EA	P	Merckem-Clerkem		–

a.   His fire cut the cable of the balloon freeing it and making the observer take to his parachute.

Casualties:

MdL Pierre Roux	N 85	P	POW	Spad VII N° 1286, probably by Ltn Otto Kissenberth, Jasta 16, (6).
S/Lt Leonard Martin	F 24	P	WIA	Sopwith
Sgt Ernst Momet &	C 13	P	WIA	Flak
Lt Roger	C 13	P	WIA	Flak, Caudron G4
S/Lt Henri Languedoc	N 12	P	KIAcc	Nieuport XXVII
Lt Sergé André	N 62	P	Injured	Spad
Brig Mathieu de Tonnac de Villeneuve	N 80	P	Injured	Nieuport XXIV
MdL Legrand &	F 204	P	Injured	
Lt Emile Mochel	F 204	O	Injured	Sopwith
Sol Rheinart	25° Cie d'Aérostiers O		Injured	All these balloons were in the
S/Lt Fernand Cons	67° Cie d'Aérostiers	XF		Soissons Sector.
		O	Injured	
S/Lt René Martin	57° Cie d'Aérostiers	XF	Injured	
		O	OK	
???	53° Cie d'Aérostiers			Attacked, not flamed.
???	52° Cie d'Aérostiers			Attacked, not flamed.

NOTE: Balloons in this secctor were claimd by Obltn Otto Schmidt (6), Ltn Fritz Kieckhäfer (1) and Vfw Kurt Petzinna (1), all of Jasta 32, as well as one by Ltn Heinrich Gontermann (24), Jasta 15.

17 July – No Claims
Casualties:

S/Lt Auguste Faidide	Sop 107	P	POW	Sopwith 1B1 N° 185, apparently became lost and landed in enemy territory.
Sgt Pierre Schmitter	N 103	P	Injured	Spad VII N° 1724
Cpl James R Doolittle	N 124	P	Injured	Nieuport XXIVbis N° 3616
Sol Dejey	SM 106	M	Injured	Sopwith
Cpl Laganne	GDE	P	Injured	Caudron G4

18 July – No Claims
Casualties:

| Lt Augustin Azais | F 50 | O | WIA | Flak, AR |
| Cpl Paul Bron | ??? | P | KIAcc | |

19 July – No Claims
Casualties:

S/Lt Marcel Gressard &	F 33	P	KIA	AR #59, ground fire,
S/Lt Lucien Le Leuch	F 33	O	KIA	X° Armée.
S/Lt Pierre Vitoux	N 82	P	WIA	Flak, Spad, 19h45.

20 July – No Claims
Casualties:

Adj Edmond Franck	GDE	P	KIAcc	Nieuport XI
MdL Pierre Charoy	N 85	P	KIAcc	Nieuport XXIV
Capt Pierre Beranger	N 83	P	Injured	Spad VII
Sgt Albert &	GDE	P	Injured	Farman 60
S/Lt Bonnin	GDE	O	Injured	DOW 29 July 1917
Lt Arbitre	C 51	O	Injured	Caudron G4
Cpl Marcel Crabère	GDE	P	Injured	VLAP

21 July

| Lt Deullin | CO | N 73 | EA | X | NE Dixmude | 1940 | 17 |
| MdL de Pracomtal | | N 102 | EA | X | | | 2 |

Adj Martin	N ???	EA	X	N Ypres		2
???	???	EA	X	N Ypres		–
Adj Hasdenteufel	N 57	EA	FTL			–
S/Lt de Sevin	N 12	EA	P			–
Lt Mallet	N 112	EA	P			–
???	???	EA	P	N Montfaucon		–
???	???	EA	P	Forêt d'Hesse		–

Casualties:

Capt Jean Lamon	N 73	P	POW	Spad VII N° 1541, probably by FwLtn Fritz Schubert, of Jasta 6, (2). Departed 16h00.
MdL Pierre de Quinsonas	???	P	KIAcc	
Sgt Gaston Rioux	GDE	P	KIAcc	Farman 61
Capt Basile Verdy	C 212	P	Injured	Morane-Saulnier Parasol
???	45° Cie d'Aérostiers			Bombed by an aircraft, not damaged.

22 July

Cpl Quette &	N 62					1
Sgt Mougeot	N 62	EA	X			1
Adj Herisson	N 75	Albatros C	POW	Faubourg-Pavé		1
MdL Le Roy de Boiseaumarie	N 78	Balloon	XF	Aure		2
MdL Sauclière	N 79	EA	X	E La Fère	0740	2
Lt Hugues	N 81	Balloon	XF	Aure		4
Lt Thiriez	N 86	Scout	X	Hannonville		2
MdL Renaux &	N 86	EA	X			1
Adj Bourdet	N 112					3
???	???	EA	X	Lierval-Laval		–
???	???	EA	X	Vacquois		–
??? a.	???	EA	X	Verdun		–
???	???	Balloon	XF			–
??? b.	DCA	Albatros	POW	Flirey		–
Lt Gérard &	F 32					–
S/Lt de Font-Reaulx	F 32	Scout	P			–
Adj Delrieu	N 83	EA	P			–
MdL Bretillon	N 79	2 seater	P	Mesnil-St Laurent		–
Adj Chauvière	N 91	EA	P			–
???	???	EA	P	Chevregny		–
???	???	EA	P	Dunkirk		–
???	???	EA	P	Dunkirk		–

a. Possibly Ltn Emil Huber, FlAbt (A) 291b, KIA Verdun.
b. Possibly DIII of Vfw Willy Kempe (1v), Jasta 34b, POW, AOK "C" Sector.

Casualties:

Lt Louis Pandevant	N 73	P	MIA	Spad VII N° 1543, probably by Obltn Kurt von Döring, Jasta 4 (4), 09h30 over the Forêt d'Houthulst.
Adj Auguste Roblin	C 46	G	WIA	DOW, Letord
Cpl Bennett Molter	N 102	P	WIA	Spad
MdL René de La Guerrande	F 70	P	WIA	AR
Capt Camille Fuzier	X° Armée	P	WIA	DOW 23 July 1917, Caudron G4
S/Lt Robert Grohin	F 35	O	KIAcc	AR
Sgt Hebert	F 204	P	KIAcc	Sopwith
Sgt Gaston Rioux	???	P	KIAcc	
MdL Gérard de Peytes de Montcabrier &	N 62	P	KIAcc	
S/Lt André Mamy	N 62	O	Injured	Sopwith
MdL Bertrand &	F 1	P	Injured	
S/Lt Mariage	F 1	O	Injured	AR
MdL Félix de St Martin &	C 219	P	Injured	
S/Lt Martinet	C 219	O	Injured	Sopwith
Sol Krauss	RGAé	M	Injured	Caudron G6
Sgt René Dubillet	GDE	P	Injured	DOW 27 July 1917, Farman 41.
MdL Desvignes &	V 109	P	Injured	
Adj Jung	V 109	G	Injured	Voisin P
Lt Contant	C 226	O	Injured	Morane-Saulnier Parasol
Adj Pierre Guidot	C 224	P	Injured	Morane Parasol

23 July

Sgt G Guérin	N 15	EA	X	E Keyem		4
Capt Derode	N 102	EA	X			6
Adj Hasdenteufel	N 57	2 seater	FTL			–
Adj M Paris	N 73	EA	P	Becelaere	1450	–
???	???	EA	P	Filain		–
???	???	EA	P	La Fère		–
???	???	EA	P	Belgium		–

Casualties:

Adj Jacques Fabre	N 68	P	KIA	Spad, probably by Ltn Heinrich Geigl, Jasta 34b, (4).	
MdL Constant Plessis	N 88	P	WIA	Spad VII, crash-landed at Saint Amand.	
MdL Arcade Tavernier &	C 27	P	WIA	Probably by Vfw H Bowski, Jasta 14,	
Lt Jean Hanus	C 27	O	OK	zlg, Caudron G4	
MdL Pierre Gracianette	F 5	P	Injured		
Sgt Achard	F 5	G	KIAcc	Farman 170 hp	
Mat Marcel Bocquin	PilSch	P	KIAcc	Hourtin, FBA 100hp	
Lt Albert de Lamberterie du Cros &	C 9	P	KIAcc		
Sol François Dumas	C 9	O	Injured	Sopwith	
Lt Le Meulais	F 45	O	Injured	Salmson-Moineau	

24 July

Cpl Bétis &	F 71				1
Sgt du Bois d'Aische	F 71	Scout	X	Cerny-en-Dormois	3
Cpl Bétis &	F 71				2
Sgt du Bois d'Aische	F 71	Scout	X	Cerny-en-Dormois	4
??? &	C 27				–
S/Lt P Heurtaux	C 27	Scout	P		–

Casualties:

Sgt Adolphe Couture	F 71	P	KIA	AR
Cpl Henri Bétis	F 71	P	WIA	AR, DOW 27 July 1917
Adj Roger Pons	F 71	P	WIA	AR
S/Lt Gagnier	F 1	O	WIA	AR
S/Lt Henri Schwander	F 218	O	WIA	AR
S/Lt Paul Heurtaux	C 27	O	WIA	Sopwith
Cpl Paul Darou &	VB 101	P	WIA	
Sgt Patel	VB 101	G	WIA	Voison LAP
Lt Mileur	VB 101	O	WIA	Bombardment of Airfield.
Cpl Edouard Moulines	N 3	P	Injured	Spad VII N° 335

25 July

Lt Malavialle		N 69	Scout	X	Ailles-Bouconville	4
Adj Martenot de Cordoux a.		N 94	Rumpler C	X	Mont Cornillet	2
Lt Lesueur &		C 17				
???		C 17	EA	X		?
Sgt Prince		N 57	2 seater	P	Verdun	–

a. Probably Gefr Bruno Jakob & Ltn Heinrich Burkert, FlAbt A 206.

Casualties:

Sgt Jean Laulhe	N 86	P	WIA	Spad
Lt Marcel Plateau	???		WIA	
Lt André Lesueur &	C 17	P	WIA	
???	C 17	O	WIA	
Lt Jacques Lefebvre des Nottes	N 86	P	Injured	Spad
Sol Frète	R 209	M	Injured	Letord

26 July

MdL du Plessis	a.	N 97	2 seater	XF	Laffaux-Feuty	1845	1
???		???	EA	P	Allemont	–
???		???	EA	P	Laon	–
Adj-Chef Fonck		N 103	Scout	P	Forêt d'Houthulst	1935	–

a. Probably Gefr Wilhelm Knerr & Uffz Willy Meyer, KIAs Laffaux.

Casualties:

Adj Etienne Mougeot	N 62	P	WIA	Spad
Sol Avenel	V 113	M	KIAcc	VLAP

Capt Jean Escudier		C 47	P	Injured	Caudron G4		
Lt Plateau		38 CA	O	Injured	Farman		
Sol Respel		F 72	M	Injured	Farman		
MdL Henri Papillon &		GDE	P	Injured			
MdL Bernaert		GDE	G	Injured	Sopwith		
Sol Pluvinage		N 62	M	Injured	Sopwith		
Cpl Marcel Bourdon		C 224	P	Injured	Morane Parasol		
???		81° Cie d'Aérostiers			Attacked, not flamed, Dunkerque Sector.		

27 July

Capt Guynemer	a.	N 3	Albatros	XF	Westroosebeke	2030	49
Adj Bajac,		N 48					3
Sgt Roques &		N 48					2
Patrol		N 69	EA	X	St Croix		–
Lt Hugues &		N 81					5
Adj Bonneau	b.	N 23	EA	X	S Cheppy		1
???		???	EA	X	Belgium		–
Sgt Dufresne &		F 14					1
???		F 14	Scout	X			?
Cpl Artigau		N 15	Albatros D	P			–
S/Lt de Rochechouart							
de Mortemart		N 23	EA	P	Verdun Sector		–
S/Lt Ortoli		N 31	EA	P	W Forêt d'Houthulst		–
MdL Renaux		N 86	EA	P	Verdun		–
???		???	EA	P	Varennes		–
???		???	EA	P	Roulers		–
???		???	EA	P	Réservoir		–

a.   Probably Ltn Fritz Vossen, Jasta 33, KIA Moorslede.
b.   Probably Ltn Erich Limpert, Jasta 21, KIA Cheppy-Wald.

Casualties:

Sgt Léon Maurin &	Sop 29	P	OK		
Lt Julien Avanti	Sop 29	O	KIA	Sopwith	
Cpl Paul Matanovitch	N 15	P	WIA/POW	DOW 28 July 1917	
Lt Pierre Mathis	N 69	P	WIA	Spad, X° Armée.	
Sgt Maurice Froger	C 42	P	WIA	Flak, Caudron G4, X° Armée.	
Cpl Jean Castiglia &	Sop 108	P	WIA		
Sol Douville	Sop 108	G	WIA	Sopwith	
Lt Raymond Langlais	???	P	KIAcc		
Sgt René Sebastiani	BM 121	O	KIAcc	Bréguet-Michelin	
Asp Louis Perriot &	F 205	P	KIAcc		
Sgt Chaume	F 205	M	KIAcc	Farman	
Cpl René Jacquemain &	C 224	P	Injured		
S/Lt Parfait	C 224	O	Injured	Morane Parasol, X° Armée.	
Capt Louis Pertusier	C 51	P	Injured	Caudron G4, X° Armée.	
Adj René Chiron &	Sop 66	P	Injured		
Sol Tondeur	Sop 66	G	Injured	Sopwith	

28 July

Capt Guynemer	a.	N 3	DFW C	X	E Forêt d'Houthulst	2050	50
Lt Exelmans &		C 17					1
Brig Lesueur		C 17	EA	X			1
Lt Verdier-Fauvety,		N 65					1
Adj A Borde &		N 65					1
MdL M Paris	b.	N 65	Rumpler C	X	Elverdinghe	1150	2
MdL Ducastel		N 154	EA	X	German lines		2
???		???	EA	X	N Ypres		–
???		???	EA	X	La Fère		–
Lt de La Tour	CO	N 26	2 seater	P	Boesinghe-Bixschoote	1030	–
Sgt Cordonnier		N 57	Balloon	P	Forêt d'Houthulst		–
Sgt Lioret		N 515	2 seater	FTL	Colmar		–

a.   Possibly Uffz Friedrich Thässler, Jasta 35b, KIA, 2000 between Oostnieuwkerke and Westroosebeke.
b.   Ltn Hans Jürgensen (O), FlAbt (A) 202, KIA, Rumpler CIV 8297/16, pilot taken prisoner.

Casualties:

Capt Alfred Auger	N 3	P	KIA	Spad VII N° 1723, at 07h30 Boesinghe, possibly by Vfw Rudolph Francke, Jasta 8, (zlg) at Bixschoote, about 3 km N Boesinghe.	

Lt Albert Deullin	N 73	P		WIA	Spad VII N° 401 at 09h00 in combat with a two-seater.
Brig Lesuer &	C 17	P		WIA	
Lt Maurice Exelmans	C 17	O		WIA	Caudron G4
S/Lt Albert Steinbach	C 228	P		KIAcc	Morane-Saulnier Parasol
Sgt André Sporrer	RGAé	P		Injured	Morane Parasol
Cpl Joseph Poullain	GDE	P		Injured	Caudron G4
MdL Léon Genot &	VC 113	P		Injured	
Sol Georges	VC 113	M		Injured	Sopwith
S/Lt Broca	C 6	O		Injured	AR

29 July

MdL Renaux,	N 86				–
Capt Vuillemin &	(1)				–
Crew from	C 11		Aviatik C	P	Verdun
???	???		EA	P	S Forêt d'Houthulst	–

(1)   CO Secteur Aéronautique 2° Corps d'Armée.

Casualties:

MdL Octave de Ginestet	N 77	P		MIA	Nieuport XXIII N° 534, by Uffz Max Kahlow, of Jasta 34b, (2).
Sgt Soleyman Nazare-Aga	N 82	P		POW	Nieuport XXIIIbis N° 3714, probably by Obltn Hans Kummetz, Jasta 1, (5) at Festieux.
Cpl Camille Desmaison &	PS 126	P		KIA	Paul Schmitt, possibly by Ltn
Cpl Felecian Ferrieux	PS 126	G		KIA	Weingarten, Jasta 1, (1).
Sgt Emmanuel Ragonnaud,	F 33	P		OK	
Cpl Edmond Moles &	F 33	G		WIA	X° Armée
Cpl Siméon Boudsocq	F 33	G		WIA	Caudron R4 N° 4077
S/Lt Jack Boulenger	F 223	P		WIA	Flak, Sopwith
Sgt Parer	V 114	M		WIA	Flak, Voisin P
Capt Bernard Christiani	F 216	P		KIAcc	
MdL Alexandre Bearbe &	PS 126	P		KIAcc	
Sol Dion	PS 126	G		KIAcc	Paul Schmitt
Sgt Alexandre Cherrie	N 82	P		Injured	Nieuport XXIVbis N° 3595, X° Armée.
Adj-Chef Napoléon Gaillard	N 77	P		Injured	Spad
Cpl Marcel Commandeur	Sop 108	P		Injured	Sopwith
S/Lt Georges Mariage	F 206	P		Injured	AR
S/Lt Alexandre Ottavy	N 94	P		Injured	
Sgt Alexandre Cherrie	N 82	P		Injured	

30 July – No Claims
Casualties:

Brig Paul Pierrard &	AL 223	P		KIAcc	
S/Lt Théo Schmoukee	AL 223	O		KIAcc	

31 July – No Claims
Casualties:

Lt Robert Geoffroy &	C 17	P		KIA	
Lt Robert Depuyper	C 17	O		WIA	Sopwith
Cpl Paul Favrouet &	F 130	P		Injured	
Sol Baudin	F 130	M		Injured	Farman 60

1 August – No Claims – No Casualties

2 August

Adj-Chef Fonck	N 103	EA		P	Belgium	–

Casualties:

S/Lt Levy	F 206	O		WIA	Sopwith

3 August – No Claims – No Casualties

4 August – No Claims
Casualties:

Lt Henri Garsault	???	P		WIA	

5 August

S/Lt Rabatel	N 3	EA	P	Forêt d'Houthulst	1655	–
Sgt Montrion &	N 48					–
Sgt Trepp	N 12	Albatros D	P	Roulers		–
Casualties:						
MdL Yves Canton	N 95	P	WIA	Shot down in flames E of Réservoir Nieuport XXIVbis		

6 August

???	???	EA	P	Laon		–
Adj Madon	N 38	EA	P			–
Casualties:						
S/Lt Paul Sauvage	N 112	P	POW	Spad VII N° 1272, apparently forced to land with motor trouble.		
Sgt Jean Girardet &	F 201	P	KIAcc			
Sol Communier	F 201	G	Injured	Sopwith		
Brig Fontaine	C 9	P	Injured	Sopwith		
MdL Emile Caillat	F 35	P	Injured	AR		
???	65° Cie d'Aérostiers			Both balloons attacked,		
???	40° Cie d'Aérostiers			not flamed, Châlons Sector.		

7 August – No Claims

Casualties:

Cpl Georges Griffon &	C 74	P	KIAcc			
Lt Richard Fanning	C 74	O	KIAcc	Caudron G6		
Adj Yves Kervadec &	GDE	P	KIAcc			
Sol Levengeur	GDE	M	KIAcc	Farman 61		
Sgt Jean Boisgard &	C 220	P	Injured			
Cpl Bodet	C 220	M	Injured	Caudron G6 N° 4645		
Cpl Plaise	PS 125	G	Injured	Paul Schmitt		

8 August – No Claims

Casualties:

MdL Gaston Valadon	SM 106	P	WIA	Sopwith		
S/Lt L'huillier &	C 104	P	KIAcc			
Lt Etienne Tétard	C 104	O	KIAcc	Sopwith		
MdL Paul Vermot	N 49	P	Injured	Nieuport XXIV		
Sgt Jean Solinhac	F 41	P	Injured	AR		

9 August

Adj A Borde	N 65	EA	X	Clerkem	0710	2
Adj-Chef Fonck	N 103	Fokker D	X	Bixschoote-Dixmude	0815	7
Adj-Chef Fonck	N 103	Fokker D	P	Bixshcoote-Dixmude	0910	–
Sgt Dhôme	N 81	EA	FTL			–
Casualties:						
MdL Pierre Falleur	N 37	P	MIA	Spad N° 1389		
Sgt Marcel Janny &	C 226	P	MIA			
S/Lt Lauvergne	C 226	O	MIA	Sopwith		
Cpl Yves Lautredou &	Sop 108	P	OK			
Sol Gustave Vaillant	Sop 108	G	KIA	Sopwith		
Cpl Roger Maillard &	Sop 108	P	OK			
Sol Georges Breton	Sop 108	G	KIA	Sopwith		
Lt Wambergue	F 60	P	WIA	Flak, AR		
MdL de la Sablonière &	C 53	P	Injured			
S/Lt Driancourt	C 53	O	Injured	Caudron G6		
S/Lt Barrière	46° Cie d'Aérostiers		XF	Probably by Ltn Heinrich		
		O	Injured	Gontermann, Jasta 15 (27).		
???	51° Cie d'Aérostiers		XF	Probably by Ltn Heinrich		
				Gontermann, Jasta 15 (28).		
???	77° Cie d'Aérostiers			Attacked not flamed, Châlons Sector.		
???	48° Cie d'Aérostiers			Attacked, not flamed, Nancy Sector.		

10 August

MdL Bannier &	N 75					1
Adj Herisson	N 75	EA	X	W Abancourt		2

Lt Lagache	N 3	EA	P	E Dixmude	1515	–
Adj-Chef Fonck	N 103	EA	P	Ypres	1715	–

Casualties:

Capt Rousseau	N 31	P	MIA	Spad XIII, probably by Lt Werner Voss, Jasta 10,(35).	
MdL Etienne Camus	N 31	P	MIA	Spad, probably by Uffz Hermann Brettel, Jasta 10, (2).	
Adj Robert Bajac	N 48	P	WIA	Spad VII N° 1589	
Cpl Jacques Ehrlich	N 154	P	WIA	Nieuport XXIVbis, strafing.	
QM Albert Biard	PilSch	P	KIAcc	Chartres	
MdL François Laforcade &	V 485	P	KIAcc		
QM Auguste Plurien	V 485	O	KIAcc	Le Tréport	
Lt Etienne Bizard CO	V 116	P	KIAcc		
S/Lt Desjardins	V 116	O	Injured	Voisin LAP	
Cpl Robert Valtat	N 88	P	Injured	Nieuport XXIII	
Brig Gerome	V 109	P	Injured	Voisin LAP	
S/Lt François Deteurtre	80° Cie d'Aérostiers		XF	Probably by Ltn Rumpel, Jasta 16b, (1).	
		O	OK		
S/Lt Georges Muetaux	34° Cie d'Aérostiers			Not flamed, probably claimed by Ltn	
		O	Injured	Emil Thuy, Jasta 21.	
Sgt Feuillette	41° Cie d'Aérostiers			Cable cut by artillery	
		O	OK	fire, Soissons Sector.	
???	78° Cie d'Aérostiers			Descended by artillery fire.	
		O	OK		

11 August

Ground fire	???	EA	X	NE Vauxaillon	–

Casualties:

Sgt Adolphe Ferrer	V 116	P	KIA	Voisin LAP	
Lt de Feydeau	C 4	O	WIA	Flak, Caudron R4	
Sgt Descoubes &	C 122	P	KIAcc		
Asp Paul Marie-St Germain	C 122	O	Injured	Caudron G6, X° Armée	
Adj Dreyfus &	F 208	P	Injured		
Lt Lalais	F 208	O	Injured	Caudron G6	
S/Lt Bérard	41° Cie d'Aérostiers			Caught in a storm, Soissons Sector.	
		O	Injured		

12 August

Adj Dramard	N 38	Balloon	XF	Hauvine	2
Capt Verdon, CO	N 78				2
Sgt Bredin &	N 78				1
S/Lt Rousset	N 93	2 seater	X	Malancourt	1
Sgt Dhôme	N 81	EA	X	Régneville	1
Lt Gigodot CO	N 153	EA	X	S St Quentin	3
MdL Moliner &	C 227				1
MdL Argelier	C 227	Scout	X	N Beaumont	1
MdL Luizet &	C 9				–
Lt Minoret	C 9	EA	P		–
Patrol	N 83	EA	P	Romague-sous-les-Côtes	–
Adj-Chef Fonck	N 103	EA	P	Belgium	–
QM Malvoisin *	CAM	2 seater	P	Forêt d'Houthulst	–

* St Pol.

Casualties:

Adj Guy Baillou	N 86	P	MIA	Spad, probably by Ltn Otto Kissenberth, Jasta 23b, (7).	
Sgt Lucien Sarrazin &	Sop 123	P	KIA		
MdL Ernest François	Sop 123	G	KIA	Sopwith N° 3085	
Adj Grinde &	VB 101	P	MIA		
Sol Balland	VB 101	G	MIA	Sopwith	
S/Lt Pierre Gautier	F ?	O	KIA		
Lt Angot	C 39	O	WIA	Caudron G4	
Sol Saboul	C 6	G	WIA	Letord	
MdL Gabriel Luizet &	C 9	P	OK		
Lt André Minoret	C 9	O	WIA	Sopwith	
Adj Marius Lebon	C 4	P	KIAcc	Caudron G4 N° 4415	
Adj Deneau	GDE	P	Injured	Nieuport XVIII	

| ??? | 74° Cie d'Aérostiers | | | Both attacked, not flamed, | | |
| ??? | 87° Cie d'Aérostiers | | | Châlons Sector. | | |

13 August – No Claims
Casualties:

S/Lt Rodolphe Sebencq	N 37	P		MIA	Spad	
Sgt Pierre Lefevre &	C 4	P		MIA	Caudron G4, XF N Beville, near Laon	
S/Lt Jacques Outhenin-					X° Armée, probably by a Jasta 15	
Chalandre	C 4	O		MIA	pilot.	
Adj Félicien Combaz,	C 219	P		MIA		
Lt Pierre Robin &	C 219	O		MIA	Letord, probably by a Jasta 15	
Cpl Fernand Lahutte	C 219	G		MIA	pilot.	
MdL Etienne Chevillard	F 41	P		WIA	Flak, AR	
Adj Marcel Nogues	N 12	P		WIA	Flak, Spad VII N° 1584	
Brig René Nacrier	F 22	P		WIA	AR	
S/Lt Plazanet	F 5	O		WIA	Sopwith	
Lt Paul Rozoy	GDE	P		Injured	Nieuport XVII	
Lt Camille Paillot &	C 227	P		Injured		
S/Lt Dussaud	C 227	O		Injured	Sopwith	
MdL Couillard	43° Cie d'Aérostiers			XF	X° Armée, these two probably	
		O		OK	claimed by Vfw Haussmann (5) &	
					Ltn Mandel, both Jasta 15.	
Adj Ducasse	71° Cie d'Aérostiers			XF		
		O		WIA		
???	67° Cie d'Aérostiers				Attacked, not flamed, Châlons	
		O		OK	Sector.	

14 August

MdL Lemelle	N 73		2 seater	XF	Forêt d'Houthulst	1630	3
MdL Lemelle	N 73		Scout	P	Forêt d'Houthulst	1630	–
???	a. ???		EA	P	N Langemarck		–

a.   Possibly Uffz Hermann Hornberger, KIA, & Vfw Kurt Boje, WIA, Schsta 12, Langemarck.
Casualties:

Cpl Oliver Chadwick	N 73	P		KIA	Spad VII N° 1429, 09h45 near	
(American)					Ferme Carnot, probably by Obltn	
					Wilhelm Reinhard, Jasta 11, (4).	
S/Lt Gustave Backle	C 226	O		WIA	Sopwith	
Cpl Roussel &	C 13	P		Injured		
S/Lt Martin	C 13	O		KIAcc	Caudron G6	

15 August – No Claims
Casualties:

Lt Delaunay	C 226	P		WIA/DOW	Sopwith
Capt René Roeckel	S/S État	P		KIAcc	

16 August

Lt Raymond	N 3	EA		X	Forêt d'Houthulst	0832	3
S/Lt Nungesser	V 116	Gotha G		X	S Forêt d'Houthulst		30
Ad-Chef Fonck	N 103	Albatros		XF	S Forêt d'Houthulst		8
???	DCA	2 EA		X			–
??? &	F 215						–
Lt Lanchy	F 215	EA		P	Verdun Sector		–
???	???	EA		P	Belgium		–

Casualties:

S/Lt Henri Rabatel	N 3	P		POW	Spad VII N° 1639,
Cpl Marcel Cornet	N 3	P		MIA	Spad VII N° 2100, these two
					probably downed by Obltn Bruno
					Loerzer, CO Jasta 26 (6) and
					Obflugmst Kurt Schönfelder, Jasta 7, (2).
MdL Seigneurie	N 103	P		WIA	Flak, Spad VII
Sol Maurice Briquet	N 70	M		KIAcc	
MdL du Peuty	F 52	G		Injured	
MdL Adolphe Lemelle	N 73	P		Injured	Spad
MdL Gustave Duverne &	C 104	P		Injured	
S/Lt Billebaud	C 104	O		Injured	Caudron G6

S/Lt Henri Coulonges &	GDE	P	Injured			
S/Lt Aubrée	GDE	O	Injured	Caudron G4		

17 August

Capt Guynemer	N 3	Albatros C	XF	S Vladsloo	0820	51
Capt Guynemer	N 3	DFW C	XF	S Dixmude	0924	52
Adj Sadron &	F 8					1
Lt Mariotti	F 8	EA	X	III° Armée-German lines		1
S/Lt Rodier,	C 9					1
Adj Douillet &	C 9					1
Sgt Grosch	C 9	EA	X			1
MdL L Rampillon	N 76	Balloon	XF	Boult		1
S/Lt Decazes	N 88	Scout	X	Courtecon	0910	2
MdL Plessis	N 88	2 seater	X	Pontavert	1010	1
S/Lt Decazes &	N 88					3
MdL Plessis	N 88	Scout	X	Craonne-Corbeny	1045	2
MdL L Rampillon	N 96	Balloon	XF	Boult	1630	1
Adj Douillet &	C 220					1
Sgt Grosch &	C 220					1
Sgt Dreyfus,	C 220					1
Sgt Serpaggi &	C 220					1
Lt Duran	C 220	EA	X			1
Sgt Pharond,	R 217					1
S/Lt Rochat &	R 217					1
Sgt Bordas	R 217	EA	X			1
???	???	EA	X	Lierval-Monampteuil		–
???	???	EA	X	Réservoir		–
???	???	EA	X	Chevregny		–
MdL Hudlet &	Sop 123					1
S/Lt Bovet	Sop 123					1
Sgt de Peyerimhoff &	Sop 123					1
S/Lt Blehaut	Sop 123					1
Brig Canivet &	Sop 123					4
Sgt Pautrat	Sop 123					1
Adj Freville &	Sop 123					1
MdL Haubtmann b.	Sop 123	2 EA	X	Fribourg-en-Brisgen		2
???	???	EA	X	Laon		–
Sgt Brétillon	N 79	LVG C	P	La Fère	1200	–
Adj Peronneau	N 81	EA	P			–
???	???	2 EA	P	Verdun Sector		–
???	???	3 EA	P	Soissons Sector		–
??? a.	???	2 seater	POW	Bourg-sur-Aisne		–

a.   Vfw Karl Hauser & Ltn Martin Wetmenn, FlAbt 280, POWs, N of Bourg-sur-Aisne.
b.   These four crews were credited with two enemy aircraft downed, each member being credited with one victory.

Casualties:

MdL Robert Lonet	N 92	P	MIA	Nieuport XXIVbis
Sgt Lucien Julien &	C 227	P	MIA	Sopwith, XF, Verdun
MdL François Argelier	C 227	O	MIA	
Adj Aimé Maneval &	Sop 123	P	KIA	Sopwith, probably by Vfw Ludwig
Cpl Georges Gaillard	Sop 123	G	KIA	Hilz, Kest 4, (1).
MdL René de Gondrecourt	C 30	P	KIA	
S/Lt René Hazera	C 30	O	KIA	Caudron G6, Flak
Sgt Requier,	F 220	P	MIA	
Lt Claude Lalias &	C 9	O	MIA	
Sol Lethuillier	F 220	G	MIA	Letord, XF Laon
MdL René Gentry &	V 114	P	MIA	
Lt Robert Mimaud-Grandchamps	V 114	O	MIA	Voisin P
Lt Raphoz	F 5		KIA	Bombardment of Airfield.
S/Lt Robert Roland-Baudoin	N 80	P	KIA	Spad N° 1566, 16h45 with two 2 seaters over Gincrey.
MdL Oliver de Hogendorp &	F 50	P	KIA	Flak
S/Lt Granier	F 50	O	KIA	Flak, AR
Sgt Pharond,	R 217	P	KIA	
S/Lt Adolphe Rochat &	R 217	O	KIA	
Sol Bordas	R 217	G	KIA	Letord, XF Châlons
Capt Jean Mutel &	F 19	P	KIA	In a car on the ground
S/Lt Liaudet	F 19	O	WIA	when hit by shell fire.

Adj Jules Godiveau	N 92	P	WIA	Flak, Nieuport XXIVbis		
Sgt Lecomte	Sop 127	G	WIA	Flak, Sopwith		
Sol Rivard	???	G	WIA	Bombardment of Airfield.		
QM Victor Pisano	PilSch	P	KIAcc	St Raphaël		
MdL Léon Laurent	N 92	P	KIAcc			
MdL Bernajuzan &	C 27	P	KIAcc			
Lt Travers	C 27	O	KIAcc	Caudron G4		
Cpl George E Turnure, Jr (American)	N 103	P	Injured	Spad VII N° 1637, Furnes		
MdL Henri Marbouty &	C 6	P	Injured	DOW 18 August 1917		
S/Lt Léon Giquel	C 6	O	Injured	Caudron G6		
MdL Martinol	C 56	P	Injured	Letord		
Sgt Jules Peureux	C 34	P	Injured	Sopwith		
Cdt Victor Chabert &	GB 1	P	Injured			
Capt Bruyère	GB 1	O	Injured	Voisin P		
MdL Martin	GDE	P	Injured	Nieuport XXII		
S/Lt Pierre Bonnier	25° Cie d'Aérostiers		XF	Both these were probably		
		O	OK	claimed by Ltn Karl Bohny,		
S/Lt Gustave Andrain	59° Cie d'Aérostiers		XF	Kest 7, (1) & (2).		
		O	OK			
???	28° Cie d'Aérostiers		XF	Both probably claimed by		
		O	OK	Ltn Heinrich Gontermann		
???	39° Cie d'Aérostiers		XF	(29 & 30), Jasta 15.		
		O	OK			
???	89° Cie d'Aérostiers			Attacked, not flamed,		
		O	OK	Nancy Sector.		

18 August

Sgt Henin	N 3	EA	XF	Forêt d'Houthulst	0745	1
Lt Chevillon	N 15	EA	X			3
S/Lt Madon	N 38	2 seater	X	Nogent l'Abbesse		13
S/Lt Testulat,	C 39					1
Lt Haentjens &	C 39					1
Sol Gisors	C 39	Scout	X			1
MdL Renauld	N 48	2 seater	XF	W Dixmude	0920	2
Lt de Turenne &	N 48					5
Adj de Guingand	N 48	Albatros D	X	Forêt d'Houthulst	0714	2
MdL M Paris &	N 65					3
Sgt Lovell	N 124	Albatros	XF	Cierges		1
MdL Flachaire	N 67	EA	X	Coucy-le-Château	0845	8
Capt E Paumier	N 76	2 seater	X	Verlet		1
Lt Manceron &	C 74					1
Lt Toussaint (Belgian)	C 75	EA	X	Belgium		1
Lt Marty a.	N 77	2 seater	X	N Cremecy	1045	4
Lt L Milliat &	N 80					2
Cpl Rheno b.	N 80	2 seater	X	Braquis	1940	1
Adj Herbelin,	N 81					4
Cpl P Guérin &	N 81					1
Sgt Taffe	N 112	EA	X	Cuissy		2
Adj van Ingelandt,	N 97					1
Brig Jumel,	N 97					1
Lt Robin &	N 97					1
MdL Presles du Plessis	N 97	EA	X	SE Chermizy	1858	2
MdL Presles du Plessis	N 97	EA	X	Montblainville		3
Adj Rotival &	C 227					1
Sgt Lemarie	C 227	EA	X	German lines		1
???	???	DFW/LVG	FTL	POWs Forêt de Coucy		–
Capt Guynemer	N 3	2 seater	P	E Dixmude	0910	–
S/Lt Madon	N 38	EA	P	Nogent l'Abbesse		–
MdL Presles du Plessis	N 97	EA	P			–
MdL Millot	Sop 111	EA	P			–
???	???	EA	P	Braquis-Etain		–
Capt E Paumier	N 76	EA	FTL			–

a.   Probably Ltn Heidschmitt & Ltn Reiher, FlAbt 12, WIAs.
b.   Probably DFW CV 5761/16, Ltn Kurt von Drigalski & Ltn Hugo Sandt, FlAbt 207, KIAs, Braquis.

Casualties:

Cpl Julian Biddle (American)	N 73	P	MIA	Spad VII N° 1300, possibly by Vfw Kaspar Rahier, Jasta 31, (1).
S/Lt André Aignan &	Sop 111	P	MIA	
Brig Paul Boudon	Sop 111	G	MIA	Sopwith
Lt Édouard Mumaud-Grandchamps	V 114	P	MIA	
Sgt Harold Willis (American)	N 124	P	POW	Spad VII N° 1615, probably by Ltn Wilhelm Schulz, Jasta 16b, (1).
Sgt Stephen Bigelow (American)	N 124	P	WIA	Spad N° 387, departed 16h35.
S/Lt Jean-Paul Favre de Thierrens	N 62	P	WIA	Spad
Adj Georges Leclerc	N 97	P	WIA	Nieuport XXIV
Lt La Mallerie &	PS 127	P	WIA	
Sol Perronet	PS 127	G	WIA	Paul Schmitt
Adj Adolphe Deroc &	C 13	P	OK	
Cpl Emile Laborne	C 13	G	WIA	
Sgt Pierre Girardot	N 37	P	KIA	Spad, Verdun Sector
LV Frantz Plenneau	PilSch	P	KIAcc	St Raphaël
Adj Jean Hamel	N 93	P	KIAcc	Nieuport XXIVbis
Cpl Ariste Pappia	GDE	P	KIAcc	Nieuport XVII
Sgt Pierre Marin	N 87	P	Injured	Nieuport XXIV
S/Lt Maurice Henriot	N 87	P	Injured	Nieuport XXIV
Cpl Roger &	PS 126	P	Injured	
Sol Delamour	PS 126	G	Injured	Paul Schmitt
S/Lt Joseph Mathieu	48° d'Cie Aérostiers O		XF	Probably by Ltn Fritz Pütter, Injured Jasta 9, (2).

---

19 August

Sgt Beauregard	N 69	EA	P	Cerisy	1145	–
Capt Franc &	N 79					1
MdL de la Dampièrre	N 79	Balloon	XF	Villers-le-Sec	1945	1
Sgt Dhôme &	N 81					2
Adj Villiars	a. N 23	2 seater	X	Souilly-Régneville		3
Capt Franc	N 79	EA	X			1
42° Sect. d'Auto Canons	DCA	EA	X			–
???	DCA	EA	X			–
Sgt Tiberghein	N 31	EA	P	E Langemarck		–
Sgt Ambrogi	N 90	EA	P			–

a. Possibly Uffz Erich Heuschkel & Ltn Eberhard Wenck, FlAbt 2, KIAs, AOK "C" Sector.

Casualties:

Sgt Georges Damez &	SM 106	P	MIA	
MdL Vitecoq	SM 106	G	MIA	Sopwith
MdL Jean Wetzel	N 86	P	MIA	Nieuport XXIV, probably by Ltn Otto Kissenberth, Jasta 23b, (9).
MdL Augustin Thevenin	N 15	P	KIA	Spad, probably by Ltn Karl Odebrett, Jasta 16b, (3).
Adj Pierre Catois	N 93	P	KIA	Nieuport XXIVbis, Bois de Forges, probably by Flakzug 183 & Flak-batterie 706.
Cpl Laborne	C 13	G	WIA	Letord
Sgt Georges Villa &	C 27	P	WIA	
OffAdm André Bouttiaux	C 27	O	KIA	Sopwith
Sgt Louis Goux	N 67	P	WIA	Spad, ground fire.
MdL Albert Coulet	C 34	P	KIAcc	Caudron G3
Sgt Adrien Chapelle	N 31	P	Injured	Spad
S/Lt Benoist	F 50	O	Injured	Caudron G3
Capt Basile Verdy	C 212	P	Injured	Caudron G4
S/Lt Jean Schoeller	38° Cie d'Aérostiers O		OK	Attacked not flamed.
Sgt Guy Benoist	48° Cie d'Aérostiers O		XF	Probably by Ltn Hans Pütter, Jasta Jasta 9, (3).
???	Cie d'Aérostiers		XF	All three flamed in the X° Armée
???	Cie d'Aérostiers		XF	Sector, probably by Ltn Heinrich
???	Cie d'Aérostiers		XF	Gonterman, Jasta 15, (32-35).

20 August

Third Battle of Verdun opens.

Capt Guynemer	a.	N 3	DFW C	XF	E Poperinghe	0905	53
Sgt G Guérin	b.	N 15	EA	X	SE Consenvoye		5
Sgt Vicaire,		F 19					1
S/Lt Lambert &		F 19					1
Sgt Hass		F 19	Scout	X	S Malancourt		1
Adj Poisard &		C 28					1
Lt Homberg		C 28	Scout	X	SW Haucourt		1
MdL M Paris		N 65	EA	X	Brabant		4
MdL Le Roy de Boiseaumarie		N 78	EA	X	Bois de Forges		3
Adj Herbelin		N 81	EA	X	Dieue		5
Lt Leps &		N 81					4
Lt Hugues		N 81	2 seater	X	Bois de Forges		6
MdL de Cazenove de Pradines		N 81	Balloon	XF	Montfaucon-sur-Meuse		2
Adj-Chef Fonck		N 103	Albatros C	XF	W Ypres	0905	9
Ground fire		???	2 EA	X	Haumont		–
Sgt G Guérin		N 15	EA	P	Haumont		–
MdL Henriot		N 65	EA	P	Samogneux		–
Sgt Dumser		N 75	EA	P	Bezonvaux		–
MdL Lemaitre		N 78	EA	P	Côte 304		–
MdL Leroy		N 78	EA	P	Côte 304		–
Adj Peronneau		N 81	EA	P	Cuizy		–
Lt Mallet		N 112	EA	P	Consenvoye		–
Cdt Ménard	CO	GC 15	EA	P	Bois de Forges		–
Sgt Pietri		N 103	EA	P	Ypres-Zonnebeke	0910	–
Lt Bues &		C 223					–
Lt Rochette		C 223	EA	FTL	Verdun Sector		–

a.   Possibly Uffz Martin Ewald & Ltn Walter Rode, FlAbt 3, KIAs, Poperinghe.
b.   Possibly Uffz Rudolf Hoffmann (KIA) and Ltn Max Pech (WIA/DOW 26 August 1917), Töter Mann, FlAbt 9w.

Casualties:

Lt Ernest Enjolras &	F 19	P	MIA	
S/Lt St Martin	F 19	O	MIA	AR
Cpl Thimothée Vila &	C 34	P	MIA	
Lt Guilland	C 34	O	MIA	Caudron G4
S/Lt Pierre Barthes	N 93	P	KIA	Spad, 09h00 E Mort Homme, probably by Ltn Otto Kissenberth, Jasta 16b (10).
Sgt René Croce-Spinelli	F 41	P	KIA	
S/Lt Chambillie	F 41	O	KIA	AR, XF Verdun Sector.
Cpl Marie Chabert &	C 13	P	KIA	XF Verdun Sector.
Capt Augustin Hubert	C 13	O	KIA	Caudron G6
Cpl Jacques Rostan	N 84	P	KIA	Spad, in flames near Ornes.
Sgt Jacques Menier	N 84	P	WIA	POW Spad, in flames, escaped during October 1918. These two probably downed by Ltn Ludwig Hanstein, Jasta 16b, (7) & Vfw Johann Neumaier, Jasta 16b, (1).
Cpl Caleb Coatsworth (American)	N 80	P	WIA	Spad
Capt Georges Aube &	C 28	P	OK	
S/Lt Pierre Billoue	C 28	O	WIA	Sopwith
Lt L'huillier	C 34	O	WIA	Letord
Sol Trillaud	F 25	M	WIA	Bombardment of Airfield.
Sol Augustin Menegaux	F 215	M	WIA	,,
Lt Leblanc	C 104	O	WIA	Caudron G4
Sgt Léon Calmon	N 49	P	Injured	Nieuport XXIVbis
MdL Camille Masson &	F 41	P	Injured	
S/Lt Genin	F 41	O	Injured	AR
MdL Marcel Lebegue	C 104	P	Injured	Caudron G4
Adj Moris Pellet	C 104	P	Injured	Caudron G6
S/Lt Claudius Forest	25° Cie d'Aérostiers			All five of these balloons
Sgt Michel Girault	31° Cie d'Aérostiers			were attacked, not flamed
???	63° Cie d'Aérostiers			in the Nancy Sector. All
???	38° Cie d'Aérostiers			observers made safe jumps.
???	48° Cie d'Aérostiers			

21 August

Lt Mendigal &	C 11					1
Lt Dagnaux	C 11	EA	X	Vauquois		1
MdL Delannoy	N 80	EA	X	Montfaucon		4
S/Lt de Bonnefoy	a. N 84	EA	X	Beaumont		6
S/Lt Dehesdin &	N 87					1
Cpl Ruamps	b. N 87	Albatros C	X	Pagny-sur-Meuse		1
Adj-Chef Fonck	N 103	2 seater	X	Dixmude	0955	10
MdL Butscher	N 151	EA	X	Burnhaupt		1
Lt Plane,	R 213					1
Sol Ledig &	R 213					1
S/Lt Boulmier	R 213	EA	X	German lines		1
Cpl Risacher	N 3	EA	P	Boesinghe-Bixschoote	0820	–
S/Lt Dezarrois	N 26	EA	P	Houthulst	0835	–
Adj Fétu	N 26	EA	P	Forêt d'Houthulst	0930	–
Adj Douchy	N 38	EA	P	N Pont-Faverger		–
Adj Joffroy	N 75	EA	P	Marre		–
Sgt Menier	N 84	EA	P	Samogneux		–
Sgt Menier	c. N 84	EA	P	Gincrey		–
???	???	EA	P	Bois de Carres		–

a. Probably Ltn Hugo Geiger, Jasta 34b, KIA N Verdun, Beaumont about 10 km N of Verdun, AOK "C" Sector.
b. Possibly Albatros CXII N 1851/17, Ltn Rudolf Littig, POW & Ltn Joseph Schwinfest, KIA, FlAbt 46, AOK "C" Sector.
c. Probably Ltn Max Wirth, Jasta 34b, KIA NW Etain, Gincrey anout 5 km NW Etain, AOK "C" Sector.

Casualties:

Lt Yves Garnier du Plessix &	C 227	P	KIA	Probably downed by Ltn Heinrich Büssing, Kest 4, (2).
Lt Charles Sainte Claire-Deville	C 227	O	KIA	Sopwith
Lt Paul Dumas	N 103	P	WIA	Spad, at 10h00
S/Lt André Dezarrois	N 26	O	WIA	Spad, at 10h00
S/Lt Alain Terme	N 68	P	WIA	Flak, Morane-Saulnier
Adj Marcel Vonflie &	C 202	P	WIA	
S/Lt André Bougault	C 202	O	WIA	Caudron G6
SM Louis Beauvir	CAM	P	KIAcc	FBA 150hp N° 534,St Tropez
SM Paul Postec	PilSch	P	KIAcc	Verdôme
Sgt Roger Lestrade	F 70	P	KIAcc	Farman 40
Asp Gustave Weltzer	F 35	O	KIAcc	Farman 40
Cpl Jean Bouie	GDE	P	KIAcc	Farman 61
S/Lt Grandperrin	C 34	O	Injured	Caudron G6
Sgt François Vacher &	VB 101	P	Injured	
Sol Edouard Salles	VB 101	G	Injured	Voisin LAP
Sol Fournerat	N 62	M	Injured	
???	87° Cie d'Aérostiers	XF		Probably by Ltn F Brandt, Jasta 19, (2).

22 August

S/Lt Madon	N 38	Albatros C	X	E Nogent l'Abbesse		14
Lt Hay de Slade	N 86	Albatros D3	X	Bois de Forges	1820	3
Adj-Chef Fonck	N 103	2 seater	XF	E Ypres	0900	11
Artillery	???	Balloon	X	E Altkirch		–
Poste 48	DCA	EA	X	Souilly		–
S/Lt Le Coq de Kerland	N 90	LVG	P	Thiaucourt		–
Sgt L de Marmier	N 112	EA	X	German lines		1
???	???	5 EA	P	Verdun Sector		–

Casualties:

Sgt André Saulière	F 205	P	MIA	AR
S/Lt Gautier	C 43	O	MIA	AR
S/Lt Janesse	F 54	O	KIA	Morane-Saulnier Parasol
Sgt Guillien	R 213	G	KIA	Letord
Sgt Cousin &	C 42	P	OK	Caudron G6, FTL at La Cense, 17h45,
S/Lt Marcel Fourment	C 42	O	WIA	X° Armée.
Sgt André Agut	N 88	P	KIAcc	Nieuport XXIVbis N° 3278
Adj Emile Dhumerelle	F 139	P	KIAcc	Farman 42
Brig Ferrand	F 130	P	KIAcc	Farman 42
Lt Georges Salze	???	P	KIAcc	
Lt Henri Garsault	F 211	P	Injured	AR
Adj Marcel Valance	F 211	P	Injured	AR

Sol Jean Guennec	Sop 123	G	Injured	Sopwith		
Asp Long	Br 209	O	Injured	Caudron G6		

23 August

???	DCA	EA	X	Bois des Caurières	am	–
Adj Douchy	N 38	EA	P	E Sommepy		–
???	a. ???	4 EA	P	Verdun Sector		–

a.   One claim was probably Vfw Konrad Poralla, Jasta 32b, WIA Dannevoux, about 20 km NNW Verdun.
      Another possible claim would be Vfw Reif (P) FlAbt 279 (A), WIA over Ft Rozeillier, near Verdun.
      Also Vfw Jahnke, Jasta 21 WIA in this sector.

Casualties:

MdL Pothier	F 215	P	WIA	AR		
Cpl Lucien Vinceneux	F 14	P	KIAcc	AR		
Cpl Paul Teulat	GDE	P	Injured	Nieuport XVII		
S/Lt Le Floch	C 17	O	Injured	Caudron G4		
Sol Raison	F 14	M	Injured	Sopwith		
???	80° Cie d'Aérostiers			Both balloons attacked by		
???	86° Cie d'Aérostiers			seven EA, not flamed:		
		O	OK	Nancy Sector.		

24 August

Cpl Maurer	N 76	EA	X			1

Casualties:

Cdt Albert Jacquin	CO	Avord	P	KIAcc		
SM Ernest Macouin &	*	CAM	P	KIAcc	Calais, Voison LAP VIII	
Mat Georges Dubois	*	CAM	M	KIAcc	N° 2217.	
MdL Pierre Campion		N 315	P	Injured	Nieuport	
Adj Jean Agostini		GDE	P	Injured	Nieuport XVII	

*   Dunkerque.

25 August

Sgt Gérard,	F 72					1
S/Lt Canouet &	F 72					1
Adj Ducrocq	F 72	Halberstadt D	XF	Pont-Girard		1
Adj Madon	N 38	EA	P	N Côte 304		–
Adj Madon	N 38	EA	P	N Côte 304		–
Sgt Ambroise-Thomas &	N 48					–
Sgt Majon de la Débuterie	N 48	EA	P	SE Langemarck		–
Adj Ferber	N 84	EA	P	Bois de Béthincourt		–

Casualties:

Brig René de Razay	N 68	P	Injured	Nieuport XXIV		
Capt Guy de Lubersac	C 11	P	Injured	Caudron G4		
MdL René Baudon	VB 101	P	Injured	VLAP		
Sgt Vacher	VB 101	P	KIAcc	VLAP		
Adj Lucien Chretienneau	CEP 115	P	KIAcc			
Sol Paul Deval &	CEP 115	G	KIAcc			
Sol Alfred Fougerolle	CEP 115	G	Injured	CEP		

26 August

Third Battle of Verdun terminated.

Sgt G Guérin	N 15	EA	X	Bois de Caures		6
Adj Naegely	N 15	EA	XF	Samogneux		2
Adj Baudrion &	F 19					1
Capt Blitz	F 19	Scout	X	Hill 304		1
Adj de Guingand &	N 48					3
Sgt Montrion	N 48	Albatros D3	X	N Dixmude		3
Sgt Boyau	N 77	Balloon	XF	Juvelize-Bourdonnaye	1530	7
Lt Hugues,	N 81					7
S/Lt Herbelin &	N 81					6
Sgt P Guérin	N 81	Albatros C	X	Ornes		2
Sgt G Guérin	N 15	EA	P	S Bois de Caures		–
Capt Vuillet	N 65	EA	P	Samogneux		–
MdL Sauclière	N 79	Albatros	P	La Fère-Danozy	1440	–
Lt Gastin	N 15	EA	P	Ornes		–

Casualties:

MdL Charles Blanchi	GDE	P	MIA	Caudron G4		

Sgt Armand Presles				Nieuport XXIVbis		
du Plessis	N 97	P	WIA	DOW 27 August 1917		
Cdt Gaston Fouceroux	(1)	P	KIAcc	Sopwith		
Adj Glaize	59° Cie d'Aérostiers		XF	Probably by Ltn Ludwig Hanstein,		
		O	Injured	Jasta 16b, (8).		
Adj Maurice Beaufeist	49° Cie d'Aérostiers		XF	These were probably claimed by		
		O	Injured	Obltn Otto Schmidt (7), &		
S/Lt Caron	93° Cie d'Aérostiers		XF	Vfw Kurt Petzinna (2) both of Jasta 29.		

(1)   CO Aviation for VII° Armée.

27 August – No Claims
Casualties:

Adj Pierre Gaudermen	N 68	P	WIA	Flak, Spad		
Cpl Archon	F 130	G	WIA	Farman 40		
S/Lt Louis Delmas	???	P	KIAcc			
Cpl Raymond Pratz	N 155	P	Injured	Nieuport XXIVbis		

28 August – No Claims
Casualties:

| Sgt Maurice Froger | C 42 | P | WIA | DOW Caudron G4 | | |

29 – 30 August – No Claims – No Casualties

31 August

Sgt Goubeau &	F 52					–
Lt Carves	F 52	Albatros D	P			–
Adj-Chef Fonck	N 103	Scout	P	Forêt d'Houthulst	1910	–

Casualties:

| Cpl Nicolas Pavlovsky | N 78 | P | Injured | Spad | | |
| Sgt Baudry | GDE | P | Injured | AR | | |

1 September

| MdL Septier & | Sop 13 | | | | | 1 |
| S/Lt van Coehorn | Sop 13 | EA | XF | Moirey | | 1 |

Casualties:

EV1 Frot	* CAM	P	POW	Spad VII, FTL in German territory with motor trouble.		
Cpl Michel	GDE	P	KIAcc	Farman 42		
S/Lt Eustice	C 9	O	Injured			

*   Dunkerque.

2 September – No Claims
Casualties:

Adj Gilbert de Guingand	N 48	P	WIA	Spad VII		
Cpl Emile Joly &	GDE	P	KIAcc			
S/Lt Panzani	GDE	O	KIAcc	Farman 60		

3 September

S/Lt de Rochechouart de						
Mortemart	N 23	EA	X	Dannevoux	1520	2
Adj Pillon	N 82	Scout	X	Molinchard	1655	5
S/Lt Madon	N 38	Albatros C	X	Nogent l'Abbesse		15
Sgt Petit-Delchet	N 69	Balloon	XF	Montaigu	1935	1
Sgt Caël	N 102	Rumpler C	X			2
Capt Heurtaux CO	N 3	2 seater	P			–
MdL Morizot &	N 23					–
S/Lt de Beauchamp	N 23	EA	P	Samogneux	1550	–
???	F 72	EA	P	Châlons-sur-Marne		–
Adj Dupré	N 102	EA	P			–
Adj-Chef Fonck	N 103	Scout	P	Poelcapelle-Ypres	1010	–
Adj-Chef Fonck	N 103	2 seater	P	Forêt d'Houthulst	1030	–
???	???	3 EA	P	Nancy Sector		–

Casualties:

| S/Lt Aimé Navarin & | VB 109 | P | MIA | | | |
| Sgt René Delaunay | VB 109 | B | MIA | Voisin VIII | | |

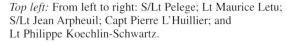

Top left: From left to right: S/Lt Pelege; Lt Maurice Letu; S/Lt Jean Arpheuil; Capt Pierre L'Huillier; and Lt Philippe Koechlin-Schwartz.

Top right: From left to right: Sgt Jules Tiberghein; S/Lt Jules Covin; Capt René Roeckel; S/Lt Jean Chaput; S/Lt Jacques Ortoli & unknown.

Middle left: Sgt Austin Crehore, an American who flew with Spa 94.

Middle centre: Sgt Elliott Cowdin (left), an American who served in Escadrilles VB 108, N 38, N 49, N 65 & N 124, and Lt Alfred de Laage de Meux, the second

in command of N 124, killed in an accident on 23 May 1917.

Middle right: MdL Marcel Paris, N 65, killed in combat 22 September 1917.

Bottom left: Nieuport No 2779 flown by Cpl Carré, N 112, made POW when he force-landed at Leffincourt, on 12 April 1917.

Bottom right: The aircraft of MdL Pierre Failleur, N 37, who evidently became lost and landed in enemy territory being taken prisoner on 9 August 1917.

Top left: Nieuport XI No 1324 of S/Lt François Raty, N 38, POW 6 July 1916.

Top right: Nieuport No 1135 of Capt Jacques de Sieyes de Veynes, CO N 26, POW on 3 July 1916.

Middle left: A group of Spa 152 pilots. From left to right: Lt Ernest Maunoury; Lt Jean Bourjade; Prince Sapia of Poland; Capt Léon Bonne CO Spa 152, and unknown.

Middle right: Sgt Upton Sullivan, one of two American members of Spa 90, alongside a Nieuport on which the squadron 'rooster' is in white (rather than customary black).

Bottom left: Sgt David Guy, an American who flew with Spa 155, Spa 156 and Spa 38.

Bottom right: Spad VII No 224 of Lt Jean Mistarlet, N 31, POW on 7 April 1917.

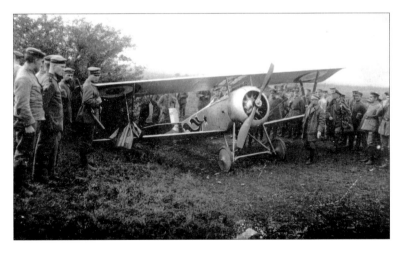

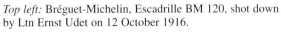

Top left: Bréguet-Michelin, Escadrille BM 120, shot down by Ltn Ernst Udet on 12 October 1916.

Top right: S/Lt Jean Bouyer, Spa 49.

Middle left: Group photo of Escadrille Spa 158 pilots.

Bottom left: Nieuport 17 No 1831 of Lt José Maria, N 77, who experienced motor trouble and was forced to land in enemy territory on 23 October 1916.

Bottom right: Lt Michel Coiffard, Spa 154, severely wounded in combat on 28 October 1918, and died the following day.

Top left: S/Lt Michel Coiffard and Adj Paul Petit, MIA 18 September 1918, of Spa 154.

Top right: S/Lt Marius Ambrogi, Spa 90, who was awarded the Chevalier de la Légion d'Honneur, Médaille Militaire and Croix de Guerre with ten palmes and one silver star.

Middle right: Capt Pierre L'Huillier, N 49, N 62 and CO Spa 150.

Bottom: From left to right: Adj Bizot; Lt Dencausse; Adj Pezon; Lt de Ginestet; Lt Renou; Capt Weiss; S/Lt Ambrogi; Adj Bordes; Lt Mallen; Lt Lemarie and Adj Mace.

Top left: Lt Gilbert Sardier, Spa 77 and Spa 48, and Capt Jean Gigodot, CO Spa 153.

Top right: The aircraft Sgt Georges Madon was flying when he became lost and landed on 5 April 1915, in Switzerland, where he was interned until he escaped.

Middle right: Adj Georges Foulon 1 victory, Spa 152.

Bottom left: S/Lt Georges Madon, Spa 38.

Bottom right: Capt Alphonse Colcomb, CO N 38.

Top left: A German aircraft downed by Adj Maurice Robert and Sgt Jean Javaud, Spa 92 on 3 May 1918.

Top right: A group of aces, from left to right: Capt Raoul Echard; Lt Charles Nungesser; Lt Georges Madon; Lt Bernard Barny de Romanet and Lt René Fonck.

Middle left: Sgt Eugène Bertin, MS 38, WIA 24 August 1915.

Middle centre: Sgt Gabriel Vallot, Spa 152.

Middle right: Cpl Eugene Bullard, an American with Spa 93.

Bottom left: First victory of Capt Jacques Leps, 16 March 1917.

Bottom right: MdL Miguel Sainz, Spa 94.

Top left: Capt Auguste Lahoulle, CO Spa 154.

Top right: A group of Spa 154 pilots.

Middle left: A group of pilots from various escadrilles.

Middle right: A group of Spa 163 pilots.

Bottom left: Adj Hector Garaud, Spa 38.

Bottom centre: S/Lt Henri Paillard, N 49, killed in combat 6 November 1916.

Bottom right: S/Lt René Cornemont, Spa 3.

Top: A group of Spa 93 pilots, from left to right:
MdL Georges Franceschi; Sgt Bernard Breton (MIA
17 June 1918); Sgt de Saint Hilaire; S/Lt Gustave
Daladier; Lt Pierre Olphe-Gaillard; Capt Adrien Moreau;
Lt Auguste Gallet; Sgt Fernand Lasne; Sgt Pierre
Ducornet; Sgt Bernard Maurice and Sgt Roger Dumont.

Middle left: Spa 48 Spad flown by Adj Jacques Roques.

Middle right: Lt Marie Majon de la Debuterie,
Spa 157/Spa 163.

Bottom left: The Morane-Saulnier, type P No 937, flown
by MdL Charles Gauthier and Soldat Abel Denis, N 31,
when down and captured on 10 July 1917.

Bottom right: Capt René Roeckel, CO F 7.

Top left: Two Spa 81 pilots, Lt Pierre de Cazenove de Pradines (left), and Lt Henri Peronneau.

Top right: The Spad VII of Lt Jean Mistarlet, Spa 31, shot down and captured on 7 April 1917.

Middle right: A Spad from Spa 81.

Bottom left: Cpl René Vandendorpe, N 152, one of the pilots who downed Zeppelin L 49 at Bourdonne-les-Bains on 20 October 1917.

Bottom right: MS 49 pilots.

Top: A group of Spa 48 pilots.

Middle left: Lt Pierre de Cazenove de Pradines tests a new model aircraft.

Middle right: Pilots of Spa 81 standing on a tank. From left to right: Adj Louis Chaigneau; Sgt Jacques Viriau and Sgt Henri Lombard.

Bottom left: Sgt Joseph Frantz (left) and his mechanic Louis Quénault. Frantz was credited with the first French air to air victory on 5 October 1914.

Bottom right: S/Lt Boillot and Lt Navarre.

Top left: Pilots of Spa 81 discussing combat manoeuvres. Front row, from left to right: S/Lt Pierre Cardon and Sgt Paul Santelli. Back row, from left to right: Adj Alphonse Malfanti; MdL Pierre Colombo and Adj Maurice Rouselle.

Top right: Sgt James A. Bayne, an American who served with Spa 85 and Spa 82, sitting on his Spad XIII in which he was killed in an accident on 8 May 1918.

Middle left: Pilots of Spa 81. From left to right: Adj Maurice Rouselle; S/Lt Pierre Cardon; Adj Alphonse Malfanti; S/Lt Levecque and S/Lt Peronneau.

Middle right: S/Lt Gaston Levecque of Spa 81.

Bottom left: Cpl John Russell Adams, an American, who served with N 95 and Spa 81.

Bottom centre: Sgt Ellison Boggs, an American with Spa 81, awarded Croix de Guerre with one Bronze Star.

Bottom right: S/Lt Marcel Dhôme, scored nine victories with Spa 81, was decorated with the Légion d'Honneur and Médaille Militaire.

Top left: Three Spa 81 aces. From left to right:
Lt Jacques Leps; Adj Maurice Rousselle and Adj Marcel
Dhôme.

Top right: Lt Pierre Cardon riding the tail of his Spad
Scout.

Middle right: Sgt Henri Lombard, Spa 81, seated in his
Spad.

Bottom left: Spa 81 pilots. From left to right: S/Lt Henri
Peronneau; Sgt Paul Guérin; Lt Jacques Leps; Lt Marcel
Dhôme and Lt Gaston Levecque.

Bottom right: Lt Cardon's plane undergoes some repairs.

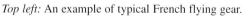

Top left: An example of typical French flying gear.

Top right: From left to right: Adj-Chief Marius Blanc; Adj Maurice Rouselle and Sgt Paul Guérin.

Middle left: Lt Pierre Le Pelve by a Spa 81 Spad. He was shot down inside German lines on 20 August 1918, but managed to regain Allied lines without being captured.

Bottom left: Adj Marcel Dhôme and Lt Henri Peronneau look through the wreckage of an aircraft.

Bottom right: Adj Pierre de Cazenove de Pradines and Adj Henri Peronneau discussing one of the victories they shared with Lt William Thaw of the Lafayette Escadrille, N 124.

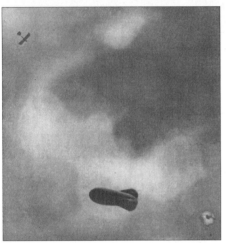

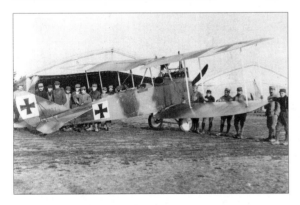

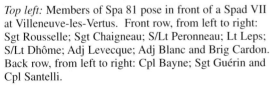

Top left: Members of Spa 81 pose in front of a Spad VII at Villeneuve-les-Vertus. Front row, from left to right: Sgt Rousselle; Sgt Chaigneau; S/Lt Peronneau; Lt Leps; S/Lt Dhôme; Adj Levecque; Adj Blanc and Brig Cardon. Back row, from left to right: Cpl Bayne; Sgt Guérin and Cpl Santelli.

Top right: Adj Maurice Rousselle, who scored five victories and was awarded the Médaille Militaire and Croix de Guerre with five palmes.

Middle left: An Albatros scout photographed at the moment it attacked a French balloon during 1918. The observer (lower right) had already jumped to escape the flames of his balloon.

Middle right: Flying boat FBA 150hp D.8 (No 323) of CAM Dunkerque, was shot down 14 April 1917 near Zeebrugge. The crew, QM Proux & Mat Prudhomme, were captured.

Bottom left: This superb Rumpler C.IV (No 1431/17) was captured 21 October 1917 on the Fère-Champenoise airfield.

Bottom right: Sgt Paul Santelli (middle) and Sgt Jacques Viriau (right) relax with another crew member.

Top left: Quarter-Master Henri Le Garrec (1 victory confirmed and several non-confirmed because they were obtained far behind the German lines) with Sopwith Triplane 14 (No F.9) at Saint Pol sur Mer in June 1917. Le Garrec was killed in aerial combat while flying Sopwith Triplane 12 (No F.15, ex-N5388 RNAS) on 3 September 1917, by Jasta 11 pilots.

Top right: Most of the Morane-Saulnier type H still in service at the start of the war were sent to Escadrille MS 31, to which this example captured in 1914, belonged.

Middle left: With 2 confirmed and 4 probable victories SM Malvoisin was probably the best chasse pilot of the French navy. Here he poses on Nieuport XVII 6

(No 1852) of CAM Dunkerque, at Saint Pol sur Mer in April 1917. Malvoisin was shot down in combat 26 May 1918, flying a Hanriot HD.2 seaplane, and ended the war in a POW camp.

Middle right: Seaplane Lévy-Besson 200hp, of CAM La Penzé (Bretagne), lost in an accident in 1918.

Bottom left & right: Two views of a Hanriot HD.2 D.30 (No 201) of the chasse seaplane escadrille at CAM Dunkerque in 1918. This seaplane was lost in an accident on 2 February 1918 at Dunkerque, killing the pilot, EV1 Daniel Pelichet. The code is painted on the right side of the fuselage and the insignia of the escadrille (a black swift in full flight) on the left side.

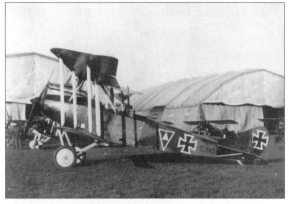

Top left: The Caudron G.3 was one of the best French artillery observation aircraft during the autumn of 1914. This captured aircraft was marked with the German Cross, but was minus its motor at the time of the photo.

Top right: On 24 October 1917, this Rumpler C.IV (No 1454/17) of Fl.Abt. (A) 209, resting at Cramaille, was downed by S/Lt Jules Covin, Spa 31, for his fourth confirmed victory.

Middle left: LVG C.V (No 9574/17, WNr 2575) was brought down by French DCA on 28 November 1917.

Middle right: EV Adelus, bareheaded, and EV1 Guierre (captured 16 September 1917) in front of a Spad VII of

the land-based escadrille de chasse of CAM Dunkerque in 1917.

Bottom left: This Nieuport XVII No 1831, of N 77, was captured after a combat with a two-seater from FlAbt 65 on 23 October 1916. The pilot, Lt Joseph Maria, had obtained three confirmed victories in 1915-1916, as an observer with N 26. He had been with N 77 only two days! In the rear is a British Handley-Page 0/100 bomber, also captured.

Bottom right: This AEG G.IV (No 1131/16) was forced to land at Monchy-Humières on 24 April 1918, by Cpl Lacout and S/Lt Descardes.

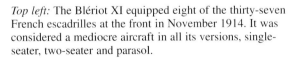

Top left: The Blériot XI equipped eight of the thirty-seven French escadrilles at the front in November 1914. It was considered a mediocre aircraft in all its versions, single-seater, two-seater and parasol.

Top right: A Fokker D-VII destroyed in 1918.

Middle left: S/Lt de Peyerimoff, a pilot of Br 123 in 1918, four confirmed victories.

Middle centre: Capitaine Daniel Fèvre, CO Escadrille C 228, shot down while flying a Morane-Saulnier type P on 19 April 1917, by Ltn Willy Daugs, Jasta 36.

Middle right: S/Lt Joseph Mathieu, 48th Cie d'Aérostiers, photographed in the nacelle of his balloon which was

flamed on 18 August 1917 by Ltn Fritz Pütter, Jasta 9.

Bottom left: Supposing that the next conflict would be a war of movement, the French high command did away with field balloon companies in 1911. It became urgently necessary to adapt the last spherical balloons again at the start of the war due to the intervention of Capitaine Saconney. This balloon regulated the fire of the 1st Heavy Artillery Rgt on the Champagne Front in 1915.

Bottom right: Lancing a captive Caquot balloon in 1917. More efficient than the German balloons, the Caquot balloons constituted one of the means of essential observation employed by the French Army up to the end of the war.

Top left: Shown in March 1917 at Dunkerque, Sopwith 130hp D.21 (No S.H.N1) was shot down in aerial combat 12 May 1917, in the North Sea. The pilot, SM Bernard Vigneau was killed.

Top right: Two pilots from CAM Dunkerque in 1917. Right, EV1 Georges Frot, captured 1 September 1917 after a forced landing in Belgium flying Spad VII No 346.

Middle left: The Nieuport XVII was one of the principal French chasse aircraft. Photographed at Saint Pol sur Mer in June 1917, 5 (No 1781) carries the insignia of the land-based chasse escadrille of CAM Dunkerque: a diving black eagle. The pilot is EV1 Frot, captured on 1 September 1917.

Middle right: Bréguet XIV B2 13 (No 128) overturned during take-off on 6 March 1918.

Bottom left: QM Amiot in front of FBA 150hp D.12 (No 422) at Dunkerque in 1917. He failed to return from a mission in the North Sea on 25 May 1917.

Bottom right: This Maurice-Farman MF.11 of an army bombardment escadrille was named Fatalitas by the crew in 1916. The gunner is QM Vacher.

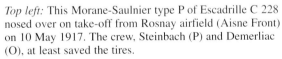

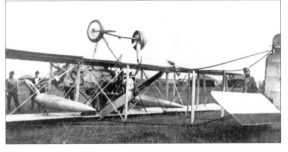

Top left: This Morane-Saulnier type P of Escadrille C 228 nosed over on take-off from Rosnay airfield (Aisne Front) on 10 May 1917. The crew, Steinbach (P) and Demerliac (O), at least saved the tires.

Top right: A Hannover CL.II (No 13369/17) of Schusta 20, on display at Stanislas Plaza in Nancy. It was downed 6 September 1918, at Bayon, by Sgt Florentin, Spa 90, for his first victory, who was himself severely wounded in the combat and died of his wounds.

Middle left: Commandant Antonin Brocard, a pilot since 1911, well-known head of the Groupe de Combat 12, les Cigognes during 1916-1917. He had two confirmed victories while commanding N 3 in 1915, and ended the war as the Under Secretary of State for Aeronautics.

Middle centre: Commandant Louis de Goÿs, an aviator before the war, became the first CO of GB 1 in November

1914. He was captured flying a Voisin on 27 May 1915, during a raid on Ludwigshafen. He escaped on 19 November 1917, and was given command of the 1re Brigade d'Aviation in 1918.

Middle right: S/Lt Georges de Ram, a remarkable observer and excellent shot, obtained four confirmed victories and several probables with Escadrilles MF 8 and N 23.

Bottom left: This N 103 Spad VII rests practically intact on German lines in 1917. It carries the first insignia of the escadrille; a red star with five branches.

Bottom right: Voisin LAP.VIII 25 (No 2058) of the land-based bombing escadrille of CAM Dunkerque, after overturning during a landing at Saint Pol sur Mer on 12 July 1917.

Top left: A mechanic poses before the wreckage of a Caudron G.6 of C 228. The crew, Sgt Barrie/Lt Grau, were killed in the accident at Rosnay, on 24 May 1917.

Top right: The Pfalz D.IIIa (No 8033/17, Wnr 1663) of Offstv Schüschke, Jasta 64w, was captured at Fléville on 27 March 1918, by Sgt Prévost of Spa 68, for his second victory.

Middle left: From left to right: LV Barbier; S/Lt Delesall (CO of the land-based escadrille de chasse of CAM Dunkerque), and S/Lt Nungesser in Spring 1917. Henri Barbier was killed in an accident at Saint Pol sur Mer on 13 July 1917, flying a Sopwith Triplane 12 (No F.12, ex-N5385 RNAS).

Middle right: The metal remains of Zeppelin L 45, downed 20 October 1917 on the shore of the Buech river,

between Lasagnea and Mison. The crew burned it before being captured. Three other Zeppelins (L 44, L 49 & L 50) were also destroyed by French DCA and chasse aircraft on this date.

Bottom left: Sgt Rédempt (P) and S/Lt Canel (O), Br 216, left to regulate heavy artillery fire on 27 June 1918. They were attacked on return from this mission by seven enemy scouts which killed the observer and wounded the pilot, who managed to escape his attackers and landed at Villers-Cotterets in the French lines.

Bottom right: The Salmson 2 A2 was, in 1918, one of the best observation aircraft in the world with the Bréguet XIV A2. N 7 of an unidentified escadrille was tested at Adlershof, after having been captured by the Germans in 1918.

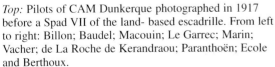

Top: Pilots of CAM Dunkerque photographed in 1917 before a Spad VII of the land- based escadrille. From left to right: Billon; Baudel; Macouin; Le Garrec; Marin; Vacher; de La Roche de Kerandraou; Paranthoën; Ecole and Berthoux.

Middle left: This two-seat Caudron G.4 (No 2235) observation aircraft fell into German hands around 1916.

Bottom left: This Spad XIII (No 497) of N 112 captured by the Germans at the end of 1917, carries the markings of the unit at the rear of the fuselage; two red bands.

Bottom right: Three officers of Escadrille C 11 in 1917. From left to right: Lt Paul Moulines (O); Capt Joseph Vuillemin (P and CO of C 11) and Capt Guy de Lubersac (O). These officers downed several enemy aircraft together, most by Vuillemin who ended the war as CO of the 12 Escadre de Bombardement and credited with 7 confirmed victories. Vuillemin later became the Commander-in-Chief of the French Air Force in 1939/1940.

Top left: The land-based bombardment escadrille of CAM Dunkerque (the most active of all the French Naval Aviation Centres during WW1) utilised Voisin bombers since it was created in February 1915. It was disestablished after its aircraft were destroyed by a German aerial bombardment of Saint Pol sur Mer on 20 September 1917. This Voisin LBP. VIII 30 (No 1826) photographed in July 1917 carried the insignia of the escadrille: a tawny owl on a blue moon, which symbolised the night bombardment of the German positions in Belgium. Its pilot was QM Le Garrec.

Top right: Adj-Chief Maurice Delépine, a chasse pilot who had two Fokker D.VIIIs confirmed and three probable victories with Spa 62 in 1918.

Bottom left: Brothers Lucien (pilot on the left) and Léon (gunner-bombardier on the right) Coupet, of Escadrille

F 25, forming one of the most famous French bombardment crews. Up to the time they were taken prisoner on 7 July 1917, on returning from a raid on Munster, Lucien had already carried out his 150th night bombardment. After the war he became chief pilot for Farman and set several world flying records.

Middle right: Entered into service as a long distance reconnaissance aircraft in 1914, the Morane-Saulnier type L became one of the first chasse aircraft the following year. This parasol (No 114) was captured during winter 1914/1915.

Bottom right: The Caudron G.6, developed in 1916, was a two-seater reconnaissance and observation plane of good quality. This example (No 1950) mostly decorated in white was equipped with Le Rhône 110hp motors.

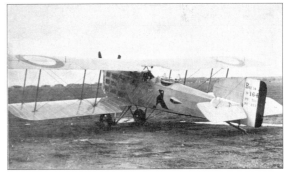

Top left: A Blériot XI one-seater (No 428) in flight in 1914. This version equipped the escadrilles called "de cavalerie" up to the start of 1915.

Top right: A crane raising the wreckage of Sopwith 130hp D.24 (No S.H.N4) of CAM Dunkerque, after an accident on 24 April 1917.

Middle left: This German two-seater bomber was shot down by French infantry at Bray Dunes in December 1914.

Middle right: QM Yves Paranthoën in front of Voisin bomber 27 of CAM Dunkeque in July 1917. This pilot

disappeared in the North Sea 30 July 1918, flying Donnet-Denhaut 200hp D.73 (No 921).

Bottom left: Seaplane FBA 150hp D.10 (No 417) of patrol escadrille from CAM Dunkerque, was downed with three other FBAs on 26 May 1917 in the North Sea. The crew, QM Amiot & EV1 Teste, were captured.

Bottom right: Escadrille Br 11 was transformed into two-seater reconnaissance aircraft, Bréguet XIV A2, at the end of 1917. This Bréguet No 164x carried the insignia of the unit, a red paper bird.

Top left, Top right & Middle left: Three views of LVG B 251/15 (WNr 361) which rests at Vieil-Arcy, after being shot down 13 April 1915.

Middle right: Commandant Maurice Happe, a pioneer of the French bombardment aviation who distinguished himself while commanding MF 29 then GB 4. One confirmed victory. A price was put on his head by the Germans who called him the Red Devil because of the colour of his aircraft. He never hesitated to question his superiors, and as a result was transferred to the Inspectorate of aviation schools in 1917. Dissatisfied, he requested to return to the war as an artillery officer on the

Italian front where he distinguished himself again as an exceptional leader of men. He returned to military aviation after the war.

Bottom left: This Nieuport XXVII bore the insignia of the Escadrille C 30 at the start of 1918. It was probably used for the protection of the two-seater observation Caudron aircraft of the unit.

Bottom right: A piece of the tail fin of LVG C (No 435) captured at Atton, near Pont-à-Mousson, 14 January 1917. The aircraft was exhibited in the Stanislas Plaza in Nancy.

Top left: Navy chasse pilots from CAM Dunkerque, at Saint Pol sur Mer in front of a Spad XIII in October 1918. From left to right, back row: SM Vacher and SM Prévost; front row: QM Bonnaud; Cne Delesalle (CO of the land-based escadrille); EV1 Popieul and SM Martin.

Top right: Adj Antoine Gallois, a pilot of Sop 111, became famous for bombing the Krupp factories in Essen on the night of 6/7 July 1917. He was accompanied by Adj Antoine Paillard and returned without a mishap to the French lines after more than seven hours in the air. Paillard was interned in Holland, due to motor problems, but escaped less than four months later.

Middle left: The Bréguet XIV B2 was probably the best single-engine bomber of WW1, and its success was known throughout the world after the war. This one, photographed in France in 1918, carries the insignia of Br 107 on the fuselage, a white, blue or gold winged serpent, and a personal insignia (a four leaf clover on a white ring) on the tail fin.

Middle right: The Caudron G.3, retired from the front in 1915, had an extraordinary career as a training aircraft, like No 4010 shown here.

Bottom left: A good view of a late Morane-Saulnier type L, around autumn 1915.

Bottom right: An Albatros C.VII downed by DCA near Dieulouard, 23 March 1917.

Top left: The Donnet-Denhaut 200hp D.40 (No 801) of the patrol escadrille of CAM Dunkerque in 1918. The Croix de Guerre with palme awarded to the unit 30 May 1917 is on the front of the hangar. Rarely publicised, the obscure and difficult work of the French navy seaplanes were nevertheless efficient because the navy losses due to torpedoes were finally reduced by 60% at the end of the war.

Top right: An original but little used triplane Lévy-Besson 200hp patrol seaplane of CAM Guernsey in 1918.

Middle right: The Maurice Farman MF.11, also known as type 1914, rendered excellent service as bombing or observation aircraft during the first two years of the war. This example is numbered 177.

Bottom left: A late Nieuport XIII (No 2137) two-seater with a Le Rhône 80hp, used as a training aircraft.

Bottom right: The Morane-Saulnier type N was replaced in the French chasse escadrilles by the Nieuport X single-seater during the summer and autumn of 1915. This Nieuport X (No 446) of N 3 was photographed during the winter of 1915/1916.

Avion allemand abattu par nos canons spéziaux près de Flirey Le 22 Juillet

Avion boche bi-moteurs abattu lors d'un combat a

Top left: S/Lt Emile Stribick, a pilot with Escadrille HF 28, who scored the second confirmed victory of the war on 24 October 1914. He claimed his second on 12 March 1916 with MF 19.

Top right: Sergeant Hott (1 victory on 13 March 1916) in front of his Farman F.40 after crash-landing at Julvécourt during the summer of 1916. This aircraft carried the first insignia of Escadrille F 228 : a star on a moon crescent.

Middle right: The Albatros D.III of Vzfw Willy Kempe, Jasta 34b, downed by anti-aircraft fire at Flirey, on 22 July 1917.

Bottom left: Paul Teste photographed in 1922, then the commander of the Aviation d'Escadre. He was an observer when captured on 26 May 1917, flying FBA 150hp D.10 (No 417) near Gravelines. He escaped in 1918.

Bottom right: The Gotha G.III from Kaghol 2 downed by two Escadrille N 3 pilots on 8 February 1917, at Bouconville, was also on display in Nancy.

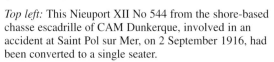

Top left: This Nieuport XII No 544 from the shore-based chasse escadrille of CAM Dunkerque, involved in an accident at Saint Pol sur Mer, on 2 September 1916, had been converted to a single seater.

Top right: The French navy had only pilot schools for seaplanes during WW1. Its land-based chasse pilots were trained at army schools, one student pilot being Fernand Vacher at the school at Pau in February 1917.

Middle left: Farman F.40 (No 2182) of artillery observation Escadrille F 228 on the airfield at Julvécourt, in autumn 1916, Verdun Front.

Bottom left: A Farman F.41bis preparing to take off from Cachy in 1916. Behind it the first Sopwith 1 A2 (No 1) of the French army, carrying the colours of escadrille N 62.

Bottom right: A well-known pilot before the war Jules Védrines in front of his Nieuport XI, christened La Vache (The Cow) in 1916. Better known for his special missions, such as landing a secret agent behind enemy lines then picking him up later, Védrines reported in 1914/1915 two victories which were not confirmed, although one of them fell in the French lines.

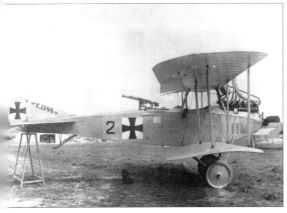

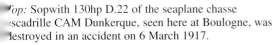

Top: Sopwith 130hp D.22 of the seaplane chasse escadrille CAM Dunkerque, seen here at Boulogne, was destroyed in an accident on 6 March 1917.

Bottom left: A good profile of Albatros C.III 2 (No 1388/16) resting on the airfield of Escadrille F 105 in 1916. On the right is a Farman F.40 of this unit.

Bottom right: The Morane-Saulnier type A1 fighter encountered problems with its Gnôme Monosoupape 150hp motor. Equipped with a less powerful Le Rhône 9 Jb, it was used as a trainer and took under this work the manufacturer's designation of MoS. 30 E1.

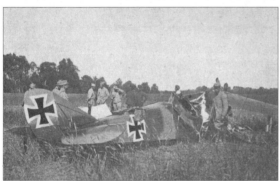

Top: The mechanics at R.G.A. at work on the Hispano-Suiza 150hp motors of Letord 1 (No 17) in 1917. Behind this aircraft are some Caudron G.4s, a Sopwith 1 A2 and a Nieuport XXIII.

Middle left: The remains of a reconnaissance Rumpler C.IV photographed after being downed on 3 June 1917 between Saint-Hilaire and Bouy.

Middle right: This DFW C.V was forced to come down at Baccarat (in Lorraine) on 13 June 1917, after being hit by French anti-aircraft fire.

Bottom left: This Caudron G.4 of Escadrille F 228 at Julvécourt, Verdun Front, during the autumn of 1916.

This plane was armed with a Colt machine-gun in the front and a Lewis in the rear, carried a blue band on the motors and the fuselage, also the escadrille insignia, a rooster profile. The tricoloured wheels were decorated with the Maltese cross.

Bottom right: This Caudron G.4 of Escadrille C 28 was photographed at la Ferme d'Alger airfield, Champagne Front, in April 1916. The cockpit was decorated with a skull and cross bones, the observer is S/Lt Henri Demerliac.

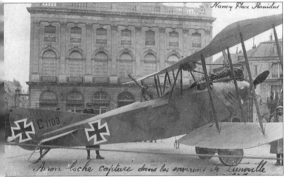

Top left: LVG C.II 5 (No 2160/15, WNr 1468) was forced to land south of Berncourt on 1 June 1916 by a Nieuport of N 31 and a Maurice-Farman of MF 44.

Top right: One of the first victories of the French aviation was this two-seater Aviatik B, shot down near Château-Thierry in March 1915, by the CO of MS 37, Capitaine Quillien.

Middle left: The AEG C.IV (No 1103/16) on display in the celebrated Stanislas Plaza in Nancy, was captured near Lunéville on 23 January 1917.

Middle right: The crews of Escadrille MF 55 talking in front of a two-seater observation Maurice-Farman MF.11, on the airfield at Vinets (Champagne) in January 1916.

Bottom: The Morane-Saulnier type P was a more powerful and better armed derivative of the first parasols type L and LA. It was used by the French Aviation Militaire during 1916/1917.

Top left: Sixteen Sopwith Triplanes were utilised by the French navy from the end of 1916 to the end of 1917, from the airfield at Saint Pol sur Mer in the suburbs of Dunkerque. This one is 17 (No F.8), seen in June 1917 with SM Vacher, who gained 3 victories during the war, standing by.

Top right: This Nieuport XVII (No 2231 of Escadrille N 62) is equipped with Le Prieur rockets in order to flame German balloons.

Middle left: The Morane-Saulnier type N was the first French single-seater fighter constructed in a series. It was equipped with a Hotchkiss machine-gun firing through the axis of the propeller by the use of deflectors, like this No 393 photographed in 1915.

Middle right: Nieuport XVII No 1490 of S/Lt Nungesser, detached to N 124 in July and August 1916. The ace had thirteen confirmed victories by the end of August.

Bottom left: A Salmson 2 A2 of Sal 18 in 1918. The insignia of the escadrille is represented by a man in black who lost his hat in the wind, on a pale blue pennant.

Bottom right: A victim of French artillery, this German two-seater crashed 4 September 1917, near Le Verguier (Aisne), in a sector occupied by British troops.

QM Henri Le Garrec		CAM	P	KIA	Dunkerque, Sopwith Triplane N° 5388 (F15) codé F 13, probably by a Jasta 11 pilot.	
Sgt Gaston Valdemarie &		F 16	P	KIA		
Asp Loth		F 16	O	KIA	AR	
Sgt Edmond Beuchat &		C 229	P	KIA		
Lt Pierre Kolb-Bernard		C 229	O	KIA	Caudron G4	
Capt Alfred Heurtaux CO		N 3	P	WIA	Spad XIII	
Sgt André Corazzini		N 91	P	KIAcc	Nieuport XXIVbis	
Lt Jules Fuzier CO		BM 121	P	KIAcc	Bréguet-Michelin IV	
Capt Louis Masse		N 96	P	Injured	Nieuport	
S/Lt Jean Dombray		Br 117	P	Injured	Bréguet	
Adj Legude		66° Cie d'Aérostiers		XF	15h35, X° Armée.	
			O	OK		
S/Lt Cabanet		70° Cie d'Aérostiers		XF	15h35, X° Armée.	
			O	OK		

4 September

Sgt Artigau		N 15	EA	X	Livry-sur-Meuse	1540	1
S/Lt Madon	a.	N 38	Scout	X	NE Beine		16
Capt Ménard &	CO	GC 15					4
Adj Douchy	b.	N 38	2 seater	XF	Vaudesincourt	0925	8
Adj Gaudermen &		N 68					1
Sgt Baudry		N 68	EA	X	N Bois de Prêtre		1
Lt Thobie &		N 95					1
Cpl Gundelach		N 95	2 seater	XF	E Pinon	1230	1
Sgt Parsons	c.	N 124	Rumpler C	X	Cheppy	0910	1
S/Lt Lufbery		N 124	EA	X	Cheppy	0915	11
QM Malvoisin	*	CAM	Albatros	X			2
???		DCA	2 seater	X	Le Verguier		–
Sgt Petit-Dariel		N 3	EA	P	Forêt d'Houthulst	0845	–
Adj Gouy du Roslan		N 84	EA	P	Forges	1015	–
Lt Robin		N 97	2 seater	P			–
Adj Dupré		N 102	EA	P			–
Sgt Schmitter &		N 103					–
Sgt Pietry		N 103	EA	P	Forêt d'Houthulst	0945	–
Lt de Sevin de Quincy		N 314	EA	P	N Forêt Château Salins		–

* St Pol.
a. Probably Obltn Erich Hahn (6v), CO Jasta 19, KIA Beine.
b. Probably Gefr Auguste Franke & Ltn Friedrich Funke, FlAbt 17, KIAs Vaudesincourt.
c. Probably Uffz Otto Meyer & Ltn Otto Stumpp, FlAbt 278 (A), KIAs Avocourt, about 3 km W Avocourt.

Casualties:

Capt Gaston Luc-Pupat		N 79	P	KIA	Spad N° 626, by MFlakZug 36 during a balloon attack.
S/Lt Jean Lasnier,		R 214	P	KIA	Letord, probably by Ltn Karl
Lt André Garret-Flandy &		R 214	O	KIA	Odebrett, Jasta 16b, (7).
Sgt Paolaggi		R 214	G	KIA	XF Verdun Sector.
Lt Louis Verdier-Fauvety		N 65	P	WIA	Spad
Lt Dominique Ciechowski		GC 13	P	WIA	Spad
MdL Naud		F 20	P	WIA	Letord
Asp Louis Potier		C 227	O	WIA	Sopwith
Brig René Lemaitre		N 78	P	KIAcc	Spad
???		48° Cie d'Aérostiers			Damaged by a bomb dropped by an aircraft.
???		72° Cie d'Aérostiers			Attacked, not flamed Dunkerque Sector.

5 September

Cpl Rounds		N 112	EA	X	E Vauquois	1745	1
Sgt Coiffard		N 154	Albatros C	XF	Le Catelet		1
S/Lt Laporte		N 15	EA	P	Bois de Montfaucon	0845	–
Lt Bastien &		F 32					–
S/Lt de Font Reault &		F 32					–
Brig Alteri &		F 5					–
S/Lt Cousin	a.	F 5	EA	P	Douaumont		–
MdL de Montrichard		N 95	2 seater	P			–
Lt Hugues &		N 81					–
Adj Herbelin		N 81	EA	P	Very	1605	–

Adj Pillon	N 82	2 seater	P	Bruyères	1115	–
Adj Bourdet,	N 112					–
Sgt Montague &	N 112					–
Sgt Reynaud	N 112	EA	P	Rouvroy	1340	–
S/Lt Lufbery	N 124	EA	P	Louvemont		–
Capt Menj CO	GC 16	EA	P	Samogneux		–
Lt de Comando &	F 33					–
S/Lt des Essarts	F 33	EA	FTL			–

a.   Possibly Ltn Moritz Raabe (O), FlAbt 284 (A), KIA Bezonvaux, about 3 km NE Douaumont.

Casualties:

Lt Nissim de Camondo &	F 33	P	KIA	
S/Lt Louis des Essarts	F 33	O	KIA	AR
Sgt Paul Bonnans	N 82	P	KIA	Nieuport XXIVbis N 3316, Bonne-Maison-La Cense, X° Armée.
MdL Jacques Thabaud-Deshoulières &	V 53	P	KIA	Caudron G6, probably by Uffz Krause, Kest 3, (1), or
Lt Marcel Mulard	V 53	O	KIA	Ltn Werner Voss, Jasta 10, (41).
Sgt Maurice Leroux &	F 215	P	KIA	Morane-Saulnier Parasol, probably
Lt Pierre Goutier	F 215	O	KIA	by Ltn Theodor Rumpel, Jasta 16b, (2).
Cpl Louis Charton	N 92	P	POW	Nieuport XXIVbis N° 4641
MdL Bourideys	BM 119	P	POW	Bréguet-Michelin IV N° 280
MdL Heer	BM 119	P	POW	Bréguet-Michelin IV
Adj Roger Leclerc	N 96	P	WIA	Flak, Nieuport
Lt Paul Gastin	N 15	P	WIA	Spad VII
Lt de Bonnaventure	F 7	O	WIA	Bréguet
S/Lt Lescure	F 223	O	WIA	AR
Cpl Alphonse Chagniat	F 216	P	Injured	Sopwith
Cpl Bouscailloux	F 41	G	Injured	Motorcycle
Cpl Bailet	F 130	P	Injured	Farman 40
Sol Emile Guignard	???	M	Injured	
Lt Gadel	47° Cie d'Aérostiers	XF		Probably by Ltn Ludwig
		O	OK	Hanstein (10), Jasta 16b.
Lt Moreaux	31° Cie d'Aérostiers			Attacked. not flamed,
		O	OK	Nancy Sector
???	33° Cie d'Aérostiers			Attacked, not flamed,
		O	OK	Dunkerque Sector.

6 September

Sgt Renaux	N 86	Scout	X	Samogneux	1010	2
Brig Cathelin &	N 96					1
Cpl Mulon	N 96	Scout	X	Aumenancourt		1
Cpl Rheno	N 80	EA	X	Samogneux	1120	2
Adj Herbelin	N 81	EA	P	S Montfaucon	1030	–
Adj Pillon	N 82	EA	P	Monthiny-Courpières		–
S/Lt Lufbery	N 124	EA	P	Bezonvaux	0955	–

Casualties:

Sgt Henri Callinet	N 86	P	MIA	Spad VII, probably by a Jasta 23b pilot.
Cpl Gaston Joblot &	F 130	P	POW	Farman 40, N° 2562,
Brig de Massia	F 130	G	POW	possibly by Flakbatterie 324.
Cpl Everett T Buckley (American)	N 65	P	POW	Spad VII N° 2118, probably by a Jasta 23b pilot.
MdL Barbe &	Sop 128	P	KIA	Sopwith N° 3253, probably by Ltn
Sol Bartaire	Sop 128	G	KIA	Wilhelm Lehmann, Jasta 5, (1).
Adj Jean Carre &	F 55	P	KIA	Sopwith, fell in no-man's land,
S/Lt Jacques Arnoux	F 55	O	WIA	Arnoux rescued 26 hours later by a French patrol.
Sgt Pierre de Cuyper	R 46	G	WIA	Letord
Sgt Henri Crémieux	R 46	O	WIA	Letord
MdL Marius Botte &	C 47	P	Injured	
MdL Vermorel	C 47	G	Injured	Caudron G4
Cpl Henri Cleroux	GDE	P	Injured	Farman 42
Sgt Maurice Allain	VB 101	P	Injured	Voisin P

7 September

Adj Quette	N 62	EA	X	NE Réservoir		2
S/Lt Busson	N 82	EA	X			1
Sgt G Guérin	N 15	EA	P	Septsarges	1800	–

Adj Pillon	N 82	2 seater	P	Pinon	1700	–
Sgt Pinot	N 84	EA	P	Very-Montfaucon	1745	–
Casualties:						
S/Lt Altairac	R 213	P	WIA	Bréguet		
Sgt Cochet	F 221	P	WIA	Sopwith		
Cpl Charles Ireland	C 224	P	Injured	Morane Parasol		

8 September

MdL Marinovitch &	N 94					1
S/Lt Parizet	N 94	Albatros DV	X	St Hilaire-le-Petit		1
MdL Bois &	N 95					1
Cpl Stehlin	N 95	2 seater	XF	Laffaux-Allemont		1
Casualties:						
Sol Gatouillat	C 104	M	KIAcc	Farman 40		
Sol Thermes	C 104	M	KIAcc	Sopwith		
S/Lt Carchereux	C 104	O	Injured	Caudron G4		
Sgt Bernard &	GDE	P	Injured			
Asp Duroux	GDE	O	Injured	Nieuport XII		
S/Lt Guette	F 204	O	Injured	Car accident		

9 September

MdL Picard &	N 83					1
MdL Humber	N 83	Scout	XF	Haumont		2
Sgt Pernelle	N 103	EA	X	NE Ypres	1525	1
Lt Privat	N 65	EA	P	Woël		–
???	???	2 EA	P	Dunkirk		–
Casualties:						
S/Lt Henri Mauduit	N 86	P	KIAcc	Spad VII		
Sgt Martinez	GDE	P	KIAcc	AR		
Sol Rignols	GDE	M	Injured			
MdL Gilbert	GDE	P	Injured	Farman 40		
MdL Rivoire	C 227	P	Injured	Sopwith		
S/Lt Berthon	93° Cie d'Aérostiers		XF	Probably by Ltn Erich		
		O	OK	Löwenhardt (4), Jasta 10.		

10 September

Sgt Quette	N 62	EA	X	Filain		3
Lt Delrieu &	N 150					2
Asp Dorizon	N 150	EA	X	N Aspach-le-Bas	1125	1
???	DCA	EA	X			–
Sgt G Guérin	N 15	EA	P	S Bois de Caures	1845	–
MdL Majon de la Débuterie	N 48	EA	P	Werkem		–
Sgt Petit-Delchet	N 69	2 seater	P	Chavignon	1700	–
S/Lt Nungesser	V 116	EA	P	Dunkirk Sector		–
???	N 150	EA	P	Filain		–
???	???	EA	P	Dunkirk		–
???	???	EA	P	Vawinay		–
Casualties:						
Capt Georges Matton	N 48	P	KIA	Spad VII N° 2416, probably by Ltn Josef Jacobs, Jasta 7, (7).		
Sgt Jules Tiberghien	N 31	P	MIA	Spad VII N° 1746, probably by Ltn Werner Voss, Jasta 10, (46).		
Adj Edmond Pillon	N 82	P	WIA	Spad VII, X° Armée.		
Adj Pierre Petit-Dariel	N 3	P	WIA	Spad VII		
MdL André Lefort	N 102	P	WIA	Spad		
Sol Lancon	F 25	M	KIAcc	Farman		

11 September

Lt Favre &	N 78					1
Sgt Bredin	N 78	EA	X	Aubérive-Prosnes		2
Sgt Caël	N 102	EA	X	E Dixmude		3
Brig G Paumier,	N 155					1
Cpl Chancerel &	N 155					1
Cpl Bettend	N 155	2 seater	XF	Moronvillers		1
S/Lt Bozon-Verduraz	N 3	2 seater	P	Forêt d'Houthulst	1620	–
Adj de Dreux	N 12	EA	P			–

S/Lt Madon	N 38	Scout	P	S Semide-Liry		–
Adj A Bordes,	N 65					–
Sgt Schlax &	N 65					–
MdL Foucher	N 65	EA	P	Béthincourt-Driancourt		–
S/Lt Rougevin-Baville	N 67	2 seater	FTL	Chevregny	0920	–
S/Lt Willemin &	N 67					–
Adj Toulze	N 67	2 seater	FTL	Itancourt	1325	–
MdL de Boigne	N 82	2 seater	P	Forêt de St Gobain		–
Sgt Pinot	N 84	EA	P	Vilosnes		–
Adj J Bordes &	N 90					–
Sgt Ambrogi	N 90	EA	P	Varviney		–
Adj Martenot de Cordoux	N 94	2 seater	P	W Beine		–
Adj Bourdet	N 112	EA	P	Bois de Consenvoye		–
Casualties:						
Capt Georges Guynemer	N 3	P	KIA	Spad XIII N° 504, claimed by Ltn Kurt Wissemann of Jasta 3, (5).		
S/Lt Robert de Bruce	N 75	P	MIA	Spad XIII, over Consenvoye		
MdL Jules Tabariès	Br 209	G	WIA	DOW 13 September 1917, Bréguet.		
Sgt Delorme	F 25	P	KIAcc	Farman		
Sol Vrot	N 37	M	KIAcc	Hit by propellor on ground.		
Capt Jean Moreau de Bonrepos	3° CA	P	KIAcc	In a car accident.		
Cpl André Chapelle	N 85	P	Injured	Nieuport		
Sgt Petitfrère	V 109	G	Injured	Voison P		
Adj René Jolly	VB 101	P	Injured	Voisin P		
Sgt Armand Weyl	RGAé	P	Injured	AR		

---

12 – 13 September – No Claims – No Casualties

---

14 September

Adj-Chef Fonck	N 103	2 seater	X	Poelcapelle	1635	12
Casualties:						
Sgt Kaminski &	F 63	P	Injured			
S/Lt Comps	F 63	O	Injured			
Sgt Lombard &	R 209	P	Injured			
S/Lt Duffaut	R 209	O	Injured			

---

15 September

Groupe de Combat 11 starts its move from the Flanders Sector back to the Champagne, VI° Armée Sector.

Adj-Chef Fonck	N 103	EA	XF	Zonnebeke-Poelcapelle	1610	13
Lt Lagache	N 3	Scout	P	Courtrai	1450	–
Adj Douchy	N 38	2 seater	P	Four de Paris		–
Adj Baron	N 103	EA	P	Poelcapelle	1355	–
Casualties:						
Sgt Berteaux	C 10	G	WIA	Letord		
MdL Jean di Meglio &	RGAé	P	Injured			
Sol Pous	RGAé	M	Injured	Morane Parasol		

---

16 September

Sgt Lacroix &	N 23					1
S/Lt de Beauchamp	N 23	Scout	X	N Bezonvaux		1
Lt Darnaud & CO	Sop 123					1
MdL Jeanniot	Sop 123					1
MdL Thuillier &	Sop 123					1
MdL Haubtmann	Sop 123	Scout	X	Stuttgart		3
S/Lt Rebourg &	N 77					1
Sgt Boyau	N 77	Balloon	XF	Haie Vauthier	1500	8
???	DCA	EA	XF	N Bermericourt		–
Adj Bellet &	Sop 129					–
Sol Sauvaget	Sop 129					–
Adj Béranger &	Sop 29					–
Sol Tixier	Sop 29					–
??? &	Sop 29					–
Sol Albrecht	Sop 29	EA	X	Legelbach		–
Adj Jailler	N 15	EA	P	Bois de Consenvoye		–
Sgt Quette	N 62	EA	P	Filain		–

MdL Sauclière		N 79	EA	P		N Ribemont	–
Adj Richard &		F 220					–
S/Lt Ambreau		F 220	EA	P		Bois de Bezonvaux	–
???		???	EA	P		Sarbourg	–
???		???	EA	P		Chamouille	–

Casualties:

Brig Jean Marquis &	Sop 131	P	MIA	Sopwiths, probably by Ltn Walter
S/Lt Paul Lavigne	Sop 131	O	MIA	Kypke, Jasta 41, (3), & Ltn Hans
Brig Emile Grandry &	Sop 131	P	MIA	Weiss, Jasta 41, (1).
Adj-Chef Jean Simon	Sop 131	G	MIA	One Sopwith N° 3161.
MdL Pierre Canivet &	Sop 123	P	POW	Sopwith N° 3154, probably
S/Lt Jean Blehaut	Sop 123	O	POW	by Vfw G Nestler, Kest 4a (1).
EV1 Gabriel Guierre, *	CAM	P	POW	Donnet-Denhaut 200HP N° 601,
EV1 Levesque & *	CAM	O	POW	codé D.40. Shot down
QM Bienvenu *	CAM	G	POW	by U-Boat UC.4, at Shouven Bank, North Sea.
MdL Pierre Thuillier &	Sop 123	P	OK	
MdL Louis Haubtmann	Sop 123	G	WIA	Sopwith
Adj Charles Béranger &	Sop 29	P	OK	
Sol Raymond Tixier	Sop 29	G	WIA	Sopwith
Sgt Robert Kaminski &	F 63	P	KIAcc	
S/Lt Marcel Comps	F 63	O	Injured	Sopwith
Lt Morisseau	C 105	O	Injured	Caudron G6
Lt Pierre Châteauvieux	C 10	P	Injured	Caudron G6
S/Lt André Perrissin-Pirasset	49° Cie d'Aérostiers		XF	Possibly by Obltn Otto Schmidt,
		O	OK	Jasta 29, (9).
S/Lt Armand Bousquet	79° Cie d'Aérostiers			Attacked, not flamed.
		O	OK	

* Dunkerque.

---

17 September

Lt Neyret,	CO	C 39					1
S/Lt Le Gallic &		C 39					1
Sol Gisors		C 39	Scout	X		Condé-dur-Suippe	2
Sgt Calmon	a.	N 49	2 seater	X		W Aspach	0820	1
S/Lt Boudoux d'Hautefeuille &		N 77					3
S/Lt Rebourg	b.	N 77	EA	XF		Forêt de Baccarat	2
Infantry fire	c.		2 seater	X		Le Crotoir Ferme	–
???	d.	DCA	2 seater	X			–
Adj Arnoux &		N 49					–
Sgt Butcher		N 49	EA	P		Aspach	1030	–

a. Possibly Flg Edgar Haustein & Ltn Hermann Grafen, FlAbt 282 (A), KIAs.
b. Possibly Gefr Berthold Gall & Obltn Heinrich Schmidt, FlAbt (A) 281, KIAs.
c. Probably Ltn Gerhard Zantz & Ltn Friedrich Junghaus, FlAbt 277 (A), KIAs.
d. Albatros CXII N 1221/17, Ltn Ludwig Roth & Ltn Walter Heiss, FlAbt 46, KIAs, Regnieville, AOK "C" Sector.

Casualties:

Brig Guillot &	F 45	P	MIA	
Lt Paul Gorge	F 45	O	MIA	Farman 60
Lt Jean de la Motte &	F 216	P	Injured	
Lt Carbonnier	F 216	O	Injured	Sopwith

---

18 September

Adj Herisson &		N 75					3
Cdt de Marancour	CO a.	GC 14	2 seater	X		S Damloup	5
S/Lt de Rochechouart de Mortemart &		N 23					–
Adj Bourdet		N 112	EA	P		Béthincourt	–
Patrol		Spa 80	EA	P		Jurnelles d'Ornes	–
Lt de Maison Rouge		N 124	EA	P		Dannevoux	–

a. Probably Flg Karl Breinig & Ltn Hermann Bagel, FlAbt 211 (A), KIAs Damloup.

Casualties:

Sgt Jean-Marie Duport	N 84	P	MIA	Spad VII, over Bois de Caures, probably by a Jasta 21 pilot.
Cpl Pierre Prost &	F 215	P	KIA	
S/Lt du Dresnay	F 215	O	KIA	Morane-Saulnier Parasol
Adj Charles Albanel &	F 24	P	Injured	
MdL Riegel	F 24	G	Injured	Sopwith

Brig Léon Payre	F 41	P	Injured	AR		
MdL de Castellane	PS 125	G	Injured	Paul Schmitt		
???	80° Cie d'Aérostiers			Both attacked, not flamed,		
???	86° Cie d'Aérostiers			Nancy Sector.		

19 September

MdL Septier &	C 13					1
S/Lt van Coehorn	C 13	Scout	X			1
Sgt Peterson,	N 124					1
Sgt Marr,	N 124					1
Sgt Desthuilliers,	F 44					1
Sgt Dauguet &	F 44					1
MdL Viallet	F 44	Albatros DV	X	Montfaucon	1540	1
Lt Dupont &	F 14					–
???	F 14	EA	P			–
S/Lt Ortoli &	N 31					–
S/Lt Covin	N 31	EA	P	Festieux		–
S/Lt Madon	N 38	EA	P	S Semide-Liry		–
Sgt Montrion &	N 48					–
Sgt Caillaux	N 48	EA	P	W Ville-au-Bois		–
Capt Sabattier de						
Vignolle, CO	N 48					–
Sgt Montrion &	N 48					–
Sgt Dousinelle	N 48	EA	P	Parfondu		–
Sgt Tassou	N 73	EA	P	Langemarck	0905	–
S/Lt de Bonnefoy	N 84	EA	P	S Avocourt		–

Casualties:

Cpl Marcel Vassal	N 80	P	MIA	Spad VII, probably by a Jasta 23b pilot.
Cpl Abrahem &	C 64	P	MIA	Caudron G4, X° Armée, probably by
Sol Mauvillier	C 64	G	MIA	Uffz Martin Mallmann, Jasta 19, (2).
S/Lt Paul Basse	C 30	O	KIA	Caudron G6
S/Lt Niels Paulli-Krause &	F 2	P	WIA	Flak, Letord, X° Armée
S/Lt Jean Poirault	F 2	O	OK	
Lt Joseph Dupont	F 14	P	WIA	AR

20 September

S/Lt de Rochechouart						
de Mortemart &	N 23					–
Adj Bourdet	N 112	EA	P	Béthincourt		–
Adj Tassou	N 73	EA	P	Langemarck		–

Casualties:

Sgt Henri Mayoussier	???	P	KIAcc	
Brig Maurice Arnal &	F 201	P	Injured	
Sol Resbeuf	F 201	M	Injured	AR
Cpl Roux	F 20	G	Injured	Caudron R4

21 September

Lt Casale,	N 23					9
S/Lt de Rochechouart						
de Mortemart &	N 23					3
Adj Melin a.	N 23	EA	X	N Douaumont		1
Sgt Montrion &	N 48					4
Sgt Dousinelle	N 48	2 seater	XF	Festieux-Coutisy	1830	1
Sgt Rodde	N 69	2 seater	X	N Chevreux	1830	3
Adj Hasdenteufel	N 57	EA	P	Ostel	1730	–
QM Malvoisin *	CAM	Albatros D	P	E Dixmude		–

a. Probably Ltn Friedrich Weber, Jasta 21, KIA Louvremont, about 6 km NW Douaumont.
* Dunkerque.

Casualties:

Sgt Hervé	GDE	P	KIAcc	Nieuport XXIII
S/Lt Louis Mathey	GDE	P	KIAcc	Nieuport XXIII

22 September

63° RA, Lt Michel &	DCA					–
S/Lt de Rochechouart						
de Mortemart &	N 23					4

Adj Herisson	N 75	Rumpler C	POW	E Cumières	1038	4
Sgt Montrion &	N 48					5
Sgt Dousinelle	N 48	Albatros C	X	NE Courtecon	1110	2
Sgt Quette &	N 62					4
Sgt L Blanc	N 62	EA	X	Courtecon		1
Brig Fontaine,	F 71					2
Lt Meunier &	F 71					1
Sgt du Bois d'Aische	F 71	Albatros D	XF	German lines		5
Brig Fontaine,	F 71					3
Lt Meunier &	F 71					2
Sgt du Bois d'Aische	F 71	2 seater	X	German lines		6
Lt Vernin	N 75	2 seater	X	Rozieler	0955	3
S/Lt Rebourg &	N 77					3
Sgt Boyau	N 77	Balloon	XF	Cirey-Bois-Bertram	1850	9
Adj Peronneau &	N 81					1
Adj de Cazenove de Pradines	N 81	Halb C X	Brimont			3
S/Lt Lufbery	N 124	2 seater	X	E Cheppy	1425	12
???	GC 15	EA	X	Grigny		–
Capt Sabattier de						
Vignolle & CO	N 48					1
Sgt Caillaux	N 48	2 seater	X	Fismes	1110	1
Sgt Quette &	N 62					–
Sgt L Blanc	N 62	EA	P	Corbeny		–
Sgt Beauregard	N 69	EA	P	Amifontaine		–
Adj-Chef Fonck	N 103	EA	P	Belgium		–
S/Lt Lufbery	N 124	EA	P	Cheppy		–
???	???	EA	P	St Mihiel		–

Casualties:

MdL Marcel Paris	N 65	P	KIA	Spad VII #1771 ??.	
MdL Raoul Huet &	C 122	P	KIA		
MdL Georges Bonneau &	VC 116	P	POW		
Sgt Decampenaert	VC 116	G	POW	Voisin LAP N° 2368.	
Lt Tessier	C 122	O	WIA	DOW, Caudron G6	
Adj-Chef Charles					
Kaciterlin &	Br 117	P	WIA	Bréguet 14	
Adj Albert Cambray	Br 117	B	OK		
S/Lt Nicodeau	F 203	O	Injured	Farman	
S/Lt Laurens	VC 116	O	Injured	VLAP	
Sgt Jacques Coll	C 104	P	Injured	Sopwith	
S/Lt Charles Tian	26° Cie d'Aérostiers	XF		Probably by Ltn Otto Förster,	
		O	OK	Jasta 15, (1).	
???	34° Cie d'Aérostiers			These three attacked, not flamed, Nancy Sector.	
???	63° Cie d'Aérostiers				
???	86° Cie d'Aérostiers			Observers jumped OK.	
???	92° Cie d'Aérostiers			Attacked, not flamed	
		O	OK	Soissons Sector.	

23 September

S/Lt Covin,	N 31					3
Adj Poreaux &	N 31					3
MdL de Freycinet	N 31	2 seater	X	Brimont	1250	1
S/Lt Testulat,	C 39					2-3
Lt Astruc &	C 39					1-2
Sol Auzat	C 39	2 EA	X	Guignicourt		1-2
Sgt Boyau	a. N 77	2 seater	X	Coincourt	1125	10
Sgt Dhôme	b. N 81	2 seater	X	NW Somme-Tourbe		3
Cpl Mulon	N 96	EA	X	Maison-Rouge		2
Adj-Chef Fonck	N 103	Albatros D	X	Forêt d'Houthulst	0910	14
Capt d'Astier de Vigerie	N 88	EA	P	Forêt de Coucy		–

a.   Possibly Vfw Stiller & Ltn Kuhne, FlAbt A 241.
b.   Probably Vfw Ferdinand Rüdersscheidt & Ltn Edwin Schwarz, FlAbt 270 (A), KIAs, Somme-Tourbe.

Casualties:

MdL Jules Petrie	N 96	P	KIA	Nieuport XXIVbis N° 4610.
Cpl Albert Mulon	N 96	P	KIA	Nieuport XXIVbis N° 3319.
				Both of these were probably victims of Ltn Walter Böning, Jasta 19, (5 & 6).

Adj Joseph Sellier &	C 28	P	KIA			
Lt Pierre Janet	C 28	O	KIA	Sopwith		
Sgt Gaston Planque	F 35	P	WIA	Flak, Letord		
Cpl Pinatel	Br 117	G	WIA	Bréguet 14		
Sgt Paul Dutherou &	F 2	P	KIAcc			
S/Lt Coreau	F 2	O	Injured	AR, X° Armée.		
Adj Louis Planson &	F 216	P	Injured			
S/Lt Jourde	F 216	O	Injured	Sopwith		
Cpl Daniel Mendaille &	C 229	P	Injured			
S/Lt Andreu	C 229	O	Injured	Sopwith		
Asp Burfin	F 59	O	Injured	AR		
Cpl Allard	MS 215	P	Injured	Morane-Saulnier Parasol		
Sgt René Marie	CEP 115	P	Injured			

24 September

Sgt Philibert	N 12	2 seater	X	Presles		1
Capt d'Aymery	N 31	EA	X	Laon		1
Adj Bertrand,	N 57					4
S/Lt Fraissinet &	N 57					1
Adj Nuville	N 57	Albatros C	X	Laval-Pompelle	1435	1
Adj Poreaux	N 31	EA	P	Etouvelle		–
Sgt Dousinelle	N 48	AEG C	P	Saliscourt	1130	–
Lt Brun	N 102	EA	P			–
Sgt R Rockwell	N 124	EA	P			–

Casualties:

Sgt Douglas MacMonagle (American)	N 124	P	KIA	Spad VII N° 2119, Thiaucourt	
Capt Guy d'Aymery	N 31	P	POW	Spad VII N° 2466, probably by Ltn.z.S Theo Osterkamp, MFJ1, (6).	
S/Lt André &	F 72	O	WIA		
Sol Couraux	F 72	G	WIA	Letord	
Cpl Michel &	F 130	P	Injured		
Cpl Szopinski	F 130	G	Injured	Farman 40	
MdL Pernet	34° Cie d'Aérostiers			Both attacked, not flamed,	
???	86° Cie d'Aérostiers			Nancy Sector, Observers OK.	

25 September

Cdt de Marancour, CO	GC 14					6
Adj Herisson &	N 75					5
Lt Vernin	N 75	Albatros C	X	NE St Mihiel	1730	4
MdL L Rampillon	N 76	2 seater	X	NW Craonne		2
Lt Hay de Slade &	N 86					4
Sgt Renaux	N 86	Albatros D3	XF	Dompierre	1230	3
???	GB 5	2 EA	X	Moinville		–
Patrol	N 86	Albatros	P	Hannonville		–

Casualties:

Sgt Maurice Becque	N 85	P	MIA	Spad N° 1114, 12h00, possibly the victim of Vfw Fischer & Ltn Wegener, FlAbt 205 (A).	
Lt Gaëtande La Brunetière	N 69	P	MIA	Spad VII, 08h45 during combat with a two-seater NW Bois de Corbeny.	
Sgt Vasseur &	Br 120	P	MIA		
S/Lt de Billy	Br 120	O	MIA	Bréguet 14	
Capt François Lafont &	F 41	P	KIA	Morane-Saulnier Parasol, probably	
Lt Henri de Nonancourt	F 41	O	KIA	by Ltn Ludwig Hanstein, Jasta 16b, (11).	
Asp Boursier	F 223	O	WIA	Sopwith	
MdL David de Conflans	F 45	P	Injured	AR	
S/Lt Vincent	F 71	O	Injured	AR	

26 September

Capt Mouronval CO a.	N 77	EA	POW			1
Patrol b.	N 75	EA	P	Forêt d'Apremont	1720	–

a.   Possibly Ltn Fischer & Ltn Ertner, FlAbt 12 flying DFW C N° 2080/17.
b.   Possibly Uffz Otto Bergen, killed, & Ltn Rein, OK, FlAbt 46, AOK "C" Sector.

Casualties:

Adj Etienne Ronserail	N 75	P	POW	Spad VII N° 10.	
MdL Georges Chaney	BM 119	P	KIA		

Sol Rammaert	BM 119	G	WIA	Bréguet-Michelin IV		
Sgt Jean Latapie &	F 14	P	WIA	Flak		
Lt Jules Roiesnel	F 14	O	KIA	Flak, Sopwith		
S/Lt Lanhumier	C 34	O	WIA	Bombardment of Airfield.		
Sgt Marc Eymery	GDE	P	KIAcc	Nieuport XXIII		
Adj Torhare &	F 60	P	Injured			
Sol Pierreni	F 60	M	Injured	Sopwith		
Brig Joseph Michelet	VB 109	P	Injured	Voisin P		
S/Lt Jules Lebeau	F 44	P	Injured	Car accident.		

27 September

Lt Deullin	N 73	EA	X	E Dixmude	1805	18
Lt Busson	N 82	EA	XF	German lines		1
Sgt Montrion	N 48	Balloon	P			–
Adj-Chef Fonck	N 103	Scout	P	Zonnebeke	1100	–
Casualties:						
Sgt Augustin Thevenin &	C 108	P	KIAcc	Sopwith		
Sol Joseph Turroc	C 108	M	Injured	DOW 28 September 1917		

28 September – No Claims

Casualties:					
MdL Noël Fontaine	N 26	P	WIA	Spad VII N° 3033, 13h00 at la Chapelle.
S/Lt Félix Challeux	???	O	WIA	
MdL Jacques Mortureux	N 26	P	Injured	Spad VII N° 1513, at 12h30.
S/Lt Florent Demarle	N 81	P	Injured	Spad VII
Sgt Louis Jousselin &	C 222	P	Injured	
S/Lt Mazet	C 222	O	Injured	Sopwith

29 September

Adj Douchy	N 38	EA	P	Four de Paris	–
Patrol	N 103	EA	P	E Dixmude	1610	–
Capt Vuillemin &	(1)				–
Crew from	C 11	EA	P	Verdun Sector	–
Capt Vuillemin &	(1)				–
Crew from	C 11	EA	FTL	Verdun Sector	–
(1) CO Secteur Aéronautique 2° Corps d'Armée.					
Casualties:					
Cpl Pierre Pelleteret &	VB 101	P	POW		
Sol Pasquinnet	VB 101	B	POW	Voisin LAP N° 2330.	
SM Ernest Gavoin	PilSch	P	KIAcc	Hourtin	
Cpl Perot	PS 127	P	Injured	Paul Schmitt	
Sgt Jean Duclos	GDE	P	Injured	Morane-Saulnier Parasol	

30 September

Lt de Sevin &	N 12					5
Adj de Dreux	N 12	EA	X			1
Lt de Sevin,	N 12					6
Adj de Dreux &	N 12					2
Adj de La Fregeolière	N 12	EA	X			1
Sgt Prou	N 26	2 seater	X	Poperinghe		1
Adj Mion,	C 27					1
S/Lt Mouchet &	C 27					1
Sol Gaillard	C 27	Scout	X	Soissons		1
Adj Bardin,	C 46					1
Sgt Wolff &	C 46					1
Cpl Ballot	C 46	EA	X	St Quentin		1
Sgt Montrion	N 48	2 seater	X	Chevy	1130	6
Lt de Turenne &	N 48					6
Sgt Montrion	N 48	Albatros C	X	Forêt de Pinon	1130	7
Capt Devese,	C 61					1
Adj Griffoul &	C 61					1
MdL Massas &	C 61					1
S/Lt Remlinger,	C 61					1
Lt Phillipe &	C 61					1
???	C 61	Scout	X	Brimont		–

Sgt Quette &	N 62					5
Sgt L Blanc	N 62	EA	X	Corbeny		2
Lt Sejourne,	N 65					1
Med-Aux Camplan &	N 65					3
MdL Le Boucher	N 65	2 seater	XF			2
Adj-Chef Fonck &	N 103					15
Adj Dupré	N 102	2 seater	XF	La Lovie	1100	2
???	GC	EA	X	Laon		–
???	GC	EA	X	Laon		–
S/Lt Coignard,	N 154					1
MdL Gassin &	PS 126					1
Sol Taulera	PS 126	Albatros D	X	St Quentin		1
S/Lt Dutrou,	C 39					–
Lt Astruc &	C 39					–
Adj Gérard	C 39	EA	P	Guignicourt		–
Sgt de Marmier	N 112	EA	P	Verdun		–
Sgt de Marmier	N 112	EA	P	Verdun		–
???	GC	2 EA	P	Soissons Sector		–

Casualties:

MdL François de Villeneuve,	R 46	P	MIA	Letord, probably by Ltn
Sgt Charles Durand &	R 46	G	MIA	Heinrich Gontermann, Jasta
Cpl Gaston Deschamps	R 46	G	MIA	15, (38).
Sgt Raoul Jourjon &	F 55	P	MIA	
Cpl de Scoraille	F 55	G	MIA	Sopwith N° 3154 ??.
S/Lt Gontier	F 55	O	WIA	Sopwith
Asp André de Baubigny &	C 39	P	WIA	
S/Lt Sadi Rassat	C 39	O	KIA	Caudron G6
Lt Laurent Aguillenty &	Sop 128	P	KIAcc	
S/Lt Vivies	Sop 128	O	Injured	Sopwith
Adj-Chef René Fonck	N 103	P	Injured	Spad XIII N° 526, landing accident, at La Lovie.
MdL Henri Petrequin	C 122	P	Injured	Caudron G6
Sgt Curtiss,	R 213	P	Injured	
S/Lt Boulmier &	R 213	O	Injured	
Cpl Courtois	R 213	G	Injured	Letord

1 October

Capt Tourangin	CO	N 89					1
S/Lt d'Hautefeuille &		N 77					4
Sgt Boyau	a.	N 77	2 seater	XF	N Champenoux	1200	11
Sgt Gilet	b.	N 86	2 seater	X	Ville-en-Woëvre	1710	2
Sgt Artigau		N 15	EA	P			–
S/Lt Jailler		N 15	EA	P	Soissons Sector		–
Sgt Jones		N 124	EA	P	Soissons Sector		–
Sgt Rodde		N 69	EA	P	S Laon		–

a.   Probably Ltn Hans Frowein & Ltn Oskar Sigg FlAbt 12, KIAs Champenoux.
b.   Probably Rumpler C IV 6752, Ltn Arno Ebersbach & Ltn Max Kingler, FlAbt 9, KIAs at Hennemont Wald, near Verdun.

Casualties:

Cpl Georges Creuze &	V 101	P	MIA	
MdL Caron de La Carrière	V 101	B	MIA	Voisin LAP
Sgt Andrew C Campbell (American)	N 124	P	KIA	Spad VII N° 4245, probably by Uffz Andreas (1) & Vfw Ritzscherle (1), of SchSt 8.
Capt François d'Astier de La Vigerie	CO	Spa 88	P	WIA	Spad VII, combat with a two-seater FTL near Vailly, possibly by Ltn Ebelt (1) & Uffz Bechert (1), FlAbt 226.
MdL Fleuret	MP 204	P	Injured	Sopwith

2 October

Sgt Rodde	N 69	EA	X	S Laon	4
Asp Defourneaux	N 78	EA	X	Suippes, IV° Armée	2
Sgt de Marmier &	N 112				–
Capt Merat	N 112	EA	P	Béthincourt	–
Lt de Maison Rouge	N 124	EA	P	NE Forêt de Pinon	–

Casualties:

S/Lt Robert de Francq	N 62	P	KIA	Spad VII N° 1633, probably by Ltn Heinrich Gontermann, Jasta 15, (39).

Adj Pierre Poisard &	C 28	P	KIA	Sopwith, probably by Ltn Otto
S/Lt Jacques Henry	C 28	O	KIA	Kissenberth, Jasta 23b, (17).
Lt Hubert	F 215	O	KIA	Morane-Saulnier Parasol
MdL Armand Mettiver	Sop ?	P	KIA	In flames.
S/Lt Eugène Montaron &	BM 119	P	MIA	
Adj Macquet	BM 119	B	MIA	Bréguet-Michelin N° 1054
MdL René Trouchaud	V 114	P	MIA	Voisin P
Sgt Berthelot &	V 110	P	POW	
S/Lt Moutillier	V 110	O	POW	Voisin P N° 20137
MdL Heuzbel	F 2	O	WIA	Flak, Letord
Sgt Denis Billas	C 17	P	WIA	
Sol Bieber	F 72	G	Injured	Letord
Lt Armand Jeannin	C 27	O	Injured	Caudron G4
Sgt Charles Quette	N 62	P	Injured	On ground
???	24° Cie d'Aérostiers			Both attacked, not flamed,
???	63° Cie d'Aérostiers			Nancy Sector.

3 October

Lt Vernin	N 75	EA	P	Le Cheppe	–

Casualties:

Sgt Guba &	V 116	P	POW	
Sol Brabant	V 116	G	POW	Voisin LAP N° 2358.
Adj Jardin	F 111	P	Interned	Sopwith
S/Lt Bloch	C 74	P	Injured	Caudron G4

4 October – No Claims

Casualties:

Lt USN Pilot	* CAM	P	MIA	Spad XIII N° 15728

*   Dunkerque.

5 October – No Claims

Casualties:

Sgt René Gaillard	Spa 3	P	KIAcc	Spad VII, collided with a RFC aircraft, 16h30 S Ypres.

6 October – No Claims

Casualties:

Capt Edouard Garcin CO	AR ?	P	KIA	

7 October

Adj Blanc &	N 31				3
Sgt Dousinelle	N 48	Scout	X	Lierval-Laval	3
???	???	EA	P	Soissons Sector	–

Casualties:

Lt Albert Ghilardelli	GDE	P	Injured	Caudron G4

8 – 9 October – No Claims – No Casualties

10 October

Infantry fire	???	2EA	X	Nancy Sector	–

Casualties:

QM Pierre Grandval	CAM	P	MIA	
QM Pierre Andries	CAM	O	MIA	
Lt René Mesguich	CAM	P	MIA	
QM André Bolle	* CAM	P	MIA	
Lt Charles Vernin	N 75	P	KIAcc	IV° Armée, Spad VII
Sgt Eugène Hanin &	C 6	P	Injured	
Sol Novi	C 6	M	Injured	Caudron G6

*   Perpignan, it is not known which pilot was with which observer.

11 October – No Claims

Casualties:

MdL Joseph Charnay &	C 27	P	KIAcc	
Lt Marc Duteurtre	C 27	O	KIAcc	Caudron G6
MdL Philippe Gohin	PS 127	P	WIA	Flak, Paul Schmitt
Lt Meunier	AR 71	O	Injured	Car Accident

12 October

Capt Franc	CO	N 79	Balloon	XF		1

Casualties:

Cpl André Chapelle		N 85	P	Injured	
Adj Maurice Beaufeist		49° Cie d'Aérostiers			Attacked, not flamed in Dunkerque Sector.

13 October – No Claims

Casualties:

Brig Lefevre &	F 230	P	WIA/POW	AR2 N° 1123, probably by
Sol Guiraud	F 230	M	WIA/POW	Ltn Ernst Hess, Jasta 19, (15).

14 October

Brig Andras de Marcy	a.	Spa 3	Albatros C	XF	Forêt d'Houthulst	1405	1
Cpl Collins	b.	Spa 103	Albatros	X	Poelcapelle	1615	1
Capt d'Harcourt,	CO	Spa 103					–
Sgt Loup,		Spa 103					–
Sgt Barault &		Spa 103					–
Cpl Turnure		Spa 103	EA	P	Forêt d'Houthulst		–
Patrols		GC 12	3 EA	P			–
???		???	EA	P	Monampteuil		–
???		???	EA	P	Anizy		–

a.   Probably Ltn Werner Hähne & Ltn Alfred Neuhaus, FlAbt 40, KIAs between Langemarck and Poelkapelle, about 3 km S of Forêt d'Houthulst.
b.   Possibly OfStv Rudolf Weckbrodt, Jasta 26, KIA Zonnebeke, about 6 km S Poelkapelle.

Casualties:

Sgt Gaston Dron	N 73	P	KIA	Spad VII N° 1760, departed 15h00.
Sgt Alfred Raveau	N 69	P	WIA	Spad, combat with a two-seater, X° Armée.
MdL Paul Pannetier	C 4	P	Injured	Caudron G6
Cpl Romieux	V 116	G	Injured	Voisin LAP
Lt Paul Raquet	27° Cie d'Aérostiers		XF	Probably by Ltn Hebler,
		O	OK	Jasta 15 (1).

15 October

Adj Vaillant	N 82	2 seater	XF	S Bois de Corbeny	1640	1
Sgt Pietri	Spa 103	EA	X	Forêt d'Houthulst	1515	1
???		DCA	Balloon	XF		1
???		???	Balloon	XF		–
Lt Hugues,	N 81					
Adj de Casenove de Pradines &	N 81					–
Adj Leveque	N 81	EA	P	Douaumont-Vaux	1510	–
Lt Bozon-Verduraz &	Spa 3					–
Adj Ambroise-Thomas	Spa 3	2 seater	P	Merckem	1655	–
???	???	EA	P	E Anizy		–
???	???	EA	P	NE Réservoir		–
???	???	EA	P	NE Réservoir		–

Casualties:

Cpl Georges Popelin	F 8	P	WIA	AR, infantry fire.
MdL Henri Lecatelinois &	PS 127	P	KIAcc	
Sol Pierre Flandin	PS 127	G	KIAcc	Paul Schmitt
Asp Prouvost &	82° Cie d'Aérostiers		XF	Probably by Ltn Heinrich
Sgt Topart		O	OK	Arntzen, Jasta 15 (8).

16 October

Lt Plane,	F 59					2
S/Lt Garrier &	F 59					1
Sgt Durieux	F 59	EA	X	Wissignicourt		1
Adj de Cazenove de Pradines,						4
Adj Simon,	N 81					1
Sgt P Guérin &	N 81					2
S/Lt Defourneaux	N 78	Scout	POW	Verdun	1225	3
Cpl Dubarry &	Spa 88					1
Sol Cabot	Spa 88	EA	X	W Foucaucourt		1
S/Lt Lufbery	N 124	2 seater	XF	Hurtebise	1015	13

DCA		???	EA	X	Bois de Holnon	–
51° Sect d'Auto-Canons		DCA	2 EA	X		–
S/Lt Pepin &		C 47				–
???		C 47	EA	P		–
Sgt Montrion		N 48	EA	P		–
???		F 58	EA	P	Belfort	–
MdL Delore	a.	N 78	EA	P	Forêt d'Hesse	1225	–
MdL Delore &		N 78				
Sgt Lemerre		N 78	EA	P	N Douaumont	1610	–
Cpl Dubarry &		Spa 88				–
Sol Cadot		Spa 88	EA	P		–
Adj Jean Éon		Sop 104				–
S/Lt Humbert		Sop 104	EA	P		–
Lt Lagache		N 112	EA	P	Béthincourt	1545	–
Cdt Ménard		GC 15	EA	FTL		1245	–
??? &		AR 20				–
Sol Latapie-Baringuet		AR 20	EA	P		–

a.   Probably Vfw Max Taucher, Jasta 34b, POW, Forêt de Hesse.

Casualties:

Capt Edouard Garcin CO	F 14	P	KIA	AR, claims for ARs made by
Sol Robert Millet	F 14	Ph	KIA	Ltn Walter Kypke, Jasta 41
Adj Raoul Chesneau &	F 58	P	KIA	(4) & Ltn Georg Schlenker,
Sgt Boitel	F 58	G	KIA	Jasta 41 (8), VII° Armée.
MdL Louis Houdusse &	F 52	P	MIA	X° Armée.
Sol Rouille	F 52	G	MIA	AR, 10h30.
Sol Massier	F 72	G	WIA	DOW 17 October 1917
Sol Joseph Latapie- Baringuet	N 20	G	WIA	
Sgt Vicario	F 40	P	WIA	IV° Armée
Sgt Degré &	F 40	G	OK	
Sol Monatte	F 40	G	WIA	Letord
S/Lt Robin	F 58	O	WIA	VII° Armée, Salmson-Moineau, FTL, probably claimed by Ltn Walter Kypke, Jasta 41 (5).
MdL Ferdinand Ropartz	Br 120	P	WIA	Bréguet
Sgt Maurice de la Morinerie &	VB 114	P	KIAcc	
S/Lt Proffit	VB 114	O	KIAcc	Voisin P
Cpl Max Edrei	Sop 13	P	Injured	Sopwith
S/Lt Christian Dauvergne	Br 120	P	Injured	Bréguet
Sol Cabot	Spa 88	G	Injured	Spad XI
Cpl Descazeneaux	GDE	P	Injured	Farman 61
Lt Maignan	MS 212	O	Injured	Morane-Saulnier Parasol
Cpl Jean Cantegil	MS 212	P	Injured	,,
Sgt Marcel Travet	MS 212	P	Injured	,,
???	64° Cie d'Aérostiers			Attacked, not flamed, in Belfort Sector.

17 October

Lt Jochaux du Plessis		N 15	Balloon	XF	Luzilly	1
Adj Blanc &		N 31				4
Adj Chartoire		N 31	Balloon	XF	Bruyères	1
Lt Marty	a.	N 77	EA	XF	Millery	1500	5
Lt Ropert		N 68	EA	X	VIII° Armée, N Jaulny	1
Sgt Rodde		N 69	Balloon	XF		5
Lt L Milliat		N 80	Balloon	XF	Vorges	2
Sgt Gohier	b.	N 85	2 seater	X	Ville-sur-Couzance	1400	1
Adj-Chef Fonck		Spa 103	2 seater	X	NW Ypres-Merken	1105	16
Adj-Chef Fonck	c.	Spa 103	2 seater	X	Forêt d'Houthulst	1120	17
Sgt Lecomte &		Spa 103				1
Sgt Turnure	c.	Spa 103	EA	X	Forêt d'Houthulst	1230	1
Lt de Geffrier &		Sop 107				1
Brig Villa		Sop 107	EA	X	Mont d'Origny	1
Sgt Faure &		Br 227				1
S/Lt Lapergue		Br 227	EA	X	German lines	1
???		???	EA	X	St Quentin	–
Sgt Artigau		N 15	2 seater	P		–

S/Lt de Romanet &	N 37					–
Brig Delannoy	N 37	EA	P	SE Ft Vaux	1510	–
Sgt Rodde	N 69	EA	P			–
Sgt Joly	N 78	EA	P	Samogneux	1625	–
Adj Ferber	N 84	Scout	P			–
Sgt Soubiran	N 124	EA	P			–
???	???	EA	P	Montfaucon		–
???	???	EA	P	Réservoir		–

a.   Probably Uffz Erich Weigert & Ltn Joseph Herkommer FlAbt 276 (A), KIAs between Millery and Nomeny.
b.   Probably Gefr Albrecht Gembler & Ltn Fritz Sanger, FlAbt 254 (A), KIAs Ville-sur-Cousances.
c.   Possibly Uffz Johannes Binsfeld & Gefr Erwin Sommer, Schusta ??, KIAs Westroosebeke, about 4 km SE Forêt d'Houlthust.

Casualties:

Sgt Marcel Montagne	N 112	P	MIA	Spad VII, probably the victim of Ltn Heinrich Kuett, Jasta 23b (1).
MdL Jean Le Dortz &	Sop 128	P	MIA	Two Sopwiths claimed, one
S/Lt Yves Jamet	Sop 128	O	MIA	by Vfw Otto Könnecke, Jasta 5 (9),
Cpl Victor Hurteau &	Sop 107	P	MIA	M Flakzug 12, near Origny.
Sol Celle	Sop 107	G	MIA	Sopwith N° 1129.
S/Lt Jean Michon &	C 47	P	KIA	
Lt Le Lapreugne	C 47	O	KIA	Caudron G6
S/Lt Pierre Vitry	Sop 214	O	WIA	Sopwith
Brig Emmanuel Colliaux	F 60	P	WIA	Flak, Sopwith
S/Lt Noël Adam	Br 213	O	WIA	Letord
Brig Edouard Chevalier	N 97	P	KIAcc	Nieuport XXIVbis
Cpl Maurice Michel &	F 130	P	KIAcc	
Cpl Henri André	F 130	G	KIAcc	Farman 40
Cpl René Espinadel	GDE	P	KIAcc	Morane Parasol XXVI
Cpl Freiss &	GDE	P	Injured	
Asp Babut	GDE	O	Injured	Caudron G4
Adj Tetard	GDE	P	Injured	Sopwith
Sgt Dereix	GDE	P	Injured	Sopwith
S/Lt Legorju	F 8	O	Injured	Letord
Sgt Trevet &	MS 212	P	Injured	FTL after combat at 11h00 between
S/Lt Chamontin	MS 212	O	Injured	Concevreux & Cormicy, X° Armée.
???	62° Cie d'Aerostiers			Both attacked, not flamed,
???	20° Cie d'Aérostiers			Nancy Sector.

18 October

Lt Delrieu	a.	N 150	Rumpler C4	X	Belfort	1115	3
Adj-Chef Fonck	b.	Spa 103	2 seater	P	Forêt d'Houthulst	1225	–
???		???	2 seater	P	W Chevregny		–

a.   Ltn August Köckmann (O), FlAbt 289b (A), WIA/POW at Belfort, died 30 October 1917, unknown pilot WIA.
b.   Possibly Obltn Otto Schmidt, Jasta 29, WIA over Oost-Vletern, about 12 km WSW Forêt d'Houthulst.

Casualties:

MdL Pierre Jolivet	N 73	P	KIA	Spad VII N° 1112, departed 08h35, probably by Ltn Walter v Bülow, Jasta 36, (24).
SM Urbain Boutin &	CAM	P	KIAcc	Donnet-Denhaut 150hp N°
Mat Marcel Dafinet	* CAM	O	KIAcc	452, Aber Wraich.
MdL Gauthier	N 49	P	Injured	Nieuport XXIV
Sgt Brichet	VC 113	?	Injured	Voisin P
MdL André Gabard &	81° Cie d'Aérostiers	XF		Probably by Ltn Helmut
S/Lt Louis Cheffrain		O	OK	Contag, Jasta 29 (1).
Sol Alfred La Rochette	29° Cie d'Aérostiers			Wounded by grenade burst

*   Brest.

19 October – No Claims
Casualties:

Lt Dupont	AR 14	P	WIA	
MdL René Maurer	N 96	P	KIAcc	Nieuport XXIVbis
Sgt Gaston	N 155	P	Injured	IV° Armée, Nieuport 24bis
Sgt Brichet	V 113	G	Injured	
Cpl Phelps Collins (American)	Spa 103	P	Injured	Spad VII N° 378.

20 October

S/Lt de Rochechouart de Mortemart	N 23	EA	XF	Bois de Forges	1700	5

Capt Darnard &	CO	VB 101					1
???		VB 101					1
S/Lt Hirsch,		N 151			Dammartin near		1
Cpl Ambrosio,	a.	N 151	Zeppelin	X	Montigny-le-Roi		1
Lt Lefevre,		N 152					1
S/Lt Lafargue,		N 152					1
MdL de la Marque,		N 152					1
Cpl Denis,		N 152					1
Cpl Gresset &		N 152					1
Cpl Vandendorpe	b.	N 152	Zeppelin	POW	Bourbonne-les-Bains		1
174 Section – 63 RAC	c.	DCA	Zeppelin	X	NE St Clément	0645	–
???		???	EA	P	Anizy-le-Château		–

NOTE: 174 Section commanded by Lt Fenouillet.
a.   Zeppelin L50, CO Ktpltn Roderich Schwonder and some crew KIAs.
b.   Zeppelin L49, CO Kptltn Hans Geyer, and 18 crew members POWs some KIAs.
c.   Zeppelin L45, CO Kptltn Waldemar Kölle and some crew KIAs.

Casualties:

MdL Robert Dagonet	N 83	P	POW	Spad VII, balloon attack, probably by Ballonzug 49.
Sgt Jean Regis	N 94	P	KIAcc	Nieuport XXVII
Sgt Roger Ploquin	N 91	P	Injured	Nieuport XXIV
MdL Lettivier,	MS 140	P	Injured	IV° Armée
Cpl Ferier &	MS 140	G	Injured	
Sol Voland	MS 140	M	Injured	Morane-Saulnier
???	31° Cie d'Aérostiers			Two of this Company's balloons attacked on the ground, not flamed. Soissons Sector.

21 October

Sgt Bouchard,		AR 8					1
Capt Jeauffreau de Lagerie &		AR 8					1
Lt Jeannissier		AR 8	EA	X	Laon		1
Adj Schurck		Spa 12	EA	X	Filain	1400	1
Asp Dubois de Gennes	a.	Spa 57	Albatros C	X	Etouvelles	1300	1
S/Lt Favre de Thierrens	a.	Spa 62	Albatros C	X	Chavignon		1
S/Lt Busson		Spa 82	EA	X	N Courtecon		1
S/Lt Fonck	b.	Spa 103	EA	X	Passchendaele	1455	18
Motor trouble	c.	???	Rumpler C4	POW	Fère-Champenoise		–

a.   Probably Ltn Ernst Tillgner & Ltn Fritz Meisinger, FlAbt 10, KIAs Chaillvois, about 4 km SW Etouvelles & 4 km N Chavignon. Which pilot should be credited is not known.
b.   Possibly Vfw Fritz Bachmann, Jasta 6, KIA E Ypres, about 9 km SW Passchendaele.
c.   N° 1431/17, possibly Vfw Brennecke & Ltn von Bernegg, FlAbt 3, POWs.

Casualties:

Cpl René Laidebeur	F 130	P	KIA	
MdL Pierre Couve	Sop 29	P	WIA	Sopwith
???	31° Cie d'Aérostiers			Attacked, not flamed.

22 October – No Claims

Casualties:

S/Lt Le Tanlay	Sop 29	P	POW	Sopwith, possibly forced to land because of motor trouble.

23 October

The Malmaison Operation commences in the area northeast of Soissons.

MdL Barancy	Spa 83	2 seater	X	Réservoir	1700	2
???	???	2 seater	FTL	Soissons Sector		–

Casualties:

Sgt Robert Brière	Spa 3	P	WIA	Flak, Spad VII N° 3035.
Capt Jacques Sabattier de Vignole	CO	N 48	P	WIA	Spad VII
S/Lt Maurice Sulphart	F 55	P	WIA	Sopwith, ground fire.
Cpl André Champod	Sop 9	P	WIA	Sopwith, ground fire.
Sgt Marchal	F 20	P	WIA	AR, ground fire.
Sgt Emile Bennehard	F 20	P	Injured	AR
Sgt Edouard St Alary	GDE	P	Injured	Sopwith
Cpl Leroux &	C 122	P	Injured	
Sol Corsetti	C 122	M	Injured	Salmson

24 October

S/Lt Covin	a.	Spa 31	Rumpler C4	POW	Cramaille		4
S/Lt Madon		Spa 38	Scout	POW	Passavant-en-Argonne		17
Capt Thiriez &	CO	Spa 86					3
Adj Hasdenteufel		Spa 57	2 seater	X	Chamouille-Laffaux		1
S/Lt Lufbery &		N 124					14
Lt Malavialle	b.	N 69	2 seater	X	Courtecon	0720	5
???	c.	DCA	EA	X	Verdun Sector		–
MdL Berthelot		N 15	Scout	P	Soissons Sector		–
MdL Beauregard		N 69	EA	P	Soissons Sector		–
Sgt Montrion		Spa 48	Scout	P			–
Adj de Guingand		Spa 48	2 seater	P			–
Patrol		GC 14	EA	P	Corbeny		–
S/Lt Lufbery		N 124	2 seater	P	Chaignon-Urcel	0925	–
S/Lt Lufbery		N 124	Scout	P	Urcel	1010	–
S/Lt Lufbery		N 124	2 seater	P	Urcel	1245	–
S/Lt Lufbery		N 124	EA	P	Challevois	1248	–
???		???	13 EA	P	Soissons Sector		–

a. Aircraft N° 1454/17, FlAbt 209 (A).
b. Probably Ltn Heinrich Breidt, Jasta 13, KIA Chevregny, about 5 km W Courtecon.
c. OfStv Otto Rössler, Jasta 23b, KIA by AA fire near Verdun.

Casualties:

Sgt Marius Bedel	Spa 57	P	MIA	Spad VII N° 1578.
Sgt Robert Collins (American)	Spa 15	P	WIA	Spad VII
Adj Marius Hasdenteufel	Spa 57	P	WIA	Spad XIII
Sgt Robert Brière	Spa 3	P	WIA	Flak, Spad VII, crash-landed.
Sgt René Fayet	GDE	P	KIAcc	Sopwith
Sol Raignault	Spa 88	G	Injured	Spad XI

25 October – No Claims

Casualties:

Cpl René Laidebeur &	F 130	P	KIAcc	
Cpl Fritsch	F 130	G	Injured	Farman 40

26 October

Sgt-Maj Tessier,		AR 20			1
S/Lt Castelain &		AR 20			1
Sol Latapie		AR 20	Scout	X	Wissignicourt	1

Casualties:

S/Lt Emile Decazes	CO	Spa 88	P	KIA	Spad VII N° 1825, over Anizy Foucaucourt, probably by KFlak 106.
Adj Louis Danglard &		F 208	P	KIA	Sopwith, probably by Ltn Konrad
S/Lt Lévy		F 208	O	KIA	Bieler, Jasta 14, (1).
MdL Louis Tachard &		F 60	P	WIA	DOW, Sopwith
Lt Jean Hardy		F 60	O	WIA	DOW 28 October 1917
Sgt-Maj Albert Tessier,		AR 20	P	OK	
S/Lt Valéry Castelin &		AR 20	O	WIA	
Sol Latapie		AR 20	G	WIA	Letord
Adj Robert Journe		Sop 204	P	Injured	On ground
Sgt Jacques Soltner		Sop 204	P	Injured	On ground

27 October

Lt Raymond	CO	Spa 3	EA	X	Forêt d'Houthulst	1535	4
S/Lt Fonck		Spa 103	EA	X	Westroosebeke	1000	19
S/Lt Letournneau		Spa 26	EA	P			–
S/Lt Fonck		Spa 103	EA	P	Forêt d'Houthulst	1520	–
S/Lt Fonck		Spa 103	EA	P	N Dixmude	1535	–
Lt Thaw		N 124	Albatros DV	P			–
???		GC	2 EA	P	Soissons Sector		–

Casualties:

MdL René Bertin,	F 8	P	KIA	Letord, probably by Ltn Konrad
Capt de Lagerie &	F 8	O	KIA	Bieler, Jasta 14, (2).
S/Lt Alexis Chambron	F 8	O	KIA	
MdL Jean Naty &	C 10	P	OK	
Capt de St Esteban	C 10	O	WIA	Caudron G6, X° Armée.

QM Jean Martin &		CAM	P	KIAcc			
QM Maurice Gibassier	*	CAM	O	KIAcc	Toulon		
Brig Roger Feissel		N 31	P	Injured	Spad VII		
Sol Legrand		Spa 78	M	Injured	Spad		
* Toulon.							

28 October

Patrol		Spa 73	Scout	P	Roulers	0715	–
S/Lt Fonck		Spa 103	EA	P	E Ypres	0945	–
Casualties: None							

29 October

Lt Blanchard,		C 11					1
Lt Cardeilhac &		C 11					1
Sgt Borel		C 11	Scout	XF	German lines		1
Sgt Garaud		Spa 38	2 seater	X	Sommepy, IV° Armée		2
Adj Gilet &		Spa 86					3
MdL Humber		Spa 83	Scout	X	Anizy		3
Sgt Haegelen	a.	Spa 103	EA	P	Westroosebeke	0930	–
???		???	EA	P	Damloup		–
???		???	3 EA	P	Laon		–
a. Possibly Vfw Josef Lautenschlager, Jasta 11, KIA Houlsterwald, about 4 km NW Westroosebeke.							

Casualties:

Sgt Paul Rodde		N 69	P	KIAcc	Rosnay		
S/Lt Brunel		C 212	O	Injured	Morane-Saulnier Parasol		
Cpl Boutet		GDE	P	Injured	Caudron G4		

30 October

Sgt Lignereux &		Sop 24					1
Lt Mangematin	a.	Sop 24	Scout	XF	S Reims		1
Adj Blanc	b.	Spa 31	Scout	X	Moulin-Didier		5
Adj Cazenove de Pradines &		Spa 81					5
Adj-Chef Péronneau		Spa 81	2 seater	X	N Verdun		2
Adj Ambrogi,		N 90					1
Adj Bordes,		N 90					1
Adj Dupré &		Spa 68					1
Brig Planiol	c.	Spa 68	DFW C	POW	Commercy	1010	1
MdL Demeuldre		Spa 84	EA	XF	Abordage		3
Adj Vieljeux,		N 93					3
MdL Guyou &		N 93					1
Adj Daladier		N 93	2 seater	X	Bois de Malancourt		4
QM Malvoisin	*	CAM	Gotha G	X	Dunkerque, at night		3
Motor Trouble		- - -	Rumpler C	POW	Pierrefitte		–
Sgt M Robert		N 92	EA	P			–
???		GC	4 EA	P	Soissons Sector		–
a. Possibly Ltn Hermann Scholl, Jasta 34b, KIA Nogent l'Abbesse, 6 km E Reims.							
b. Possibly Ltn Anton Warmuth, Jasta 34b, KIA Filain, in operational area of Spa 31.							
c. Probably Vfw Leonhard Endress & Ltn Lehnerer, FlAbt 46, on DFW CV N 126/17, POWs, AOK "C" Sector.							
* Dunkerque.							

Casualties:

Cpl Hippolyte Fabre	N 92	P	MIA	Nieuport XXIVbis, probably by Ltn Alfred King, Jasta 40 (2).	
S/Lt Robert Masson &	Br 210	P	OK		
S/Lt Georges Moro	Br 210	O	KIA	Bréguet 14	
Sgt Théodore Cancel &	C 18	P	OK	IV° Armée, FTL during	
S/Lt Petit	C 18	O	WIA	combat, Caudron G6.	
S/Lt Chauvin	AR 72	O	WIA	Flak, Letord	
Sgt René Montrion	N 48	P	WIA	Combat with 7 EA	
MdL René Autin &	F 16	P	Injured	IV° Armée	
S/Lt Bellay	F 16	O	Injured	AR	
MdL Berthomieux	AR 230	G	Injured	AR	

31 October

Sgt H Jones	N 124	EA	FTL		–
Casualties:					
Sol Dupont	GDE	P	Injured	Sopwith	

Between 21 to 31 October 1917, DCA downed two enemy aircraft.

1 November

Adj G Guérin		N 15	EA	XF	SE Chevrigny	1240	7
Sgt Artigau &		N 15					2
MdL Calamai	a.	N 15	Rumpler C	X	SE Chevrigny	1245	1
Adj Variot	b.	N 94	2 seater	XF	Souain		2
Adj Van Ingelandt		N 97	2 seater	X	Etain		1
Cpl Wilmart &		N 155					1
Adj Guiraut		N 155	Albatros D	X	German lines		1
DCA	c.	???	DFW C	X	Châlons Sector		–
Adj Schlax &		N 65					–
MdL Le Boucher		N 65	Albatros	P			–
Sgt de Marmier		N 112	2 seater	P	Watronville		–
???		N 155	EA	P			–
???		???	2 EA	P	Soissons Sector		–
Motor trouble	d.	???	Albatros D	POW	Pont Rouge		–

a.   Probably Gefr Josef Kremp & Vfw Josef Leppich, Schsta 18, KIAs Laon, about 8 km N Chevregny.
b.   Possibly Ltn Friedrich Hahn & Ltn Karl Mangold, FlAbt 297b (A), KIAs Souain.
c.   Possibly Flg Ernst Graef & Ltn Max Bartel, FlAbt 206 (A), KIAs Dontrien, about 30 km N Châlons.
d.   Albatros DV N° 2218/17.

Casualties:

MdL Vernaudon	N 112	P	MIA	II° Armée, Spad, probably by Vfw Diessner & Ltn Lange, FlAbt 36.
Cpl Geronimus Wilmart (Argentine)	N 155	P	KIA	Nieuport XXIV, probably by Ltn Otto von Breiten-Landenberg of Jasta 9, (3).
Lt Jean Le Gorju &	Sop 132	P	KIA	Sopwith N° 3150, possibly by Ltn
S/Lt Chauvin	Sop 132	O	KIA	Georg Schlenker, Jasta 41, (9).
Brig Jean de Civille	AR 16	P	WIA	Flak
Cpl Rayez	Sop 131	G	WIA	Flak, Sopwith
S/Lt Chauvin	Let 219	O	WIA	Flak, Letord
S/Lt Marcel Couvert &	Sop 222	P	Injured	
S/Lt Mazert	Sop 222	O	Injured	Sopwith, crash-landing.
MdL Alexandre Leduc	GDE	P	Injured	Nieuport XXIII
Adj Pierre Desmond	N 85	P	Injured	On ground
S/Lt Xavier Pollet	Br 117	O	Injured	
Adj Maurice Bex	65° Cie d'Aérostiers		XF	Both of these probably claimed by
		O	OK	Ltn Fritz Pütter, Jasta 9, (4 & 5).
S/Lt Fernand Cons &	67° Cie d'Aérostiers		XF	
Asp Emile Lenglet		O	KIA	
	52° Cie d'Aérostiers			All 4 balloons attacked in
Adj Charles Guggenheim	57° Cie d'Aérostiers			Châlons Sector, last two not flamed. One of the attacking planes was hit DCA fire N of the Butte de Mesnil, and was also attacked by Adj Dramand, Spa 38 & a Morane from Escadrille 54.

2 November – No Claims
The Malmaison Operation ends.
Casualties:

MdL Bertrand &	AR 1	P	Injured	VII° Armée
Lt Hautier	AR 1	O	Injured	AR

3 November
A two-motor Gotha was forced to land near Blanc-Nez, in the Dunkerque Sector, the four occupants, Vfw Hermann Kirch, Uffz Wilhelm Schmidt, Ltn Martin Schünke and Uffz Wilhelm Voss, of KG 3 were all dead. This is listed as 3 November in the Résumés but as 4 November in von Eberhardt's listing of Luftstreitkräfte personnel killed or died.
Casualties:

MdL Paul Chavane de Dalmassy	???	P	KIAcc	
Adj Gérard &	C 51	P	KIAcc	
Sol Kintzeler	C 51	M	Injured	Sopwith

4 November – No Claims – No Casualties

5 November

???	???	EA	P	Esnes	1430	–
???	???	EA	P	Esnes	1430	–

Casualties:

Lt Dumas	Spa 103	P	WIA	Spad
Lt Alexandre Marty	N 77	P	Injured	VIII° Armée, Spad, crash-landing.
Adj Claudius Schiavazzi &	C 53	P	Injured	
MdL Vaisselet	C 53	G	Injured	Caudron G6
Asp Jon	AR 72	O	Injured	On ground
???	61° Cie d'Aérostiers			Attacked, not flamed, Nancy
		O	OK	Sector.

6 November – No Claims
Casualties:

Cpl Jacques Fontaine-Desjardins,	F 71	P	KIAcc	
Adj Samana &	F 71	R	KIAcc	
Sol Brusq	F 71	M	KIAcc	AR
Asp Moles	MS 140	O	Injured	Morane-Saulnier Parasol

7 November

MdL Berthelot	N 15	EA	P			–
Adj Herbelin	N 81	EA	P			–

Casualties:

Sgt Rachat &	F 50	P	WIA	VII° Armée, AR, infantry
Lt Thomas	F 50	O	OK	fire.

8 November

Capt Deullin	CO	Spa 73	Pfalz DIII	X	Hollebeke	1045	19
???		???	Rumpler C	P	Forêt de Pinon		–

Casualties:

Brig Paul Teulat	F 41	P	Injured	Morane-Saulnier Parasol

9 November

Sgt Meige	Spa 102	EA	X	Forêt d'Houthulst	1
Sgt Meige	Spa 102	EA	P	E Dixmude	–

Casualties:

Asp Edouard Chausamy	N 49	P	POW	VII° Armée, Spad XVI & N° 6006, probably became lost and FTL in
Adj Camille Fleurot	N 49	G	POW	enemy territory.
S/Lt Pierre Constantini	N 102	P	POW	Spad, probably by Ltn Josef Jacobs, Jasta 7 (10).
S/Lt Henri Salvetat	GDE	P	Injured	Nieuport XXIII
S/Lt Devaux	GDE	P	Injured	AR

10 November – No Claims
Casualties:

Lt Antoine de Dampierre	???	P	KIAcc	
MdL André Soubies &	RGAé	P	Injured	
Sol Monteil	RGAé	M	Injured	Sopwith

11 November

Adj G Guérin	a.	Spa 15	Rumpler C	XF	N Courtecon	1435	8

a.   Probably Uffz Emil Herrlich & Ltn Kurt Flintzer, FlAbt 277 (A), KIAs Braye-en-Laonnois, about 7 km SW Courtecon.

Casualties:

MdL Landelle	???	M	KIAcc	
Cpl Prosper Sirey &	Sop 123	P	KIAcc	
Sol Moulon	Sop 123	M	Injured	Sopwith

12 November

Lt Battesti	a.	Spa 73	EA	X	Forêt d'Houthulst	1045	3
Adj Peronneau	b.	Spa 81	2 seater	X	Courouvre		3
Capt Derode	CO	Spa 102	EA	P	Dunkirk Sector		–

a.   Possibly Ltn Georg Behnisch, FlAbt 211 (A), KIA Houthulsterwald.
b.   Probably Vfw Gustav Dietrich & Ltn Heinrich Kumkell, FlAbt 279 (A), KIAs at Courouvre, AOK "C" Sector.

Casualties:

Capt Duval	Spa 73	P	KIAcc	Spad VII N° 1641 at 14h30.	
EV1 Louis Maraval	PilSch	P	KIAcc	St Raphaël	
Cpl André Arcelin	N 93	P	Injured	Nieuport XXIVbis	

13 November

Sgt Garaud	Spa 38	EA	X	Sommepy	3
Adj Dramard	Spa 38	EA	X		3
Adj Dramard	Spa 38	EA	X		4
MdL Henriot &	Spa 65				2
MdL Lienhard	a. Spa 65	Albatros	POW	Dannemarie	1400	1
Cpl Biddle &	Spa 73				–
Sgt Turnure	Spa 103	Scout	P	Passchendaele	1600	–
???	???	EA	P	Fleury-Bezonvaux	–
???	???	2 EA	P	Soissons Sector	–

a.   Probably Uffz Theodor Seffig, Jasta 34b, POW, in German 7° Armee Sector opposite French VI° Armée.

Casualties:

S/Lt Jacques Pelletier	Sop 17	O	KIA	Sopwith
MdL Louis Rampillon	N 76	P	WIA	Spad
Adj Jean Dramard	Spa 38	P	KIAcc	Spad
Adj Maurice Croissant &	Br 202	P	KIAcc	
S/Lt Emile Richard	Br 202	O	KIAcc	Bréguet 14
Adj Carlier	GDE	P	KIAcc	Caudron G4
MdL Baptiste Boyer	N 315	P	Injured	
MdL Jean Bouyer	N 49	P	Injured	VII° Armée, Nieuport XXIV
Adj Charles Casin	N 90	P	Injured	Nieuport XXIV
Cpl Robert &	???	P	Injured	
S/Lt Lardillon	???	O	Injured	Sopwith
Adj Léon Berthon,	AR 8	P	Injured	
Lt Jeannissier &	AR 8	O	Injured	
Sol Guyezant	AR 8	G	Injured	Letord
Adj Henri Gilig	GDE	P	Injured	AR
Cpl Marcel Simenel	GDE	P	Injured	AR

14 November

Sgt Counord,	N 151				1
Sgt Aumaitre &	N 151				1
Sgt Chambel	a. N 151	DFW C	POW	Elbach	1
???	???	EA	P	Heimsbrunn	–

a.   Possibly Gefr Schmalfuss & Ltn Moering, FlAbt 223s (Lb), POWs, Dammerkirch.

Casualties:

Cpl Meunier &	Sop 29	P	WIA	VII° Armée
Sol Louis Fréchin	Sop 29	G	KIA	Sopwith

15 November

Motor trouble	a. ???	2 seater		Senozan	1000	–

a.   Probably Vfw Blümlein & Ltn Aign, FlAbt 46b, POWs, AOK "C" Sector, reason unknown. The destroyed their aircraft.

Casualties: None

16 November – No Claims

Casualties:

MdL Canivet &	AR 19	P	Injured	
Sol Celles	AR 19	M	Injured	AR
S/Lt Meunier	Br 7	O	Injured	Bréguet 14

17 November – No Claims

Casualties:

MdL Quintard	???	P	KIAcc	Sopwith
MdL Antoine Huguet &	V ??	P	KIAcc	
Cpl Virebayre	V ??	O	KIAcc	Voisin
Capt Meffre	(1)	P	Injured	FTL

(1)   Commandant of the Belfort Sector air service.

18 November – No Claims
Casualties:

MdL Louis Paoli	Spa 73	P	Interned	Spad VII N° 1832. Departed 10h00, landed at Bergen op Zoom, Holland. Escaped 9 January 1918 and rejoined Spa 73 on 7 March 1918.
Sgt Barclay de Tholey	GDE	P	KIAcc	Caudron G4

19 November – No Claims
Casualties:

Capt Oscar de Montiero-Torres	Spa 65	P	MIA	Spad N° 4268, probably by Ltn Rudolf Windisch, Jasta 32b, (6).

20 November – No Claims – No Casualties

21 November

Lt Roederer	Spa ???	EA	X		–
Casualties:					
Lt François Roederer	Spa ???	P	KIA		
MdL Emmanuel Baussier	Pau	P	KIAcc		

22 November

Ground fire	???	EA	X		–
Brig Chabrier	N 315	Scout	P	VII° Armée Sector	–
???	???	2 seater	P	S Laval	–
Casualties:					
S/Lt André Vangeon	V 113	O	KIAcc	Voisin	
Lt Jean de La Motte de La Motte-Rouge	N 96	P	Injured	Nieuport XXIV	
Brig Liontel	BM 119	P	Injured	BM IV	

23 November

S/Lt Bernard	Spa 15	EA	P	Courtecon	1130 –
Casualties:					
S/Lt Jacques Bernard	Spa 15	P	WIA		
Sol Gillet	PS 125	G	Injured		
Sgt Dabny Horton &	C 17	P	Injured		
Sol Abrial	C 17	M	Injured	Sopwith	
Brig René Le Tilly &	N 313	P	Injured		
Cpl Bocquet	N 313	G	Injured	Sopwith	
Lt Alane &	AR 50	P	Injured		
Sol Le Hello	AR 50	M	Injured	Caudron G3	

24 November – No Claims
Casualties:

Cpl Gaston Flattet &	Sop 51	P	Injured	
Sol Varnet	Sop 51	M	Injured	
Cpl Simon &	GDE	P	Injured	
Sol Feinturier	GDE	M	Injured	Caudron G4
S/Lt Pierre Perrody	35° Cie d'Aérostiers			Attacked not flamed.
		O	Killed	

25 November – No Claims
Casualties:

Lt Duesaul	Br 227	O	Injured	Letord

26 November

Belfort Sector	DCA	EA	P	Thann	–
Casualties:					
Adj-Chef Gazave	Spa 37	P	MIA	II° Armée, Spad N° 1389, probably FTL in enemy territory due to motor trouble.	
MdL Alexis Lendresse	N 152	P	KIAcc	VII° Armée, Nieuport XXIVbis	
MdL de Beauvoir	GDE	P	Injured	Nieuport XXIII	
Brig Derrien	GDE	P	Injured	AR	
Cpl Alphonse Chagniat	Sop 216	P	Injured	Sopwith	

27 November

Navagational error	a.	???	LVG CV	POW	N Ham-Auroir	–

a. NCO pilot, officer observer, the aircraft was in good condition.

Casualties:

S/Lt Pierre Parrody	35° Cie d'Aérostiers			Attacked, not flamed.
		O	Killed	

28 November

???	a.	DCA	LVG CV	POW	–

a. N° 9574/17.

Casualties:

MdL Marius Lacrouze	???	P	KIAcc	
Cpl Charles Pascal	GDE	P	Injured/DOW 30 November 1917, Spad	
Cpl France	GDE	P	Injured	Nieuport XXIII

29 November – No Claims

Casualties:

Cpl Pierre Blain	N 89	P	POW	Nieuport XXIVbis #3656, departed at 14h45, probably by Flak-batterie 527, VIII° Armée.
Sol Chopin	V 116	M	Injured DOW	
S/Lt Clément Payen	N 79	P	WIA	
Cpl Charles Trinkard	N 68	P	KIAcc	Spad
Lt Claude Celerier &	Br 66	P	KIAcc	
MdL Museur	Br 66	G	KIAcc	Bréguet
MdL Henri Aumaitre &	V 116	P	KIAcc	
MdL Roger Dupille &	C 228	P	KIAcc	
S/Lt Gomez-Vaëz	C 228	O	Injured	Morane-Saulnier Parasol
Adj Gaston Planque	F 35	P	KIAcc	Letord
Sol Papon	F 35	M	Injured	Letord
Sol Albert Grouillière	V 116	M	Injured DOW	VLAP
Capt Jean Viennot	Br 7	P	Injured	VII° Armée, DOW 30 November 1917,
Lt Dauvin	Br 7	O	OK	Bréguet 14.
Sgt Jean Dedieu	Spa 26	P	Injured	Spad XIII N° 1865, collided with a Voisin taking off.
Sol Monteil	Br 227	G	Injured	Letord

30 November – No Claims

Casualties:

S/Lt René Merle &	F 208	P	Injured	
S/Lt Gillot	F 208	O	Injured	Sopwith

1 December

Sgt Bouyer	N 49	EA	X	VII° Armée Sector	3

Casualties:

Brig Reingeissen &	C 10	P	POW	Caudron G6 N° 2993, probably by
Asp Goguet	C 10	O	POW	Vfw Karl Thom, Jasta 21s, (14).
Capt Marcel Guillou	Spa 81	P	KIAcc	II° Armée, Spad VII

2 December

S/Lt G Guérin	Spa 15	EA	XF	Vaudesson	1010	9
Sgt Vidal,	N 88					1
MdL Rousseaux,	N 88					6
Brig Wurtz,	N 88					1
Cpl Cabot &	N 88					2
S/Lt Lufbery	a. N 124	2 seater	XF	S Ployart	1005	15
S/Lt Lufbery	N 124	2 seater	X	Laval	1125	16
???	???	EA	P	Bourgogne-Brimont		–
???	???	EA	P	Laval		–
???	???	2 seater	P	E Bois de Forges		–

a. Possibly Ltn Erich Pohl and Ltn Otto Heilmann, FlAbt 255s (A), KIAs over Chemin-des-Dames, about 10 km south of Ployart-Laval.

Casualties:

Sgt Théophile Joly	N 78	P	POW	Spad VII N° 1774, 2° Armée
Cpl Leo Benoit	Spa 84	P	Injured	Spad VII
Cpl Bazergue &	Sop 13	P	Injured	
Sol Meunier	Sop 13	G	Injured	Sopwith

3 December

Capt Sabattier de Vignolle &		CO	Spa 48					2
Adj Caillaux	a.		Spa 48	Aviatik C	X	Ostel-Chavonne		2
Lt Jaille	b.		Spa 75	Albatros D3	X	Filain	1040	2
Lt Jaille			Spa 75	Albatros D	P	Soupir	1041	–
Capt Verdon			N 96	2 seater	P	Fresnes		–
Lt Thaw			N 124	Rumpler C	P			–
???			GC	EA	P	Monampteuil		–
???			GC	EA	P	Urcel		–
???			GC	EA	P	Lavannes		–
???			???	EA	P	NE Laon		–

a. Probably Ltn Hans Mayer (P) FlAbt 10, KIA Chavonne.
b. Probably Vfw Otto Pelz, Jasta 32b, KIA Verneuil, about 10 km SE Filain.

Casualties:

Sgt Gaston Malfait	GDE	P	Injured	Nieuport XXIVbis
MdL Julien Lapalu	N 96	P	Injured	Nieuport XXIVbis

4 December

Cpl Vandendorpe	a.	N 152	2 seater	POW	Champ-le-Dec		2
???	b.	DCA	EA	X	Nancy-Sector		–
???		???	EA	P	Lizy-Soissons		–

a. Possibly Vfw Albrecht & Ltn Bach, FlAbt 46, POWs, AOK "C" Sector.
b. Probably Ltn Laibrecht & Ltn Wolfgang Paulus, FlAbt 46, POWs, AOK "C" Sector.

Casualties:

Brig Paul Renault	Avord	P	KIAcc	
Cpl Nobuo Yamanaka &	Spa 77	P	KIAcc	VIII° Armée, Spad XI
MdL Nacotte	Spa 77	G	Injured	DOW 27 Dec 1917
Cpl René Vandendorpe	N 152	P	Injured	VII° Armée, Nieuport XXIV
S/Lt Camille Bouisett	GDE	P	Injured	Nieuport XXIV
MdL Jacques Jourdanet &	F 50	P	Injured	VII° Armée, Letord, shot
S/Lt Villegoureix	F 50	O	Injured	down, crash-landed during combat.
Cpl Delporte	F 50	G	OK	

5 December

Lt de Châteauvieux &		C 10					1
S/Lt Tocker		C 10	EA	X	Corbeny		1
Cpl C Biddle	a.	Spa 73	2 seater	X	Langemarck	1045	1
Lt Hugues,		Spa 81					8
Adj Herbelin &		Spa 81					7
Adj Levecque	b.	Spa 81	2 seater	X	Ft Rozellier		1
S/Lt Hay de Slade		Spa 86	Rumpler C	X	Anizy	1140	5
Sgt Marinovitch		N 94	Rumpler C	POW	Mourmelon-Baconnes		2
Sgt Van Den Bosch		N 94	Albatros C	X	Sommepy		1
???	c.	???	2 seater	POW	VII° Armée, Melisey		–
Sgt Collins		Spa 103	EA	P	Forêt d'Houthulst	1115	–
???		???	EA	P	Laon-Soissons		–

a. Possibly Fldwbl Hermann Seidel, Jasta 26, KIA Westroosebeke, about 5 km NE Langemarck.
b. Probably Gefr Kaufmann & Ltn Kaminski, FlAbt 244s (A), WIAs Acremont, about 8 km SW Ft Rozellier.
c. FlAbt (A) 289, crew two officers.

Casualties:

Sgt Marcel Puy &	Spa 42	P	KIA	Spad XI, N° 6007, III° Armée
Lt Jean Mathe-Dumaine	Spa 42	O	WIA	DOW 6 December 1917
Cpl Robert Douvry	BM 112	G	KIA	Bombardment of Airfield.
Sgt Krutzberger &	C 18	P	KIAcc	Caudron G6
Cpl Falcon	C 18	G	KIAcc	
QM Henri Picard	PilSch	P	KIAcc	Hourtin, FBA 100hp, his corpse retrieved 26 April 1918.
Adj Robert	V 110	P	Injured	Voisin P
Adj Louis Peignat	Sop 221	P	Injured	Sopwith
Lt Pierre Pascal &	BM 119	P	Injured	
Sgt Joseph Roth	BM 119	B	Injured	BM IV
S/Lt Cezilly	F 45	O	Injured	Letord
Sgt Gaston Soleau	V 109	P	Injured	

6 December

S/Lt Favre de Thierrens	Spa 62	Fokker D	X	Colligis		2
MdL de Tonnac de Villeneuve	Spa 80	2 seater	XF	Forêt de St Gobain	0840	1
Adj Martin,	Spa 76					–
Lt de Jumilhac,	Spa 76					–
Adj Barbazet &	Spa 76					–
Lt Ribout	Spa 76	Scout	P	Lavannes		–
???	GB 5	2 EA	P	Hagondange		–

Casualties:

Brig Lucien Bonnet	Sop 60	P	WIA	Sopwith, ground fire.	
Brig Traibault	GDE	P	Injured	Nieuport XXIV	
Brig Henri Sacerdotte &	Sop 39	P	Injured		
Sol Auzat	Sop 39	G	Injured	Sopwith	
Sgt Paul Vieu &	V 109	P	Injured		
Sgt Petit	V 109	G	Injured	Voisin P	
Adj Magnier &	F 25	P	Injured		
Lt Manificat	F 25	O	Injured	Farman 60	

7 December

The Third Battle of Ypres ends.

Sgt Bouyer	N 49	Scout	X	E Burnhaupt	4
Sol Michel	AR 5	EA	P		–
Brig Machetay,	F 50				–
S/Lt Mouillard &	F 50				–
Sol Michel	F 50	Scout	P		–

Casualties:

Brig René Machetay,	F 50	P	KIA	VII° Armée, Letord, probably by	
S/Lt Maurice Mouillard	F 50	O	KIA	Uffz Walther, Jasta 76b, (1).	
Sol René Michel	F 50	G	KIA		
QM Joseph Sondumavais &	CAM	P	MIA		
SM Frédéric Tachet *	CAM	O	MIA	Port Vendras	
Adj Etienne Combret	GDE	P	Injured	Spad	
Cpl Favier	GDE	P	Injured	Sopwith	
Lt Jean Vachon,	Sop 39	P	OK	Letord, FTL during combat	
S/Lt Ganne &	Sop 39	O	OK	and destroyed by enemy	
Sgt Settelem	Sop 39	G	OK	artillery.	
S/Lt Gilbert &	51° Cie d'Aérostiers		XF	VII° Armée, probably by Ltn Hans	
Asp Grandjean		O	OK	Weiss, Jasta 41, (2).	

*   Perpignan.

8 December

Adj Renauld	Spa 48	EA	X		2

Casualties:

Lt Paul Tourtel	N 103	P	KIAcc	Spad XIII, Crépy-en-Valois
QM Emile Barat *	CAM	P	KIAcc	Sopwith 130hp codé D.24.

*   Dunkerque.

9 December

Sgt Bouyer &	N 49					5
S/Lt Hirsch	a. N 151	2 seater	X	Masseveaux		2
???	DCA	EA	P	Aspach, VII° Armée		–
???	???	Balloon	P	Septsarges		–

a.   Possibly Ltn Dagobert Jäger & Ltn Wilhelm Leonhard, FlAbt 289b (A), KIAs, near Belfort.

Casualties:

Adj Pierre Cazenove				II° Armée, Spad XIII, probably by
de Pradines	Spa 81	P	WIA	Ltn Walter Böning, Jasta 76b, (9).

10 December

Lt Hugues,	Spa 81					9
Adj Herbelin &	Spa 81					8
S/Lt Leps	Spa 81	Albatros C	X	N Recicourt		5
VIII° Armée	DCA	Rumpler CV	X	Montenoy-Nancy		–
Patrol	Spa 80	EA	P	Louvemont-Anizy	1105	–
???	Sop 9	Scout	P	Grandelain		–

Casualties:

Adj Paul Malençon &	C 56	P	KIA	Caudron G6s, probably
S/Lt Julien Ballureau	C 56	O	KIA	downed by Ltn Otto Homuth,
MdL Jean Agostini &	C 56	P	KIA	Jasta 23b (3) and Vfw
S/Lt Moinville	C 56	O	KIA	Johann Neumaier, Jasta 16b (3).
Lt Paul Tarel &	AR 230	P	KIAcc	
Sol Dussaussoy	AR 230	M	KIAcc	
S/Lt Robert Dubois	Spa 68	P	KIAcc	Spad
Adj Robert	V 110	P	Injured	Voisin P
Sgt Georges Contal	92° Cie d'Aérostiers		XF	Ltn Georg
		O	OK	Strasser, Jasta 17 (6).

11 December

Groupe de Combat 12 departed the Flanders Sector for the Champagne, VI° Armée Sector.

Adj Dhôme	a.	Spa 81	EA	XF	Bois de Cheppy	4
???	b.	DCA	EA	XF	Manonviller	–
???	c.	???	EA	P	Louvemont	–

a. Probably OfStv Friedrich Berwald & Obltn Hermann Hofmann, FlAbt 278s (A), KIAs Montfaucon, about 8 km NE Bois de Cheppy.
b. Probably Gefr Georg Hofmann & Ltn Otto Hellmuth, FlAbt 199b, KIAs Manonviller.
c. Possibly a crew from FlAbt 289 (A) which was FTL near Melissy.

Casualties:

Adj Gilbert Triboulet	Spa 57	P	KIAcc	Spad XIII N° 1955
Sgt Charles Caigne	???	P	KIAcc	
Sgt Paul Vigen	GDE	P	Injured	Farman

12 December

Sgt Garaud	Spa 38	Rumpler C	X	Louvercy	4
Cpl Walcott	Spa 84	2 seater	X	St Souplet	1
Sgt Demeuldre	Spa 84	Albatros	P		–

Casualties:

Cpl Benjamin Walcott (American)	N 84	P	KIA	Spad VII N° 6024, probably by Ltn Otto von Breiten-Landenberg, Jasta 9, (4).
SM Georges Fressanges	PilSch	P	KIAcc	Ambérieu
Cpl Alfred Chambalu &	Sop 106	P	Injured	
Sol Lemire	Sop 106	M	Injured	
Cpl Roblot	39° Cie d'Aérostiers			All three attacked, not flamed,
???	92° Cie d'Aérostiers			Soissons Sector.
???	94° Cie d'Aérostiers			All observers OK.

13 December

Sgt Bouyer	a.	Spa 49	EA	XF	Montbéliard	6

a. Probably Vfw Schorner & Ltn Sahm, FlAbt 289b (A), Rumpler C #8273, KIAs between Montbéliard and Oberelsasse.

Casualties:

Brig Charles Caigne	GDE	P	KIAcc	Farman 40
S/Lt Alfred Lebègue &	61° Cie d'Aérostiers		XF	Probably by Vfw Karl Schattauer,
Adj Albert Depoux		O	OK	Jasta 16b (2).

14 December – No Claims – No Casualties

15 December

Cpt Sabattier de Vignolle,	CO	Spa 48					3
Adj Renauld,		Spa 48					3
Adj de Guingand &		Spa 48					4
S/Lt Delannoy	a.	Spa 80	2 seater	XF	Nauroy-Prosnes	0930	5
Adj-Chef Laplasse	b.	Spa 75	2 seater	XF	Saint-Mard	1125	1
Adj Dhôme	c.	Spa 81	Rumpler C	XF	S Ville-sur-Cousance		5
Sgt Demeuldre		Spa 84	Albatros C	X	W Hans		4

a. Possibly Vfw Leo Streiber & Ltn Eduard Kropff, FlAbt 206 (A), KIAs in Champagne Sector.
b. Probably Uffz Rudolf Kausmann & Uffz Wilhelm Befort, Schutzstaffel 18, KIAs Braye, about 10 km NW of St Mard.
c. Probably Ltn Paul Hoffmann & Ltn Bodo Heyne, FlAbt 273 (A), KIAs Ville-sur-Cousance.

Casualties:

S/Lt Henri Astor	Spa 80	P	POW	Spad VII, Chevregny-Juvincourt, 10h15, probably by Ltn Scheller, Jasta 19, (2).
Cpl Roger Beynet &	F 54	P	Injured	
Sol Bayen	F 54	M	Injured	AR

16 December – No Claims
Casualties:

Lt Paul Fabel	AR ??	P	KIA	
Brig Gaston Coriol	N 85	P	Injured	Nieuport XXIV
Capt René de Lavergne	31 CA	P	Injured	Nieuport XXIV

17 December – No Claims
Casualties:

Capt Mathieu Tenant de La Tour CO	Spa 26	P	KIAcc	Spad XIII, 15h20, Auchel
Cpl François Monpas &	AR 40	P	Injured	
S/Lt Gaston Biasini	AR 40	O	Injured	AR

18 December – No Claims – No Casualties

19 December

Patrol	Spa 57	EA	P	Voult-sur-Suippe	–
Patrol	Spa 80	2 seater	P	Anizy-le-Château	–

Casualties: None

20 December – No Claims
Casualties:

Sol Clamens	Spa 84	M	Injured	Nieuport XXIV

21 December

Adj-Chef Péronneau	a.	Spa 81	DFW C	X	Fort de Genicourt	4
Sgt Demeuldre		Spa 84	DFW C	P		–
S/Lt Dreyfus &		Br 220				–
S/Lt Servanty		Br 220	EA	P		–
??? &		???				–
Sgt Borel		???	EA	P		–

a.   POWs.
Casualties:

Sgt François Borel	???	G	WIA

22 December

S/Lt G Guérin,		Spa 15				10
Sgt Garaud &		Spa 38				5
MdL Henriot	a.	Spa 65	2 seater	POW	Louvercy	3
S/Lt Madon		Spa 38	Scout	XF	N Selles	18
Sgt Demeuldre		Spa 84	DFW C	X	St Jean-sur-Tourbe	5
Adj Marinovitch		N 94	Rumpler C	X	N Pont Faverger	3
S/Lt Nazarre-Aga &		Br 66				1
Sgt Boudier		Br 66	Scout	X	German lines	1
DCA		???	EA	X	Grugies	–
??? &		GB 1				–
S/Lt Maguet &		Sop 108				1
Sgt Mespleine &		Sop 108				1
Sgt Balignac		Sop 108	EA	X	Asfeld	1

a.   Probably Ltn Bruno Grosse, POW & Ltn Adolf Gerhardt, KIA, FlAbt 251 (A), Mourmelon-le-Petit, about 3 km E Louvercy.
Casualties:

Sgt Mespleine &	Sop 108	P	WIA/POW	Bréguet 14 N° 1202, probably by
Sgt Balignac	Sop 108	G	WIA/POW	Uffz Herbert Boy, Jasta 14, (1).
Capt Bloch &	Sop 216	P	POW	Sopwith N° 4130, probably
Sol Frieur	Sop 216	M	POW	by Ltn A Wünsch, Jasta 22, unconf.
MdL Honoré Battut	AR 40	P	WIA	Flak
S/Lt Hubert Petry	Spa 62	O	Injured	Bréguet
Adj Armand Lutiau &	Sop 226	P	Injured	
Sol Lemaitre	Sop 226	M	Injured	Sopwith

23 December

S/Lt G Guérin &		Spa 15				11
Sgt Artigau	a.	Spa 15	DFW C	X	Beine-Bois de Berru	3
S/Lt Madon &		Spa 38				19
Sgt Garaud	b.	Spa 38	2 seater	X	Tahure	6
Sgt Frick,		Spa 78				1
S/Lt Mouquet &		Spa 78				1
Lt Hugues		Spa 81	2 seater	XF	Bois de Landricourt	1

Sgt Demeuldre		Spa 84	DFW C	X	N Hurlus	6
Adj de Kergolay	c.	N 96	Albatros DV	X	Fresnes	1
???	d.	DCA	AEG G.IV	POW	Achiet-le-Grand	–
S/Lt Guérin &		Spa 15				–
Sgt Artigau		Spa 15	DFW C	P	Berru	–
S/Lt Madon		Spa 38	EA	P	Heurtregiville	–
S/Lt Madon		Spa 38	EA	P	Beine	–
Patrol		N 83	EA	P	Chevregny	1335	–
???		???	EA	P	SW Jarry	–
???		???	EA	P	Montfaucon	–

a. Probably Ltn Willy Müller & Ltn Max Winterfeldt, FlAbt 248 (A), KIAs, SE Reims.
b. Probably Ltn Adolf Schleiper (O) FlAbt A 271, KIA Tahure, pilot severely wounded.
c. Possibly Ltn Ernst Hess (17v), Jasta 19, Albatros DVa #5347/17, KIA Fresnes.
d. AEG G.IV N° 1125/16, in late evening, probably OfStv Paul Hintersatz, Ltn Schuster & Fw Junemann, came down at Acy, flying a Friederichshafen, POWs.

Casualties:

Brig Baron &	Sop 251	P	POW	Sopwith, probably by Vfw Weber (3)
Asp Rebut	Sop 251	O	POW	& Vfw Ritscherle Schutzstaffel 8.
S/Lt René Dutrou &	Let 39	O	WIA	
Sol Tissier	Let 39	G	WIA	Letord
Brig Emmanuel Augier	Spa 65	P	Injured	Spad VII
MdL Louis Weber	AR 254	P	Injured	
S/Lt Fichot	AR 32	O	Injured	
Sol Louis Remy	???	M	Injured	Letord 1, N° 130.
Adj Albert de Kergolay	N 96	P	OK	Shot down and crashed near front lines – not harmed.

---

24 December

Adj Bourdet	Spa 112	2 seater	X	Dompierre	4

Casualties:

Lt Carpin	AR 56	O	WIA	Ground fire.

---

25 – 26 December – No Claims – No Casualties

---

27 December – No Claims

Casualties:

MdL Léo Rayer	N 94	P	KIAcc	Nieuport XXIVbis
Cpl Robert	GDE	P	KIAcc	Nieuport XXIVbis
MdL Gérard Faure	N 82	P	Injured	Nieuport XXIV
Sgt Léon Van Den Bosch	N 94	P	Injured	

---

28 December – No Claims

Casualties:

Sgt Georges Burlaton &	Br 66	P	POW	Bréguet 14B2 N° 1168, probably
S/Lt Debrus	Br 66	O	POW	became lost and FTL in enemy territory.

---

29 December

Adj Naudin		Spa 26	EA	X	Châlons Sector	2
MdL Berthelot		Spa 15	DFW C	P	Butte de Souain	–
S/Lt de Guingand		Spa 48	2 seater	P	Sault St Rémy-Roizy	–
DCA	a.	???	EA	X	French lines	–

a. Probably Vfw Otto Rosenfeld, Jasta 41, POW, shot down during a balloon attack.

Casualties:

Cpl Henri Guitreau &	???	P	Injured	
S/Lt Boisseau	???	O	Injured	AR
Sgt Pierre Prieur	51° Cie d'Aérostiers		XF	VII° Armée. Probably by Vfw Otto
		O	OK	Rosenfeld, Jasta 41 (8).

---

30 December – No Claims

Casualties:

S/Lt Francois Rey	AR 14	O	KIA	
Cpl Monnier	AR 230	P	Injured	

---

31 December

Patrol	Spa 48	3 EA	P	–

Casualties:

SM Henri Prigent	PilSch	P	KIAcc	FBA 150hp N° 31, St Raphaël

French Combat Log 1918

1 January

S/Lt G Guérin	a. Spa 15	2 seater	X	Nogent l'Abbesse		12
Sgt Garaud	Spa 38	EA	X	Sommepy		7
MdL Marinovitch	N 94	EA	X	Beine	1415	4
Adj de Kergolay &	N 96					2
Sgt de La Forest Divonne	b. N 96	EA	X	S Billy-sur-Aisne	1125	1
Sgt J N Hall	c. N 124	Albatros D	X	E Forêt de Brimont		1
Patrol	Spa 75	2 seater	P	Fressancourt	1500	–
Patrol	Spa 86	2 seater	P	Pinon	1130	–

a.   Probably Ltn Karl Koelschtzky & Ltn Robert Wiegard, RHBZ 1, KIA Nogent l'Abbesse.
b.   Possibly Ltn N Hillmann & Ltn H Predöhl, FlAbt (A) 261, KIAs Montreux.
c.   Possibly Uffz Albert Meinhardt, Jasta 21s, KIA Betheny, SE Brimont.

Casualties:

Lt Jean du Crest	N 79	P	MIA	III° Armée, departed 13h00
Cpl Cotton &	Spa 42	P	MIA	
Sol Balairy	Spa 42	G	MIA	III° Armée

---

2 January – No Claims – No Casualties

---

3 January

S/Lt G Guérin	a. Spa 15	EA	X	Nogent l'Abbesse		13
Adj Peronneau	b. Spa 81	EA	XF	E St Mihiel		5
S/Lt Boyau	Spa 77	Balloon	XF	Benay		12
Sgt Demeuldre	Spa 84	EA	XF	Forêt de Brimont		7
S/Lt Coiffard	Spa 154	Scout	X	NE St Quentin	1245	2
Sgt Duvaut &	Br 209					1
Sol Delcey	Br 209	Scout	X	Monceau-les-Leups		1
Patrol	Spa 3	EA	P	Corbeny-Craonne	1510	–
Patrol	Spa 73	EA	P	Réservoir	1310	–
Patrol	Spa 86	2 seater	P	Anizy	1130	–
???	Spa 31	EA	P	Lavannes		–

a.   Probably Ltn Fritz Schultz (O), RHBZ 1, KIA Nogent l'Abbesse.
b.   Possibly Ltn Josef Lampart & Ltn Alexander Zipperer, FlAbt 46b, KIAs, Wald de Apremont, about 10 km SE St Mihiel.

Casualties:

Adj Georges Bourdet	Spa 112	P	KIA	Spad N° 2018, probably by Ltn von Seelen & Ltn Quentin, FlAbt (A) 257.
Cpl Charles Nicolas	N 94	P	WIA	DOW 4 January 1918, Nieuport, IV° Armée, FTL near Auberive.
Sgt Duvaut,	Br 209	P	OK	
Sol Delcey &	Br 209	G	OK	
S/Lt Letanche	Br 209	O	WIA	Bréguet
MdL François Meauze	N 99	P	Injured	Nieuport
Lt Degrelle &	F 25	P	Injured	
Sol Terrier	F 25	M	Injured	Voisin R
Sgt André Catrice	67° Cie d'Aérostiers		XF	IV° Armée, probably by Vfw Erich Thomas, Jasta 9, (1).
		O	OK	
???	62° Cie d'Aérostiers			Attacked, not flamed,
		O	OK	Nancy Sector.
S/Lt Marc Desache	72° Cie d'Aérostiers			Attacked, not flamed.
		O	OK	Châlons Sector.

---

4 January

S/Lt Madon	Spa 38	Scout	X	Pont-Faverger		20
Adj Sardier &	Spa 77					3
Sgt Ruamps	N 87	EA	X	N Arracourt	1615	2
Adj Peronneau &	Spa 81					6
Adj Dhôme	Spa 81	2 seater	XF	Bois de Forges		6
Sgt Bouyer	a. Spa 49	EA	P	VII° Armée		–
S/Lt Parizet	N 94	2 seater	P	NW Sommepy		–
Sgt Denizot &	N 152					–
Sgt Hahn	N 152	EA	P	VII° Armée		–

a.   Possibly DFW CV N° 6175, FlAbt 199b.

Casualties:

S/Lt François Kermina	Sop 131	P	MIA	
Sol Rey	Sop 129	G	WIA	Flak
MdL Raymond Douay	N 90	P	KIAcc	
Cpl Daisson	N 157	P	KIAcc	
Sgt Louis Breuils	C 222	P	KIAcc	Sopwith
Lt Beaute	Sop 131	P	Injured	
???	79° Cie d'Aérostiers	XF		VII° Armée, probably by Ltn Hans
		O	OK	Weiss, Jasta 41, (3).
Brig Jacques Duteurtre	83° Cie d'Aérostiers	XF		III° Armée
		O	OK	

---

5 January

Cpl Popelin &		Sal 8				1
Capt Rudy		Sal 8	Scout	X	Monempteuil	1
S/Lt Madon		Spa 38	EA	P	N Nogent l'Abbesse	–
Capt Lamy	CO	Spa 65	EA	P	St Hilaire-le-Petit	–
MdL Bannier		Spa 75	Albatros D3	P	Vauxillon	1605 –

Casualties:

Sgt Rochet &	F 25	P	POW	Probably by Flakzug 406,
Sgt Tramoni	F 25	G	POW	Vfw Köhler.
Lt Anquier &	BM 118	P	POW	Voisin N° 2546, possibly
Sol Plossut	BM 118	M	POW	by KFlak 83, Ltn Keerl.
Brig Jouve	N 157	P	WIA	DOW 6 January 1918. Probably by Ltn Walter Ewers, Jasta 77b, (5), VII° Armée.
MdL Hyppolite Cavieux	Spa 76	P	Injured	
???	AR			VIII° Armée, FTL in French lines during combat, crew not harmed.
S/Lt Millet &	64° Cie d'Aérostiers	XF		VIII° Armée, probably by Vfw Franz
Sgt Aubry		O	OK	Piechulek, Jasta 41, (2).
Asp Maurice Prouvost	82° Cie d'Aérostiers	XF		III° Armée, 15h05, probably by Ltn
		O	OK	Erich Löwenhardt, Jasta 10, (9).

---

6 January

Cpl Hitchcock	a.	N 87	2 seater	X	St Maurice	1130	1
Adj Ambrogi &	a.	N 90					2
S/Lt Le Coq de Kerland		N 90	2 seater	X	N Regneville	1000	2
Cpl Woodward		N 94	Albatros	X	Manre		1
Adj Dousinelle		Spa 48	EA	P	Brimont	1910	–
Patrol		Spa 48	EA	P	Amifontaine	1025	–
S/Lt Martin &		Spa 76					–
Sgt H Rampillon		Spa 76	Scout	P	Nogent l'Abbesse	1530	–

a.   Probably Uffz Höschle & Ltn Hentschel of Rb-Truppe, who got them is not known, claims in same vicinity.

Casualties:

MdL Henri Durand	N 89	P	POW	VIII° Armée, Nieuport XXIV N° 5449, FTL at Emmerich, becauseof motor trouble, after attacking a balloon at Bourdonnay.
Adj Marcel Croize-Fourcelet &	Sop 123	P	MIA	Probably by Ltn Georg
Sol Legors	Sop 123	G	MIA	Schlenker, Jasta 41, (11).

---

7 January – No Claims – No Casualties

---

8 January – No Claims

Casualties:

Adj Jean Eon &	Sop 104	P	WIA	Flak
S/Lt Humbert	Sop 104	O	WIA	Flak

---

9 January – No Claims – No Casualties

---

10 January

Three crews	a.	AR 4	Scout	X	–

a.   Including S/Lt A Thomas (O)(1), S/Lt L Blanchot (O)(1) & S/Lt Dufresne (P)(1).

Casualties:

S/Lt Gotrait	Sop 221	O	WIA		
Asp Jean Chalambel	N 82	P	Injured		
S/Lt Choux	Sop 214		Injured		

11 January – No Claims
Casualties:

Sgt Paul Lenis	Sop 214	P	KIAcc

12 January

Patrol	Spa 57	Scout	P	Berru	1120 –
???	GC	EA	P	Bois de Forges	–

Casualties:

Sgt Joseph Leboucher	Spa 65	P	POW	Spad N° 4267, possibly by Ltn Fritz Pütter, Jasta 9, (6), IV° Armée.
Sgt Salah Siamer	Spa 124	P	Injured	Spad
Adj André Lelarge	C 56	P	Injured	Caudron G6
???	53° Cie d'Aérostiers		XF	These two balloons were
		O	OK	destroyed by Vfw Erich
S/Lt Georges Zengerlin	65° Cie d'Aérostiers		XF	Thomas (2) and Ltn Fritz
		O	OK	Pütter (6) of Jasta 9, IV° Armée.
???	62° Cie d'Aérostiers			Attacked, not flamed, Nancy Sector.

13 January

Patrol	Spa 75/80	Rumpler C	P	Juvincourt	1545 –

Casualties:

Capt de Saint-Ceran CO	C 41	P	Injured	Spad XI
Adj Eugène Jacquinot	GDE	P	Injured	Spad
Sgt Paul Gaudin	N 95	P	Injured	
Cpl Launay	GDE	P	Injured	Nieuport
MdL Fernand Delreux	F 25	P	Injured	

14 January

Capt Tourangin & CO	Spa 89				–
Sgt Massol	Spa 89	EA	P	Forêt de Parroy	1300 –
??? &					–
Sol Hincelin	Sop 132	EA	P		–
Sgt Denis &	Spa 152				–
Sgt Hahn	Spa 152	EA	P	Belfort Sector	–
Adj Gros	Spa 154	EA	P		–

Casualties:

Sgt Louis Silbermann &	Sop 132	P	MIA	These two a/c probably downed
Sgt Liauzu	Sop 132	G	MIA	by Vfw Josef Schwendemann
Brig Victor Piel &	Sop 129	P	KIA	(2) & Vfw Hermann Reisch, Jasta 41,
MdL Ruse	Sop 129	G	POW	3374, (1).
Sol René Hincelin	Spa 132	G	WIA	
Lt Jean de La Motte de La Motte-Rouge	N 96	P	KIAcc	Nieuport
Sol Lafont	GDE	M	Injured	
MdL Jean Bernheim	36° Cie d'Aérostiers		XF	Nancy Sector, probably by Ltn Fritz
		O	OK	Pütter, Jasta 9, (8).

15 January – No Claims
Casualties:

Mat Jean Le Kernec	*	EP	O	Injured	DOW, FBA 150HP N° 44
Adj Marcel Dussous		RGAé	P	Injured	
S/Lt Goulut		V 114	O	Injured	Voisin R

*   St Raphaël.

16 January

???	DCA	EA	X	–

Casualties: None

17 & 18 January – No Claims – No Casualties

19 January

Sgt Mereau &		C 10					1
S/Lt Brager		C 10	EA	X	Paissy		1
Lt de Rochechouart de Mortemart	a.	Spa 23	EA	X	Dieppe		6
Asp Dubois de Gennes		Spa 57	Scout	X	Warmerville	1110	2
Patrol		Spa 76	2 seater	P	Beine	1205	–
Cpl Hitchcock &		Spa 87					2
Cpl Wellman	b.	Spa 87	2 seater	X	Lunéville	1300	1
MdL Marinovitch &		N 94					5
Cpl Crehore	c.	N 94	Albatros DV	X	Manre-Beine		1
S/Lt Fonck		Spa 103	Scout	X	Bois de Chaume	1425	20
S/Lt Fonck		Spa 103	Scout	X	Samogneux	1435	21
Cpl Winter,		N 156					1
S/Lt Belloc &		N 156					1
Cpl Putnam		N 156	EA	X	Nogent l'Abbesse		1

a. Possibly Uffz Karl Schneider (P), FlAbt 291b (A), KIA, Maucourt, about 5 km N Dieppe.
b. Had just downed MdL Paul Miot, N 87, probably Uffz Weiss, WIA, & Ltn Martin of FlAbt 199 (A).
c. Possibly Vfw Martin Mallmann, Jasta 19.

Casualties:

Adj Henri Variot	N 156	P	MIA	IV° Armée, possibly by Ltn Fritz Pütter, Jasta 9, (9)
MdL Paul Miot	N 87	P	KIA	VIII° Armée, probably by Uffz Weiss (1) & Ltn Martin (1) FlAbt (A)199.
S/Lt Albert Borrel	Br 218	O	WIA	VIII° Armée, DOW 20 January 1918, Nieuport.
Lt Prinsac	C 18	O	WIA	IV° Armée, AR
Sgt Henri Burlet	AR 1	P	WIA	Flak, VIII° Armée, AR
Sgt Georges Plez	GDE	P	KIAcc	Spad
Sgt Alfred Guyot	RGAé	P	KIAcc	Nieuport
Sgt Raymond Blondy	???	P	KIAcc	
MdL Marcel Woog &	C 6	P	KIAcc	
S/Lt Camion	C 6	O	KIAcc	Caudron G6 N° 5175
Capt José Dos Santos Liete	Spa 124	P	Injured	
Adj Foulon	AR 50	P	Injured	
Sol Leblanc	AR 39	M	Injured	
S/Lt Muret	C 229	O	Injured	Sopwith
Lt René Itier,	CEP 115	P	Injured	
Adj Nungesser &	CEP 115	P	Injured	
Sol Noël	CEP 115	M	Injured	Caproni
S/Lt Maurice Platel	24° Cie d'Aérostiers		XF	Nancy Sector, possibly by Ltn Otto
		O	OK	Hohmuth, Jasta 23b, (4).

20 January

Lt de Sevin &	CO	Spa 26					7
MdL Fontaine		Spa 26					1
Sgt Mouton &		AR 35					1
Lt Deullin	a.	AR 35	Scout	X	Samogneux-Magenta	1040	1
???		DCA	Friedrichshafen				–
				POW	Belgian Lines		–
???		DCA	EA	X			–
Patrol		Spa 57	EA	P	Roizy		–
Cpl Hitchcock &		N 87					–
Cpl Wellman		N 87	Rumpler C	P	Nancy Sector		–
Adj Pietri		Spa 103	EA	P	Sivry-sur-Meuse		–
???		???	EA	P	St Marie-aux-Mines		–

a. Possibly Ltn Fritz Schönberger, Jasta 16b, WIA near Verdun, 12 km SSE Samogneux.

Casualties:

S/Lt Maurice Barbey	N 23	P	WIA	Spad
Sgt Félix Durand	Spa 80	P	WIA	
Cpl Harry F Johnson	N 98	P	WIA	Probably by Ltn Hans Rolfes, Jasta 45, (2)
Cpl Raymond Blondy	???	P	KIAcc	
Lt Chanut	Spa 64	O	Injured	Spad XI
Cpl Henry A Batchelor	Spa 103	P	Injured	Spad
Cpl Georges Laurendin	GDE	P	Injured	Nieuport
Sgt Georges Misery	N 315	P	Injured	DOW 28 January 1918.

Adj Rémy	73° Cie d'Aérostiers			Broke loose in high winds, headed	
		O	OK	for German lines. Observer jumped	
				to avoid capture.	

21 January

| Patrol | a. | Spa 57 | EA | P | Roisy | – |
| Lt Nungesser | | Spa 65 | EA | P | | – |

a.   Possibly Gefr Josef Mayer, Jasta 32b, KIA 11h50, Mars-sous-Bourcq.

Casualties:

Sgt Paul Riche &		AR 262	P	POW		
Lt Drouet		AR 262	O	POW	AR N° 309, IV° Armée	
Adj Pierre Teurlay		GDE	P	KIAcc	Nieuport	
Brig Jean Matignon		N 89	P	Injured		
Cpl Rebière &		AR 58	P	Injured		
Capt Homassen		AR 58	O	Injured	AR	

22 January – No Claims

Casualties:

Adj Ludovic Pams &		Br 11	P	WIA		
Capt de Lubersac	CO	Br 11	O	WIA		
Lt Francis Gloaguen		Sal 18	O	WIA	Flak, AR, IV° Armée	
Cpl Dumaresq Spencer		N 150	P	KIAcc		

23 January – No Claims

Casualties:

| Cpl Fernand Lehnert & | | Sop 43 | P | Injured | | |
| Sol Christophe | | Sop 43 | M | Injured | | |

24 January

Adj Majon de la Debuterie		N 87	Rumpler C	XF	Gondrexange	1
DCA	a.	???	DFW C	POW	Belfort Sector	–
Sgt Joubert &		AR 58				–
S/Lt Dechery		AR 58	Albatros	P	VII° Armée	–

a.   The occupants were officers, and the aircraft was intact.

Casualties:

Sgt Paul Joubert &		AR 58	P	KIA	VII° Armée, probably by Ltn	
S/Lt Dechery		AR 58	O	KIA	Wilhelm Schulz, Jasta 41, (4).	
Lt Paul de Minteguiaga &		C 47	P	Injured	DOW, Beauzé, 15h30.	
S/Lt Paul Marcaggi		C 47	O	KIAcc	Caudron G6	
S/Lt Pierre Morel		N 84	P	KIAcc	Spad, IV° Armée	
Cpl Léon Estève		AR 70	P	Injured		
Asp Cuche &		BM 121	P	Injured		
Asp Lataste		BM 121	O	Injured		
MdL Henri Larue &		BM 121	P	Injured		
S/Lt Carles		BM 121	O	Injured		

25 January

Lt Berlioz &	CO	AR 1				1
S/Lt Gaudy	a.	AR 1	Albatros D3	XF	VII° Armée	1
Lt Goux,		C 10				1
Brig Guérin &		C 10				1
Sgt Gaumont		C 10				1
Adj de St Savin &		C 10				1
Lt Tongas		C 10	EA	X	Colligis	1
Adj Duret		Spa 67	Albatros D	X	Béthincourt	1515 1
Lt Parizat,		Spa 94				2
Cpl Bonnet,		Spa 94				1
Lt Laganne &		Spa 94				1
MdL Bessières		Spa 94	Scout	X	Fontaine-en-Dormois	1
??? &		DCA				–
Adj Merle		Spa 313	Gotha G	X	Dunkerque Sector	1
???		DCA	EA	X		–
???		DCA	EA	X		–
Brig Beney		Spa 67	Albatros D	P	Fort Choisel	1450 –
S/Lt Thomas		Spa 88	EA	P	Nogent l'Abbesse	–
Sgt M Robert		N 92	EA	P		–

Patrol	Spa 86	EA		FTL	N Anizy	1145 –

a.   Possibly Vfw Hermann Reisch, Jasta 41, KIA Ammerzweiler, on VII° Front.

Casualties:

S/Lt Auguste Jacob &	AR 1	P	MIA	VII° Armée, possibly Ltn Georg	
Adj Jean Jacob	AR 1	O	MIA	Michaelis, Jasta 41, (1).	
MdL Pierre Menandais &	AR 32	P	KIA	Flak, SW Dommartin.	
Lt Bessec	AR 32	O	KIA	Flak	
Adj Eugène Monges &	Spa 212	P	POW	Spad XI N° 6249, FTL in	
Sol Chenal	Spa 212	M	POW	enemy lines at Neufchâtel.	
Brig Philip Beney	Spa 67	P	WIA	DOW 26 January 1918, Spad, FTL	
				W Ft Choisel, 14h50, probably by	
				Ltn Otto Kissenberth, Jasta 23b, (18).	
Cpl Polonceau	PS 127	P	WIA	Bréguet	
Sgt Jean Duclos &	Spa 102	P	KIAcc		
Sol Longuet	Spa 102	M	KIAcc	Spad XI	
MdL Fernand Rayne &	Spa 34	P	Injured	DOW 26 January 1918	
Asp Boissaud	Spa 34	O	KIAcc	Spad XI	
Lt Jean Chotard	Spa 64	P	Injured	Spad XI	
MdL T Faure & (KIA)	80° Cie d'Aérostiers		XF		
???		O	KIA		
Sgt Auguste Guaquière &	55° Cie d'Aérostiers		XF	All three by Ltn Friedrich Röth,	
Sgt Bretonnèche				Jasta 23b, (1 – 3).	
		O	Injured	All in II° Armée Sector.	
Lt Louis Bigot &	59° Cie d'Aérostiers		XF		
Asp Louis Villarino		O	OK		
MdL Couillard &	43° Cie d'Aérostiers		XF	By Ltn Heinrich Arntzen, Jasta 50,	
MdL Clément		O	OK	(7).	

---

26 January

???	a. DCA	2 seater	POW	Forêt de Remiremont	–

a.   Obltn (P) WIA, and other crewman WIA.

Casualties:

MdL Jacques Lemaitre &	Sop 214	P	KIAcc	
S/Lt Douffiagues	Sop 214	O	KIAcc	Sopwith
Lt Jean Monnet	GDE	P	KIAcc	

---

27 January

S/Lt Madon	a. Spa 38	2 seater	X		N Ville-sur-Tourbe	21
Capt Paumier, CO	N 156					1
Lt Belloc,	N 156					2
Adj Barriot &	N 156					1
Cpl Putnam	N 156	Albatros C	XF		Vaudesincourt	2
Patrol	Spa 12	EA	P		Lavannes	–
Patrol	Spa 94	EA	P		IV° Armée	–
Patrol	Spa 155	EA	P		IV° Armée	–

a.   Possibly Vfw Anton Schmitz & Ltn Albert Kickert, FlAbt 19, KIAs, Mont-devant-Laffey.

Casualties:

Lt Raoul Belloc	N 156	P	POW/DOW	Nieuport N° 5964, FTL near
				Vaudesincourt during combat, probably
				by Ltn Fritz Pütter, Jasta 9, (10).
Cpl Monatte	Spa 40	G	WIA	IV° Armée, Letord
Sgt Julien Lacroix	Spa 23	P	Injured	
MdL Pierre Chabert	GDE	P	Injured	Spad XI
Brig Clerc	GDE	P	Injured	Spad XI
Cpl Jean Dalaunay	N 156	P	Injured	
Cpl Louis Feuillatre	GDE	P	Injured	Sopwith
Cpl Robert Donze	N 314	P	Injured	
???	28° Cie d'Aérostiers		XF	VII° Armée, probably by Ltn Hans
		O	OK	Weiss, Jasta 41, (4).

---

28 January

Sgt Pilgler,	Sal 51				1
Lt Bellet &	Sal 51				1
MdL Leplant	Sal 51	EA	X	Craonne-Beine	1
Patrol	Spa 42	EA	P	Craonne	–
Patrol	N 96	EA	P	Ferme Médéah	–

Casualties:

S/Lt For &	C 18	P	KIA	Flak, N St Hilaire, Caudron G6, probably
S/Lt Auguier	C 18	O	KIA	by K Flak-batterie 3, Ltn Petzke.
Adj Denis Durand &	Br 7	P	WIA	Flak
Lt Jules Tison	Br 7	O	OK	
Asp Maurice Dumant	Spa 86	P	KIAcc	
Lt Garin	17 CA	O	Injured	Sopwith
MdL Jean Balland	PS 127	P	Injured	
Lt Bernard Abadie	PS 127	P	Injured	
???	AR 268			AR1, Motor hit in combat forced to crash-land.
???	57° Cie d'Aérostiers		XF	IV° Armée, probably by
		O	OK	Ltn Joachim Huth, Jasta 14, (1).
???	85° Cie d'Aérostiers			Attacked, not flamed, Châlons Sector.

---

29 January

Lt de Turenne &	CO a.	Spa 12				7
Adj Bernard de La Frégeolière		Spa 12	Albatros D3	XF	Allemant	2
Adj Volmerange		Spa 38	EA	X	Aure-Marvaux	1
Adj Babo		Spa 38	EA	P	Varicourt	
Adj Roques &		Spa 48				–
S/Lt Bajac		Spa 48	Rumpler C	P		–
Lt Nungesser		Spa 65	Albatros	P		–
Patrol		GC 11	Scout	P	NE Jouy	–

a.   Vfw Christian Brunnengräber, Jasta 13, KIA, had just flamed the balloon of the 45° Cie Aérostiers.

Casualties:

Sgt Louis Divi	C 46	G	WIA	Letord
Sgt Henri Roulie	RGAé	P	KIAcc	Sopwith
S/Lt Charles de Chevreuse	GDE	P	KIAcc	Sopwith
Sol Lacheze	???	M	KIAcc	
SM Alexandre Morin	* CAM	P	KIAcc	Donnet-Denhaut 150HP N° 604, at La Pallice.
MdL Lesueur &	Sop 255	P	KIAcc	
Sol Leroy	Sop 255	M	Injured	
S/Lt Eugène Lasselain	Sop 222	P	Injured	
Lt Mello-Viera	GDE	P	Injured	DOW 31 January 1918, Sopwith
Adj Berlioux &	RGAé	P	Injured	
Sol Perey	RGAé	M	Injured	Caudron R11
Lt Fabre	GDE	P	Injured	AR N° 1187
MdL Chouineau	???	P	Injured	AR
MdL Valensi &	Sal 122	P	Injured	
Sol Brunel	Sal 122	M	Injured	
???	45° Cie d'Aérostiers		XF	VI° Armée, probably by Vfw
		O	OK	Christian Brunnengräber, Jasta 13, (1).

*   La Pallice.

---

30 January

Sgt Mereau,	(P)	C 10				2
Sgt Boutique,	(P)	C 10				1
Adj Naty,	(P)	C 10				1
Adj de Saint-Savin	(P)	C 10				1
Lt Goux,		C 10				1
Lt Tongas,	(O)	C 10				1
Lt Desbief,	(O)	C 10				1
Sgt Graumont	(O)	C 10				1
Lt Mevellec	(O)	C 10				1
Sgt Gabel &	(G)	C 10				1
Brig A Guérin	(G)	C 10	Fokker DrI	X	La Neuville	1
S/Lt Covin,		Spa 31				5
S/Lt A Borde,		Spa 65				3
MdL Lienhard &		Spa 65				2
Sgt Gérard		Spa 65	EA	X	Beine	1
S/Lt Herbelin		Spa 81	EA	X	La Pompelle	9
Sgt Vergnes &		AR 464				1
Cpl Billard	a.	AR 464	DFW CV	X	Chelles-Vincennes	1

Sgt Artigau	Spa 15	Rumpler C	P	La Pompelle	–
Patrol	GC 13	2EA	P	„	–

a.   CRP unit, DFW CV N° C5950/16, Crew two Ltn, WIA/POWs, night victory.

Casualties:

MdL Raymond Vanier	Spa 57	P	WIA	Possibly by Vfw Mikat, Jasta 14, (1).	
Sgt Emile Decagny	GDE	P	Injured	AR	
Brig Gaston Gueuedet	GDE	P	Injured	Sopwith	

31 January – No Claims

Casualties:

IGM Jean Alcide	SC Aéro	P	KIAcc	Rouen	
Cpl Mathieu	???	M	KIAcc	Coudebec	

The night of 30-31 January a DFW C V was forced to land between Chelles and Vaires, and was destroyed by the occupants, see above.

Dates of these claims are not known at this time:

Adj Mouguet	Spa 78	EA	XF	French lines	1
??? &	Spa 62				–
Lt Brousse	Spa 62	EA	P	German lines	–

1 February – No Claims

Casualties:

Cpl Flamme	AR 1	P	Injured	AR	

2 February

Adj de Marmier &	Spa 112					1
Sgt Reynaud	Spa 112	2 seater	X	S Altkirch		1
S/Lt Coiffard	Spa 154	2 seater	X	Juvincourt	1210	3
S/Lt G Guérin	Spa 15	EA	P	Beine		–
???	Br 66	Scout	P	Sissone		–
???	AR 230	Albatros	P	Belfort Sector		–

Casualties:

Adj Robert Ragaz &	Br 66	P	KIA	In flames possibly by Ltn	
MdL Duffrène	Br 66	G	KIA	Konrad Bieler, Jasta 14 (4).	
Cpl L'Heureux &	AR 59	P	POW	AR N° 1614, probably by K-Flak-	
Sol Dubret	AR 59	G	POW	batterie 126, Ltn Heiderich.	
Brig Joseph					
Pollaud-Duillaud	GDE	P	KIAcc	Sopwith	
EV1 Daniel Pelichet	* CAM	P	KIAcc	Hanriot HD.2 N° 201, codé D.30.	
Lt Léonce Sorbier &	N 88	P	KIAcc		
Sgt Gibert	N 88	G	Injured	Spad XI	
Sgt Marien	Sop 219	G	Injured		
MdL Charbonnier	C 18	P	Injured	Caudron G6 N° 5271, AA fire.	
???	57° Cie d'Aérostiers		XF	IV° Armée, probably by Vfw Erich	
		O	OK	Thomas, Jasta 9.	
S/Lt Pierre Bacalou &	45° Cie d'Aérostiers		XF		
1/Lt Doherty, USBS		O	OK		

*

3 February

S/Lt G Guérin	a. Spa 15	EA	X	Beine		14
S/Lt G Guérin &	Spa 15					15
Sgt Artigau	Spa 15	2 seater	X	Nogent l'Abbesse		4
S/Lt Covin	Spa 31	Fokker DrI	X	Pontgirard		6
S/Lt Madon	Spa 38	Scout	X	Bétheniville		22
S/Lt Madon	Spa 38	2 seater	X	Caurel		23
S/Lt Demeuldre	b. Spa 84	2 seater	XF	St Souplet		8
S/Lt Demeuldre &	Spa 84					9
Sgt Prouvost	Spa 84	2 seater	XF	Prunay		1
Cpl Lee &	N 96	EA	X			1
Lt Barthe	N 96	2 seater	X	Orainville	1125	1
Adj Vial	N 315	2 seater	X	Wittelsheim		2
Capt Verdon	CO N 96	EA	P			–
Capt Verdon	CO N 96	EA	P			–
S/Lt de Kergolay	N 96	EA	P			–
S/Lt Gaillard	N 158	EA	P	Vaucelles		–
Sgt Artigau	Spa 15	2 seater	P			–

Sgt Artigau	Spa 15	2 seater	P		–

a. Probably Uffz Otto Gumz & Ltn Karl Otto, FlAbt (A) 203, KIA, Beine.
b. Possibly Uffz Willi Grunewald, FlAbt 251 (A), KIA, St Souplet.

Casualties:

MdL Georges Pouillard	N 96	P	KIA	Spad XIII, N° 16241, near Orainville, probably the victim of Vfw Herbert Boy Jasta 14, (2) who claimed a Spad at Aguilcourt, about 6.5 km NW of Orainville.
S/Lt Henri Leau	Sop 123	P	KIA	St Die
MdL Armand Mettivier &	Sop 260	P	WIA/POW	Sopwith N° 2505, probably by Ltn Konrad von Bülow, Jasta 19, (2).
S/Lt Hervé Picard-Destelan	Sop 260	O	KIA	
Sgt Baillon	Br 128	P	Injured	
Cpl Boucher &	46° Cie d'Aérostiers	XF		Soissons Sector, possibly by Ltn
S/Lt Joussaume		O	OK	Siegfried Büttner, Jasta 22s, (2).

4 February

S/Lt Gaillard	N 158	EA	P	Vaucelles	–
???	Sop ??	Albatros	P	Thann	–

Casualties:

S/Lt Baillodz &	Sop 17	P	KIA	These two Sopwiths probably downed by Ltn Konrad Bieler, Jasta 14, (3) and Ltn Ulrich Fischer, Jasta 22s, (1).
S/Lt Rousseau	Sop 17	O	KIA	
Sgt Henri Cordonnier &	Sop 129	P	KIA	
Cpl Allais	Sop 129	G	KIA	
Sgt Georges Bourie	Sop 134	P	KIAcc	
Sol Béchet	Sop 134	G	Injured	
Cpl Joseph Raymond &	???	P	KIAcc	
Sol Clauzet	???	M	Injured	
Cpl Lefeubre	AR 58	P	Injured	

5 February

Adj Gaudermen &	Spa 68					2
Adj P Baudry	Spa 68	Albatros D	X		Thiaucourt	2
Lt Fonck	Spa 103	2 seater	X		Avocourt	1205	22
Sgt Duvall &	GB 5					1
2/Lt Thompson, USAS	a. GB 5	Albatros D3	XF		Sarrebruck	1
???	b. DCA	Rumpler C	POW		Lérouville	–
Sgt Clément &	Br 117					1
Sgt Gueriaud	Br 117					1
1/Lt Wilson, USAS &	Br 117					1
Sgt Vaudelon	Br 117					1
S/Lt D'jobert &	Br 120					1
???	Br 120	Albatros D	X		Sarrebruck	1
Patrol	Spa 57	Albatros	P		Fresnes	1445	–
S/Lt Willemin	Spa 67	2 seater	P		Moulinville	1245	–
Adj Gaudermen &	Spa 68					–
Adj P Baudry	Spa 68	Albatros D	P		Thiaucourt	–
Adj Gaudermen &	Spa 68					–
Adj Baudry	Spa 68	Albatros	P		Thiaucourt	–
???	GB	2 Scouts	P		Sarrebruck	–

a. Possibly the Albatros D3 of Ltn Vetter, Kest 3, WIA near Lansdorf. First aerial victory credited to a USAS airman.
b. Rumpler C.4, occupants taken prisoner, Nancy Sector.

Casualties:

Cpl William H. Tailer	Spa 67	P	KIA	13h30 near Montzéville.
S/Lt Henri Leau	Sop 123	P	MIA	
Brig Mars	GDE	P	KIAcc	AR
MdL Joseph du Verne	???	P	KIAcc	
Brig Raymond &	AR 259	P	KIAcc	
Sol Clauzet	AR 259	M	Injured	VIII° Armée
Sgt Gendron	GDE	P	Injured	AR

6 February

Brig Chabrier	N 315	Scout	X		Belfort Sector		1
???	DCA	EA	X			a.m.	–

Casualties:

Brig Albert Chabrier	N 315	P	WIA	VII° Armée	
Cpl Claude	Br 213	P	Injured		
Lt Pierre Pascal	GB 7	P	Injured	Voison	
S/Lt Girard	GB 7	P	Injured	Voisin	

7 February – No Claims
Casualties:

QM René Dubourg	* EP	P	KIAcc	FBA 150HP, N° 532	

*   St Raphaël.

8 February

Sgt Chavannes	a. Spa 112	Albatros DV	X	Belfort Sector	1

a.   Probably Ltn Georg Michaelis, Jasta 41, KIA, at Füllern.

Casualties:

Sgt Herschel McKee	N 314	P	POW	Nieuport XXIV N° 5340, VIII° Armée hit by Flak over Château-Salins.	
Lt Henri Decoin	Spa 77	P	Injured		
Lt Chapon &	58° Cie d'Aérostiers			Attacked, not flamed,	
MdL Larquier		O	OK	Nancy Sector.	

9 February

???	GC 11	Rumpler C	FTL	Neufchâtel-sur-Aisne	1100 –
Lt de Turenne	CO Spa 12	EA	P	N Reservoir	–

Casualties:

Lt Maxime Maret &	Sop 9	P	KIAcc		
Sol Lavalette	Sop 9	M	Injured		
Cpl Théodore Petrognani	GDE	P	Injured	Nieuport	

10 February

S/Lt Bourjade	N 152	EA	P	Ban-de-Sapt	–

Casualties:

Adj Hans-Christian Welling-Bielsen	Sop 221	P	KIAcc		
S/Lt Paul Cotrait	Sop 221	O	Injured	Spad XI	

11 February

Sgt Gaillard &	Br 35				1
Lt Peyron	Br 35	Albatros D	X	Verdun	1
Adj Leclerc	Spa 102	EA	X	Goin	1
MdL Monnier &	AR 230				1
S/Lt Taron &	AR 230				1
S/Lt Goeury &	AR 230				1
S/Lt Berger	AR 230	Albatros D	X	VII° Armée	1
MdL Monnier &	AR 230				–
S/Lt Taron &	AR 230				–
S/Lt Goeury &	AR 230				–
S/Lt Berger	AR 230	Albatros D	P	VII° Armée	–

Casualties:

Adj Jean Desbaus &	Sop 60	P	WIA/POW	Sopwith N° 3504, probably by	
S/Lt Turinas	Sop 60	O	WIA/POW	Ltn Wilhelm Schulz, Jasta 41, (2).	
Brig Frédéric Monnier &	AR 230	P	WIA	VII° Armée, probably by a Jasta-	
S/Lt Taron	AR 230	O	WIA	76b pilot.	
Adj Julien Lanjard &	Spa 42	P	KIAcc		
Lt Pierre de Lignières	Spa 42	O	KIAcc	Spad XI	
Sgt André Fridberg	AR 70	P	Injured		
Lt Auvray	Spa 140	O	Injured	Letord N 263, IV° Armée.	
S/Lt Henri Parizy	82° Cie d'Aérostiers		XF	Nancy Sector, probably by Ltn	
		O	KIA	Niebecker, Jasta 43, (2).	
1/Lt James Wallace USBS	26° Cie d'Aérostiers		XF	VII° Armée, probably by	
		O	OK	Ltn Erich Raabe, Jasta 41, (1)	
???	27° Cie d'Aérostiers		XF	VII° Armée, probably by	
		O	OK	Ltn Hans Weiss, Jasta 41, (5).	

12 February

Cpl Boisnard &	Sal 225				1
Lt Fraisse	Sal 225	Scout	X	German lines	1

Lt Nungesser	Spa 65	EA	P	Nauroy-Beine	–
Lt de Sevin de Quincy	N 314	Albatros D3	FTL		–
Lt de Sevin de Quincy	N 314	Balloon	P	La Neuveville	–

Casualties:

Adj Adolphe Baranovitch	Spa 78	P	KIA	VII° Armée, combat with three two-seaters, probably by Obltn Schmid & Gefr Braun, FlAbt (A) 289,
Cpl Louis Bardoulat	N 162	P	MIA	VII° Armée, by Vfw Bauschke & Ltn Buse, FlAbt (A) 218,
Lt Henri Schwander	Spa 112	P	WIA/POW	VII° Armée, Spad VII N° 1268, probably by Ltn Hans Weiss, Jasta 41, (5).
Cpl Francisquet Boisnard &	Sal 225	P	OK	
Lt Pierre Fraisse	Sal 225	O	WIA	Salmson, VIII° Armée
MdL Rochard & *	CI	P	KIAcc	
Sol Souffrand *	CI	M	KIAcc	
MdL Merle des Isles &	V 114	P	KIAcc	
Cpl Viennois	V 114	G	Injured	
Sgt Georges Bernardeau	Sop 134	P	Injured	
Sol Boudon	Spa 153	M	Injured	
Sgt Gros	Sop 5	P	Injured	
Adj Henri Maque *	CI	P	Injured	
Lt Pierre Bacalou &	45° Cie d'Aérostiers		XF	Probably by Ltn Heinrich
2/Lt Doherty, USAS		O	OK	Arntzen, Jasta 50, (9).

*   Sommessous.

---

13 February – No Claims
Casualties:

MdL Georges Pouillard	MF ?	P	MIA	
Cpl André Ricard	GDE	P	Injured	Nieuport
Sgt André Autiquet	CAP 130	P	Injured	Bréguet

---

14 February – No Claims
Casualties:

S/Lt Chabagny	Spa 140	O	WIA	Spad XI, IV° Armée.
MdL Roche	AR 40	P	WIA	Flak, IV° Armée.
MdL Aimé Chardin &	C 18	P	KIAcc	
Asp Bucquet	C 18	O	KIAcc	Caudron G6.
Lt Jean Wambergue &	N 214	P	KIAcc	
MdL Armand Rosset	N 214	G	KIAcc	Sopwith

---

15 February

S/Lt Madon	Spa 38	EA	P	Liry-Marvaux	–
S/Lt Gaillard	N 158	EA	P		–

Casualties:

MdL Alexandre Brétillon	Spa 79	P	WIA	La Fère
Cpl Drunel &	Spa 34	P	Injured	
Lt Corsanini	Spa 34	O	Injured	Spad XI
MdL Alexandre Leduc	N 92	P	Injured	Nieuport
S/Lt Allegrie &	??? Cie d'Aérostiers			Attacked, not flamed, probably by
1/Lt Allport, USBS		O	OK	Ltn Siegfried Büttner, Jasta 22s, (3).

---

16 February

Lt Bozon-Verduraz &	Spa 3					1
Lt de la Rochfordière	Spa 3	EA	X	E Damloup	1135	1
S/Lt Wertheim	Spa 84	2 seater	X	Dontrien		1
MdL Discours &	Spa 87					1
MdL Gasser a.	Spa 87	DFW C	X	N Xures	1030	1
??? b.	???	LVG C.V	POW	Catigny		–
??? c.	???	FdH G.III	POW			–
S/Lt Gaillard	N 158	2 seater	P	Vaucelles		–
Patrol	GC 13	3 EA	P			–

a.   Possibly Uffz Franz Traitteur & Ltn Josef Dechant, FlAbt (A) 199, KIAs, AOK 19 Sector.
b.   N° 9812/17, possibly from BG7/BSt23.
c.   Friedrichman N° 326/17, probably from BG1/BSt1.

Casualties:

Adj Martial Gilet	Spa 86	P	WIA

Sol Dabanovitch	Sop 123	G	KIAcc			
Cpl Thomas	Spa 54	M	KIAcc	Hit by propeller.		
S/Lt Sadi Coignard	Spa 154	P	Injured	DOW 28 February 1918.		
Sgt Joseph Sauvignet	Sop 134	P	Injured	DOW 27 February 1918.		

17 February

Lt Bozon-Verduraz		Spa 3	2 seater	X	Montfaucon	1215	2
MdL Lamur		Spa 62	Balloon	XF			1
Sgt Prévost		Spa 68	EA	X			1
Lt de Nompère de Champagny		Spa 86	EA	XF	NW Reservoir		1
VII° Armée	a.	DCA	2 seater	X	St Die		–
???		DCA	EA	X			–
???	b.	???	2 seater	POW			–
S/Lt Madon		Spa 38	EA	P	Lavannes		–
Sgt Garaud		Spa 38	EA	P	Cornillet		–
???		???	2 EA	P			–
Sgt Grenez		N 99	AEG	FTL	Hattigny		–

a.   Probably Ltn Nikolaus Ohlweiler & Ltn Theodor Ott, FlAbt 10, KIAs St Die.
b.   For unknown reasons this two-seater landed in French territory where the occupants were taken prisoner.

Casualties:

Lt Clément Plane,	AR 32	P	MIA	Letord, AA fire, probably
S/Lt René Garrier &	AR 32	O	MIA	by Flakbatterie 563, OfStv
MdL Mail	AR 32	G	MIA	von Kolada.
Cpl Robert Sevault	???	P	KIA	
S/Lt Houpert	C 47	O	WIA	
Cpl Francisquet Comby	N 98	P	KIAcc	
Lt Graffin	DPTA	O	KIAcc	
Cpl Pierre Bourgeois	N 68	P	Injured	Spad
Lt Georges Bourseul	Spa 63	P	KIAcc	Spad XI
Lt Bonneton	Spa 63	O	Injured	DOW 19 February 1918
???	27° Cie d'Aérostiers		XF	Probably by Ltn Schulte,
		O	OK	Jasta 50, (1).
2/Lt Thomas Barrow USBS	88° Cie d'Aérostiers			Attacked, not flamed.

18 February

Lt Jaille,	Spa 75					3
S/Lt Hérisson,	Spa 75					6
Adj Chrétien &	Spa 75					1
MdL Freycinet	Spa 31	2 seater	X	Missy-sur-Aisne		2
S/Lt Fonck	Spa 103	Albatros D	X	Bezonvaux	1300	23
S/Lt Madon	Spa 38	EA	P	IV° Armée		–
S/Lt Madon	Spa 38	EA	P	IV° Armée		–
S/Lt Fonck &	Spa 103					–
three other pilots	Spa 103	2 seater	P	Bezonvaux		–

Casualties:

Sgt Edward J. Loughran	N 84	P	KIA	IV° Armée, Spad, S Minaucourt.
S/Lt Maurice Finat &	Spa 20	P	WIA	VII° Armée, Spad XI, probably by
Sgt Roux	Spa 20	G	WIA	Ltn Karl Odebrett, Jasta 42, (8).
MdL Charles Champagne	CEP 115	P	KIAcc	
MdL Henri Langlois	CEP 115	P	KIAcc	
S/Lt Rouanet	AR 268	O	Burned	Signal Flare exploded.
Brig Marcel Colombel	V 114	P	Injured	
Sol Gauthier	Spa 53	M	Injured	

19 February

Cpl Baylies	a.	Spa 3	2 seater	XF	N Forges	1315	1
Cpl Burello		Spa 23	EA	X			1
S/Lt Rochechouart de Mortemart		Spa 23	EA	X			7
Capt Vachon &	CO	Sop 39					1
Lt Roques		Sop 39					1
Sgt Lemarie &		Spa 42					1
Sgt Geroux		Spa 42					1
Adj Pigier &		Sal 51					1

???		Sal 51	Scout	X	German lines	1
Sgt Garaud	b.	Spa 38	EA	X	Prunay	8
Adj Caillaux,		Spa 48				3
S/Lt Bajac &		Spa 48				4
Adj Roques		Spa 48	Rumpler C	XF	Nogent l'Abbesse	3
Adj Bouyer	c.	Spa 49	Scout	X	Pfetterhausen	7
S/Lt Fonck	a.	Spa 103	Albatros C	X	Montfaucon	1205 24
???		DCA	EA	X		–
Lt Nungesser		Spa 65	EA	P		–

a. Possibly Obltn Hans Karl Frhr von Wolfskeel-Reichenberg, Jasta 34b, KIA over Mort Homme.
b. Possibly Vfw Adolf Schulz & Ltn Erich Richter, FlAbt (A) 203, KIAs, Prunay.
c. Possibly OfStv Albers and Ltn Hirsching, FlAbt (A) 276, or Vfw Machens & Ltn Rotenhöfer, FlAbt (A) 218, MIAs, in AOK "A" Sector.

Casualties:

Cpl Auguste Perry &	PS 126	P	MIA	Bréguet, probably by Ltn	
Lt Huguet	PS 126	O	MIA	Wolfgang Güttler, Jasta 13, (8).	
S/Lt Eve	Sop 269	O	WIA		
S/Lt Roques	Sop 39	O	WIA		
Cpl Jean Andraud	N 162	P	Injured	DOW 12 March 1918, Nieuport XXIV.	
Sol Monier	GB 8	M	Injured		
Cpl Jean Damilleville	N 100	P	Injured		
???	27° Cie d'Aérostiers	XF		VII° Armée, probably by	
		O	OK	Ltn Albert Dietlen, Jasta 41, (4).	

20 February

Lt Bozon-Verduraz &		Spa 3				3
Lt de la Rochefordière		Spa 3	2 seater	XF	Les Eparges	1120 2
Lt Raymond	CO	Spa 3	2 seater	X	N Vauquois	1640 5
Capt Pinsard	CO	Spa 23	Albatros	X	Forêt d'Apremont	17
S/Lt Sardier &		Spa 77				4
S/Lt Boyau		Spa 77	Balloon	XF	Vaxy	0735 13
S/Lt Madon		Spa 38	EA	P	Vivère	–
S/Lt Bourjade		Spa 152	Balloon	P		–
???		???	EA	P		–

Casualties:

Cpl Jean Six		N 159	P	POW	Nieuport XXIVbis N° 3305, probably by Ltn Niebecker, Jasta 43, (3), VIII° Armée
MdL François		N99	P	WIA	Groundfire, VIII° Armée.
QM Hervé Fave	*	EP	P	KIAcc	
EV1 Charles Fleury,	**	CAM	P	KIAcc	La Hève,
QM Eugène Julien &	**	CAM	M	KIAcc	Dirigible N° VA 3.
SM Jean Folini	**	CAM	R	KIAcc	
MdL Gaston Méchin &		Sop 131	P	Injured	
Cpl Michel		Sop 131	G	Injured	

* Châteauroux.
** Le Havre.

21 February

MdL Berthold	Spa 15	Rumpler C	P	Epoye	–
???		GB	EA	P	–

Casualties:

Sgt Henri Jacquemin	Spa 80	P	Injured	

22 February – No Claims
Casualties:

Lt José Cabrita	Sop 208	P	Injured	Bréguet

23 February

S/Lt J Schneider &	Spa 49				1
S/Lt H Schneider	Spa 49	EA	X	Aspach	1
French Artillery	???	Balloon	XF		–

Casualties:

Sgt Joseph Piton &	AR 274	P	KIA	VII° Armée, XF
Lt Jean Daguillon	AR 274	O	KIA	
S/Lt Henri Schneider	N 49	P	WIA	DOW 24 February 1918, Spad, probably by Ltn Walter Ewers, Jasta 77b, (6), VII° Armée.

24 February – No Claims
Casualties:

S/Lt Raymond Arnault &	Sop 29	P	KIA	
Cpl Henri Rouanet	Sop 29	G	KIA	Bréguet N° 1346
Adj André Lévy &	Sop 29	P	KIA	
Cpl Jean Albrecht	Sop 29	G	KIA	Bréguet N° 1354
Sgt Baron &	Sop 29	P	WIA	
Adj Orain	Sop 29	G	WIA	Bréguet, claimed by Jasta 41 pilots, Ltns Hans Weiss (8), Georg Schlenker (12) & Albert Dietlen (5).
Lt Charles Houssemand	Avord	P	KIAcc	
Adj Morel	Spa 20	P	Injured	Spad XI, VII° Armée
Brig Jacques Champion	N 82	P	Injured	
Cpl Huguet	4° Armée	P	Injured	

25 February – No Claims – No Casualties

26 February

S/Lt Fonck		Spa 103	2 seater	X	S Montfaucon	1010	25
S/Lt Fonck	a.	Spa 103	2 seater	X	Dieppe	1025	26
S/Lt Bucquet	b.	Spa 3	Balloon	XF	Belleray	–
???		???	EA	P		–

a.   Possibly Uffz Paul Hess, Jasta 42, KIA, Pannes, AOK "C" Sector.
b.   This was a small balloon carrying leaflets and was not confirmed as a victory.

Casualties:

Lt Robert Sénéchal	N 83	P	MIA	Spad, in flames near Paissy.
MdL Emile Robert &	Sop 51	P	MIA	
S/Lt François Dorlencourt	Sop 51	O	KIA	Salmson
S/Lt Pierre Marin	N 87	P	KIA	VIII° Armée, Nieuport N° 5690, by Erich Weiss, Jasta 33 (1).
S/Lt Poevilliers	12 CA	R	KIA	Bombardment of airfield
Asp Murat	Sal 1	O	WIA	VII° Armée, FTL during combat.
S/Lt Jean Durand,	R 46	P	KIAcc	
Sgt Castagnier &	R 46	R	KIAcc	
Adj-Chef Robert Mazeron	R 46	G	KIAcc	Caudron
Lt Jean Tourtay	MS 156	P	KIAcc	Morane
Sgt Alexandre Dumollard &	GDE	P	Injured	
Sgt Delgay	GDE	O	Injured	AR
Adj Maurice Cabe	GDE	P	Injured	Sopwith
Sgt Niepceron	Sop 106	P	Injured	
S/Lt Joseph Cussonneau	33° Cie d'Aérostiers		XF	Probably by Gefr Rudolf
		O	WIA	Kassner, Jasta 65, (1).
???	55° Cie d'Aérostiers		XF	II° Armée, 14h00, near the Forêt de
		O	OK	Hesse, probably by Ltn Konrad Schwartz, Jasta 22s, (1).
MdL Christian Oudard	59° Cie d'Aérostiers		XF	II° Armée, 14h00, near the Forêt de
		O	OK	Hesse, probably by Vfw Paul Färber, Jasta 22s, (2).
S/Lt André Lebouc &	90° Cie d'Aérostiers		XF	V° Armée, probably by Ltn Schulte,
S/Lt Flett (USBS)		O	OK	Jasta 50, (2).
2/Lt Thomas Barrow USBS	88° Cie d'Aérostiers			Attacked, not flamed, 80 bullet holes in balloon.

Two other balloons were attacked without success.

27 February – No Claims
Casualties:

Cpl Marcel Janet	GDE	P	MIA	Nieuport XXIVbis N° 4713, possibly by Obltn Paul Blumenbach, Jasta 12, (1).

28 February – No Claims
Casualties:

Cpl Jean Valder	GDE	P	Injured	AR
MdL Jacques Chameroy	GDE	P	Injured	

The date of this February victory cannot be established at this time:
S/Lt Paul Baudry,   Spa 68

| Adj Pierre Baudry & | Spa 68 | | | German lines. | |
| MdL Planiol | Spa 68 | Scout | X | Conf 14 Mar 18 (14.446) | |

1 March

Adj Montrion	Spa 48	2 seater	X	Nogent l'Abbesse	8
Sgt Quiles	Spa 48	EA	P	N St Hilaire-le-Petit	–
Sgt Quiles	Spa 48	EA	P	Manre	–
1/Lt Baer, USAS	103rdUS	EA	P	St Souplet	–

Casualties:

Brig Collin &	Sop 231	P	KIAcc		
S/Lt Gauvin	Sop 231	O	KIAcc		
Cpl Gasperi	N 89	P	Injured	Spad	
Cpl John F. Randall	N 158	P	Injured	Morane	
MdL René Ropert	N 158	P	Injured	Morane	
Sgt Jean Barnier	GDE	P	Injured	AR	
Lt Pierre Bacalou &					
2/Lt Fred Morgan, USBS	?? Cie d'Aérostiers		XF	Hptm Adolf von Tutschek	
		O	OK	CO JGII (25).	

2 March – No Claims – No Casualties

3 March – No Claims
Casualties:

| Lt Perruch de Velma & | Sop 231 | P | Injured | | |
| S/Lt Stehle | Sop 231 | O | Injured | | |

4 March – No Claims – No Casualties

5 March

Adj-Chef Peronneau &	Spa 81				7
S/Lt Herbelin	Spa 81	2 seater	XF	Challevois	1040	10
Adj de Marmier &	Spa 112				2
Sgt Chavannes	Spa 112	DFW C	X	Munster-Colmar	2
Adj de Marmier &	Spa 112				3
Sgt Chavannes	Spa 112	DFW C	X	Munster-Colmar	3
Brig Stahl	Spa 150	DFW C	X	Cernay	1
Ran out of petrol	a. DCA	Albatros DV	POW	Bras	1345	–
???	b. DCA	EA	XF	Massif de Berru	–

a.   Gefr Lothmann, Jasta 65, POW, SE Bras, Albatros DVa N° 5695.
b.   Probably Uffz Albert Matz & Ltn Georg von Döring, FlAbt 212 (A), KIAs at Berru.

Casualties:

Cpl Debras &	Sop 281	P	POW	Sopwith N° 2629, possibly	
Sol Honin	Sop 281	G	POW	by Flakbatterie 535.	
MdL Raymond Gaumont &	C 10	O	WIA		
Cpl André Guérin	C 10	G	WIA	Letord III	
MdL Marcel Chapaut	???	P	KIAcc		
Cdt Robert Massenet					
de Marancour CO	GC 14	P	Injured	Spad	
Capt Léon Bonne	N 98	P	Injured	Nieuport XXIV	
MdL Maurice Bizot	N 90	P	Injured	Nieuport XXIV	
Cpl Cordier	Sop 281	P	Injured		
Brig Jacques Duteurtre	80° Cie d'Aérostiers		XF	Probably by Ltn Helmut	
		O	WIA	Contag, Jasta 65, (4).	

One other balloon attacked but not flamed.

6 March

Adj Garaud	Spa 38	2 seater	X	Main-de-Massiges	9
Adj Douchy	a. Spa 38	EA	X	Main-de-Massiges	9
S/Lt Madon	Spa 38	EA	P	Monts	–
Adj Leclerc &	Spa 102				–
Capt Derode CO	Spa 102	EA	P		–
Patrol	Spa 12	Hannover CL	FTL	Evergnicourt	–

a.   Possibly Ltn Erich Bahr, Jasta 11, KIA Nauroy-Etricourt, operating area of Spa 38.

Casualties:

| S/Lt Henri Dorizon | Spa 150 | P | KIA | Spad XIII, probably by Ltn Walter | |
| | | | | Böning, Jasta 76b, (10), VII° Armée. | |

Name		Unit		Fate	Notes	
Brig Paul Brun		Spa 151	P	KIA	Probably by Ltn Walter Böning, Jasta 76b,(11), VII° Armée.	
Sgt Thomas Hitchcock, Jr. (American)		Spa 87	P	WIA/POW	Spad VII N° 1765, probably by Ltn Georg Weiner, Kest 3, (2), AOK 19. Escaped 28 August 1918, into Switzerland, then to France.	
Cpl Jean Lafay		Spa 93	P	MIA	Spad, probably by Vfw Günther Dobberke, Jasta 45, (1).	
Cpl Fernand Deltour		N 152	P	KIA	VII° Armée, Nieuport, probably by Ltn Albert Dietlen, Jasta 41, (6).	
Adj Albert Tessier,		Spa 20	P	KIA	VII° Armée, Letord, probably by	
Asp Delorme &		Spa 20	O	KIA	Ltn Hans Weiss, Jasta 41,	
Cpl Appert		Spa 20	G	KIA	unconfirmed.	
Sgt Ombredanne &		AR 253	P	KIA	Probably by Vfw Konrad	
Cpl Nguyen-Xuan-Nha		AR 253	G	KIA	Brendle, Jasta 45, (1).	
Lt Girbal		GDE	P	KIAcc	AR	
MdL Delayre		GDE	P	KIAcc	AR	
Cpl Huard &		AR 267	P	KIAcc	AR N° 1417	
S/Lt Granger		AR 267	O	Injured	DOW 7 March 1918	
Cpl Lourme		7° Armée	P	Injured		
Cpl Marteau &	*	CI	P	Injured		
Asp Boivin	*	CI	O	Injured	Sopwith	
Sgt André Leclair		N 92	P	Injured	Nieuport XXIV	
???		56° Cie d'Aérostiers		XF	IV° Armée, probably by Ltn	
			O	OK	Paul Jäger, Jasta 9, (1).	
S/Lt Gustave Lemaitre &		87° Cie d'Aérostiers		XF	IV° Armée, probably by Ltn	
1/Lt Sidney I Howell, USBS			O	OK	Erich Thomas, Jasta 9 (4).	

*   Sommessous.

7 March

Name		Unit		Fate	Notes	
Cpl Baylies		Spa 3	EA	X	NE Courtecon	2
???		DCA	EA	X		–

Casualties:

Name		Unit		Fate	Notes	
S/Lt Martin Trepp		Spa 12	P	MIA	Nieuport	
Brig Glenisson &		Br 127	P	POW		
Cpl Taulera		Br 127	G	POW	Bréguet 14 N° 1206	
Sgt Gabariel Liesta		AR 58	P	KIAcc	VII° Armée, AR	
Mat Louis Guégan	*	CAM	P	KIAcc	Hanriot HD.2 N° 231, codé D.36.	
Sgt Didier		RGA'	P	Injured	DOW 8 March 1918, Sopwith	
Cpl Dejan		GDE	P	Injured	Sopwith	

*   Dunkerque.

8 March

Name		Unit		Fate	Notes	
Lt Goux,		C 10				2
Sgt Gaumont &		C 10				1
Brig Guérin		C 10	Albatros D3	X	Grandelain-Malval	2
Adj Garaud		Spa 38	2 seater	X	St Martin l'Heureux	10
S/Lt J Milliat &		Spa 80				1
MdL Delmetz		Spa 80	2 seater	X	Berrieux-Prouvais	1
S/Lt Demeuldre		Spa 84	Rumpler C	X	Forêt de Coucy	10
Ground fire		???	Albatros D3	X	Belfort	–
???	a.	DCA	FdH	X	Forêt de Compiègne	2145 –
???		Sal ??	EA	P	Crepy	–
1/Lt Wilcox		103rdUS	EA	P		–

a.   Crew of four KIAs, probably including Ltn Leo von Heydebreck (P) & Hptm Fritz Eckstein (O), BG 5, KIAs Compiègne.

Casualties:

Name		Unit		Fate	Notes	
MdL Connin &		Br 107	P	MIA		
Sol Cador		Br 107	G	MIA	Bréguet N° 1277 ??.	
Cpl Michel &		Br 107	P	MIA		
MdL Hertzog		Br 107	G	MIA	Bréguet N° 1278.	
Sgt Aureléin Larroucau		Br 107	P	KIA		
Brig Bouet		Br 107	G	KIA	Bréguet N° 1272	
Cpl Wallace Winter		MS 156	P	KIA	Nauroy, Morane-Saulnier N° 1512, probably by Ltn Julius Keller, Jasta 21s, (1).	
Capt Jean de Fontenillat &	CO	C 17	P	KIA	Flak	

Lt Gaubert		C 17	O	WIA	Flak, Sopwith 1A2	
Sgt Guignaud &		AR 274	P	OK	VII° Armée, FTL during combat.	
Lt Barrère		AR 274	O	WIA	AR	
Lt Goux,		C 10	P	OK		
MdL Raymond Gaumont &		C 10	O	WIA		
Cpl Guérin		C 10	G	WIA	Letord III	
Sgt Blanchard &		C 21	P	KIAcc		
Sol Jouvance		C 21	M	Injured	AR	
Sgt Cortes		GDE	P	Injured	Morane Parasol	

9 March

Lt Madon	a.	Spa 38	2 seater	XF	Pont-Faverger		24
Lt Madon	b.	Spa 38	Scout	X	Pomacle		25
Cpl Bosson		Spa 62	EA	XF	Clacy-Thirret		1
Adj Ruamps &		N 87		X			3
MdL Wellman		N 87	Rumpler C	X		1630	2
Adj Ruamps		N 87	Albatros DV	X	US Lines	1630	4
S/Lt Déjobert &		Br 120					2
???		Br 120	EA	X			?
S/Lt Madon		Spa 38	EA	P	Lavannes		–
Adj Garaud		Spa 38	EA	P	St Pierre-à-Arnes		–
Cpl Bosson		Spa 62	EA	P			–
Cpl Bosson		Spa 62	EA	P			–
Cpl Dalet		N 87	2 seater	P	E Blamont	1445	–
MdL Wellman		N 87	Albatros DV	P	US Lines	1635	3
1/Lt Baer		103rdUS	EA	P			–
???		???	EA	P			–

a. Possibly Vfw Ernst Schiemann & Ltn August Daniel, FlAbt 270 (A), KIAs Bemont Ferme.
b. Possibly Ltn Joachim Nissen, Jasta 52, KIA, Malmaison.

Casualties:

Sgt Curtet &	C 47	P	MIA	Salmson, possibly by Ltn
S/Lt Posse	C 47	O	MIA	Karl Odebrett, Jasta 42, (9).
Capt James E Miller CO	95thUS	P	KIA	Spad N° 3144, Nerrieux
MdL Henri Clément &	Sop 277	P	OK	
S/Lt Poissonnier	Sop 277	O	WIA	Flak
Adj Poitou	V 116	P	Injured	

10 March

???	???	EA	X		–
S/Lt Madon	Spa 38	2 seater	P	N Sommepy	–
Adj de Marmier &	Spa 112				–
Sgt Chevannes	Spa 112	EA	P	Swiss Border	–
Capt Collins, USAS	103rdUS	EA	P	Epoye	–
???	103rdUS	EA	P	Nauroy	–

Casualties:

Adj Eugène Vallod	Spa 86	P	KIA	Malmaison, by Hptm Adolf von Tutschek, CO JGII, (27).
S/Lt Got	Sop 276	O	WIA	
Lt Emile Brantonne	Spa 153	P	OK	Shot down in flames over Laval, but landed OK.
Lt Damelincourt,	C 74	P	OK	
Lt Girard &	C 74	O	WIA	
Sol Bodin-Donnat	C 74	G	WIA	Caudron
Lt Duhart	GDE	P	Injured	AR
Capt Francois Coli CO	N 62	P	Injured	Spad VII
Lt Pierre Coubris	N 160	P	Injured	
Adj Bernard Breton	N 93	P	Injured	
MdL Dusseau	Sop 231	O	Injured	Sopwith 1A2

11 March

S/Lt G Guérin		Spa 15	EA	X	Berry-au-Bac		16
Adj Garaud		Spa 38	EA	X	Aubérive-Dontrien		11
Adj de Marmier &		Spa 112					4
Sgt Chavannes	a.	Spa 112	Rumpler CIV	POW	S Petit-Croix		4
1/Lt Baer		103rdUS	Albatros D	X	Cernay-les-Reims		1
???	b.	DCA	Gotha G	XF	Château-Thierry	p.m.	–
???	c.	DCA	2 motor	X	N Soissons	p.m.	–

???	d.	DCA	Gotha G	XF	Essones	p.m.	–
???		???	2 seater	X	Meaux	p.m.	–
Capt Collins		103rdUS	2 seater	P	IV° Armée		–
S/Lt G Guérin &		Spa 15					–
Adj Artigau		Spa 15	2 seater	P	NE Berry-au-Bac		
S/Lt G Guérin &		Spa 15					–
Adj Artigau		Spa 15	2 seater	P	NE Berry-au-Bac		
Capt Pinsard	CO	Spa 23	EA	P	Gremilly		–
Sgt Bruley		Spa 23	EA	P	Damvillers		–

a.   Possibly Vfw Fritz Gramms & Ltn Hans Kraus, FlAbt 289b (A), POWs.
b.   Crew of four POWs.
c.   Crew of three POWs.
d.   Crew of three KIAs, including Hptm Schoebler, Bogohl VII, 3 Kasta.
NOTE: BG 2 is known to have had five airmen taken prisoner this date: Ltn Georg Kretschmer (P), Ltn Piachnow (P), Ltn Karl Pott (O), Uffz Franz Schober (G), and Uffz Witte (G).

Casualties:

Brig Abdon Borca &		AR 58	P	OK	
Asp Benjamin Girardot		AR 58	O	WIA	Flak, VII° Armée
Cpl Staquet &		AR 40	P	WIA	Flak IV° Armée, FTL W Prosnes.
S/Lt Beucler		AR 40	O	WIA	Flak, Probably by Flakzug 86 Ltn Goebel.
Lt Pinchart		Sop 250	O	WIA	Bombardment of airfield
MdL Louis Bringay		GDE	P	KIAcc	Nieuport
Lt Legrende		GDE	P	KIAcc	Caudron G3
MdL Benoit	*	CI	P	Injured	AR
MdL Paul Basset		AR 201	P	Injured	
Cpl André Boudinaud		GDE	P	Injured	Sopwith

*   Sommesssous.

---

12 March

Lt Mazimann,		Spa 57					1
S/Lt Nuville &		Spa 57					2
S/Lt Hasdenteufel	a.	Spa 57	DFW C	X	Fresnes		2
Cpl Bosson		Spa 62	Fokker DrI	X	Crepy-en-Laonnois	1405	2
Lt Nungesser		Spa 65	EA	X	Craonne		31
Sgt Bruley &		Spa 23					–
MdL de Bailly		Spa 23	2 seater	P	Azannes		–
Adj Garaud	b.	Spa 38	EA	P	Marquises		–
MdL Bizot,		Spa 90					–
Cpl Sullivan &		Spa 90					–
Cpl Pezon		Spa 90	2 seater	FTL	Château-Salins	1515	–
1/Lt Baer		103rdUS	Scout	P	Vitry-les-Reims		–

a.   Possibly Ltn Schreibler & Ltn Peter Frhr von und zu Mentzingen, BG 2/BSt 1, KIAs Château-Thierry, about 12 km SW of Fresnes-en-Tardenois.
b.   Possibly Ltn Oskar Ehricht & Ltn Karl Mösenthin, FlAbt (A) 252w, KIAs St Clémens-à-Arnes, about 15 km NE Marquises.

Casualties:

Brig Petros &		V 125	P	MIA	IV° Armée
MdL de Castellane		V 125	G	MIA	Voisin R
Lt Denis &		AR 40	P	OK	
S/Lt Betge-Lagarde		AR 40	O	KIA	IV° Armée, AR
Capt Phelps Collins		103rdUS	P	KIA	IV° Armée, Spad
S/Lt André Derode		Pau	P	KIAcc	
Adj Mosir		Spa 83	P	Injured	
S/Lt Pagnier &		Sop 251	P	Injured	
Lt Yves Onno		Sop 251	O	Injured	Sopwith 1A2
Cpl Claverie &		Sop 263	P	Injured	
S/Lt Chapuillot		Sop 263	O	Injured	
Sol Latour		Sop 8	M	Injured	AR
S/Lt Menissier		GDE	P	Injured	Morane-Saulnier

---

13 March

Adj-Chef Laplasse		Spa 75	2 seater	X	Septvaux		2
S/Lt Bucquet		Spa 3	Scout	P	Guignicourt	1250	–
Sgt Bruley		Spa 23	EA	P	Ornes		–
Lt Letourneau		Spa 26	Scout	P	Asfeld	1310	–
Adj-Chef Baron		Spa 103	Scout	P	S Nogent l'Abbesse	1350	–

Casualties:

Cpl Chaputs &		V 114	P	MIA	
S/Lt Contine		V 114	O	MIA	II° Armée

Cpl Charles Dugay &	Sop 278	P	KIA			
2/Lt Richard L Whitner	Sop 278	O	KIA	IV° Armée, Sopwith		
Capt René Itier	Spa 112	P	KIAcc	Spad XIII		
Cpl Pierre Méry &	Sop 141	P	KIAcc		Collided	
S/Lt Boelm	Sop 141	O	KIAcc	Sopwith		
Cpl Claude &	GDE	P	KIAcc	Voisin P		
Sgt Lafargue	GDE	G	Injured	Voisin P		
Adj Georges Longère	N 86	P	Injured	Spad		
Brig Cantegril	Spa 212	P	Injured	Spad XI		
S/Lt Petit	Spa 213	O	Injured	Spad XI		
S/Lt Canal	Sop 60	P	Injured			
MdL Poitte &	Sop 231	P	Injured			
S/Lt Ducasse	Sop 231	O	Injured	Sopwith 1A2		
MdL Robert Berthelot	AR 44	P	Injured	AR		
Capt Henri Ballyguier CO	CEP 115	P	Injured	Caproni		
S/Lt Albert Depoux	61° Cie d'Aérostiers		XF	II° Armée, probably by		
		O	OK	Uffz Erich Meyer, Jasta 45, (1).		
Lt Tiau	26° Cie d'Aérostiers		XF	VII° Armée, probably by Ltn Hans		
		O	OK	Weiss, Jasta 41, (10).		
S/Lt Georges Magnan	53° Cie d'Aérostiers		XF	IV° Armée, probably by Ltn Erich		
		O	OK	Thomas, Jasta 9, (5).		
???	57° Cie d'Aérostiers			IV° Armée, both attacked		
???	72° Cie d'Aérostiers			not flamed. Observers OK.		

14 March

S/Lt G Guérin	Spa 15	EA	P			–
Sgt Putnam	MS 156	Albatros	P	Nauroy		–
Casualties:						
Cpl Chapius &	V 114	P	MIA	Voisin R, probably by O Flakzug		
S/Lt Contini	V 114	O	MIA	83 & O Flak S zug 121.		
Brig Nicolay	Sop 285	P	Injured			
Lt Rousset	GDE	O	Injured	Voisin P		
Lt Le Maignen	Escad 1	O	Injured			
S/Lt Emile Ponge	85° Cie d'Aérostiers		XF	IV° Armée, probably by Ltn		
		O	Injured	Erich Thomas, Jasta 9, (6).		
Lt Gaston Sauvage &	57° Cie d'Aérostiers			IV° Armée, attacked, not		
Adj Charles Guggenheim		O	OK	flamed.		
One other balloon attacked, not flamed.						

15 March

Adj Quette	Spa 62	EA	X	Orgeval		6
S/Lt Fonck	Spa 103	2 seater	X	Berméricourt	1015	27
S/Lt Fonck	Spa 103	2 seater	X	N Courtecon	1725	28
Sgt Schmitter	Spa 103	2 seater	X	Vorges-Lierval	1730	1
Sgt Putnam	MS 156	Rumpler C	X	Beine		3
S/Lt Madon	Spa 38	EA	P	Selles		–
S/Lt Baudry	Spa 68	Albatros	P	S Vigneulles	0830	–
???	Sop 252	EA	P	VII° Armée		–
Casualties:						
Sgt Gacon &	Sop 252	P	KIA	VII° Armée, Sopwith N° 3476 probably		
S/Lt Malot	Sop 252	O	KIA	by Ltn Walter Böning, Jasta 76b, (12),		
Sgt Martin	Sal 61	G	WIA			
S/Lt Jean Macé	Sal 61	O	WIA			
S/Lt Caulier	GDE	P	KIAcc	Spad		
MdL Berthier	N 99	P	KIAcc			
Cpl Jean Bert &	Sop 251	P	Injured			
Lt Legorju	Sop 251	O	Injured	Sopwith 1A2		
Cpl Cavillon	V 25	P	Injured			
Cpl Marcus &	Sop 252	P	OK	VII° Armée, shot down		
S/Lt Guérineau	Sop 252	O	OK	between lines.		

16 March

Sgt Baylies	a.	Spa 3	Scout	XF	Chevrigny	1735	3
S/Lt Levrier-Coffard &		Spa 38					1
1/Lt Baer, USAS		103rdUS	Albatros C	XF	Nogent l'Abbesse		2
S/Lt Demeuldre		Spa 84	Rumpler C	X	NE Anizy		11
S/Lt Fonck		Spa 103	2 seater	XF	Nogent l'Abbesse	1150	29

Sgt Baux		Spa 103	Albatros DV	XF	Vitry-les-Reims	1750	1
Adj Garaud	b.	Spa 38	2 seater	P	Vitry-les-Reims		–
Adj Pendaries		Spa 67	2 seater	P	S Challerange	1420	–
S/Lt Letourneau		Spa 26	2 seater	FTL	N Fismes		–

a.   Possibly Ltn Walter Riedel (O), FlAbt 209 (A), KIA near Soissons, about 15 km SW of Chrevigny.
b.   Probably Ltn Paul Jäger, Jasta 9, KIA Berru, about 3 km SE Witry-les-Reims.

Casualties:

S/Lt François de				Spad XIII N° 2167, probably by Ltn Arno
Rochechouart de Mortemart	Spa 23	P	MIA	Benzler, Jasta 65, (3), at Consenvoye.
Cpl Raymond d'Argence &	Spa 62	P	POW	Spad XI N° 6084, probably
Cpl Ledig	Spa 62	G	POW	by Ltn Bleibtrau, Jasta 45, (1).
MdL Jung	GDE	P	KIAcc	Nieuport
Brig Morin &	C 228	P	KIAcc	
Lt Paul Chatel	C 228	O	Injured	Spad XI N° 4032.
Cpl Pierre Depaulis	Spa 88	P	Injured	Spad
Adj René Feuilette	41° Cie d'Aérostiers	XF		IV° Armée, probably by Ltn
		O	OK	Erich Thomas, Jasta 9, (7).
Adj Paul Marion	44° Cie d'Aérostiers	XF		IV° Armée, probably by Ltn Erich
		O	OK	Thomas, Jasta 9, (8).
S/Lt Jean Desbouts &	36° Cie d'Aérostiers	XF		II° Armée, probably by Ltn Hans
Adj André Bry		O	OK	Hans Rolfes, Jasta 45, (3).
???	?? Cie d'Aérostiers	XF		II° Armée, probably by Gefr
		O	OK	Rudolf Kassner, Jasta 65, (3).

One other balloon attacked, not flamed.

---

17 March

MdL Artigaut &		Br 11					1
Asp Legrain &		Br 11					1
Sgt Boyard &		Br 11					1
S/Lt Delaporte	a.	Br 11	Albatros DV	X	Avocourt		1
Adj Courtois		Spa 12	Balloon	XF	Laon		1
Adj Mion		Spa 67	2 seater	X	Montaigu-Marchaix	1140	2
Adj Plessier &		Spa 87					1
MdL Gasser		Spa 87	Rumpler C	X	Haute-Riouville	1145	2
MdL Lemaire &		N 90					1
Cpl Geoffroy	b.	N 90	DFW C	X	Bézange	1130	1
S/Lt Fonck		Spa 103	2 seater	X	N Menneville	1820	30
MdL Lambert &		Br 213					1
S/Lt Maguères		Br 213	Scout	X	German lines		1
S/Lt Demeuldre		Spa 84	Albatros D	P			–
MdL Wellman		N 87	Albatros D	P			–
MdL Wellman		N 87	Albatros D	P			–
Sgt Loup		Spa 103	Albatros D3	P	Laval	1820	–
S/Lt Fonck		Spa 103	2 seater	P	Nogent l'Abbesse	1750	–
1/Lt Baer, USAS		103rdUS	EA	P	Ft Brimont		–

a.   Possibly Ltn Gotthilf Pleiss, Jasta 9, POW, Forêt de Hesse.
b.   Probably Vfw Paul Formelle & Ltn Rudolf Schmitz, FlAbt 12, KIAs Arracourt.

Casualties:

MdL Joseph Réchède	Spa 75	P	POW	
MdL Courtois	Spa 12	P	MIA	Spad VII N° 1195.
MdL Valadon &	Sop 106	P	KIA	VII° Armée, XF
S/Lt Bessec	Sop 106	O	KIA	Sopwith
Lt Dumont	C 47	O	WIA	
S/Lt Marie Nicolle-Malpas	Br 213	O	WIA	Bréguet
S/Lt Gaston Rousset	Spa 124	P	KIAcc	⎫
S/Lt Henri Vimal du			Collided	
Monteil	Spa 124	P	KIAcc	⎭
Sol Thomas	Spa 95	M	Injured	
Adj Pain &	Br 218	P	Injured	
S/Lt Falco	Br 218	O	Injured	
Sol Haessens	GDE	M	Injured	AR
MdL Cormelier	VB 101	P	Injured	Voisin P
MdL Houdard	59° Cie d'Aérostiers	XF		II° Armée, Probably by Uffz
		O	OK	Erich Meyer, Jasta 45 (2).

Four other balloons attacked. not flamed.

18 March

Adj Baudrion &		AR 19				2
Asp Jaboulay		AR 19	Scout	X	Boureuilles	1
1/Lt Larner, USAS	a.	Spa 86	Pfalz DIIIa	X	Condé-sur-Suippe	1
???	b.	DCA	2 seater	X	Cumières	–
???	c.	DCA	2 seater	X	Bray-Dunes	–
MdL Wellman		N 87	Albatros D	P		–

a. Probably Uffz Kurt Straube (1v), Jasta 66, KIA, Aguilcourt, about 3 km SE of Condé-sur-Suippe.
b. Probably Uffz Alfred Schulz, KIA & Ltn Wilhelm Schütte, FlAbt 9, who died of his wounds at Cumières.
c. Occupants POWs, they burned their aircraft.

Casualties:

Capt Jean Lavidalie &	CO	Br 131	P	POW	Bréguet 14B2 N° 1479, probably by
S/Lt Eugène Le Bouter		Br 131	O	POW	Vfw Josef Schwendemann, Jasta 41, (4).
Adj Corentin Carré &		Sop 229	P	KIA	Probably by Flak-
Sol Joseph Perrin		Sop 229	G	KIA	batterie 128, Vfw Seitz.
MdL Henri Adenot		N 315	P	WIA	VII° Armée, Nieuport 27, possibly
					Ltn Albert Dietlen, Jasta 41, (7).
Sgt Lucien Mestivier		Spa 102	P	KIAcc	
MdL Bernard de					
Pontavice de Hussey		Spa 68	P	KIAcc	
Sgt Victor Avard		Chartres	P	KIAcc	
Sgt René Moreau &		C 56	P	KIAcc	
Sgt Lafosse		C 56	G	Injured	Caudron G6
MdL Charbonnier &		Sal 18	P	Injured	
S/Lt Francis Gloaguen		Sal 18	O	Injured	Salmson N° 335
Cpl Quenel		GDE	P	Injured	Voisin P
S/Lt Léon		73° Cie d'Aérostiers		XF	VIII° Armée, probably by Vfw
			O	OK	Gustav Wandelt, Jasta 43, (1).

19 March

MdL Gasser,		Spa 87				3
Adj Duhomme &		Spa 87				2
Adj Ruamps	a.	Spa 87	Rumpler C	X	Bois de Blamont	1045	5

a. Probably from FlAbt 276 (A), FTL near Reichental.

Casualties:

Sgt Pierre Bruley		Spa 23	P	KIA	Spad VII N° 5309, probably by FlAbt 36.
S/Lt Cattaret		V 110	P	KIAcc	
Capt Verdy	CO	V 110	P	Injured	Voisin R

20 March

Adj Vial		N 315	2 seater	X	3

Casualties: None

21 March

The Great German Offensive (Operation Michel) also known as the Second Battle of the Somme commences between Arras and Noyon, with the French VI° Armée on right flank of British 5th Army which received the main thrust of the attack.

Adj Bannier &		Spa 75				2
S/Lt Bamberger		Spa 75	2 seater	X	Chaillevois	1
Adj Baron,		Spa 103				1
Adj Tasque &		Spa 103				1
Sgt Baux	a.	Spa 103	Rumpler C	POW	Rilly-la-Montagne	1340	2
S/Lt Lutzius &		Spa 153				1
MdL Arrault	b.	Spa 153	Scout	X	N Nauroy	1
S/Lt Barcat &		Spa 153				1
S/Lt de Guingand		Spa 48	Albatros	XF	Rilly-la-Montagne	1808	5
II° Armée		DCA	EA	X	Dieppe	–
II° Armée	c.	DCA	EA	POW	Neuvilly	–
Adj Garaud		Spa 38	EA	P	Nogent l'Abbesse	–
Adj Garaud		Spa 38	EA	P	Nogent l'Abbesse	–
S/Lt Madon		Spa 38	EA	P	Ripont	–

a. Probably Ltn Michael Frhr von Korff & Gefr Willi Speier, & Ltn Frhr von Zedlitz und Neulich, BG3/BSt16, POWs.
b. Possibly Flg Franz Matuszewsky, Jasta 73, KIA Nauroy.
c. Possibly Ltn Herbert Kohl, Jasta 34b, POW, S Bellicourt.

Casualties:

S/Lt Jules Covin		Spa 31	P	WIA	DOW at Beaudrieux.

MdL William Wellman	Spa 87	P	WIA	Flak, Nieuport XXVII, over Forêt de Parroy.	
S/Lt Rouille	Br 209	O	Injured		
???	??? Cie d'Aérostiers		XF	Probably by Ltn Heinrich	
		O	OK	Arntzen, Jasta 50 (10).	

One other balloon attacked, not flamed.

22 March

MdL Delaye,	Spa 157					1
Cpl Eoff &	Spa 157					1
Brig Lantierie	Spa 157	Scout	X	Souain		1
???	a. DCA	Gotha	X	French lines		–
Adj Naudin	Spa 26	2 seater	P	Nogent l'Abbesse	1715	–
S/Lt Madon	Spa 38	EA	P	Caurel		–
S/Lt Madon	Spa 38	EA	P	Epoye-Pont Faverger		–
Sgt Schmitter &	Spa 103					–
Sgt Hoeber	Spa 103	Scout	P	Berry-au-Bac	1515	–
S/Lt Fonck	Spa 103	2 seater	P	Nogent l'Abbesse	1715	–
???	GC	EA	P			–

a.   Three occupants POWs.

Casualties: None

23 March

Lt de Turenne,	CO	Spa 12				8
Adj Decugis &		Spa 12				1
Adj Philibert		Spa 12	2 seater	X	La Fère	2
Lt Lahoulle &		Spa 57				1
Lt Chaput	a.	Spa 57	Albatros DV	X	Coucy-le-Château	13
Lt Chaput,		Spa 57				14
Lt Lahoulle &		Spa 57				2
S/Lt Haegelen	b.	Spa 100	Albatros DV	X	Coucy-le-Château	3
S/Lt Demeuldre &		Spa 84				12
Sgt Prouvost		Spa 84	2 seater	X		2
Sgt Quintard		Spa 88	Balloon	XF	Morieuloix	1
Lt de Sommyèvre		Spa 93	Balloon	XF		1
Capt Lemaitre,		EM GC 16				1
Adj de Marmier &		Spa 112				5
Sgt Chavannes	c.	Spa 112	Rumpler C	XF	Frapelle, VII° Armée	5
IV° Armée		DCA	EA	X	Cornillet	–
???		GC	2 EA	X		–
S/Lt Daubail		Spa 83	Scout	P		–
???		GC	3 EA	P		–

a.   Possibly Ltn Hans Unger, Jasta 22s.
b.   Possibly Ltn Erich Thomas, Jasta 22s.
c.   Probably Vfw Bänsch & Ltn Ehmann, FlAbt 10, KIAs, near Avricourt, AOK "A" Sector.

Casualties:

Lt Pierre Lecoq	Spa 62	P	KIA	Spad VII
Adj Eugène Simon	Spa 81	P	MIA	Ground fire.
MdL Maillet &	Spa 215	P	MIA	Spad XI, probably by Vfw
S/Lt Tomberlaine	Spa 215	O	MIA	Walter Schäfer, Jasta 66, (2).
S/Lt Jean-Paul Favre de Thierrens	Spa 62	P	WIA	
Adj Gaston Tasqué	Spa 103	P	KIAcc	
Sgt Chartron &	Sop 235	P	KIAcc	
Sol Delcorps	Sop 235	M	KIAcc	
MdL Lalanne	AR 230	P	KIAcc	
Sgt Mendaillie &	Sop 229	P	Injured	
Asp Bidault	Sop 229	O	Injured	Sopwith 1A2
MdL Castelain &	VB 101	P	Injured	
Sol Goreau	VB 101	G	Injured	
S/Lt Etienne	72° Cie d'Aérostiers			IV° Armée, both attacked,
S/Lt André Pate	85° Cie d'Aérostiers			not flamed, observers OK.

One other balloon attacked, not flamed.

24 March

S/Lt G Guérin &	Spa 15		17

Patrol	Spa 15	Balloon	XF	Forêt de St Gobain		–
MdL Berthelot	Spa 15	EA	X	Forêt de St Gobain		1
Lt Augier de Moussac &	Spa 49					1
Adj Calmon a.	Spa 49	DFW C	POW	S Dannemarie		2
Capt Mouronval, CO	Spa 77					2
Lt Battle &	Spa 77					1
S/Lt Barbaza	Spa 77	Balloon	XF	N Quessy		2
Adj Brétillon	Spa 79	Scout	XF	Germaine		2
Cpl Gaudin	Spa 79					1
Cpl Vilbois &	Spa 79					1
S/Lt Cournaud	Spa 79	EA	X	St Simon, III° Armée		1
Lt Lanez	Spa 87	Albatros D3	X	Forêt de Parroy	1640	1
MdL Discours	Spa 87					2
MdL Gasser &	Spa 87					4
Lt Reverchon b.	N 99	2 seater	X	Avricourt-Igney	1530	1
MdL Gassin &	Br 126					2
Sgt Damiette &	Br 126					2
Lt Bargeaud &	GB 3					1
Sgt Leroux	GB 3	Scout	X	W Lassigny-le-Grand		1
Cpl Carbone &	Br 128					1
Sol Mallet &	Br 128					1
MdL Courtine &	GB 3					1
Sol Guinard	GB 3	Scout	X			1
Lt Gamerdinger &	GB 3					1
Sol Lucien	GB 3	EA	X			1
Sgt Brouet &	Br 128					1
MdL Monard	Br 128	EA	X			1
S/Lt G Guérin	Spa 15	2 seater	P	Forêt de St Gobain		–
S/Lt Madon	Spa 38	EA	P	Nogent l'Abbesse		–
Adj Garaud	Spa 38	EA	P	Nogent l'Abbesse		–
MdL Pezon &	N 90					
Sgt Mace	N 90	Scout	P	Parroy		–
???	GC	EA	P			–
???	GB	6 EA	P			–
???	AO	EA	P			–

a.   FlAbt A 282.
b.   Possibly Vfw Rudolf Franz and Ltn Wilhelm Lepp, FlAbt 199b, KIAs at Amenoncourt, about 2 km SW Igney.

Casualties:

MdL Cheudet &	Br 126	P	MIA	
Asp Emile Roux	Br 126	G	MIA	
Cpl Jouy &	Sop 234	P	MIA	III° Armée
S/Lt François Touchfeu	Sop 234	O	MIA	
Adj Porcher &	Sal 13	P	WIA	
Sol Jules Delplanque	Sal 13	G	KIA	Letord, VIII° Armée
Lt Jacques Brossollet	Sop 277	O	WIA	
MdL Lalanne	AR 230	P	KIAcc	
MdL Jacques Wurtz	Spa 88	P	Injured	
MdL Marcel Danel	Spa 91	P	Injured	Spad VII
Sol Cardoux	Spa 150	M	Injured	
Sol Maréchal	Spa 150	M	Injured	
Lt Salvetat	AR 259	P	Injured	

25 March

Adj Chrétien	Spa 75	Balloon	XF	Fressancourt	2	
Lt Hay de Slade &	Spa 86					6
1/Lt Larner, USAS	Spa 86	2 seater	XF	Noyon, III° Armée	1040	2
??? a.	DCA	Albatros C	X	Lac Noir		–
???	DCA	2 seater	X	Lac Noir		–
Brig Antoine &	Sal 27					1
S/Lt Mouchet	Sal 27	Albatros D	X	Urbach		2
S/Lt Dupuich	Spa 68	EA	P	Bourdonnay	1140	–
???	Spa 86	EA	P	Bois Geline		–
MdL Jeanot &	Sal 27					–
S/Lt Piat &	Sal 27					–
MdL Dussing &	Sal 27					–
Sol Gegarde	Sal 27	EA	P	Urbach		–

a.   Probably Sgt Walter Lübke & Ltn Hans Röchling, FlAbt (A) 243, KIAs Sairis, in Alsace.

Casualties:

Cpl Soussenin	Sop 255	P	KIA	Sopwith 1A2
Sol Jarrige	Sop 255	G	Injured	
Sgt Cassales &	Br 205	P	KIAcc	
Sol Fays	Br 205	M	KIAcc	
Lt Orban	Sop 232	O	KIAcc	
Lt de Garbinski	Sop 232	O	KIAcc	
S/Lt Miquel	GDE	P	KIAcc	Sopwith
QM Pierre Fichot	* EP	P	KIAcc	FBA 100HP

*   Hourtin.

26 March

Adj Garaud	a.	Spa 38	Rumpler CVII	POW	Châlons-sur-Marne		12
Lt Laganne &		Spa 94					2
Cpl Martin		Spa 94	2 seater	X	Caurel	1130	1
???	b.	???	Rumpler C	POW	Mont St Martin		–

a.   N° 6484/17, FlAbt (A) 270.
b.   FlAbt 23, landed in French lines, aircraft intact.

Casualties:

Capt Pol Moulines &	Escad 1	P	KIA	
S/Lt Jean Lecreux	Br 127	O	POW	Bréguet 14 N° 1524.
Adj Hector Garaud	Spa 38	P	WIA	
Sgt Casanas &	Br 205	P	KIAcc	
Sol Fay	Br 205	M	KIAcc	

27 March

Patrol		Esc 1	EA	XF			–
Patrol		Esc 1	EA	XF			–
Lt Poupon &		Spa 37					1
Sgt Marot		Spa 37	Balloon	XF			1
Sgt Prevost	a.	Spa 68	Pfalz DIII	POW	Fleville		2
MdL Gasser		Spa 87	Balloon	XF	Ommerey		5
Adj Ruamps,		Spa 87					6
Adj Bizot &		N 90					1
Adj Mace		N 90	Scout	X	Lagarde-Parroy	1710	1
Adj Ruamps,		Spa 87					7
Adj Bizot &		N 90					2
Adj Mace		N 90	EA	X	Lagarde-Parroy	1900	2
Major Thaw,	CO	103rdUS					3
Capt J N Hall &		103rdUS					2
1/Lt Ford		103rdUS	Scout	X	St Etienne-à-Arnes		1
Capt J N Hall		103rdUS	Scout	X	Sommepy		3
S/Lt Bourjade		Spa 152	Balloon	XF	Guebersschweiler	1215	1
S/Lt Ambrogi &		N 90					–
S/ Lt Le Coq de Kerland		N 90	2 seater	FTL	Louvigny-sur-Seilles		–
Adj Plouquin		Spa 91	2 seater	P	Maucourt-Guiscard		–
Capt J N Hall		103rdUS	EA	P	St Etienne-à-Arnes		–
Major Thaw	CO	103rd US	EA	P			–

a.   Probably OffStv Schüschke, Jasta 64w, Pfalz DIIIa 8087/17.
NOTE: In the AOK 19 Sector three German balloons were attacked but not flamed, those of BZug 71, 11h40, BZug 211, 11h45 and BZug 72, 16h20.

Casualties:

S/Lt André Willemin	Spa 67	P	MIA	Spad VII, departed between 16h00 & 16h30, III° Armée.
S/Lt Paul Van Ingelhandt	Spa 97	P	MIA	
Brig Voirin &	Sop 279	P	KIA	III° Armée
Asp Jean Breuil	Sop 279	O	KIA	SE Cuvilly
MdL Jules Bertrand &	Sal 10	P	OK	
S/Lt Charles Luguet	Sal 10	O	WIA	
Cpl Etienne Carbone &	Br 128	P	OK	
Sol Arsène Matte	Br 128	G	WIA	Flak
Sgt Dhenin &	Sop 279	P	WIA	III° Armée
S/Lt Michel	Sop 279	O	WIA	
Sol Debière	Sal 10	G	Injured	DOW 27 March 1918.
Sol Massenet	Sal 10	M	Injured	
Cpl Marie Blachon &	Sal 10	P	Injured	

???		28° Cie d'Aérostiers		Attacked, not flamed.		

28 March

Sgt Boudou		Spa 48	EA	X	Dammery	1
Adj Sallares		Spa 86	Scout	X	Boulogne-la-Grasse	1
S/Lt Fonck		Spa 103	2 seater	XF	E Montdidier	1030	31
???		Esc 2	EA	P		–
???		Esc 2	EA	FTL		–

Casualties:

S/Lt Lucien Coulon	Spa 96	P	MIA	Spad VII	
Brig Gay	Spa 96	P	MIA	Spad VII N° 1019.	
Cpl Jean Magnies &	Sal 28	P	MIA	III° Armée, departed 13h40	
Sgt Jean Eyrolles	Sal 28	O	MIA		
Adj Jean Brut &	Sop 9	P	MIA		
Adj Escoffre	Sop 9	O	MIA		
Lt Servais	Spa 89	P	MIA	Spad VII	
Lt Joseph Pozzo di Borgo	Spa 57	P	POW	Spad N° 3072.	
S/Lt Billoue	C 28	O	KIA	III° Armée, Salmson, ground fire, FTL near Le Tronquoy.	
S/Lt Clément Payen	Spa 79	P	WIA	III° Armée	
Asp Baer	Br 208	O	WIA	III° Armée	
Lt Joseph Battle CO	Spa 103	P	WIA	Ground fire, III° Armée.	
Cpl Emile Limousis	N 84	P	KIAcc	Spad	
Sol Pacaud	Spa 96	M	KIAcc	Spad VII	

29 March

Capt Tourangin & CO	Spa 89					2
Patrol	Spa 89	Scout	X	Chauny		–
S/Lt Fonck	Spa 103	Scout	X	E Montdidier	1830	32
S/Lt Fonck	Spa 103	Scout	X	E Montdidier	1835	33

Casualties:

S/Lt Lucien Servais	Spa 89	P	MIA	Spad VII, probably by Ltn Dieter Collin, Jasta 22s, (6).
Cpl Léon Sigaud	Sal 52	P	MIA	III° Armée
S/Lt Jean du Peuty	Sal 52	O	MIA	
Lt Jacques de Sommyèvre	Spa 93	P	WIA	
Asp Guilleaume	Sop 281	O	WIA	
Sol Louis Mallet	Br 128	G	WIA	
Adj Mayerhoffer	Br 111	P	WIA	
Cpl Talabot	GDE	P	Injured	Spad XI
Cpl Orsini	GDE	P	Injured	Nieuport

30 March

S/Lt G Guérin,		Spa 15				18
S/Lt Cordonnier &		Spa 15				2
S/Lt Bernard		Spa 57	2 seater	XF	N Montdidier	0845	1
S/Lt G Guérin,		Spa 15				19
S/Lt Hérisson &		Spa 75				7
Adj Delaruelle	a.	Spa 75	Scout	XF	SW Bourguignon	1
S/Lt M Nogues		Spa 73	Scout	X		1
S/Lt Déjobert &		Br 120				3
???		Br 120	EA	XF		?
Lt Ribière &		Br 209				1
Lt Letanche		Br 209	Scout	X	Roye-Montdidier	1
???		???	Balloon	XF	Fressancourt	–

a.   This EA was attacking the 92° Cie Balloon, probably Uffz Hellmuth Krätaschmer, Jasta 48, flying a Pfalz, who was shot down and taken prisoner south of Bourguignon.

Casualties:

Sgt Landragin &	Br 127	P	MIA	
Lt Le Courtaulx de Molay	Br 127	O	MIA	
MdL Audinot &	Br 127	P	MIA	
Asp Hellouin de Senival	Br 127	O	MIA	
Adj Caraval &	Br 66	P	MIA	
Sgt Baudier	Br 66	G	MIA	
MdL Edouard Guillory	Spa 86	P	POW	Spad 7 N° 3216, probably by Vfw Friedrich Neubauer, Jasta 63, (2).
Sgt Robert Barriat &	Sal 52	P	Injured	III° Armée, hit by flak,

S/Lt Langlois	Sal 52	O	Injured	Crash-landed.		
MdL Campana	Sop 237	P	KIAcc			
???	Sop 237	O	Injured			
???	64° Cie d'Aérostiers		XF	6° Corps d'Armée, probably by Ltn		
		O	OK	Fritz Pütter, Jasta 68, (18).		

31 March

Lt Poupon,		Spa 37				2
S/Lt Barny de Romanet &		Spa 37				2
MdL Coupillaud	a.	Spa 37	Albatros	XF	Rollot	1
Adj Gourdon &		Spa 37				1
Cpl Francisquet		Spa 37	EA	X	German lines	1
Lt Nungesser &		Spa 65				32
Sgt Gérard		Spa 65	Scout	XF	Lagny	2
S/Lt Wertheim &		Spa 84				2
Sgt Delcuze	b.	Spa 84	Fokker DrI	XF	Orvillers	1800	1
S/Lt Wertheim &		Spa 84				3
Sgt Delcuze	b.	Spa 84	Fokker DrI	X	Orvillers	1800	2
Brig Buc		N 159	EA	P		–
Sgt Jouneau &		Br 111				1
Sgt Bisch		Br 111	EA	X	Guerbigny	1
???		GB 6	EA	P		–
???		GC 15	2 EA	P		–
???		GC 19	EA	P		–

a.   Probably Vfw Friedrich Neubauer, Jasta 63, KIA Rollot.
b.   Probably Uffz Rupert Merkle & Uffz Jon Santjer, Jasta 63, KIAs. Hainvillers, about 3 km NW Orvillers.

Casualties:

Cpl Amblard	N 100	P	MIA	Spad VII, probably by Ltn	
				Hans Kürner, Jasta 19, (4)	
Cpl Villatte &	Sop 141	P	MIA		
S/Lt Balvet	Sop 141	O	MIA		
Adj Jean Balland &	Br 127	P	MIA		
Cpl Guy Polonceau	Br 127	G	MIA		
Sgt C W Kerwood &	Br 117	P	POW	Over Montdidier, probably by	
Sgt Biot	Br 117	G	MIA	Ltn Walter Jumpelt, Jasta 19, (2).	
Sgt Jean-Marie Jouneau &	Br 111	P	MIA		
Sgt Bisch	Br 111	G	MIA	Bréguet	
S/Lt François d'Alton &	Spa 268	P	KIA	III° Armée	
S/Lt François Balet	Spa 268	O	KIA	Assainvillers-Ayencourt	
Brig Lalier &	Spa 63	P	KIA	Flak	
S/Lt Robert Favre	Spa 63	O	KIA	Flak, Spad XI	
Adj Paul Thuries	Spa 57	P	POW	Spad XIII, probably by Hermann	
				Becker, Jasta 12, (8).	
S/Lt Pierre Vieljeux	Spa 93	P	POW	Spad VII, NE Montdidier	
Adj Roger Tassou	Spa 73	P	WIA	Spad VII, FTL.	
Sgt Derré &	Sop 279	P	WIA		
S/Lt de La Heignant	Sop 279	O	WIA		
Adj Fabre	Sal 28	P	WIA	Flak, Salmson 2A2, III° Armée	
MdL Mouchot	Sop 105	?	Injured		
Cpl Jean Lefebvre &	Sop 234	P	Injured		
MdL Matenas	Sop 234	O	Injured		

During the period 21 – 31 March 1918 the date of the following victory cannot be ascertained at this time:

Adj Doux &		Br 111				1
Adj Matheron		Br 111	EA	X		1

At a date prior to 31 March 1918 the following claim was also made:

Adj Bohan &		Spa 212				–
S/Lt Cotton	a.	Spa 212	Scout	P	German lines	–

a.   One of two scouts that had just flamed a French balloon.

1 April

Capt de Sevin	CO a.	Spa 26	EA	X	Fignières	1415	8
S/Lt Resel,		R 46					1
Adj Poggioli &		R 46					1
Sgt-Maj Armenault		R 46	EA	XF			1
S/Lt Martenot de Cordoux &		Spa 94					3

Lt Bechon	b.	Spa 155	Albatros DV	X	Chaulnes-Montdidier	3
Lt Lahoulle &	CO	Spa 154				3
Sgt Moissinac		Spa 154	Balloon	XF	Fresnoy-en-Chaussée	1
Sgt Moissinac		Spa 154	EA	X	Fresnoy-en-Chaussée	2
???	c.	DCA	EA	X	Soissons Sector	–
Two pilots		Spa 75	EA	P	Lassigny	–
Patrol		Spa 86	EA	P	Cailleaux	–
S/Lt Martenot de Cordoux	d.	Spa 94	EA	P	Montdidier	–
Cpl Mabereau &		Spa 26				–
Cpl Loup		Spa 103	Fokker DrI	P	Bois de Tilleloy	1445 –
Lt Bechon		Spa 155	EA	P	Montdidier	–

a.   Possibly Ltn Richard Grüter, Jasta 17, KIA Montdidier.
b.   Possibly Ltn Paul Hoffmann, Jasta 12, WIA, Montdidier, DOW 2 April 1918.
c.   This EA had just attacked the 49° Cie balloon, probably Ltn Rudolf Kommoss, Jasta 50, KIA during a balloon attack. His aircraft broke up in the air and pieces hit the parachute of the balloon observer causing his parachute to fold.
d.   Possibly Ltn Paul Hoffmann, Jasta 12, WIA over Montdidier, died same day.

Casualties:

S/Lt Jacques Bernard	Spa 15	P	MIA	
Lt René Bechon	Spa 155	P	MIA	Spad VII
Sgt Laurent Peyzaret	RGAé	P	MIA	Sopwith
Cpl Houston Woodward	Spa 94	P	KIA	Spad 7 N° 1419, probably by Ltn Johannes Klein, Jasta 15, (4).
Lt Maurice Houdaille &	AR 272	P	KIA	AR1, III° Armée, XF, probably by
Lt Pierre Gagnier	AR 272	O	KIA	OfStv Emil Bergmann, Jasta 22s, (1)
Sgt Dherre &	Sop 279	P	WIA	
Lt Theignau	Sop 279	O	WIA	
Cpl Oyarsabal	GDE	P	Injured	AR
Sgt Mandavy	Br 120	G	Injured	
Sol Chambe	Sop 231	M	Injured	
Cpl Lefevre &	Sop 234	P	Injured	
MdL Matenas	Sop 234	O	Injured	
Adj Roger Pineau &	49° Cie d'Aérostiers		OK	Attacked and damaged, not
Sgt Gaston Verneuil		O	KIA	flamed, note c. above.
???	89° Cie d'Aérostiers		XF	Probably by Ltn Hans Pippart, Jasta 13, (9).
Lt Caron	93° Cie d'Aérostiers		XF	Possibly by Ltn Hans Böhning,
		O	OK	Jasta 79, unconfirmed. III° Armée.

2 April

Capt Franc,	CO	Spa 79				2
Sgt S/Lt Bourguin &		Spa 79				1
Sgt Rousseau		Spa 79	Scout	X	Beuvraignes	1
Adj Naudin		Spa 26	Fokker DrI	P	S Montdidier	1130 –
Patrols		Spa 3/67	Fokker DrI	P	N Montdidier	1800 –
Patrol		Escad 1	Rumpler C	FTL	Montdidier	–

Casualties:

Cpl Jean Godrie	Spa 79	P	KIA	Assainvillers-Montdidier, by Flak Groupe Brimont.
Cpl Martin	Spa 3	P	MIA	Departed 17h00, during combat with Fokker Triplanes near Montdidier.
Brig Henri Pesque &	V 119	P	WIA	
Sol Gontrand Owen	V 119	G	KIA	
Brig Usser	AR 262		WIA	
Cpl Albert Bézard	V 109	P	WIA	Sopwith
Sgt René Meyer	Spa 86	P	KIAcc	Spad VII
Cpl Yves Busser	Sal 1	P	Injured	
Brig Lelong	V 125	G	Injured	

3 April

S/Lt Bourjade &		Spa 152				2
Brig de Freslon		Spa 152	Balloon	XF	Willer	1
Sgt Petit		Spa 154	Albatros D	X	Marcelcave	1
75° Cie Aérostiers	a.	DCA	Scout	POW		–
???		Escad 2	2 EA	XF		–
Patrol		Spa 3	2 seater	P	Faverolles-Piennes	0715 –
Sgt Vincent	b.	Spa 26	EA	P	Lignières	1030 –
Capt de Sevin	CO b.	Spa 26	EA	P	Lignières	–
Sgt Prévost		Spa 68	2 seater	P	Coincourt	1215 –

1/Lt Baer, USAS	103rdUS	Scout	P		Monts	–
1/Lt Baer, USAS	103rdUS	Scout	P		Monts	–

a. Probably Vfw Hurrle, Jasta 45, POW 08h50 at Bailly.
b. Probably Ltn Ernst Hensel, Jasta 62, WIA over Courtemanche & Ltn Paul Quast, Jasta 63, KIA over Montdidier, each about 4 km S of Lignières.

Casualties:

Sgt Pierre Devaulx	Spa 26	P	MIA	Spad VII, Montdidier, probably by Ltn Fritz Pütter, Jasta 68, (16).
Sgt Perdriel &	V 101	P	KIA	
Asp Meynial	V 101	O	KIA	Voisin Renault
Sol Rameau	Sop 276	G	KIA	
Cpl Claude Bernard	Spa 67	P	WIA	Spad, probably by Obltn Theodor Cammann, CO Jasta 74, (2).
Brig Besnard	V 125	P	KIAcc	
Adj Allain &	V 101	P	Injured	
S/Lt Lefroid	V 101	O	Injured	Voisin Renault
Sol René Van Spranghe	V 109	G	Injured	
Lt Jochyms	Sal 27	O	Injured	Letord
Sgt Charles Debas	69° Cie d'Aérostiers	XF		Probably by Sgt Pfänder,
		O	OK	Jasta 69, (3).
1/Lt T P Atkinson	62° Cie d'Aérostiers			Attacked, not flamed
		O	OK	

---

4 April

S/Lt Matrat &		Spa 154				1
Adj Gros	a.	Spa 154	Albatros D	XF	Plessier-Rosainvillers	2

a. Uffz Erich Gürgenz, Jasta 46, flying Albatros DVa 7161/17 "STROPP", KIA at Marcelcave.

Casualties: None

---

5 April

Sgt Rousselle	Spa 81	Balloon	XF	Chauny	1
S/Lt Herbelin	Spa 81	Balloon	P	Caumont	–
MdL Gasser &	N 87				–
MdL Discours	N 87	Hannover C	FTL	Lay	–

Casualties:

S/Lt Georges Poreaux	Spa 31	P	WIA	Spad XIII N° 1908
Adj Alfred Guyot	Spa 81	P	WIA	
Sgt Giraud	Sop 281	G	WIA	
Brig David	Sop 141	P	WIA	
Sol Georges Raignault	Sal 39	G	WIA	
MdL Robert Mazurel	Sal 8	P	WIA	
Lt Burlé &	Sal 8	O	WIA	
Cpl Guyetant	Sal 8	G	WIA	Letord
S/Lt Bastien	Br 107	O	WIA	
S/Lt Jean-Paul Favre de Thierrens	Spa 62	P	Injured	Spad XI
S/Lt Nicolle-Malpas	Br 213	O	Injured	

---

6 April

Lt Goux,		Sal 10					2
Sgt Schmidt &		Sal 10					1
Lt de La Croix de Laval		Sal 10	Scout	X	German lines		1
Lt Leps	CO	Spa 81	EA	XF			6
Capt Papin &	CO	Br 126					1
Sgt André &		Br 126					1
Sgt Briand &		Br 126					1
S/Lt Estrayer		Br 126	EA	X	Verpilliers		1
IV Armée		DCA	EA	X			–
1/Lt Baer, USAS	a.	103rdUS	Scout	XF	Sommepy	1855	3
Capt de Sevin	CO		Spa 26	EA	P	Lignières	
1135	–						
S/Lt Douladoure &		Sal 28					–
Sgt Lom		Sal 28	EA	P	NE Soissons		–
Sgt Gérard		Spa 65	EA	P	Beaucourt-en-Santerre		–
S/Lt Herbelin		Spa 81	EA	P	Caumont		–
S/Lt Coadou		Spa 88	EA	P	S Piennes		–
1/Lt Baer, USAS		103rdUS	Scout	P			–
Patrol		103rdUS	Scout	P			–

Patrol		GB	EA	P	Verpillières	–

a.   Possibly Uffz Georg Erdmann, Jasta 73, KIA at 19h30 between Sommepy & St Marie-à-Py.

Casualties:

MdL Pierre Cardon		Spa 81	P	WIA	Spad VII	
Sgt François Rispal &		Sal 105	P	KIA		
S/Lt Bergère		Sal 105	O	KIA		
Cpl Herman Whitmore		Spa 77	P	POW	Spad VII, probably by OfStv Otto Sporbert, Jasta 62, (1).	
Lt Louis Goux,		Sal 10	P	OK	Letord L.2, III° Armée, FTL N of Latrule, a/c badly damaged and unusable. Possibly claimed by Ltn Karl Menckhoff, Jasta 72, (22).	
Lt de La Croix de Laval		Sal 10	O	WIA		
Sgt Léon Schmidt		Sal 10	G	KIA		
Adj Marius Portet		Spa 100	P	KIAcc	Spad VII	
Lt Renault &		V 121	P	Injured		
MdL Blanchon		V 121	G	Injured		

7 April

| Adj Chauvière | a. | Escad 2 | EA | P | SE Thennes | – |

a.   Possibly Ltn Franz Trommer (O), FlAbt (A) 206, KIA, S Amiens, Thennes about 15 km SE Amiens.

Casualties:

S/Lt Louis Mouy &		C 74	P	MIA	Caudron G6, probably by
S/Lt Laroche		C 74	O	MIA	Ltn Fritz Pütter, Jasta 68, (18).
S/Lt François d'Alton &		AR 268	P	KIA	
S/Lt Balet		AR 268	O	KIA	
Cpl Bigey		Spa 228	P	WIA	Flak, Spad XI
S/Lt David		Sop 279	O	WIA	
Sol Cousin		RGAé	M	Injured	
Lt Gérard &		???	P	OK	FTL near Servais, after combat with
Lt Cherier		???	O	OK	three EA and hits by shrapnel.

8 April – No Claims – No Casualties
The Second Battle of the Somme (Operation Michel) is concluded.

9 April

Lt M Nogues,		Spa 73				2
Lt de Girval,		Spa 73				1
Adj M Paris &		Spa 73				2
Sgt Travet		Spa 73	EA	X	Moreuil	1

Casualties:

SM Georges Landraud	*	CAM	P	KIAcc	Lévy Besson 200HP N° 16.
Cpl Fernand Dauvergne &		Sop 276	P	KIAcc	
Sol Besson		Sop 276	M	Injured	

*   Cherbourg.

10 April

???		DCA	EA	X		–
Infantry fire		???	EA	X		–
Lt Achard &		Spa 78				–
MdL Pavlovsky		Spa 78	EA	P	E Montdidier	–

Casualties:

Cpl Grebil &		Br 129	P	MIA	Possibly by Ltn Rudolf Windisch, CO
Asp Edmond Carron		Br 129	G	MIA	Jasta 66, (15).
SM François Pouliquen	*	CAM	P	KIA	FBA 150HP N° 567 codé H.2 in English Channel.
Sgt Sauvaget		Br 129	G	KIA	
Lt Durand		Spa 286	P	Injured	Spad XI

*   Le Havre.

11 April

Sgt Baylies	a.	Spa 3	2 seater	X	Courtemanche	1330	4
Adj Artigau		Spa 15	Rumpler C	X	Rollot-Bois de Bus		5
Capt Dupuy	CO	Spa 31	Fokker DrI	X	SE Montdidier		1
Asp Dubois de Gennes		Spa 57	Albatros D3	X	Mailly-Raineval		3
Brig Lacombe &		Spa 75					1
S/Lt Hérisson	b	Spa 75	Pfalz DIII	POW	Margueglise		8
Lt Hugues	CO	Spa 95	2 seater	X	Mesnil-St Georges		11

S/Lt Louvat	Spa 153	Balloon	XF	Barisis		1
Sgt Rue &	Br 209					–
Sgt Huet	Br 209	EA	X	Orvillers-Borel		–
Adj Montrion	Spa 48	Pfalz	P			–
??? &	Br 123					–
Cpl Roy	Br 123	EA	P			–
Patrol	Spa 80	Albatros	P	Hainvillers		–
Patrol	Escad 28	EA	P			–

a.   Possibly Flg Gottfried Aberle & Ltn Wilhelm Schuleit, FlAbt (A) 271, KIAs Montdidier, about 2 km S Courtemanche.
b.   Probably Ltn Wilhelm Buchstett, Jasta 79b, POW.

Casualties:

S/Lt Jules Milliat	Spa 80	P	POW	Spad VII, probably by Vfw Rudolf Francke, Jasta 8, (10), III° Armée.	
Ltn Pierre Besançon	Spa 163	P	WIA	Possibly by Ltn Gustav Dörr, Jasta 45, (2)	
Capt Pierre L'Huillier CO	Spa 150	P	KIAcc	Spad VII	
S/Lt Deliège	Sop 285	O	Injured	Sopwith 1A2	
Sol Soulatges	Spa 212	M	Injured	Spad XI	
Adj Fourcade	Br 217	P	Injured		
MdL Rey	Sal 32	G	Injured		
Lts Jacquart & Frixon	33° Cie Aérostiers,		XF	VI° Armée, probably by Ltn Fritz	
		O	OK	Höhn, Jasta 21s, (2).	

12 April

Sgt Baylies		Spa 3	2 seater	X	Gratibus	0650	5
MdL Berthelot		Spa 15	Balloon	XF	Mézières		2
Adj Artigau		Spa 15	2 seater	X	S Grivesnes		6
Lt Brusco,		R 46					1
S/Lt Blitz &		R 46					1
Sgt Delaporte		R 46	EA	XF			1
Lt Chaput &	CO	Spa 57					15
Asp Dubois de Gennes	a.	Spa 57	2 seater	X	Fontaine-sous-Montdidier		4
Lt Nuville,		Spa 57					3
MdL Roquefeuil &		Spa 57					1
Adj Hasdenteufel		Spa 57	Rumpler C	XF	NE Bois de Hangard		3
S/Lt Fraissinet		Spa 57	Aviatik C	X	Hangard		2
Lt Koenig Belliard de Vaubicourt &		Spa 84					2
S/Lt Demeuldre		Spa 84	2 seater	X	Le Plessier		12
S/Lt Desmond	b.	Spa 85	EA	X			2
S/Lt G Thomas &		Spa 88					1
MdL Quintard		Spa 88	2 seater	XF	Coulemelle		2
Sgt Fleury		Spa 95	2 seater	X			1
S/Lt Guertiau,		Spa 97					5
MdL Legagneux &		Spa 97					1
Cpl Cheyne		Spa 97	Balloon	XF			1
Sgt Lenoir &		Spa 99					1
Sgt Grenez		Spa 99	Balloon	XF	Petitmont	1100	1
Adj Leclerc &		Spa 102					2
Cpl Delaville		Spa 102	EA	XF	Courtigny		1
Lt Fonck		Spa 103	Scout	XF	Montdidier	1815	34
Lt Fonck		Spa 103	2 seater	XF	S Moreuil	1840	35
Sgt Brouet &		Br 128					2
MdL Monard		Br 128	Scout	X	Septvaux		2
S/Lt Waddington,		Spa 154					2
MdL Moissinac &		Spa 154					3
MdL Fuchs		Spa 154	2 seater	XF	Mailly-Raineval		1
Lt Chambarière	CO c.	Spa 162	Balloon	XF	Xammes	1605	1
MdL Boudouin &		Sop 271					1
Lt Boisse	d.	Sop 271	EA	POW	N Gury		1
Cdt de Marancour	CO	GC 14	2 seater	XF	Ressons-sur-Matz		7
Capt Biddle	e.	103rdUS	Halb C	X	SE Corbeny	1130	2
1/Lt Baer		103rdUS	Albatros D	X	Proyart	1217	4
Adj Artigau		Spa 15	2 seater	P			–
Capt de Sevin &	CO	Spa 26					–
Patrol		Spa 26	2 seater	P	Marcelcave	1745	–
Lt Marinier &		AR 45					–
Lt Porteu de La Morandière		AR 45	EA	P			–

Lt Brusco,	R 46					–
S/Lt Blitz &	R 46					–
Sgt Delaporte	R 46	EA	P			–
Capt Franc,	Spa 79					–
Lt Koffmann,	Spa 79					–
Sgt Luseau &	Spa 79					–
S/Lt Bourquin	Spa 79	Fokker DrI	P		Verpillières	–
Maj Lufbery	CO	94thUS	Albatros D3	P	Xivray	1215	–
Patrol	Spa 94	Scout	P		Villers-Bretonneux	–
Sgt Putnam	MS 156	Scout	P		St Hilaire-le-Petit	–
Sgt Putnam	MS 156	Scout	P		St Hilaire-le-Petit	–
Lt Chambarière	CO	Spa 162	Balloon	P	Beney	–
???	???	EA	P		Piennes	–

a.   Possibly Ltn Fritz Pollandt (O), FlAbt (A) 237, KIA, Fontaine-Montdidier.
b.   Possibly Gefr Ernst Bareth & Ltn Paul Helbig, FlAbt 254 (A), KIAs Montdidier, about 5 km east of Mesnil-St Georges.
c.   Probably Bz 59, Cirey, Armee-Abteilung "A".
d.   Probably Ltn Erich Ziffer, Jasta 69, POW at Péronne-Chauny.
e.   Probably Uffz Helmut Suhrmann (P) & Ltn Theodor Krubeck, FlAbt (A) 201, KIAs Corbeny.

Casualties:

MdL Roger Busch	Spa 94	P	MIA	Spad VII N° 3191, by Ltn Ulrich Neckel, Jasta 12, (9).
MdL Georges Paumier	Spa 155	P	MIA	Spad VII, probably by Ltn Fedor Hübner, Jasta 4, (1).
Brig Joubert	Spa 155	P	MIA	Spad XIII, probably by Ltn Viktor von Rautter, Jasta 4, (3).
Brig Yves Sallandrouze &	Sal 10	P	MIA	III° Armée, Montdidier
Sol Albert Lorthioir	Sal 10	G	MIA	Salmson 2A2
Lt François de La Croix Laval	Sal 10	O	Injured	collided Salmson 2A2
Cpl Schuyler Lee	Spa 96	P	KIA	Spad VII, probably by Hptm Wilhelm Reinhard, JGI,(12).
MdL Maxime Matignon	Spa 89	P	KIA	Spad VII
Sgt Robert &	Br 111	P	OK	
Sgt Frelières	Br 111	G	KIA	
Lt Paul Rozoy	Spa 88	P	WIA	Spad VII
Brig Bardy &	Br 111	P	WIA	
Sgt Léo Delhommeau	Br 111	G	WIA	
Sgt Gaston Ouillie	Sal 6	P	WIA	Salmson 2A2, III° Armée
Cpl Charles Farey	N 152	P	KIAcc	Nieuport XXVII
Cpl Renoux,	V 114	P	KIAcc	
Sol Perruchot &	V 114	G	KIAcc	
Sgt-Maj Trouve	V 25	G	KIAcc	
Lt Jean Ducruzel &	V 121	P	KIAcc	
Brig ???	V 121	G	Injured	
Cpl Clément	Sop 280	P	KIAcc	
S/Lt Cambier	Sop 280	O	Injured	Sopwith N° 489
Sgt Julien Barberousse	Spa 86	P	Injured	Spad XIII
Cpl Jean Lagrue	Spa 85	P	Injured	
Cpl René Hummel	Spa 93	P	Injured	
Cpl Bedet &	Sop 60	P	Injured	
Sol Auverlot	Sop 60	M	Injured	Sopwith 1A2
S/Lt Cottin	Esc 22	P	Injured	Caudron G3
Cpl Meunier	Spa 38	M	Injured	By Propeller
Capt Ruggerone &	CO	GB Ital	P	Injured	
Cpl de Sanctis	GB Ital	G	Injured	
Lt Venditti	GB Ital	O	KIAcc	Caproni
Adj Auguste Renard	45° Cie d'Aérostiers	XF		Balloons 45 & 46 claimed
	O	OK		by Ltn Arno Benzler (4) &
MdL Raynard	46° Cie d'Aérostiers	XF		Vfw Stein (1) of Jasta 45.
	O	OK		VI° Armée.
Lt Gustave Audrain	59° Cie d'Aérostiers			Attacked, not flamed.
	O	KIA		Parachute caught on cable.
Lt Jean Herbert	23° Cie d'Aérostiers			Claimed by Ltn Fritz Höhn,
S/Lt Eugène Reb	O	OK		Jasta 21s, (3).
???	26° Cie d'Aérostiers			Attacked, not flamed.

13 April

S/Lt Bouvard &	Br 209		1

Sgt Delcey	Br 209	EA	X	Conchy-le-Pots		1
Ground fire	???	EA	X	Pont l'Evéque		–
Casualties:						
Brig Lagoutre	V 121	G	WIA			
Sgt Thomas &	V 110	P	Injured			
S/Lt Casteignau-Gaumont	V 110	O	Injured	DOW		
MdL Raymond Dubray	N 99	P	KIAcc	Nieuport XXIV		
Sgt Brude	Sop 283	P	Injured			
MdL Pratte &	Sop 270	P	Injured			
S/Lt Kurzenne	Sop 270	O	Injured			

14 April

1/Lt Campbell	a. 94thUS	Pfalz DIIIa	POW	Toul	0853	1
1/Lt Winslow	b. 94thUS	Albatros DVa	XF	Toul	0851	1
???		DCA	EA	X		–

a.   Vfw Anton Wroniecki, Jasta 64w, WIA/POW.
b.   Uffz Heinrich Simon, Jasta 64w, POW.

Casualties:					
S/Lt Arnoux de Maison					
Rouge	Spa 78	P	WIA	DOW 29 May 1918	
S/Lt Robert Levi	Spa 78	O	WIA		

15 April – No Claims – No Casualties

16 April – No Claims
Casualties:

Sgt René Lusseau	Spa 79	P	KIA	Spad, III° Armée
Cpl André Ricard &	Sal 225	P	KIA	Salmson 2A2, III° Armée, probably
S/Lt Paul Pruvot	Sal 225	O	KIA	Ltn Julius Buckler, Jasta 17, (31).
Cpl René Hummel	Spa 93	P	WIA	
Sgt Roger Dumont	Spa 93	P	Injured	Spad XIII
Sgt Barthe	GDE	P	Injured	AR

17 April

Sgt Ouillie &	Sal 6				1
S/Lt Chenard &	Sal 6				1
Adj Gelin &	Sal 6				1
Lt Arnaud &	Sal 6				1
S/Lt Boitieux &	Sal 6				1
S/Lt Picard	Sal 6	Scout	XF	Boulogne-la-Grase	1
Casualties:					
Sgt Gaston Ouillie	Sal 6	P	WIA	III° Armée.	
MdL René Nacrier &	AR 254	P	KIAcc		
Lt Augustin Podevin	AR 254	O	Injured		

18 April

Adj Damenez,	R 46				1
S/Lt Tison &	R 46				1
Adj Astoin &	R 46				1
Lt Hostein,	R 46				1
Lt Petyst de Morcourt &	R 46				1
MdL Baratciart	R 46	EA	X		1
Casualties:					
Adj Roger Leclerc	Spa 102	P	KIAcc	Spad XIII	
MdL Lelache &	Sop 277	P	KIAcc		
Sol Deguise	Sop 277	M	KIAcc		
MdL Laude &	V 109	P	Injured	DOW 20 April 1918	
Cpl Rodier	V 109	G	Injured		
MdL Charbonnier	Sal 18	P	Injured		

19 April

| DCA | a. ??? | EA | X | | – |

a.   Probably Uffz Peter Baumler & Gefr Michael, Schusta 22, POWs, S Rouvrel, pilot WIA by flak and FTL.

Casualties:				
Sgt Armand Oppel &	V 125	P	MIA	
Sol Dulon	V 125	G	MIA	

MdL Valles &	Br 111	P	MIA			
Adj Gauthier	Br 111	M	MIA			
MdL Lanciaux	V 113	P	WIA			
Asp Clarac	Br 128	O	WIA	Flak		
Brig Petit	Sop 232	P	KIAcc			
Brig Coulomb	V 121	G	Injured			
Sgt Guillaumont &	V 113	P	Injured			
MdL Gaisbault	V 113	G	Injured			
Sgt Henri Royer	Spa 77	P	Injured	Spad VII		
Sgt Jarnach	RGAé	P	Injured			
MdL Maurice Bechet &	CEP 115	P	Injured			
Sol Louis Lagneau	CEP 115	G	Injured	Caproni		
MdL Lanciaux	GB 8	P	Injured			

20 April

Lt Bozon-Verduraz	Spa 3	2 seater	X	Hangard-Thennes	1005	4
S/Lt G Guérin &	Spa 15					20
S/Lt Cordonnier	Spa 15	Rumpler C	X	NE Montdidier		3
Lt Rougevin-Baville &	Spa 67					1
Adj Pillon	Spa 67	2 seater	X	Moreuil-Sauvillers	0940	6
Sgt Jacob &	Spa 157					1
Sgt Connelly	Spa 157	Balloon	XF	Selles		1
Major Thaw & CO	103rdUS					4
1/Lt Turnure	103rdUS	Balloon	XF	Montaigu	1812	2
Major Thaw CO	103rdUS	Scout	XF	Nogent l'Abbesse	1827	5

Casualties:

Lt Charles Boudoux			Spad XIII, probably by Ltn		
d'Hautefeuille CO	Spa 100	P	MIA	Hans Pippart, Jasta 19, (10).	
Brig Lesbroussart &	V 101	P	KIA		
Brig Chapel	V 101	G	KIA	Voisin Renault #2761.	
Sgt Victorien Bordes &	Sal 61	P	WIA		
S/Lt Jean Griffoul	Sal 61	O	WIA	Salmson, III° Armée	
S/Lt Laneyrie	Sop 104	P	WIA	Ground fire	
Cpl Charasse	V 121	P	WIA		
Cpl Narbey	GDE	P	Injured	DOW 29 April 1918 Spad VII	
Sgt Boissie	GDE	P	Injured	AR	
Sol Mounard	Sal 225	M	Injured		
Cpl Albert Guerrier	Sop 234	P	Injured		
Adj Breyer &	45° Cie d'Aérostiers		XF		
Cpl Guyot		O	OK		
Adj Renard	75° Cie d'Aérostiers		XF	Both claimed by Ltn Fritz	
		O	OK	Höhn, Jasta 21s, (5-6).	

21 April

S/Lt Bucquet	Spa 3	2 seater	XF	Contoire-Roye	1215	3
S/Lt Bouzac &	Spa 12					2
Adj Decugis	Spa 12	Albatros	X	Dives		2
S/Lt Bozon-Verduraz,	Spa 3					5
S/Lt Duret,	Spa 67					2
Adj Mion &	Spa 67					3
MdL Ouvrard de Linière	Spa 67	2 seater	XF	Thory-Rouvrel	0815	1
Sgt Gérard &	Spa 65					3
MdL Lienhard a.	Spa 65	2 seater	X	W Etelfay		3
S/Lt Chaput & CO	Spa 57					16
S/Lt Wertheim	Spa 84	Pfalz DIII	X	S Rollot		4
Lt Jochaux du Plessis,	Spa 15					2
S/Lt Hasdenteufel &	Spa 57					4
Adj Petit-Delchet b.	Spa 57	EA	X	Lignières		1
Lt Le Roy de Boiseaumarie &	Spa 78					4
Sgt Rouvin	Spa 78	Scout	X	Lassigny,		1
S/Lt Castelli	Spa 102	EA	XF	SE Moreuil		2
S/Lt Brussaux &	Sop 269					1
Lt Mognot c.	Sop 269	Albatros DV	POW			1
???	???	Balloon	XF	Hangest-en-Santerre	1800	–
Infantry fire	???	EA	X			–
Patrol	Spa 3	2 seater	P	Roye	1205	–
Capt C Biddle	103rdUS	EA	P			–

???		???	3 EA	P			–

a. Possibly Gefr August Penske & Gefr Johannes Straub, Schsta 33, KIAs, Montdidier, about 3 km SW Etelfay.
b. Possibly Ltn Otto Wille & Ltn Willibald Richter, FlAbt (A) 223, KIAs Ancre-Montdidier, about 6 km S Lignières.
c. Possibly Ltn Rudolph Abt, Jasta 69, POW near Collezy.

Casualties:

Sgt Paul Marie	Spa 12	P	MIA	Spad VII N° 5404 Collided⎤
Cpl Donald E Stone	Spa 12	P	MIA	Spad VII N° 5358 Collided⎦
(American)				
MdL David de Conflans &	Br 220	P	MIA	Bréguet 14, probably by
Asp Millardet	Br 220	O	MIA	Ltn Ulrich Neckel, Jasta 12, (10).
Sgt Henri Jarry	Spa 150	P	KIA	Spad VII, III° Armée
Cpl Lafarge &	Sop 269	P	KIA	Sopwith 1A2, probably by
S/Lt Ponsard	Sop 269	O	WIA/DOW	Uffz Wilhelm Zorn, Jasta 60, (6).
Sgt Renaud Bernard				
de La Fregeolière	Spa 12	P	WIA	Spad VII N° 3192
Cpl Marcel Gavot &	V 119	P	KIAcc	
Lt Besson	V 119	O	Injured	
MdL Barthélemy Lantieri	Spa 157	P	Injured	Spad VII
Cpl Marlière	Spa 67	M	Injured	
Cpl Henri Delberghe &	Sop 283	P	Injured	
Sol Jabally	Sop 283	M	Injured	
Cpl Richard	GDE	P	Injured	DOW 24 April 1918
Adj Beaunier &	46° Cie d'Aérostiers			Deflated by artillery fire
MdL Chotard		O	OK	Observers jumped safely.

22 April

S/Lt G Guérin	a.	Spa 15	2 seater	XF	Royaucourt		21
Cpl Boyer		Spa 97	Balloon	XF	N Contoire		1
S/Lt Fonck		Spa 103	2 seater	X	Assainvillers	1805	36
DCA		???	EA	X	Dunkerque		–
Became lost		???	EA	POW	Beaurepaire		–
Adj Artigau		Spa 15	DFW C	P			–
Sgt Loup &		Spa 103					
Sgt Baux		Spa 103	Scout	P	Montdidier		–
Sgt Loup &		Spa 103					
Sgt Baux		Spa 103	Scout	P	Montdidier		–

a. Possibly Vfw Karl Peiling & Ltn Franz Späth, FlAbt (A) 203, KIAs,Montdidier-Rocquencourt, about 10 km NW Royaucourt.

Casualties:

MdL Fabre	V 121	P	WIA	
Cpl Deplante	V 121	P	WIA	
Lt Charlouty	Sal 286	O	WIA	
Cpl Eugène Bouvier	GDE	P	KIAcc	Spad VII
Cpl Dufloux	GDE	P	KIAcc	Nieuport XXIVbis
Cpl Dinsmore Ely	???	P	KIAcc	
Sgt de Laguerie &	Spa 212	P	Injured	
Sol Roland	Spa 212	M	Injured	Spad XI
Brig Gouverneur	GDE	P	Injured	AR
MdL Chaffaud	GDE	P	Injured	AR
Brig Chomel	GDE	P	Injured	AR

23 April

Sgt Gérard &		Spa 65					4
MdL Gentil		Spa 65	2 seater	X	N Ployron		1
Sgt Gérard		Spa 65	2 seater	X	Rollot		5
S/Lt G Thomas	a.	Spa 88	2 seater	X	Esclainvillers		2
Lt Marty	b.	Spa 90	Hannover CL	XF	Pagny-sur-Meuse	1115	6
Cpl Guillaume &		AR 272					1
Asp Barbaut	c.	AR 272	Albatros D3	POW	III° Armée		1
Cdt Vuillemin &	CO	Esc 12					4
Lt Dagnaux	d.	Esc 12	Rumpler C	X	Montigny-Ravenel		3
???		DCA	Albatros D	FTL	Mont St Simon		–
1/Lt Baer &		103rdUS					5
1/Lt Wilcox		103rdUS	Albatros C	X	St Gobain	0955	1
Sgt Putnam		MS 156	3 EA	P			–
Patrol		GC 18	2 seater	P	W Moreuil		–
Patrol		Spa 68	EA	P	Thiaucourt		–

Patrol	e. Br 127	EA	P	N Moreuil	–
Patrol	AR 272	Albatros	FTL	St Simon	–

a.   Probably Uffz Otto Schenke & Obltn Georg Schmidt, FlAbt (A) 254, KIAs Esclainvillers.
b.   Probably Ltn Heinrich Ohler & Ltn Otto Hickmann, FlAbt (A) 242, KIAs Pagny-sur-Meuse, AOK 19 Sector.
c.   Probably Uffz Wilhelm Zorn, Jasta 60, POW after combat with Bréguets.
d.   Probably Uffz Konrad Kayler & Ltn Hugo Schumann, FlAbt 39, KIAs Montigny.
e.   Possibly Uffz Emil Dassenies, Jasta 13, KIA at Moreuil.

Casualties:

Lt Abadie &	Br 127	P	MIA	
Lt Mativon	Br 127	O	MIA	
Capt Georges Flouch & CO	Sal 225	P	KIA	III° Armée, W Chevincourt
Lt Henri de Barres	Sal 225	O	KIA	Salmson 2A2, possibly by Ltn Heinrich Arntzen, Jasta 50, (11).
Sgt Edmond Hebert &	AR 272	P	KIA	
S/Lt Jean Bajard	AR 272	O	KIA	AR1, III° Armée
Sgt Marcou	???	P	WIA	Flak
Cpl Ivan Caster	V 116	P	WIA	
Cpl Tilloy &	AR 272	P	OK	III° Armée
Asp Léon Barbaut	AR 272	O	WIA	FTL during combat.
MdL Edmond Cazeaux &	AR 272	P	WIA	
Lt Gaudy	AR 272	O	WIA	AR1, III° Armée
MdL Pinatel	Br 117	G	WIA/DOW	
Adj Henri Tiffagnon	Spa 151	P	KIAcc	
MdL Vasel	Spa 38	P	Injured	Spad XIII
Lt Lautier	Sop 252	O	Injured	
Sol Jousse	Sop 255	M	Injured	

24 April

S/Lt Descardes &	???				1
Cpl Lacout	a. ???	AEG G.IV	POW	Monchy-Humières, at night	1

a.   All three occupants taken prisoner, aircraft N° 1131/16.

Casualties:

Asp Henri Cessieux	Spa 77	P	Injured	Spad VII

25 April

MdL Hamot &	Spa 49			–
Adj Bouyer	Spa 49	Scout	P	Carspach
Sgt Gérard	Spa 65	Fokker DrI	P	–

Casualties:

Adj Eon	Sop 104	P	WIA	Ground fire.
SM Jacques Monier	* EP	P	KIAcc	
Cpl Gelot	GDE	P	Injured	Sopwith
S/Lt Beroo,	Sal 13	P	OK	
Lt Van Coehorn &	Sal 13	O	Injured	
Sgt Muller	Sal 13	G	OK	Letord N° 64

*   St Raphaël.

26 April – No Claims

Casualties:

MdL Lanciaux	V 113	P	WIA	
LV Emile Le Voyer &	* CAM	P	KIAcc	
Mat Antoine Chambriard	CAM	O	KIAcc	Tellier 200HP, N° 125.
Sgt Jean Rouvin	Spa 78	P	KIAcc	Spad VII
Brig Georges Lecoq	Spa 84	P	Injured	Spad VII
Lt Georges Parizet	Spa 81	P	Injured	Spad XIII

*   Tréguier.

27 April

S/Lt G Guérin	a. Spa 15	DFW C	X	N Moreuil	22
Major Lufbery	CO 94thUS	EA	P		–

a.   Probably Flg Otto Behringer, Schsta 22b, KIA, Morisel, about 2 km W of Moreuil.

Casualties:

Lt Maurice Nogues	Spa 73	P	Injured	Spad XIII

28 April – No Claims

Casualties:

Cpl Archambault &	Spa 63	P	KIAcc

| Sol M J Cuenot | | Spa 63 | M | | Injured | Spad XI | | |
| MdL Albert Armangue | | Spa 77 | P | | Injured | Spad VII | | |

29 April

| 1/Lt Rickenbacker & | | 94thUS | | | | | | 1 |
| Capt J N Hall | a. | 94thUS | Pfalz DIII | X | | Mortmare | 1810 | 4 |

a.   Probably from Jasta 64w.

Casualties:

???		C 74	?		MIA			
Sgt Roger Narbey		???	?		KIAcc			
Sol Thomas		Spa 68	M		Injured			

30 April

| Infantry fire | a. | 3 Armée | 2 seater | X | | Le Monchel | | – |

a.   Possibly Ltn Hans Wolf & Ltn Bernhard Ziegler, FlAbt (A) 295b, KIAs Montdidier-Le Monchel.

Casualties:

MdL Pillas		GDE	P		KIAcc	Voisin P		
Cpl Marchal		GDE	P		KIAcc	Voisin P		
Lt Edouard Garcin		Spa 38	P		Injured			
Asp Mole		Br 123	G		Injured			
Sgt Cheyroux &		Sal 74	P		Injured	DOW 2 May 1918		
Sol Corbi		Sal 74	M		Injured			

April dates unknown:

| Cpl Jean Lefebvre & | | Sop 234 | P | | Injured | | | |
| MdL Pierre Matenas | | Sop 234 | O | | Injured | | | |

1 May – No Claims

Casualties:

Capt Meiffre		33 CA	P		KIA	AR, ground fire, aircraft		
Lt Ménétier		33 CA	O		OK	landed by observer.		
S/Lt Charles du Tertre		Spa 68	P		WIA	DOW 2 May 1918, Spad VII VIII° Armée		
Lt Edmond Chamboredon		N 314	P		WIA	Flak, VIII° Armée, Nieuport 27.		
Sgt .... ssard		V 116	P		Injured			

2 May

Sgt Baylies		Spa 3	Rumpler C	X		Assainvillers	1320	6
S/Lt Fraissinet		Spa 57	Aviatik C	X		Dormart-sur-le-Luce		3
S/Lt Nogues		Spa 57	Albatros D	X		Mailly-Raineval		3
Lt Hay de Slade	a.	Spa 86	Pfalz DIII	XF		Morlancourt		7
S/Lt Claret de Fleurieu		Spa 95	2 seater	X		Plessier		1
S/Lt Martin &		Br 111						1
Lt Frichon		Br 111	EA	XF		Fouquescourt		1
S/Lt Louvat,		Spa 153						2
S/Lt Barcat,		Spa 153						2
Sgt Morel &		Spa 153						1
Lt Lahoulle	CO b.	Spa 154	Pfalz DIII	X		Montdidier		4
33° Section d'Autos-canons		DCA	Halb CLII	X		Méry	p.m.	–
	c.	DCA	Halb CLII	X		Méry	p.m.	–
III° Armée		DCA	EA	X		Godenvillers	p.m.	–
III° Armée		DCA	EA	X		Conchy-le-Pots	p.m.	–
???		GC	EA	X		Saulshoy-les-Davenscourt		–
???		GB	EA	X		Chaulnes		–
1/Lt Meissner		94thUS	Albatros C	X		Martincourt	1203	1
Lt Nungesser		Spa 65	EA	P				–
Lt Nungesser		Spa 65	EA	P				–
MdL Mony		Spa 82	EA	P		Amifontaine		–
Adj Gasser &		Spa 87						–
Cpl Muzart		Spa 87	2 seater	P		Blamont		–
MdL Pezon		Spa 90	Scout	P				–
Patrol		Br 128	Fokker DrI	P		Avricourt		–
S/Lt Barcat &		Spa 153						–
S/Lt Louvat	d.	Spa 153	Pfalz	P		Montdidier		–

Patrol	(1)	d.	GC 12	EA	P		Montdidier	1835	–
Sgt Baylies			Spa 3	2 seater	P			p.m.	–
1/Lt Blodgett			95thUS	EA	P		Montsec		–

a. Possibly Ltn Stoy, Jasta 10, WIA W Péronne, Morlancourt about 20 km W Péronne.
b. Possibly Vfw Philipp Jopp, Jasta 79b, KIA Montdidier.
c. Probably Vfw Willy Sonnenberg, KIA, & Gefr Stolz, WIA, Schsta 8.
d. Possibly Ltn Fritz Edler von Braun, Jasta 79b, WIA Montdidier.
(1) Claimed by one pilot from GC 12 and patrols from three other GCs.

Casualties:

Asp Jean Cabannes &	Br 126	P	MIA	Bréguet 14 N° 1306, probably by
Sgt Eugène Muracciole	Br 126	G	MIA	Ltn Hans Pippart, Jasta 19, (11).
Capt Michel Mahieu & CO	V 114	P	MIA	
Lt Rivalleau	V 114	O	MIA	Voisin N° 5597
S/Lt Richard Cathelin	Spa 154	P	KIA	Spad VII
Adj André Bussienne	Spa 86	P	POW/WIA	Spad VII N° 3288
Sgt René Nicolas	Spa 86	P	POW	Spad VII N° 3305
Cpl René Brisset	Spa 86	P	POW	
Lt Gouilloud	Br 214	O	WIA	V° Armée, Bréguet.
Cpl André Pointe	Spa 151	P	KIAcc	Spad VII
Brig Cheillant	GDE	P	Injured	Spad VII
Sol Bonnefoy	Spa 153	M	Injured	
Sgt Albert Morel &	Br 132	P	Injured	
Sol Séguy	Br 132	M	Injured	

3 May

Sgt Baylies &		Spa 3					7
MdL Dubonnet	a.	Spa 3	2 seater	XF		Montdidier	1725	1
Cpl Bacque		Spa 23	EA	X		Bois de Brieulles		1
Adj M Paris	b.	Spa 73	EA	X		S Villers-Bretonneux		3
S/Lt Bouisset &		N 87					1
MdL Duhomme	c.	N 87	Rumpler C	X		E Goincourt	1045	1
Adj Gasser		N 87	Albatros D3	XF		Arracourt	1910	6
Sgt Warnotte		Spa 88	Balloon	XF		Marquivillers		1
Adj M Robert &		N 92					4
MdL Javaud		N 92	Rumpler C4	POW		French Lines		1
Lt Hugues & CO		Spa 95					12
Sgt Fleury		Spa 95	2 seater	XF		Hailles		2
Cpl Lacouture		Spa 95	2 seater	X		Villers-Bretonneux		1
MdL Quiles &		Spa 48					1
S/Lt Brunel	b.	Spa 95	2 seater	POW		Gentelles-Amiens		1
Adj Doux &		Br 111					2
Adj-Chef Thévenin		Br 111	EA	X		Chipilly		1
Adj Doux &		Br 111					3
Adj-Chef Thévenin		Br 111	EA	X		Chipilly		2
MdL de Freslon &		N 152					2
Cpl Vallot	d.	N 152	2 seater	X		Raon l'Etape		1
VII° Armée	e.	DCA	EA	X		Poureux-Jarmenil	1100	–
???		DCA	EA	X		Hailles		–
Capt Peterson		94thUS	Scout	XF		Amenoncourt	1040	–
Adj Gasser		N 87	Albatros D	FTL				–
Adj Dousinelle		Spa 48	EA	P				–
S/Lt Brunel	c.	Spa 95	2 seater	P		Picardie		–
Lt Hugues & CO		Spa 95					–
Sgt Fleury	c.	Spa 95	2 seater	P		Picardie		–
???		Escad 1	2 EA	P				–
???		Escad 2	3 EA	P				–
???		GC 16	EA	P		NE Noyon		–

a. Probably Ltn Willi Karbe & Ltn Erich Meuche, FlAbt 245 (A), KIAs Montdidier.
b. One possibly Vfw Karl Peez, WIA/POW/DOW & Gefr Michael Lang (G), Schsta 31b, KIA Moreuil, about 11 km S Villers-Bretonneux.
c. One probably Flg Hans Buck, POW, & Ltn Alfred Scharf, KIA, FlAbt 276Lb, AOK "A" Sector.
d. Possibly Ltn Seit & Lt Martin, FlAbt (A) 199, WIAs, FTL after combat, AOK 19 Sector.
e. Pilot KIA, observer WIA.

Casualties:

MdL Jean Vialla	Spa 96	P	MIA	Spad VII
S/Lt Omer Demeuldre	Spa 84	P	MIA	Spad VII, Monchel, combat with a 2 seater
Sgt Désiré Mabereau	Spa 26	P	KIA	Spad VII N° 3802, Moreuil, departed 12h00, possibly by Ltn Carl Galetschky, Jasta 48, (3).

MdL Jacques Charnet &	Br 111	P	KIA			
Sgt André Teissedre	Br 111	G	KIA	Bréguet 14B2 N° 1457.		
Sol Jeudi	Spa 102	G	KIA	Flak, Bréguet		
MdL Moreau &	Br 44	P	KIA	Flak		
Adj Noël	Br 44	G	KIA	Flak		
MdL-Chef Gabriel Rochas &	Br 218	P	KIA	Probably by Ltn Viktor v Rautter,		
Cpl Jean L'Heritier	Br 218	G	KIA	Jasta 4, (4).		
2/Lt Charles W Chapman, Jr	94th US	P	KIA	VIII° Armée, Nieuport 28 N° 6138, Autrepierre, probably by Obltn Erwi Wenig, CO Jasta 80b, (2). AOK 19 Sector.		
Sgt Eugène Warnote	Spa 88	P	POW	Spad VII N° 5488		
Cpl Jean Guéry	Br 131	G	WIA			
S/Lt Montaufray	Sal 122	O	WIA	VIII° Armée, DOW 4 May 1918.		
Lt Henri Arnaud	Sal 6	O	WIA	III° Armée, Salmson 2A2,		
Asp Lécuyer	Sop 282	O	WIA	Flak, III° Armée, Sopwith		
Sgt Alfred Raveau	Spa 163	P	KIAcc	Spad VII N° 5491		
EV2 Olivier de Parscau du Plessis	* CAM	O	KIAcc	Tellier 200HP, N° 136.		
Adj ... dirert &	???	P	KIAcc			
Sol ... croix	???	M	KIAcc	Spad XI		
Cpl Fernand Bourjournier &	Br 236	P	KIAcc			
S/Lt Gieules	Br 236	O	Injured			
Capt Raymond Bailly CO	GC 20	P	Injured	Spad		
Asp Chanouy	Sop 282	O	Injured			
2/Lt Gundersen, USAS	Sal 51	O	Injured	Caudron R11		
Lt Weiss & Asp Tricot	67° Cie Aérostiers		XF	III° Armée, Probably by Ltn Julius		
		O	OK	Buckler, Jasta 17, (33).		
S/Lt Raymond Lériche	88° Cie Aérostiers		XF	Probably by Ltn Rudolf		
		O	OK	Windisch, Jasta 66, (18).		

*   Boulogne.

---

4 May

S/Lt Cordonnier	Spa 15	Scout	X	NE Montdidier		4
Capt Pinsard	Spa 23	Balloon	XF	Bois de Brieulles	1745	18
Lt Nungesser	Spa 65	2 seater	X	N Bouissancourt		33
Lt Nungesser	Spa 65	2 seater	X	S Marquivillers		34
Cpl Mevius	Spa 77	Scout	XF	Faverolles-Montdidier		1
S/Lt Bourjade a.	N 152	Balloon	XF	Gueberswihr	1135	3
Sgt Gérard	Spa 65	2 seater	P	Chaudun		–
Lt Nungesser	Spa 65	EA	P	Marquivillers		–
S/Lt Leroy de Boiseaumarie &	Spa 78					–
Adj Bredin	Spa 78	Albatros D3	P	Le Quesnoy-en-Santerre		–
Patrol	Spa 78	EA	P	Lignières		–
Patrol	GC 12	EA	P	Lignières	1610	–

a.   Possibly BZug 36 attacked at 12h40 but not flamed, AOK 19 Sector.

Casualties:

Brig Laraud	Spa 77	P	MIA	Probably by Ltn Arthur Rahn, Jasta 19, (6)		
Sgt Jean Mathieu &	Br 132	P	MIA			
Sol Francis Potier	Br 132	G	MIA			
M Yves Le Creurer	* CAM	P	KIA	Hanriot HD.2 N° 226, codé D.30, off Nieuport.		
M Jean-Pierre Salaun	* CAM	P	KIA	Hanriot HD.2, codé D.35. Both of these pilots were probably claimed by Ltn z S Poss (2) and FlgMt Hubrish (1), Sea Front Staffel 2.		
Sgt Boreau &	Br 129	P	KIA	Bréguet 14, possibly by Ltn Moritz		
2/Lt Raymond B Parker, USAS		O	KIA	Bretschneider-Bodemer, Jasta 6, (2).		
Adj Faivre	Br 129	P	OK			
Lt Marie Ste Chapelle	Br 129	O	KIA	Bréguet 14B2		
Cpl Thomas Buffum	Spa 77	P	POW	Spad N° 3411, probably by Ltn Hans Pippart, Jasta 19, (12).		
S/Lt Lucien Gauthier	Spa 62	P	POW	Spad VII		
Cpl Marcel Dupont	Spa 26	P	WIA	Spad VII		
Cpl Vallée &	AR 272	P	KIAcc			
Asp Vincent	AR 272	O	KIAcc			

S/Lt Fernand Ducos	Sop 285	P	KIAcc	Sopwith 1A2		
Brig Lanquelin &	Spa 54	P	KIAcc	Spad XI		
Lt Bouchaud	Spa 54	O	Injured	DOW 5 May 1918		
Cpl Thébaud	Br 234	P	Injured			
Cpl Jean Defosses	Sop 269	P	Injured			
Sol Marius Bousquet	Sop 269	G	Injured			
* Dunkerque.						

5 May

| ??? | Esc 2 | EA | P | Faverolles | – |
Casualties:
| Sgt Virot & | GDE | P | KIAcc | | |
| Sol Pedoussant | GDE | M | Injured | Sopwith | |

6 May

Adj Parsons	Spa 3	2 seater	X	W Montdidier	1715	2
Lt Verdier-Fauvety,	Spa 65					2
Adj Camplan &	Spa 65					4
MdL Giovetti	Spa 65	2 seater	X	Etelfay		2
Sgt Royol &	Br 131					1
Lt Dutourleau	Br 131	Scout	X	German lines		1
???	Escad 1	EA	XF			–
???	Escad 2	EA	X	Etelfay-Lignières		–
???	Escad 2	EA	X	Gratibus		–
Adj Artigau	Spa 15	Fokker DrI	P	Montdidier		–
???	???	EA	FTL			–
???	Escad 2	EA	P	Courtemanche		–
???	Escad 2	5 EA	P			–
Patrol	Spa 88	EA	P			–

Casualties:

Lt Maurice Barthe	CO	Spa 96	P	MIA	Spad XIII, probably by Ltn Hans Pippart, Jasta 19, (13).
Sgt Jean-Marie Royol &		Br 131	P	MIA	Bréguet 14s, probably by
Lt André Dutourleau		Br 131	O	MIA	Ltn Wilhelm Schwartz (3) &
Lt Jean Pavinet &		Br 131	P	MIA	Ltn Robert Hildebrandt (4),
Cpl René Monier		Br 131	G	MIA	Jasta 13.
Lt Jean Chaput		Spa 57	P	WIA/DOW	Spad VII, possibly by Ltn Hermann Becker, Jasta 12, (10).
Cpl André Patrat &		Br 131	P	WIA	DOW 6 June 1918
Lt de Lasteyrie du Saillant		Br 131	O	KIA	
S/Lt Gilbert Caron &		93° Cie d'Aérostiers			Not flamed, probably claimed by
MdL Bloze			O	OK	Fldw Karl Schmückle, Jasta 21s, (3).
S/Lt Perucat		87° Cie d'Aérostiers			Attacked, not flamed.
			O	OK	

7 May

| 1/Lt Rickenbacker | a. | 94thUS | Pfalz DIII | X | Pont-à-Mousson | 0805 | 2 |
a.   Ltn Willi Scheerer, Jasta 64w, WIA/DOW Vieville-en-Haye, about 9 km WNW Pont-à-Mousson.

Casualties:

Cpl Joseph Deom,	Let 74	P	MIA	Letord, probably by Flak-
S/Lt Nelson-Pautier &	Let 74	O	MIA	batterie 503, OfStv Mobe.
Asp Cochet	Let 74	O	MIA	
Capt James N Hall	94thUS	P	POW	VIII° Armée, Nieuport 28, N° 6153, by Ltn Friedrich Hengst, Jasta 64w. (1).
Cpl Dufour &	Sop 279	P	KIA	
S/Lt David	Sop 279	P	WIA	
Brig Le Sanne &	Sal 280	P	KIAcc	
S/Lt Rime	Sal 280	O	Injured	Sopwith N° 691
Sol Gehant	Spa 73	M	Injured	

8 May

| 1/Lt Baer | a. | 103rdUS | 2 seater | X | Mont Kemmel | 1028 | 6 |
| 1/Lt Baer | | 103rdUS | Scout | X | Mont Kemmel | 1738 | 7 |
a.   Possibly Uffz Paul Fritz & Ltn Ulrich Haupt, FlAbt 240 (A), KIAs Wytschaete, about 6 km ENE of Mont Kemmel.

Casualties:

| Adj Henri Renault | Spa 86 | P | KIA | Spad VII, by a Sopwith Camel of N° 4 Sqn, AFC, between Bailleul and Hazebrouck. |

Sgt Albert Ferrat		Spa 80	P	KIA	Spad VII, Bray-Dunes, probably by by Ltn.z.S Theo Osterkamp, MFJ2, unconfimed.		
MdL Singlas &		AR 274	P	KIAcc			
Sgt Clausier		AR 274	O	Injured			
Adj Charles-Lavauzelle		Br 224	P	Injured			
Sol Delhumeau		Br 224	G	Injured	DOW 23 May 1918		

9 May

Sgt Baylies		Spa 3	Halb CL2	X	Braches-Gratibus	1930	8
Lt Fonck		Spa 103	2 seater	X	S Moreuil	1600	37
Lt Fonck		Spa 103	2 seater	X	S Moreuil	1600	38
Lt Fonck		Spa 103	2 seater	XF	Moreuil	1605	39
Lt Fonck		Spa 103	2 seater	X	Montdidier	1820	40
Lt Fonck		Spa 103	2 seater	XF	Hargicourt	1855	41
Lt Fonck		Spa 103	2 seater	XF	Braches	1856	42
???		Spa 3	EA	P	Ayencourt	1455	–
???		Escad 1	EA	P			–
???		Escad 2	EA	P	SE Montdidier		–
???	a.	Escad 2	EA	P	W Gratibus		–
???	a.	Escad 2	EA	P	N Gratibus		–

a.   Probably Uffz Otto Kutter and Ltn Ernst Schulze, Jasta 48, KIAs near Montdidier, about 5 km SE Gratibus.

Casualties:

MdL Léon Génot &	Br 107	P	WIA	Bréguet 14 N° 1434, probably by		
S/Lt Jardin	Br 107	O	OK	Vfw Fritz Rumey, Jasta 5, (16).		
Adj Lardeich	Br 208	P	WIA			
Asp Chazal	Sal 59	O	WIA			
1/Lt James A Bayne	Spa 81	P	KIAcc	Spad XIII		
MdL Charles Delaville	Br 224	P	Injured	DOW, Spad XI		
Cpl Laffont	GDE	P	Injured	Spad		
Cpl Daniel	GDE	P	Injured	Nieuport		

10 May

Sgt Baylies &		Spa 3					9
MdL Clément		Spa 3	2 seater	X	Faverolles	1725	1
MdL Dubonnet		Spa 3	EA	X	Montdidier	1725	2
Adj Bertrand &		Sal 10					1
Brig Thomas		Sal 10	EA	X	Rollot		1
Sgt Leclerc &		Br 107					1
Sgt Maillard &		Br 107					1
Sgt Scellier &		Br 128					1
Cpl Mathieu		Br 128	EA	X			1
Lt Hervieu &		Br 128					1
MdL Gaussen		Br 128	EA	X			1
Sgt Stary &		Br 128					1
Cpl Santos		Br 128	EA	X			1
Capt Bloch &	CO	R 46					–
Crew		R 46	Scout	P			–
Adj Mion		Spa 67	EA	P	Wiencourt-Cayeux	1600	–
???		Escad 1	EA	P			–
???		GC	EA	P	Coucy-le-Château		–

Casualties:

Adj Henri Chan	Spa 94	P	MIA	Spad XIII, probably by Ltn Josef Veltjens, Jasta 15, (12).	
Brig Paul Teulat	Spa 97	P	MIA	Spad XIII	
Lt Maurice Sulphart	Spa 12	P	KIA	Spad XIII Collided	
Cpl Edmond Charlier	Spa 12	P	KIA	Spad VII Collided	
Sgt Mollon,	Sal 61	P	OK	III° Armée, FTL near	
S/Lt Masse &	Sal 61	O	OK	Lassigny, during combat,	
S/Lt François Marquer	Sal 61	O	KIA	Letord Type 5, III° Armée	
Adj Emile Doux	Br 111	P	KIA	Bréguet 14B2 N° 1408, probably by	
1/Lt Ralph M. Noble, USAS	Br 111	O	KIA	Ltn Paul Wenzel, Jasta 6, (2).	
Sol Dutour	Spa 95	M	KIAcc	Spad	
Lt Jacquemont	IV° Armée	O	KIAcc	Salmson	
Brig Victor Vial &	Br 219	P	KIAcc		
S/Lt Gustave Briot	Br 219	O	KIAcc		

11 May

S/Lt Bourjade,	N 152					4
Cpl Vallot,	N 152					2
Cpl Bebely &	N 152					1
Cpl Marsaudon	N 152	Balloon	XF	Willer	0835	1
Casualties:						
Cpl Wehlen	Sal 58	P	MIA	VII° Armée, Salmson, probably by		
Lt Peyre	Sal 58	O	MIA	Ltn Hermann Stutz, Jasta 71, (3).		
S/Lt Georges Durmeyer	Spa 80	P	KIA	Spad XIII		
1/Lt Paul W Eaton	103rdUS	P	POW	Spad XIII, SE Ypres.		
S/Lt Gabriel Guérin	Spa 15	P	WIA	Spad VII		
Brig ... elle-Larant	AR 272	P	KIAcc			
Sol ... ngiand	AR 272	M	KIAcc			
Cpl Karl Compère-Morel	Spa 85	P	Injured	Spad VII		
Cpl Le Carpentier	GDE	P	Injured	Nieuport XXIV		
Cpl Daudrel	GDE	P	Injured	Nieuport XXIV		
Capt Biaruilanges CO	Sop 222	P	Injured			

12 May

Adj Dhome &	Spa 81				7
Lt de Turenne CO	Spa 12	Albatros	X	Guerbigny	9
S/Lt Nogues	Spa 57	Scout	X	Lassigny	4
Casualties:					
1/Lt Richard A Blodgett	95thUS	P	KIA	VIII° Armée, Nieuport 28 N° 6141.	
Adj Roger Ronserail	Spa 81	P	Injured	Spad XIII	
Cpl Molard	Spa 73	M	Injured	Spad	

13 May

???	GC	EA	X	La Neuville	0632	–
Casualties:						
MdL Masse &	Sop 55	P	WIA	DOW 14 May 1918		
Sol Peltier	Sop 55	G	OK			
MdL Collin	GDE	P	KIAcc	Spad VII		
Sgt Maurice Brugère	Spa 88	P	Injured	Spad VII		
Sol Guillet	Sop 141	G	Injured			
Cpl Jouve	GDE	P	Injured	Nieuport XXIV		

14 May

Sgt Choel,	Spa 124				1
Sgt Grillot &	Spa 124				1
Adj Bentejac a.	Spa 124	Rumpler C	X	Pontfaverger	1
Adj Marinovitch	Spa 94	2 seater	P	Moreuil	–
Sgt Fleury	Spa 95	2 seater	P	Villers-aux-Erables	–
???	Escad 2	EA	P	Neuville-sur-Bernard	–
Patrol	Sal 10	Pfalz	P	III° Armée	–

a.   Possibly Vfw Barth & Ltn Ernst Klump, FlAbt 252w (A), WIAs St Etienne-à-Arnes, about 10 km ENE Pontfaverger.

Casualties:

2/Lt Cyril N Angell &	12thUS	P	KIA	VIII° Armée, Raulescourt
2/Lt W K B Emerson	12thUS	O	KIA	Salmson 2A2
Brig Pierre Thomas	Sal 10	G	WIA	III° Armée, Salmson 2A2
Sgt Desmons &	V 110	P	KIAcc	
Sol Fievet	V 110	G	KIAcc	
Lt Jean Baudry	Spa 68	P	Injured	
Brig David	GDE	P	Injured	Salmson 2A2
???	27° Cie d'Aérostiers	XF		Both flamed by
		O	OK	Ltn Josef Jacobs, Jasta 7,
Adj A Lavaille &	50° Cie d'Aérostiers	XF		(18) & (19).
Sgt L Perin		O	OK	

15 May

Capt Sabattier de						
Vignolle & CO	GC 18					4
Brig Ouvrard de Lignières	Spa 67	Scout	XF	Dompierre	0825	2
Lt Bozon-Verduraz &	Spa 3					6
MdL Moulines	Spa 3	2 seater	X	Assainvillers	1135	1
Adj Berthelot,	Spa 15					3

Lt Laporte &	Spa 15	2 seater	POW	Gamelin		1
Capt de Sevin, CO	Spa 26					9
S/Lt de Tascher &	Spa 26					1
Adj Antoine	Spa 26	2 seater	X	Assainvillers	1225	1
Lt Dombray &	Spa 26					1
Lt Letoureau	Spa 26	EA	X	Rubescourt	1225	1
Lt Houlette &	Sal 52					1
Lt Schmitt	Sal 52	Fokker DrI	XF	Ham		1
S/Lt Favre de Thierrens	Spa 62	LVG C	XF	Monampteuil		3
Lt Nungesser &	Spa 65					35
Adj Camplan a.	Spa 65	2 seater	XF	Erchau		5
S/Lt Sardier,	Spa 77					5
Lt Decoin &	Spa 77					1
Sgt Gelin	Spa 77	Albatros D	XF	Montdidier		1
S/Lt Sardier &	Spa 77					6
Sgt Gelin	Spa 77	Albatros D	XF	Montdidier		2
S/Lt Sardier &	Spa 77					7
Sgt Gelin	Spa 77	Albatros D	X	Montdidier		3
Capt Franc CO	Spa 79	2 seater	X	Grisolles, III° Armée		3
Lt Leps & CO	Spa 81					7
Sgt Cardon	Spa 81	Balloon	XF			1
Sgt Cardon &	Spa 81					2
MdL Chaigneau	Spa 81	Balloon	XF			1
MdL Chaigneau	Spa 81	Balloon	XF			2
Cpl Tyson	Spa 85	EA	X	Aure-Montdidier		1
Adj Marinovitch b.	Spa 94	2 seater	X	Esserteaux		6
Sgt Fleury &	Spa 95					3
S/Lt Claret de Fleurieu	Spa 95	2 seater	X	Lagny-Caudon		2
Lt Robin	Spa 97	Balloon	XF	Mézières		1
Sgt Pietri	Spa 103	EA	X	Moreuil	1955	2
Lt Barcat &	Spa 153					3
Adj Artigau	Spa 15	Rumpler C	XF	Thory-Moreuil		7
MdL Moissinac	Spa 154	Scout	X	NW Assainvillers		4
Sgt Castiglia &	Br 111					1
MdL Douville &	Br 111					1
MdL Loustallot &	Br 111					1
Lt Vercherin &	Br 111					1
S/Lt Gallois &	Br 111					1
Adj Matheron	Br 111	Scout	XF	Harbonnières		1
Same crews	Br 111	EA	P			–
???	GC	EA	XF		0855	–
???	GB	EA	X			–
???	Escad 2	EA	XF	Ferme Belle-Assise		–
Capt Peterson	94thUS	Rumpler C	X	Thiaucourt	1205	3
Capt Peterson	94thUS	Rumpler C	X	Thiaucourt	1210	4
???	DCA	EA	X			–
Patrol	Spa 62	2 EA	P			–
???	Spa 103	EA	P	Demuin	2000	–
Sgt Putnam &	Spa 156					–
Cpl Guy	Spa 156	EA	P	Sommepy		–
Cpl Guy	Spa 156	EA	P	Nogent l'Abbesse		–
Capt Biddle	103rdUS	2 seater	P	Ypres		–
???	GB	2 EA	P			–
???	Escad 2	2 EA	P	Moreuil		–
???	Escad 2	2 Scouts	P	Cantigny		–
???	Escad 2	2 seater	P	Rubescourt		–
???	Escad 2	Pfalz	P	Gratibus		–
???	Spa 79	2 seater	P	Noyon		–
???	Spa 79	Scout	P	E Noyon		–

a. Probably Ltn Albrecht Spiess (P), FlAbt 15, KIA Erchau.
b. Probably Ltns von Bülow & Fricke, unit unknown.

Casualties:

Cpl Joseph Vittet &	Spa 79	P	MIA	III° Armée, departed 09h05 Bréguet,
Sgt Jean Grimal	Spa 79	G	MIA	probably the victim of a JG II pilot.
Adj Millot &	Br 111	P	MIA	
Sgt Lavergne	Br 111	G	MIA	Bréguet 14B2
Cpl Armand Daraspe &	Sal 230	P	MIA	

Sol Tardy	Sal 230	G	MIA	
S/Lt Fouquet &	V 121	P	KIA	
Sol Davout	V 121	G	KIA	
S/Lt Charles Matrat	Spa 154	P	POW	WIA/DOW Spa XIII N° 2194, probably by Ltn Hans Böhning, Jasta 79, (10).
Lt Jean Chotard &	Spa 265	P	KIA	Spad XI, probably by Ltn
Asp Jean Fropo	Spa 265	O	WIA/DOW	Rudolf Windisch, Jasta 66, (29).
???	Sal 230	P	OK	
Lt Edouard Henry	Sal 230	O	KIA	
MdL Marcel Guerre	Br 111	G	KIA	
MdL Marcel Cordier	Spa 84	P	WIA	
Adj André Petit-Delchet	Spa 57	P	WIA	Ground fire.
Sgt Degre	Spa 140	P	OK	
S/Lt Chapagny	Spa 140	O	WIA	Spad XI
Sgt Joubert &	V 121	P	WIA	
Lt Mongin	V 121	O	WIA	
Adj Chevalier	Br 127	G	WIA	
S/Lt Jacques Xambo	Br 127	P	WIA	
S/Lt François Paul	Spa 79	O	WIA	III° Armée, Bréguet
Capt Charles W Biddle	103rdUS	P	WIA	DAN, Ypres.
Cpl Emile Boucheron	MS 158	P	KIAcc	Morane XXIX
QM Georges Pacatte	* EP	P	KIAcc	
Sgt Leichler &	V 113	P	Injured	
Sgt Georges Prévot	V 113	G	Injured	
Sgt Girard	GDE	P	Injured	Nieuport XXIII
Cpl Bedet	Sop 60	P	Injured	Sopwith 1A2
S/Lt Paul	Spa 70	O	Injured	
Lt Champsaur	71° Cie d'Aérostiers		XF	
		O	KIA	
???	29° Cie d'Aérostiers			Attacked, not flamed.
Adj Maurice Damanez,	R 46	P	OK	Shot down and crash-landed
S/Lt Paul Tison &	R 46	O	OK	No one was harmed.
Adj André Astoin	R 46	G	OK	

*   St Raphaël.

---

16 May

Lt Bozon-Verduraz,	Spa 3					7
Sgt Risacher &	Spa 3					1
Sgt Moulines	Spa 3	2 seater	XF	Faverolles		
0940	2					
Adj Parsons	Spa 3	2 seater	X	Mesnil-St Georges	0945	3
Capt de Sevin & CO	Spa 26					10
Lt Puget	Spa 26	Albatros C	X	NE Montdidier	1045	1
S/Lt Sardier &	Spa 77					8
Adj Guerrier	Spa 77	Balloon	XF			1
Sgt Frick &	Spa 78					1
Sgt Petit	Spa 78	EA	X	III° Armée		1
Sgt Nichols	Spa 85	EA	XF	Cappy		1
S/Lt Ambrogi &	Spa 90					3
S/Lt Dencausse a.	Spa 90	2 seater	XF	Nomeny	1100	1
Lt Hostein,	R 46					2
Lt Petyst de Morcourt &	R 46					2
MdL Baratciart &	R 46					2
Adj Damenez,	R 46					2
S/Lt Tison &	R 46					2
Adj Astoin &	R 46					2
British Patrol		EA	POW			
Adj Parsons	Spa 3	2 seater	P	Rollot-Orvillers	1000	–
Adj Pillon	Spa 67	2 seater	P	Fontaine	0645	–
MdL Pezon	Spa 90	Scout	FTL	Goincourt	1015	–
Adj Naudin	Spa 103	2 seater	P	Mézières	1910	–
Patrol	Spa 157	Scout	P	Sommepy		–
Patrol	GC 20	EA	P	Boinville	1005	–
???	Escad 2	2 EA	P			–
???	???	EA	P	St Mihiel		–
???	???	Scout	P	Sommepy		–

a.   Probably Ltn Günther Amlinger & Ltn Robert Kamm, FlAbt 242w (A), KIAs Raucourt, about 6 km N of Nomeny, AOK 19 Sector.

Casualties:

S/Lt Charles Albanel	Spa 3	P	MIA	Spad XIII, departed 08h00.		
Cpl Karst &	???	P	MIA			
Cpl Métairie	???	G	MIA			
Brig Bouzet &	AR 264	P	KIA	Probably by a Jasta 1		
Asp William Arnaud	AR 264	O	KIA	pilot.		
Brig Jean Faur &	Sal 18	P	KIA			
Cpl Marcel Leyat	Sal 18	G	KIA			
Sgt Adolphe Silvain	Spa 85	P	POW	Spad VII, these two were probably		
MdL Jean Lagrue	Spa 85	P	WIA	Spad claimed by Ltn Ludwig Leur		
				(6) & Ltn Max Näther (1) of Jasta 62.		
MdL Astier &	V 110	P	WIA			
Sgt Levergue	V 110	G	WIA			
Sgt Paul Laveissière	AR 264	P	KIAcc			
Sgt Ginoux	AR 264	P	KIAcc			
S/Lt Pierson	Sop 269	O	Injured			
Asp Pierson	Sop 269	O	Injured			
Adj Marcel Mezergues &	CEP 115	P	Injured			
Sol Fabre	CEP 115	M	Injured	Caproni		
Cpl Gazelle	GDE	P	Injured	Nieuport		
Sgt Gabriel	84° Cie d'Aérostiers	XF		VII° Armée, 16h15, probably by		
		O	OK	Obltn Hasso v Wedel, Jasta 75, (2).		

17 May

Adj Veau	Spa 62	2 seater	X			1
Adj Quette	Spa 62	Scout	X			7
S/Lt Pendaries	Spa 67	2 seater	X	NE Moreuil	1140	5
Adj Planiol &	Spa 68					3
MdL Baudry	Spa 68	Balloon	XF	Amelecourt	1815	4
Adj-Chef Gaillard	a. Spa 77	EA	X	N Montdidier		1
S/Lt Ambrogi &	Spa 90					4
MdL Pezon	b. Spa 90	Balloon	XF	Juville	1800	1
S/Lt Claret de Fleurieu	Spa 95	EA	X	German lines		2
MdL Drouillh &	Spa 103					1
Sgt Loup	Spa 103	Pfalz D	X	Montdidier	1330	1
Sgt Courdec &	Spa 152					1
Cpl Hertier	Spa 152	Balloon	XF	Ferette	1035	1
S/Lt Majon de la Débuterie	Spa 163	EA	X			2
???	DCA	2 seater	POW	Francisières		–
1/Lt Rickenbacker	94thUS	Albatros DV	X	Ribecourt	1824	3
Capt Peterson & CO	95thUS					5
1/Lt Hambleton	c. 95thUS	LVG C.VI	X	St Mihiel	2100	1
Sgt Lederlin	Spa 163	EA	FTL	Mont St Quentin		–
Sgt Dubonnet	Spa 3	Scout	P	S Gratibus	1845	–
Adj Baron	Spa 3	2 seater	P	Courtemanche	1910	–
Adj Artigau	Spa 15	Rumpler C	P	Roye		–
Adj Bajac	Spa 48	EA	P			–
Adj Roques	Spa 48	EA	P			–
Adj Pillon	Spa 67	2 seater	P	Moreuil	1120	–
???	Escad 2	2 Rumpler C	P	E Montdidier		–
???	Escad 2	Rumpler C	P	Lassigny		–
???	Escad 2	EA	P	Montdidier		–
???	Escad 2	EA	P	Guerbigny		–
???	Escad 2	EA	P	Mézières		–
???	Escad 2	EA	P	Courtemanche		–

a.   Probably Ltn Heinrich Zürn, Jasta 62, KIA Gratibus, about 6 km NNE of Montdidier.
b.   Probably Bz 143.
c.   N° 14512/17, FTL at Woinville, with engine on fire.

Casualties:

Cpl Serge Kiriloff	Spa 155	P	MIA	Spad VII, possibly by Ltn		
				Fritz Imme, Jasta 42, (1).		
Cpl Karet &	Sal 225	P	MIA	III° Armée		
Cpl Metaride	Sal 225	G	MIA			
Brig Bevalet &	Sal 5	P	KIA	XF Arracourt, by Obltn		
S/Lt Gaillard	Sal 5	O	KIA	Erwin Wenig, CO Jasta 80b, (3).		
MdL Michel Mohr	Br 117	B	KIA			
Adj Michelaut &	Br 120	P	KIA	Probably by a		
Lt du Sapin	Br 120	O	POW	Jasta 6 pilot.		

S/Lt Tanner &	Br 120	P	KIA	Bréguet 14B2 N 2009, probably by
MdL Attal	Br 120	G	WIA/POW	either Ltn Hans Kirschstein (14) or
				Ltn Johann Janzen (7), of Jasta 6.
S/Lt Bergé &	V 121	P	POW	
MdL Lusven	V 121	B	POW	
Capt Marcel de Flers CO	Br 209	P	WIA	III° Armée, Bréguet
Cpl Dubois	Sal 39	P	WIA	
Sgt Longo	Sal 28	Ph	WIA	
Adj André Astoin	R 46	G	WIA	Caudron R11
1/Lt Richard A Blodgett	95thUS	P	KIAcc	Nieuport 28
S/Lt Brager	Sop 282	O	Injured	Bréguet
Cpl Boulle	Br 229	P	Injured	
Cpl Boutin	GDE	P	Injured	Spad VII
Cpl Laffont	GDE	P	Injured	Nieuport 27
Cpl Dourel	GDE	P	Injured	Nieuport 27

18 May

Lt Paumier	CO	Spa 37	Albatros	X			1
Adj Bouyer &		Spa 49					8
MdL Hamot		Spa 49	Scout	XF	Burnhaupt	0950	1
Adj Pillon		Spa 67	2 seater	X	E Montdidier	0930	7
Adj Picard		Spa 83	Balloon	XF			2
Lt Hay de Slade		Spa 86	2 seater	X	E Langemarck		8
Adj Vial		N 315	Scout	X	W Soultz	0940	4
MdL Chabrier		N 315	Scout	X	Burnhaupt	0948	2
1/Lt Campbell	a.	94thUS	Rumpler C	X	Bonzée-en-Woëvre	0930	2
???		DCA	EA	X			–
Lt Puget,		Spa 26					–
Adj Naudin &		Spa 26					–
Lt de Sevin	CO	Spa 26	2 seater	P	Framicourt	0820	–
Lt de Sevin,	CO	Spa 26					–
Adj Naudin &		Spa 26					–
Lt Puget		Spa 26	Scout	P	Framicourt	0820	–
Lt de Sevin &	CO	Spa 26					–
Sgt Garnier		Spa 103	EA	FTL	German Lines		–
???		Escad 2	2 seater	P	Marquivillers		–
???		Escad 2	Scout	P	Courtemanche		–
???		Escad 2	EA	P	E Longuevaisne		–
???		Escad 2	EA	P	Homble		–
???		Escad 2	EA	P	Champien-Bâlatre		–
???		Escad 1	EA	P			–

a.   Probably Ltn Isselstein, (O), FlAbt (A) 279, WIA.

Casualties:

Sgt Chanussot	Br 45	P	MIA	Bréguet 14B2, probably by Ltn Hans
Adj Legrand	Br 45	G	MIA	Kirschstein, Jasta 6, (15).
MdL Robert Petit	Spa 78	P	MIA	III° Armée, Spad VII
Sgt César Viez &	Br 45	P	KIA	Bréguet 14B2, probably by Ltn
MdL Lamarre	Br 45	G	KIA	Josef Veltjens, Jasta 15, (13).
MdL Jacques Bendix &	Br 107	P	WIA/DOW	
Cpl Alix Decourbe	Br 107	G	KIA	
Sgt Renaud	N 315	P	WIA	VII° Armée, Nieuport 27, possibly by Vfw
				Donhauser & Ltn Hempler, FlAbt 10.
Lt Niels Paulli-				
Krause-Jensen &	Spa 2	P	WIA	Spad XI, possibly by OfStv
Capt Eugène Fay	Spa 2	O	KIA	Walter Beyer, Jasta 42, (2).
S/Lt Lagrave	Sop 287	O	WIA	Flak, probably by Flak-batterie 710.
Sgt Maurice Rousselle	Spa 81	P	Injured	
Sgt Denis Decharnia	Br 227	P	Injured	
Cpl Sèguy &	Sal 252	P	Injured	
Lt Jeannin	Sal 252	O	Injured	
Sgt Chaussinand &	Spa 284	P	Injured	DOW 23 May 1918
Lt Legrand	Spa 284	O	Injured	DOW 22 May 1918

19 May

| Adj Parsons, | Spa 3 | | | | | 4 |
| MdL Denneulin & | Spa 3 | | | | | 1 |

Sgt Chevannes	b.	Spa 3	2 seater	X	Montdidier	1220	1
Sgt Dupré	a.	Spa 68	Rumpler C	POW	Filain	1100	2
Adj Coadou		Spa 88	EA	X	Grisolles		1
Brig Lacombe		Spa 75	Scout	X	Contoire		1
MdL Marinovitch &	c.	Spa 94					7
S/Lt Claret de Fleurieu		Spa 95	Rumpler C	X	SE Moreuil		3
Lt Fonck		Spa 103	Albatros	X	Faverolles		
0940		43					
Sgt Brugère		Spa 103	Scout	X	NE Montdidier	0950	1
Lt Fonck		Spa 103	2 seater	X	Grivesnes	1000	44
S/Lt Barcat &		Spa 153					4
MdL Arrault		Spa 153	Scout	POW	Moreuil		2
Capt Deullin	CO	GC 19	Albatros	X	E Montdidier	1845	20
1/Lt Campbell	d.	94thUS	Rumpler C	X	Voisogne, VIII° Armée	1130	3
Lt Fonck		Spa 103	Scout	P	NW Montdidier	0950	–
S/Lt Bourjade		Spa 152	Balloon	P	Nüsserbourg		–
???		???	EA	P	Flanders		–
???		???	2 seater	P	Gratibus-Gondry		–
???		Escad 1	EA	P			–

a. Probably Reihenbildtruppe, AOK "C" Sector, Gefr Otto Kirschbaum & Ltn Kurt Scheibe, POWs.
b. Possibly Uffz Walter Graaf & Sgt Christian Hofele, unit unknown, KIAs Montdidier.
c. Possibly Ltn Kurt Riege, FlAbt 241 (A), KIA Moreuil.
d. Probably Ltn Wilhelm Bayer & Ltn Ludwig Kämmerer, FlAbt 298b (A), KIAs Flirey, AOK "C" Sector.

Casualties:

Lt Philibert Dumarche	Spa 91	P	MIA	Spad VII, possibly by Ltn Franz Hemer, Jasta 6, (10).	
Cpl Sidney Drew	Spa 31	P	MIA	Spad VII N° 3284.	
Adj Pierre Baudry	Spa 68	P	KIA	VIII° Armée, Spad XIII, possibly by Uffz Martens & Ltn Jägenberg, unit N° 678.	
Capt Desbains	Spa 55	O	WIA	Flak, Spad XI	
Adj Geoffroy	RGAé	P	KIAcc	Spad	
MdL René Dumuys &	V 113	P	KIAcc		
S/Lt Bréville	V 113	O	KIAcc		
Cpl Auguste Laulhe	Spa 2	P	KIAcc		
Lt Jean Piorault	Spa 2	O	KIAcc	Spad XI	
Cpl Ricaux &	V 110	P	Injured		
Brig Blanchard	V 110	G	Injured		

20 May

Adj Parsons		Spa 3	2 seater	X	Gratibus	0915	5
Adj Naudin		Spa 26	2 seater	X	Onvillers	1110	3
MdL Montange		Spa 155	2 seater	X	German lines		1
MdL Montange		Spa 155	Scout	X	German lines		2
Lt Bouvard &		Br 209					2
Lt Letanche &		Br 209					2
Brig Bonnaire &		Br 209					1
Lt du Caylar		Br 209	Pfalz D	X	Conchy-les-Pots	1830	1
Adj Fournier &		Br 209					1
Lt Villemaud &		Br 209					1
Adj Prieur &		Br 209					1
Sgt Delcey		Br 209	Pfalz	X	Conchy-les-Pots	1100	1
Capt Peterson	CO	95thUS	2 seater	X	Pont-à-Mousson		6
???		DCA	EA	X			–
Lt Madon	CO	Spa 38	Fokker	P	Manre		–
Adj Martenot de Cordoux		Spa 94	Scout	P			–
Patrol		Spa 112	EA	P			–
???		Escad 2	2 seater	P	Abbecourt		–
???		Escad 2	2 seater	P	Tilloloy		–

Casualties:

Cpl Lapicotière	Spa 155	P	MIA	Spad XIII, possibly by Ltn Konrad Schwartz, Jasta 22s, (4).	
Sgt Mouel	Br 123	M	Killed	Airfield bombardment.	
Sgt Sylvain Boineau	Spa 38	G	Injured	Bréguet	
Sol Malfait	Spa 38	M	Injured		
Sol Rousseau	Spa 99	M	Injured		
S/Lt Serre	Sal 19	O	Injured		
Sgt Tesserau &	Sop 251	P	Injured		
S/Lt Sciandra	Sop 251	O	Injured		

21 May

Lt Sondermayer (Serb)	Spa 3	2 seater	X	Montdidier	0807	1
S/Lt Hérisson &	Spa 75					9
Brig Lacombe	Spa 75	Scout	X	SE Ypres		2
Adj Ruamps &	Spa 87					8
Sgt Legrand	Spa 87	Scout	X	Gogney	1800	1
1/Lt Baer,	103rdUS					8
1/Lt Baker,	103rdUS					1
1/Lt Ford &	103rdUS					2
1/Lt Wilcox	103rdUS	Albatros	X	W Ypres	1850	2
52° Cie d'Aérostiers	DCA	2 seater	FTL	Montjay, N Besme		–
S/Lt Ambrogi,	Spa 90					–
MdL Pezon &	Spa 90					
Sgt Mace	Spa 90	2 seater	P	Juville		–
MdL de Gaillard de La Valdène	Spa 95	2 Scouts	P			–
Adj Baron,	Spa 103					–
Adj Pietri &	Spa 103					–
S/Lt Lecomte	Spa 103	EA	P	Gratibus-Fignières	1350	–
???	EdeA	EA	P	Flanders		–
???	Escad 1	2 EA	P			–

Casualties:

S/Lt Paul Tison	R 46	O	WIA	DOW 22 May 1918, Caudron R11	
Sgt Marcel Houel	Br 123	G	KIA		
MdL Marie Houbault	Spa 102	P	KIAcc	Spad VII	
1/Lt Harry F W Johnson (American)	Spa 163	P	KIAcc	Spad VII N° 1649	
S/Lt Latour	Sop 285	P	KIAcc	Sopwith 1B2	
Lt Henri Bavière &	Sal 8	P	KIAcc		
S/Lt Levy	Sal 8	O	KIAcc		
Sgt Autiquet	VB 101	P	KIAcc	Voisin B	
Sol Chevreau	Sal 1	M	KIAcc		
Lt Tadia Sondermeyer (Serb)	Spa 3	P	Injured	Caught fire in the air, FTL severely burned.	
Adj Touery	Sal 22	P	Injured		
MdL Grosnier	8° Armée	P	Injured	AR	

22 May

Lt Reverchon &	Spa 31					2
S/Lt Portron	Spa 31	2 seater	X	Bouillancourt		1
S/Lt Nuville &	Spa 57					4
Adj Petit-Delchet	Spa 57	Albatros D	X	Malpart		2
S/Lt Battesti	Spa 73	EA	X	Biaches		4
MdL Santelli	Spa 81	Balloon	XF			1
Lt Leps &	CO Spa 81					8
Sgt P Guérin	Spa 81	Albatros	XF	Lamotte-en-Santerre		3
1/Lt Rickenbacker	94thUS	Albatros DV	X	Flirey	0912	4
1/Lt Buford	95thUS	2 seater	X	Flirey		1
1/Lt Baer	103rdUS	Albatros	X	Laventie, DAN	0945	9
Lt Madon	CO Spa 38	Albatros	P	St Geneviève		–
Lt Madon	CO Spa 38	Albatros	P	St Geneviève		–
???	Escad 1	2 EA	P			–
???	Escad 2	4 EA	P			–
???	EdeA	2 EA	P			–
III° Armée-de Creil a.	DCA	AEG	POW	Verberie	0100	–

a.　During the night of 21-22 May a two motor AEG was hit by DCA fire and FTL, immediately torching their aircraft. Crew possibly Vfw Lüdke, Ltn Schiffer & Uffz Wallerand, BG 3, all POWs at Villers-au-Bois.

Casualties:

Cpl Félix Gibier	Spa 12	P	MIA	Spad VII N° 5815, probably by Ltn Hermann Schmidt, Jasta 69, (2).
S/Lt Desgardes &	V 116	P	MIA	Voisin N° 2739, probably by Ltn Fritz Thiede, Jasta 24s, (2).
Cpl Lacout	V 116	G	MIA	
1/Lt Paul B Kurtz	94thUS	P	KIA	VIII° Armée, Nieuport 28, N° 6185.
1/Lt Ernest A Giroux	103rdUS	P	KIA	DAN, Spad XIII N° 2282,
1/Lt Paul F Baer	103rdUS	P	POW	DAN, Spad VII N° 3173, both probably claimed by Vfw Debenitz (1) & Ltn Hans Müller (5) Jasta 18.

S/Lt Jourdain &	Br 107	P	WIA		
Sgt Pierre Vandecasteele	Br 107	O	OK		
Sgt Amoudric du Chaffaut	Sop 141	P	KIAcc		
Cpl Jean Druilles	Spa 79	P	Injured	III° Armée, Spad	
Brig Truchot	GDE	P	Injured	Nieuport	
Adj Faure	Br 227	P	Injured		
Lt Moreau	Sal 33	O	Injured		
MdL Piger	GDE	P	Injured	Voisin X	
Cpl Martellat &	Sop 55	P	Injured		
S/Lt Sosthène de La Rochefoucauld	Sop 55	O	Injured	Sopwith 2A2	
Sgt Georges Crossnier	Spa 87	P	Injured	AR	

23 May

Adj Brétillon	a.	Spa 49	EA	X	Hamegicourt		3
Lt Leps &	CO	Spa 81					9
MdL Santelli		Spa 81	Balloon	XF	Villers-Bretonneux	0715	2
MdL Santelli		Spa 81	Balloon	XF			3
Adj Marinovitch &		Spa 94					–
Lt de Fleurieu		Spa 95	2 seater	P			–

a.   Possibly Uffz Richard Jentzsch, Jasta 71, KIA Habsheim.

Casualties:

MdL Charles Kühling	Spa 15	P	MIA	Spad XIII, combat with a two-seater. Possibly by Ltn Heller & Vfw Runau, unit unknown.
Cpl Henri Davione	Spa 85	P	KIAcc	Spad VII
Adj Hourdouille	Sop 41	P	KIAcc	
Cpl Paul Mouginor	GDE	P	KIAcc	Salmson
Lt Lautier	Sop 252	O	Injured	
MdL Blocq	Br 231	P	Injured	Bréguet 14A2

24 May – No Claims – No Casualties

25 May

S/Lt Favre de Thierrens	Spa 62	EA	X	Ambrief	4

Casualties:

Cpl Turquin	Spa 96	M	Injured	Spad VII
Lt Leray	Sal 1	O	Injured	

26 May

???	DCA	EA	P	Flanders	–

Casualties:

Cpl Laroze &	Spa 276	P	KIAcc	
Sol Bebert	Spa 276	G	Injured	Spad XI
Cpl Karl Compère-Morel	Spa 85	P	Injured	
Sgt Pelot	Spa 67	M	Injured	
Sgt Catouillat	Br 238	P	Injured	
Asp d'Aubigny &	49° Cie d'Aérostiers			VI° Armée, attacked not,
S/Lt Perissin-Pirasset		O	OK	flamed.

27 May

The German Offensive on the Aisne (Operation Blücher), also known as the Third Battle of the Aisne and the Battle of Chemin-des-Dames, begins between Noyon and Reims.

Adj Berthelot &		Spa 15					4
Adj Artigau		Spa 15	DFW C	XF	Comin-Bourg		8
Lt Madon	CO a.	Spa 38	EA	X	Condé-sur-Suippe		26
Lt Madon	CO b.	Spa 38	EA	X	Condé-sur-Suippe		27
Sgt Bosson		Spa 62	2 seater	X		1420	3
S/Lt Souleau &		Spa 76					1
MdL Cavieux		Spa 76	Scout	X			1
S/Lt de Boigne,		Spa 82					5
Adj Rimbaud &		Spa 82					3
MdL Faure		Spa 82	Scout	XF	Craonne		1
Lt Hay de Slade		Spa 86	2 seater	XF	Mont Kemmel		9
Adj Gasser	c.	Spa 87	EA	XF	Reherrey	1130	7
Cpl Gérard &		Br 217					1

Lt Charlet		Br 217	EA	X	Guiscart		1
Cpl Gérard &		Br 217					2
Lt Charlet		Br 217	Scout	X	Rambercourt		2
Cpl Gérard &		Br 217					3
Lt Charlet	d.	Br 217	2 seater	X	Rambercourt		3
1/Lt Campbell	e.	94thUS	Pfalz DIII	X	Montsec	1006	4
1/Lt Buford,		95thUS					2
1/Lt Fisher,		95thUS					1
1/Lt Curtis &		95thUS					1
1/Lt McLanahan	f.	95thUS	2 seater	X	St Mihiel-Flirey	1735	1
1/Lt Mitchell	f.	95thUS	2 seater	X	Mont Sec		1
???	g.	???	Rumpler C	POW	Sergy		–
Sgt Ventre		???	EA	P	Coucy-le-Château		–
S/Lt Majon de La Débuterie &							–
Sgt Guillet		Spa 163	3 EA	P	Brimont-Bourgogne		–
Patrol		Spa 151	EA	P	Lassigny		–
???		???	3 EA	P	Flanders		–
1/Lt Mitchell		95thUS	EA	FTL			–

a. Possibly Vfw Willy Glander & Ltn Kurt Haese, FlAbt (A) 244s, KIAs Amifontaine, about 12 km NNW of Condé-sur-Suippe.
b. Possibly Uffz Wilhelm Weniger & Ltn Fritz Freit, FlAbt (A) 252w, KIAs Brimont, about 12 km SSE of Condé-sur-Suippe.
c. Probably Ltn Max Thässler & Obltn Karl Röchling, FlAbt 276 Lb, KIAs Lunéville.
d. Probably Hptm Rudolf Frhr von Esebeck (1v), CO Jasta 17, KIA Noyon.
e. Probably Ltn Walter Fritzsche, Jasta 65, KIA Montsec.
f. Probably Ltn Hans Behringer & Ltn Wilhelm Ortegel, FlAbt 46b, KIAs Varneville, which USAS pilot got them ???
g. Aircraft landed intact in the Aisne Sector.

Casualties:

Sgt Louis Des Salles &		Br 126	P	MIA	Probably by Ltn
Sgt Jean Lingueglia		Br 126	G	MIA	Viktor v Rautter, Jasta 4, (14).
1/Lt Willard D Hill		94thUS	P	WIA	VIII° Armée, Nieuport 28, Ltn Fitzner & Vfw Thiedje, Jasta 65, each claimed a Spad in this sector.
S/Lt Etienne Mougeot		Spa 62	P	WIA	Spad VII
Capt Nely d'Oissel &		Sop 55	P	WIA	Sopwith A2, probably by
S/Lt Bernard Lancrenon		Sop 55	O	WIA	Ltn Rudolf Otto, Jasta 74, (2).
Capt Wiedemann		Sal 8	P	WIA	Salmson 2A2
S/Lt Hubert Knipping		Sal 8	P	WIA	Salmson 2A2
Lt Paul Desbief		Sal 10	O	WIA	III° Armée, Salmson 2A2.
EV1 Georges Arne	*	CAM	P	KIAcc	Hanriot HD.2 N 230, codé D.34.
Lt Picot &		Sop 251	P	Injured	
S/Lt Madon		Sop 251	O	Injured	
Adj Meunier &		Br 221	P	Injured	
Sgt Bouchu		Br 221	O	Injured	
Adj Beaunier &		46° Cie d'Aérostiers			These two observers and three
Sgt Boucher +			O	POW	telephonists of the other balloon were
three telephonists		29° Cie d'Aérostiers			taken prisoner while riding in transport
				POW	vehicles on the ground. VI° Armée

Sector.
* Dunkerque.

28 May

Sgt Baylies	Spa 3	Scout	X	Courtemanche	0815	10
Patrol	Spa 23	EA	X	Ivoiry		–
Sgt Mattel &	Sal 33					1
Lt Salomon &	Sal 33					1
Sgt Leray &	Sal 33					1
Cpl Dallon	Sal 33	Scout	XF	Bouillancourt	0815	1
Cpl Piednonel,	Sal 51					1
Lt du Peloux &	Sal 51					1
MdL du Pontavice de Heussey &	Sal 51					1
MdL Leplane &	Sal 51					1
Sgt Nozat &	Sal 51					1
Sgt Ferrin	Sal 51	EA	X	Cense		1
Adj Veau,	Spa 62					2
Sgt Bosson,	Spa 62					4
Sgt Dupont &	Spa 62					1
Adj Blanc	Spa 62	2 seater	X		1355	3
Adj Quette	Spa 62	2 seater	X			8

Adj Camplan	a.	Spa 65	2 seater	POW	W Dampleux	0830	6
Lt Romatet		Spa 76	LVG C	POW	Longpont		1
MdL Santelli &		Spa 81					4
Adj Malfanti		Spa 81	Balloon	XF	Ivoiry		1
Sgt Armanet		Spa 160	EA	X	Ances		1
Lt Arpheuil		Spa 151	2 seater	X	Ressons-sur-Matz		1
IV° Armée	b.	DCA	Halb C	POW	Linthelles		–
???		DCA	EA	X	Maisonneuve		–
MdL Mattei		R 46	EA	X			1
1/Lt Hambleton &		95thUS					1
1/Lt W Taylor		95thUS	2 seater	X	Thiaucourt	1615	1
1/Lt Rickenbacker		94thUS	Albatros C	X	St Baussant	0931	5
S/Lt Boyau		Spa 77	Albatros DV	P	Maisonneuve		–
Patrol		Spa 78	Scout	P	Noyon		–
Broke loose		???	Balloon		Aulnay-Vertus		–
???		???	Scout	P	Noyon		–
???		???	EA	P			–

a. Possibly Flg Ackermann & Flg Jeschke, SchSta 5, POWs.
b. FlAbt 44, became lost and landed in Allied lines.

Casualties:

Adj Louis Blanc	Spa 62	P	MIA	Spad VII	
Brig Pourrez &	Sop 278	P	MIA		
Sol Bernard	Sop 278	G	MIA		
Sgt Gentine &	Sop 278	P	WIA		
Asp Benard	Sop 278	O	WIA		
MdL Leplant	Sal 51	G	WIA	Salmson 2A2	
1/Lt John A Hambleton	95thUS	P	WIA	VIII° Armée, Nieuport 28.	

29 May

Sgt Baylies		Spa 3	Scout	X	Faverolles		
0815							11
Lt Bozon-Verduraz		Spa 3	2 seater	X	Faverolles-Etelfay	0815	8
Sgt Prouvost		Spa 12	EA	XF			3
S/Lt Boyau		Spa 77	Balloon	XF	Dole		14
S/Lt Boyau &		Spa 77					15
S/Lt Sardier		Spa 77	Albatros DV	X	Ville-en-Tardenois		9
MdL Ducornet		Spa 93	Pfalz	XF			1
Lt Gallet		Spa 93	Balloon	XF	St Marguerite		1
Adj Daladier		Spa 93	Balloon	XF	Vauxillon		5
S/Lt Claret de Fleurieu		Spa 95	EA	X	German lines		4
Sgt Cancel,		Spa 99					1
Sgt Lenoir &		Spa 99					2
Sgt Madinier		Spa 99	Balloon	XF	Lagery		1
Cpl Nordhoff &		Spa 99					1
Patrol		Spa 99	EA	X			–
Capt Rocard &	CO	Br 128					1
Lt de Loisy		Br 128	EA	X			1
2/Lt Ponder,		Spa 163					1
1/Lt Cassady,		Spa 163					1
Cpl Dequeker		Spa 163	LVG C	X	Savigny	1330	1
MdL Barbier &		Sop 260					1
S/Lt Resel		Sop 260	EA	XF	La Neuvillette		1
Patrol		GC 21	EA	X	Savigny		–
???	b.	DCA	Gotha	X	Fransactel		–
S/Lt Boyau		Spa 77	Albatros	P			–
???		GC	5 EA	P			–

a. Possibly Ltn Günther Keitsch, Jasta 74, KIA Reims, about 3 km SE of La Neuvillette.
b. Night of 29-30 May.

Casualties:

Sgt Rémy Morel	Spa 153	P	MIA	Spad VII N° 5727, possibly Ltn Gerhard Schulte, Jasta 50, (3).
1/Lt Carter L. Ovington	Spa 98	P	MIA	Spad VIIs, collided in mid-air
Sgt Léon Hoor	Spa 98	P	MIA	during combat, possibly claimed by Ltn Josef Veltjens, Jasta 15 (14), and Ltn Georg von Hantelmann, Jasta 15, u/c.
Sgt André Gelin	Spa 77	P	MIA	Spad XIII, possibly by Obltn Rudolph Berthold, CO JG II, (30).
MdL Tussing &	Sal 27	P	MIA	
Lt Camille Lemmery	Sal 27	O	WIA/POW	Salmson 2A2

Name		Unit	Type	Result	Location		Score
Cpl Clarence Shoninger		Spa 99	P	POW	Spad, Fismes, probably by Ltn Karl Bolle, Jasta B, (12).		
MdL Elien Duru &		Br 237	P	OK			
S/Lt Louis Sarrauste de Menthière		Br 237	O	KIA	Ground fire		
S/Lt Henri Claret de Fleurieu		Spa 95	P	WIA	Spad		
Lt Desmolles		Sop 281	O	WIA	Flak		
Adj Fernand Monin		Sop 260	P	WIA			
Lt Louis Resal		Sop 260	O	WIA			
Sgt Tirlet		Br 107	G	WIA			
S/Lt Paul Albert		Sal 14	O	WIA	Bombardment of airfield.		
Cpl Louis Thomas		Spa 89	P	Injured	Spad VII		
Sol Laurent		Spa 153	M	Injured			

30 May

Name		Unit	Type	Result	Location		Score
Capt Pinsard	CO	Spa 23	Balloon	XF	Dannevoux		19
Lt Barny de Romanet &		Spa 37					3
MdL Lostalot		Spa 37	Balloon	XF	Fère-en-Tardenois		1
Sgt Boinet		Spa 37	EA	X	N Fère-en-Tardenois		1
S/Lt Nuville &		Spa 57					5
Asp Dubois de Gennes		Spa 57	Balloon	XF	E Saponay		5
Sgt Bosson		Spa 62	Albatros	X	Ivord	1410	5
Adj Quette		Spa 62	2 seater	X			9
S/Lt Plessis		Spa 65	EA	XF	Beauzard		4
Sgt Mony		Spa 82	Balloon	XF	Villemoyenne		1
Capt Moreau,	CO	Spa 93					3
S/Lt Duchaussoy,		Spa 93					1
Adj Breton &		Spa 93					3
Adj Guyou		Spa 93	Balloon	XF	Grouy-Vrigny		2
MdL Legagneux &		Spa 97					2
MdL Coupillaud		Spa 97	Balloon	XF	W Saponay		2
MdL Moissinac &		Spa 154					5
S/Lt de Mirman		Spa 154	EA	X			1
Lt Lahoulle &	CO	Spa 154					5
MdL Moissinac		Spa 154	Fokker D7	X			6
Lt Lahoulle &	CO	Spa 154					6
MdL Moissinac		Spa 154	Fokker D7	POW			7
Lt Majon de La Débuterie,		Spa 163					3
Brig Marsaux,		Spa 163					1
Cpl Sedillon &		Spa 163					1
Cpl Bertrand		Spa 163	2 seater	X	Bourgogne		1
Sgt Guillet &		Spa 163					1
Cpl Lederlin		Spa 163	LVG C	X	Epernay-Reims		1
???		???	EA	X	Armentières		
1/Lt Rickenbacker		94thUS	Albatros C	X	Jaulny	0738	6
1/Lt Meissner	a.	94thUS	Albatros DV	X	E Thiaucourt	0755	2
1/Lt Mitchell,		95thUS					2
1/Lt Hambleton,		95thUS					2
1/Lt Buckley,		95thUS					1
1/Lt Casgrain &		95thUS					1
1/Lt McKeown		95thUS	2 seater	X	Apremont, VIII° Armée	0800	1
1/Lt McKeown		95thUS	EA	X	Vigneulles	0805	2
Capt de Sevin,	CO	Spa 26					–
S/Lt Puget &		Spa 26					–
Adj Vincent		Spa 26	EA	P	Rollot	1805	–
Lt Le Barbu &	CO	Br 29					–
Sgt Schwartz		Br 29	EA	P			–
Escad 2		???	6 EA	P			–
???		???	EA	P	Coulonges		–

a. OfStv Tiedje, Jasta 65, collided with Meissner's Nieuport and claimed it as his second victory.

Casualties:

Name	Unit	Role	Result	Details
Cpl Robert Sarkis	Spa 84	P	POW	Spad VII, probably by Obltn Bruno Loerzer, CO JGIII, (25).
MdL Maurice Fuchs	Spa 154	P	MIA	Spad VII N° 3635, probably by Ltn Johann Janzen, Jasta 6, (9).
MdL Jacques Lostalot	Spa 37	P	MIA	Probably by Ltn Fritz Pütter, Jasta 68, (24).

Name	Unit	Crew	Fate	Notes
Lt Cyrille Le Barbu & CO	Br 29	P	MIA	Bréguet 14B2, probably by
Sgt Victor Schwartz	Br 29	G	MIA	Ltn Hans Pippart, Jasta 19, (14).
Adj Jimbeau &	???	P	MIA	
S/Lt Bauget	???	O	MIA	Lhéry
Capt Pierre Mouronval CO	Spa 77	P	KIA	Spad XIII, probably by Ltn Walter Blume, Jasta 9 (9).
1/Lt Wilfred Casgrain	95thUS	P	POW	VIII° Armée, Nieuport 28, probably by FlAbt 46b.
MdL-Chef Gérard Faure	Spa 82	P	WIA	Spad XIII
Lt Rey	Spa 212	O	WIA	Spad XI
Cpl Claveau	Sop 55	P	WIA	Salmson 2A2
Capt Robert CO	Sal 106	P	WIA	Flak
S/Lt Bancon	VB 118	O	KIAcc	
Capt Janet &	Br 206	P	KIAcc	
S/Lt Côte	Br 206	O	KIAcc	
Sol Huber	Br 128	M	KIAcc	
S/Lt Menissier	Br 128	P	Injured	
Sgt Boinet &	VB 118	P	Injured	
Asp Bancon	VB 118	O	Injured	DOW
???	88° Cie d'Aérostiers	XF		
		O	OK	

31 May

Name	Unit	Type	Result	Location	Time	Score
Patrol	Spa 3	2 seater	X	Montdidier	1045	–
Sgt Baylies &	Spa 3					12
MdL Dubonnet	Spa 3	2 seater	XF	Montdidier	1045	3
S/Lt de Dreux &	Spa 12					3
Adj Philibert	Spa 12	EA	X	Romigny		3
Adj Berthelot	Spa 15	DFW C	X	Grottes		5
Sgt Quiles	Spa 48	Fokker	X	Bergny		2
S/Lt de Guingand a.	Spa 48	Fokker DrI	X	S Soissons		6
Lt Mazimann,	Spa 57					2
S/Lt Fraissinet &	Spa 57					4
S/Lt Nogues	Spa 57	EA	X	Eterpilly		5
S/Lt Favre de Thierrens &	Spa 62					5
Adj Tissier	Spa 78	EA	X	Lassigny, III° Armée		1
Sgt Rousselle &	Spa 81					2
MdL Cardon	Spa 81	Balloon	XF	Juvigny		3
Lt Leps & CO	Spa 81					10
MdL Santelli	Spa 81	Balloon	XF	Juvigny-Soissons		5
Sgt Nichols &	Spa 85					2
Sgt Tyson	Spa 85	EA	X	Vailly		2
Adj Daladier c.	Spa 93	Fokker DrI	X	Chaudun		6
Adj Marinovitch d.	Spa 94	2 seater	X	Villers-Cotterêts	0500	8
S/Lt Martenot de Cordoux &	Spa 94					4
Adj Marinovitch	Spa 94	Fokker DrI	X	Amly	p.m.	9
Sgt Paulnier,	Spa 98					1
S/Lt Jobert &	Spa 98					1
Lt Cauboue CO	Spa 98	Balloon	XF	St Thierry		2
Sgt Paulnier,	Spa 98					2
S/Lt Jobert &	Spa 98					2
Lt Cauboue CO	Spa 98	Balloon	XF	Prouilly		3
Sgt Aleppe &	Spa 98					1
Cpl Geiger	Spa 98	Balloon	XF	Branscourt		10
Sgt Michaudet &	Spa 112					1
Lt Viguier	Spa 112	EA	X	Lassigny		1
Adj de Marmier	Spa 112	EA	X	Lassigny		6
??? &	Br 117					?
Adj Cambray	Br 117	EA	X			1
S/Lt Barancy	Spa 124	2 seater	X	Dravigny-Branscourt		3
Capt d'Humières CO	Spa 124	Balloon	XF	St Thierry-Courmont		1
S/Lt M Robert	Spa 124	Scout	X	Prouilly		2
S/Lt Paillard & (1)	Br 132					1
S/Lt Calbet (1)	Br 132	EA	XF			1
MdL Rivoire &	Br 132					1
Sgt Bougeard	Br 132	EA	X			1
Sgt Veil	Spa 150	2 seater	X	Lassigny		1

MdL A Thélot &	Spa 151					1
Lt Arpheuil	Spa 151	2 seater	XF	Lassigny		2
Sgt Gatineau &	Spa 157					1
MdL Froissard	Spa 157	EA	X	Bouleuse		1
Sgt Baugham	Spa 157	EA	X	Jonchery		1
MdL Froissard &	Spa 157					2
Sgt Gatineau	Spa 157	Balloon	XF	Jonchery		1
MdL François,	Br 219					1
Sgt Depardieu &	Br 219					1
Cpl Jouano	Br 219	2 seater	X	Ivord		1
Adj Guillot &	GB 5					1
Lt Duverger	GB 5	EA	X	Soissons		1
Cpl Hutin &	GB					1
???	GB	EA	XF			?
1/Lt Campbell d.	94thUS	Rumpler C	X	Bois Brûlé	0810	5
??? e.	???	Rumpler C4	POW	S Noyon		–
Lt Madon CO	Spa 38	Albatros	P	Jonchery-Muizon		–
Sgt Boudou	Spa 48	EA	P			–
Lt Dumont	Spa 85	EA	P			–
Capt Etienne CO	N 315	EA	P	Burnhaupt		–
???	Escad 2	Balloon	P			–
???	Escad 1	3 EA	P			–
GB	Escad 1	3 EA	P			–
1/Lt Taylor	94thUS	EA	P	Thiaucourt	0750	–

a.   Possibly Ltn Edouard Stratmann, Jasta 9, POW Villers-Cotterêts, about 20 km SW Soissons.

b.   Possibly Ltn Viktor von Rautter, Jasta 4, KIA Soissons, about 8 km ENE of Chaudun.

c.   Probably Uffz Hippolyt Kaminski, KIA, & Ltn Bake, OK, FlAbt 264 (A), Villers-Cotterêts.

d.   Possibly Sgt Richard Strunk & Ltn Erich Külz, FlAbt (A) 242, KIAs, AOK 19 Sector.

e.   III° Armée Prisoner Interrogation Report, Vfw & Ltn/ WIA, FlAbt 226, shot down at 08h45 S of Noyon, POWs. Shot down by three French chasse planes.

(1)   Both these men are pilots, it is not known if their gunners were also credited with the shared victory.

Casualties:

Lt Antoine Arnoux de Maison Rouge	Spa 78	P	MIA	III° Armée, Spad XIII.
MdL Maurice Porteret &	Br 131	P	MIA	
Sgt Valentin Tonda	Br 131	G	MIA	Bréguet 14
Cpl Alan Ash	Br 134	P	MIA	
Sol Roget Letot	Br 134	G	MIA	Bréguet 14
S/Lt Charles Baranger &	Br 29	P	MIA	Bréguet 14B2
Sgt Wolf	Br 29	G	MIA	These two probably downed
Sgt Hypollyte Martin &	Br 29	P	MIA	by JG I pilots.
Sol Jean Galbrun	Br 29	G	MIA	Bréguet 14B2
Cpl René Lecomte &	Br 129	P	MIA	
MdL Garciete	Br 129	G	MIA	Bréguet 14B2
Sgt Clément Duval &	Sal 61	P	MIA	III° Armée, Lassigny,
S/Lt Jean Martin	Sal 61	O	MIA	Salmson 2A2
Sgt Costeau &	Br 44	P	MIA	
S/Lt Petit	Br 44	O	MIA	Bréguet 14B2
Cpl Berthelot &	VR 119	P	MIA	
Sol Lapierre	VR 119	B	MIA	
Lt Viron	Sal 106	O	MIA	
Lt Roger Goubeau	Spa 76	P	KIA	
Sgt Alfred Pelton	Spa 97	P	KIA	
Adj Julien Gourdon	Spa 96	P	WIA	Spad XIII, ground fire.
Cpl Vion	II° Armée	P	Injured	Spad
Sol Saudit	Spa 73	M	Injured	Spad
Asp Jean Dubois de Gennes	Spa 57	P	WIA	Spad VII
S/Lt Postangue	Spa 53	O	WIA	Spad XI
Capt Eudes	Sal 106	O	WIA	Salmson 2A2
S/Lt Sieper	Sal 52	O	WIA	
Cpl Bailly &	Sal 18	O	WIA	
S/Lt Loth	Sal 18	O	WIA	
S/Lt Louis Jourde	Br 216	O	WIA	Ground fire
Lt Bertelère	Br 216	O	WIA	Ground fire
MdL Vimneral	???	P	WIA	
???	??? Cie d'Aérostiers			Attacked, not flamed, the attacking aircraft was shot down by a RAF patrol, Flanders Sector.

During May 1918, French DCA was credited with 28 confirmed and 20 probable aircraft downed.
Unknown dates for claims in May 1918:

MdL Perrotin &	Spa 212				1
???	Spa 212	EA	X		?
Lt Grimardia	Spa 98	EA	P		–

1 June

Adj Artigau		Spa 15	DFW C	X	Villers-Cotterêts	9
Lt Barny de Romanet		Spa 37	2 seater	X	Villers-Cotterêts	4
Lt Madon	CO	Spa 38	Albatros D	X	S Reims	28
Lt Madon	CO	Spa 38	Albatros D	X	Betheny	29
Lt Madon &	CO	Spa 38				30
Lt Casale		Spa 38	Balloon	XF	Reims-Epernay	10
Sgt Dupont		Spa 62	Scout	X		2
S/Lt Boyau		Spa 77	Pfalz	X	Epieds	17
Capt Lagache	CO	Spa 78	2 seater	X	Compiègne	1
Adj Martenot de Cordoux		Spa 94	2 seater	X	Parcy	5
??? &		Br 123				?
S/Lt Powell		Br 123	EA	X		1
Capt d'Argueeff		Spa 124	Scout	XF	Puisieux	7
Lt Barancy		Spa 124	Scout	X	Puisieux	4
Lt Arpheuil		Spa 151	2 seater	POW	St Léger-au-Bois	3
Lt Hirsch		Spa 151	2 seater	X	SW Villers-Cotterêts	3
Sgt Putnam		Spa 156	2 seater	X	Ferme de Godat	4
Lt Chambarière &	CO	Spa 162				2
Adj Halm		Spa 162	Balloon	XF	Vezilly	1
Brig Nestler		Spa 162	Balloon	XF		1
1/Lt Turnure		103rdUS	Balloon	XF	NE Armentières 1503	3
Escad 2		GC	EA	X	Aisne	–
Escad 1		BG	3 EA	X		–
???		DCA	EA	X		–
Adj Naudin		Spa 26	EA	P	Montdidier 1010	–
Adj Marinovitch		Spa 94	Fokker DrI	P	Longpont	–
Adj Marinovitch		Spa 94	Fokker DrI	P	Longpont	–
Sgt Cote &		Sop 251				–
2/Lt Miller, USAS		Sop 251	Scout	P		–
Lt Janère		Spa 461	EA	P	Vieray	–
Escadre 1		GC	3 EA	P		–
Escadre 1		GC	EA	P	Coucy-le-Château	–
Escadre 1		GB	EA	P	Neuilly-St Front	–

Casualties:

Cpl Paul Bertrand	Spa 163	P	MIA	Spad VII N° 5596, SE Soisson probably by Vfw Fritz Jacobsen, Jasta 73, (4).
Cpl York	???	P	MIA	
MdL Eugène Perrigot &	Br 237	P	MIA	
S/Lt Lescure	Br 237	O	MIA	Bréguet 14A2
Cpl Gaston Herzog &	Br 134	P	MIA	
Sol Etienne Beau	Br 134	G	MIA	
Cpl Jean Portois &	Br 108	P	MIA	
Capt Henri Vallet	Br 108	O	MIA	
Cpl Callame &	Br 119	P	MIA	
Sgt Drossner	Br 119	G	MIA	IV° Armée, Bréguet
Sgt Castaings	Sop 278	P	MIA	Sopwith 1A2
Lt Burgue	???	P	MIA	V° Armée, N Château-Thierry.
MdL Alan Nichols	Spa 85	P	WIA	DOW 2 June 1918, Spad, combat with 2 seater, possibly by Uffz Haberland (1) & Ltn Kasperait (1), FlAbt (A) 216.
Cpl Louis Charton	Spa 124	P	WIA	Spad N° 5837, S Reims, probably by OfStv Werner Schluckebier, Jasta 73 (1).
Capt Georges Perrin-Pelletier	Br 214	P	OK	
Lt Moraillon	Br 214	O	WIA	Bréguet 14 N° 4644.
S/Lt Hennoque	Br 216	O	WIA	
S/Lt Clifford R Powell	Br 123	O	WIA	
Capt d'Argueeff	Spa 124	P	WIA	

S/Lt Morraglia &		Br 120	P	WIA	
??? Mauler		Br 120	O	OK	Bréguet 14B2
Adj Aubertin		Sal 106	P	WIA	
S/Lt Tiberghein &		Sop 55	P	WIA	
S/Lt Sosthène de la Rochefoucault		Sop 55	O	Injured	
Sgt Cote &		Sop 251	P	OK	
2/Lt Charles Miller (American)		Sop 251	O	WIA	
Sgt Yves de Castéran		Spa 91	P	KIAcc	Spad VII
Sgt Roger Vetillard &		Br 108	P	KIAcc	
Sgt Bourlon		Br 108	G	Injured	
MdL Pierre Cousin		Spa 153	P	Injured	Spad XIII
Sgt Eugène Prouvost		Spa 12	P	Injured	Spad XIII N° 3501.
Brig Bottot		Br 45	P	Injured	
S/Lt Paté		54° Cie d'Aérostiers		XF	III° Armée
			O	OK	
Adj Haentjens &		33° Cie d'Aérostiers			Attacked, not flamed.
Sgt Simon			O	OK	

2 June

Adj Philibert		Spa 12	EA	X			4
Sgt Burello		Spa 23	Balloon	XF	Ivoiry		2
Lt Madon	CO	Spa 38	EA	X	Reims	0600	31
Lt Madon	CO a.	Spa 38	EA	X	Reims	0700	32
Sgt Bosson		Spa 62	Albatros	X			6
Sgt Dupont		Spa 62	Scout	X			1
??? &		Br 66					?
2/Lt Schaffer, USAS		Br 66	EA	X			1
Sgt Putnam,		Spa 38					5
Adj Daladier &		Spa 93					7
Adj Guyou	b.	Spa 93	Albatros C	XF	Villers-Cotterêts		3
Sgt Baux		Spa 103	2 seater	X	NE Moreuil		3
S/Lt Coudouret &		Spa 103					6
Sgt Hoeber		Spa 103	Albatros D	X	Carlepont	1605	1
MdL Oudart &		Br 111					1
???		Br 111	EA	X			?
Patrol		Spa 112	Scout	X	Ribecourt		–
S/Lt Barcat &		Spa 153					5
MdL Halberger		Spa 153	Balloon	XF	E Thory		1
S/Lt Waddington &		Spa 154					3
MdL Barbreau		Spa 154	Balloon	XF	Igny l'Abbesse		1
Sgt Putnam,		Spa 156					6
Cpl Schenck &		Sal 288					1
S/Lt Rancurel	b.	Sal 288	Albatros	X	N Reims		1
Sgt Meyer		Spa 160					1
Sgt Chantegrel	c.	Spa 160	Hannover C	X	Epinal		1
Capt Petit &	CO	GB 5					1
MdL Lepers &		GB 5					1
Sgt de Jobert &		Br 120					1
Sgt Guignard		Br 120	EA	XF	Monnes		1
Lt Lemaitre &	CO	Br 120					1
Adj Roussel &		Br 120					1
Sgt Deschamps &		GB 5					1
Cpl Gauthier		GB 5	EA	XF	Monnes		1
Brig Bastard &		GB 9					1
Sol Lebrun		GB 9	Scout	X	Faverolles		1
Lt Allegret &		Br 117					1
Lt Garret		Br 117	EA	XF	Neuville-St Front		1
S/Lt de Peyerimhoff &		Br 123					2
Sgt Le Thuaut		Br 123	EA	X	Nanteuil		1
MdL Rivoire &		Br 132					2
Sgt Bougeard		Br 132					1
Lt Gros &		Br 132					2
S/Lt Weismann		Br 132	Scout	XF	German lines		2
???		GB	2 EA	X			–
???	d.	DCA	Staaken R	X	Nanteuil-le-Haudoin		–

???	e.	DCA	2 seater	POW	Epernay	0930	–
VII° Armée		DCA	2 seater	X	Epinal		–
1/Lt Hunter, USAS		103rdUS	2 seater	X	Mont Kemmel	1725	1
Sgt Tyson		Spa 85	EA	P	Troesnes		–
Sgt Ferguson		Spa 96	Fokker DrI	P	Villers-Cotterêts		–
Patrol		Spa 103	Albatros D	P	Carlepont	1605	–
Cpl Schenck &		Sal 288					–
S/Lt Rancurel		Sal 288	EA	P	N Reims		–
Cpl Schenck &		Sal 288					–
S/Lt Rancurel		Sal 288	EA	P			–
GC Escad 2			EA	P	Aisne		–
Escadre 2		GC	2 Balloons	P	Aisne		–
Escadre 1		GC	3 EA	P			–
???		Spa 112	EA	P	Ribecourt		–
???		GB	2 EA	P			–
MdL Rivoire &		Br 132					–
Sgt Bougeard		Br 132	Scout	FTL			–

a. Possibly Gefr Adolf Schneider, Jasta 1, KIA Reims.
b. Possibly Ltn Heidenreich, Jasta 6, POW.
c. Probably Ltn Julius Frhr von Seher-Thoss & Ltn Friedrich Baumann, FlAbt 12, KIAs, between Epinal and Dombasle, AOK 19 Sector.
d. Brought down at night, all eight crew members taken prisoner.
e. DFW C.V N° 433/18, probably Ltn Arnold Wichum, & Ltn Ulrich Emanuel, FlAbt 237, POWs.

Casualties:

Capt Maurice Rebreget	Spa 62	P	MIA	Spad VII, probably by Vfw Alfred Hübner, Jasta 36, (2).
S/Lt Anquetil &	Sal 17	P	MIA	
Lt Braud	1er CA	O	MIA	Salmson, X° Armée
Cpl Louis Poulhes &	Br 226	P	MIA	
Sol Audoynaud	Br 226	G	MIA	Bréguet 14A2
MdL Edgard Léger-Belair	Br 131	P	MIA	
Sgt Jean Lehmann	Br 131	B	MIA	
Sgt Marcel Commandeur &	Br 108	P	MIA	
Sgt Marcel Hedman	Br 108	G	MIA	
Cpl Guillaume Rampillon des Magnius	Spa 112	P	KIA	III° Armée, Spad VII.
Lt Fernand Penot &	Sal 24	P	KIA	III° Armée, S La Ferté
Lt Leseur	Sal 24	O	KIA	Milon, Salmson 2A2.
S/Lt Baptiste Istria &	Br 129	P	KIA	
Cpl Pierre Charvet	Br 129	G	KIA	
2/Lt Phillip W Davis	94thUS	P	KIA	VIII° Armée, Nieuport 28 N° 6193, Richemont, 15h12, probably by Ltn Hengst, CO Jasta 64w, (3), AOK "C".
MdL Ernest Rivoire &	Br 132	P	WIA	FTL near French lines
Sgt Pierre Bougeard	Br 132	G	WIA	
Cpl Gavoret	Spa 155	P	WIA	Spad XIII
S/Lt Dureuil	Spa 286	O	WIA	Flak, VII° Armée, Spad XI, possibly by Flakzug 107.
Sgt Lahemade	Sal 171	G	WIA	Salmson 2A2, V° Armée
Lt de Mondredon CO	Sal ???	P	WIA	Salmson 2A2, III° Armée ground fire.
1/Lt Frank O'D Hunter	103rdUS	P	WIA	DAN, Mont Kemmel
S/Lt Muret	Br 229	O	WIA	V° Armée, Bréguet,
MdL Edouard Bossard &	Sop 260	P	WIA	Flak, V° Armée
1/Lt Tillman, USAS	Sop 260	O	Injured	
Lt Eymann &	???	P	WIA	
Lt Garnier	???	O	WIA	
S/Lt Paul Jobert	Spa 98	P	WIA	Spad VII
Lt Bertezène	???	O	WIA	
S/Lt Rancurel	Sal 288	O	WIA	V° Armée, Salmson
2/Lt Edgar A Lawrence	147thUS	P	KIAcc	
Lt Maitre	Sal 17	P	KIAcc	Spad VII,
Sol Lemonnier	R 46	M	Injured	
Sol Gobard	R 46	M	Injured	
Lt Lesprit	AR 262	O	Injured	AR N° 347.
Lt Brisset	86° Cie d'Aérostiers			Attacked, not flamed.
		O	Injured	
Adj Haentjens &	23° Cie d'Aérostiers			VI° Armée, attacked, not
Sgt Simon		O	OK	flamed. Hit 15 times.

3 June
Third Battle of the Aisne ends.

Sgt Rousselle		Spa 81	2 seater	X	Aisne		3
Adj Malfanti,		Spa 81					2
Sgt P Guérin &		Spa 81					4
MdL Cardon		Spa 81	Balloon	XF	Aisne		4
MdL Poisson		Spa 83	Balloon	XF	E Chaudun	0850	1
MdL Gaudry		Spa 95	2 seater	X	Aisne		1
Sgt Lacouture		Spa 95	2 seater	X	Aisne		2
Escad 1		GB	2 EA	X	Aisne		–
1/Lt Sewell	a.	95thUS	2 seater	X	NW Dieulouard	0845	1
S/Lt de Peyerimhoff &		Br 123					3
Sgt Le Thuaut		Br 123	EA	X	Betz		2
??? &		Br 123					?
Sgt Le Thuaut		Br 123	EA	X			3
Adj Marinovitch &		Spa 94					–
Adj Martenot de Cordoux		Spa 94	2 seater	P	La Ferte Milon		–
Escad 2		GC	EA	P	Aisne		–
Patrol		GC 14	2 seater	FTL	Chaudun	0855	–
???	b.	???	Pfalz DIII	POW	N Bois de Cossu		–

a.   Probably a crew from FlAbt 254 (A), POWs.
b.   Ltn Josef Weckerie, Jasta 79b, POW, motor hit during combat.

Casualties:

Sgt Pierre Burello	Spa 23	P	MIA	Spad XIII N° 1927, probably by Ltn Otto Fitzner, Jasta 65, (5), AOK "C" Sector.
Cpl Charles Gueret	Spa 93	P	MIA	Spad XIII, probably by Ltn Erich Löwenhardt, Jasta 10, (26).
MdL Xavier Moissinac	Spa 154	P	MIA	Spad XIII N° 753, N Dormans
Sgt Pierre Meunié	Spa 95	P	MIA	
Spad Sgt Marc Pontet	Spa 37	P	MIA	Spad VII
Sgt Jean Heuzey	Spa 89	P	MIA	Spad VII
S/Lt Jacques Xambo &	Br 127	P	MIA	Probably by a
Cpl Guillain	Br 127	G	MIA	Jasta 6 pilot.
Lt Bernard de Lille de Loture &	Br 127	P	MIA	Probably by a
Sgt Georges Grisval	Br 127	G	MIA	Jasta 6 pilot.
Cpl Georges Félix &	Sop 278	P	KIA	
S/Lt Nuguet	Sop 278	O	KIA	Sopwith 2A2
Adj Hyppolyte Ordonneau	Br 127	O	KIA	
S/Lt Maurice Brunel	Spa 95	P	WIA	
Sgt Centine &	Sop 278	P	WIA	
Asp Bernard	Sop 278	O	WIA	
Adj Duprinz	Br 127	G	WIA	DOW 7 June 1918.
Lt Richet	Br 117	P	WIA	
S/Lt Thonier	Br 117	O	WIA	
MdL Burelle	Br 127	P	WIA	
S/Lt Leveque	Br 127	O	WIA	
Sgt Perot	Br 116	P	WIA	
S/Lt Garnier de Biolt	Br 123	P	WIA	
Sgt Robert	Escad 1	P	KIAcc	Sopwith A2
Sgt Bourgeat	Sal 252	P	KIAcc	Salmson 2A2
Lt Rechenmann	Sal 252	O	Injured	Salmson 2A2
Sgt Derboux	Sal 17	P	Injured	Salmson 2A2
Adj Proton	Spa 65	M	Injured	DOW 4 June 1918.
Capt Bourges	V 110	P	Injured	
Sgt Vacher	V 110	G	Injured	
Sgt André &	V 118	P	Injured	
S/Lt Gelon	V 118	O	Injured	
MdL René Trouchaud	Spa 68	P	Injured	Spad VII
Lt Payen	78° Cie d'Aérostiers	XF		Probably by ObFlgMt Kurt
		O	WIA	Schönfelder, Jasta 7, (10).

4 June

Adj Quette	Spa 62	EA	X		10
Sgt Damidaux	Spa 62	EA	X		1
Sgt Bosson &	Spa 62				7

S/Lt Favre de Thierrens	Spa 62	Albatros DV	X	Aisne		6
S/Lt Terlez &	Br 66					1
Lt Guinegot	Br 66					1
Sgt Beaumel &	Br 66					1
Adj Osmond	Br 66	EA	X	French lines		1
S/Lt Boyau &	Spa 77					17
S/Lt Sardier	Spa 77	Balloon	XF			10
S/Lt Boyau &	Spa 77					18
S/Lt Sardier	Spa 77	Balloon	XF			11
??? &	Br 111					?
S/Lt Pobey	Br 111					1
??? &	Br 111					?
Adj-Chef Thévenin	Br 111	EA	X	Aisne		3
Capt Derode CO	Spa 99	EA	X	German lines		7
Capt Derode CO	Spa 99	EA	P			–
MdL Halberger &	Spa 153					–
MdL Arrault	Spa 153	2 seater	P	Vislaine-Boiry		–
Escad 1	GB	2 EA	P			–
Patrol	GC 21	EA	P	Villers-Cotterêts		–
Sgt Bourgeois	Spa 68	Balloon	P			–
???	???	*	FTL	SW of Soissons		–

*   What the French called un avion Géant Zeppelin, this aircraft was destroyed by the occupants.

Casualties:

Sgt Marcel Letellier &	Sal 203	P	MIA		
S/Lt Marcel Nicodeau	Sal 203	O	MIA	Salmson 2A2, Faverolles	
Lt René Vogelin &	Br 279	P	MIA		
Asp Charles Wesbecher	Br 279	O	MIA	Sopwith 1A2	
S/Lt Guy Passerat de La Chapelle &	Br 108	P	MIA		
S/Lt Xavier de Masin	Br 108	O	MIA		
Cpl Edouard Fénioux &	Br 279	P	MIA		
Cpl Adolphe Barbarin	Br 279	G	MIA	III° Armée, Sopwith 1A2,	
Capt Jean Derode CO	Spa 99	P	KIA	Spad XIII	
Sgt Emile Champagnole &	Sal 106	P	KIA		
S/Lt François Lasvignes	Sal 106	O	KIA	Salmson 2A2	
Sgt Viltard de Laguerie &		P	OK		
Lt Etienne Charlot	Spa 212	O	KIA	V° Armée, Spad XI	
Capt Henri Paumier CO	Spa 37	P	KIA	Bombardment of airfield.	
Cpl La Barrière	Spa 95	M	KIA	Bombardment of airfield.	
Adj Wenceslas Pilat	Spa 124	P	WIA	Spad XIII, probably by Ltn Heinrich Drekmann, Jasta 4, (3).	
Sgt Emile Damidaux	Spa 62	P	WIA	Spad VII	
Sgt Samson	Spa 55	P	WIA	Spad XI, ground fire.	
Sol Gaillard	Sal 17	G	WIA	Salmson 2A2	
Lt Got	Sop 260	O	WIA	Sopwith, ground fire.	
Sol Cessens	Spa 73	M	WIA	Bombardment of airfield.	
MdL André Courtieu	Spa 96	P	WIA	Bombardment of airfield.	
2/Lt Edgar A Lawrence	147thUS	P	KIAcc	Nieuport 28	
Lt Ferez	Sal 52	O	Injured	Salmson	
MdL Terzi &	V 119	P	Injured		
MdL Carré	V 119	G	Injured		
Sgt André Boinet	Spa 37	P	Injured	Spad XIII	
Sgt-Maj Niord	GDE	P	Injured	Spad VII	
Lt Joseph Voland &	Sop 281	P	Injured		
Capt Henri Legrende	Sop 281	O	Injured	Sopwith 1A2	
S/Lt Alfred Van der Brule	27° Cie d'Aérostiers	O	KIA	Flak	
???	88° Cie d'Aérostiers		XF	Probably by Obltn Oskar v Bönigk, Jasta 21s, (18).1er Corps d'Armée Sector.	
		O	OK		

Three other Balloons XF, observers OK.

---

5 June

Sgt Putnam	Spa 38	Albatros DV	X	Fère-en-Tardenois		6
Adj-Chef Dousinelle	Spa 48	2 seater	X	Soissons		4
Lt Nungesser	Spa 65	2 seater	X	W Château-Thierry		36
MdL Trémeau	Spa 83	EA	X	Chaudun	0855	1
Adj Marinovitch &	Spa 94					10

S/Lt Martenot de Cordoux	Spa 94	2 seater	X	E Faverolles		6
Lt Viguier &	Spa 112			III° Armée		2
Sgt Issaly a.	Spa 112	2 seater	X	Margny-les-Compiègne		1
Capt Lahoulle, CO	Spa 154					7
S/Lt Waddington,	Spa 154					4
S/Lt Gros &	Spa 154					3
MdL Barbreau	Spa 154	Balloon	XF	Trigny	1800	2
Adj Viquier,	Spa 157					1
Sgt Baugham &	Spa 157					2
Sgt Connelly	Spa 157	Pfalz	X	Villers-Cotterêts		2
1/Lt Cassady, USAS	Spa 163	Albatros DV	X	Epieds		2
Lt Dupont &	Br 219					1
Sgt Murien &	Br 219					1
MdL Clairin &	Br 219					1
MdL Goujois	Br 219	EA	X	VI° Armée		1
1/Lt Campbell &	94thUS					6
1/Lt Meissner b.	94thUS	Rumpler C	X	Eply	1000	3
Sgt Putnam	Spa 38	Albatros D	P	Fère-en-Tardenois		–
Sgt Putnam	Spa 38	Albatros D	P	Fère-en-Tardenois		–
Sgt Putnam	Spa 38	Albatros D	P	Fère-en-Tardenois		–
Sgt Putnam	Spa 38	Albatros D	P	Fère-en-Tardenois		–
S/Lt de Marmier	Spa 112	Albatros D	P			–
Patrol	GC 14	EA	P	Vertefeuille	0855	–
Patrol	Spa 83	EA	P	Ambleny	0840	–
Patrol	GC 21	EA	P			–
Escad 2	GC	EA	P	Aisne		–
Patrol	GC 18	EA	P			–
Brig Marsaux	GC	EA	P			–

a.   Probably Sgt Ernst Rasch, FlAbt 223 (A), KIA Margny.
b.   Probably Ltn Löschmann (O), FlAbt 12, WIA.

Casualties:

Brig Sabatier	Spa 157	P	MIA	Spad VII
Sgt Bernard	Spa 62	P	MIA	Spad VII N° 7216
S/Lt Charles Quette	Spa 62	P	MIA	Spad VII N° 5603
Cpl Bibault	???	P	MIA	
Lt Mouille &	V 109	P	MIA	
Adj Pauly	V 109	G	MIA	Voisin R
Lt Dijeaux &	???		MIA	
MdL Picinbono	???		MIA	
Sgt Perrin	Sal 51	G	KIA	Salmson 2A2
Cpl Arthur Blumenthal &	Br 227	P	KIA	Bréguet 14, probably by Ltn Hans
Lt Charles de Coopmann	Br 227	O	KIA	Kirchstein, Jasta 6, (22).
MdL Marie Coutel &	Br 129	P	KIA	
Sgt Lescoeur	Br 129	G	KIA	
1/Lt Karl H Eymann USAS	Br 129	O	KIA	
S/Lt Lionel de Marmier	Spa 112	P	WIA	III° Armée, Spad XIII.
Sgt Marius Grebil	Br 129	P	WIA	
Brig Moine	Br 129	G	WIA	
S/Lt Pouget	Br 129	O	WIA	
Lt Pierre Allegret	Br 117	P	WIA	
MdL André Duriez	Spa 26	P	KIAcc	Spad XIII N° 3247
Sgt Hannesse	RGAé	P	KIAcc	Farman
EV1 Félix Poeyarre *	EP	P	KIAcc	
Brig Flechon	GDE	P	Injured	Spad
S/Lt Ferez	Sal 52	O	Injured	
MdL Terzi	???		Injured	
MdL Carré	???		Injured	
Sgt James H Baugham	Spa 157	P	OK	Spad, shot down inside German lines but managed to regain Allied lines.
Cpl Marcel Girardeau	Spa 163	P	OK	Spad VII N° 5572, probably by Ltn Hans Kirchstein, Jasta 6, (21). Shot down inside French lines.
??? Marsaux French	Spa 163	P	OK	Spad VII N° 5575, shot down inside
???	45° Cie d'Aérostiers		XF	lines near Château-Thierry.
		O	Injured	
S/Lt Le Mare	39° Cie d'Aérostiers		XF	III° Armée, Aisne Sector.
		O	OK	
Adj Lacombe	90° Cie d'Aérostiers		XF	VI° Armée, Aisne Sector, 10h00.
		O	OK	

Sgt Cordillat, OK &		21° Cie d'Aérostiers	XF	VI° Armée, Aisne Sector,	
Adj L Humbert		O	WIA	14h00. DOW 6 June 1918.	
Adj Auvray &		28° Cie d'Aérostiers	XF	VI° Armée, Aisne Sector,	
S/Lt Ledent		O	OK	20h00.	
???		??? Cie d'Aérostiers		Attacked, not flamed,	
		O	OK	Flanders Sector.	

NOTE: In the Aisne Sector balloons were claimed by Ltn Justus Grassmann, Jasta 10 (1); Obltn Oskar v Bönigk, Jasta 21s, (9); Ltn Max Näther, Jasta 62, (3); Ltn Wilhelm Schulz, Jasta 66, (6).

*   Biscarosse.

6 June

Capt Pinsard	CO	Spa 23	2 seater	X	Ornes		20
Lt Madon	CO	Spa 38	2 seater	X	Rosnay-Gueux		33
S/Lt de Guingand &		Spa 48					7
Adj Montrion		Spa 48	Balloon	XF	Catigny		9
Sgt Gérard		Spa 65	EA	X	Longpont		6
Lt Leps,	CO	Spa 81					11
MdL Cardon &		Spa 81					5
Sgt Rousselle		Spa 81	Balloon	XF	NW Soissons		4
Sgt Rousselle		Spa 81	Balloon	XF			5
MdL Conraux		Spa 83	Scout	X	W Coucy	1750	1
Adj Vidal,		Spa 88					2
S/Lt Haegelen,		Spa 100					4
MdL Schuster &		Spa 100					1
Sgt Ouizille		Spa 100	Balloon	XF	Courpoil-Le Charmel		1
Lt Parfait &	CO	Spa 161					1
Cpl Rollin		Spa 161	EA	X	Ville-en-Tardenois	1500	1
S/Lt Basuyaux		Spa 62	EA	P			–
Patrol		Spa 83	EA	P	Bois de Coucy	1751	–
Adj M Robert		Spa 92	2 seater	P	Fère-en-Tardenois		–
Sgt Rand		Spa 158	EA	P			–
Patrol		GC 11	EA	P		0450	–
Patrol		GC 11	EA	P		0455	–
Patrol		GC 11	EA	P		0500	–
Escad 1		GC	4 EA	P			–
Escad 2		GC	Balloon	P			–
Escad 2		GC	EA	P			–

Casualties:

Sgt Louis Durin		Spa 92	P	MIA	IV° Armée, Spad XIII
Sgt Jean Bouilliant		Spa 69	P	MIA	X° Armée, Spad VII, probably by a Jasta 15.
MdL Picinbono &		???	P	MIA	
Lt Digeaux		???	O	MIA	IV° Armée
Cpl Jean Vaivre		Sal 275	G	KIA	
Adj René Pascaud		Spa 158	P	WIA	III° Armée, Spad
Asp Valtier		Sal 104	O	WIA	
S/Lt Rivier		Sop 55	O	WIA	
1/Lt Douglas Campbell		94thUS	P	WIA	VIII° Armée, Nieuport 28
1/Lt Charles L Miller		Sop 251	O	WIA	
Adj Alexandre		GDE	P	KIAcc	Nieuport
Brig Durand Touche		Spa 67	P	Injured	Spad XIII
Lt de Fonds Lamothe &		Spa 64	P	Injured	
S/Lt Ytasse		Spa 64	O	Injured	Spad XI
MdL Robert Pourpe		Sal 18	P	Injured	
???		??? Cie d'Aérostiers		XF	Aisne Sector
		O	OK		

Two balloons in the Picardie Sector were attacked but not flamed.

7 June

Adj Artigau		Spa 15	DFW C	X	NW Château-Thierry	10
S/Lt de Guingand,		Spa 48				8
Adj Montrion &		Spa 48				10
Adj Caillaux		Spa 48	Balloon	XF	Vezaponin	4
S/Lt Haegelen,		Spa 100				5
MdL Schuster &		Spa 100				2
Sgt Ouizille		Spa 100	Balloon	XF	Aougny	2
??? &	a.	DCA				

Sgt Le Roy de Boiseaumarie	Spa 78	Fokker DrI	POW	St Leu d'Esseurant	5
Lt Madon	CO Spa 38	2 seater	P	W Courcy	–
Le de La Rochefordière,	Spa 94				–
MdL Caulier,	Spa 94				–
Cpl Martre &	Spa 94				–
S/Lt Martenot de Cordoux	Spa 94	2 seater	P		–
???	GC	2 EA	FTL	German lines	–

a.   N° 1147/17, Flg Wilhelm Schade, Jasta 41.

Casualties:

Cpl Christiani &	Br 236	P	MIA	V° Armée	
S/Lt Baillaud	Br 236	O	MIA	Bréguet 14A2 N° 319	
S/Lt de Vaugelas	???	P	MIA		
Sgt Shukunosuke Kobayashi				X° Armée, Spad VII, 18h00	
	Spa 86	P	KIA	N Montgobert, probably by Ltn Hans Kirschstein, Jasta 6, (24).	
Sgt Lavernes	N° 463/CRP	P	KIA	Nieuport, Villers-Cotterêts	
Cpl Jean-Marie Martre	Spa 94	P	WIA/POW	Later escaped.	
S/Lt Pierre Le Roy de Boiseaumarie	Spa 78	P	WIA	III° Armée, Spad XIII.	
Sgt Pierre Hannesse	???	P	KIAcc		
S/Lt Paul Menissier	GB ?	P	KIAcc		
Sgt Antoine Bayle	Spa 91	P	Injured		
Brig Renault	GDE	P	Injured	Spad	
Asp Morin	GDE	P	Injured	Spad	
Cpl Palau	GDE	P	Injured	Nieuport 27	
Lt Weiller	Sop 261	O	Injured		
S/Lt Michel	V 110	P	Injured		
Lt Ternynck	84° Cie d'Aérostiers		XF	VII° Armée, Probably by Vfw Karl	
		O	OK	Schmelcher, Jasta 71, (2).	
S/Lt Etienne Bourgogne	45° Cie d'Aérostiers		XF	X° Armée, at 16h00	
		O	Injured		
Adj Roger Étienbied	43° Cie d'Aérostiers		XF	V° Armée, 06h40, probably by Ltn	
		O	OK	Heinrich Otto, Jasta 10, (1).	
???	??? Cie d'Aérostiers		XF	Aisne Sector	
???	??? Cie d'Aérostiers		XF	Aisne Sector	
???	??? Cie d'Aérostiers			Attacked, not flamed,	
		O	OK	Picardie Sector.	

8 June

MdL Darche &	Sal 8					1
S/Lt Mariotti &	Sal 8					1
MdL Boullo &	Sal 8					1
MdL Dufour-Bourru &	Sal 8					1
Cpl Poirier &	Sal 8					1
Sgt Ratel	Sal 8	Fokker DrI	X	Nauroy		1
Adj Arnoux	a. Spa 49	Balloon	XF	Ferrette	0946	2
S/Lt Vidal &	Spa 88					2
Adj Delzenne	Spa 88	EA	X	Muizon		1
Lt Marty	b. Spa 90	2 seater	X	W St Die	0815	7
Sgt Lachat	Spa 124	Fokker DrI	X	Prier		2
Capt Aron &	CO Br 134					1
Lt Brunet	c. Br 134	LVG CV	POW	Rouges Eaux		1
S/Lt Casale	Spa 38	EA	P	N Berru		–
S/Lt d'Estainville	Spa 87	EA	P	Bouleuse		–
Patrol	Sal 8	EA	P	X° Armée		–

a.   Probably Balloonzug 212, at Altpfirt.
b.   Probably Vfw Gerhardt, POW, & Ltn Franz Burkart, KIA, FlAbt 10, LVG CV N° 1772/18.
c.   LVG C.V N° 2993.

Casualties:

MdL Paul Maurice	Br 132	G	WIA	DOW, Bréguet	
Sol Charles Chaudun	Br 132	G	WIA	Bréguet	
S/Lt Henri Barancy	Spa 124	P	WIA	VI° Armée, Spad, possibly by Vfw Otto Rosenfeld, Jasta 41, (10).	
Cpl Lucien Moreau	Br 132	P	KIAcc	Bréguet	
Lt Andrieux	73° Cie Aérostiers		XF	VI° Armée, probably by Ltn Fritz	
		O	OK	Friedrichs, Jasta 10, (10).	

9 June

Lt Dumas		Spa 12	Balloon	XF	Aisne	1
Adj Berthelot		Spa 15	DFW C	X	Bois de Chaux	6
MdL Marinovitch		Spa 94	2 seater	X	St Paul-aux-Bois	1010	11
1/Lt Wilcox &		103rdUS				3
1/Lt Merrick		103rdUS	2 seater	X	Wulverghem	1023	1
Sgt Baugham		Spa 157	EA	X	N Château-Thierry	0545	3
III Armée		DCA	EA	X		–
Patrol		GC 11	Scout	P	Brimont	0715	–
Patrol		R 46	3 EA	P		–
Two seater crew		Spa 76	EA	P	Tagnon	1000	–
Sgt Rand		Spa 158	Scout	P		–
Sgt Rand		Spa 158	Scout	P		–
Lt Parfait &	CO	Spa 161				
Patrol		Spa 161	EA	P	Villers-Franqueux	1800	–
Patrol		Br ???	Scout	P		–
Patrol		GC 16	Fokker DrI	P	Mont Renauld, III° Armée	–
Patrol		EdA	2 EA	P		–

Casualties:

Brig Marcel Gloux		Spa 158	P	MIA	III° Armée, Spad
Lt Jean Dehesdin	a.	Spa 159	P	MIA	Spad VII
Sgt Villard	a.	Spa 159	P	MIA	Spad VII
MdL Jacques Nestler	a.	Spa 162	P	MIA	Spad VII
Adj Jean Grenez	a.	Spa 99	P	MIA	Spad XIII N° 4418.
Sgt Joseph Poullain		Spa 88	P	MIA	Spad XIII, probably by Ltn Heinrich Kroll, Jasta 24s, (26).
MdL Ropartz &		Br 120	P	MIA	
Lt Menaud		Br 120	O	MIA	
MdL Boulanger &		Br 120	P	MIA	
Sgt Millioud		Br 120	G	MIA	
Lt Alexandre Marty		Spa 90	P	KIA	Spad XIII, Plainfaing, 09h00.
Cpl Pierre Chan		Spa 94	P	POW	Spad VII, probably by Obltn Hermann Göring, Jasta 27, (20).
Cpl Jenn &		Br 45	P	POW	
S/Lt Tisnes		Br 45	O	POW	Bréguet 14A2 N° 2085
Sgt Maurice Laurent &		Sal 10	P	KIA	III° Armée, Courcelles
Lt Jules Mevellec		Sal 10	O	WIA	Salmson 2A2
Cpl Marcel Gérard &		Br 217	P	KIA	III° Armée, in flames
S/Lt Alfred Tallot		Br 217	O	WIA	
Sgt Benoit Savot		Spa 88	P	WIA	Spad XIII, probably by Ltn Heinrich Kroll, Jasta 24s, (27).
Cpl Elie Le Roy	a.	Spa 159	P	WIA	
S/Lt Victor du Tremblay	a.	Spa 159	P	WIA	Spad XIII
Adj Claude Beauregard		Spa 69	P	WIA	X° Armée, FTL, Spad VII.
S/Lt François Robert		Sop 271	O	WIA	III° Armée, Sopwith 1A2,
Lt Robert Solot		Sal 58	O	WIA	DOW, VI° Armée, Salmson, ground fire.
MdL Henri Laplace		Spa 77	P	Injured	Spad XIII
MdL de Maulde &		Br 219	P	Injured	
Lt Porion		Br 219	O	Injured	
Sgt-Maj Gilibert		???	P	Injured	
MdL Lafont-Raploum &		Sal 288	P	Injured	V° Armée, Salmson, crash-laanded
Asp Fleury de Flassieux		Sal 288	O	Injured	after combat, near Reims.
1/Lt F S Adams &		1st Bal Co USBS			Attacked, not flamed.
Lt d'Argent (French)			O	OK	

a.   These pilots were probably the victims of Jadgeschwader I pilots who claimed a total of five Spads this date.

10 June

Lt Lavergne		Spa 87	Balloon	XF	Freslon-Bouleuse	1
MdL Halberger &		Spa 153				2
MdL Parresse	a.	Spa 153	EA	X	Ressons-sur-Matz	1
Adj Miserolle		Spa 92	EA	P	Nogent l'Abbesse	–
Patrol	b.	Spa 94	Fokker DrI	P	Villers-Bretonneux	–
???		???	EA	P		–

a.   Probably Ltn Walter Balzer, Jasta 44s, KIA Ressons-sur-Matz.
b.   Possibly Lfw Willi Gabriel, Jasta 11, shot down, not harmed.

Casualties:

Sgt Alfred Ambrosio	Spa 151	P	MIA	III° Armée, Spad VII.
S/Lt Jean Pequin	Spa 69	P	POW	WIA, Spad VII N° 5553.
Adj Raymond Legrand	Spa 87	P	WIA	IV° Armée, Spad VII, FTL near Verzenay.
MdL Ondet &	Br 216	P	WIA	
Adj Bethemy	Br 216	O	WIA	Bréguet 14A2
Brig Bernada	Br 11	P	WIA	Bréguet 14A2
Sol Boury	Sal 72	M	Injured	

11 June

Adj Naudin		Spa 26	Scout	X	Mortemert-Rollot	1645	4
Adj Binoche &		Spa 48					1
S/Lt Dousinelle		Spa 48	Halb CL	X	N Compiègne		5
Cpl Mercier &		Spa 48					1
S/Lt Dousinelle		Spa 48	Halb CL	X	Fanières		6
Capt d'Indy	CO	Spa 67	2 seater	X	Reims-Fécamp	1830	1
Brig Clairac		Spa 84	EA	XF	S Gury		1
Patrol		Br 126	EA	XF	Cuvilly		–
British Ground Fire	a.	???	Fokker	POW			–
Patrol		Sal 13	EA	P			–
Adj Naudin		Spa 26	EA	P	Antheuil	1615	–
Adj Roques &		Spa 48					–
S/Lt de Guingand		Spa 48	2 seater	P	La Neuville-sur-Ressons		–
Patrol		GC 16	2 EA	P			–
???		???	EA	P			–

a.   Vfw Josef Degen, Jasta 6, French POW Camp.

Casualties:

Lt Guy de La Rochefordière	CO	Spa 94	P	KIA	Spad XIII, probably by Ltn Kurt Hetze, Jasta 13, (1).
S/Lt Pierre Cramoisy		Spa 159	P	KIA	Spad VII, Méry, probably by Ltn Franz Büchner, Jasta 13, (4).
Sgt Maurice Laurent		???	P	KIA	
Lt Guy d'Anglejean		Br 126	O	KIA	
Adj Gonnet &		Sal 10	P	OK	
Lt Joseph Brun		Sal 10	O	KIA	III° Armée, Salmson 2A2.
Capt Pierre Pène &	CO	Sal 10	P	KIA	
Lt Luguet		Sal 10	O	WIA	III° Armée, Salmson 2A2.
Cpl Auber &		Br 282	P	OK	III° Armée, FTL during
Lt Charles Posth		Br 282	O	KIA	combat, Bréguet.
Sgt Edouard Mieille		Spa 87	P	WIA	Spad VII
Sgt Louis Piatte &		Sop 270	P	WIA	
S/Lt Louis Kurzenne		Sop 270	O	WIA	III° Armée, Sopwith 1A2.
Cpl Marius Clément		Br 132	G	WIA	
Sgt Robert Maillard		Br 107	G	WIA	
Asp Fernand Camus		Br 217	O	WIA	III° Armée, Bréguet.
2/Lt J H Ackerman (American)		Spa 73	P	WIA	
Sgt Gaget,		V 125	P	KIAcc	
Adj Laugerotte &		V 125	O	KIAcc	
Sol Ribois		V 125	M	KIAcc	

12 June

Lt Pique &		Sop 36					1
Cpl Mathieu &		Sop 36					1
Lt Krieg &		Sop 36					1
Sgt Chatagnon		Sop 36	Scout	X	Cormicy		1
Lt Madon	CO	Spa 38	Fokker	X	Fismes		34
Lt Carretier &		Sal 39					1
S/Lt Ganne		Sal 39	Pfalz	X	Château-Thierry		1
Lt Carretier &		Sal 39					2
S/Lt Ganne		Sal 39	Pfalz	X	Château-Thierry		2
Adj Quiles &		Spa 48					3
Adj Roques	a.	Spa 48	Fokker D7	X	Ressons-sur-Matz	1840	4
S/Lt Battesti		Spa 73	EA	X			5
Patrols		GB	3 EA	X			–
Patrol	b.	Spa 86	EA	P	W Soissons	1530	–

Patrol	Spa 161	EA	P	Cormicy	–
Patrol	GB	EA	P		–
Patrols	GC	3 EA	P	Picardie	–
III° Armée	GEA	EA	P		–

a.   Probably Ltn Ernst, Jasta 69, POW Courcelles, about 10 km NE of Ressons- sur-Matz.
b.   Possibly Ltn Fritz Loerzer, CO Jasta 26, POW at Cutry, about 7 km SW of Soissons.

Casualties:

Sgt Marcel Bossard &	Br 127	P	MIA	
Sgt Honoré Leyre	Br 127	G	MIA	
Cpl Mathieu &	Sop 36	P	OK	VI° Armée
S/Lt Jacques Pique	Sop 36	O	KIA	Sopwith 1A2 N° 2456.
1/Lt Blanchard B Battle	91st US	P	POW	Salmson 2A2 N° 753,
Capt Joseph F Williamson	91st US	O	POW	FTL, reason unknown.
Lt Albert Charette &	Spa 266	P	KIA	Spad XI
Asp André Weismann	Spa 266	O	WIA	DOW 13 June 1918
Cpl Jacques Monod	Spa 96	P	WIA	DOW 28 June 1918
Adj Joseph Fontan	Spa 53	P	OK	X° Armée, Spad XI, ground fire.
Lt Bernast	Spa 53	O	WIA	
Sgt Marcel Seclin	Spa 228	P	WIA	Spad XI
Asp Camus	Br 217	O	WIA	
S/Lt Cousin	Sal 259	O	WIA	Salmson 2A2
S/Lt Paul Ganne	Sal 39	O	WIA	
Sgt Roche &	Br 214	P	KIAcc	
S/Lt Muller	Br 214	O	KIAcc	Bréguet 14 N° 4656.
Lt Dorizon	Sal 263	O	Injured	
Capt L'hôtel	2 CA	P	Injured	DOW, Sopwith 1A2.

Three balloons unsuccessfully attacked in the Aisne Sector.

---

13 June

Sgt Chevannes &		Spa 3					2
MdL Dubonnet		Spa 3	Balloon	XF	La Boissière	1115	4
Sgt Massicot &		Spa 12					1
Brig Rabeau		Spa 12	EA	X	N Château-Thierry		1
Lt de Turenne	CO	Spa 12	Pfalz DIII	X	Bezuet-Soissons	1715	10
Lt Leclerc		Spa 98	EA	X	Dommiers		1
Capt d'Argueeff		Spa 124	Rumpler C	X	Monnes		8
Sgt Gaudry		Spa 155	Balloon	XF			1
1/Lt Meissner,		94thUS					4
1/Lt T Taylor &		94thUS				0815	1
2/Lt Winslow	a.	94thUS	Hannover CL	X	Thiaucourt		2
1/Lt Phyler		27thUS	Hannover CL	X	Lorry	0830	1
1/Lt McArthur,		27thUS					1
2/Lt Clapp &		27thUS					1
1/Lt Rucker		27thUS	Albatros	X	Lorry		1
Lt Nungesser		Spa 65	3 seater	P			–
Lt Nungesser		Spa 65	3 seater	P			–
Patrol		GC 11	2 EA	P			–
Patrol		GC 12	2 seater	P	Ressons-sur-Matz	0840	–
Patrol		GC 21	EA	P	Monnes, VI° Armée		–
Escad 1		GC	EA	P			–
1/Lt Schaffner &		91stUS					–
2/Lt Bender		91stUS	Pfalz	P			–

a.   Possibly Sgt Fritz Mohr, WIA/DOW 19 June 1918, & Ltn Kurt von Bruckner, FlAbt 46b, KIA Thiaucourt.

Casualties:

Cpl Henri Lacombe	Spa 75	P	MIA	X° Armée, Spad XIII.
Cpl Chapel	Spa 98	P	MIA	VI° Armée, Spad VII.
Brig François Aleppe	Spa 98	P	MIA	VI° Armée, Spad VII.
Lt Edmond Friedel	Escad 2	P	POW	Spad VII
MdL André Delannoy	Spa 37	P	WIA/POW	Spad XIII
S/Lt Robert Masson &	Br 35	P	MIA	X° Armée, Bréguet 14A2,
S/Lt René Ruf	Br 35	O	MIA	12h55, Dommiers, probably Ltn Walter Blume, Jasta 9, (10).
Sgt Cyrus Chamberlain	Spa 98	P	KIA	VI° Armée, Spad VII, la Ferte Milon.
Brig Maxime Ouizille	Spa 100	P	POW	Spad VII N° 3332, probably by Obltn Bruno Loerzer, CO JG I, (26).
1/Lt William H Phyler	27thUS	P	POW	VIII° Armée, Nieuport 28 N° 6218, probably by Flg Bünning, Kest 3, (1).
Sgt Emile Lecarpentier	Spa 12	P	WIA	

Adj Emile Strohl	Spa 77	P	WIA	Spad XIII		
Sgt Fernand Massicot	Spa 12	P	WIA	Spad XIII		
Lt Prat	Sal 14	O	WIA			
S/Lt Paul Lapeyre	GDE	P	KIAcc	Nieuport		
Adj Dulac	GDE	P	KIAcc	Caproni		
MdL Morin	GDE	P	KIAcc	Caproni		
Brig Henri Rabeau	Spa 12	P	OK	V° Armée, FTL after combat.		

14 June

S/Lt Bamberger &	Spa 75					2
MdL Beaulieu	a. Spa 75	Fokker	POW	Soucy		1
Lt Romatet	Spa 76	Scout	X	W Reims	1930	2
Capt d'Argueeff	Spa 124	2 seater	X	German lines		9
Lt Brantonne &	Spa 153					1
MdL Halberger	Spa 153	Fokker D7	XF	St Pierre Aigle		3
Sgt Ropert	Spa 158	Scout	X	NW Ressons-sur-Matz		1
Lt Prévost	Spa 163	Fokker DrI	X	Villers-Cotterêts		1
Lt Majon de la Débuterie	Spa 163	Fokker	X	Villers-Cotterêts	1945	4
Capt Echard CO	GC 22	Fokker DrI	X	Cernay-les-Reims		6
Patrol	GC	Fokker	X	Soucy		–
1/Lt Putnam, USAS &	Spa 38					–
Sgt Bricq	Spa 38	EA	P	NW Reims		–
1/Lt Putnam, USAS &	Spa 38					–
Sgt Bricq	Spa 38	EA	P	NW Reims		–
1/Lt Putnam, USAS &	Spa 38					–
Sgt Bricq	Spa 38	EA	P	NW Reims		–
Patrol	Spa 69	EA	P	Dommiers	1750	–
MdL Chayne	Spa 97	EA	P			–
S/Lt Barcat	Spa 153	Fokker D7	P	St Pierre Aigle		–
MdL Halberger	Spa 153	Fokker D7	P	St Pierre Aigle		–
MdL Gangeron &	Spa 156					–
Adj Van den Bosche	Spa 156	EA	P	Ville-en-Tardenois		–
Patrol	Spa 161	2 seater	P	Villers-Agron	1830	–
Patrols	GC	2 EA	P			–

a.   Probably Ltn Busso von Alversleben, Jasta 21s, who had just flamed the balloon of the 45° Cie Aérostiers, POW, Villers-Cotterêts, DOW 15 June 1918.

Casualties:

Sgt Hare	GDE	P	MIA	Letord
S/Lt Marie Majon de la Débuterie	Spa 163	P	POW	VI° Armée, Spad XIII.
Cpl Robert L Moore &	Br 29	P	POW	Probably by Ltn Karl Bolle, CO
Lt Guy Giguel	Br 29	O	KIA	Jasta "B", (16).
Adj Edouard Muller &	Br 104	P	WIA	
S/Lt Léonard Goursat	Br 104	O	KIA	
S/Lt Henri de Pracomtal	Spa 99	P	KIAcc	Spad XIII
Sgt Antoine Madinier	Spa 99	P	KIAcc	Spad XIII
S/Lt Raymond Carré	29° Cie d'Aérostiers	XF		Aisne Sector
		O	OK	
	45° Cie d'Aérostiers	XF		X° Armée, probably by Ltn
		O	OK	Busso von Alversleben, Jasta 21s, (1), see a. above
	85° Cie d'Aérostiers	XF		X° Armée
		O	OK	

NOTE: One of the above balloons had its cable cut by a French aircraft.

15 June

Sgt Putnam	a. Spa 38	2 seater	X	La Neuvillette		7
Sgt Putnam	Spa 38	Balloon	XF	Mercy		8
Lt Leps CO	Spa 81	Balloon	XF			12
Cpl Martre	Spa 94	Fokker D7	X	Moulins-Touvant		1
X° Armée	???	2 seater	XF	Gueux-Thillois	1740	–
IV° Armée	CA	2 seater	X	Valsery		–
Sgt Shaffer	Spa 38	EA	P	La Neuvillette		–
Capt Deullin CO	GC 19	EA	P			–
Patrol	Spa 26	EA	P	Monchel	1920	–
Patrol	GC	EA	P	Picardie		–

a.   Probably Uffz Martin Höntsch & Gefr Wilhelm Naraska, SchSta 22b, KIAs at St Thierry, about 3 km NW La Neuvillette.

Casualties:

Cpl Jean-Marie Martre	Spa 94	P	MIA	Spad VII, probably by Ltn Karl Menckhoff, Jasta 72, (35).	
Sgt Grude &	Sal 70	P	WIA	DOW 17 June 1918	
Lt Rue	Sal 70	O	OK	X° Armée	
Cpl Charles Hautecoeur	Spa 85	P	KIAcc	Spad VII	
Lt Théophile Laplyre	???	P	KIAcc		
Cpl Henri Schildknecht &	???	P	KIAcc		
Sgt Delbos	???	G	KIAcc	Sopwith	
Lt Cachet	GDE	P	Injured	Caudron G3	
Lt Quenot	Sal 6	O	Injured	Salmson 2A2	
S/Lt Gilbert de Guingand	Spa 48	P	OK	Shot down behind enemy lines by AA fire, but managed to regain Allied lines.	
???	Cie d'Aérostiers		XF	Aisne Sector	
???	Cie d'Aérostiers		XF	Aisne Sector	
???	Cie d'Aérostiers		XF	Aisne Sector	
Adj Catrice	67° Cie d'Aérostiers			Attacked, not flamed,	
		O	Injured	Picardie Sector.	

16 June

MdL Voedts &		Sal 18				1
S/Lt Mairey		Sal 18	Scout	XF	French lines	1
MdL Voedts &		Sal 18				2
S/Lt Mairey		Sal 18	Scout	X	German lines	2
MdL Moreux &		Spa 53				1
S/Lt Saulnier		Spa 53	EA	XF	French lines	1
Lt Bergé &		Spa 92				1
Adj Miserolle		Spa 92	Scout	XF	N Taissy, E Reims	1
Lt Lahoulle &	CO	Spa 154				8
S/Lt Henot	a.	Spa 154	Scout	POW	SW Taissy	1
Patrol		EdA	EA	X		–
Lt Berge &		Spa 92				1
Adj-Chef Miserolle		Spa 92	Scout	XF	N Taissy	1

a. Probably Vfw Willi Peters, Jasta 66, SW Taissy, POW, he had just unsuccessfully attacked the balloon of the 76° Cie d'Aérostiers, V° Armée Sector.

Casualties:

MdL ???	C 46	P	WIA	Caudron R11, probably by	
Brig Picard &	C 46	G	WIA	Uffz Otto Rosenfeld, Jasta	
Sgt Léon Condamine	C 46	G	WIA	41, (11).	
S/Lt Gabolde	Br 205	O	WIA	Shrapnel, on ground.	
Sol Audry	Br 205	M	WIA	Shrapnel, on ground.	
MdL Gervais Voedts &	Sal 18	P	WIA		
S/Lt Mairey	Sal 18	O	OK		
S/Lt Demery	Sal 18	P	WIA	Bomb blast.	
Sgt Feugère	Spa 314	P	KIAcc	Spad XIII	
MdL Jean Allaert,	C 227	P	KIAcc		
S/Lt Laurier	C 227	O	KIAcc		
MdL Jean Buisson	C 227	G	KIAcc	Caudron R11	
MdL Royer	Spa 156	P	Injured	Spad N° 5408.	
Sgt Bragou	Br 257	P	Injured		
Cpl Miot	???		Injured		
???	83° Cie d'Aérostiers		XF	X° Armée, probably by OfStv Paul	
		O	OK	Aue, Jasta 10, (7).	
???	76° Cie d'Aérostiers			V° Armée, NOT flamed, probably claimed by Vfw Willi Peters, Jasta 66, (2), see a. above.	
Adj Bucquet	62° Cie d'Aérostiers		XF	VI° Armée	
		O	OK		

One other balloon was attacked but not flamed in the Picardie Sector.
Two other balloons were attacked but not flamed in the Aisne Sector.

17 June

Adj Caillaux,	Spa 48				5
Adj Montrion &	Spa 48				11
Adj Roques	Spa 48	Halb CL2	XF	Chaudun	5
S/Lt Gaudermen &	Spa 68				3
Sgt Sinclaire	Spa 68	Albatros D	XF	German lines	1

Sgt E Régnier		Spa 89	2 seater	XF	W Ricquebourg		1
Lt Chambarière	CO	Spa 162	Balloon	XF			3
Lt Chambarière	CO	Spa 162	Balloon	XF			4
Adj Breton		Spa 93	EA	XF	German lines		3

Casualties:

MdL Luc Dol	Spa 162	P	MIA	Spad XIII, probably by Ltn Franz Brandt, Jasta 26, (5).
S/Lt André Guersant	Spa 162	P	MIA	Spad VII, possibly by Vfw Josef Schwendemann, Jasta 41, (6).
Sgt Frank Baylies	Spa 3	P	KIA	Spad XIII. By Ltn Wilhelm Leusch, Jasta 19, (2), Montdidier-Onvillers.
Cpl Colanbo	Spa 81	P	MIA	Spad
Adj Bernard Breton	Spa 93	P	POW	Spad VII, FTL mechanical problems, escaped October 1918.
MdL Georges Franceschi	Spa 93	P	POW	Spad XIII, probably by Ltn Rudolf Klinke, Jasta 27, (8), escaped in October.
Lt Picat	???	O	KIA	
Lt Guérin &	V 116	P	KIAcc	
Cpl Henniot	V 116	G	KIAcc	
Adj Louis Marot	Spa 37	P	Injured	Spad XIII
Cpl Arnault	Spa 37	P	Injured	Spad XIII
Adj Saisset	Spa 228	P	Injured	Spad XI
Brig Jean Meyer	Spa 151	P	Injured	Spad VII
MdL Grisset	39° Cie d'Aérostiers	XF		III° Armée, probably by Vfw Emil
		O	OK	Schäpe, Jasta 33, (3).
Sgt Guyot	70° Cie d'Aérostiers			III° Armée, not flamed
		O	Injured	
Adj Lamcombe	90° Cie d'Aérostiers			VI° Armée, attacked, not
		O	OK	flamed.

18 June

Adj Prêtre	a.	Spa 67	2 seater	X	Le Frêtoy	0645	1
Adj-Chef Laplasse		Spa 75	Balloon	XF	Moulin-le-Comte		3
Lt Hay de Slade		Spa 86	2 seater	X	Gravençon		10
Cpl Mathieu &		Sop 141					1
Cpl Guillet		Sop 141	Albatros D	X	NE Parroy		1
Lt de Nompère de Champagny	CO	Spa 163	Scout	X	Le Charmel		2
Escad 2		GC	EA	XF			–
Patrol		Spa 57	EA	P	Cormicy-Bouleuse	1330	–
Escad 2		GC	EA	P			–

a.   Had just flamed a French balloon.

Casualties:

MdL Pierre Rouxel	Spa 100	P	MIA	Spad XIII, probably by Ltn Georg von Hantelmann, Jasta 15, (4).
Sgt Mallet	Spa 100	P	MIA	Spad VII, probably by OfStv Karl Thom, Jasta 21s, (18).
MdL Victor Beauchène	Spa 89	P	MIA	Spad XIII
MdL Soulac &	Sal 59	P	WIA	
MdL Couret	Sal 59	O	KIA	
Sgt Ercole Balzac	Spa 69	P	WIA	X° Armée, Spad, FTL at La Ferté sous Jouarre, after combat.
S/Lt Lavoinne	Br 226	O	WIA	V° Armée, Bréguet 14A2.
Cpl Pierre Mathieu &	Sop 141	P	OK	
Cpl Henri Guillet	Sop 141	G	WIA	VIII° Armée, Sopwith
MdL Anthelme Dufour-Bourru	Sal 8	G	WIA	Flak, DOW 22 June 1918.
Cpl Coquard	GDE	P	KIAcc	Spad VII
Sgt-Maj Boom	56° Cie d'Aérostiers	XF		X° Armée, 13h50, probably by Ltn
		O	OK	Martin Demisch, Jasta 58, (3).
Sgt Cordaillat &	21° Cie d'Aérostiers			VI° Armée, attacked, not
Asp Vallier		O	OK	flamed.

19 June – No Claims

Casualties:

Cpl Freval	???	P	KIAcc	Spad VII
S/Lt Auguste Vasilesco	Spa 37	P	KIAcc	Spad XIII

Sol Pouily		Sal 56	G	DOW	Salmson	
Lt Jean Desquenne	EM	GC 13	P	Injured	Spad	
Lt Volland		Spa 55	O	Injured	Car accident	
???		74° Cie d'Aérostiers	XF		III° Armée	
			O	OK		

20 June

Asp Bos &		Sop 270				1
Cpl Digeon	a.	Sop 270	Scout	X	French lines	1

a.   Probably Vfw Ludwig Bergmann, Jasta 79b, KIA Autheuil.

Casualties:

MdL Moliargues &	Sal 259	P	KIA	VI° Armée
Lt Cousin	Sal 259	O	WIA	Salmson 2A2
Asp Alexandre Bos	Sop 270	P	KIA	
Cpl Marcel Digeon	Sop 270	G	WIA	Sopwith 1A2
S/Lt Tuly	Spa 20	O	WIA	Flak, Spad XI
S/Lt Raymond Carré	29° Cie d'Aérostiers	XF		
		O	OK	

21 June – No Claims

Casualties:

MdL Gaujour &	Sal 40	P	WIA	IV° Armée
S/Lt Joseph Philippe	Sal 40	O	WIA	DOW, Salmson 2A2 N° 3029
Brig Guenechau &	Let 64	P	KIAcc	
Sol Gave	Let 64	M	KIAcc	Letord 2
Sgt Delmée	GDE	P	Injured	Bréguet

22 June – No Claims

Casualties:

Adj Bralat &	Br 11	P	MIA	Armée, Bréguet 14, probably by Ltn
S/Lt Lemoine	Br 11	O	MIA	Erich Löwenhardt, Jasta 10, (28).
Cpl Paul Mulot	Spa 77	P	KIAcc	Spad VII
Sgt Michaudet	GDE	P	KIAcc	Nieuport
Sgt de Gembiki	GDE	P	KIAcc	Nieuport
Cpl Apostolakis	GDE	P	Injured	Spad VII
Lt Louis Koenig Beillard				
de Vaubicourt	CO	Spa 100	P	Injured

23 June

Sgt d'Epenoux &		Br 11				1
Lt Cardeilhac &		Br 11				2
Sgt Boyard &		Br 11				2
S/Lt Coffin		Br 11	EA	X		1
Lt Hostein,		R 46				3
Lt Pavy &		R 46				1
MdL Baratciart		R 46	EA	X	Picardie	3
S/Lt Fraissinet		Spa 57	Halb C	X	S Reims	5
Adj Gasser	a.	Spa 87	Fokker D7	X	N Bezannes	8
1/Lt Cassady, USAS		Spa 163				3
Sgt Lederlin &		Spa 163				2
Sgt Guillet	b.	Spa 163	Halb CLII	POW	La Ferté Gaucher	2
Adj Poulet &		Br 219				1
S/Lt Varloup		Br 219	EA	X		1
III° Armée	c.	DCA	EA	POW	Gournay-sur-Aronde	–
S/Lt Nogues		???	EA	X	Aisne	–
V° Armée		???	Fokker DrI	X	SW Reims	0750 –
Patrol		Spa 62	2 EA	P	VI° Armée	–

a.   Possibly Uffz Ernst Bielefeld, Jasta 60, KIA Reims, about 5 km NE Bezannes, but see 24 June entry.
b.   Probably Vfw Eilemann & Vfw Richter, Schutzstaffel 26b, POWs.
c.   Possibly Ltn Max Schick, Jasta 76b, POW, Albatros DVa #5765/17.

Casualties:

Sgt Albert Voisin	Spa 62	P	MIA	VI° Armée, Spad VII N° 7231 possibly by
				Ltn Alois Heldmann, Jasta 10, (7).
Cpl Crettre &	Sal 41	P	MIA	
S/Lt Pillot	Sal 41	O	MIA	VIII° Armée, Salmson N° 5036.
Lt Pierre Tournadre &	Br 216	P	KIA	X° Armée, Bréguet, probably by
Sol Pic	Br 216	G	KIA	Ltn Ernst Udet, Jasta 4, (31).

Sgt Jean Vinouze	Spa 85		P		WIA	Spad, Villers-Cotterêts.		
Cpl Léon Morisaux &	Sal 6		P		WIA	X° Armée, Salmson 2A2,		
S/Lt Henry Picat	Sal 6		O		WIA	DOW 25 June 1918.		
S/Lt Roger Bousquet	Sop 271		O		WIA	Sopwith 1A2, III° Armée.		
S/Lt d'Arrigade	GDE		P		KIAcc	Nieuport		
Sgt Maurice Jacquelin	Spa 98		P		Injured	Spad XIII		
S/Lt Marchand &	Br 237		P		Injured			
Sol Forest	Br 237		M		Injured	Bréguet 14A2		
Brig Denait	V 116		P		Injured	Voisin		
???	??? Cie d'Aérostiers					Attacked, not flamed,		
			O		OK	Aisne Sector		

24 June

Lt Nuville &	Spa 57							6
Adj Petit-Delchet	Spa 57	a.	Rumpler C	XF		Reims	0710	3
Sgt E Régnier,	Spa 89							2
Sgt Dreyfus &	Spa 89							1
Sgt L Thomas	Spa 89		2 seater	POW		Tricot		1
Sgt Gillet &	GB 3							1
Sgt Duhamel	GB 3		EA	X		Aisne		1
???	CA		2 seater	XF				–
1/Lt Raymond	27thUS		2 seater	X		Thiaucourt	0920	1
Sgt Fleury	Spa 95		2 seater	P				–
Patrol	GC 21		EA	P		VI° Armée		–
???	GC		2 seater	P		Picardie		–
???	CA		Albatros	P				–

a.   Vfw Ernst Bielefeld, Jasta 60, was a passenger in this aircraft, V° Armée records identify the unit of the passenger, but Jasta 60 records note him to be lost on 23 June.

It is quite possible that this crew was Uffz Rudolf Schubert and Ltn Walter Vaditz, FlAbt 229 (A), KIAs Reims.

Casualties:

Adj Sechet &	Sal 280	P	MIA	VI° Armée,
S/Lt Temple	Sal 280	O	MIA	Salmson 2A2 N° 5042
Sgt Samuel Cachard &	Br 128	P	MIA	
Sgt Jules Morel	Br 128	G	MIA	Bréguet 14B2
S/Lt Triollet &	Br 107	P	MIA	
Sgt Boyreau	Br 107	G	MIA	Bréguet 14B2
Brig Lamy &	Br 121	P	MIA	
Lt Gibelin	Br 121	O	MIA	IV° Armée
Capt François Fageol &	20° CA	P	KIA	X° Armée, 09h15,
Lt Marie Faure	20° CA	P	KIA	Salmson 2A2
Sgt André Scellier	Br 128	P	WIA	
1/Lt Amos L Hopkins	12thUS	O	WIA	
1/Lt Armin F Herold	12thUS	O	KIAcc	
Capt Elliott P Hinds	12thUS	P	KIAcc	Dorand
Sgt Ladislas Gembricki	???	P	KIAcc	
2/Lt James F Ashenden	147thUS	P	Interned	Nieuport 28 N° 6212, Switzerland

25 June

S/Lt Nogues	Spa 57		Scout	XF		Bois de Belleau	1110	6
S/Lt Nuville &	Spa 57							7
S/Lt Hasdenteufel	Spa 57	a.	Fokker D7	XF		S Dormans	1810	5
Adj Gérard	Spa 65		EA	X		Chaudun	1825	7
Adj Balzac	Spa 69		2 seater	X		German lines		2
S/Lt Ambrogi &	Spa 90							5
MdL Pezon	Spa 90	b.	Balloon	XF		Goin-en-Moselle	1740	2
Lt Fonck	Spa 103		Halb C	X		Contoire	1800	45
Lt Fonck	Spa 103		Fokker D7	X		Villers-aux-Erables to		46
Lt Fonck	Spa 103		Fokker D7	X		W Fescamps	1835	47
Lt Mézergues &	Br 131							5
MdL Miclet	Br 131		EA	X				2
??? &	Br 134							?
Cpl Callois	Br 134							1
MdL Meillant &	Br 134							1
MdL Bras	Br 134		EA	X		Verpilliers	1750	1
S/Lt Bourjade	Spa 152		Balloon	XF		St Etienne-à-Arnes		5
Cpl Bertho	Spa 161		Fokker DrI	X		N Cernay	1915	1
Sgt Villetard de Laguerie &	Spa 212							1

Lt Augiex		Spa 212	2 seater	X	V° Armée Sector	1
Major Hartney &	CO	27thUS				5
1/Lt McArthur		27thUS	Albatros	X	Lorry, VIII° Armée	2
Major Hartney &	CO	27thUS				6
1/Lt McArthur		27thUS	Rumpler C	X	Lorry, VIII° Armée	3
Patrol		Spa 69	EA	P	St Pierre Aigle	–
MdL Paoli		Spa 75	EA	P	NE Villers-Cotterêts	–
Lt Hugues &	CO	Spa 95				–
S/Lt de Montrichard		Spa 95	2 seater	P		–
Sgt Fleury &		Spa 95				
MdL Gaudry		Spa 95	2 seater	P		–
Patrol		GC 11	EA	P	Rocourt	1110 –
Patrol		GC 11	EA	P	Dormans	1810 –
Patrols		???	2 EA	P		–
???		???	Balloon	P		–

a.   Possibly Ltn Wilhelm Schulz, Jasta 37, who had just unsuccessfully attacked a balloon in the V° Armée Sector, KIA Dormans.
b.   Probably Balloonzug 152, AOK 19 Sector.

Casualties:

Brig Yves Adam &	Br 134	P	MIA	
Asp André Desages	Br 134	O	MIA	Bréguet 14B2 N° 1655
Lt Albert Mézergues &	Br 131	P	WIA	
Sgt Henri Miclet	Br 131	G	KIA	Bréguet 14B2
1/Lt Warren T Hobbs	103rdUS	P	KIA	DAN, Spad XIII, SE Ypres.
Adj-Chef Pierre Galgani	Spa 57	P	WIA	Spad VII N° 2330, probably by Vfw Gondermann, Jasta 66, (3). V° Armée, FTL after combat.
S/Lt Pierre Desmond	Spa 85	P	WIA	Spad, Dommiers-Corcy
Sgt Vernon Booth	Spa 96	P	WIA	DOW 10 July 1918, Spad XIII, probably by Ltn Ernst Udet, Jasta 4, (34).
Cpl Edouard Aury	Spa 96	P	WIA	Spad VII, probably by Ltn Ernst Udet, Jasta 4, (35).
Adj Touret &	Sop 285	P	WIA	Flak
Sol Dargaud	Sop 285	G	WIA	Flak, VII° Armée, Spad XI.
MdL Georges Davier &	Br 226	P	OK	
MdL Jean Lyvet	Br 226	O	WIA	V° Armée, DOW, Bréguet 14A2.
Cpl Albert Lethuaire	Br 134	G	WIA	Bréguet 14B2
MdL Louis Bras	Br 134	G	WIA	Bréguet 14B2
Asp Robert Falquerho	Br 134	O	WIA	Bréguet 14B2
Sol Dargaud	Sop 285	G	WIA	DOW 28 June 1918, Sopwith
MdL Lendret	???	O	WIA	DOW 25 June 1918.
1/Lt Hathaway &	90thUS	P	KIAcc	
1/Lt Maynor	90thUS	O	KIAcc	Sopwith
Cpl Paul Breuil	???	P	KIAcc	
Cpl Guignard &	???	P	KIAcc	
Lt Girard	???	O	KIAcc	
Capt Hinde &	???	P	KIAcc	
Lt Henderson	???	O	Injured	
Adj Porquet &	Br 222	P	Injured	
S/Lt Robinet	Br 222	O	Injured	Bréguet 14A2
Sgt Faure	Br 279	P	Injured	Bréguet 14
Brig Brame	Br 279	P	Injured	Bréguet 14
Sgt Touery	V 22	P	Injured	
Cpl Foucon	Spa 38	P	Injured	
Cpl Rouquette	GDE	P	Injured	DOW 29 June 1918, Nieuport
S/Lt Roman	???	O	Injured	
Sgt Gabriel	84° Cie d'Aérostiers		XF	VII° Armée, probably by Gefr
		O	OK	Johann Diebold, Jasta 71, (1).
S/Lt Paillat &	55° Cie d'Aérostiers		XF	V° Armée, 18h35, probably by Ltn
Adj Prieur		O	OK	Fritz Friedrichs, Jasta 10, (14).

26 June

Adj Arnoux	a.	Spa 49	Balloon	XF	Tagsdorff	
0910	3					
Adj Damidaux,		Spa 86				2
Sgt Lanier &		Sal 8				1
S/Lt Lechat		Sal 8				1
??? &		Sal 8				?
S/Lt Mariotti		Sal 8	Fokker DrI	X	Chauny	2
Capt d'Argueeff		Spa 124	2 seater	XF	German lines	10

S/Lt Douillet &	Spa 124					2
Sgt Siamer	Spa 124	2 seater	X	German lines		1
Adj Ruamps	Spa 87	EA	P			–
Adj Ruamps	Spa 87	EA	P			–
Patrol	GC 14	EA	P			–
Patrol	GC 21	2EA	P	VI° Armée		–

a.   Probably Balloonzug 205.

Casualties:

S/Lt Henri de Mirman	Spa 154	P	MIA	Spad XIII N° 8284, XF, probably by Vfw Josef Schwendemann, Jasta 41, (7).	
Asp Chevalier &	???	P	MIA		
Lt Grenié	???	O	MIA		
1/Lt Herbert A. Wardle	Ferry	P	POW	FTL in Germany.	
Sgt Lucien Lanier &	Sal 8	P	WIA		
S/Lt Camille Lechat	Sal 8	O	WIA	X° Armée, Salmson 2A2.	
MdL Désiré Baratciart	R 46	G	WIA		
Brig Roux &	Sop 251	P	WIA		
Lt Legorju	Sop 251	O	WIA	X° Armée, Sopwith 1A2.	
S/Lt Louis de Mailly-Nesles d'Orange	Spa 112	P	WIA	Bombardment of airfield.	
S/Lt Marius Hasdenteufeul	Spa 57	P	KIAcc	Spad VII N° 7262	
Cpl Blaise,	???	P	KIAcc		
Lt Jourdain &	???	O	KIAcc		
Asp Denys	???	O	KIAcc	Voisin R	
Brig Guignard &	V 119	P	KIAcc		
S/Lt Girard	V 119	O	KIAcc		
MdL Claude Buerrier	Spa 91	P	Injured	DOW, Spad VII	
Cpl Charles Giraudet	Spa 163	P	Injured	Spad VII N° 5144, crash-landing, motor trouble.	
Adj-Chef Constantin Miserolle	Spa 92	P	Injured		
S/Lt Roman	Spa 228	O	Injured	Spad XI	
Cpl Bouffange &	???	P	Injured		
Sol Hesseyre	???	M	Injured	Bréguet 14B2	
Cpl Michel	???	P	Injured		
MdL Wissenberger	59° Cie d'Aérostiers		XF	VI° Armée, probably by Sgt Friedrich Schumacher, Jasta 10, (2).	
		O	OK		
Cpl Graville	62° Cie d'Aérostiers			VI° Armée, attacked, not	
		O	OK	flamed.	

One other balloon was unsuccessfully attacked in the Aisne Sector.

---

27 June

S/Lt Boyau	Spa 77	Balloon	XF			19
S/Lt Cayol	Spa 84	Balloon	XF			1
S/Lt Vidal &	Spa 88					3
Adj Delzenne	Spa 88	Balloon	XF			2
Lt Fonck	Spa 103	Halb C	XF	Morisel	0810	48
Lt Fonck	Spa 103	2 seater	X	N Moreuil	0815	49
III° Armée	a. DCA	EA	POW	Picardie		–
MdL Dubonnet	Spa 3	2 seater	P	Gratibus-Fignières	0907	–
Sgt Hoeber	Spa 103	2 seater	P	Rollot-Montdidier	0830	–
Lt Fonck	Spa 103	2 seater	P	NE Moreuil	1845	–
Lt Letellier	Spa 152	EA	P	Villers-Franqueux		–
Patrol	GC 16	EA	P	Ressons-sur-Matz		–
Escad 1	GC	EA	P	Picardie		–
Escad 2	GC	EA	P			–
Escad 2	GC	Balloon	P			–
???	???	EA	P			–

a.   Probably Vfw Stadly, Jasta 62, flying Albatros DVa #7285/17, who had just flamed the balloon of the 41° Cie, POW/DOW.

Casualties:

MdL Jean Goffre	Spa 99	P	MIA	Spad XIII
S/Lt Jean Vidal	Spa 88	P	MIA	Spad XIII, probably by OfStv Karl Thom, Jasta 21s, (19).
S/Lt Douladoure &	Sal 28	P	MIA	
S/Lt Marchand	Sal 28	O	MIA	Salmson 2A2
Brig Emile Thevenoux	Sal 10	P	MIA	III° Armée, Rollot
Brig André Juin	Sal 10	G	MIA	Salmson 2A2 N° 270

Sgt Rédempt &	Br 216	P	WIA	FTL at Pisseleux,		
S/Lt Jean-Baptiste Canal	Br 216	O	WIA/DOW	Bréguet 14A2.		
Sgt Caudron	Sal 252	P	WIA	Flak, IV° Armée, Salmson.		
S/Lt René Gaillard	Spa 158	P	KIAcc			
Cpl d'Epinay	Spa 75	P	Injured	Spad VII		
Asp Scheurer	Br 234	O	Injured	Bréguet 14A2		
MdL Barret	GDE	P	Injured	DOW 28 June 1918.		
Sgt Tharasse &	???	P	Injured	Landing accident.		
Sgt Pauthe	???	O	Injured			
Sgt Birr	41° Cie d'Aérostiers		XF	III° Armée, probably by		
		O	WIA	Vfw Stadly, Jasta 62, (1).		
	83° Cie d'Aérostiers			X° Armée, Probably by Ltn Heinrich Drekmann, Jasta 4,(6).		
Lt Baudouin &	75° Cie d'Aérostiers		XF	III° Armée		
Lt Lanthiner		O	OK			
Sgt Guyot	70° Cie d'Aérostiers			III° Armée, attacked, not		
		O	OK	flamed.		
Lt de Bernardi	85° Cie d'Aérostiers			III° Armée, attacked, not		
		O	OK	flamed.		
???	??? Cie d'Aérostiers			Attacked, not flamed		
		O	OK	Aisne Sector.		

28 June

MdL Pallier	Spa 15	EA	XF	Near Montdidier		1
Lt Dombray &	Spa 26					2
Adj Naudin	Spa 26	Scout	XF	Bois de Fay	2015	5
Lt Poupon, CO	Spa 37					3
Sgt Morin &	Spa 37					1
Sgt Francisquet	Spa 37	2 seater	X	NE Ambleny	0820	2
Lt Hostein,	R 46					2
Lt Pavy &	R 46					2
MdL Baratciart	R 46	Scout	XF	E Cutry		2
S/Lt Dousinelle,	Spa 48					7
Adj Binoche &	Spa 48					2
Brig Patry	Spa 155	Scout	X	Dommiers	0615	1
S/Lt Dousinelle,	Spa 48					8
Adj Binoche &	Spa 48					3
MdL Danglade	Spa 48	2 seater	X	Vercefeuille	0700	1
Lt Augier de Moussac	Spa 49	2 seater	X	Hericourt		2
S/Lt Nogues &	Spa 57					7
Adj Bocquentin	Spa 57	2 seater	XF	Bois de Pateuil		1
Sgt Priollaud	Spa 65	EA	XF			1
Adj Gérard	Spa 65	Albatros D	XF	Chaudun		8
S/Lt Plessis &	Spa 65					5
MdL Giovetti	Spa 65	EA	X	Valpriez		3
Adj Henriot	Spa 65	EA	X	Chaudun		4
Sgt Dreyfus,	Spa 89					2
Sgt E Régnier &	Spa 89					3
Sgt L Thomas	Spa 89	2 seater	X	NE of Paris		2
S/Lt C Robin	Spa 93	Scout	X	N Longpont		1
MdL de Gaillard de La Valdène	Spa 95	2 seater	XF	Dommiers	0540	5
S/Lt Bourjade	Spa 152	Balloon	XF	St Pierre-à-Arne		6
S/Lt Pelissier,	Spa 155					4
Sgt Degorge &	Spa 155					1
Sgt Gaudry	Spa 155	Balloon	XF	Chaudun		1
Lt Ribault &	Br 224					1
Adj Arcaute &	Br 224					1
S/Lt Payart &	Br 224					1
Adj-Chef Moreau	Br 224	EA	X	Aisne		1
S/Lt Pellerin &	Br 224					1
S/Lt Jean-Marie	Br 224	EA	X	Aisne		2
Navigation error a.	???	Albatros DV	POW	Charmantray		–
DCA Ecouen (Lt Weil) b.	DCA	FdH III	X	Forêt de Laigue night		1
Sgt Ventre	Spa 82	EA	P			–
Patrol	GC 12	2 seater	P	Courtemanche	0745	–
Patrol	GC 21	EA	P	VI° Armée		–

X° Armée	EdA	2 EA	P			–
Escad 1	???	3 EA	P			–

a.   Ltn Siegfried, Jasta 37, Albatros DV N° 4526/17, POW.
b.   Night of 28-29 June this two motor aircraft landed in French territory, and the three occupants were taken prisoner. Aircraft N° 5, Bogohl I, Uffz (P) WIA, Ltn (O) WIA/DOW, & VFW (G) OK, WIA, ???.

Casualties:

Adj Christian Schlumberger	Spa 162	P	MIA	Spad XIII
Adj René Montrion	Spa 48	P	MIA	Spad VII, balloon attack.
Cpl Camille Javet	Spa 159	P	MIA	Spad XIII
Sgt Pierre Lafargue	Spa 159	P	MIA	Spad XIII
Lt Maurice Patret	Spa 159	P	MIA	Spad VII
Asp Marion &	Br 224	P	MIA	X° Armée, XF, Longpont
Lt Jacques Franceschi	Br 224	O	MIA	Bréguet 14B2
Capt Marcel Doumer CO	Spa 88	P	KIA	Spad XIII
Sgt Antony Girard &	Sal 253	P	KIA-Flak	X° Armée
Lt Henri Garréard	Sal 253	O	KIA-Flak	Salmson 2A2
Cpl Georges Joblot	Spa 88	P	POW	Spad XIII
Cpl Lucien Filhol	Spa 36	G	WIA	Spad 2 seater
MdL Frantz Divoy	Spa 159	P	WIA	DOW, Spad VII, possibly by Ltn Eberhardt Mohnicke, Jasta 11, (8).
Sgt Marius Ventre	Spa 82	P	WIA-Flak	X° Armée, Spad XIII.
MdL Désiré Baratciart	R 46	G	WIA	Caudron R11
Cpl Henri Caussidery	Spa 20	P	KIAcc	Spad XI
Brig Lepage	GDE	P	KIAcc	Voisin P
Cpl Henri Coquart	???	P	KIAcc	
Sgt Comby &	Spa 64	P	Injured	DOW Spad XI
S/Lt Tavan	Spa 64	O	Injured	DOW 29 June 1918
S/Lt Rey	Sal 273	O	Injured	Salmson 2A2
S/Lt Mauret	51° Cie d'Aérostiers		XF	Probably by Ltn Max
		O	Injured	Näther, Jasta 62, (8).
Adj Auclerc &	63° Cie d'Aérostiers		XF	Probably by Uffz Friedrich
Adj Maurice Guibillon		O	Injured	Engler, Jasta 62, (2).

Three other balloons were attacked, but not flamed, in the Picardie Sector.

---

29 June

Sgt Fabre	Spa 38	EA	X		Nogent l'Abbesse	1
S/Lt Nogues	Spa 57	Halb C	XF		Bouleuse-Rosnay	1855	8
S/Lt Haegelen	Spa 100	EA	X			6
S/Lt Bourjade	Spa 152	Scout	X		N Rosnay	7
Sgt Thuillier,	Br 44					1
Lt Fine &	Br 44					1
Lt de Nompère de Champagny CO	Spa 163	Pfalz DIII	X		Château-Thierry	3
???	DCA	EA	X		Aisne	–
???	DCA	EA	X		Aisne	–
Lt Madon CO a.	Spa 38	Fokker	P		Betheny	–
Lt Madon CO	Spa 38	Pfalz	P		Betheny	–
Sgt Planiol	Spa 68	Fokker D7	P		Aisne	–
Adj Sinclaire	Spa 68	Fokker D7	P		Aisne	–
S/Lt Gaudermen	Spa 68	Fokker D7	P		Aisne	–
Patrol	GC 21	EA	P			–
???	CA	EA	P		Aisne	–
Motor Trouble? b. ???	Rumpler C	POW			VII° Armée	–

a.   Possibly Gefr Friedrich Bär, Jasta 81, KIA Reims, Betheny about 3 km N of Reims.
b.   Possibly Ltn Werner von Bülow & Ltn Graf Bethusy, FlAbt 23s (Lb), POWs, forced to land in Allied lines, cause unknown.

Casualties:

S/Lt Jean Lavergne	Spa 87	P	MIA	
Sgt Mivière &	Sal 74	P	MIA	Flak, VIII° Armée
Capt Saumande	36 CA	O	MIA	Salmson, probably by Flak-batterie 761.
MdL Jean Planiol	Spa 68	P	KIA	Spad VII, Faverolles
Cpl Jean Mandray	Spa 103	P	KIA	Spad VII, probably by Ltn Alfred Fleischer, Jasta 17, (1). 18h45 at Villers-Tournelles.
Lt Eugène Letellier	Spa 152	P	POW	IV° Armée, escaped, 3 July 1918, and rejoined Spa 152. Probably by Vfw Josef Schwendemann, Jasta 41, (8).
Asp Pierre Cour	Sal 52	O	WIA	X° Armée, Salmson 2A2.

Sgt Emile Thuillier &		Br 44	P	WIA		
S/Lt Pierre Fine		Br 44	O	WIA	Bréguet 14A2	
MdL Paul Barret		???	P	KIAcc		
Cpl Henri Dabat		Pau	P	KIAcc		
QM Marcel Guy &	*	CAM	P	KIAcc	Colp Janet FBA 150HP	
SM Alphonse Poulmarch	*	CAM	O	KIAcc	N° 607.	
Qm Ambroise Lalanne	*	CAM	P	KIAcc	Hourtin	
Brig André Delaby		Spa 151	P	Injured	Spad VII	
MdL Ginestet &		Sal 4	P	Injured		
2/Lt Peck, USAS		Sal 4	O	Injured	Salmson 2A2	
Brig Calvet &		Sal 253	P	Injured		
Lt Maixandeau		Sal 253	O	Injured	Salmson 2A2	
Lt Rey		???	O	Injured	Salmson	
Sgt Huntzbuchler &		Br 131	P	Injured		
Sgt Rayez		Br 131	G	Injured		
Sgt Perrin		GDE	P	Injured	AR	
Sol Lhomme		Sal 6	M	Injured		

*   Toulon.

30 June

Lt Poupon &	CO	Spa 37					4
Lt Barny de Romanet		Spa 37	Fokker D7	X	Chouy	1910	5
Lt Poupon &	CO	Spa 37					5
Sgt Morin		Spa 37	Fokker	X			2
Lt Madon	CO b.	Spa 38	Fokker DrI	X	Pont Faverger		35
Lt Nungesser		Spa 65	Fokker	X	Moreuil-le-Monthe	1845	37
Adj M Robert		Spa 92	Scout	X	Bouleuse		5
MdL Schuster		Spa 100	Fokker D7	X	Chirmont-Epagny	1100	3
S/Lt Bourjade		Spa 152	Balloon	XF	Marvaux-Rosières	1145	8
S/Lt Maunoury		Spa 152	Balloon	XF	St Marie-à-Py		2
MdL Barbreau,		Spa 154					3
MdL Ehrlich &		Spa 154					1
S/Lt Coiffard		Spa 154	Balloon	XF	Beauvardes	0650	4
S/Lt Coiffard,		Spa 154					5
S/Lt Gros &		Spa 154					4
Adj Petit		Spa 154	Balloon	XF	Courpoil	1750	2
S/Lt Sardier,		Spa 77					12
S/Lt Haegelen,		Spa 100					7
Sgt Perrotin &		Spa 212					2
Lt Augeix &		Spa 212					2
Sgt Oge &		Spa 212					1
Sgt Jaubert	a.	Spa 212	Fokker D7	XF	Bois de Bonval	0950	1
1/Lt Putnam	b.	139thUS	Rumpler C	X	N Régneville	1820	10
Lt Madon	c.	Spa 38	EA	P	Nogent l'Abbesse		–
Adj Gasser		Spa 87	Fokker D7	P	Moronvillers		–
Adj M Robert		Spa 92	EA	P	Faverolles		–
S/Lt Haustin		Spa 92	EA	P			–
Capt Echard	CO	GC 22	EA	P	Faverolles		–
Patrol		GC 16	EA	P	III° Armée		–
Patrol		GC	2 seater	P	Vauxbin-Berzy		–
Escad 1		GC	3 EA	P	Picardie		–
???		GC	EA	P	Aisne		–

a.   Crashed in French lines, Uffz Heinrich Piel (2v), Jasta 13, Fokker D7 N° 373/18, reported as 29 June in German records.
b.   Probably Sgt Eduard Bohlen & Ltn Gebhard Schia, FlAbt 31, KIAs Vieville- en-Haye, AOK "C" Sector.
c.   Possibly a JG I pilot, Ltn Lothar Feige, Jasta10 & Ltn Friedrich Hoffmann, Jasta 11, KIAs, in Spa 38 operating area.

Casualties:

S/Lt Jean Lavergne		Spa 87	P	MIA	IV Armée, Spad.
Lt Bernard de Girval		Spa 73	P	KIA	Spad XIII N° 8352, over Queuneviers
Adj Edmond Pliez &		Sal 28	P	KIA	Salmson 2A2, probably by
S/Lt André Mars		Sal 28	O	KIA	Ltn Albert Wunsch, Jasta 67, (1).
2/Lt John Wilford		USAS	P	KIA	
S/Lt Houpert		Sal 47	O	WIA	
Sgt Pierre Thomas		Sal 6	G	WIA	III° Armée, Salmson 2A2,
MdL Domec		Spa 75	P	WIA	X° Armée, Spad VII.
Adj René Pascaud		Spa 158	P	WIA	Spad, possibly by Ltn
					Felix Bornträger, Jasta 49, (1).
Lt Marcel Berge		Br 209	O	Injured	Bréguet 14A2
Capt Fourchet		???		Injured	

Lt Graffe		69° Cie d'Aérostiers		XF	V° Armée, probably by Ltn Justus Grassmann, Jasta 10, (2).		
Adj Couillard		43° Cie d'Aérostiers		XF	V° Armée, probably by Ltn Fritz Friedrichs, Jasta 10, (18).		
S/Lt Lebouc		54° Cie d'Aérostiers		XF	VI° Armée, probably by Ltn Fritz Friedrichs, Jasta 10 (19).		
Adj Pourrat		90° Cie d'Aérostiers		XF	VI° Armée, probably by Sgt Friedrich Schumacher, Jasta 10, (3).		
???		??? Cie d'Aérostiers		XF	Flanders Sector.		
			O	OK			
Lt Veiss		67° Cie d'Aérostiers			III° Armée, attacked, not		
			O	OK	flamed.		

June 1918 victory claims with dates unknown:

MdL Jacquot &		Br 131					
???		Br 131	Scout	X			1
Lt Génin		Spa 461/CRP					
			Scout	P			–
Lt Génin		Spa 461/CRP					
			Scout	P			–

During the first week of June 1918 French DCA shot down 13 enemy aircraft.
From 13 to 17 June 1918, French DCA claimed four more enemy aircraft.

1 July

Sgt Guy		Spa 38	Rumpler C	X	Cornillet		1
Lt Madon,	CO	Spa 38					36
Lt Vitoux &	CO	Spa 76					3
Lt Romatet	a.	Spa 76	Rumpler C	POW	Breuil		3
Lt Vitoux	CO	Spa 76	EA	X			4
Lt Boyau &		Spa 77					20
S/Lt Haegelen		Spa 100	Balloon	XF			8
S/Lt Peronneau &		Spa 81					8
S/Lt de Cazenove de Pradines		Spa 81	2 seater	X	Reims		6
Adj Marinovitch		Spa 94	Rumpler C	X	Monnes	1715	12
S/Lt Gros,		Spa 154					5
Adj Petit,		Spa 154					3
MdL Ehrlich &		Spa 154					2
S/Lt Coiffard		Spa 154	Balloon	XF	Courmont	1715	6
1/Lt Fish, USAS		???	EA	X			1
Escad 2		???	EA	P	Picardie		–

a. Probably from BG5.

Casualties:

Lt Henri Dupont &		Br 219	P	KIA	VI° Armée, Bréguet 14B2.		
S/Lt Schalbar		Br 219	O	KIA	N° 851, probably by Ltn Ernst Udet, Jasta 4, (37). Forêt de Villers-Cotterêts.		
1/Lt Henry G MacLure		139thUS	P	POW	Spad VII N° 7137, engine failure.		
Sgt James H Baugham		Spa 98	P	WIA	DOW 2 July 1918, Spad.		
Lt Parlier		Br 7	O	WIA	Flak		
Ltn Emile Hochard		Spa 75	P	KIAcc	Spad VII		
Lt Delas &		???	P	KIAcc			
Sgt d'Haze		???	G	KIAcc	Bréguet 14B2		
Sgt Beau		GDE	P	KIAcc	AR		
S/Lt Bernard du Fresne		Sal 14	P	Injured			
Capt Landormy &		Br 238	P	Injured			
Lt Garnier		Br 238	O	Injured			
Adj André		25° Cie d'Aérostiers		XF	Probably by Sgt Friedrich		
			O	OK	Schumacher, Jasta 10 (4).		

2 July

Lt Robin		Spa 97	Balloon	XF			2
???		GC	Balloon	XF	Moulin-le-Courmont		–
2/Lt McArthur,		27thUS					4
1/Lt Hoover,		27thUS					1
1/Lt Schmitt,		27thUS					1
1/Lt Grant,		27thUS					1

1/Lt Norton &	27thUS					1
1/Lt Hudson	27thUS	Pfalz D	X	Verville	0715	1
2/Lt McArthur,	27thUS					5
1/Lt Hoover,	27thUS					2
1/Lt Schmitt,	27thUS					2
1/Lt Grant,	27thUS					2
1/Lt Norton &	27thUS					2
1/Lt Hudson	27thUS	Pfalz D	X	Entrépilly	0745	2
2/Lt O'Neill,	147thUS					1
2/Lt Parry,	147thUS					1
2/Lt Bronson,	147thUS					1
1/Lt Stevens,	147thUS					1
2/Lt McDermott &	147thUS					1
2/Lt Porter	147thUS	Fokker	X	Château-Thierry	1730	1

Casualties:

1/Lt Walter B Wanamaker	27thUS	P	POW	VI° Armée, Nieuport 28 N° 6347, probably by Ltn Ernst Udet, Jasta 4, (39).
1/Lt Edward B Elliott	27thUS	P	KIA	VI° Armée, Nieuport 28 N° 6234, probably by Ltn Erich Löwenhardt, Jasta 10, (33).
Sgt Louis Kernévez	Spa 163	P	KIA	Spad VII, N° 1281, Chezy-sur-Marne, probably by Vzfw Konrad Brendle, Jasta 45, (3).
MdL Jean Graillot	Spa 159	P	KIA	Spad XIII
MdL Jean Cassagne &	Sal 27	P	WIA	DOW
Sgt Maurice Gaillard	Sal 27	G	WIA	DOW, Salmson 2A2
MdL Mercier	Sal 27	G	KIA	Salmson 2A2
S/Lt Caze	Sal 27	O	KIA	Salmson 2A2
Capt Eugène du Vaincey	Spa 255	O	KIA	
S/Lt Comte Henri d'Hunolstein &	Sop 36	P	KIA	VI° Armée, Sopwith N° 9366,
Lt Cambefort	Sop 36	O	OK	aircraft crash-landed by observer.
1/Lt Howard G Mayes	91stUS	P	POW	VIII° Armée, Salmson N° 591,
1/Lt Frank F Schilling	91stUS	O	KIA	probably by Ltn Fitzner, Jasta 65, (6), AOK "C".
Adj Emile Quiles	Spa 48	P	WIA	Spad XIII
S/Lt Paul Croc	Spa 83	P	KIAcc	Spad VII
Adj François Lamy	Spa 85	P	KIAcc	Spad XIII
Sgt Gautier,	V 121	P	KIAcc	
Sol Letroupe &	V 121	M	KIAcc	
Sol Senot	V 121	M	KIAcc	
Cpl Gonnon	V 110	B	KIAcc	

3 July

Adj Gasser	Spa 87	Albatros	X	Forêt de Ris	1830	9
Sgt Fos &	Spa 152					1
Brig Marsaudon	Spa 152	2 seater	XF	Villers-Agron	2015	1
Escad 2	GC	Fokker	X	Aisne		–
Sgt E Régnier	Spa 89	Rumpler C	P			–

Casualties:

Adj Georges Lienhard	Spa 65	P	MIA	Spad XIII, both brought down Vfw
Adj Jacques Gérard	Spa 65	P	MIA	Spad XIII N° 8341 Franz Hemer (12) & Ltn Werner Nöldecke (1) Jasta 6.
Lt Comte Sanche de Gramont de Coigny CO	N 471/CRP	P	MIA	Spad, probably by Ltn Ernst Bormann, Jasta B, (1), VI° Armée.
MdL Jean de Laubier	Spa 77	P	MIA	Spad VII, probably by Ltn Werner Preuss, Jasta 66, (3).
Adj Gillet &	Br 128	P	MIA	Bréguet 14B2, probably by Ltn
Sgt Fernand Duhamel	Br 128	G	MIA	Heinrich Drekmann, Jasta 4, (7).
Sgt Fernand Figon &	Sal 17	P	KIA	
Lt Pierre Ehrhardt	Sal 17	O	KIA	Salmson 2A2, X° Armée
Cpl Gaudellière	R 240	G	KIA	Caudron R11
Sgt Guernet	Spa 31	P	WIA	DOW
Sgt Legoff	Br 128	P	WIA	
Sgt Santos	Br 128	G	WIA	

Adj Camille Guérard &	Br 205	P	OK			
S/Lt Joseph Houillon	Br 205	O	WIA	X° Armée		
Sgt Stary	Br 128	G	WIA	Bombardment of airfield		
MdL Georges Lerche	???	P	KIAcc	Spad VII		
Brig Jean Dessalces	Spa 83	P	KIAcc	Spad VII		
Cpl Enteric &	???	P	KIAcc			
Asp Bouckaert	???	O	KIAcc	AR		
Adj Coache	RGAé	P	KIAcc			
Sol Champchou	V 119	M	KIAcc			
Capt Partridge	V 119	P	Injured	Voisin R		
Sgt Bouchayer	RGAé	P	Injured			
Sgt Derobert	RGAé	P	Injured	Spad XVI		

4 July

S/Lt Chartoire,	Spa 31					2
Adj Deley &	Spa 31					1
MdL Gerbault	Spa 31	2 seater	X	Romigny	1730	2
S/Lt Nogues &	Spa 57					9
Adj Petit-Delchet	Spa 57	Balloon	XF	Coemy	1910	4
Sgt Fos	Spa 152	EA	P	Chatillon-sur-Marne		–
Casualties:						
Lt Debeyer	Br 11	O	WIA	Bréguet 14B2		
MdL de Percy	???	P	KIAcc			
???	45° Cie d' Aérostiers			X° Armée, 17h45, probably		
		O	OK	Sgt Karl Schlegel, Jasta 45, (2).		

5 July

S/Lt Boyau	Spa 77	Balloon	XF	Ville		21
S/Lt Boyau	Spa 77	Scout	X	Ville		22
S/Lt Haegelen	Spa 100	Balloon	XF	Fecamps		9
S/Lt Bourjade,	Spa 152					9
Sgt Robert &	Spa 152					1
Cpl Lac	Spa 152	Balloon	XF	Hauvine		1
S/Lt Coiffard,	Spa 154					7
Adj Petit &	Spa 154					4
MdL Ehrlich	Spa 154	Balloon	XF	Sapincourt	0548	3
Adj Risser &	Br 217					1
Lt Charlet &	Br 217					4
Cpl Richard &	Br 217					1
Cpl Ferrier	Br 217	EA	X	Machemont		1
VII° Armée	a. DCA	EA	X	Baccarat		–
1/Lt Mitchell,	95thUS					3
1/Lt Heinrichs &	95thUS					1
1/Lt Sewall	95thUS	Fokker	X	Château-Thierry		2
1/Lt Simonds &	147thUS					1
2/Lt O'Neill	147thUS	Pfalz DIII	X	Château-Thierry	0930	2
2/Lt Raible	147thUS	Pfalz DIII	X	Château-Thierry	0930	1
Lt Madon	CO Spa 38	Scout	P	Caurel		–
Lt Bonneton	Spa 69	EA	P	Ribecourt-Noyon	1000	–
S/Lt Boyau	Spa 77	EA	P	Aisne		–
???	Sal ??	Albatros	P	Aisne		–

a.   Probably Ltn Hans Beiche & Ltn Hans Albrecht Frhr von Digeon von Monteton, FlAbt (A) 281, KIAs by Flak, AOK "A" Sector.

Casualties:

1/Lt Sidney P Thompson	95thUS	P	POW	VI° Armée, Nieuport 28, probably by Obltn Karl Bolle, CO Jasta B, (20).	
1/Lt Carlyle Rhodes	95thUS	P	POW	VI° Armée, Nieuport 28, probably by Ltn Hermann Frommherz, Jasta B, (5).	
S/Lt Preaux	Sal 4	O	WIA		
1/Lt Benjamin P Harwood	12thUS	O	WIA	Salmson 2A2	
2/Lt Stephen W Thompson	12thUS	O	WIA	Salmson 2A2	
Lt Auguste Gallet	Spa 93	P	KIAcc	Spad VII	
MdL René Le Reide	PilSch	P	KIAcc	Avord	
Sgt Maison,	R 240	P	Injured		
Cpl Gaudillière &	R 240	G	KIA		
Cpl Blond	R 240	G	Injured	Caudron R11	

Lt Richard	67° Cie d'Aérostiers			Probably by Ltn Paul Schwirzke,		
		O	OK	Jasta 68, (1).III° Armée.		

6 July

Lt Carretier &	Sal 39					3
S/Lt Ganne	Sal 39	EA	X	VI° Armée		3
Adj Prince &	Spa 57					1
Cpl Peyrouse	Spa 57	2 seater	XF	S Bligny	0550	1
S/Lt d'Estainville	Spa 87	2 seater	X			2
Patrol	Sal 18	EA	P	V° Armée		–

Casualties:

MdL Vilain	Br 234	P	WIA	VI° Armée		
Sgt Goimard &	Sal 18	P	OK			
Cpl André Rafaitin	Sal 18	G	WIA	V° Armée		
S/Lt Carretier &	Sal 39	P	OK			
S/Lt Georges Rodier	Sal 39	O	WIA	Flak, Salmson 2A2		
1/Lt Roger Clapp &	96thUS	P	KIAcc			
Sgt Robert J Dunn	96thUS	M	KIAcc			
Brig Gabriel Pachy	Spa 81	P	Injured			
Asp Mesh	Br 217	O	Injured			
Cpl Lemeunier	C.I.Perthe	P	Injured			
Asp Chevalier &	,,	O	Injured			
Adj Lechien	,,	G	Injured	Voisin R		
Adj Bocquet	62° Cie d'Aérostiers			VI° Armée, attacked,		
		O	Injured	not flamed.		
1/Lt Leo M Murphy & *	2nd Bal Co USBS		XF	VI° Armée, probably by Sgt		
1/Lt Malcolm A Sedgwick		O	OK	Karl Schlegel, Jasta 45, (3).		

*   First American balloon shot down in flames during the war.

7 July

Adj-Chef Delépine	Spa 62	EA	X	VI° Armée		1
Lt Le Coq de Kerland,	Spa 82					3
S/Lt Flers &	Spa 82					1
Sgt Ventre	Spa 82	Fokker DrI	X	St Pierre Aigle		1
S/Lt Flers	Spa 82	Fokker DrI	X	St Pierre Aigle		2
S/Lt G Thomas	Spa 88	Fokker DrI	X	Corcy	1905	3
Adj Gasser,	Spa 87					10
Lt Henot &	Spa 154					2
MdL de Vuillemin a.	Spa 154	Rumpler C	POW	Rilly-le-Montagne	0915	1
S/Lt Coiffard	Spa 154	Balloon	XF	Courcelles	0900	8
Sgt Imbert &	N 314					1
Sgt Castings b.	N 314	Balloon	XF	Marieulles	1845	1
Cdt Vuillemin & CO	Escad 12					5
Lt Chalus	Escad 12	Rumpler C4	X	Corcy		2
V° Armée	???	Rumpler C	X	Le Charmel		–
VIII° Armée	???	Rumpler C	XF	Serey St Martin		–
1/Lt Cates &	94thUS					1
1/Lt Coolidge	94thUS	Rumpler C	XF	Grisolles	0950	1
1/Lt Cook,	94thUS					1
1/Lt Green &	94thUS					1
1/Lt Loomis	94thUS	EA	X			1
1/Lt McKeown c.	95thUS	EA	X	Château-Thierry	1010	2
1/Lt McKeown	95thUS	EA	X	Château-Thierry	1015	3
V° Armée	GC	EA	P	Bouleuse	0650	–
V° Armée	GC	EA	P	Betheny-Fresnes	0900	–
V° Armée	GC	EA	P	Breuil-Chambry	1855	–

a.   Possibly Ltn Böhmer (P), FlAbt 261 (Lb), POW Reims, about 10 km N Rilly-le-Montagne.
b.   Balloon N° 55, attacked by two Spads at 19h45, observer Vfw Schmeer, was burned during his descent, AOK 19 Sector.
c.   Possibly Vfw Otto Rosenfeld (13v), Jasta 41, KIA Coincy, about 12 km N of Château-Thierry.

Casualties:

Sgt François Castaings	N° 314	P	KIA	Spad XIII N° 4715, probably by	
				MFlak 69, AOK 19 Sector during a	
				balloon attack.	
1/Lt William W Chalmers	94thUS	P	POW	Nieuport 28 N° 6181, Château-	
				Thierry probably by a Jasta 26 pilot.	
1/Lt Stuart E McKeown	95thUS	P	POW	Nieuport 28, probably by a Jasta 26 pilot.	
S/Lt Champsaur	???	O	WIA	Ground fire.	

| Sol Boudret | | Br 206 | M | Injured | Bréguet 14B2 | | |
| ??? | | 90° Cie d'Aérostiers | | | VI° Armée, probably by Ltn Erich Raabe, Jasta 41, (4). This balloon trap was carrying 150 kg of explosives in its basket but the explosion didn't affect the attacking plane. | | |

8 July

S/Lt Cordonnier		Spa 15	Scout	X	Vierzy	0950	5
Capt Pinsard	CO	Spa 23	Balloon	XF	Boinville		21
Adj Bouyer &		Spa 49					9
MdL Hamot		Spa 49	Rumpler C	XF	Burnhaupt	0907	2
S/Lt Nuville		Spa 57	2 seater	XF	N Tingneux	0915	8
MdL Conraux		Spa 83	Scout	X	Louatre		2
Sgt Issaly		Spa 112	EA	XF	III° Armée		2
S/Lt Vial		Spa 152	2 seater	X	Ste Geneviève		5
S/Lt Vial		Spa 152	EA	X			6
S/Lt Bourjade		Spa 152	Balloon	XF	Ivoiry		10
2/Lt Ponder, USAS		Spa 163	2 seater	X	Sommepy		2
Capt Weiller &	CO	Br 224					3
S/Lt Payart &		Br 224					2
Adj-Chef Moreau &		Br 224					2
Cpl Marquet		Br 224	Scout	X	Villers-le-Petit-Blanzy		1
Capt Weiller &		Br 224					4
S/Lt Payart &		Br 224					3
S/Lt Guidot &		Br 224					1
???		Br 224	Scout	X	E Ambley		?
Capt de Luppe		Spa 83	EA	P			–
???		GC	2 EA	P	Aisne		–

Casualties:

Sgt Dudley Tucker		Spa 15	P	MIA	Spad VII, possibly by Obltn Oskar Frhr von Boenigk, Jasta 21s, (13).
S/Lt Maurice André		Spa 86	P	MIA	Spad VII, E Cutry, probably by Vfw Richard Schneider, Jasta 19, (1).
MdL Alphonse Hays &		Br 224	P	MIA	X° Armée
Asp Maxime Girard		Br 224	O	MIA	Bréguet 14A2
2/Lt Maxwell O Parry		147thUS	P	KIA	VI° Armée, Nieuport 28 N° 4264, probably by Ltn Fritz Friedrichs, Jasta 10, (21).
Sgt Camille Issaly		Spa 112	P	WIA	Spad VII, III° Armée
Adj Henri Chevalier		Spa 49	P	WIA	Spad VII, VII° Armée, ground fire.
Lt Baumont &		C.I. Perthe	P	KIAcc	
Sol Montalant		„	G	KIAcc	Bréguet 14B2
Adj Bertrand		Sal 10	P	OK	
S/Lt Mathusière		Sal 10	O	Injured	
Cpl Berger		GDE	P	Injured	Spad
Sgt Larefait &		Spa 215	P	Injured	
S/Lt Paul Gouy		Spa 215	O	Injured	Spad XI
Cpl Edouard Pinot		Spa 84	P	Injured	
Lt Marcel Regnault		Spa 79	P	Injured	Bréguet 14A2
Cpl Rivière		C.I. Perthe	P	Injured	Spad VII
Sol Haenssens		C.I. Perthe	M	Injured	Sopwith
Sgt Ferte &		„	P	Injured	
Adj Simonet		??? Cie d'Aérostiers			Attacked by two Albatros, not flamed.

9 July

Lt Kauffmann &		Spa 79				1
Adj Lesec		Spa 79	EA	XF	Ressons	1

Casualties:

EV1 François Michel	*	CAM	P	MIA	Spad codé 3, North Sea	
Sgt François Bourbon &		Br 202	P	MIA	Flak, III° Armée	
S/Lt Louis Colas		Br 271	O	MIA	Flak, Bréguet 14A2	
EV1 François Michel		Navy	P	POW	FTL German territory.	
Cpl Deprez		GDE	P	KIAcc	Nieuport XXIV	
Sgt Romanet		???	P	Injured	Spad	
Asp Monsacre		GDE	P	Injured	Spad XI	

* Dunkerque.

10 July

Lt Bonneton		Spa 69	EA	X	Noyon-Ribecourt	3
S/Lt Haegelen,		Spa 100				10
MdL Gaudry &		Spa 100				1
S/Lt Nuville		Spa 57	2 seater	XF	Baslieux	1055	9
1/Lt Roosevelt		95thUS	Fokker	X	Bouvardes	1
Lt Daurat &	CO	Br 134				–
???		Br 134	Scout	P		–

Casualties:

Cpl Pichereau	RGAé	P	MIA	
Maj Harry M Brown	96thUS	P	POW	
2/Lt Harold A MacChesney	96thUS	O	POW	Bréguet 14B2 N° 4012
1/Lt Robert C Browning	96thUS	P	POW	
1/Lt James E Duke, Jr	96thUS	O	POW	Bréguet 14B2 N° 4015
1/Lt Henry C Lewis	96thUS	P	POW	
1/Lt Caxton H Tichenor	96thUS	O	POW	Bréguet 14B2 N° 4020
1/Lt Durwood L McDonald	96thUS	P	POW	
2/Lt Alfred R Strong	96thUS	O	POW	Bréguet 14B2 N° 4003
1/Lt George I Patterman	96thUS	O	POW	
1/Lt Herbert D Smith	96thUS	P	POW	Bréguet 14B2 N° 4005
1/Lt Joseph M Mellen	96thUS	P	POW	
2/Lt Rowan H Tucker	96thUS	O	POW	Bréguet 14B2 N° 4019
Lt Didier Daurat	CO	Br 134	P	WIA	Bréguet 14B2
Sgt Noël		GDE	P	Injured	Sopwith

All these Bréguets of the 96th Bombardment Squadron, USAS, became lost and landed intact on a German airfield where the crews were taken prisoner.

11 July

Lt Le Coq de Kerland	CO	Spa 82	EA	X		4
Lt Le Coq de Kerland	CO	Spa 82	EA	X		5
MdL Dequeker		Spa 163	Scout	X		2
Lt Fraslon &		Spa 315				1
MdL Uteau	a.	Spa 315	Scout	X	Altkirch	1750	1
Cdt Vuillemin &	CO	Escad 12				6
Lt Dagnaux		Escad 12	EA	X		4
1/Lt Tobin &		103rdUS				0750	1
1/Lt Jones	b.	103rdUS	2 seater	XF	Thiaucourt	1
S/Lt Prévost		Spa 163	EA	P	Sommepy	–
???	c.	GC	2 seater	P		–

a.   Possibly Gefr Johann Diebold, Jasta 71, WIA Fontaine, 17h10.
b.   Probably OfStv Franz Trautmann, WIA, & Uffz Jucknat, FlAbt 279 (A), FTL between the lines, AOK "C" Sector.
c.   Possibly Uffz Kastner & Ltn Kurz, FlAbt 46Lb, WIAs, AOK "C" Sector.

Casualties:

Cpl Henri Bayde	Spa 163	P	WIA	Spad VII N° 5554, crash-landed near Tahure.
Adj Maisonnave	???	P	KIAcc	Biscavosse.
Capt François Laurent	Spa 85	P	Injured	

12 July

S/Lt Coiffard,		Spa 154				9
S/Lt Waddington &		Spa 154				5
MdL Ehrlich		Spa 154	Albatros D	X	Rosnay	0655	4
Capt Homo &	CO	Br 235				5
S/Lt Guérin	a.	Br 235	Albatros D	XF	W Bois de Vrigny	0650	1
V° Armée		GC	EA	X	W Bois de Vrigny	–
II° Armée		Br ??	EA	X	Tresauvaux	–
1/Lt Putnam		139thUS	2 seater	P		–
Cpl Pauly &		Br 266				–
2/Lt Urband USAS		Br 266	Scout	P	VII° Armée	–
Sgt Poncet &		Reco				–
???		Reco	Scout	P		–

a.   Probably Uffz Karl Röttgen, Jasta 39, KIA Vrigny.

Casualties:

1/Lt Gilbert N Jerome	Spa 90	P	KIA	Probably by Obltn Hans Schleiter, Jasta 70 (3), VIII° Armée.
QM Eugène Kerfanto &	*	CAM	P	KIA	Camaret, Tellier 200HP

EV Henri Fayout	*	CAM	O	KIA	N° 73.	
Lt Boulay		??? Cie d'Aérostiers			Attacked by an Albatros,	
			O	OK	not flamed.	
Sgt Pierre Poncet &		Reco	P	OK	Shot down during combat.	
???		Reco	O	OK		

13 July – No Claims
Casualties:

Brig Clerc &		Sal 5	P	OK	
Sgt Gérard		Sal 5	G	KIA	
Lt Philippe Carré de Busserole		Sal 106	O	WIA	DOW 16 July 1918 Salmson 2A2
Brig Georges Lecoq		Spa 84	P	KIAcc	Spad XIII
Capt Georges Raymond CO		Spa 3	P	Injured	DOW 4 October 1918, Spad XIII.

14 July

S/Lt Cousin &		Spa 157			1
Patrol		Spa 157	EA	X	–
V° Armée		31 DCA	EA	X	Gueux	–
Escadre 2		GC	EA	P	–

Casualties:

Cpl Roger de Elduezabel &	Br 233	P	MIA	Bréguet 14B2, probably by Ltn
Lt Le Gallic	Br 233	O	MIA	Erich Löwenhardt, Jasta 10, (39).
1/Lt Quentin Roosevelt	95thUS	P	KIA	Nieuport 28 N° 6177, probably by Uffz Carl Gräper, Jasta 50, (1).
S/Lt Barthelemy	Sal 280	O	WIA	Salmson 2A2
Sol Diligent	Spa 73	M	Injured	
Adj Laurent Veau	Spa 62	P	Injured	Spad VII
Adj-Chef Maurice Delépine	Spa 62	P	Injured	Spad VII

15 July
The last German Offensive, The Second Battle of the Marne, or the Battle of Reims (Operation "Friedenstrum" – Peace Offensive), commenced this date.

Lt de Turenne &	CO	Spa 12					11
Asp Herlemont		Spa 12	Fokker D7	X	Château-Thierry	2030	1
Lt Barny de Romanet		Spa 37	DFW C	X	Laval		6
S/Lt Nuville,		Spa 57					10
Adj Vanier &		Spa 57					1
S/Lt Fraissinet	a.	Spa 57	Albatros C	X	Fleury-la-Rivière	0455	6
Lt Tarascon		Spa 62	Albatros	X	Villers-Cotterêts		12
S/Lt Pinard &		Br 66					1
1/Lt Shaffer USAS		Br 66	Scout	XF	Aisne		4
S/Lt Boyau		Spa 77	Fokker D7	X	SE Dormans	1550	23
Adj Dhome,		Spa 81					9
Adj Malfanti,		Spa 81					3
MdL Santelli &		Spa 81					6
Sgt Boggs		Spa 81	Balloon	XF	N Main de Massiges		1
Capt Tourangin &	CO	Spa 89					3
S/Lt Daubail		Spa 89	Fokker	X	Chatillon	1540	1
Sgt Crehore		Spa 94	2 seater	X	Vouziers	1020	2
Adj Marinovitch,		Spa 94					14
Lt Carbonnel &		Spa 94					1
MdL Ducornet		Spa 93	Rumpler C	X	Moronvillers	1020	2
Sgt Martin &		Spa 94					2
Sgt Grimouille		Spa 94	Rumpler C	XF	Moronvillers	1020	1
Adj Lucas &		Spa 97					1
S/Lt Herbelin		Spa 97	2 seater	X	French lines		11
MdL Camus &		Spa 100					1
Sgt Morel d'Arleux		Spa 100	Scout	X	Picardie		1
MdL Burke &		Br 132					1
Cpl Vidal		Br 132	Scout	XF	Marcilly	1930	1
Cpl Gloaguen &		Br 132					1
??? &		Br 132					?
Lt Gros &		Br 132					1
Adj Lasserre		Br 132	Scout	XF	Jaulgonne		1
S/Lt Bourjade		Spa 152	Balloon	XF	Champagne		11

S/Lt Bourjade		Spa 152	Balloon	XF	Champagne	12
S/Lt Bourjade		Spa 152	Balloon	XF	Main de Massiges	13
Capt Lahoulle,	CO	Spa 154				9
S/Lt Coiffard,		Spa 154				10
Adj Chevalier &		Spa 154				1
Sgt Abbott		Spa 154	Balloon	XF	Goussancourt	1030	1
Capt Lahoulle,	CO	Spa 154				10
S/Lt Coiffard &		Spa 154				11
Adj Chevalier		Spa 154	Balloon	XF	Goussancourt	1032	2
S/Lt Coiffard,		Spa 154				12
MdL Ehrlich &		Spa 154				5
S/Lt Gros		Spa 154	Balloon	XF	S Le Charmel	1905	6
Capt Lahoulle	CO	Spa 154	Balloon	XF	N Goussancourt	1905	11
Adj Viguier &		Spa 157				2
MdL Froissard		Spa 157	Scout	X		3
Lt Senart		Spa 157	EA	X		2
S/Lt Givon,		R 240				3
Asp Roques &		R 240				1
Sgt Coolen		R 240	EA	X	Aisne	1
Lt Cauchy &		GB 9				1
Sgt Dervan		GB 9	Scout	X	Aisne	1
Capt Petit &	CO	GB 5				2
MdL Lepers		GB 5	Fokker D7	XF	Aisne	4
Sgt Fabre		???	EA	X		–
???		Escad 12	EA	X	Aisne	–
MdL de St Sulpice &		Sal 16				–
S/Lt Carayon		Sal 16	EA	P	Aisne	–
Adj Dormal &		Sal 51				–
Lt Guillon		Sal 51	EA	P		5
MdL Cavieux		Spa 76	EA	P	Chavenay	1300	–
Sgt Crehore		Spa 94	EA	P		–
Adj Marinovitch		Spa 94	Scout	P		1010	–
MdL de Gaillard de La Valdène		Spa 95	2 seater	P	St Hilaire-le-Petit	–
Lt Gros &		Br 132				–
Adj Lasserre		Br 132				–
Cpl Gloaguen &		Br 132				–
???		Br 132	EA	P	Champagne	–
2/Lt Abernathy		147thUS	Fokker	P		–
S/Lt Bourjade		Spa 152	Balloon	P		–
Lt Henriot		Spa 161	EA	P	Ville-en-Tardenois	1200	–
Patrol		GC 21	EA	P		–
Escadre 2		GC	3 EA	P	Champagne	–
???		???	6 EA	P	Champagne	–
???		GC	EA	P	Aisne	–
???		GC	Balloon	P	Aisne	–

a.   Probably Sgt Wilhelm Hentchel & Lt Erwin Müller, POWs.

Casualties:

Sgt Rolland &	AR 267	P	MIA	
Brig Desmoulin	AR 267	G	MIA	AR LIA2, IV° Armée
Lt Marcel Guillot &	Br 29	P	POW	
Sgt Beraud	Br 29	G	WIA/POW	Bréguet 14B2
Cpl René Petitberghien	Spa 87	P	KIA	Spad XIII
MdL Pierre Schuster	Spa 100	P	KIA	Spad XIII, Comblizy
Sgt Marcel Denis	Spa 162	P	WIA	DOW, Spad XIII, possibly by Uffz Reinhold Neumann, Jasta 36, (1).
Lt Delord &	Br 234	P	KIA	
S/Lt Fontaine	Br 234	O	KIA	Bréguet 14A2
S/Lt Vacher &	Sal 14	P	KIA	
Asp Marnier	Sal 14	O	KIA	Salmson, Jonchery, XF.
1/Lt Manderson Lehr &	Br 117	P	KIA	Bréguet 14B2, crash-landed by
S/Lt Carles	Br 117	O	Injured	Carles. Possibly by Vfw Erich Buder, Jasta 26, (4).
1/Lt Richard W Moody	Br 129	O	WIA	DOW
Cpl René Tognard	Spa 161	P	WIA	Spad VIII, V° Armée
Capt Augustin Lahoulle	Spa 154	P	WIA	Spad VII, V° Armée
MdL Raymond Merklen	Spa 154	P	WIA	Spad XIII, V° Armée

Adj Marcel Gasser	Spa 87	P	WIA	Spad VII
Adj Pierre Igert	Spa 100	P	WIA	Spad XIII
S/Lt Charles Besson	AR 270	O	WIA	AR LIA2, ground fire
MdL Bouvard &	AR 267	P	WIA	IV° Armée.
S/Lt Soule	AR 267	O	WIA	AR LIA2, ground fire
Sgt Lassaigne &	Br 222	P	WIA	FTL, V° Armée
S/Lt Chastaing	Br 222	O	WIA	DOW Bréguet 14B2
Sgt Gros &	Br 222	P	WIA	FTL after combat
S/Lt Mazet	Br 222	O	WIA	Bréguet 14B2, V° Armée
MdL Vilain	Br 234	G	WIA	Bréguet 14A2
Lt Laugier	63 SPAé	O	WIA	Salmson 2A2, V° Armée
MdL Marcel de St-Sulpice &	Sal 16	P	WIA	
S/Lt Jean Carayon	Sal 16	O	WIA	Salmson 2A2, V° Armée
MdL Durand &	Sal 4	P	WIA	
S/Lt Pierre Prélot	Sal 4	O	WIA	Salmson 2A2, ground fire
Cpl André Rafaitin	Sal 16	G	WIA	Salmson
Sgt Glenn N Sitterly	R 46	P	OK	Caudron R11, probably by Ltn Kurt
Sgt-Maj Henri Lacassagne &	R 46	G	WIA	Jacob, Jasta 36, (5).
Sol William MacKerness (American)	R 46	G	WIA	
Sol Delcroix &	R 240	G	WIA	
Sol Renauld	R 240	G	WIA	Caudron R11
SM Marie Amiot	SC Aéro	P	KIAcc	Seine FBA
Sgt Louis Della-Via &	Spa 69	P	OK	
S/Lt Bonfils	Spa 69	O	Injured	Bréguet 14A2
Asp Bastie	GDE	P	Injured	Nieuport XXVII
S/Lt Carles	Br 117	P	Injured	Bréguet 14A2
S/Lt A Guy	44° Cie d'Aérostiers		XF	
		O	OK	
S/Lt Fleury &	21° Cie d'Aérostiers		XF	IV° Armée
Asp Cordaillat		O	OK	
Lt Verdier	37° Cie d'Aérostiers			VIII° Armée, balloon
		O	Injured	attacked, not flamed.
1/Lt Glenn Phelps &	2nd Bal Co, USAS		XF	Villers-sur-Marne, this same balloon had
1/Lt Roy K Patterson		O	OK	been attacked earlier and not flamed.

16 July

Lt de Turenne,	CO	Spa 12					12
MdL Beaunée &		Spa 12					1
Cpl Haller	a.	Spa 12	Albatros C	X	S Reims		1
Lt Barny de Romanet,		Spa 37					7
Adj Lienhart &		Spa 37					1
MdL Francisquet		Spa 37	DFW C	X	Champagne		3
Lt Nungesser		Spa 65	Scout	X	Mericourt	1325	38
S/Lt Battesti &		Spa 73					6
S/Lt Claude-La Fontaine		Spa 73	EA	X			2
Sgt Rouanet &		Spa 98					1
Sgt Vauquelin		Spa 98	2 seater	X	Ville-en-Tardenois		1
Sgt Rouanet		Spa 98	Balloon	XF	Gratreuil		2
Lt Cauboue	CO	Spa 98	Balloon	XF	SE Tahure		4
Lt Fonck		Spa 103	2 seater	XF	Dormans	1710	50
Lt Fonck		Spa 103	2 seater	XF	S Dormans	1712	51
MdL Ehrlich		Spa 154	Balloon	XF	Anthenay	1345	6
Adj Bohan &		Spa 212					1
Lt Cassé		Spa 212	EA	XF	Grand-Roy		1
MdL Lhomme &		Br 227					1
Lt Allanic &		Br 227					1
Sgt Lemarie		Br 227	Albatros D	XF	N Andechy		2
???		GC	EA	X	Aisne		–
1/Lt Tobin	b.	103rdUS	Pfalz DIII	XF	Vieville-en-Haye	1015	2
1/Lt Sewell &		95thUS					3
1/ Lt Curtis		95thUS	2 seater	X	Crezancy		2
1/Lt Vann		95thUS	Albatros C	X	Champaillet		1
1/Lt Miller		27thUS	Balloon	XF	S Coupeils	1415	1
1/Lt Miller		27thUS	Balloon	XF	S Le Charmel	1815	2

1/Lt Vasconcelles	27thUS	Rumpler C	X	W Dormans	1810	1
2/Lt Clapp	27thUS	Rumpler C	X	Mezy		2
2/Lt Porter,	147thUS					1
2/Lt Simonds &	147thUS					2
2/Lt Jones	147thUS	Fokker	X	Dormans	1415	1
S/Lt Casale &	Spa 38					–
Cpl Foucon	Spa 38	EA	P	Pont Faverger		–
Patrol	Spa 163	2 Balloons	P			–
1/Lt Tobin	103rdUS	Pfalz DIII	P	Vieville-en-Haye		–
1/Lt Cassard	147thUS	EA	FTL	Dormans		–
2/Lt Simonds	147thUS	2 seater	FTL	Dormans		–
???	GC	3 EA	P	Aisne		–
???	GB	EA	P	Aisne		–

a. Possibly Sgt Hentschel & Ltn Müller, FlAbt(A)222, POWs.
b. Possibly Flg Franz Schlotter & Ltn Walter Reuss, FlAbt 31, KIAs, AOK "C" Sector.

Casualties:

MdL Emile Vieil	Spa 161	P	MIA	Spad VII, V° Armée
Cpl Roger Guitoger	Spa 96	P	MIA	Spad VII
Lt Lacoste &	V 116	P	MIA	
MdL Boissel	V 116	G	MIA	Voisin R10
Cpl Louis Gloaguen &	Br 132	P	POW	WIA Bréguet 14 N° 4,
Cpl René Burckel	Br 132	G	MIA	hit by flak.
1/Lt Malcolm B Gunn	27thUS	P	KIA	Nieuport 28 N° 6302, VI° Armée, probably by Uffz Schneck, Jasta 9(1).
1/Lt Daniel W Cassard	147thUS	P	KIA	Nieuport 28 N° 6210, VI° Armée, Dormans, probably by Ltn Walter Blume, CO Jasta 9, (13).
1/Lt John W Van Heuval	91stUS	P	WIA	Pont-à-Mousson
2/Lt Frederick K Hirth	91stUS	O	KIA	Salmson 2A2
Brig Vautrot &	Sal 27	P	KIA	
S/Lt Joseph Jannon	Sal 27	O	WIA	IV° Armée
S/Lt André Barcat	Spa 153	P	KIA	Spad XIII, Malmy, probably by Jasta 19 pilots.
S/Lt Georges Lutzius	Spa 153	P	KIA	Spad XIII, Vrigny, probably by Jasta 19 pilots.
Adj-Chef Castets &	Br 236	P	KIA	IV° Armée, Bréguet 14A2, probably
S/Lt Laharrague	Br 236	O	KIA	by Ltn Franz Büchner, Jasta 13,(10).
1/Lt Robert F Raymond	27thUS	P	POW	Nieuport 28, VI° Armée probably by Obltn Bruno Loerzer, CO JG III,(26).
Adj Jules Bohan &	Spa 212	P	WIA	
Lt Eugène Cassé	Spa 212	O	WIA	Spad XI, V° Armée
Lt Le Gad	R 239	O	WIA	Caudron R11
MdL Hervé du Pontavice de Hussey &	Sal 51	P	KIAcc	
Sol Albert Léchappé	Sal 51	G	KIAcc	Salmson 2A2, V° Armée
Brig Edouard Deraisme &	Spa 278	P	KIAcc	X° Armée
S/Lt Pasquet	Spa 278	O	Injured	Spad XVI
Brig Davis	GDE	P	Injured	Nieuport XXVII
Sol Poyat	C.I.Perthe	G	Injured	Collision
Sol Pittion	C.I.Perthe	G	Injured	Collision
Adj Ruyer &	Sop 285	P	Injured	
1/Lt ??? USAS	Sop 285	O	Injured	
Lt Beix	65° Cie d'Aérostiers		XF	IV° Armée, probably by Vfw
		O	OK	Richard Rübe, Jasta 67, (3).
Lt Sauvage	57° Cie d'Aérostiers			IV° Armée, attacked, not
		O	OK	flamed, hit 63 times.
???	49° Cie d'Aérostiers		XF	Probably by Obltn Oskar v
		O	OK	Boenigk, Jasta 21s, (15).

Two other balloons were attacked but not flamed in the Champagne Sector.

17 July

Lt Madon	CO	Spa 38	Scout	X	Main de Massiges	0716	37
Lt Madon	CO	Spa 38	Scout	X	Gueux		38
S/Lt Nogues &		Spa 57					10
Cpl Rotureau		Spa 57	Balloon	XF	N Anthenay	0716	2
S/Lt Boyau		Spa 77	EA	X	NE Nesle-le-Repons		24
Sgt Guillaume &		Spa 77					1

1/Lt Davis, USAS		Spa 77	EA	X	St Agnan		1
S/Lt Bourjade		Spa 152	Balloon	XF	S Nauroy		14
S/Lt Coiffard,	CO	Spa 154					13
MdL Ehrlich &		Spa 154					7
Sgt Hubert		Spa 154	Balloon	XF	NE Moronvillers	0530	1
S/Lt Coiffard,	CO	Spa 154					14
MdL Ehrlich &		Spa 154					8
Sgt Hubert		Spa 154	Balloon	XF	Moronvillers	0535	2
S/Lt Waddington &		Spa 154					6
MdL Barbreau		Spa 154	Balloon	XF	Beine	0845	4
Adj Pigier,		R 239					2
Lt Decaze &		R 239					4
Adj Pousse		R 239	Scout	XF	Fère-en-Tardenois	2015	1
2/Lt McArthur		27thUS	2 seater	X	Chassins		6
2/Lt Roberts		27thUS	2 seater	X	SW Dormans		1
IV° Armée	a.	???	FDH	X	Melette		–
Lt Madon	CO	Spa 38	EA	P	IV° Armée		–
Lt Madon	CO	Spa 38	EA	P	IV° Armée		–
Patrol		Spa 31	EA	P	V° Armée		–
Patrol		Spa 57	EA	P	V° Armée		–
Patrol		Spa 103	2 seater	P	Curchery-Bois de Roi		–
Patrol		Spa 103	2 seater	P	Jonchery-Champlat	0830	–
Lt Pitault &		Br 134					–
Brig Poulalion		Br 134	Scout	P			
S/Lt Bourjade		Spa 152	Balloon	P	NE Vaudesincourt		–
Sgt Heritier		Spa 152	Balloon	P	N Moronvillers		–
S/Lt Prévost &		Spa 163					–
MdL Dequeker		Spa 163	Scout	P	Main de Massiges		–
Lt Génin		Spa 461/CRP	EA	P			–
Escadre 2		GC	2 EA	P			–

a. Friedrichschafen GIII N° 774/18, BG II.

Casualties:

Adj Auguste Baux	a.	Spa 103	P	MIA	Spad XIII N° 2683, shot down by a two-seater over Curchery, at 08h45.
Sgt Foin &		Spa 140	P	MIA	Spad XI, probably by Ltn Alfred
S/Lt Borg		Spa 140	O	MIA	Lenz, Jasta 22s, (5). IV° Armée.
Sgt Albert Rochard &		Br 132	P	MIA	
S/Lt Emile Delaire		Br 132	O	MIA	
Sgt Gaston Renard &		Br 134	P	MIA	
MdL Pascal Chadefaux		Br 134	G	MIA	
Sgt Raymond Cornu &		Br 134	P	MIA	
Sgt Julien Simonnot		Br 134	G	MIA	
1/Lt Henry G MacClure		139thUS	P	POW	Spad VII N° 7137 "9" VIII° Armée, probably by Flg Oeltschner, Jasta 64w (1), AOK "C" Sector.
Sgt Goimard &		Sal 16	P	OK	
S/Lt Antoine Poli		Sal 16	O	KIA	Salmson 2A2
Sgt Marcel Gottlieb &		Br 132	P	KIA	
Sgt Léon Renard		Br 132	G	WIA	POW
Lt Amédée Pitault &		Br 134	P	OK	
Brig André Poulalion		Br 134	M	WIA	DOW, Bréguet
Sgt Alfred Dubois		Sal 39	P	WIA	Flak, Salmson 2A2
Adj François Pousse		R 239	G	WIA	
Cpl Rateau		Br 238	P	Injured	Bréguet 14A2
Adj Ruyer		GDE	P	Injured	Sopwith
Lt Guidal		C.I.Perthe	P	Injured	Spad XIII
S/Lt André Caniaux		76° Cie Aérostiers			Attacked, not flamed,
			O	WIA	

a. Gefr Johann Baur & Ltn Georg Hengl FA 295, who claimed two Spads over Courton Wood, 1000hrs.

---

18 July

The Second Battle of the Marne terminates, and the Allies counter-attack in what was known as the Aisne-Marne Operation, also the Battle of Château-Thierry, began in the same area.

??? &		Sal 17				?
S/Lt Guinouard		Sal 17	EA	POW		1
MdL Fouilhaux &		Sal 53				1
S/Lt Prengrueber		Sal 53	EA	X	Soissons	1

Adj Hudellet		Spa 75	Balloon	XF	Oulchy-le-Château	2
S/Lt Barbaza &		Spa 77				3
MdL Armangué		Spa 77	EA	X	Armentières	1
MdL de Tonnac de						
Villeneuve		Spa 80	Scout	X	Aisne	2
Lt Desprez		Spa 83	EA	X	NE Soissons	1
Lt Fonck		Spa 103	EA	X	Cuchery	1120	52
Lt Fonck		Spa 103	EA	X	Cuchery	1130	53
Adj Parcejoux &		Sal 106				1
S/Lt Guérineau		Sal 106	2 seater	X	E Tahure	1
S/Lt Chavannes	a.	Spa 112	Fokker D7	X	Rozières-sur-Crise	6
S/Lt Douillet		Spa 124	Scout	X	Navarin-Sommepy	3
S/Lt Dupuy &		Br 131				1
Sgt Gautier &		Br 131				1
Sgt Emmanuelli &		Br 131				1
Asp Ulrich		Br 131	Fokker D7	X	Villemoyenne	0825	1
Lt Thuillier &		Br 131				2
Lt Fischer &		Br 131				1
Sgt Jacquot &		Br 131				1
Adj Lebrand	b.	Br 131	Fokker D7	X	Neuilly-St Front	0835	1
Lt de Sevin de Quincy	CO	Spa 151	Scout	X			2
S/Lt Coiffard &	CO	Spa 154				15
MdL Ehrlich		Spa 154	Balloon	XF	Forêt de Ris	0915	9
MdL Barbreau &		Spa 154				5
Sgt Abbott		Spa 154	Balloon	XF	Forêt de Ris	0915	2
S/Lt Coiffard,	CO	Spa 154				16
S/Lt Waddington &		Spa 154				7
S/Lt Gros		Spa 154	Rumpler C	X	E Bois de Beine	0945	7
IV° Armée		???	Balloon	XF	Aubérive	1555	–
1/Lt Calkins USAS &		Br 129				1
1/Lt Bourchers USAS		Br 129	EA	X			1
Patrol		Spa 3	Scout	P	Chaumuzy	1615	–
Lt Madon	CO	Spa 38	2 seater	P	N Main de Massiges	–
Cpl Foucon		Spa 38	Fokker	P	Main de Massiges	–
Patrol		Spa 69	EA	P		–
S/Lt Poirier		Spa 99	EA	P		–
??? &		Br 134				–
Cpl Callois		Br 134	EA	P		–
??? &		Br 279				–
S/Lt Duplastre		Br 279	Scout	P	Aisne	–
X° Armée		CA	EA	P	Aisne	–
???		GC	Balloon	P		–
???		GB	4 EA	P		–
???		GC	4 EA	P		–

a.   Possibly Gefr Ludwig Müller, Jasta 10, KIA Chaudun, about 5 km W of Rozières-sur-Crise.
b.   Possibly Ltn Moritz Bretschneider-Bodemer (6v), Jasta 6, KIA Grand-Rozoy, about 12 kn NNE of Neuilly-St-Front.

Casualties:

Lt Pierre Daire	Spa 159	P	MIA	Spad XIII, probably by Ltn Karl Bolle, Jasta B, (24).
Sgt Bernhardt &	Br 210	P	MIA	
S/Lt L'Etang	Br 210	O	MIA	Bréguet 14A2 N° 696.
Capt Maurice Aron & CO	Br 104	P	MIA	X° Armée
Lt Harle	Br 104	O	MIA	Bréguet 14B2
Cpl Reby	Br 104	P	MIA	Bréguet 14B2
S/Lt Jean Bourhis	Spa 80	P	KIA	Spad XIII, probably by Ltn Alois Heldmann, Jasta 10, (8), X° Armée, N Chaudun.
1/Lt Lawrence D Layton (American)	Spa 77	P	KIA	Spad
S/Lt Marcel Gasser	Sal 8	O	KIA	Ground fire.
S/Lt Pierre Nodet	Sal 8	O	KIA	
Cpl Louis L. Byers	Spa 38	P	POW	Spad XIII, IV° Armée
MdL Glenn Sitterly,	R 46	P	OK	
??? &	R 46	G	OK	
Sgt Marcel Faivre	R 46	G	KIA	Caudron R11
Cpl Georges Cumont	Spa 75	P	WIA	Spad VII, X° Armée
S/Lt Jean Debard	Spa 82	P	WIA	Spad XIII
MdL Louis Quet	Spa 266	P	OK	

S/Lt Merot		Spa 266	O	WIA	Spad XI, X° Armée		
Sgt Adrien Pauquet		Spa 55	P	WIA	Spad XVI, X° Armée		
S/Lt Jean Etève		Spa 42	O	WIA	Spad XIA2, X° Armée		
S/Lt Duplastre		Br 279	O	WIA	Bréguet 14A2, X° Armée		
Adj Eugène Lebraud		Br 131	G	WIA			
Adj René Germain &		Br 132	P	WIA			
Sgt Pierre Dionnet		Br 132	G	WIA			
Sgt Paul Danton		Br 134	P	OK			
Asp Gaston Camot		Br 134	O	WIA	Flak		
Sgt Caccia		Br 11	P	WIA	Bréguet 14A2		
MdL Mouchot &		Sal 105	P	WIA	DOW		
MdL Cirotteau		Sal 105	O	WIA	DOW Salmson 2A2, V° Armée		
MdL Masurel &		Sal 8	P	WIA			
Lt Lafeuille		Sal 8	O	WIA	Salmson 2A2, X° Armée		
Cpl Laserre &		Sal 16	P	OK	Salmson 2A2		
S/Lt Alexandre Perugia		Sal 16	O	WIA	DOW 20 July 1918		
Adj-Chef Louis Majorel		Sal 52	P	OK			
Lt André Péronne		Sal 52	O	WIA			
Adj Marcel Thierry &		Sal 18	P	OK			
S/Lt Lavedrine		Sal 18	O	WIA	Salmson 2A2		
S/Lt Jean Arnoux &		Sal 253					
S/Lt Georges Derre		Sal 253	P	WIA	Salmson 2A2, X° Armée		
1/Lt Floyd E Evans		88thUS	P	WIA	Salmson 2A2, ground fire.		
Cpl Bordes &		Br 226	P	WIA			
MdL Jus		Br 226	O	OK	V° Armée		
S/Lt Arcady Novocieloff		PilSch	P	KIAcc	Hourtin		
Brig René Dupart,		R 46	P	Injured			
S/Lt Raymond Crémieux &		R 46	O	Injured	Landing accident.		
Sol Pelletier		R 46	G	Injured	Caudron R11		
Sgt Grandon		Br 211	P	Injured			
S/Lt François		Br 287	O	Injured	Bréguet 14A2		
Adj Petitjean		Br 238	P	Injured	Bréguet 14A2		
S/Lt Mazerat		49° Cie d'Aérostiers		XF	V° Armée, probably by Ltn		
			O	OK	Herbert Mahn, Jasta 72s, (1).		
Lt Jacquart		33° Cie d'Aérostiers			X° Armée		
			O	Injured			
Lt Brisset		36° Cie d'Aérostiers			II° Armée		
Lt Desbouis					Observers landed safely.		
Lt Clément		86° Cie d'Aérostiers			II Armée		
???		76° Cie d'Aérostiers			V° Armée, attacked 12h30,		
			O	OK	not flamed.		

19 July

Capt Pinsard	CO	Spa 23	Balloon	XF	Bois de Epoye		22
Patrol		Spa 31	Fokker	X	Forêt de Fère	0730	–
Patrol		Spa 31	Fokker	X	Forêt de Fère	0730	–
Adj Bouyer &		Spa 49					10
MdL Hamot	a.	Spa 49	Albatros D	X	Guerweiler	0610	3
Adj Bouyer &		Spa 49					11
MdL Hamot		Spa 49	Albatros D	X	Sulz	0615	4
Adj Vanier		Spa 57	2 seater	X	Cuperly	0900	2
MdL Renault &		Spa 62					1
Lt Mamy		Spa 62	Scout	X			1
Lt Achard		Spa 78	Scout	X	Crécy-Mont		4
Adj Santelli		Spa 81	Balloon	XF			6
Adj-Chef Sallares		Spa 86	Scout	X	W Buzancy		2
Lt G Guérin	CO	Spa 88	2 seater	X	S Vierzy	1645	23
Lt Fonck		Spa 103	Fokker D7	XF	Châtillon	0630	54
Lt Fonck		Spa 103	Fokker D7	XF	Châtillon	0632	55
Lt Fonck		Spa 103	2 seater	X	Dormans	1555	56
S/Lt Bourjade		Spa 152	Balloon	XF	Tahure		15
S/Lt Collet &		Spa 461/CRP					1
Adj Delaye		Spa 461/CRP	2 seater	X			1
1/Lt Miller		27thUS	Fokker D7	X	St Rémy	1400	3
2/Lt McArthur		27thUS	EA	X	Norey	1400	7
1/Lt Dawson		27thUS	EA	X	Oulchy	1400	1
1/Lt Hill		27thUS	EA	X	Château-Thierry		1

Adj Artigau		Spa 15	Fokker DrI	P		–
Capt Pinsard	CO	Spa 23	EA	P	Cernay-en-Dormois	–
Patrol		Spa 31	EA	P		0730 –
Patrol		Spa 31	EA	P		0730 –
Sgt Bosson		Spa 62	EA	P		–
Sgt Damidaux		Spa 62	EA	P		–
Patrol		Spa 69	EA	P		–
Patrol		Spa 76	EA	P	Dormans	1920 –
Patrol		Spa 82	EA	P		–
S/Lt d'Estainville		Spa 87	EA	P	St Hilaire-le-Grand	–
MdL Chambaz		Spa 92	EA	P	Prosnes	–
Lt Bergé &		Spa 92				–
MdL Le Duc		Spa 92	EA	P	Marquises	–
Sgt Priollaud		Spa 159	EA	P		–
French pilot &		Spa 285				–
2/Lt Powell		99thUS	Rumpler C	FTL	Ban de Sapt	–

a.   Probably Vfw Karl Schmelcher, Jasta 71, KIA Gebweiler.

Casualties:

Sgt Stephen Tyson	Spa 85	P	MIA	Spad XIII, possibly by Ltn Erich Löwenhardt, Jasta 10, (43).
S/Lt Paule	Spa 99	P	MIA	Spad XIII
Cpl Alfred Dereix &	Br 221	P	MIA	VII° Armée
Cpl Delong	Br 221	G	MIA	Bréguet 14B2
Lt Georges Winter	Spa 85	P	MIA	Possibly by Vfw Wilhelm Seitz, Jasta 8, (7).
SM Joseph Budin	CAM	P	MIA	Palavas
Adj Maurice Robert	Spa 92	P	KIA	Spad XIII, IV° Armée
Adj Joseph Jullière &	Spa 53	P	KIA	X° Armée, E Saconin
Capt Raoul Le Poupon	Spa 53	O	KIA	Spad XI
Lt Roger Lapergue	Br 219	O	KIA	Bréguet 14A2
Adj Pierre Magdelaine &	Br 216	P	KIA	
Capt Henri Denis &	Sal 40	P	KIA	Salmson 2A2, IV° Armée, observer
Lt Chappius	Sal 40	O	OK	landed the aircraft unharmed.
S/Lt Léon Bourjade	Spa 152	P	WIA	Spad XIII, IV° Armée
MdL Maurice Renault &	Spa 62	P	WIA	
Lt André Mamy	Spa 62	O	OK	
S/Lt François Plessier	Spa 84	P	WIA	Spad XIII
S/Lt Jean Schneider	Spa 314	P	WIA	Spad XIII, VIII° Armée, possibly by Uffz Zenk & Ltn Kaeb, FlAbt (A) 199, AOK 19 Sector.
MdL Charles Chambaz	Spa 92	P	WIA	Spad, IV° Armée
S/Lt Andrieu	Br 216	O	WIA	Bréguet 14A2
Sgt Gisors	Sal 39	G	WIA	Salmson 2A2
MdL Belin	???	G	WIA	
MdL Camille Grangeron	Spa 156	P	WIA	Spad VII
Cpl Jean Dalaunay &	Spa 156	P	WIA	
Lt Joseph Aribaut	Spa 156	O	OK	
1/Lt Lawrence Richards	95thUS	P	WIA	Spad
1/Lt Ralph S Schmitt	27thUS	P	WIA	Nieuport 28
Lt Langrand	Sal 39	P	KIAcc	Salmson 2A2
MdL Jacques Neyret &	Spa 64	P	KIAcc	Spad XI, collided with another
Lt Chanut	Spa 64	O	KIAcc	aircraft which landed OK.
Sgt Maurice Sover	???	P	KIAcc	
S/Lt Louis Poirier	Spa 99	P	Injured	Spad XIII
Adj Clément &	86° Cie d'Aérostiers		XF	II° Armée probably by Vfw
Lt Desbouis		O	OK	Richard Rübe, Jasta 67, (2).
Lt Brisset	36° Cie d'Aérostiers		XF	II° Armée Probably by Ltn
		O	OK	Hans Quartier, Jasta 67, (1).
Adj Guggenheim	57° Cie d'Aérostiers		XF	IV° Armée probably by
		O	WIA	Uffz Haur, Jasta 68, (1).
S/Lt Chinot & Lt Vieban	72° Cie d'Aérostiers		XF	IV° Armée, probably by
		O	OK	Vfw Jeep, Jasta 58, (1).
Lt Vieban	50° Cie d'Aérostiers		XF	IV° Armée probably by Uffz
		O	OK	Friedrich Engler, Jasta 62, (3).
Sgt Leclerc	92° Cie d'Aérostiers		XF	V° Armée, probably by Vfw
		O	OK	Karl Schlegel, Jasta 45, (6).
S/Lt Legube	66° Cie d'Aérostiers			IV° Armée, attacked, not
		O	Injured	flamed.

20 July

S/Lt Casale		Spa 38	Fokker D7	X	Ville-en-Tardenois	0920	11
MdL Conraux		Spa 83	Scout	X	Aisne		3
Capt de Luppe	CO	Spa 83	EA	X	Ploisy		1
Lt Letu &		Spa 151					1
Lt Arpheuil		Spa 151	2 seater	XF	St Léger-aux-Bois		4
S/Lt Maunoury &		Spa 152					3
S/Lt Vial		Spa 152	2 seater	X	Faverolles		
1005	7						
S/Lt Maunoury &		Spa 152					4
S/Lt Vial		Spa 152	Rumpler C	X	Nogent l'Abbesse	1015	8
1/Lt Miller		27thUS	Fokker D7	X	Braisnes	1930	4
1/Lt Miller		27thUS	Fokker D7	X	Braisnes	1940	5
???	a.	DCA	Rumpler C	POW	Oulchy-le-Château		–
???		DCA	Fokker D7	X	Oulchy-le-Château		–
S/Lt Maunoury &		Spa 152					
S/Lt Vial		Spa 152	2 seater	P	Faverolles-Jonchery		–
Lt Meline		Spa 3	Fokker DrI	P	Vezilly	1600	–
Patrol		Br 224	EA	P	X° Armée		–
Patrol		GC 22	2EA	P			–
Escadre 1		GC	EA	P			–
???		GC	2 EA	P	Champagne		–
1/Lt Putnam		139thUS	EA	P	Bourloncourt		–
Cdt de Marancour	CO	GC 14	EA	P			–

a.   Pilot WIA, observer KIA.

Casualties:

Sgt André Bosson	Spa 62	P	MIA	Spad VII	
Brig René Vignes	Spa 151	P	MIA	Spad VII	
Adj Théodore Cancel	Spa 99	P	MIA	Spad XIII	
1/Lt John McArthur	27thUS	P	MIA	Nieuport 28 N° 6293, probably by a Jasta 27 pilot.	
Lt Georges Mazimann CO	Spa 159	P	KIA	Spad XIII, probably by Obltn Bruno Loerzer, CO JGIII, (27).	
Lt Henri Garsault &	Br 211	P	KIA	X° Armée, XF, Bréguet 14B2,	
S/Lt Alphonse Charasse	Br 211	O	KIA	probably by Ltn Helmut Brünig, Jasta 50, (3).	
1/Lt Herman Boldt	90thUS	O	KIA	Salmson, ground fire	
1/Lt Zenos R Miller	27thUS	P	POW	Nieuport 28, probably by a Jasta 27 pilot.	
1/Lt Fred W Norton	27thUS	P	WIA	DOW, Nieuport 28 N° 6296, probably by a Jasta 27 pilot.	
S/Lt Camille Monteillet	Sal 6	O	WIA	Flak, Salmson 2A2	
MdL Mignis &	Sal 4	P	WIA		
Lt Pardot	Sal 4	O	WIA		
S/Lt Louis Crémont &	Sop 251	P	WIA		
Lt Eugène Mansillon	Sop 251	O	WIA	X° Armée	
S/Lt Sciandra	???	O	WIA	X° Armée	
Brig Raoul Dupart,	R 46	P	WIA		
Sol Pelletier &	R 46	G	OK		
???	R 46	G	KIA	Triplace	
Sgt Louis Thomas	Spa 89	P	KIAcc	Spad XIII	
Cpl Juraud	GDE	P	KIAcc	Salmson 2A2	
Lt Nougues	Br 238	O	Injured	Bréguet 14A2	
Cpl Valette	GDE	P	Injured	Sopwith	
Adj Ruyer &	???	P	Injured		
Lt Hallan	???	O	Injured	Sopwith	
Lt St Etienne	72° Cie d'Aérostiers			IV° Armée, not flamed.	
		O	Injured		
Adj Finet	??? Cie d 'Aérostiers			Attacked, not flamed.	
		O	Injured		
Lt Magniez	??? Cie d' Aérostiers			Attacked, not flamed.	
		O	WIA		
Adj Georges Poirier	59° Cie d'Aérostiers		XF	VI° Armée, probably by	
		O	OK	Ltn Richard Wenzl, Jasta 6, (7).	
S/Lt Forest	25° Cie d'Aérostiers			V° Armée, probably by Vfw	
		O	OK	Karl Schlegel, Jasta 45, (10) not flamed. This balloon did catch fire in its bed at 17h50.	

21 July

Cpl Dalaunay &		Spa 156					–
Lt Aribaut		Spa 156	EA	P			–
Cpl Dalaunay &		Spa 156					–
Lt Aribaut		Spa 156	EA	P			–
Cpl Chorier &		Sal 55					1
Lt Astruc	CO	Sal 55	Scout	X	Aisne		3
S/Lt Boyau	a.	Spa 77	EA	XF	S Soissons	1905	25
Lt Hay de Slade		Spa 86	Fokker D7	XF	SE Belleu	1745	11
Adj Loup &		Spa 103					2
Sgt Drouilh		Spa 103	Fokker D7	X	Chambrecy	1800	2
MdL Oudart &		Br 111					2
Sgt Paillard		Br 111	EA	X			1
S/Lt Coiffard	CO	Spa 154	2 seater	X	Champlat	1805	17
Adj Abraham &		Br 224					1
S/Lt Danhiex		Br 224	Scout	X	Venizel-Bellau		1
Capt Menj	CO	GC 16	Scout	X			3
Lt Sardier &	CO	Spa 48					–
S/Lt de Guingand		Spa 48	EA	P			–
Adj Loup		Spa 103	Fokker	P	Ville-en-Tardenois	1808	–
Sgt Drouilh		Spa 103	Fokker	P	Bouleuse	1810	–
Escadre 12		GB	EA	P	Villers-sous-Châtillon		–

a. Possibly OfStv Otto Esswein (12v), Jasta 26, KIA Hartennes, about 15 km S of Soissons.

Casualties:

Sgt François Hugues	Spa 26	P	MIA	Spad XIII, 18h00	
Lt Henri Fellonneau	Spa 77	P	MIA	Spad XIII	
Capt Vaucey	Spa 255	O	KIA	Spad XVI, ground fire, X° Armée.	
Sol Clerc	Br 279	G	KIA		
Sgt Lenoir	Spa 103	O	WIA	Spad XIII, 18h00	
Lt Bollon	Spa 36	O	WIA	Spad XVI, ground fire	
S/Lt Fabre	Sal 52	O	WIA	Salmson 2A2, ground fire, X° Armée.	
S/Lt de Hargues	Br 237	O	WIA		
Capt Louis Thébault	CO	Br 210	P	WIA	X° Armée
Sol Meillat	Br 279	G	WIA	Bombardment of airfield.	
Adj Machie	CAP 130	P	Injured	Bréguet, bomb exploded on landing.	
Asp Fichet &	R 240	O	Injured		
Cpl Lailhager	R 240	G	Injured	Caudron R11	
MdL Roger Bouzerand	CEP 115	P	Injured	Caproni, bomb exploded	
MdL Robert Pinguely	CEP 115	P	Injured	while landing.	

22 July

Adj Artigau		Spa 15	Rumpler C	X	Ville-en-Tardenois	0745	11
S/Lt Canivet &		Sal 19					1
???	a.	Sal 19	2 seater	X	S Champfleury	0920	?
1/Lt Blake &		Br 29					1
2/Lt Porter		Br 29	Fokker D7	XF	Conflans		1
S/Lt Dousinelle		Spa 48	EA	X			9
S/Lt Pendaries &		Spa 67					6
Sgt Jaubert		Spa 67	2 seater	X	Ville-en-Tardenois	0545	1
Lt Decoin	CO	Spa 77	EA	X	Le Charmel	1500	2
S/Lt Boyau &		Spa 77					26
Sgt Guerrier		Spa 77	Balloon	XF			2
S/Lt Boyau &		Spa 77					27
Sgt Guerrier		Spa 77	Balloon	XF			3
S/Lt Boyau		Spa 77	EA	X	Fresnes	1530	28
S/Lt Guertiau		Spa 97	EA	X	Cuisles-Basileux		6
Capt Battle	CO	Spa 103	Balloon	XF	E Epoye	0700	2
??? &		Br 111					?
Sgt M Lévy		Br 111	EA	X			1
S/Lt de Peyerimhoff &		Br 123					2
Sgt Le Thuaut &		Br 123					4
Sgt Le Braz &		Br 123					1
Sgt Guillot		Br 123	EA	X			1
Lt Pascal &	CO	Br 129					1
Sgt Delhommeau		Br 129	Fokker DrI	X	Châlons-sur-Marne	1700	1
Sgt Roques &		Br 129					1
Asp Lambert		Br 129	EA	X			1

1/Lt Calkins &	Br 129					2
1/Lt Borchers	Br 129	Scout	X			2
S/Lt Vanthieghem &	Br 134					1
???	Br 134	Scout	X			?
Capt Gigodot, CO	Spa 153					4
Adj Arrault &	Spa 153					3
Cpl Villeneuve	Spa 153	2 seater	X	Aisne		1
Sgt Dossisard &	Br 219					1
Sgt Jouanno	Br 219	EA	X	Aisne		2
Sgt Pithois,	R 239					1
Sgt Caillot &	R 239					1
Asp Foch	R 239	Scout	XF	French lines		1
S/Lt Givon &	R 240					4
Sgt Coolen &	R 240					2
MdL Gault &	R 240					1
Asp Davantes	R 240	EA	X			1
Sgt Vicaire,	R 240					1
Asp Roques &	R 240					2
Sgt Chayle	R 240	EA	X	German lines		1
???	b. ???	Rumpler C	POW	Sommeland		–
Lt Madon	Spa 38	Fokker	P	Nogent l'Abbesse	0915	–
Adj Binoche &	Spa 48					–
S/Lt de Guingand	Spa 48	Fokker	P			–
Sgt Rejon	Spa 62	EA	P			–
S/Lt Pendaries	Spa 67	EA	P	Ville-en-Tardenois	0545	–
Adj Marinovitch &	Spa 94					–
MdL Bessières	Spa 94	Rumpler C	P	Epernay		–
Adj Marinovitch	Spa 94	Rumpler C	P	Epernay		–
Lt Fonck	Spa 103	Fokker D7	P	Cuisles-Basileux	1810	–
Lt Fonck	Spa 103	Fokker D7	P	Cuisles-Basileux	1810	–
Escadre 1	GB	EA	P			–
Escadre 2	GC	2 EA	P	Aisne		–

a.   Probably Gefr Johann König & Ltn Erich Joachimbauer, FlAbt 296b (A), KIAs, at Champfleury.
b.   Rumpler C IV N 7917/17, possibly OfStv Karl Witterstädter & Ltn Karl Lau, FlAbt 202 (A), POWs.

Casualties:

S/Lt Charles Robin	Spa 93	P	MIA	Spad XIII, Faverolles, possibly by Ltn Hans Pippart, Jasta 19, (21).	
Cpl Pichney	Spa 100	P	MIA	Spad VII	
Sgt Pierre Pithois	C 239	P	MIA		
Asp Foch &	C 239	O	WIA		
Sgt-Maj Henri Caillot	C 239	G	KIA	Caudron R11, DOW	
MdL Richard Mevius	Spa 77	P	KIA	Spad VII N° 5152, Jaulgonne, possibly by Vfw Christian Mesch, Jasta 26, (4).	
Sgt Vicaire,	R 240	P	WIA	Caudron R11, probably by	
Asp René Roques &	R 240	O	WIA	Ltn Hans Pippart, Jasta 19 (20).	
Sgt Chayle	R 240	G	WIA		
1/Lt William W Palmer	94thUS	P	WIA	Spad, Oulchy-le-Château	
Cpl Clave	C.I.Perthe	P	KIAcc		
Asp Jaubert		O	KIAcc		
Adj Finet	69° Cie d'Aérostiers			X° Armée, probably by a	
		O	Injured	Jasta 50 pilot.	
1/Lt Leo C Ferrenback &	4th Balloon Co, USBS		XF	VIII° Armée, 12h13, probably by	
1/Lt Paul N A Roony		O	OK	Ltn Neitzer, Jasta 65, (1).	
MdL Bonnemaison	82° Cie d'Aérostiers		XF	VIII° Armée, 12h20, probably by	
		O	OK	Ltn Otto Fitzner, Jasta 65, (7).	
S/Lt Léonard &	37° Cie d'Aérostiers			VIII° Armée, 20h00	
S/Lt Marchal	"	O	OK	Attacked, not flamed.	
???	??? Cie d'Aérostiers			Attacked, not flamed,	
		O	OK	Aisne Sector	

---

23 July – No Claims
Casualties:

Sgt Daniel Desgouttes	Spa 86	P	KIA	Spad XIII, probably by Vfw Dietrich Averes, Jasta 81, (2), X° Armée.	
2/Lt Ralf A Floyd	Ferry	P	POW	Salmson, FTL in Germany.	

S/Lt Castex		Spa 289	P		WIA	Spad XVI	
Lt Evins		???			WIA	Ground fire, V° Armée.	
Adj Gasquet &		V 116	P		KIAcc		
Cpl Clerbeaux		V 116	G		Injured		
Sgt Claisse		67° Cie d'Aérostiers					
			O		WIA	Flak	

---

24 July

S/Lt Dumas		Spa 12	Balloon	XF	Aisne	1830	1
Lt Achard		Spa 78	2 seater	X	Crécy-Mont		5
S/Lt Basuyaux,		Spa 92					1
S/Lt Austin &		Spa 92					1
S/Lt Haegelen	a.	Spa 100	2 seater	POW	Avise	1545	11
MdL Ehrlich		Spa 154	Balloon	XF	Pouilion	0735	10
2/Lt White		147thUS	Albatros DV	X	Château-Thierry	1705	1
2/Lt White		147thUS	Albatros DV	X	Château-Thierry	1707	2
1/Lt Healy,		147thUS					1
2/Lt Abernathy,		147thUS					1
2/Lt O'Neill,		147thUS					3
2/Lt Jones &		147thUS					2
2/Lt Porter		147thUS	Fokker D7	X	Bois de Fère	1735	2
1/Lt Healy,		147thUS					2
2/Lt Abernathy,		147thUS					2
2/Lt O'Neill,		147thUS					4
2/Lt Simonds,		147thUS					3
2/Lt Jones &		147thUS					3
2/Lt Porter		147thUS	Fokker D7	X	Bois de Fère	1735	3
VIII° Armée	b.	DCA	Fdh	X	Sozey-les-Bois	0010	–
Lt Fonck		Spa 103	EA	P	Châtillon	1130	–
???		???	6 EA	P	Aisne		–

a.   Possibly Vfw Fuss & Flg Dittmar, FlAbt 297b (A), POWs.
b.   FdH G III N 180/17, Ltn Hubert Huther, Gefr Jacob Hoffmann, Sgt Vanner & Flg Neck, BG8/BSt25, POWs.

Casualties:

Lt Jean Dumas	Spa 12	P	MIA	Spad
Sgt Piler &	V 121	P	MIA	
S/Lt Le Forestier	V 121	O	MIA	Voisin Renault
MdL André Conraux	Spa 83	P	POW	X° Armée, Spad XIII N° 8262, probably by Ltn Hermann Frommherz, Jasta B, (8).
Cpl Bendix	Spa 99	P	POW	Spad VII N° 5214, probably by OfStv Gustav Dörr, Jasta 45, (17).
2/Lt R A Floyd, USAS	Sal ??	P	POW	Became lost and landed on a German airfield, AOK 19.
Lt Albert Achard	Spa 78	P	WIA	Spad XIII
Adj Fabien Lambert	Spa 62	P	WIA	Spad VII
Cpl Ludovic Corne	???	P	WIA	
MdL Fatin &	Sal 256	P	KIAcc	
S/Lt Habasque	Sal 256	O	Injured	Salmson 2A2
S/Lt Ernest Maunoury	Spa 152	P	Injured	Spad XIII N° 1506
Sol Vigliano	Spa 162	M	Injured	
Brig Alfred Rousse	Spa 163	P	Injured	Spad N° 5790
Sgt Schneider &	???	P	Injured	
S/Lt Descousis	???	O	Injured	Salmson
Sol Gillet	Br 233	M	Injured	
Lt Caron	??? Cie d'Aérostiers			Attacked, not flamed,
		O	OK	Aisne Sector.
Cpl Bouillot	??? Cie d'Aérostiers			Attacked, not flamed,
		O	OK	Aisne Sector.

---

25 July

Sgt Clément &	Sal 40						1
Cpl Bouillon	Sal 40	EA	X		Champagne		1
MdL Monthiers	Spa 86	2 seater	XF		NE Bois d'Ecurry		1
V° Armée	???	EA	X		NW Gueux	1900	–
1/Lt Sewell,	95thUS						4
1/Lt Heinrichs,	95thUS						2
1/Lt Knowles	95thUS						1

1/Lt Puryear &	95thUS					1
1/Lt Gill	95thUS	Rumpler C	X	Villeneuve-sur-Fère		1
1/Lt Avery	a. 95thUS	Fokker D7	POW	Château-Thierry		1
1/Lt Knowles	95thUS	Fokker D7	X	Bouvardes		2
1/Lt Healy &	147thUS					2
2/Lt Raible	147thUS	Fokker D7	X	Bois de Fère		3
S/Lt Faucillon &	Sal 51					–
???	Sal 51	Scout	P			–
Patrol	Spa 62	EA	P			–
Lt Delrieu	Spa 152	EA	P	Gueux	1030	–
Escadre 2	GC	EA	P			–
???	GC	EA	P	Aisne		–
???	GC	EA	P	Champagne		–

a. Obltn Carl Menckhoff, CO Jasta 72, (39v), POW Château-Thierry.
b. Possibly Ltn Friedrich Graf Frhr von Hehenau, Jasta 11, WIA Cugny, about 12 km W of the Bois de Fère.

Casualties:

Sgt Pierre Rejon	Spa 62	P	MIA	
1/Lt Grover C Vann	95thUS	P	KIA	Spad XIII N° 15017
1/Lt Alfred N Joerg &	12thUS	P	KIA	
2/Lt Alford T Bradford	12thUS	O	KIA	Salmson 2A2
Adj-Chef Bonjean	C.I.			Sommesous
	,,	P	KIA	Bombardment of airfield.
Adj Berger	,,	P	KIA	,,
Cpl Bonneville	,,	P	KIA	,,
Adj Tardies	,,	P	WIA	,,
Adj Vaille	,,	P	WIA	,,
Sgt Delannoy	,,	P	WIA	,,
Cpl Mouthiez	,,	P	WIA	,,
Brig Chedin	,,	P	WIA	,,
Sol Henri Beckerick	Br 219	G	WIA	
S/Lt Forgues	???	?	WIA	Ground fire.
Cpl Combadières	GDE	P	Injured	AR
Sol Busson	Spa 73	M	Injured	
S/Lt Victor Fournier	Br 260	P		Intoxicated by gas during a low level mission.
Lt Roger &	Sal 51	P	OK	V° Armée, FTL at Rilly-la-
Sgt Rigal	Sal 51	G	OK	Montagne, after combat.
S/Lt Jean Robert de Beauchamp	Spa 75	P	OK	Spad XIII, probably by Ltn Heinrich Drekmann, Jasta 4 (10). FTL in German lines but managed to escape.
???	59° Cie d'Aérostiers		XF	VI° Armée, probably by Ltn Gerold
		O	OK	Tschentschel, Jasta 72s, (3).
1/Lt Ray W Thompson	1st Bal Co USBS		XF	VI° Armée, probably by Vfw
		O	OK	Karl Schlegel, Jasta 45, (10).
S/Lt Lucien Hézard	68° Cie d'Aérostiers			
		O	Injured	

---

26 July

Lt Achard	Spa 78	3 seater	XF	Soissons	6
III° Armée	a. DCA	DFW C	POW	Ployron	–
Lt Achard	Spa 78	Scout	P	Soissons	–

a. III° Armée Prisoner Interrogation Report, Uffz Neuendorf & Ltn Golgiehn, FlAbt 232, POWs.

Casualties:

Sgt Edmond Durel &	Br 207	P	POW	IV° Armée
S/Lt Roland	Br 207	O	POW	Bréguet 14A2
1/Lt George W Puryear	95thUS	P	POW	Nieuport 28,
S/Lt Gloaguen	Sal 18	O	WIA	Salmson 2A2, ground fire.
QM Gabriel Chollet	PilSch	P	KIAcc	Ambérieu
???	21° Cie d'Aérostiers		XF	Probably by Vfw Kurt Deland, Jasta
		O	OK	Jasta 54s, (3), IV° Armée Sector.
???	??? Cie d'Aérostiers		XF	Aisne Sector, Pouillon,
		O	OK	at 05h59, V° Armée Sector.
???	??? Cie d'Aérostiers		XF	Courceles-Sapincourt, at
		O	OK	07h05, V° Armée Sector.
Sgt Blondeau	27° Cie d'Aérostiers			V° Armée, attacked, not
		O	OK	flamed.
???	46° Cie d'Aérostiers			An artillery salvo hit this balloon unit

at 04h15 and killed 9 men and
wounded 25 others, V° Armée.

27 July

Adj Petit-Delchet	Spa 57	Balloon	XF	N Caurel	0835	5
??? &	Br 129					–
Sgt Rey	Br 129	EA	P			–
X° Armée	11 CA	EA	P			–
Patrol	GC 16	Balloon	P	X° Armée		–

Casualties:

1/Lt Walter R Lawson	91stUS	O	WIA		
Lt Paul Antoni	Spa 92	P	WIA	FTL near Marfaux, V° Armée, departed 18h15.	
Brig Levamis &	GDE	P	Injured		
Brig Gautier	GDE	O	Injured	Sopwith	

28 July

1/Lt Miller &	12thUS					1
1/Lt Thompson	a. 12thUS	EA	X	Fère-en-Tardenois	1900	2
1/Lt Miller &	12thUS					2
1/Lt Thompson	a. 12thUS	EA	X	Fère-en-Tardenois	1905	3
Infantry	b. VI° Armée	Halberstadt	X	Fère		–
Patrol	GC 16	Balloon	P	Aisne		–
Sgt Daussin &	Sal 52					–
S/Lt Philies	Sal 52	Scout	P	German lines		

a.　Possibly Uffz Wilhelm Mittelbachert (P), Sgt Paul Osswald (P), Ltn Walter Knobel (O) & Gefr Wilhelm Wilde (G), SchSta 33, KIAs, Villers- sur-Fère.
b.　Uffz Helmut Michael & Gefr Christian Meyer, SchSta 8, POWs.

Casualties:

S/Lt Antoine Cordonnier	Spa 15	P	MIA	Spad VII, probably by Ltn Erich Löwenhardt, Jasta 10, (45), Fère-en Tardenois.
1/Lt John C Miller &	12thUS	P	WIA	DOW. These two Salmson 2A2s
1/Lt Stephen W Thompson	12thUS	O	KIA	probably the victims of Ltn Karl
2/Lt Alfred B Baker &	12thUS	P	POW	Bolle (27) & Ltn Hermann Frommherz.
2/Lt John C Lumsden	12thUS	O	KIA	(10), both Jasta B.
Cdt Houdemon	X° Armée	P	WIA	Spad VII
MdL Duhau	Sal 72	P	WIA	Salmson 2A2, ground fire.
Cpl Heroguez	Sal 4	G	WIA	
Sol Boisson	R 240	G	KIAcc	Caudron R11
MdL Pierre	???	P	KIAcc	
MdL Lambs &	Sal 18	P	Injured	
S/Lt Paul Baumann	Sal 18	O	Injured	Salmson 2A2
S/Lt Maurice Brunel	Spa 95	P	Injured	Spad VII
Adj André Petit-Delchet	Spa 57	P	KIAcc	Spad XIII

29 July

Patrol	R 46	Fokker D7	X			–
Sgt Rougerie,	R 239					1
??? &	R 239					?
Sgt Cézard	R 239	EA	X	Aisne		1
???	R 240					?
??? &	R 240					?
Sgt Coolen	R 240	EA	X	French lines		2
1/Lt Brooks	139thUS	Pfalz DIII	X	Buxières		1
Adj-Chef Artigaut &	Br 11					–
S/Lt Legrain	Br 11	Fokker D7	P	Aisne		–
S/Lt Bergot	Spa 73	Scout	P	Aisne		–
Lt Douillet &	Spa 124					–
Sgt Siamer	Spa 124	2 seater	P	Moronvillers		–
1/Lt Cassady, USAS	Spa 163	2 seater	P	Cornillet	1745	–
Escadre 1	GB	EA	P	Aisne		–
Escadre 2	GC	3 EA	P	Aisne		–

Casualties:

Cpl Charles Gabouillet &	Spa 278	P	MIA	
Lt Albert Rapilly	Spa 278	O	MIA	Spad XVI, X° Armée
MdL Jean Tornare &	Br 210	P	KIA	X° Armée

S/Lt René Goriot	Br 210	O	WIA	Bréguet 14CA
Adj-Chef Marcel Artigaut	Br 11	P	OK	
S/Lt Legrain	Br 11	O	WIA	Bréguet 14A2
Cpl Laujac &	Br 216	P	WIA	X° Armée, FTL
S/Lt Delageneste	Br 216	O	OK	Bréguet 14A2
MdL Le Gorju	Br 287	P	WIA	DOW 30 July 1918
S/Lt Aberton	Br 269	O	WIA	DOW 30 July 1918
Lt Blanc	???		WIA	
Adj Heroguez	???		WIA	Flak
Adj-Chef Martin Roussel	Br 120	G	WIA	Flak
Sol Margery	Spa 95	M	Injured	
S/Lt Delval &	Br 120	P	Injured	
S/Lt Delaunay	Br 120	O	Injured	

30 July

Lt de La Poeze &		EM GC 14					1
S/Lt Bamberger	a.	Spa 75	Scout	X	Soissons		3
Lt Romatet,		Spa 76					4
Adj Martin &		Spa 76					1
Adj Barreau	b.	Spa 76	LVG C	POW	Eterpilly	1200	1
S/Lt Ambrogi &		Spa 90					6
MdL Bizot		Spa 90	Balloon	XF	Grange-en-Haye	1845	3
V° Armée		???	EA	X	S Lagery	1600	–
Escadre 1		GC	2EA	P	Aisne		–
Escadre 2		GC	EA	P	Aisne		–
Patrol		Spa 69	EA	P	X° Armée		–
???		GC	EA	P	Aisne		–

a.   Possibly Ltn Heinrich Drekmann (11v), Jasta 4, KIA Grand-Rozoy, about 20 km S of Soissons.
b.   Possibly Vfw Christian Spering & Ltn Walter Jacobi, Fl Abt 266 (A), POWs.

Casualties:

QM Yves Paranthoen &	* CAM	P	MIA	Donnet-Denhaut, 200HP, N° 921,
Mat Laurent Le Tynevez	CAM	M	MIA	codé D.73. North Sea.
Cpl Georges Cabanel	Spa 83	P	WIA	DOW 31 July 1918.
				Spad VII, X° Armée
S/Lt Couec	C.I.			Sommesous
		O	WIA	Bombardment of airfield.
Lt Cadeilhan	,,	O	WIA	,,
Asp Dore	,,	O	WIA	,,
1/Lt Walter R Lawson	91stUS	O	WIA	Flak, Salmson 2A2.
Capt Bourges	F 110	P	Injured	Farman 50.
Capt Charles Tavera CO	Spa 49	P	OK	VII° Armée, 10h00, FTL during combat.
Adj Roger &	64° Cie d'Aérostiers			VIII° Armée, 16h21,
Cpl Prud'homme		O	OK	attacked, not flamed.
1/Lt James A Higgs, Jr &	7th US Bal Co			Attacked, not flamed.
Adj Petit-Jean (French)		O	OK	

*   CAM.

31 July

Capt Pinsard	CO	Spa 23	Balloon	XF	Lançon		23
Adj Naudin,		Spa 26					6
Adj Usse &		Spa 26					1
Sgt Vincent		Spa 26	Albatros	X	Gratibus	1940	1
Lt Madon	CO	Spa 38	Fokker D7	X	S Lhéry	1600	39
S/Lt Peronneau &		Spa 81					9
S/Lt de Cazenove de							
Pradines	a.	Spa 81	2 seater	X	Cormontreuil		7
1/Lt Cates		94thUS	Fokker	X	Oulchy-le-Château		1
S/Lt Peronneau		Spa 81	EA	P	Sillery		–
Adj Naudin,		Spa 26					–
Adj Usse &		Spa 26					–
Sgt Vincent		Spa 26	Albatros	P	Maresmontier		–
???		18 CA	EA	P	X° Armée		–

a.   FlAbt 286, pilot KIA, Observer WIA.

Casualties:

Lt Blanchard	Spa 20	O	KIA	Spad XI
1/Lt Gilford C Davidson	Spa 100	P	KIA	Spad

1/Lt John H Stevens		147thUS	P	KIA	Nieuport 28 N° 6300, possibly by Ltn Johannes Klein, Jasta 15, (11).		
1/Lt Alan F Winslow		94thUS	P	POW	Spad XIII N° 15067, probably by Ltn Emil Rolff, Jasta 6, (2).		
1/Lt Paul H Montague		95thUS	P	POW	Spad XIII		
Brig Coppon		Spa 20	G	WIA	Spad XI		
Sgt Lucien Lacouture		Spa 95	P	WIA			
Sgt Jacques Pilleux		Spa 89	P	KIAcc	Spad XIII		
Sgt René Dubarry		Spa 88	P	KIAcc	Spad XIII		
Cpl Coursin		Spa 75	P	KIAcc	Spad VII		
Sgt Manuel &		Spa 261	P	KIAcc			
Sol Fabureau		Spa 261	M	Injured	Spad XI		
Sol Anguille		Spa 95	M	Injured			
Sgt Fernand Halb &		Sal 19	P	OK	Hit by ground fire, FTL.		
???		Sal 19	O	OK			
Adj Bocquet		62° Cie d'Aérostiers					
			O	Injured			

Victory claims with unknown dates during July 1918.

Sgt Lods		Br 117	EA	X			1
Sgt Duveau		Br 29	EA	X			1

1 August

S/Lt Portron &		Spa 31					2
Adj Deley		Spa 31	Balloon	XF	Epoye	0940	2
S/Lt Coadou	a.	Spa 88	Fokker D7	X	Villemoyenne	1415	2
Lt Bonneton		Spa 69	Balloon	XF	Aisne		4
Adj Girod		Spa 73	Fokker	X	Septmonts		1
S/Lt Camplan		Spa 84	Scout	X			7
Lt Fonck		Spa 103	2 seater	X	E Bois de Hangard	1100	57
S/Lt Coiffard &	CO	Spa 154					18
MdL Ehrlich		Spa 154	Balloon	XF	N Sommepy	0900	11
S/Lt Coiffard &	CO	Spa 154					19
MdL Ehrlich		Spa 154	Balloon	XF	N Sommepy	0902	12
S/Lt Coiffard &	CO	Spa 154					20
MdL Ehrlich		Spa 154	Balloon	XF	N Sommepy	0905	13
S/Lt Wadddington,		Spa 154					8
S/Lt Barbreau &		Spa 154					6
Adj Chevalier		Spa 154	Balloon	XF	N Sommepy	0940	3
MdL Lhomme,		Br 227					2
S/Lt Allanic &		Br 227					2
Cpl Monteil		Br 227	Fokker D7	X	NE Montdidier		1
MdL Lhomme,		Br 227					3
S/Lt Allanic &		Br 227					3
Cpl Monteil		Br 227	Fokker D7	X	NE Montdidier		2
Capt Biddle,	CO	13thUS					3
1/Lt Freeman,		13thUS					1
1/Lt Stovall &		13thUS					1
1/Lt Seerley		13thUS	Albatros D3	X	Vieville-en-Haye	1850	1
Capt Biddle,	CO	13thUS					4
1/Lt Freeman,		13thUS					2
1/Lt Stovall &		13thUS					2
1/Lt Seerley		13thUS	Albatros D3	X	Vieville-en-Haye	1852	2
1/Lt Hudson,		27thUS					3
1/Lt Vasconcelles &		27thUS					2
1/Lt Nevius	b.	27thUS	Rumpler C	X	Fère-en-Tardenois	0810	1
1/Lt Hudson		27thUS	Rumpler C	X	Saponay	0811	4
1/Lt Hudson,		27thUS					5
1/Lt Vasconcelles &		27thUS					3
1/Lt Roberts		27thUS	Fokker DII	X	Fère-en-Tardenois	0815	2
1/Lt Cates,		94thUS					3
1/Lt Cook &		94thUS					1
1/Lt Loomis		94thUS	Fokker D7	X	Bois de Dole	1005	1
1/Lt Tobin		103rdUS	2 seater	X	Prinz Würtemberg	1018	3
1/Lt Meissner &		147thUS					5
1/Lt Brotherton		147thUS	Fokker D7	X	Fère-en-Tardenois	1330	1
S/Lt Volmerange &		Spa 38					–

Adj Garaud	Spa 38	EA	P	Ville-en-Tardenois	0945	–
Sgt Fabre &	Spa 38					–
Sgt Shaffer	Spa 38	EA	P	Champigny-Thillois	1000	–
Patrol	Spa 69	EA	P	X° Armée		–
MdL Cauvet &	Br 229					
Sol Kuchelbecker	Br 229	Fokker D7	P	St Thierry	0925	–
Lt Fonck	Spa 103	Fokker D7	P	Moreuil	1120	–
1/Lt Cassady,	Spa 163					–
Sgt Connelly &	Spa 163					–
Sgt Cook	Spa 163	2 seater	P	Monts	1150	–
1/Lt Tobin	139thUS	EA	P	S Metz	1100	–
Patrol	GC	EA	P	Picardie		–
Patrol	GC 15	EA	P	Dole		–
Patrol	GC 16	EA	P	X° Armée		–

a.   Probabaly Ltn Walter Lehmann, Jasta 10, WIA/POW, Fère-en-Tardenois.
b.   Posssibly Uffz Theodor Scharmann & Ltn Heinz Wenner, FlAbt 276 Lb, POWs.

Casualties:

Adj-Chef Raszewski	Spa 96	P	MIA	Spad VII, probably by Obltn Oskar von Boenigk, CO Jasta 21s, (17).
Cpl Georges Perrin	Spa 73	P	MIA	Possibly by Ltn Lothar von Richthofen, Jasta 11, (31).
S/Lt Eugène Camplan	Spa 84	P	WIA	Spad XIII
Adj Bonnafous &	Spa 215	P	KIA	
S/Lt Revel	Spa 215	O	KIA	Spad XI, II° Armée
S/Lt Gourmaud	Spa 215	P	KIA	
S/Lt Berger	Spa 215	O	KIA	Spad XI, II° Armée
Lt Blanchard	Spa ???	O	KIA	Spad XVI
MdL André Lebrun &	Spa 62	P	KIA	
Lt Robert Brumaule des Allées	Spa 62	O	KIA	Bréguet 14
Adj Forquet &	Sal 106	P	KIA	Flak
S/Lt Penigaud	Sal 106	O	KIA	Flak. Salmson, V° Armée
1/Lt Charles B Sands	27thUS	P	KIA	Nieuport 28 N° 6275
1/Lt Oliver T Beauchamp	27thUS	P	KIA	Spad XIII N° 15143
1/Lt John L Hunt	27thUS	P	KIA	Nieuport 28 N° 6259
1/Lt Richard C Martin	27thUS	P	POW	
1/Lt Clifford McElvain	27thUS	P	POW	Spad XIII
1/Lt Arthur L Whiton	27thUS	P	POW	Nieuport 28
1/Lt Walter P Miller &	1stUS	P	KIA	
2/Lt James J Sykes	1stUS	O	KIA	Salmson N° 792
1/Lt Ernest G Wold	1stUS	P	WIA	
2/Lt James C Wooten	1stUS	O	KIA	Salmson N° 1101
Capt Davenne	Spa 140	O	KIA	Bombardment of airfield
Adj Thiery	Spa 140	G	KIA	at Matougues.
Cpl Fontaine	Spa 140	P	KIA	,,
S/Lt ... affert	R 214	P	WIA	,,
Sgt ... ampe	R 214	P	WIA	,,
Cpl ... heulpin	R 214	P	WIA	,,
Asp de Curel	R 214	O	WIA	,,
Sgt ... aurin	R 214	G	WIA	,,
Cpl Ambroise Bicaisse	R 213	G	WIA	,,
1/Lt Earl N Spencer	1st US	O	WIA	Salmson
S/Lt Langlois	Sal 52	O	WIA	Salmson, ground fire
Sgt Cottard	R 214	P	WIA	DOW 8 August 1918
Sgt Coppon	Spa ??	G	WIA	Spad XVI
Cpl André Hoguet	Spa 96	P	KIAcc	Spad XIII
Lt Gabriel Guérin CO	Spa 88	P	KIAcc	Spad XIII
Sgt Drossner	V 112/119	B	KIAcc	Voisin X
Cpl ... angres	GDE	P	KIAcc	Voisin X
Sgt Le Ray &	Sal 33		KIAcc	
Lt Salomon	Sal 33	O	KIAcc	Salmson 2A2
Adj Beauvraignes,	R 213	P	KIAcc	
Sgt Allombert &	R 213	O	KIAcc	
Sol Carrolet	R 213	G	KIAcc	Caudron R11, IV° Armée
MdL Pontavie &	Sal 51	P	KIAcc	
Sol Lechappe	Sal 51	G	KIAcc	Salmson, V° Armée
Sol Guillet	R 46	M	Injured	Caudron
Sol ... ery	R 240	G	Injured	Caudron R11

??? ... ros		CIACB	P	Injured	Spad VII	
Capt François Rageau		V 112/119	P	Injured		
Cpl Fernand Halb		Sal 19	P	OK		
S/Lt Serre		Sal 19	O	Injured	Salmson 2A2, II° Armée	

2 August

MdL Uteau		Spa 315	Balloon	XF	Saulewald	2
Lt Bozon-Verduraz		Spa 94	EA	P		–
Casualties:						
S/Lt Delval		Br 120	P	KIAcc		
Adj Guyot		Sal 70	G	Injured	Salmson 2A2	

3 August

Lt Guyou &		Spa 37				5
MdL Martin		Spa 37	EA	X		1
Lt Rondot		Spa 48	Scout	X	Thillois	1
MdL de Gaillard de La Valdène		Spa 95	2 seater	XF	Jonchery-Fismes	6
S/Lt Coiffard &	CO	Spa 154				21
S/Lt Barbreau		Spa 154	Balloon	XF	N Sommepy	1935	7
S/Lt Coiffard &	CO	Spa 154				22
S/Lt Barbreau		Spa 154	Balloon	XF	N Sommepy	1937	8
Lt Madon	CO	Spa 38	Fokker D7	P	N Fismes	1930	–
S/Lt Clain &		Sal 263				–
S/Lt Aime		Sal 263	Scout	P	Muizon	–
Casualties:						
S/Lt Paul Conheau &		Spa 278	P	OK		
Asp André Bénard		Spa 278	O	WIA	Spa XVI, FTL after combat.	
Adj ... auger		F 110	P	Injured		
MdL René Panigot &		Br 223	P	OK	FTL N Bezannes, after combat	
S/Lt Jules Bonnaz		Br 229	O	OK	against 8 Albatros scouts.	
???		45° Cie d'Aérostiers		XF	X° Armée, probably by Vfw	
			O	OK	Max Kuhn, Jasta 21s, (3).	
Lt Jacques Gauthier		52° Cie d'Aérostiers			Attacked, not flamed.	
			O	OK		

4 August

Lt Madon	CO	Spa 38	EA	P	N Betheny	1945	–
Patrol		Spa 103	Balloon	P	La Boissière	0950	–
???		Spa ??	Fokker	P	Aisne	–
Casualties:						
Sgt Gratien Verrier		Spa 76	P	MIA	Spa XIII	
Cpl Besson		Br 44	P	WIA	Bréguet	
Cpl Larcher		Spa 63	P	KIAcc	Spad XI	
Lt Georges Madon	CO	Spa 38	P	Injured	Spad	
???		68° Cie d'Aérostiers		XF	X° Armée	
			O	OK		

5 August

MdL de Gaillard de La Valdène		Spa 95	2 seater	P		–
Casualties:						
Cpl Bordessoul &		Br 226	P	MIA	V° Armée, Bréguet 14A2,	
Asp de Chatellus		Br 226	O	MIA	probably by K Flakbatterie 126.	
Sgt-Maj Marguet		V 25	P	KIAcc	Caudron C.23	
Sol Lardens		C.I.Perthe	M	KIAcc	Caudron C.23	
Lt de Lattre		Br 133	O	Injured		

6 August – No Claims

Casualties:						
S/Lt Bonnamy &		Spa 285	P	WIA		
S/Lt Hendle		Spa 285	O	WIA	Spad XVI	
Sol Louis Chaput		Sal 13	M	Injured	Salmson	
1/Lt W S Anderson		1st Balloon Co, USBS		XF	VI° Armée, probably by Vfw Karl	
			O	OK	Schlegel, Jasta 45, (9).	

7 August

Sgt Shaffer	Spa 38	Balloon	XF	St Thierry		1
Adj-Chef Delépine,	Spa 62					2
Lt Brousse (O) &	Spa 62					1
Sgt Virard	Spa 62	Fokker D7	X	German lines		1
Asp Viort &	Spa 62					1
Sgt Réjon (O)	Spa 62	Fokker D7	X	German lines		1
MdL Bizot	Spa 90	Balloon	XF	Juville	1752	4

Casualties:

Cpl Mourgues &	Spa 212	P	WIA	DOW 9 August 1918.	
Adj Bender	Spa 212	O	KIA	Spad XI	
Cpl Placide	GDE	P	KIAcc	Voisin P	
Sgt Gilormini	V 121	P	Injured		
Lt de Brullon &	Br 223	P	Injured		
Asp Robert	Br 223	O	Injured		
Asp Léon Viort	Spa 62	P	OK	FTL in German lines after combat, escaped to French lines.	
1/Lt Phelps &	2nd Balloon Co, USBS		XF	VI° Armée, probably by Obltn	
1/Lt Montgomery		O	OK	Oskar von Bönigk, Jasta 21s, (20).	
Lt Dumas & Asp Bonnet	54° Cie d'Aérostiers		XF	VI° Armée, probably by Sgt Max	
		O	OK	Kuhn, Jasta 21s, (4).	

8 August

S/Lt Boyau &	Spa 77					29
MdL Lentz-Mitchell	Spa 77	Rumpler C	XF	Ressons-sur-Matz	1815	1
S/Lt Boyau	Spa 77	2 seater	XF	Piennes	1815	30
S/Lt Boyau	Spa 77	Balloon	XF	Cury	1820	31
Adj Bizot	Spa 90	Balloon	XF	Vazy-Amelecourt	0501	5
???	GC	2 EA	P	Picardie		–

Casualties:

Cpl Georges Raymond	Spa 57	P	MIA	V° Armée, Spad VII 5467, departed at 16h15.	
Brig Antoine Lentz-Mitchell	Spa 77	P	KIA	Flak, Spad XIII N° 8500.	
Adj Pierre Morin	Spa 37	P	WIA	DOW 16 August 1918.	
S/Lt Jean Vial &	Spa 289	P	WIA	Ground fire	
Lt Regagnon	Spa 289	O	WIA	Ground fire, Spa XVI.	
S/Lt Georges Jaussaud	Spa 21	O	WIA	Flak, Spad XVI, III° Armée	
Lt Canaud	C.I. Perthe	P	KIAcc	Spad VII	
Cdt Barthelemy &	???	P	OK		
S/Lt Tignolet	???	O	Injured	Sopwith, VIII° Armée	

9 August

S/Lt Risacher	Spa 3	Scout	X	Bouchoir	1730	2
1/Lt Blake, USAS &	Br 29					2
2/Lt Porter, USAS	Br 29	Fokker D7	P	Lassigny		2
Lt Poupon, CO	Spa 37					6
Lt Barny de Romanet,	Spa 37					8
S/Lt Guyou &	Spa 37					6
Sgt Coupillaud	Spa 37	EA	X	Mortemer		3
Lt Loubignac,	Spa 93					1
Lt Olphe-Gaillard &	Spa 93					2
MdL Ducornet	Spa 93	Balloon	XF	Orvillers		3
S/Lt Haegelen &	Spa 100					12
1/Lt Stephenson, USAS	Spa 100	Balloon	XF	Roye	1115	1
S/Lt Waddington,	Spa 154					9
Adj Chevalier &	Spa 154					4
2/Lt Treadwell, USAS	Spa 154	Fokker D7	X	Cormontreuil	0845	1
Capt Battle CO a.	Spa 103	Scout	X	Etelfay	1930	3
Adj Naudin	Spa 26	Scout	P	S Mortemer	1650	–
Sgt Dupont	Spa 62	EA	P			–
???	Br 129	EA	P	Picardie		–
???	GC	2 EA	P	Aisne		–

a. Possibly Ltn Egon Patzer, Jasta 36, KIA Montfaucon, about 5 km S of Etelfay.

Casualties:

Brig Henri Pathais	Spa 153	P	MIA	Spad XIII N° 2268, possibly by Ltn Gutsche, Jasta 36, (1).	

Sgt André Martin	Spa 94	P	MIA			
Sgt Leger &	Spa 289	P	KIA			
Lt Flamming	Spa 289	O	KIA	Spad XVI		
Sgt Pollet &	Spa 289	P	KIA			
S/Lt Bouvier	Spa 289	O	KIA	Spad XVI		
S/Lt Pierre Wertheim	Spa 84	P	WIA	Spad, FTL after combat.		
S/Lt Saint-Martory	Sal 32	P	WIA	Salmson 2A2		
Lt Grisoni	Sal 225	O	WIA	Salmson, DOW 10 August 1918.		
1/Lt Charles R Blake, USAS &	Br 29	P	OK			
2/Lt Earl W Porter, USAS	Br 29	O	WIA	Bréguet 14B2		
S/Lt Marcel Herbert &	Spa 21	P	Injured	III° Armée, crash-landed after a combat.		
S/Lt Maurice Masson-Regnault	Spa 21	O	Injured	Spad XVI		
Sgt Pierre Robert	Spa 152	P	Injured	Salmson 2A2 N° 8243.		

10 August

Capt Stoffels d'Haurefort &	Sal 33					1
S/Lt Chasles	Sal 33	Scout	X	Picardie		1
Patrol	R 46	EA	X	Picardie		–
Lt Marques & CO	Br 108					1
S/Lt Maquet &	Br 108					1
Sgt Duro &	Br 108					1
1/Lt Reedy, USAS &	Br 108					1
S/Lt Fouan &	Br 108					1
MdL Douville	Br 108	Scout	X	Picardie	1655	1
Adj Ehrlich	Spa 154	Balloon	XF	Brimont	1630	14
Sgt Rotival,	Br 227					3
S/Lt Allanic &	Br 227					4
Cpl Monteil	Br 227	Fokker D7	XF	Picardie		3
S/Lt Grillon	R 239					1
Sgt Haarbleicher &	R 239					1
???	R 239	Scout	X	Picardie		?
IV° Armée	DCA	EA	X			–
1/Lt Buckley &	95thUS					2
1/Lt Avery	95thUS	Fokker	X	Bazaches		2
1/Lt Tobin　a.	103rdUS	Fokker D7	X	Thiaucourt	2020	4
Capt Bridgman &	139thUS					1
1/Lt McCormick	139thUS	Rumpler C	X	Xivray	1925	1
III° Armée　b.	???	Scout	POW	Cuvilly		–
S/Lt Caël	Spa 3	Fokker D7	P	Carrepuis	1145	–
Patrol	Spa 12	Scout	P	St Thierry	1745	–
???	GC	Balloon	P	E Roye		–

a.　Probably Flg Herbert Koch, Jasta 64w, KIA Thiaucourt.
b.　Probably Ltn Muhs, Jasta 12, shot down and taken prisoner near Cuvilly, at 11h15.

Casualties:

Sgt Geneste &		Sal 33	P	MIA	Salmson 2A2, probably by
S/Lt Mallet		Sal 33	O	MIA	Bavarian Flakzug 121.
Lt Condefort		???	P	MIA	
Sgt Tinot		66 APAé	G	MIA	
QM Marcel Lefevre &	*	CAM	P	MIA	Lévy Besson, 200 HP N° 118
SM Dominique Novel	*	CAM	M	MIA	
1/Lt Irby R Curry, USAS		95th US	P	KIA	Spad XIII N° 15009.
Sgt Tisseau		Spa 36	P	WIA	Spad XVI, DOW 23 August 1918.
MdL Arondel		Sal 33	P	WIA	DOW
S/Lt Cabirol		Sal 33	O	WIA	Salmson 2A2
Adj Bertrand		Sal 10	P	WIA	Salmson 2A2, ground fire
Sgt Mercier &		R 239	G	WIA	
Asp Foch		R 239	G	WIA	Caudron R11
MdL Billon		Sal 236	G	WIA	Salmson 2A2
Sgt Moyon &		Sal 28	P	WIA	
S/Lt Coint-Bavarot		Sal 28	O	WIA	Salmson 2A2
Sol Bérard		???	G	WIA	
1/Lt Clarence Gill, USAS		95thUS	P	WIA	Nieuport 28
S/Lt Georges Thurel		Br 201	O	WIA	
Sgt Robert Thibaudier		Spa 313	P	KIAcc	
SM Pierre Belhomme &	*	EP	P	KIAcc	
SM Eugène Bourdic	*	EP	O	KIAcc	

QM Jean Odinot	***	EP	P	KIAcc			
Capt Kahn &		???	P	Injured			
Capt Robinot		???	O	Injured			
S/Lt Gustave Fournier		47° Cie d'Aérostiers	XF	Probably by Uffz Kurt Pietzsch, Jasta 58, (1).			

* Cherbourg.
** Pilot School St Raphaël.
*** Pilot School Amberieu.

---

11 August

S/Lt de Dreux		Spa 12	Fokker D7	X	Pavy	1015	4
Capt Pinsard	CO	Spa 23	Balloon	XF	Mangiennes		24
Sgt Lebroussard		Spa 26	Scout	X	Grivillers	2015	1
S/Lt Puget &		Spa 26					2
Sgt Pelletier		Spa 26	Scout	XF	Grivillers	2015	1
S/Lt Portron		Spa 31	Fokker	XF	NE Crugny	1810	3
Lt Madon	CO	Spa 38	Fokker D7	X	E Soissons	1630	40
Lt Brusco,		R 46					2
Sgt Delaporte &		R 46					2
Cpl Caumes		R 46	Fokker D7	X	Noyon		1
Cpl Plomion,		R 46					1
2/Lt Burger, USAS &		R 46					1
MdL Leroy de Présale		R 46	Fokker D7	X	Noyon		1
S/Lt Plessis,		Spa 65					6
MdL Maine &		Spa 65					1
Sgt Descamps		Spa 65	Balloon	XF	Rethonvillers		1
Adj Henin &		Br 66					1
??? &		Br 66					?
??? &		Br 66					?
Sgt Jardin		Br 66	EA	X			1
S/Lt Le Coq de Kerland		Spa 82	Fokker D7	X	Lassigny-Chauny		6
Adj-Chef Bousquet &		Br 108					1
Lt Guinegot &		Br 108					1
Sgt Castiola &		Br 108					1
Cpl Pirio &		Br 108					1
MdL Lhert &		Br 108					1
Sgt Frossard		Br 108	Scout	X			1
Lt G Hall &		Br 111					1
??? &		Br 111					
MdL Oudart &		Br 111					3
Sgt Paillard		Br 111	EA	X			2
S/Lt Kaciterlin &		Br 117					1
Adj-Chef Cambray		Br 117	SS DIII	X			2
MdL Deschamps &		Br 120					1
MdL Galand		Br 120	Scout	X			1
??? &		Br 129					?
Sgt Rey		Br 129	EA	X			1
S/Lt Coiffard	CO	Spa 154	Fokker D7	X	NW Jonchery	1930	23
S/Lt Coiffard &	CO	Spa 154					24
Adj Ehrlish		Spa 154	Balloon	XF	Caurel-Beine	1945	15
S/Lt Coiffard &	CO	Spa 154					25
Adj Petit		Spa 154	Fokker D7	X	Beine	1955	5
Sgt Proullard		Spa 159	EA	X	Picardie		2
S/Lt Meyer		Spa 160	Aviatik C	X	NE Commercy		3
2/Lt Ponder, USAS,		Spa 163					3
1/Lt Cassady, USAS &		Spa 163					4
1/Lt Cook, USAS		Spa 163	2 seater	X	Bétheniville	1205	1
Sgt Roger &		R 239					1
Adj Pousse		R 239	Scout	X	Picardie		2
S/Lt Medard &		Sal 288					1
Lt Garnier &		Sal 288					1
Sgt Danière &		Sal 288					1
Sol Feneyrols		Sal 288	Scout	X	Champigny		1
Patrol		Spa 12	2 seater	FTL	N Bouffignereux		–
Patrol		Spa 12	Fokker D7	P	N Vesle River	1015	–
Patrol		Spa 26	2 seater	P	Roiglise	0925	–
MdL Brunet		Spa 31	Fokker D7	P	Breuil-Courlandon	1810	–

Sgt Millot	Spa 90	Albatros D	P			–
S/Lt Delaitre &	Br 123					–
S/Lt Molé	Br 123	2 seater	P			–
Patrol	Spa 124	EA	P	Ripont	0730	–
Patrol	Spa 154	Fokker D7	P	Fismes-Jonchery	1015	–
Patrol	Spa 154	Fokker D7	P	Chenay	0930	–
Patrol	GC 14	EA	P	Chasseny	0940	–
Patrol	GC 14	EA	P	S Bazoches	1530	–
Patrol	GC	Balloon	P	Aisne		–
???	GB	4 EA	P	Picardie		–

Casualties:

Adj Max Coupillaud	Spa 37	P	MIA	Spad XIII, probably by Ltn Ulrich Neckel, Jasta 13, (24).	
MdL Robert Martin	Spa 37	P	MIA	Spad XIII, probably by Ltn Hermann Becker, Jasta 12, (13).	
MdL de Maulde &	Br 219	P	MIA		
S/Lt Varloud	Br 219	O	MIA	Bréguet 14	
S/Lt Kaciterlin &	Br 117	P	MIA	Bréguet 14, probably by	
Adj-Chef Alberet Cambray	Br 117	O	MIA	Gefr Felder, Jasta 19, (1).	
Lt Barberet &	Br 108	P	MIA		
Adj Jean-Marie Rivière	Br 108	O	MIA	Bréguet 14B2	
Brig Paul Flamen,	R 239	P	MIA	Caudron R11, probably by	
Sgt Marcel Richer &	R 239	G	MIA	Ltn Josef Veltjens, Jasta 15, (28).	
Sol Pierre Crapel	R 239	G	MIA		
S/Lt Robert Segond	Spa 89	P	WIA		
MdL Fey,	R 239	P	WIA	Caudron R11, probably by	
Sol Marcel Martin &	R 239	G	WIA	Ltn Josef Veltjens, Jasta 15, (27).	
MdL Ernest Gayet	R 239	G	WIA		
Sol Lamouche	R 240	G	WIA		
Sol Berard	R 240	G	WIA		
Sol Murot	R 240	G	WIA		
MdL Robert Sedillon	Spa 163	P	Injured	Spad XIII	
Sol Berra	Spa 95	M	Injured	Spad XIII	
Sgt Sauvage &	Spa 2	P	Injured		
Lt de Roscoat	Spa 2	O	Injured	Spad XVI	
Lt Janissier	Sal ??	O	Injured	Salmson	
1/Lt B T Burt &	7th US Bal Co		XF	VIII° Armée, probably by OfStv	
Sgt H O Nicholls		O	OK	Wilhelm Kühne, Jasta 18, (5).	
Adj Jean-Marie Durand	83° Cie d'Aérostiers		XF		
		O	OK		

12 August

Adj Garaud		Spa 38	Fokker D7	X	Vitry	1945	13
Lt Sardier	CO	Spa 48	Fokker D7	X	Catigny		13
Lt Ménard		Spa 85	2 seater	XF	Noyon		1
Sgt Dumont,		Spa 93					1
Cpl Doerr &		Spa 93					1
Lt Olphe-Gaillard		Spa 93	Balloon	XF	NE Roye	1730	3
Capt Lefevre,	CO	Spa 96					5
1/Lt Vernam, USAS,		Spa 96					1
Sgt Degrott &		Spa 96					1
Sgt Courtier		Spa 96	Balloon	XF	Thilloy		1
Adj Berthier,		Spa 98					1
Cpl Eubriet,		Spa 98					1
Cpl Bougen &		Spa 98					1
Cpl Bouilly		Spa 98	2 seater	X	Moronvillers	1930	1
Lt Varocquier &		Br 221					1
S/Lt Bourdier	a.	Br 221	Scout	X	VII° Armée	1620	1
S/Lt Fieuvet &		Br 232					1
MdL Merftrat &		Br 232					1
Sgt Fellot &		Br 232					1
S/Lt Henry &		Br 232					1
MdL Grer &		Br 232					1
MdL Jolimoy		Br 232	Scout	X	St Thierry	1650	1
MdL Uteau &		Spa 315					3
MdL Bertrou		Spa 315	Balloon	XF	Saulewald	0655	1
IV° Armée		54 AC	LVG C	X	Hill 147	1100	–

Patrol	Spa 12	Balloon	P	Nogent l'Abbesse	0600	–
Adj Garaud	Spa 38	Fokker D7	P	NE Reims		–
Patrol	Spa 124	EA	P	Tahure	1930	–
Patrol	Spa 163	EA	P	Beausejour	1930	–
Patrol	GC 16	EA	P	S Noyon		–
Patrol	GC 18	EA	P			–
Patrol	CRP	EA	P	III° Armée		–

a. Probably Gefr Johann Janiszewski, Jasta 75, KIA Romagny.

Casualties:

MdL Georges Roque	Spa 156	P	MIA	Spad VII, probably by Vfw Rudolf Francke, Jasta 8, (13).	
Sgt Raoul Vatta	Spa 84	P	MIA	Spad XIII, probably by Vfw August Jühe, Jasta 8, (3).	
MdL Jacques Perles &	Br 232	P	MIA	V° Armée, Bréguet 14A2,	
MdL Honoré Pons	Br 232	O	MIA	XF St Thierry, at 18h45.	
MdL Louis Paoli	Spa 73	P	KIA	Spad XIII N° 8803, at Crépy-en-Valois.	
Sgt Michel Bertrou	Spa 315	P	KIA	VII° Armée, Spad VII, probably by Ltn Hesse, Jasta 75, (1).	
MdL Costerisant &	Br 229	P	OK		
S/Lt Auzou	Br 229	O	WIA	Bréguet 14A2, V° Armée Lt Dumas,	
	???	O	WIA	Flak	
S/Lt Albert Brissot	Sal 13	O	WIA	Salmson 2A2, ground fire	
Lt Jean Mace	Br 209	O	WIA	Bréguet F40, ground fire	
S/Lt François Gélin &	Sal 4	P	KIAcc		
S/Lt Maurice Picard	Sal 4	O	Injured	Salmson 2A2	
MdL Roupnel &	Sop 280	P	OK		
S/Lt Marande	Sop 280	O	Injured	Sopwith	
???	68° Cie d'Aérostiers		XF	X° Armée, probably by Ltn	
		O	OK	Fritz Reimer, Jasta 26, (3).	
S/Lt Lacaille	89° Cie d'Aérostiers			VIII° Armée, 17h50, not flamed.	
		O	OK	probably claimed by Ltn Romeis, Jasta 80, (1).	
Mdl Louis Paoli	Spa 73	P	KIA	Possibly by Ltn Werner Peckmann, Jasta 3, (2).	

---

13 August

Adj Delelée		Spa 82	Balloon	XF	Ostel	1300	2
S/Lt Famin		Spa 86	2 seater	X	Soissons	0920	2
Lt Rozoy &	CO	Spa 88					1
Adj Quintard		Spa 88	2 seater	X	Nampcel	1005	3
Sgt Connelly,		Spa 163					3
Mdl Féry &		Spa 163					1
Cpl Onillon		Spa 163	2 seater	X	St Martin l'Heureux		1
Sgt Coquiard &		Sal 288					1
S/Lt Garoby		Sal 288	EA	X	La Neuvillette		1
MdL Chabrier &		Spa 315					3
MdL Mesny		Spa 315	Scout	X	Mulhouse		1
S/Lt Fraissinet		Spa 57	2 seater	P	Bazoches	1030	–
MdL Chabrier &		Spa 315					–
MdL Mesny		Spa 315	Scout	P	Mulhouse		–
Patrol		GC 19	EA	P	Picardie		–

Casualties:

MdL Saglier &	Sal 59	P	MIA		
S/Lt Durin	Sal 59	O	MIA	Salmson 2A2	
Lt Marinier &	Br 45	P	MIA	Bréguet 14A2, probably by	
Lt Forteu de La Morandière	Br 45	O	MIA	Ltn Egon Koepsch, Jasta 4, (6).	
Sgt Jean Jolivet	Spa 98	P	KIA	Spad XIII	
Brig Emile Brume	Spa 154	P	KIA	Spad VII N° 11018, S Reims	
Lt Lehou	13 CA	O	WIA	III° Armée, ground fire	
Sgt Raoul Viret &	Sal 270	P	WIA	DOW, Salmson 2A2,	
Lt Roger Audugé	Sal 270	O	WIA	Thiescourt, ground fire.	
Sgt Candoin	Spa 157	P	KIAcc		
MdL Marcel Denizot	Spa 161	P	KIAcc	Spad VII	
Brig Wagner	CIACB	P	KIAcc	Spad VII	
Cpl Sarrazin &	Br 29	P	KIAcc		
Sol Artigue	Br 29	M	KIAcc		
Lt Mattei	GDE	P	KIAcc	Voisin-Renault	

Brig Foulot &		F 110	P	KIAcc			
S/Lt Raberdel		F 110	O	KIAcc	Voisin		
Lt Des Fonts		C 121	P	KIAcc	Caudron C.23		
S/Lt Astier		F 110	P	KIAcc	Caudron C.23		
Lt François Neyrand &		V 113	P	KIAcc			
Sgt Marcel Berube		V 113	O	Injured	Voisin X		
S/Lt René Lehoucke		Br 283	O	Injured			
Cpl Hamiaux		CIACB	P	Injured	Caudron C.23		
Sgt Jean Gilormini		V 121	P	Injured			
Lt Canivet &		Sal 19	P	Injured			
Lt Desmaroux		Sal 13	O	Injured	Salmson 2A2		

14 August

Adj Berthelot		Spa 15	Rumpler C	X	Chavigny	1040	7
Capt Pinsard &	CO	Spa 23					25
Lt Simeoni		Spa 23	Balloon	XF	Buisson-Chaumont		1
Adj Bouchard &		Br 45					1
Lt Pollet		Br 45	Scout	X	German lines		1
Adj Brétillon		Spa 49	Rumpler	X			4
Lt Nungesser		Spa 65	Balloon	XF		am	39
Lt Nungesser		Spa 65	Balloon	XF		am	40
Lt Nungesser		Spa 65	Balloon	XF		pm	41
Lt Nungesser		Spa 65	Balloon	XF		pm	42
S/Lt Lemaire,		Spa 90					4
S/Lt J Bordes &		Spa 90					2
Adj Mace	a.	Spa 90	DFW C.V	POW	Lunéville	0630	3
Lt Fonck		Spa 103	2 seater	X	S Roye	1110	58
Lt Fonck		Spa 103	2 seater	X	Gruny-Cremery	1120	59
Lt Fonck	b.	Spa 103	2 seater	X	Gruny-Cremery	1120	60
Lt Hay de Slade	CO	Spa 159	EA	X	SE Morsain	1015	12
Escadre 1		GC	2 EA	P	Picardie		–
Patrols		GC	2 Balloons	P	Picardie		–
Patrols		GC 14	2 EA	P	Aisne		–
???		GB	EA	P			–

a.   DFW C.V N° 2379/18, probably Uffz Stamer & Ltn Georg Kolb, FlAbt 242.
b.   Possibly Uffz Alfred Arnold & Ltn Curt Friedrich, FlAbt 232 (A), KIAs Chaulnes.

Casualties:

Lt Puig &		CEP 115	P	MIA	Caproni		
MdL Pelichet		CEP 115	P	MIA	Caproni		
Sgt Calibert &		Sal 122	P	MIA	VIII° Armée		
MdL Simonnet		Sal 122	O	MIA	Salmson 2A2		
Lt Bouchet		Spa 51	O	KIA	Spad XVI, V° Armée, probably by Ltn Helmut Brünig, Jasta 50, (6).		
Lt Alfred Palats &		Spa 62	P	KIA			
Lt Paul Brousse		Spa 62	O	KIA	Bréguet		
Lt Vuillame		1er CAC	Ph	KIA			
Lt Maurice Loubignac		Spa 93	P	POW	Spad XIII, Roye		
Adj Fernand Bouchard &		Br 45	P	OK			
Lt Bernard Pollet		Br 45	O	WIA	Bréguet 14A2		
MdL Joseph Nollet		Spa 68	P	WIA	Spad VII		
Lt Jacques Leps		Spa 81	P	WIA			
Sgt Guiet &		Br 237	P	WIA			
S/Lt Constant		Br 237	O	WIA			
Sgt Cousin &		Br 221	P	OK			
S/Lt Lenoir		Br 221	O	WIA	Bréguet 14, VII° Armée		
Sgt Marchal		Sal 8	G	WIA	DOW		
Mat Roger Cazaux		EP *	P	KIAcc	FBA, St Raphaël		
Cpl Sicre de Pont-Brune		GDE	P	Injured	Bréguet		
Sgt Palette &		Spa 55	P	Injured	DOW 16 August 1918.		
Sol Arsigny		Spa 55	G	Injured	Spad XVI		
???		91° Cie d'Aérostiers		XF	X° Armée, probably by Ltn Max Kuhn, Jasta 21s, (7).		

*   Pilot School, St Raphaël.

15 August

Sgt Manichon &		Spa 15					1
Sgt Douillet		Spa 77	EA	X	Ribecourt	0930	1
Lt Barny de Romanet,		Spa 37					9

MdL Daniel &	Spa 37					1
Adj Marot	Spa 37	Fokker D7	X			2
MdL Dupart,	R 46					1
2/Lt Lake, USAS &	R 46					1
Sol Mondème	R 46	Fokker D7	XF	Ferme d'Attiche	0945	3
Capt L. Séjourné	Spa 65	EA	X	Carlepont	0625	1
Lt Nungesser,	Spa 65					43
Adj Henriot &	Spa 65					5
Sgt Millot	Spa 65	EA	X			1
Lt Bonneton	Spa 69	Balloon	XF	Pontoise	0630	5
Adj Hudellet	Spa 75	2 seater	X	NE Soissons	1105	3
Cpl Teyssonneau,	Spa 157					1
MdL Bois &	Spa 157					1
Adj Vanier	Spa 57	2 seater	XF	N Châlons	0925	3
1/Lt Cassady, USAS,	Spa 163					5
Sgt Connelly &	Spa 163					4
Sgt Penevynck	Spa 163	Fokker D7	X	Ste Marie-à-Py		1
Patrol	R 239	EA	X	Picardie		–
Escadre 1	GC	EA	X	Picardie		–
MdL Pardo	Spa 38	EA	P	Marizon		–
Lt Nungesser	Spa 65	Balloon	P	Picardie		–
Patrol	Spa 124	EA	P	La Pompelle		–
MdL Farradet	Spa 157	EA	P	N Reims		–
1/Lt Cassady, USAS,	Spa 163					–
Sgt Connelly &	Spa 163					–
Sgt Penevynck	Spa 163	Fokker D7	P	Ste Marie-à-Py		–
Escadre 1	GC	EA	P	Picardie		–
Escadre 2	GC	EA	P	Picardie		–
Patrols	GC	3 EA	P	Aisne		–

Casualties:

Adj Charles Loilier,	R 46	P	MIA	Caudron R11, probably by	
2/Lt Paul Penfield &	R 46	O	MIA	Vfw Gustav Klaudat, Jasta	
MdL François Anceau	R 46	G	MIA	15 (1).	
Sgt Joseph Delin	Spa 157	P	MIA	IV° Armée, Spad VII	
Brig René Dupart,	R 46	P	KIA	Caudron R11, probably by	
Adj Germain Goulin &	R 46	G	KIA	Ltn Karl Odebrett, Jasta	
Sol William McKerness	R 46	G	KIA	42, (13).	
MdL Marcel Heimann	Spa 102	P	KIA		
Brig Emile Brume	Spa 154	P	KIA	Spad VII, Moulin	
Sol Arthur Topart	R 240	G	WIA	Caudron R11	
MdL Pierre Pomarel &	Sal 70	P	OK		
Lt Rue	Sal 70	O	WIA	DOW, Salmson 2A2	
Cpl Lietard,	CIACB	P	Injured		
Adj Verdon &	CIACB	G	Injured		
Sol Godin	CIACB	G	Injured	Voisin-Renault	

16 August

MdL Dubonnet &		Spa 3					5
Capt de Sevin	CO	Spa 26	2 seater	X	Gruny	1130	11
MdL Dubonnet &		Spa 3					6
Capt Battle	CO	Spa 103	2 seater	X	Carrepuis	0915	4
Adj-Chef Sallares		Spa 86	Scout	X	W Braisne		3
S/Lt Schmitter &		Spa 103					2
Adj Baron		Spa 103	2 seater	X	St Mard	1100	2
Infantry fire		???	EA	X	Champagne		–
Escadre 1		GC	EA	P	Picardie		–
MdL Dubonnet		Spa 3	Scout	P	Amy-Candor	0900	–
MdL Denneulin		Spa 3	Scout	P	Estrées-Denicourt	1940	–
S/Lt Pendaries		Spa 67	2 seater	P	Margny-aux-Cerises	1015	–
S/Lt Schmitter &		Spa 103					–
Adj Baron		Spa 103	Scout	P	SW Roye	1100	–
???		GC	2 EA	P	Aisne		–

Casualties:

Adj Jules Moulais	Spa 88	P	MIA	Spad XIII
MdL Edouard Gaultie	Spa 88	P	MIA	Spad XIII
MdL Maurice Lechanteur	Spa 87	P	MIA	Spad
Cpl Georges Groet &	???	P	MIA	

S/Lt Mautalen	???	O	MIA	Farman, II° Armée
Lt Marie Dujarric	Br 220	O	KIA	
Cpl Chaussard &	Sal 61	P	KIA	
S/Lt Roy	Sal 61	O	KIA	Salmson 2A2, III° Armée
S/Lt Fabre	Br 227	O	KIA	Bombardment of airfield
S/Lt Jean Caël	Spa 3	P	POW	Spad XIII N° 4848, probably by Obltn Ernst Udet, Jasta 4, (56).
MdL Velten	???		WIA	Bombardment of aifield
Brig Jean Rebattet	Sal 270	P	WIA	Salmson, III° Armée
Sgt Henri Sedwick-Berend	Spa 91	P	KIAcc	Spad VII
Sgt Nathanael Duffy	Spa 96	P	Injured	
Sgt Lucien Armanet	Spa 160	P	Injured	
???	27° Cie d'Aérostiers	O	Injured	
Lt Guieu	41° Cie d'Aérostiers			III° Armée, not flamed
		O	OK	

17 August

Capt Bladinières &	CO	Spa 75				1
Adj-Chef Laplasse		Spa 75	Balloon	XF	Blérancourt	4
Adj-Chef Laplasse		Spa 75	Balloon	XF	Cuts	5
S/Lt Bollinger &		Spa 76				1
Lt Mantcewitch		Spa 76	Fokker D7	X	Vitry-les-Reims	1
MdL Poisson		Spa 83	Balloon	XF	Aisne	2
Capt Gastin,	CO	Spa 84				6
Lt Cayol,		Spa 84				2
Sgt Faurel &		Spa 84				1
Sgt Panel		Spa 84	EA	X	Dreslincourt	1015	1
Adj Marinovitch		Spa 94	Fokker D7	X	Roye	14
Adj Marinovitch		Spa 94	2 seater	X	Roye	15
Lt Bozon-Verduraz	CO	Spa 94	2 seater	X	Roye	9
??? &		Br 217				?
Sol Bordas		Br 217	EA	X		1
Adj Naudin		Spa 26	Scout	P	Carrepuis	0600	–
S/Lt Garin		Spa 152	Balloon	P	Hermoniville	–
???		GC	2 EA	P	Aisne	–
???		GC	EA	P	Picardie	–
???		GC	Balloon	P	Champagne	–

Casualties:

MdL Patay	Spa 26	P	MIA	Spad VII N° 3257, departed at 14h40, possibly by Uffz Vahldieck, Jasta 50, (1).
Sgt Veyer	Spa 100	P	MIA	Spad XIII
Sol Géraud Bordas	Br 217	G	KIA	
Lt Jules Dupuis	Spa 21	O	WIA	Spad XVI, III° Armée
Sgt Mereau &	Sal 10	P	OK	
S/Lt Ferruit	Sal 10	O	WIA	Ground fire.
Adj Thierry &	Sal 18	P	Injured	DOW 20 August 1918.
Lt Bonnafé	Sal 18	O	OK	Salmson 2A2
S/Lt Clément	??? Cie d'Aérostiers			
		O	WIA	

18 August

311 Infantry Rgt	IV° Armée	EA	XF		–
MdL Hervé Chambrun de Rosemont,					–
Adj Vaysse &	Spa 85				–
Cpl Rousseau	Spa 85	2 seater	P	N Roye	–
Adj Petit	Spa 154	Balloon	P	Picardie	–

Casualties:

MdL Hervé Chambrun de Rosemont	Spa 85	P	POW	WIA/DOW, Spad XIII
S/Lt Pierre Paquier &	AR 268	P	KIA	AR1, probably by Ltn Ernst
Lt Marcel Tournaire	AR 268	O	WIA	Bormann, Jasta B, (3).
MdL Cambon	Spa 23	P	WIA	Sopwith, ground fire.
Cpl Kjell Nyegaard	Spa 15	P	KIAcc	Spad XIII
Sol Georges Maupied	Br 209	M	Injured	Bréguet F40

S/Lt Declety		94° Cie d'Aérostiers O		OK	III° Armée, attacked not flamed, probably claimed Ltn Siegfried Büttner, Jasta 61, (11).		

19 August

Escadre 1		GC	Balloon	XF	Picardie		–
Escadre 2		GC	EA	P	Picardie		–

Casualties:

MdL Maurice Gaulier		Spa 94	P	MIA	Spad XIII, probably by Ltn Alfred Fleischer, Jasta 17, (3).		
Sgt Auguste Carle		Spa 79	P	POW	Spad XIII, FTL in enemy territory because of motor malfunction.		
Adj Eugène Guillemet		Spa 15	P	WIA	Spad VII		
MdL Defos &		Spa 60	P	KIAcc			
Lt Mayer		Spa 60	O	Injured	Spad XVI		
Sol Gonnier		Spa 96	M	Injured	Spad XIII		
S/Lt Emile Martinet		61° Cie d'Aérostiers O		OK	II° Armée, not flamed, probably claimed by Vfw Thilo Boelcke, Jasta 67, (3).		

20 August

Capt Pinsard	CO	Spa 23	Balloon	XF	Mangiennes	1840	26
MdL Lambotte &		Spa 26					1
Capt d'Indy	CO	Spa 67	2 seater	POW	Armancourt	1735	2
S/Lt Bollinger &		Spa 79					2
1/Lt Lovett, USAS		Spa 79	2 seater	X	NE Fismes		1
Adj de Tonnac de Villeneuve,		Spa 80					3
S/Lt Delannoy &		Spa 80					6
S/Lt Compagnion		Spa 80	Halb C	XF	Aisne		1
Adj de Tonnac de Villeneuve, &		Spa 80					4
S/Lt Delannoy		Spa 80	Halb C	POW	Aisne		7
S/Lt Devilder,		Spa 83					1
Sgt Fouquet &		Spa 278					1
S/Lt Got		Spa 278	Scout	X	Aisne		1
Lt Ménard,		Spa 85					2
Capt Lefevre &	CO	Spa 96					6
Lt Fauquet-Lamaitre		Spa 96	Scout	X	Picardie		1
Sgt Dumont,		Spa 93					2
MdL Ducornet &		Spa 93					4
Lt Olphe-Gaillard		Spa 93	Balloon	XF	Epagny		4
Sgt Dumont,		Spa 93					3
MdL Ducornet &		Spa 93					5
MdL Maurice		Spa 93	Balloon	XF	Epagny		1
Capt Echard	CO	GC 22	Balloon	XF	Concevreux	1900	7
86° Cie d'Aérostiers		II° Armée	EA	X			–
Escadre 1		GB	EA	X	Picardie		–
Adj Peti		Spa 154	EA	P	Picardie		–
Escadre 1		GC	EA	P	Picardie		–
S/Lt Metayer &		Br 108					–
???		Br 108	EA	P			–

Casualties:

MdL Etienne Crouan &		V 25	P	MIA	Voisin-Renault N° 2966,		
S/Lt Poissonier		V 25	O	MIA	both crews probably by		
MdL G Lepicier &		V 25	P	MIA	Ltn Fritz Anders, Jasta		
Sgt E Mangot		V 25	G	MIA	73, (3) & (4).		
Cpl Meyer		Spa 68	P	MIA	Spad		
Lt Edgar Marques &		Br 108	P	MIA			
S/Lt Georges Maguet		Br 108	O	MIA	Bréguet 14B2		
S/Lt Pierre Dufayet &		Br 127	P	MIA			
S/Lt Fernand Castets		Br 127	O	MIA	Bréguet 14B2		
Adj Dominque Emmanuelli		Br 131	P	MIA			
S/Lt Charles Ulrich		Br 131	O	MIA			
Lt Raymond Castaignet		Spa 155	P	MIA	Spad XIII, probably by Ltn Franz Büchner, Jasta 13, (19).		

Capt Désiré Dubois de La Sablonière & CO	Spa 255	P	KIA	
S/Lt Daumery	Spa 255	O	KIA	Spad XVI, X° Armée
Lt Louis Verdier-Fauvety	Spa 65	P	KIA	Bombardment of airfield
S/Lt Marcel Dupic	Sal 6	O	WIA	Salmson, X° Armée
MdL Désiré Baratciart	R 46	G	WIA	Caudron R11
S/Lt Thomas	Spa 95	P	WIA	Spad
Sgt Lucien Gaillard &	V 109	P	WIA	
Cpl Pierre Noir	V 109	G	WIA	
MdL Maurice Diringer	Spa 278	P	WIA	Flak
MdL Jules Viget	Spa 278	O	WIA	Flak
MdL Gaudry	Spa 155	P	Injured	Spad XIII, DOW 22 August.
Lt Pierre Lepelve	Spa 81	P	OK	Spad, shot down behind German lines, but managed escape to Allied side safely, bringing two prisoners with him.
S/Lt Pujau	71° Cie d'Aérostiers		XF	X° Armée, probably by Ltn
		O	OK	Friedrich Noltenius, Jasta 27, (2).
S/Lt Emile Martinet	86° Cie d'Aérostiers		XF	II° Armée, probably by Vfw Thilo
		O	OK	Boelcke, Jasta 67, (4), 11h20.

21 August

Adj Deley	Spa 31	Balloon	XF	Bonflignereux	1845	3
S/Lt Guyou &	Spa 37					7
Sgt Boinet	Spa 37	EA	X	Picardie		2
Asp Discours	Spa 87	Balloon	X	N Merval	0740	3
S/Lt Ambrogi &	Spa 90					8
Adj Bizot	Spa 90	Balloon	XF	Vaxy	1330	6
MdL Ducornet,	Spa 93					6
MdL Maurice,	Spa 93					2
Cpl Doerr	Spa 93	Balloon	XF	N Noyon		2
Adj Ondet	Spa 94					1
S/Lt Martenot de Cordoux	Spa 94	Fokker D7	X	W Soissons		7
Sgt Robin &	Sal 105					1
Lt Chatellier &	Sal 105					1
Sgt Piron &	Sal 105					1
Sol Vernier	Sal 105	Fokker D7	XF	Bouvancourt		1
Sgt Robin &	Sal 105					2
Lt Chatellier &	Sal 105					2
Sgt Piron &	Sal 105					2
Sol Vernier	Sal 105	Fokker D7	XF	Bouvancourt		2
Patrol	Br 126	EA	X	N Pierrefonds	1650	–
Brig Rivoire &	Br 127					1
Cpl Poirot	Br 127	EA	XF	Picardie		1
S/Lt Brouet &	Br 128					2
Adj Monard	Br 128	EA	X	S Pierrefonds	1710	2
S/Lt Waddington	Spa 154	Scout	XF	Caudry		10
Sgt Rand,	Spa 158					1
MdL Proal &	Spa 158					1
Cpl Lasourdy	Spa 158	2 seater	XF	N Noyon		1
Lt Madon CO	Spa 38	2 seater	P	Oeuilly-Maizy	1115	–
Lt Madon CO	Spa 38	Fokker D7	P	Chavonne	1240	–
MdL Chayne	Spa 97	EA	P			–
Adj Montel &	Br 123					–
???	Br 123	EA	P			–
S/Lt Champetier de Ribes &	Br 228					–
Lt Bey	Br 228	Scout	P			–
Patrol	GC 14	EA	P	X° Armée		–
Escadre 2	GC	Balloon	P	Picardie		–
???	GC	3 Balloons	P	Aisne		–
Casualties						
Lt Benjamin Trefault	Sal 72	O	WIA	Ground fire		
Lt Pirre Chatellier	Sal 105	O	WIA	Salmson		
Adj Dejean de St Marcel	Br 131	P	WIA			
MdL Jean-Baptiste Gurby	Br 131	O	WIA	Bréguet 14B2		
Lt Jean Rouxel	Spa 23	P	KIAcc	Spad XIII		
MdL Jean Javaud	Spa 160	P	KIAcc	Spad XIII		
Brig Legrand,	R 242	P	KIAcc			

Sol Demercy &	R 242	G	KIAcc	
Sol Rombach	R 242	G	KIAcc	Caudron R11
Cpl Groslet &	Spa 258	P	KIAcc	
Cpl Perthuisot	Spa 258	G	KIAcc	Spad XVI
S/Lt Jean Vuillemin	X° Armée	P	Injured	Farman 60
Sgt Crunelle	???	G	Injured	
S/Lt Bonin &	Br 222	P	OK	FTL near Bezannes, after
MdL Laporte	Br 222	O	OK	a combat.
Lt Gabard	33° Cie d'Aérostiers		XF	X° Armée, probably by Vfw
		O	OK	Karl Schlegel, Jasta 45, (17).
Cpl Gaitz-Hocki	83° Cie d'Aérostiers		XF	X° Armée, probably by Vfw
		O	OK	Karl Schlegel, Jasta 45, (18).
Cpl Aboucaya &	25° Cie d'Aérostiers		XF	II° Armée, probably by Vfw
Asp Depoux		O	OK	Richard Rübe, Jasta 6, (4).

22 August

Capt de Turenne &	CO	Spa 12					13
Sgt Saxon		Spa 12	Balloon	XF	S Cuiry	1500	1
Capt Pinsard	CO	Spa 23	Balloon	XF	Romagne		27
Lt Poupon &	CO	Spa 37					7
Lt Barny de Romanet		Spa 37	2 seater	X	Soissons		10
Adj Boudou		Spa 48	2 seater	X	Picaradie		1
Lt Bonneton		Spa 69	Balloon	XF	Vauxillon		6
Adj-Chef Laplasse		Spa 75	Balloon	XF	St Gobain		6
Adj-Chef Laplasse		Spa 75	Balloon	XF	St Gobain		7
Adj-Chef Laplasse		Spa 75	Balloon	XF	St Gobain		8
S/Lt Payen,		Spa 79					1
MdL Couez &		Spa 79					1
S/Lt Sittler		Spa 79	EA	X	N Roiglise		1
Adj Delmetz		Spa 80	2 seater	X	Aisne		2
S/Lt Levecque		Spa 81	Balloon	XF	Picardie		2
S/Lt Chevannes	a.	Spa 112	Scout	X	Chiry-Ourscamps		7
Capt Jannekeyn &	CO	Br 132					1
S/Lt Weismann		Br 132	Scout	X			3
S/Lt Waddington,		Spa 154					11
S/Lt Gros &		Spa 154					8
S/Lt Condemine		Spa 154	Balloon	XF	E Caudry	1200	1
Lt Hay de Slade	CO	Spa 159	EA	X	Bieuxy	1955	13
Sgt Lusinchi &		Br 207					1
???		Br 207	EA	X	German lines		?
Adj Tison &		Spa 315					1
Sgt Boishardy		Spa 315	Balloon	XF	Pulversheim	0745	1
CRP	c.	DCA	Gotha G	X	Near Paris		–
Patrol		Spa 12	2 seater	P	Marquises-Nauroy	1920	–
Capt Hugues	CO	Spa 95	2 seater	P	Hombleux		–
Adj Tison &		Spa 315					–
Sgt Boishardy		Spa 315	EA	P	Pulversheim		–
???		GC	Balloon	P	Picardie		–

a.   Either Uffz Bödinghaus or Sgt Starost, Jasta 66, both POWs at Ribecourt, about 8 km SW Chiry-Ourscamp.
b.   Probably Uffz Paul Bucheim & Ltn Paul Hohenschutz, FlAbt 46Lb, KIAs Joinville-Marne.
c.   Crew of three POWs.

Casualties:

MdL Anot &	V 116	P	MIA	Voisin Renault N 2995,
MdL Roberini	V 116	O	MIA	night victory, claimed by
				Ltn Fritz Anders, Jasta 73, (5).
Adj-Chef Antoine Laplasse	Spa 75	P	KIA	Spad XIII
Sgt Jean Gentil	Spa 75	P	KIA	Spad XIII
MdL Joseph Brouillet	Br 283	P	WIA	Bréguet
Sol Louis Le Roy de Presale	R 46	G	WIA	Caudron R11
Cpl Leroy	Spa 78	M	WIA	Bomb blast
Brig Rivet,	F 110	P	KIAcc	
MdL Villiers &	F 110	G	KIAcc	
MdL Renelier	F 110	G	KIAcc	Voisin-Renault
Sol Marnaut	Spa 155	M	KIAcc	Spad XIII
Sgt Gaudry	Spa 155	P	Injured	Spad XIII, DOW 28 August 1918.

S/Lt Pujau	87° Cie d'Aérostiers		XF	X° Armée, probably by Ltn		
		O	OK	Siegfried Büttner, Jasta 61, (13).		
???	93° Cie d'Aérostiers		XF	X° Armée, probably by Vfw		
		O	OK	Albert Haussmann, Jasta 13, (12).		

23 August

S/Lt Bouzac,		Spa 12					3
MdL Beaunée &		Spa 12					2
Cpl Maurio		Spa 12	Balloon	XF	Geneviève	0755	1
S/Lt Poreaux		Spa 31	Fokker	X	N Ventelay	0900	3
S/Lt d'Aboville,		Spa 86					1
S/Lt Famin &		Spa 86					3
Cpl Simonet	a.	Spa 86	Fokker D7	X	Blérancourt		1
S/Lt G Thomas,		Spa 88					4
Adj-Chef Delzenne &		Spa 88					3
MdL Barré		Spa 88	2 seater	X	Crouy	1020	1
S/Lt Lemaire,		Spa 90					3
Adj Bizot &		Spa 90					7
Sgt Bisonnade	b.	Spa 90	LVG C	X	Autrepierre		1
S/Lt Brouet &		Br 128					4
Adj Monard &		Br 128					4
Sgt Carbone &		Br 128					2
Cpl Mallet		Br 128	Scout	X	Picardie		2
Adj Sarrabezolles &		Br 128					1
Asp Clarac		Br 128	Scout	X	Picardie		1
S/Lt Cehe &		Sal 259					1
Lt Thabourey		Sal 259	EA	X	Crécy-au-Mont		1
Sgt Noppe	c.	Spa 315	2 seater	X	Thann-Cernay		1
Lt Pressac,		R 241					1
S/Lt Banse &		R 241					1
Cpl Hautelin		R 241	Fokker	X	Maizières		1
V° Armée	d.	DCA	DFW C	POW	Crugny	1030	–
Sgt Stanley		Spa 23	2 seater	P	II° Armée		–
???		GC	2 EA	P			–

a.   Probably Flg Hermann Jander, Jasta 24s, POW/DOW Blérancourt.
b.   Probably Ltn Ulrich & Ltn Kurt Jeschonneck, FlAbt 281 (A).
c.   Pilot KIA, observer, probably Ltn Zeigler, WIA/POW, FlAbt 290b (A),
d.   Possibly Uffz Ackenhausen & Flg Amzehnhoff, SchSta 13, POWs Chipilly.

Casualties:

Cpl Marchal	Spa 31	P	MIA	V° Armée, Spad VII N° 3331.	
				Departed 07h55, possibly Ltn	
				Wilhelm Seitz, Jasta 8 (10).	
Cpl Lardent &	???		MIA		
S/Lt de La Geneste	???		MIA		
Cpl Gaston Sachet	Spa 67	P	KIAcc	Spad VII N° 3359	
MdL Bonnet	???	P	KIAcc	Sopwith	
Cpl Ranceau	Br 238	P	Injured	Bréguet 14A2	
Lt Gilbert Caron	93° Cie d'Aérostiers		XF		
		O	OK		

24 August

S/Lt Rousset.	Br 43					1
Asp Pernet &	Br 43					1
MdL de La Fourcade						
de Tauzia	Spa 80	2 seater	POW	Chavigne		1
S/Lt Brétillon	Spa 49	EA	X			5
S/Lt G Thomas,	Spa 88					5
Adj-Chef Delzenne &	Spa 88					4
Sgt Chacornau	Spa 88	2 seater	X	S Fresnes	1745	1
Patrol	GC 14	EA	P	X° Armée		–
Patrol	GC 16	EA	P	III° Armée		–
X° Armée	CA	EA	P			–
???	CA	EA	POW			–

Casualties:

Adj Ercole Balzac	Spa 69	P	Injured	Spad XIII

25 August

Adj Usse	Spa 26	2 seater	X	SW Meharicourt	1125	2
Lt Pressac,	R 241					1
S/Lt Banse &	R 241					1
Cpl Hautelin	R 241	Scout	X	Omery		1
V° Armée a.	DCA	Fokker D7	POW	Ferme Attiche		–
Lt Madon CO	Spa 38	Fokker D7	P	Vauxcère	1650	–
Patrol	Spa 67	Balloon	P	Margny-sur-Cerises	1825	–
Adj Ruamps	Spa 87	Fokker DrI	P	N Soissons	1255	–
Escadre 2	GC	2 EA	P	Aisne		–
X° Armée	GC	EA	P	Aisne		–

a.   Probably Ltn Friedrich Wilhelm Dieves, Jasta 45, Fokker D7 N° 4162/18.

Casualties:

Brig Pierre Fournillon &	Sal 18	P	KIA	Salmson 2A2, probably by Vfw Hans	
Asp Victor Bogry	Sal 18	O	KIA	Donhauser, Jasta 17, (3), X° Armée.	
Cpl Foltzer &	Br 44	P	WIA		
Sol Thorin	Br 44	G	WIA	Bréguet 14A2	
MdL Jean Sinoir	Spa 78	P	WIA	Spad VII	
Capt Paul Rozoy CO	Spa 88	P	WIA	Spad XIII	
Sgt Emile Noppe	Spa 315	P	WIA	Spad VII, at Bourguignon	
Sgt Cussac &	Br 44	P	Injured		
S/Lt Guillemin	Br 44	O	KIAcc		
Cpl ... et	GDE	P	KIAcc	Salmson 2A2	
Lt Georges Bonnigal	Sal 72	?	Injured		
MdL André Recoque	Spa 87	P	Injured	Spad XIII	

26 August

Sgt Shaffer	Spa 38	EA	X	Aisne	2

Casualties:

Brig Beausoleil &	Br 275	P	WIA	
Lt Cotard	Br 275	O	KIA	Ground fire
Cdt Patart	???	O	Injured	

27 August

Asp Bonneau	Spa 48	Balloon	XF	Laffaux		1
S/Lt Brétillon	Spa 49	EA	X	Mulhouse	1015	6
DCA 39 AA	X° Armée	Fokker D7	X			–
??? a.	DCA	AEG G.IV	POW	Varennes-Brétigny		–

a.   AEG C.IV N° 548/18.

Casualties:

Adj Ludovic Hannebique	Spa 93	P	MIA	Spad XIII, probably by Vfw Hans Donhauser, Jasta 17, (7).
Lt Yves de Keraval	Spa 261	O	KIA	Spad XVI, ground fire.

28 August

S/Lt Guertiau	Spa 97	EA	X			7
Adj Tison &	Spa 315					2
Sgt Boishardy	Spa 315	Balloon	XF	Wasserbourg	0850	2
Capt Etienne CO	Spa 315	Scout	P	Riespach		–
Adj Tison &	Spa 315					–
Sgt Boishardy	Spa 315	Scout	P	Riespach		

Casualties:

Asp Viort	Spa 62	P	MIA	
Sgt Emile Damideau	Spa 62	P	MIA	
Asp Triquera &	Br 217	P	Injured	
S/Lt Geille	Br 217	O	Injured	Bréguet 14A2
S/Lt Boulay	42° Cie d'Aérostiers			VII° Armée, attacked not
		O	OK	flamed.
1/Lt Jonathan Lane &	5th US Bal Co		XF	VIII° Armée, these two American
1/Lt John S Burrell		O	OK	balloons probably by Ltn Weisshaar,
1/Lt S V Clark &	9th US Bal Co		XF	Jasta 65, (1) & (2).
Cpl L S Balay		O	OK	
1/Lt G R Nixon	6th US Bal Co		XF	VIII° Armée, probably by OfStv
		O	OK	Kühne, Jasta 18, (6).

29 August

Name		Unit	Type	Result	Location	Time	Score
Adj Parsons		Spa 3	2 seater	X	Morchain-la-Somme	0800	6
Lt Mougin,		Br 29					1
MdL Fauvau,		Br 29					1
Asp Weill,		Br 29					1
Sol Perris,		Br 29					1
S/Lt Hudlet &		Br 29					1
MdL Haubtmann		Br 29	EA	X	Champagne		2
1/Lt Noonan, USAS &		Br 29					1
1/Lt Noring		Br 29	EA	X			1
??? &		Br 66					?
Adj Correges		Br 66	Scout	X			1
S/Lt Haegelen &		Spa 100					13
Brig Gérin		Spa 100	Balloon	XF	NE Chauny	0730	1
V° Armée		DCA	DFW C	POW	Crugny	1030	–
Sgt Carteron,		R 240					1
Sgt Gagne &		R 240					1
Adj Buisson		R 240	Scout	X	Semide		2
???		R 240					?
S/Lt Varet &		R 240					1
Lt Mauger		R 240	2 seater	X	German lines		1
??? &		Br 108					?
S/Lt Hammond &		Br 108					1
S/Lt Metayer &		Br 108					1
S/Lt Bonfils		Br 108	EA	X	German lines		1
Sgt-Maj Leteneur &		Br 111					1
Asp Etcheberry		Br 111	EA	X	German lines		1
Asp Briaumont &		Br 129					1
Asp Clausse		Br 129	Scout	X	German lines		1
???,		R 240					?
??? &		R 240					?
Sgt Coolen		R 240	2 seater	X			3
S/Lt Levrier		Spa 38	Fokker D7	P	Berry-au-Bac	1745	–
Adj Herbert		Spa 38	Fokker D7	P	Réservoir	1750	–
??? &		Br 66					–
Sgt Jaunaut &		Br 66					–
??? &		Br 66					–
S/Lt Schaeffer		Br 66	EA	P			–
MdL de Gaillard de La Valdène		Spa 95	Fokker D7	P			–
Capt Lefevre	CO	Spa 96	Scout	P			–
Capt Lefevre	CO	Spa 96	Scout	P			–
???		GB					–
Sgt Ceysson		GB	EA	P			–
???		GC	EA	P	Aisne		–
MdL Diringer &		Spa 278					–
???		Spa 278	Scout	FTL			–

Casualties:

Name		Unit		Result	Notes
MdL Gabriel Chayne		Spa 97	P	MIA	Spad XIII
Lt Richter &	CO	Br 117	P	MIA	Bréguet 14B2, hit by bombs
Sgt Marcel Lods		Br 117	G	MIA	dropped by a higher formation.
S/Lt Maurice Bonfils		Br 108	O	KIA	Bréguet 14B2
Lt Louis Brusco,		R 46	P	KIA	Flak, Caudron R11, probably by
S/Lt Henri Blitz &		R 46	O	KIA	Flak, Flakbatterie 756.
Adj Léon Delaporte		R 46	G	KIA	Flak
Sgt Marcel Jaunaut		Br 66	G	WIA	Bréguet 14B2
Capt André Darnaud	CO	Br 123	P	WIA	Bréguet 14B2
Capt Charles Lefevre	CO	Spa 96	P	WIA	Spad XIII
Sgt Eugène Panel		Spa 84	P	WIA	Spad XIII, ground fire
S/Lt Henri Claret de Fleurieu		Spa 95	P	WIA	
Lt Margot		Spa 289	O	WIA	Spad XVI
S/Lt Léon Mauger		R 240	O	WIA	Caudron R11
Lt Halley		???		WIA	
Lt Schaffer		???		WIA	
Asp Kalucq		???		WIA	
MdL ...ouguard		GDE	P	KIAcc	Spad VII
Adj Toutain &		Spa 102	P	KIAcc	

Lt Xavier de Magallon						
d'Argens	Spa 102	O	KIAcc	Bréguet 14B2		
Lt Petit	29° Cie d'Aérostiers		XF	X° Armée, probably by Vfw		
		O	WIA	Hermann Behrends, Jasta 61, (2), 10h20.		
S/Lt Lecot	87° Cie d'Aérostiers		XF	X° Armée, probably by Vfw		
		O	OK	Hermann Behrends, Jasta 61, (3), 10h20.		

30 August

S/Lt Delaitre,	Br 123					1
S/Lt Molé &	Br 123					1
Cpl de Peyerimhoff,	Br 123					1
Capt Durand, CO	Br 123					1
Adj Joffre &	Br 123					1
Sgt Pinardel	Br 123	EA	X	Picardie		1
S/Lt Bourjade &	Spa 152					16
S/Lt Maunoury	Spa 152	Balloon	XF	Chavonne	0820	5
S/Lt Gros	Spa 154	Balloon	XF			9
Adj Naudin	Spa 26	2 seater	P	Bois de Chaptire	0845	–
S/Lt G Thomas &	Spa 88					–
Patrol	Spa 88	Balloon	P	Laffaux		
Patrol	GC 21	2 seater	P	Souain-Tahure	0715	–
Patrol	GC 21	Scout	P	Moronvillers	1040	–

Casualties:

Adj Bourgine	Br 271	P	WIA	Flak, Bréguet 14A2	
Sgt Tardieu &	Spa 289	P	WIA	DOW 4 September 1918	
Lt Margot	Spa 289	O	WIA	Spad 2	
Lt Durand	???	O	WIA		
Sgt ... ervade	X° Armée	P	KIAcc		
S/Lt Lacaille &	89° Cie d'Aérostiers		XF	VIII° Armée, probably by	
S/Lt Viron		O	OK	Ltn Lidl, Jasta 78b, (1).	

31 August

Adj Joffre &	Br 123					2
Adj Pinardel	Br 123	EA	X	Aisne		2
S/Lt Risacher	Spa 159	Scout	X	Forêt de St Gobain	1830	3
S/Lt Risacher	Spa 159	Scout	X	Forêt de St Gobain	1835	4
MdL Sicaut,	R 240					1
Sol Gagne &	R 240					1
Sol Vanderhaeghen	R 240	Scout	XF	Picardie		1
Patrol of R11s	???	EA	X	Aisne		–
Escadre 2	GC	EA	P			–
Escadre 2	GB	EA	P			–
???	GC	EA	P			–
???	EdA	EA	P			–

Casualties:

Cpl Grandpierre	Spa 77	P	MIA	Spad XIII, in flames.	
MdL Albert Toussaint	Spa 89	P	MIA	Spad VII	
Sgt Guillot	Sal 72	P	WIA		
Lt Malrait &	???	P	WIA	Ground fire	
Sgt Parodi	???	G	WIA	Ground fire	
Adj Tyl	Spa 96	P	Injured	Spad VII	
Adj-Chef Clément &	Br 117	P	Injured		
Adj-Chef Albert Guériaud	Br 117	G	Injured	Bréguet 14B2	
Cpl Jamot &	Br 274	P	Injured	DOW	
Sol Laine	Br 274	M	Injured		
Sgt Gelandais	Br 287	P	Injured	Bréguet 14B2	
Lt Stadler	GDE	P	Injured	Spad XVI	
Sgt Lelandie &	???	P	Injured		
Asp Jourdanes	???	O	Injured		
Lt Dillard	???	O	Injured	Bréguet	

During August 1918, French DCA units claimed 29 enemy aircraft as either destroyed or probably destroyed.

Unknown dates for victories during August 1918:

Adj Briand &	Br 126		
S/Lt Estrayet	Br 126	EA	X
MdL Nadat &	Br 128		

???		Br 128	EA	X			

1 September

Sgt Veil		Spa 150	EA	X	Flavy-le-Meldeux		2
Lt Stickney &		Spa 150					1
Sgt Bagarry		Spa 150	EA	X	Flavy-le-Meldeux		1
S/Lt Bourjade &		Spa 152					17
S/Lt Maunoury		Spa 152	Balloon	XF	Pont-Arcy	1840	6
S/Lt Bourjade		Spa 152	EA	P	Fismes		–
S/Lt Bourjade		Spa 152	EA	P	Fismes		–
Patrol		Spa 103	Scout	P	S Fréniches		–
Patrol		Spa 103	Scout	P	S Fréniches		–
Casualties:							
Cpl Revolte &		V 106	P	MIA	Probably by VFW		
Sol Robin		V 106	G	MIA	Friedrich Poeschke, Jasta, 53, (2).		
Adj Proust		29° Cie d'Aérostiers			X° Armée, probably by Vfw		
			O	OK	Karl Schlegel, Jasta 45, (20).		

2 September

MdL Galand &		Spa 2					1
Lt Heuzeel		Spa 2	Fokker D7	X	Basileux-Fismes	1535	1
Adj Dutrey &		Spa 20					1
Sgt Latapie-Barinquet		Spa 20	Fokker D7	X	La Neuvillette	1030	2
S/Lt Clavel &		Spa 20					1
Lt Puisieux		Spa 20	Fokker D7	X	N La Neuvillette		1
MdL Verges &		Spa 34					1
Lt Barat		Spa 34	EA	X	Coucy-la-Ville		1
Lt Bonneton		Spa 69	Balloon	XF	Pontavert		7
Lt Bonneton	k.	Spa 69	Fokker D7	X	Beaurieux		8
Adj Bizot &		Spa 90					8
S/Lt Dencausse	a.	Spa 90	Balloon	XF	Geline	0900	2
Lt Ambrogi,		Spa 90					9
Adj Bizot &		Spa 90					9
Adj Pezon	b.	Spa 90	Balloon	XF	Juvelize	0930	3
S/Lt Pretre,		Spa 91					2
MdL de Caso &		Spa 91					1
Cpl Lebland	c.	Spa 91	2 seater	X	Crécy-au-Mont	0730	1
Adj Lucas		Spa 97	Balloon	XF			1
Adj Pillon		Spa 98	Scout	X	Servon		8
Sgt Rozes		Spa 99	EA	X	Sorny	1800	1
Sgt-Maj Leteneur &		Br 111					2
Asp Etcheberry		Br 111					2
S/Lt de Carheil &		Br 111					1
Adj-Chef Thevenin,		Br 111					2
MdL Hugon &		Br 111					1
Adj Thomas,		Br 111					1
Adj Loustallot &		Br 111					1
Lt Oise,		Br 111	Scout	X	Basileux	1500	1
Adj Bentejac &		Spa 124					2
Sgt Grillot		Spa 124	Balloon	XF	Manre		2
Lt Bergé &	CO	Spa 124					2
Sgt Caton		Spa 124	Balloon	XF	Bois de la Taille		1
MdL Montange		Spa 155	2 seater	X	Vauxillon		3
MdL Montange		Spa 155	Balloon	XF	Bauris		4
Lt Hay de Slade	CO	Spa 159	EA	X	W Terny-Sorny	1045	14
Adj Cousin		Spa 163	2 seater	X	Tahure-Aubérive		2
Patrol	d.	GC 14	DFW C	X	X° Armée		–
X° Armée		39 SAC	Fokker D7	X			–
X° Armée	e.	DCA	DFW C	X	Servenay	1700	–
52° Cie d'Aérostiers	f.	DCA	Albatros DV	POW	Prosnes		–
IV° Armée	g.	DCA	Fokker D7	POW	Dommartin-la-Plancette		–
II° Armée	h.	DCA	DFW	POW	Foucaucourt		–
V° Armée	i.	DCA	Fokker D7	POW	Bouleuse		–
VI° Armée	j.	DCA	DFW C	X	Arcy-Ste Restitue		–
S/Lt Cabirol &		Sal 288					1
Lt Hequet &		Sal 288					1
MdL Danière &		Sal 288					1

Sol Gruley	Sal 288	Fokker	X	S Trigny	1045	1
Patrol	Spa 38	EA	P	Réservoir		–
Patrol	Spa 124	Balloon	P	Bouconville		–
Patrol	???	EA	P	S Trigny		–
MdL Brochon &	Spa 140					–
S/Lt Japy	Spa 140	2 seater	P			–
???	GB	2 EA	P	Aisne		–
???	???	2 EA	P	Picardie		–

a.   Probably Bz 62, AOK 19.
b.   Probably Bz 36, AOK 19.
c.   Ltn Konrad Brendle (9v), Jasta 45, KIA, Crécy-au-Mont.
d.   This aircraft had just attacked the balloon of the 68° Cie d'Aérostiers.
e.   DFW N° 4429/18.
f.   Probably Ltn Hans Quartier (2v), Jasta 67, POW at Prosnes.
g.   Probably Uffz Karl Pabst, Jasta 50, Fokker D7 #2012, KIA Charleville, near Ste Menehould.
h.   DFW N° 8008/18, Vfw Thiessen, FlAbt 216, POW.
i.   Probably Flg Ludwig Prillwitz, Jasta 81, POW.
j.   Ltn Emil Tauchnitz, POW, & Uffz Otto Reichert, WIA/DOW, FlAbt 225.
k.   Possibly Ltn Gottfried Clausnitzer (1v), Jasta 72, who had just flamed the balloon of the 72° Cie.

Casualties:

MdL Henri Billiet	Spa 99	P	MIA	
Sgt Deglise &	Spa 20	P	MIA	V° Armée, Spad 2, 10h30, possibly
Lt Brasseur	Spa 20	O	MIA	by Ltn Gustav Dörr, Jasta 45, (25).
Sgt Poiss	Br 289	P	MIA	Probably by Ltn Hermann
Cpl Gamin	Br 289	O	MIA	Habich, Jasta 49, (2).
Capt Philippe Champtier				
de Ribes & CO	Br 207	P	KIA	Landed safely by
Sol Peret	Br 207	G	OK	the gunner.
Capt Henry Lamasse & CO	Br 224	P	KIA	
S/Lt Guibert Jean-Marie	Br 224	O	KIA	X° Armée
MdL Verges &	Spa 34	P	KIA	Landed by observer.
Lt Barat	Spa 34	O	Injured	X° Armée, Spad 2, probably by Ltn
				Werner Preuss, Jasta 66, (13).
Lt Gabriel Thomas	Spa 88	P	WIA	
S/Lt Camille Bouisset	Spa 87	P	WIA	
Sgt Louis Juge	Spa 38	P	WIA	
Adj Maurice Bizot	Spa 90	P	WIA	VII° Armée, balloon attack.
Cpl Raymond Perrier	Spa 87	P	WIA	
MdL Poitte	Spa ??	P	WIA	
S/Lt René d'Aux	Spa 159	P	WIA	
Adj Fernand Dutrey &	Spa 20	P	OK	V° Armée, Spad 2, possibly
Sgt Joseph				by Ltn Gustav Dörr, Jasta
Latapie-Barinquet	Spa 20	G	WIA	45, (24).
Lt Victor Fournier &	Br 260	P	WIA	
Sol Lucien Guimbertau	Br 260	G	KIA	
Cpl Fournier &	Br 289	P	WIA	
Lt de Boeuxis	Br 289	O	OK	X° Armée
MdL Hoppelt	Br 104	O	WIA	X° Armée
Cpl Maurel &	Spa ??	P	WIA	
Lt du Boueric	Spa ??	O	OK	Spad 2
Capt de la Teillias &	Spa 215	P	KIAcc	
Cpl Lateix	Spa 215	O	Injured	
S/Lt Fontan &	Spa 53	P	OK	X° Armée, Spad 2, FTL
S/Lt Bolzinger	Spa 53	O	OK	during combat.
S/Lt Gravier	52° Cie d'Aérostiers	XF		II° Armée, probably by Ltn Hans
		O	OK	Quartier, Jasta 67, (2), see f. above.
S/Lt Lamaud	81° Cie d'Aérostiers	XF		II° Armée probably by Uffz
		O	OK	Baumgarten, Jasta 67, (2).
S/Lt Gilbert Brutus	72° Cie d'Aérostiers	XF		IV° Armée, probably by Ltn
		O	OK	Gottfried Clausnitzer, Jasta 72s, (1).
Asp Simondi	27° Cie d'Aérostiers	XF		V° Armée, probably by Ltn
		O	OK	Krayer, Jasta 45, (3).
Lt Yves Hernot	89° Cie d'Aérostiers	XF		VIII° Armée, probably by
		O	Injured	Gustav Bürck, Jasta 54s, (3).
1/Lt G C Carroll &	3rd Bal Co, USBS	XF		VIII° Armée, probably by Obltn
1/Lt H P Niebling		O	OK	Gottleib Rasberger, Jasta 80, (1),
				AOK 19.
???	34° Cie d'Aérostiers	XF		VIII° Armée probably by Ltn Josef
		O	OK	Filbig, Jasta 80, (2). AOK 19.

Lt Gibert		42 Cie d'Aérostiers			VII° Armée, attacked, not		
			O	OK	flamed, 14h50.		

3 September

Lt Schneider		Spa 15	Balloon	XF	N Fismes	0930	1
Lt Madon	CO	Spa 38	Scout	X	N Fismes	1645	41
Adj Guerrier,		Spa 77					4
MdL Thévenot,		Spa 77					1
Cpl Maria &		Spa 77					1
Brig Coquelin		Spa 77	Balloon	XF			1
Adj Guerrier		Spa 77	Balloon	XF			5
Adj-Chef Delzenne		Spa 88	Balloon	XF			5
Adj Pezon	a.	Spa 90	Balloon	XF	Goin-en-Moselle	1730	4
Lt Prêtre		Spa 91	Scout	XF	Noyon	1210	3
MdL Courtieu		Spa 96	2 seater	X			2
Sgt Mailhes &		Spa 96					1
Sgt Hutreau		Spa 96	2 seater	X			1
MdL de Freslon		Spa 152	Balloon	XF	Concevreux	0830	3
X° Armée		73 SAC	EA	X			
Patrol		Spa 31	Fokker	P	Muizon	1705	–
Lt Madon	CO	Spa 38	Scout	P	N Fismes	1630	–
Patrol		Spa 103	2 seater	P	Quesmy	1750	–
Patrol		Br 203	2 seater	P	X° Armée		–
Patrol		GC 14	EA	P	X° Armée		–
Escadre 2		GC	2 EA	P			–
???		GC	2 EA	P	V° Armée		–
X° Armée		73 SAC	Fokker	P			–

a.   Probably Bz 152, flamed at 17h40 in AOK 19 Sector.

Casualties:

Cpl Roger Pradel		Spa 96	P	MIA	Probably by Vfw Hans Donnhauser, Jasta 17, (5).
Cpl André Dumont		Spa 91	P	KIA	Probably by a Jasta 61 pilot.
Brig Robert Hazemann		Spa 15	P	WIA	Flak
Cpl Raymond Chambert		Spa 15	P	WIA	
Lt Paul Schneider		Spa 15	P	WIA	
Cpl van Troyen &		Sal ??	P	WIA	
Adj Langlois		Sal ??	O	WIA	
1/Lt D Schaeffer		Br 66	O	WIA	
S/Lt F Wachter		Br 210	O	WIA	X° Armée, Bréguet
IGM Chéri Halbronn		SC Aéro	P	KIAcc	Scout, at Buc.
Lt Georges Madon	CO	Spa 38	P	Injured	
Adj Chaule Chaudy		76° Cie d'Aérostiers		XF	V° Armée, probably by Ltn Gustav
			O	OK	Wember Jasta 61, (1), 09h05.
Adj Joseph Branche		44° Cie d'Aérostiers		XF	Probably by Uffz Friedrich
			O	OK	Engler Jasta 62, unconf.
S/Lt Paul Phalempin		26° Cie d'Aérostiers		XF	Aisne Sector.
			O	OK	
Sgt Gaitz-Hocki		83° Cie d'Aérostiers			X° Armée, attacked, not
			O	OK	flamed.

Three other balloons were attacked in the Aisne Sector, but not flamed.

4 September

Adj Berthelot,		Spa 15					8
Sgt Fourcade &		Spa 15					1
Sgt Barat		Spa 15	EA			1135	1
Sgt Theiller &		Sal 19					1
Lt Delagoutte		Sal 19					1
Sgt Tucci &		Sal 19					1
Sgt Esnault		Sal 19	Scout	X	German lines		1
S/Lt Volmerange		Spa 38	2 seater	X	Lavannes	1200	2
Capt de Luppe &	CO	Spa 83					2
S/Lt Devilder		Spa 83	Balloon	XF	Filain		2
S/Lt Coadou,	CO	Spa 88					3
Adj-Chef Delzenne &		Spa 88					6
Adj Pinot		Spa 84	Scout	POW	Juvigny	1815	1
Adj Jacquot		Spa 100	Scout	X	Breuil-sur-Vesles	1145	1
S/Lt Bourjade,		Spa 152					18

S/Lt Maunoury &	Spa 152					7
Cpl Manson	Spa 152	Balloon	XF	Pont Arcy	0645	1
Escadre 2	GC	Balloon	XF			–
Sgt Fabre	Spa 38	EA	P	Grandelain	1200	–
MdL C Chambaz	Spa 92	Fokker	P			–
Sgt Couderc	Spa 152	Balloon	P	Concevreux	0730	–
Escadre 2	GC	2EA	P	Aisne		–
???	R 242	EA	P	VII° Armée		–
???	CA	4 Fokkers	P			–

Casualties:

MdL René Trouchaud	Spa 68	P	KIA	Probably by a Jasta 45 pilot.
MdL Camille Chambaz	Spa 92	P	POW	Probably by Ltn Werner Peckmann, Jasta 9, (3). Escaped a few days later.
Capt Jean de Luppe CO	Spa 83	P	POW	X° Armée, probably by Vfw Arthur Korff, Jasta 60 (4).
Sgt Gauthier &	Br 9	P	WIA	Flak, Bréguet N° 6309, aircraft
Sgt Mulot	Br 9	O	OK	crash-landed by observer.
Lt Hoppelt	Br 104	O	WIA	
Sgt Tardieu	Br 289	P	WIA	
S/Lt Malot &	???	P	WIA	
S/Lt Chevrel	???	O	WIA	DOW
Adj Jules Jacquot	Spa 100	P	OK	FTL during combat.
Cpl Aboucaya &	25° Cie d'Aérostiers		XF	II° Armée, probably by Ltn
Cpl Guilbert		O	OK	Berling, Jasta 45, (3).
Adj Boitard	26° Cie d'Aérostiers		XF	V° Armée, probably by Vfw Karl Schlegel, Jasta 45, (21), 12h04.
Sgt Euriburt	27° Cie d'Aérostiers		XF	V° Armée, probably by Uffz
		O	OK	Heinrich Haase, Jasta 21s, (3), 09h50.
???	43° Cie d'Aérostiers			Probably by Uffz
		O	OK	Baumgarten, Jasta 67, (3).
Sgt Godefroy	69° Cie d'Aérostiers			V° Armée, attacked not
		O	Injured	flamed.
S/Lt Derudder	??? Cie d'Aérostiers			Attacked, not flamed,
		O	Injured	Picardie Sector.

---

5 September

S/Lt Haegelen,	Spa 100					14
Brig Gerin &	Spa 100					2
Sgt Peuch	Spa 100	Balloon	XF	Boult-sur-Suippes	1545	1
Artillery a.	???	Balloon	XF	Altfirt		–
Sgt Grillot	Spa 124	EA	P	Monts		–
Patrol	GC 21	2 EA	P	Monts		–
???	EdA	3 EA	P	Monts		–
Patrol	GC 14	Scout	P	Vauxillon		–

a.   Bz 212, XF, AOK "B" Sector.

Casualties:

1/Lt Russell C McCormick	Spa 164	P	WIA	Probably by Ltn Karl Ritscherle, Jasta 60, (6).
Lt Antoine Mantcewitch	Spa 76	P	Injured	
Cpl Gaillard &	???	P	Injured	
Asp Marielle	???	O	OK	
Sgt Fernand Halb &	Sal 19	P	OK	FTL after being hit by
???	Sal 19	O	OK	flak.
S/Lt Gustave Fournier	47° Cie d'Aérostiers		XF	VI° Armée, probably by Vfw
		O	OK	Karl Schlegel, Jasta 45, (20).
S/Lt Paul Phalempin	26° Cie d'Aérostiers			Attacked, not flamed,
		O	WIA	Flak, Aisne Sector.

---

6 September

MdL Serusclat &	Sal 18			X° Armée		1
Sgt Maréchal	Sal 18					1
Adj Sola &	Sal 18					1
Lt Picart	Sal 18	Scout				1
Sgt Rouzaud &	Sal 18					1
Sol Martin	Sal 18	Scout	P	German lines		1

MdL Florentin	a. Spa 90	2 seater	POW	Bayon	1215	1
Adj Corso &	Spa 124					1
Adj Bentejac	Spa 124	2 seater	X	W Dontrien	1930	3
Sgt Connelly &	Spa 163					5
MdL Morvan	Spa 163	Fokker D7	X	Navarin	0830	1
Adj Guiraut	CRP/Spa 462	2 seater	POW	W Coucy-le-Château		3
IV° Armée	???	Balloon	XF	Manre	0910	–

a.   Probably Uffz Weisser & Uffz Wilhelm Scharg, SchlaSta 20, POWs Bayon, AOK "C" Sector. Hannover CL.II N° 13369/17.

Casualties:

Lt Salvetat &	Br 269	P	MIA	X° Armée, Bréguet, probably by
S/Lt Decousis	Br 269	O	MIA	Ltn Martin Haenichen, Jasta 53 (2).
Cpl Georges Nal &	Sal 18	P	KIA	X° Armée, probably by
Sol Jeandemange	Sal 18	O	KIA	Ltn Hans Rolfes, Jasta 45 (15).
Sgt Armand Blovac &	Br 260	P	KIA	V° Armée, probably by
Lt Pierre Millot	Br 260	O	KIA	Ltn Max Näther, Jasta 62, (12).
S/Lt Sébastien Tourné	Spa 75	P	WIA	X° Armée, FTL Attigny.
MdL Joseph Perraud	Spa 83	P	WIA	X° Armée, posssibly
				by Uffz Willy Dost, Jasta 21s, (3).
MdL Gérard Florentin	Spa 90	P	WIA	DOW VIII° Armée, possibly by Ltn
				Martin Haenichen, Jasta 53, (3).
MdL Ballidoz &	Sal 17	P	OK	X° Armée, Salmson,
Lt Le Floch	Sal 17	O	WIA	DOW probably by Ltn Buddeberg,
				Jasta 50, (2).
Sgt Jean Loumain	Spa 162	P	KIAcc	
Lt Charotte	68° Cie d'Aérostiers		XF	X° Armée, probably by Ltn
		O	OK	Hans Rolfes, Jasta 45, (14).
Sgt Gaitz-Hocki	83° Cie d'Aérostiers		XF	X° Armée, probably by Ltn
		O	OK	Berling, Jasta 45, (2).
S/Lt Phalempin	26° Cie d'Aérostiers			V° Armée, attacked, not
		O	Injured	flamed.

Two other balloons attacked. but not flamed, Aisne Sector.

---

7 September

S/Lt Austin	Spa 92	Balloon	XF	Beaurieux	0730	2
S/Lt Douillet &	Spa 124					4
Sgt Caton	Spa 124	Fokker D7	X	W Dontrien		2
S/Lt Coiffard, CO	Spa 154					26
S/Lt Condemine &	Spa 154					2
Sgt Peillard	Spa 154	Balloon	XF			1
S/Lt Ambrogi,	Spa 90					–
S/Lt Dencausse &	Spa 90					–
Adj Pezon	Spa 90	2 seater	P	Baccarat		–
???	EdA	EA	P	III° Armée		–

Casualties:

Sgt Thomas &	Spa 140	P	MIA	Spad 2, probably by Ltn
S/Lt Moles	Spa 140	O	MIA	Hermann Habich, Jasta 49, (3).
Adj Videcoq &	Spa 47	P	MIA	Spad 2, probably by Vfw
Lt Broca	Spa 47	O	MIA	Josef Hohly, Jasta 65 (5).
Adj Chenard &	Br 221	P	KIA	VII° Armée, probably by
S/Lt Plébert	Br 221	O	KIA	Ltn Hermann Stutz, Jasta 71 (4).
MdL Clerc &	Sal 5	P	KIA	VIII° Armée, probably by
S/Lt Thirion	Sal 5	O	WIA	Ltn Oliver von Beaulieu-Marconnay,
				Jasta 19 (14).
2/Lt David W Lewis	Spa 79	P	WIA	III° Armée
S/Lt Dontrien Lamprou	Spa 87	P	WIA	
Lt Jean Mongin	Br ??	P	WIA	
???	??? Cie d'Aérostiers			Attacked, not flamed,
		O	OK	Aisne Sector.

---

8 September – No Claims

Casualties:

S/Lt Pierre Artur	R 46	O	KIA	Caudron R11
Lt Vedi &	7 CA	P	Injured	X° Armée, shot down by ground fire
Lt Boulloud	7 CA	O	OK	W Prosner, between lines, regained
				French lines OK.

9 September – No Claims
Casualties:

Brig Albert Tournie	Spa 95	P	KIAcc	Spad

10 September

Adj Petit-Delchet	Spa 57	EA	P		–

Casualties:

Brig Dupont,	R 46	P	KIA	
S/Lt Roger Arrault &	R 46	O	KIA	
Brig Gaudin de Villaine	R 46	G	KIA	Caudron R11

11 September – No Claims – No Casualties

12 September
St Mihiel Offensive commences.

Lt Renon &	Br ??				1
Lt Giquel	Br ??	Scout	XF	German lines	1
1/Lt Nelson (USAS) &	Br 131				1
2/Lt Newel (USAS)	Br 131	Balloon	XF		1

Casualties:

Cdt Rochard &	GB 3	P	MIA	Bréguet, probably by Vfw Robert
Lt Louis Carrelet de Lousy	GB 3	O	MIA	Mossbacher, Jasta 77b, (3).
Sgt Charles Godin &	Br 132	P	MIA	Probably by Ltn Franz Büchner,
MdL Paul Aligros	Br 132	G	MIA	Jasta 13, (26).
Sgt Etienne Carbone &	Br 128	P	MIA	Probably by Ltn Grimm,
Cpl Louis Mallet	Br 128	G	MIA	Jasta 12, (3).
Lt Georges Mariage &	Br 29	P	KIA	These two Bréguets were
S/Lt Jean Lavidalie	Br 29	O	KIA	brought down by the
Lt Marie de Quatrebarbes &				explosions of the bombs
	Br 129	P	KIA	they dropped from a low
Sgt Delhommeau	Br 129	G	KIA	altitude.
Lt Robert Remon &	Br ??	P	WIA	
Lt Giquel	Br ??	G	WIA	
Cpl André Cren	Spa 81	P	KIAcc	

13 September

S/Lt Martenot de Cordoux,	Spa 94					8
Lt Laganne &	Spa 94					3
Lt Carbonnel	a. Spa 94	Fokker D7	X	Vieville-en-Haye	1720	2
MdL Montange	a. Spa 155	Scout	X	Chambley	1750	5
Sgt Puistienne &	Spa 155					1
Cpl Chartier	a. Spa 155	Scout	X	Haumont	1750	1
Adj Fleury	Spa 95	Fokker D7	P	Ancy		–
Escadre 1	???	3EA	P			–

a.   Possibly Ltn Eugen Kelber, Jasta 12, KIA W Longeville, or Ltn Paul Wolff, Jasta 13, POW, AOK "C" Sector.

Casualties:

Brig Paul Boulard	Spa 155	P	MIA	Probably by Obltn Oskar von
				Boenigk, CO JGII, (23).
Cpl de Kermal &	Br 225	P	MIA	II° Armée, probably by Ltn Oliver von
S/Lt Girard	Br 225	O	MIA	Beaulieu-Marconnay, Jasta 13, (15).
Sgt Gaston de la Guerande	Spa 102	P	POW	
S/Lt Charles Dufour	Br 29	O	WIA	
Sgt Metarie	Br 225	G	WIA	II° Armée, Bréguet.
Sgt Raymond Noël	Spa 85	P	KIAcc	
???	71° Cie d'Aérostiers		XF	Hit by artillery fire.

14 September

Sgt Duval &	Spa 23					1
Sgt Bacqué	Spa 23	Balloon	XF	Etraye		2
S/Lt Resal, CO	R 46					1
Sgt-Maj Lacassagne &	R 46					1
Sol Pompougnac	R 46	Scout	X	German lines		1
Sgt Bourgeois	Spa 68	EA	XF	Jonville	0910	1
S/Lt Boyau,	Spa 77					32
Cpl Corsi &	Spa 77					1
S/Lt Haegelen	Spa 100	Balloon	XF	Etraye	1745	15

Capt Mezergues &	CO	Br 131					5
Asp Collin		Br 131					1
MdL Jacquot &		Br 131					2
MdL Gautier		Br 131	Scout	X	German lines		2
1/Lt Nelson (USAS) &		Br 131					2
2/Lt Newel (USAS)		Br 131	Scout	X	German lines		2
MdL Pradel de Lamaze &		Br 131					1
Sgt Rayez		Br 131	Scout	XF	German lines		1
S/Lt Truchement &		Br 131					1
Asp Hogenbille &		Br 131					1
Sgt Deupuis &		Br 131					1
Cpl Magnenot		Br 131	Scout	XF	German lines		1
Capt Jannekeyn &	CO	Br 132					2-5
Lt Weissmann		Br 132	Fokker D7	XF		0930	2-5
Brig Vollet &		Br 132					1-4
Sol Malacrida		Br 132	Fokker D7	X		0935	1-4
Sgt Bridelance &		Br 132					1-4
Lt Pechine		Br 132	Fokker D7	X			1-4
S/Lt Paillard &		Br 132		(1)			2-5
Sgt Hincelin		Br 132	Fokker D7	X			1-4
MdL Halberger &		Spa 153					4
MdL Aubailly	a.	Spa 153	Balloon	XF	Goin	1640	1
S/Lt Coiffard,	CO	Spa 154					27
S/Lt Condemine &		Spa 154					3
Cpl Lisle		Spa 154	Balloon	XF	Gernicourt	1345	1
S/Lt Coiffard,	CO	Spa 154					28
S/Lt Condemine &		Spa 154					4
Cpl Lisle		Spa 154	Balloon	XF	Cormicy	1350	2
Lt Senard	CO	Spa 160	Fokker	X	X° Armée		3
Adj Charvat &		Spa 315					1
MdL Uteau		Spa 315	2 seater	X			4
Pilot,		GC 18					–
Lt Ambrogi,		Spa 90					–
Lt Lemaire &		Spa 90					–
Adj Mace	b.	Spa 90	EA	P	German lines		–
S/Lt Schroeder &		Spa 95					–
Sgt Lacouture		Spa 95	2 seater	P	Vittonville		–
Lt Couderc		Spa 152	EA	P	Pont-Arcy	0920	–
Patrol		Spa 154	Fokker	P	Bouvancourt	1300	–
Patrol		Spa 26	2 seater	P	E Châtillon	0845	–
Patrol		GC 16	EA	P			–
Escadre 2		???	EA	P	Woëvre		–

a.   Possibly Bz 152, flamed at 17h35, AOK 19 Sector.
b.   Possibly Ltn Eugen Siempelkamp (5v), CO Jasta 64w, WIA, AOK "C" Sector.
(1)   These crews shared in all four victories according to citations received.

Casualties:

Sgt Georges Fuoc	Spa 160	P	MIA	X° Armée, probably by Ltn Werner Preuss, Jasta 66 (16).
MdL Alain de Freslon	Spa 152	P	MIA	V° Armée, NW Fismes, possibly by Ltn Karl Maletsky, Jasta 50, (2).
Lt Pierre Many	Spa 150	P	MIA	
S/Lt Adolphe Calbet &	Br 132	P	MIA	
Sgt Elie Destieux	Br 132	G	MIA	By JGII
Lt Jehan de Villèle &	Br 132	P	MIA	
Brig Georges Valat	Br 132	G	MIA	By JGII
Brig Raymond Fontaine &	Br 132	P	MIA	
Sol Marcel Pillot	Br 132	G	MIA	By JGII
Brig Henri Mestre &	Br 132	P	MIA	
Asp Edouard Grand	Br 132	G	MIA	By JGII
S/Lt Teilhac &	Br 131	P	MIA	
Cpl René Jacquet	Br 131	G	MIA	By JGII
Sgt Roger Landreaux &	Br 243	P	WIA	II° Armée, probably by
Lt Sabirini	Br 243	O	KIA	OfStv Hasenpusch, Jasta 67, (2).
MdL Gaston Boeglin,	R 46	P	MIA	Caudron R11, by Jasta 65
Sgt Ernest Monfils &	R 46	G	MIA	
Sol Emmanuel Ruet	R 46	G	MIA	
Brig Joseph Dubuisson,	R 46	P	MIA	Caudron R11, by Jasta 65

Sgt Jean Mantel	R 46	G	MIA	
Sol Paul Vincent	R 46	G	MIA	
MdL Pierre de Villeneuve	Spa 153	P	KIA	Spad VII N° 5905, probably by Ltn Hans Müller, Jasta 18, (11).
Capt Raymond Bailly CO	GC 20	P	POW	Spad
Sgt Pierre Le Roy de Boiseaumarie	Spa 78	P	POW	
Sgt Julien Bonnet	Br 287	P	OK	V° Armée, FTL Fismes –
S/Lt Jounin	Br 287	O	KIA	Vauxcère, 14h00. Probably by Ltn Ulrich Könnemann, Jasta 45, (3).
Adj Giafferi &	Sal 280	P	KIA	V° Armée, probably by
Lt Arquis	Sal 280	O	KIA	OfStv Gustav Dörr, Jasta 45, (26).
S/Lt Ernest Gendreau	Spa 83	P	WIA	X° Armée, Spad
Sgt Charles Descamps	Spa 65	P	WIA	
Adj Aimé Vincent	Spa 26	P	WIA	
1/Lt C L Nelson (USAS) &	Br 131	P	OK	
1/Lt J M Newel (USAS)	Br 131	O	WIA	
MdL Bernard &	Br 231	P	OK	
Lt Toucane	Br 231	O	WIA	
MdL Jus	Br 226	G	WIA	X° Armée, Bréguet
Lt Paul Resal, CO	R 46	P	WIA	
Sgt-Maj Henri Lacassagne	R 46	G	WIA	
Sol Henri Pompougnac	R 46	G	OK	Caudron R11
S/Lt Boret	25 Cie d'Aérostiers		XF	II° Armée, probably by
		O	OK	Uffz Hans Marwede, Jasta 67, (2).
Adj André Lurcat	30° Cie d'Aérostiers		XF	II° Armée, probably by Uffz
		O	OK	Hans Marwede, Jasta 67, (3).
Cpl Guilbert	31° Cie d'Aérostiers		XF	II° Armée, probably by Uffz
		O	OK	Hans Marwede, Jasta 67, (4).
Adj Claude Chaudy	76° Cie d'Aérostiers		XF	V° Armée, probably by Ltn
		O	OK	Max Näther, Jasta 62, (13), 15h35.
Asp Bixiaux	29° Cie d'Aérostiers		XF	X° Armée, probably by Ltn
		O	OK	Wember, Jasta 61, (4).
???	57° Cie d'Aérostiers			IV° Armée, attacked not
		O	OK	flamed.
S/Lt Delorme &	84° Cie d'Aérostiers			VII° Armée, attacked, not
Adj Gabriel		O	OK	flamed, 18h00.
Sgt Desrumeaux	??? Cie d'Aérostiers			Attacked, not flamed,
		O	OK	Champagne Sector.

15 September

Lt Jallois &	Sal 19					1
Lt Delagoutte &	Sal 19					2
S/Lt Canivet &	Sal 19					2
Lt Despamoux &	Sal 19					1
Sgt Halb &	Sal 19					1
S/Lt Serré	Sal 19	Fokker D7	X	Saint Thierry		1
Lt Jallois &	Sal 19					2
Lt Delagoutte &	Sal 19					3
S/Lt Canivet &	Sal 19					3
Lt Despamoux &	Sal 19					2
Sgt Halb &	Sal 19					2
S/Lt Serré	Sal 19	Fokker D7	X	Saint Thierry		2
S/Lt Nogues	Spa 57	Balloon	XF	Bois de Buttes	1850	11
S/Lt Nogues	Spa 57	Balloon	XF	Craonne	1855	12
S/Lt Boyau,	Spa 77					33
Lt Decoin, CO	Spa 77					3
S/Lt Barbaza &	Spa 77				1230	4
Adj-Chef Strohl	Spa 77	Balloon	XF	La Haie des Allemands		1
S/Lt Boyau,	Spa 77					34
Lt Decoin, CO	Spa 77					4
S/Lt Barbaza &	Spa 77					5
Adj-Chef Strohl	Spa 77	Balloon	XF	Foulgrey	1250	2
Lt Ambrogi &	Spa 90					10
Adj Mace	Spa 90	Balloon	XF	Bourdonnay	0700	4
Lt Lemarie &	Spa 90					3
Lt de Ginestet	a. Spa 90	EA	X	Raon l'Etape	1100	1

Adj Pezon		Spa 90	Balloon	XF	Avricourt	1130	5
Cpl Chollet		Spa 92	2 seater	X	N Vieil-Arcy		
1300		1					
Adj Daladier,		Spa 93					8
Sgt Meyneil &		Spa 93					1
MdL Prarond		Spa 93	Balloon	XF	Chambley	0945	1
MdL Sainz		Spa 94	Balloon	XF	Goin	0930	1
Sgt Corcelle		Spa 97	Fokker D7	X	Lorry	1630	2
Sgt York		Spa 97	Fokker D7	XF	Preny	1630	1
S/Lt Guertiau,		Spa 97					8
Adj Lucas &		Spa 97					2
Sgt Corcelle		Spa 97	EA	X			1
S/Lt Haegelen &		Spa 100					16
Sgt Douzant		Spa 100	Balloon	XF	Château-Chehery	1520	1
S/Lt Haegelen &		Spa 100					17
MdL Peuch		Spa 100	Balloon	XF	Brieulles		2
S/Lt Bourjade &		Spa 152					19
S/Lt Maunoury		Spa 152	Balloon	XF	Ailles	0730	8
S/Lt Bourjade &		Spa 152					20
S/Lt Maunoury		Spa 152	Balloon	XF	Hurtebise	0750	9
S/Lt Coiffard,	CO	Spa 154					29
S/Lt Condemine &		Spa 154					5
Adj Ehrlich	b.	Spa 154	Balloon	XF	Brimont	1230	16
S/Lt Coiffard,	CO	Spa 154					30
S/Lt Condemine &		Spa 154					6
Adj Ehrlich	c.	Spa 154	Balloon	XF	Cormicy	1233	17
S/Lt Coiffard,	CO	Spa 154					31
S/Lt Condemine &		Spa 154					7
Adj Ehrlich		Spa 154	Balloon	XF	Gernicourt	1235	18
Sgt Jacob		Spa 157	EA	X	N Servon	1640	2
Escadre 2		???	Balloon	XF			–
Lt Jallois &		Sal 19					–
Lt Delagoutte		Sal 19					–
S/Lt Canivet &		Sal 19					–
Lt Despamoux		Sal 19					–
Sgt Halb &		Sal 19					–
S/Lt Serré		Sal 19	Fokker D7	P	Saint Thierry		–
Adj Garaud		Spa 38	2 seater	P	Hermonville	1030	–
MdL de Gaillard de							
La Valdène		Spa 95	EA	P	St Die		–
Adj Fleury		Spa 95	2 seater	P	Forêt de Mondon		–
Patrol		Spa 98	EA	P			–
S/Lt Condemine		Spa 154	Balloon	P			–
Patrol		GC 14	EA	P	X° Armée		–

a.   Probably Ltn Friedrich Gerke & Ltn Willy Beck, FlAbt 281 (A), KIAs Raon l'Etape.
b.   Probably BZug 43, XF, 1130, AOK "A" Sector.
c.   Probably BZug 26, XF, 1130, AOK "A" Sector.
NOTE: The balloons of Bz 211 (07h25) and 152 (1028), observer Ltn Kralewski, were flamed in the AOK 19 Sector.

Casualties:

Sgt Henri Bernon	Spa 92	P	MIA	Probably by Ltn Franz Büchner, Jasta 13, (27).
S/Lt Lucien Martin	Spa 97	P	MIA	Possibly by Vfw Schneck, Jasta 9, (2).
MdL Raymond Merklen	Spa 154	P	KIA	Flak, V° Armée, Spad XIII N° 6708, 16h30, Cormicy.
Adj Edouard Stahl	Spa 150	P	KIA	Probably by Ltn Rudolf Rienau, Jasta 19, (4).
Lt Mathieu de Robien CO	???		KIA	Night bomber Escadrille.
Cpl Jean Rouanet	Spa 98	P	POW	IV° Armée, 18h00, E Cernay.
Sgt Louis Fabel	Spa 95	P	POW	Probably by Ltn Scheller, Jasta 19, (4).
S/Lt Louis Gros	Spa 154	P	WIA	V° Armée, Spad N° 4929, FTL at Lhéry, probably by Ltn Oliver von Beaulieu-Marconnay, Jasta 19, u/c.
MdL Bernard &	Br 231	P	OK	
Lt Toucanne	Br 231	O	WIA	X° Armée, Bréguet.
??? &	???	P	WIA	
Asp Gustave Cormier	???	O	WIA	
Adj Charles Gauthier	Spa 80	P	KIAcc	X° Armée, collided in mid-air with Lt Feschi, Spa 80, who landed safely.
S/Lt Marcel Nogues	Spa 57	P	OK	V° Armée, FTL at Goussancourt, after combat.

???	54° Cie d'Aérostiers	XF	V° Armée, probably by Ltn
	O	OK	Meixner, Jasta 45, (2).
Sgt Bosc	29° Cie d'Aérostiers	XF	X° Armée, probably by Ltn
	O	OK	Hans v Freden, Jasta 50, (8).
S/Lt Aasche	33° Cie d'Aérostiers	XF	X° Armée, probably claimed by Vfw
	O	OK	Arthur Korff, Jasta 60, (5), not flamed.
Adj Dunard	83° Cie d'Aérostiers	XF	X° Armée, probably by Ltn
	O	OK	Fritz Höhn, Jasta 60, (11).
S/Lt Gustave Lemaître	87° Cie d'Aérostiers	XF	X° Armée, Probably by Ltn
	O	OK	Hans v Freden Jasta 50, (9).

Two other balloons were attacked, not flamed, in the Aisne Sector.

---

16 September

S/Lt Nuville &	Spa 57					11
Adj Vanier	Spa 57	2 seater	X	Breuil	1215	4
S/Lt Boyau &	Spa 77					35
Asp Cessieux	a. Spa 77	Balloon	XF	Marville	1117	1
Lt Ambrogi,	Spa 90					11
Adj Pezon &	Spa 90					6
Cpl Rivière	b. Spa 90	Balloon	XF	Cirey	1030	1
S/Lt Daladier &	Spa 93					9
Adj Delage	Spa 93	LVG C	XF	NE Juvelize	1025	1
S/Lt Haegelen &	Spa 100					18
MdL Peuch	Spa 100	Scout	X	Sept-Sarges	1200	3
S/Lt Pelissier	c. Spa 155	2 seater	X			5
DCA (Lt Weil)	d. DCA	Gotha GV	X	Ecouen-Gonesse	0258	2
???	DCA	2 seater	X	Forêt de Compiègne	Nite	–
S/Lt Philibert	Spa 12	Fokker	P	Revillon	1650	–
Adj Naudin	Spa 26	Fokker D7	P	Ornes-Azannes	1825	–
S/Lt Casale	Spa 38	Fokker D7	P	Concevreux	0700	–
Lt Lanez	Spa 87	Fokker D7	P	Allemont	0800	–
Adj Pezon &	Spa 90					
Lt Ambrogi	e. Spa 90	2 seater	P	Allarmont	1035	–
S/Lt Coudouret	Spa 103	2 seater	P	Damvillers	1315	–
Escadre 1	???	EA	P			–
Escadre 2	???	EA	P			–

a.   Possibly BZug 59.
b.   Probably BZug 141, XF, Juvigny-Cirey, AOK "A" Sector.
c.   Possibly Vfw Franz Padberg & Ltn Springorum, FlAbt (A) 279, slightly injured after being shot down and crash-landing, AOK "C" Sector.
d.   Uffz Josef Wach, Ltn Horst von Olearius & Sgt Max Zrocke, BG 4/19, KIAs at Gonesse.
e.   Possibly from FlAbt 10, crash-landed, AOK "A" Sector.

Casualties:

Sgt Gros &	Br ??	P	MIA	
Lt Carré	Br ??	O	MIA	
Sgt Foiny &	Br 229	P	MIA	
Cpl Kucher Becker	Br 229	G	MIA	II° Armée
Adj Emile Lemedeyer	Spa 12	P	KIA	V° Armée, Spad N° 5464, 16h50.
S/Lt Maurice Boyau	Spa 77	P	KIA	Probably by Ltn Georg von Hantelmann, Jasta 15, (14).
Cpl Albert Goujat	Spa 93	P	KIA	NE Pont-à-Mousson, shot down by Flak, AOK "A".
Cpl Rivière	Spa 90	P	POW	St Ludwig, evidently by Flakzuges 98, Bz 155, AOK "B" Sector.
Cpl René Walk	Spa 77	P	POW	Probably by AA fire protecting Bz 152, AOK 19 Sector.
MdL G Ravault,	F 114	P	POW	Probably by Fritz Anders,
Ltn Adj Deaux &	F 114	G	POW	Jasta 73 unconfirmed.
S/Lt Bombezin	F 114	O	KIA	
Asp Henri Cessieux	Spa 77	P	WIA	FTL French lines.
MdL Veron	Navy	P	KIAcc	
Sgt René Garin &	Sal 253	P	OK	FTL after being hit by
Lt Jean Fargeaud	Sal 253	O	OK	ground fire.
Cpl C J Leverrier	50° Cie d'Aérostiers	XF		IV° Armée, 11h30, probably
	O	KIA		by a Jasta 47w pilot.
???	??? Cie d'Aérostiers			Attacked, not flamed,
	O	OK		Aisne Sector.

17 September

Adj Marot &	Spa 37					3
Adj Lienhart	Spa 37	2 seater	XF		1630	2
S/Lt Hérisson &	Spa 75					10
Sgt Le Tilly	Spa 75	2 seater	X	Soissons-Vailly	1800	1
S/Lt Hérisson &	Spa 75					11
Sgt Baralis	Spa 75	Fokker D7	X	Soissons-Vailly		1
S/Lt Haegelen &	Spa 100					19
Lt Poulin	Spa 100	Balloon	XF		1615	1
???	DCA	EA	X			–
Patrol	GC 14	2 Fokker D7s	P	X° Armée	1619	–
Patrol	GC 23	EA	P			–
Escadre 1	???	EA	P			–

Casualties:

S/Lt E Carnell &	Br 111	P	MIA	Probably by Ltn	
Sgt A Puel	Br 111	G	MIA	Georg Weiner, Jasta 3, (7).	
Cpl Dubourg &	???	P	KIA		
Adj Huart	???	O	KIA		
MdL Kienne &	Br 269	P	KIA	Flak, Bréguet N° 6314, aircraft	
Sgt Sauton	Br 269	G	WIA	landed safely by gunner.	
Asp Mokel	Br 255	O	WIA	X° Armée, Bréguet.	
MdL Levadoux	Spa 100	P	Injured		
Adj Léonard Flament	33° Cie d'Aérostiers		XF	X° Armée, probably by Vfw	
		O	OK	Arthur Korff, Jasta 60, (6).	
MdL Tronquom	46° Cie d'Aérostiers		XF	V° Armée, 15h30.	
		O	Injured		

Two other balloons were attacked, not flamed, in the Aisne Sector.

18 September

Asp Bonneau	Spa 48	Balloon	XF	Onville		2
1/Lt Sinclair, USAS &	Spa 68					2
S/Lt Gaudermen	a. Spa 68	Halb C	X	Jonville	1645	4
Adj E Régnier,	Spa 89					4
Lt Fedoroff,	Spa 89					5
Sgt Lasnes,	Spa 89					2
Cpl Havard,	Spa 89					1
Sgt Stanley &	Spa 23					1
2/Lt Luke, USAS	27th US	2 seater	X	Belrupt		13
Adj Ehrlich,	Spa 154					19
Adj Petit &	Spa 154					6
Sgt Peillard	Spa 154	Balloon	XF	Brimont	1805	2

a.   Probably Ltn Ernst Höhne & Ltn Ernst Schulz, FlAbt 36, KIAs.

Casualties:

Adj Jacques Ehrlich	Spa 154	P	POW	V° Armée, Spad N° 7921, departed 16h50.
Adj Paul Petit	Spa 154	P	POW	V° Armée, WIA/DOW, Spad N° 15060, departed 16h50.

19 September

Lt Delrieu,	Spa 150					4
Sgt Veil &	Spa 150					3
MdL Lebigre	Spa 150	Halb C	X	Rezonville	0900	1

Casualties:

Cpl Jean Fontelle	Spa 89	P	MIA	Near Verdun
Sgt Marcel Choel	???	P	WIA	

20 September

S/Lt Pelissier	Spa 155	EA	X		6
S/Lt Condemine	Spa 154	Balloon	P		–
S/Lt Condemine	Spa 154	2 seater	P		–
Patrol	Br 132	EA	P		–
Patrol	GC 14	EA	P	X° Armée	–

Casualties:

Three GB 1 aircraft missing, probably downed by Jasta 73 pilots who claimed three Voisins downed this date, crews unknown.

21 September

S/Lt Coadou	CO	Spa 88	EA	X	N Cernay	4
VII° Armée	a.	???	2 seater	X	N St Die	–
Escadre 1	a.	???	EA	P	Woëvre	–
S/Lt Cousin		Spa 163	EA	P	Tahure	–

a.　Possibly Uffz Schlater & Ltn Erwin Sklarek, FlAbt 2, KIAs, or Flg John & Ltn Eduard Reichenwallner, FlAbt 46Lb, KIAs, AOK "C" Sector. Aircraft completely burned.

Casualties:

Sgt Frédéric Claudet	Spa 151	P	KIA	Spad
Sgt Pierre Millot	Spa 65	P	WIA	
S/Lt Bernard &	Br 221	P	OK	
Sgt Darbonnens	Br 221	G	WIA	VII° Armée, Bréguet.
Cpl Prost	Spa 23	P	KIAcc	
Lt Jean Charlet	Br 217	O	KIAcc	
Sgt Henri Fourcade	Spa 15	P	Injured	
Sgt Sauvage &	Spa 2	P	OK	
Sol Garricq	Spa 2	M	Injured	Crash-landing.

22 September

Adj Mace	a.	Spa 90	Balloon	XF	Geline	1004	5
Adj Mace	b.	Spa 90	Balloon	XF	Juvelize	1007	6
Cpl Tailler		Spa 124	Fokker	X	German lines		1
Patrol		Spa 69	EA	P	X° Armée		–
Sgt Decatoire		Spa 92	Balloon	P	Gernicourt	0740	–

a.　Probably Bz 62, AOK 19 Sector.
b.　Probably Bz 36, AOK 19 Sector.

Casualties:

1/Lt E M Powell, USAS	Br 123	O	WIA	Probably by Ltn Karl Odebrett, Jasta 42, (14).

23 September

Lt Denis &		Sal 40				1
S/Lt Beucler		Sal 40	EA	X	Mont-sans-Nom	1

Casualties:

Cpl Latil &	Sal 28	P	MIA	II° Armée, probably by Ltn Oliver von
Sgt Saloman	Sal 28	G	MIA	Beaulieu-Marconnay, CO Jasta 19, (20).
S/Lt Bernard Schroeder	Spa 95	P	WIA	
Cpl Alfred H Stanley	Spa 23	P	Injured	

24 September

S/Lt Nuville &		Spa 57					12
MdL Imhoff		Spa 57	EA	X	Cernay-en-Dormois		1
Capt Lagache,	CO	Spa 78					2
Sgt Tscheoberle,		Spa 78					1
Sgt Le Fustec &	a.	Spa 78					1
Patrol		Spa 26	2 seater	X	Massiges	1800	1
S/Lt d'Estainville		Spa 87	Balloon	XF	Bourgogne	0745	3
Capt Hay de Slade	CO	Spa 159	EA	X	N Suippes		15
45° Cie d'Aérostiers	b.	DCA	Fokker D7	POW	E Suippes	1630	–
Lt Casale &		Spa 38					–
Adj Garaud	c.	Spa 38	Fokker D7	P	Pevy-Prouilly	1810	–
Patrol		Spa 67	Fokker D7	P	Châlons	1200	–
S/Lt Dencausse		Spa 90	EA	P			–
Patrol		GC 12	Scout	P	Rouvroy-Cernay	1805	–
Patrol		GC 14	EA	P	X° Armée		–
Escadre 2		???	2 EA	P			–

a.　Possibly Vfw Wilkens & Ltn Rudolf Kaehne, FlAbt 29, KIAs, AOK "C" Sector.
b.　Probably Ltn Wilhelm Meyer, Jasta 47w, Fokker D7 N° 4522/18, POW Suippes.
c.　Had just flamed a balloon at 18h10??.

Casualties:

Sgt Delporte &	Sal 263	P	KIA	IV° Armée, probably by Vfw
S/Lt Burfin	Sal 263	O	KIA	Friedrich Poeschke, Jasta 53, (8).
MdL Charles Bettend	CRP/Spa 462	P	KIA	
S/Lt Bouillanne &	Br ??	P	OK	
Sgt Junot	Br ??	G	WIA	
Adj-Chef Pain &	Sal 218	P	WIA	

???	Sal 218	O	WIA		
Adj Pierre Couillard	43° Cie d'Aérostiers		XF	V° Armée, probably by Sgt	
(4th jump)		O	OK	Max Kuhn, Jasta 21s, (9).	
Adj Auguste Renard	45° Cie d'Aérostiers			IV° Armée, probably claimed by Ltn	
		O	OK	Wilhelm Meyer, Jasta 47w.	
S/Lt Marcel Brière	75° Cie d'Aérostiers		XF	X° Armée, probably by Uffz	
		O	OK	Heinrich Haase, Jasta 21s, (4).	
Asp Bixiaux	29° Cie d'Aérostiers			Attacked, not flamed.	
		O	OK		

25 September

Adj Priollaud	Spa 159	Scout	X	Ornes	3
Escadre 2	???	4 EA	P		–
Casualties:					
Cpl Pierre Abebes	Spa 88	P	MIA	Probably by Ltn	
				Rudolf Fuchs, Jasta 77b, (1).	
Adj Fabiani &	Br ??	P	MIA	Probably by Uffz	
S/Lt Lormail	Br ??	O	MIA	Karl Treiber, Jasta 5, (3).	
Lt Paul Bizard,	F 114	P	MIA	Probably by Ltn	
Capt Garnier &	F 114	O	MIA	Fritz Anders, Jasta 73,	
Asp Rives	F 114	G	MIA	(7).	
Sgt Chauffeur &	Sal 47	P	KIA	II° Armée, probably by Ltn	
MdL Alby	Sal 47	G	KIA	Friedrich Hengst, Jasta 64w, (3).	
S/Lt Paul Bertel	Spa 84	P	Injured		
???	??? Cie d'Aérostiers			Attacked, not flamed,	
		O	OK	Woëvre Sector.	

26 September

Meuse-Argonne Offensive starts.

Adj Parsons,		Spa 3					6
MdL Denneulin &		Spa 3					2
Lt Pendaries		Spa 67	Fokker D7	X	S Tahure	1800	6
Sgt Saxon &		Spa 12					2
Cpl Haller		Spa 12	Balloon	XF	N Sommepy	0820	2
Capt de Turenne,	CO	Spa 12					14
S/Lt Schurck &		Spa 91					3
Adj E Régnier		Spa 89	Fokker D7	POW	Ville-sur-Tourbe	0800	5
Capt de Turenne,	CO	Spa 12					15
S/Lt Herlemont &		Spa 12					2
Sgt Maurio		Spa 12	Balloon	XF	Ste Geneviève	1845	2
Adj Berthelot		Spa 15	DFW C	X	N Montfaucon	1410	9
S/Lt Guyou &		Spa 37					8
Adj Lienhart		Spa 37	Balloon	XF	N Cernay		3
S/Lt Guyou &		Spa 37					9
Adj Lienhart		Spa 37	2 seater	XF			4
Adj Lienhart &		Spa 37					5
Adj Marot		Spa 37	EA	X	Butte de Mesnil		4
Lt Body de La Chapelle		Spa 37	EA	X			1
Adj Damenez,		R 46					2
Sgt Jourde &		R 46					1
Cpl Gallotte		R 46	Scout	X			1
S/Lt Nogues &		Spa 57					13
Cpl Beaume		Spa 57	Balloon	XF	NE Sommepy	1645	1
S/Lt Gaudermen,		Spa 68					5
Adj Prévost &		Spa 68					3
Cpl Chirac		Spa 68	Scout	X	W Ville-sur-Tourbe		1
S/Lt Coadou		Spa 88	Scout	X	French lines		5
S/Lt Daladier,		Spa 93					10
Adj Delage &		Spa 93					2
MdL Meyniel		Spa 93	Balloon	XF	N Sommepy		2
S/Lt Daladier		Spa 93	EA	X			11
S/Lt de Lostalot-Bachové		Spa 97					2
Adj Joubert &		Spa 97					1
MdL Gaston		Spa 97	Balloon	XF	St Hilaire		1
1/Lt Eypper, USAS		Spa 98	2 seater	X	NE Bouconville	1545	1
Lt Fonck		Spa 103	Scout	XF	St Marie-à-Py	1145	61
Lt Fonck		Spa 103	Scout	XF	St Souplet	1145	62

Lt Fonck		Spa 103	Halb C	X	Perthes-les-Hurlus	1210	63
Lt Fonck		Spa 103	Fokker D7	X	St Souplet	1810	64
Lt Fonck		Spa 103	Fokker D7	X	E Souain	1820	65
Lt Fonck		Spa 103	Fokker D7	X	E Souain	1820	66
Sgt Kamisky		Spa 124	Balloon	XF	Sechault	1530	1
Sgt Caudry		Spa 165	Fokker D7	X	Souain	1755	1
??? &		Br 214					1
S/Lt Henry		Br 214	Scout	X	French lines		1
Brig Delage		Br 234					1
Asp Paturet		Br 234	EA	X	N Montfaucon		1
Adj Parsons		Spa 3	Fokker D7	P	Aubérive-Souain	1745	–
Adj Naudin		Spa 26	Scout	P	Grateuil	1015	–
Lt Pendaries		Spa 67	Fokker D7	P	S Tahure	1800	–
Adj Brugère		Spa 103	Fokker D7	P	N Souain	1820	–
Adj Corso &		Spa 124					–
Sgt Kamisky		Spa 124	Scout	P	E Sechault	1050	–
Cpl Tailler		Spa 124	Scout	P	Manre-Aure	1705	–
Patrol		Br 132	EA	P			–
MdL Dequeker		Spa 163	2 seater	P	Monthois	1510	–
Lt Barancy	CO	Spa 164	Fokker D7	P	Massiges	0827	–
Lt Robert		Spa 164	Fokker D7	P	Massiges	0827	–
Lt de Romanet	CO	Spa 167	Fokker D7	P	Navarin	1720	–
Lt Robert &		14 CA					–
Lt Dupuy		14 CA	Scout	P	St Souplet		–
???		???	7 EA	P			–

Casualties:

Sgt Roger Callinet		Spa 89	P	KIA	Probably by Vfw Alfons Nagler, Jasta 81, (7).
Sgt Meynadier		R 239	P	KIA	
S/Lt Richard &		Br 234	P	KIA	
Lt Sacquin		Br 234	O	WIA	II° Armée
Brig Georges Delage &		Br 234	P	WIA	
Asp Paturet		Br 234	O	WIA	II° Armée
Capt Schulenberger	CO	Br 9	P	WIA	IV° Armée
Asp Pacquet		Br 9	O	WIA	IV° Armée
Sgt Victor Jacquin		Spa 265	P	WIA	IV° Armée
Adj Vitrac		Br 207	?	WIA	IV° Armée
Lt René Henry		Br 232	P	OK	
Lt Henri Fieuvet		Br 232	O	WIA	IV° Armée
Lt Edouard Body de La Chapelle		Spa 37	P	WIA	DOW
Sgt Henri Lemaire &		Sal 16	P	WIA	Flak
Lt Champagnet		Sal 16	O	OK	V° Armée
MdL Robert Neveux &		Sal 16	P	WIA	
S/Lt Guinard		Sal 16	O	OK	V° Armée
Cpl Elie Boutin		Spa 315	P	Injured	VII° Armée, shot up in combat and crashed, AOK "B" Sector.
Lt Hayer &		Spa 213	P	Injured	Spad 2, probably by Ltn
Cpl Chausden		Spa 213	G	Injured	Walter Blume, Jasta 9, (26).
Lt Jean Philippe Nèpre		19° Cie d'Aérostiers		XF	IV° Armée, probably by Ltn
			O	OK	Hermann Habich, Jasta 49 (4).
S/Lt Defleury &		21° Cie d'Aérostiers		XF	IV° Armée, probably by Ltn
S/Lt Vallier			O	OK	Fritz Höhn, Jasta 60, (12).
Adj André Lurcat		30° Cie d'Aérostiers		XF	IV° Armée, probably by Ltn
			O	OK	Hans v Freden, Jasta 50, (10).
???		39° Cie d'Aérostiers		XF	1st Army, AEF, Sector.
S/Lt Henri Lovat		31° Cie d'Aérostiers			Attacked, not flamed, Woëvre Sector.

27 September

MdL Frémiot &		Br 29				1
Lt Coubaz		Br 29				1
Lt Charmess &		Br 29				1
Sgt Lascourreges		Br 29	Scout	X		1
Sgt Corsi &		Spa 77				2
MdL Thévenod		Spa 77	Balloon	XF		2
Capt Tourangin,	CO	Spa 89				4
Adj E Régnier &		Spa 89				6

Sgt Lasnes	Spa 89	2 seater	X	Sommepy-Marne		2
Adj Fleury &	Spa 95					4
Sgt Lacouture	Spa 95	EA	X	German lines		3
Capt Koenig Belliard de Vaubicourt, CO	Spa 100					2
Lt Poulin,	Spa 100					2
Sgt Corale &	Spa 100					1
Sgt Hummell	Spa 100	EA	XF			1
Lt Fouan &	Br 108					2
Asp Blanc &	Br 108					1
Adj Robyn &	Br 108					1
Adj Douville	Br 108	EA	X			1
Capt d'Argueeff &	EM GC 21					11
Lt Marolle	EM GC 21	Fokker D7	X	N Cernay		1
Sgt Guillet a.	Spa 163	Pfalz	X	Sommepy	1735	3
Lt Thiberge	EM IV° Armée	EA	X	Grateuil		2
MdL de Gaillard de Valdène	Spa 95	EA	P			–
S/Lt Coudouret	Spa 103	Rumpler C	P	NE Sommepy	1730	–
Lt Metayer &	Br 108					–
Asp Millet	Br 108	Scout	P			–
??? &	Br 129					–
Lt Briset	Br 129	EA	P			–

a.   Possibly Vfw Heinrich Brobowski, Jasta 53, POW Sommepy.

Casualties:

MdL Joseph Thévenod	Spa 77	P	MIA	Probably by Ltn Max Näther, Jasta 62, (17).	
Lt Delephine	GB 4	P	KIA		
Sgt Henri Gantois	Spa 100	P	WIA	Probably by Vfw Dietrich Averes, Jasta 81, (8).	
Lt Cuvelier	Spa 60	P	WIA	Flak, IV° Armée, Spad 2.	
Lt Roger Metayer &	Br 108	P	WIA	Probably by Vfw Alfons Nagler,	
Asp René Millet	Br 108	G	WIA	Jasta 81, (8).	
Sgt-Maj Charles Leteneur &	Br 111	P	WIA		
Asp Auguste Etchberry	Br 111	O	WIA		
Cpl Gabriel Pachi	Spa 81	P	KIAcc		
MdL Louis Beudin	CI	P	Injured		
Sgt François Compagnon	31° Cie d'Aérostiers		XF	IV° Armée, probably by Ltn Hans	
Sgt Henri Bonnières		O	OK	von Freden, Jasta 50, (12), 16h55.	

28 September

The Battle of Flanders commences.

S/Lt Portron,	Spa 31					4
S/Lt Chartoire &	Spa 31					3
MdL Jacquet	Spa 31	Fokker D7	X	N Bois de Bouc	1145	1
Adj Henriot	Spa 65	EA	XF	N Sommepy	1512	6
Sgt Damhet	Spa 65	EA	XF	N Sommepy		1
Adj Delage	Spa 93	Scout	XF			3
Lt Fonck	Spa 103	2 seater	X	E Sommepy	1030	67
Capt d'Argueeff	EM GC 21	2 seater	X	Manre	1010	12
Capt d'Argueeff	EM GC 21	2 seater	X	Séchault	1520	13
Lt de Sevin de Quincy	CO Spa 151	2 seater	XF	Sommepy	1645	3
S/Lt Coiffard	CO Spa 154	Balloon	XF	SW Semide	0900	32
MdL Onillon	Spa 163	Balloon	XF	Challerange	0930	2
Sgt Connelly	Spa 163	Balloon	XF	Challerange	1115	6
S/Lt Romatet,	CO Spa 165					5
S/Lt Decugis &	Spa 165					3
Lt Besse	Spa 165	Balloon	XF	Orfeuil	0845	1
Sgt Chauffaux	Spa 3	2 seater	P	Ste Geneviève	1130	–
Adj Prévost	Spa 68	EA	P			–
Lt Bergé	CO Spa 124	EA	P	N Bois de Forges	1200	–
S/Lt Coiffard	CO Spa 154	Fokker	P			–
Lt Romatet	CO Spa 165	Fokker D7	P		0700	–
S/Lt Hueber &	Br 257					–
???	Br 257	Fokker	P			–
???	???	EA	P	Flanders		–

Casualties:

Cpl Gérard	Spa 62	P	MIA	Probably by Uffz	

				Konrad Boness, Jasta 53, (1).		
Cpl Gaulhiac	Spa 62	P	MIA	Probably by Ltn Wolff, Jasta 60, (1).		
MdL Roger Milhan	Spa 65	P	MIA	Probably by Jasta 72s		
Adj Montel &	Br 123	P	MIA			
Sgt Fautrat	Br 123	G	MIA			
Cpl Moser &	Br 9	P	WIA/POW			
S/Lt Henri Le Conte des Loris	Br 9	O	POW	IV° Armée		
Lt Gilles	Br 269	O	KIA	IV° Armée		
Sgt Bal &	Sal 252	P	KIA	IV° Armée, probably by Vfw		
S/Lt Nouvellon	Sal 252	O	KIA	Friedrich Poeschke, Jasta 53, (4).		
S/Lt Gaston Jeanniot	Br 123	O	WIA	Flak		
Sgt Roux	Br 282	P	OK			
Asp Bertrand	Br 282	O	WIA			
Lt Louis Mailloux	Br 55	O	WIA	Ground fire.		
MdL Emmanuel Colliaux &	Br 209	P	KIAcc	Bréguet F40		
Lt Marcel Laville	Br 209	O	KIAcc			
Sgt Bourgeois	Spa 65	P	Injured			
Lt Robert Weiss	67° Cie d'Aérostiers		XF	IV° Armée, probably by Ltn		
		O	OK	Fritz Höhn, Jasta 60, (15).		

29 September

S/Lt Waddington	Spa 31	Fokker D7	XF	Orfeuil	0945	12
Sgt Rotureau	Spa 57	2 seater	X	N Aubérive	1740	2
Adj Drozière &	Spa 69					1
Sgt Fugier	Spa 69	Balloon	XF			1
Adj-Chef Delzenne	Spa 88	Scout	X	E Monthois	1825	7
MdL Ducornet	Spa 93	Balloon	XF	Machault		7
MdL Meyniel	Spa 93	Scout	XF			3
Sgt Bellat &	Br 127					1
Asp Steiner	Br 127	EA	X			1
S/Lt Cousin	Spa 163	2 seater	X	Sechault	1545	3
Sgt Lucot,	R 240					1
Sol Devillers &	R 240					1
Sol O'Farrel	R 240	Scout	X	German lines		1
Sgt Savaurel &	Sal 8					–
Sgt Petit	Sal 8	EA	P			–
Capt de Turenne CO	Spa 12	Scout	P	NE Sommepy	1015	–
Lt Herlemont	Spa 12	Scout	P	NE Sommepy	1030	–
Lt Madon CO	Spa 38	2 seater	P	Chevrigny	1515	–
Lt Le Petit	Spa 67	EA	P	Sommepy	1135	–
Adj Discours	Spa 87	Balloon	P	Parisy	1210	–
Adj Paulinier &	Spa 98					–
MdL Champavier	Spa 98	Fokker	P	Vaux-les-Mouron	1720	–
S/Lt Bourjade	Spa 152	Balloon	P	Hermoniville	1750	–
MdL Julien	Spa 156	Fokker D7	P	Macahult	1800	–
Sgt Paden	Spa 163	Fokker	P	Machault	1545	–
Sgt Lederlin	Spa 163	Fokker	P	Challerange	1550	–
Lt Hervieux &	Br 128					–
???	Br 128	EA	P			–
??? &	Br 127					–
Sgt Touchet	Br 127	EA	P			–
???	???	EA	P	Aisne		–
Escadre 2	???	2 EA	P	Champagne	–	
???	GB	5 EA	P			–

Casualties:

Sgt Kalley &	Spa 42	P	MIA	IV° Armée, Spad 2, probably by	
Lt Kervadoe	Spa 42	O	MIA	Uffz Otto Bieliet, Jasta 66 (1).	
Capt Paul Reverchon CO	Spa 31	P	KIA	Probably by Ltn Hans v Freden, Jasta 50, (13).	
MdL de Bellencourt &	Spa 34	P	WIA	Spad 2, possibly by Ltn	
S/Lt François Le Clerc de Bussy	Spa 34	O	WIA	Theo Osterkamp, MJFII, (29).	
Adj Gustave Naudin	Spa 26	P	WIA	During morning hours.	
Adj Coudreau	Br 8	P	WIA	IV° Armée	
Sgt Prosper Bellat &	Br 127	P	OK		
Asp Pierre Steiner	Br 127	O	WIA		

S/Lt Henri Arnould	Spa 84	P	KIAcc			
Adj Toutain	Spa 102	P	KIAcc			
S/Lt Robert Waddington	Spa 31	P	Injured			
MdL Pierre Burke &	Br 132	P	Injured			
Cpl Elie Vidal	Br 132	G	Injured			

30 September

Sgt Onillon,	Spa 163					3
Sgt Paden &	Spa 163					1
Sgt Lefevbre	Spa 163	2 seater	X	Cernay	1823	1
MdL Jallot &	Sal 27					–
???	Sal 27	EA	P			–
Cpl Heine &	Spa 164					–
Cpl Gerain	Spa 164	EA	P	Challerange	1823	–

Casualties:

Adj Albert Montel &	Br 123	P	MIA	Probably by Ltn Franz Ray,		
Sgt Marcel Poclet	Br 123	G	MIA	Jasta 49 (17).		
Cpl Limay Heine	Spa 164	P	KIA	Probably by Vfw Alfons Nagler, Jasta 81, (9).		
Capt Marcel Morize CO	Br 207	P	WIA	V° Armée, ground fire.		
Sgt Gramaud	Spa 155	P	KIAcc			
Adj Coudero &	Sal 106	P	OK	IV° Armée, FTL at Mont Murat,		
S/Lt Zuber	Sal 106	O	OK	during combat, probably by Ltn Hermann Habich, Jasta 49, (5).		

Date unknown, September 1918.

S/Lt René Dalquie	???	?	KIAcc			

1 October

Adj Parsons	Spa 3	2 seater	XF	N Sommepy	1510	8
S/Lt Portron &	Spa 31					5
MdL Libault	Br 11					1
S/Lt Marrec	Br 11	Scout	X	Orfeuil	1550	1
S/Lt Fraissinet a.	Spa 57	Halb CL	XF	Aure	1800	7
S/Lt Fraissinet &	Spa 57					8
Sgt Graignac	Spa 57	Halb CL	XF	N Sommepy	1805	1
Adj Rimbaud &	Spa 82					3
Cpl Gravis	Spa 82	Scout	X	Flanders		1
Lt Pellet	Spa 85	2 seater	POW	Champagne	1745	2
S/Lt Coadou & CO	Spa 88					6
Sgt Serne	Spa 88	EA	X	N Sommepy		1
Sgt Sansom &	Spa 103					1
Adj Drouilh	Spa 103	Scout	X	NW Sommepy	1245	3
Patrol	Br 120	EA	X			–
S/Lt Bourjade &	Spa 152					21
S/Lt Maunoury	Spa 152	Balloon	XF	Orainville	1350	10
S/Lt Bourjade &	Spa 152					22
S/Lt Maunoury	Spa 152	Balloon	XF	Orainville	1355	11
Capt Hay de Slade CO a.	Spa 159	EA	XF	Aure	1800	16
Capt Hay de Slade CO	Spa 159	EA	XF	NE Sommepy		17
Cpl de Lombardon	Spa 167	2 seater	X	N Béthéniville	1405	1
Adj Artigau	Spa 15	Scout	P	Champagne		–
MdL Legron	Spa 98	Scout	P	Lancon	0745	–
Sgt Sansom &	Spa 103					–
Adj Drouilh	Spa 103	Scout	P	NW Sommepy	1245	–

a.   Probably Vfw Theodor Schäfer & Vfw Alfred Hädrich, SchSta 34, KIAs Aure.

Casualties:

Sgt Paul Joubert	???	P	KIA	Collided with another a/c.		
Asp Paret &	Spa 55	P	WIA	IV° Armée		
Lt Volland	Spa 55	O	WIA	Spad XVI, ground fire.		
Asp Roger Lavalley	Br 202	O	WIA	Flak		
Sgt Icard	Spa 315	P	KIAcc	Spad		
Cpl Denis Vincent	Spa 92	P	KIAcc	Spad VII		
Cpl Ory	Sal 33	P	Injured	Salmson 2A2		
Sol Vignolet	GDE	M	Injured	DOW		
???	83? Cie d'Aérostiers			V° Armée, 18h00. probably by		
		O	OK	Sgt Max Kühn, Jasta 21s,(10).		

???		??? Cie d'Aérostiers			Attacked, not flamed,		
		O		OK	Aisne Sector.		

2 October

Name		Unit	Type		Location	Time	No.
Lt Garros		Spa 26	Fokker D7	X	Ste Marie-à-Py	1245	4
Adj Prévost	a.	Spa 68	Scout	X	Cuisy		4
Lt Pellet &		Spa 85					3
Sgt Rousseau		Spa 85	Balloon	XF	N Semide		1
Adj Delage		Spa 93	Balloon	XF	Sommepy		4
Adj Delage		Spa 93	Balloon	XF	Machault		5
Adj Delage		Spa 93	Fokker D7	XF	Champagne		6
Lt Lemaitre &	CO	Br 120					2
Adj Rousel &		Br 120					1
Adj Guillon &		Br 120					1
MdL Galand		Br 120	Scout	X	Champagne		2
Asp Briaumont &		Br 129					2
Asp Brunet		Br 129	Scout	X	Champagne		1
S/Lt Coiffard	CO	Spa 154	2 seater	X	St Etienne-à-Arnes		33
Cpl Huillet		Spa 161	Scout	X	Flanders		1
Brig Coriol &		Br 211					1
S/Lt Théry		Br 211	EA	X	French lines		1
Sgt Carteron,		R 240					2
MdL Buisson &		R 240					3
Sol Raymond		R 240	Scout	XF	Semide		1
Capt de Sevin &	CO	Spa 26					–
Lt Garros		Spa 26	Fokker D7	P	Ste Marie-à-Py	0910	–
Sgt Lachat		Spa 124	EA	P	Brécy	1600	–
Escadre 2		GC	2EA	P			–

a.   Possibly Uffz Max Niemann, Schusta 21, POW, shot down at Malancourt, about 5 km S of Cuisy.

Casualties:

Name	Unit	Role	Status	Notes
Sgt Henri Durand	Spa 150	P	KIA	V° Armée, Spad VII, probably by Ltn Walter Blume, Jasta 9 (27).
S/Lt Robert Decugis	Spa 165	P	MIA	Spad XIII N° 3597, and
Sgt Georges Louison	Spa 165	P	MIA	Spad XIII N° 11133, these two collided during combat probably claimed by Vfw Dietrich Averes (9) & Alfons Nagler (10) Jasta 81, IV° Armée.
Sol Druon	Sal 14	G	MIA	Salmson 2A2
Asp Maily	Br 117	B	MIA	Bréguet 14B2
S/Lt Jean Morraglia	Br 127	P	WIA	Bréguet 14B2
S/Lt Falgarone	Br 250	O	WIA	V° Armée, Bréguet.
MdL Tétart	Br 281	P	OK	
Sgt Giraud	Br 281	G	WIA	II° Armée, Bréguet 14A2.
Asp Weil	Br 29	P	WIA	Bréguet 14
Adj Laporte	???	P	WIA	Ground fire.
S/Lt Poirier &	V 121	P	KIAcc	
MdL Baras	V 121	G	Injured	Voisin X
Sgt Hortale &	Br 202	P	Injured	
S/Lt Mongin	Br 202	O	Injured	Bréguet 14A2
???	31° Cie d'Aérostiers			IV° Armée, probably by Ltn
	O		OK	Fritz Höhn, Jasta 41, (20).
???	??? Cie d'Aérostiers			Cable cut by French two-
	O		OK	seater, crews unharmed.

3 October

Name		Unit	Type		Location	Time	No.
Capt Chevillon	CO	Spa 15	EA	XF	E Vaudesincourt		4
Capt de La Perelle &		Spa 15					1
S/Lt Serge		Spa 15	EA	X	St Hilairel		1
MdL Brillaud		Spa 26	Fokker D7	X	E Sommepy	1435	1
Lt Le Petit		Spa 67	Fokker D7	X	Dontrien	1450	1
Cpl Gravis		Spa 82	EA	X	Flanders		2
Lt Le Coq de Kerland	CO	Spa 82	Fokker D7	X	Roulers		7
MdL Rousseau		Spa 84	EA	X	Moronvillers	1452	1
MdL Rouchaud,		Spa 84					1
MdL Marnat &		Spa 84					1
MdL Cordier		Spa 84	Fokker D7	X	Moronvillers		1
Lt Bozon-Verduraz	CO	Spa 94	EA	X			10

S/Lt Bourjade &	Spa 152					23
S/Lt Garin	Spa 152	Balloon	XF	Cherest	1540	1
S/Lt Condemine	Spa 154	Balloon	XF	Bétheniville	0900	8
Sgt Patry	Spa 155	EA	X	Champagne		2
Lt Barny de Romanet & CO	Spa 167					11
Cpl de Lombardon	Spa 167	Fokker D7	XF	St Pierre-à-Arnes	1010	2
S/Lt Martel	Spa 313	Fokker D7	X	Flanders		1
Asp Nicodeau &	Spa 315					1
Adj Ferte	Spa 315	Balloon	XF	Pulversheim		1
S/Lt Coiffard & CO	Spa 154					–
S/Lt Condemine	Spa 154	2 seater	P	S Dontrien	0845	–
Lt Madon CO	Spa 38	EA	P	Condé-sur-Suippe	1045	–
Patrol	Spa 82	EA	P	Flanders		–
S/Lt Martenot de Cordoux a.	Spa 94	Fokker D7	P	St Martin l'Heureux		–
Adj Bentejac &	Spa 124					–
Sgt Grillot	Spa 124	2 seater	P	Brecy-Olizy	1320	–
Lt Dumont	Spa 85	EA	P	Champagne		–
???	9?CA	Fokker D7	P	Savigny		–
Escadre 1	GC	EA	P	Champagne		–
???	GB	EA	P	Champagne		–
???	GC	EA	P	Aisne		–

a.   Probably Ltn Fritz Höhn, Jasta 41, KIA St Martin l'Heureux.

Casualties:

MdL Maurice Lesueur	Spa 313	P	KIA	Spad VII
Brig Bourgoin	Spa 156	P	MIA	IV° Armée, Spad VII, probably by Ltn Franz Kirchfeld, Jasta 73 (5).
Cpl Tallet	Spa 155	P	MIA	Spad VII
Brig Carton	Spa 100	P	MIA	Spad XIII
Cpl Raymond Desouches	Spa 159	P	MIA	Spad VII, probably by Vfw Dietrich Averes, Jasta 81, (10).
Cpl Henri Fouriex	Spa 82	P	MIA	Spad VIIs, four claimed by Jasta
Cpl Louis Rolland	Spa 82	P	MIA	40 pilots, Lts Degelow (22),
Brig Edmond Pirolley	Spa 82	P	MIA	Rosenstein (6), Gilly (5) and Vfw Groll (3), over Roulers.
Cpl Guy &	Br 214	P	MIA	
S/Lt Dhers	Br 214	O	MIA	Bréguet 14A2
Cpl Puyaubert &	Br 128	P	MIA	
Asp Goyot	Br 128	O	MIA	
Adj Dieudonne &	Sal 106	P	MIA	IV° Armée, Salmson 2A2, probably
Lt Hamon	Sal 106	O	MIA	by OfStv Gustav Dörr, Jasta 45 (30).
MdL Armand Rousseau	Spa 84	P	KIA	Spad VII
MdL Roger Maindron &	Br 282	P	KIA	III° Armée
Brig Emile Billet	Br 282	G	KIA	Bréguet 14A2
Cpl Chatelain &	V 101	P	KIA	
Asp Ouin	V 101	O	KIA	Voisin-Renault
Sgt Walter J Shaffer	Spa 38	P	WIA/POW	Spad VII, ground fire.
Sgt Emile Breton	Spa 84	P	POW	
MdL Edmond Féry	Spa 163	P	WIA	DOW 10 October 1918 IV° Armée, Spad VII.
MdL Robert Brillaut	Spa 26	P	WIA	IV° Armée, Spad XIII.
Lt Hubert Dumont	Spa 85	P	WIA	Spad XIII
Sgt Tucci	Br 250	P	WIA	V° Armée, Bréguet.
Cpl Jacques	Spa 91	P	KIAcc	Spad VII
Sgt Adolphe du Bois d'Aische	GDE	P	Injured	Spad VII
Cpl Larousse	Br 215	P	Injured	Bréguet 14A2
Adj de Balmann	V 113	G	Injured	Voisin X
S/Lt Hector Garaud	Spa 38	P	OK	FTL during combat, and strafed on the ground.
???	51° Cie d'Aérostiers		XF	Probably by Vfw Richard
		O	OK	Rübe, Jasta 67, (5).
S/Lt René Prévost	51° Cie d'Aérostiers		XF	IV° Armée
		O	OK	
Lt Robert Weiss	67° Cie d'Aérostiers		XF	IV° Armée, probably by Ltn
		O	WIA	Karl Ritscherle, Jasta 60, (8).
Sgt Blondeau	??? Cie d'Aérostiers			Attacked, not flamed,
		O	OK	Champagne Sector.

S/Lt Vital Joy	43° Cie d'Aérostiers		XF	V° Armée, Aisne Sector.		
	O		OK			
???	??? Cie d'Aérostiers		XF	Aisne Sector.		

4 October

Sgt Belin &	Sal 27					1
Adj Lemmery	Sal 27	2 seater	XF	Château de Bemont	1535	1
S/Lt Joublin &	Sal 40					1
Lt Chappuis &	Sal 40					1
MdL Brochon &	Spa 140					1
S/Lt Crosnier	Spa 140	Fokker D7	X	Moronvillers	1715	1
S/Lt Daladier	Spa 93	Balloon	XF	W Machault	1155	12
Adj Delage	Spa 93	EA	X	German lines		7
Cdt Vuillemin & CO	Esc 12					7
Adj Borel	Br 127	Fokker D7	X	Semide	1200	3
S/Lt Bourjade &	Spa 152					24
Adj Manson	Spa 152	Balloon	XF	Orgeval	0720	2
S/Lt Gérard,	R 242					1
Sgt Fortin &	R 242					1
Cpl Ravaux &	R 242					1
Brig Daulouet,	R 242					1
Sgt Pibart &	R 242					1
Sol Andille	R 242	EA	X	Vosges		1
??? a.	DCA	Fokker D7	X	Argonne		–
S/Lt Nautet &	Br 213					–
S/Lt Massini	Br 213	EA	P	Cerbon	1630	–
Escadre 2	GC	EA	P	Champagne		–

a.   Three Fokker D7s claimed shot down by 68° Section d'Auto-Canons (66° RA).

Casualties:

Sgt Wolff &	Spa 265	P	MIA	IV° Armée, Spad XI, probably by
Lt Jourdain	Spa 265	O	MIA	Wilhelm Frickart, Jasta 65 (10).
Cpl Alphonse Lambert	Spa 93	P	MIA	Spad XIII, possibly by Jasta 17.
Adj Pierre Delage	Spa 93	P	MIA	Spad VII, pilots Ltn Bohny (6),
				Ltn Kaiser (1) or Ltn Fleischer (3)
				all at St Morel.
Lt Artemus Gates, USN #	CAM	P	POW	Spad XIII N° 15728.
Sgt Eugène Tourane	Spa 83	P	POW	Spad XIII, St Quentin.
S/Lt Suder	Sal 106	O	WIA	IV° Armée, DOW 6 October 1918,
				Salmson 2A2, ground fire.
S/Lt Pierre Gérard	R 242	P	WIA	VII° Armée, Caudron R11,
Sgt Fortin &	R 242	G	WIA	probably by Uffz Stehling,
Cpl Maurice Ravaux	R 242	G	WIA	Jasta 69 (1), AOK "B".
Cpl Desmoulins	GDE	P	KIAcc	Sopwith
Cpl Bonneau &	???	P	Injured	
Lt Duflos	???	O	Injured	
???	??? Cie d'Aérostiers			During night of 3-4 Oct, this balloon was
				damaged by a bomb dropped from an
				EA, one sentry was killed. Picardie Sector.

\#   Secretary of the U.S. Navy during WWII.

5 October

MdL Libault &	Br 11					1
S/Lt Coffin	Br 11	Fokker D7	X	N Monts-Chery		1
Sgt Rousselle,	Spa 81					6
Lt Lemarie,	Spa 81					1
Adj Guyot &	Spa 81					1
MdL Gallant	Spa 81	Balloon	XF			1
Adj Marinovitch	Spa 94	Fokker D7	XF	E Challerange	1130	16
Lt Fonck	Spa 103	2 seater	X	Liry-Marvaux	1730	68
Lt Fonck	Spa 103	Fokker D7	X	St Clément	1740	69
Capt d'Argueeff	EM GC 21	2 seater	X	Orfeuil	1815	14
Adj Dossisard &	Br 219					1
MdL Barelle	Br 219	EA	X			1
Adj de Faucamberge &	Br 267					1
S/Lt Plantier	Br 267	EA	X	Champagne		1
Lt Dombray	Spa 26	2 seater	FTL	Bétheniville	1600	–
MdL Lambotte	Spa 26	2 seater	P	Aure-Manre	1710	–

Cpl Prévost	Spa 68	EA	P	Bourgogne	1800	–
Lt Fonck	Spa 103	Scout	P	St Etienne-à-Arnes	1800	–
Lt Fonck	Spa 103	Scout	P	Orfeuil	1800	–
Capt d'Argueeff	EM GC 21	2 seater	P	NE Autry	1125	–
Sgt Lachat	Spa 124	2 seater	P	N Monthois	1735	–
Sgt Guillet,	Spa 163					–
Sgt Onillon &	Spa 163					–
Sgt Cook	Spa 163	Fokker	P	NE Marvaux	1500	–
S/Lt Gerbault	Spa 165	Fokker	P	N Sommepy	1330	–
Escadre 1	GC	4 EA	P	Champagne		–
Escadre 2	GC	3 EA	P	Champagne		–
Infantry fire	???	EA	P	VII° Armée		–

Casualties:

Sgt Lucien Costes	Spa 168	P	MIA	V° Armée, Spad XIII.
S/Lt Roland Garros (1)	Spa 26	P	KIA	Spad XIII N° 15403, probably by Ltn Hermann Habich, Jasta 49, (6).
MdL Carlin &	Sal 27	P	MIA	IV° Armée, Salmson 2A2s, possibly
Sol Catineau	Sal 27	G	MIA	by Ltns K Bohny (7) & J Buckler
MdL Rey &	Sal 27	P	KIA	(34), Jasta 17.
Lt d'Exea-Doumerc	Sal 27	O	KIA	(2 AR2s in this sector).
MdL Icaré &	Br 222	P	KIA	V° Armée, at Marzilly,
Lt Choupaut	Br 222	O	KIA	Bréguet 14A2.
Cpl Jules Vernier	Sal 105	G	WIA	DOW, V° Armée
MdL Valentin Libault &	Br 11	P	WIA	IV° Armée
S/Lt Maurice Coffin	Br 11	O	WIA	Bréguet 14A2
Sgt Pierre Capelet &	Sal 264	P	WIA	V° Armée, FTL Brimont,
S/Lt Jean Lagarde	Sal 264	O	OK	probably by OfStv Gustav Dörr, Jasta 45, (31) (AR2 at Brimont).
Brig Delaunay &	CIACB	P	KIAcc	
Sol Cerier	CIACB	M	KIAcc	Voisin
Lt Busk	Spa 2	O	Injured	Spad XVI
Sol Lesneux	???	M	Injured	
???	51° Cie d'Aérostiers			IV° Armée, probably by Ltn
		O	OK	Gustav Wember, Jasta 61 (3).
???	54° Cie d'Aérostiers			X° Armée, probably by Sgt
		O	OK	Max Kuhn, Jasta 21s, (12).
???	76° Cie d'Aérostiers			Attacked, cable cut and balloon set
		O	OK	adrift, came down in French lines.

One other balloon was attacked in the Aisne Sector, but not flamed.

(1)   Departed at 09h30, MIA at 11h15 during combat with three Fokker D7s SW of Vouziers. It appeared that the synchronisation of his Vickers machine-guns, which he had specially modified, malfunctioned and shot his propeller, breaking it, and he was unable to defend himself.

6 October

S/Lt Brétillon	Spa 49	Scout	XF	Soppe	1040	7
Sgt Daussin &	Sal 52					1
S/Lt Lucques	Sal 52	Scout	X			1
Brig Pature dit Binet	Spa 97	EA	X	Falaise		1
S/Lt Cousin	Spa 163	2 seater	X	Machault	0940	4
MdL Legros &	Sal 230					1
S/Lt Ferry	Sal 230	Scout	X	Bétheniville	1630	1
Adj de Faucamberge &	Br 267					2
S/Lt Thinat	Br 267	2 seater	X	La Neuville	0630	1
Adj Bajac	Spa 48	EA	P			–
Adj Bentejac	Spa 124	2 seater	P	Mouron	1320	–
S/Lt Cousin	Spa 163	2 seater	P	Machault	0950	–
MdL Morvan	Spa 163	Scout	P	Suippe	0940	–
MdL Morvan	Spa 163	Scout	P	Machault	0950	–
S/Lt Agaccio &	Sal 230					
Asp Gosse	Sal 230	2 seater	P	St Clément-à-Arne		–
VII° Armée	GC	EA	P	Vosges		–
Ground fire	VII° Armée	EA	P			–

Casualties:

Sgt Georges Boudet	Spa 95	P	MIA	Spad VII, probably by a Jasta 61 pilot.
Cpl Jean Maupoil	Spa 80	P	MIA	Spad VII
S/Lt Vicaro &	Br 267	P	MIA	IV° Armée, Bréguet 14A2, probably by a
S/Lt Cardey	Br 267	O	MIA	Jasta 49 pilot, N Pont-Faverger.
Sgt Dupuy &	Br 208	P	KIA	Bréguet 14A2, probably by

FRENCH AIR SERVICE WAR CHRONOLOGY

Name	Unit	Role	Fate	Location	Time	No.
Lt Guinet	Br 208	O	WIA	Jasta 49 pilot.		
Lt Pierre Jacob	Spa 20	O	WIA	IV° Armée, Spad XVI.		
Adj Ange Poggioli	R 46	G	WIA			
Sol André Dupuis	R 46	G	WIA	Caudron R 11		
Sol Géry Waeselynck	R 46	G	WIA			
Sgt Antoine	GDE	P	KIAcc	Spad XIII		
Sgt Désiré Munerot	Spa 65	P	KIAcc	Spad XIII		
Cpl Baumgartner	Spa 97	P	Injured	Spad XIII		
Sgt Lanaud	52° Cie d'Aérostiers			II° Armée, attacked, not		
		O	OK	flamed.		

7 October

Name	Unit					No.
Adj Arnoux,	Spa 49					4
MdL Girard &	Spa 49					1
MdL Simonin	Spa 49	Rumpler C	X	Burnhaupt		1
Casualties: None						

8 October

Name	Unit					No.
Sgt Bodin	Spa 62	EA	X	Flanders		1
S/Lt Bourjade &	Spa 152					25
Sgt Garin	Spa 152	Balloon	XF	Chamouille	1645	2
Adj Champod &	Spa 285					1
S/Lt Elissagaray &	Spa 285					1
S/Lt Fonde de Niort &	Spa 285					1
S/Lt Montaudie	Spa 285	Fokker D7	XF	SW Avaux	1630	1
Casualties:						
MdL Couturier &	Sal 24	P	MIA	Salmson 2A2, possibly by		
Adjudant Guinsard	Sal 24	G	MIA	Ltn Werner Preuss, Jasta 66, (19).		
Lt Vedie	Spa 235	P	WIA	IV° Armée, Spad 2, ground fire.		
Sol Pellini	Sal 24	G	WIA	Salmson 2A2		
S/Lt Benjamin Girardot	Sal 58	O	WIA	Salmson, ground fire		
S/Lt Boulommier	Br 213	O	WIA	Flak		
Adj Argobast	???	P	WIA	Flak		
Sgt Gieger	Br 281	P	Injured	Bréguet 14A2		
Sgt Laurent	Br 66	P	Injured			
Cpl Deiller	GDE	P	Injured	Sopwith		
???	26° Cie d'Aérostiers		XF	IV° Armée		
		O	OK			
Sgt Gravier	61° Cie d'Aérostiers			II° Armée, attacked, not		
		O	OK	flamed.		

9 October

Name	Unit					No.
Adj Berthelot	Spa 15	EA	X	Bantheville	1640	10
Adj Berthelot	Spa 15	EA	X	Bantheville	1645	11
Lt Sardier, CO	Spa 48					14
Sgt Denomaison &	Spa 48					1
Sgt Grimouille	Spa 94	Rumpler C	X	Semide		2
Adj Franc &	Spa 69					2
Lt de Boigne	Spa 69	2 seater	X	German lines		6
Cpl Froussard	Spa 84	EA	X	Machault	1545	1
S/Lt Coadou a.	Spa 88	Scout	X	Montfaucon	1640	7
S/Lt Le Comte &	Spa 88					2
Cpl Cantener a.	Spa 88	EA	X	Campagne		1
Lt Fedoroff	Spa 89	Scout	XF	Damvillers		6
S/Lt Prêtre	Spa 91	Scout	X	Champagne		4
Adj Marinovitch	Spa 94	Rumpler C	X	Semide	1530	17
Lt Bozon-Verduraz & CO	Spa 94					11
Lt Laganne	Spa 94	2 seater	X	Bétheniville		4
Brig Froussard	Spa 94	2 seater	X	Machault	1545	1
Lt Luciani,	Br 108					1
Lt Mongin,	Br 108					1
S/Lt Nazare-Aga,	Br 108					2
Adj Douville,	Br 108					3
Adj Caulliez &	Br 108					1
Adj Hugues	Br 108	Fokker D7	XF	Champagne		1
Sgt Lhert,	Br 108					1

Sgt Frossart,		Br 108				1
Sgt Birio,		Br 108				2
Asp Roux,		Br 108				1
Sgt Gillet &		Br 108				1
Sol Sallas		Br 108	Fokker D7	XF	Champagne	1
Cpl Groléas &		Br 127				1
Sol Floissac		Br 127	EA	X	Champagne	1
Asp Desmoulins &		Br 29				1
Sol Terres		Br 29				1
MdL de Savy &		Br 29				1
Lt Chardenot		Br 29				1
MdL Bourrey &		Br 29				1
Asp Pesset		Br 29				1
MdL Cesbron &		Br 29				1
Adj Besset		Br 29	EA	X	Champagne	1
MdL Borel &		Br 129				1
Asp Bras &		Br 129				1
Asp Briaumont &		Br 129				2
Asp Brunet &		Br 129				2
MdL Boucher &		Br 129				1
Asp Alcouffe		Br 129	EA	X	Champagne	1
MdL Gault,		R 240				2
Adj Pilleron &		R 240				1
Sol Guillet		R 240	Scout	X	Champagne	1
MdL Gault,		R 240				3
Adj Pilleron &		R 240				2
Sol Guillet		R 240	Scout	X	Champagne	2
Cpl Pileyre,		R 240				1
Sol Delcroix &		R 240				1
Sol Moulin		R 240	Scout	X	Champagne	1
Sgt Carteron,		R 240				3
Asp Fichet &		R 240				1
Asp Gras		R 240	Scout	X	Champagne	1
Patrol		Spa 69	EA	P	Laval	–
???		GC	5 EA	P		–
???		EdA	EA	P	Flanders	–

a.   Possibly Ltn Gerhard Hoffmann and Uffz Paul Drybusch, Jasta 68.

Casualties:

Sgt Le Mercier &	Br 238	P	MIA	Bréguet 14A2 #5450, posssibly by
Cpl Charles	Br 238	G	MIA	Uffz Dannemann, Jasta 56, (2).
Cpl Ballou &	Br 238	P	MIA	Bréguet 14A2 possibly by Vfw
Cpl Feignier	Br 238	G	MIA	Krebs, Jasta 56, (1).
Cpl Charles Daladier &	Br 29	P	MIA	Possibly by OfStv
Sol Eugène Corbisier	Br 29	G	MIA	Gustav Dörr, Jasta 45, (32).
Brig Raymond Tertain	Spa 89	P	KIA	Spad VII
Asp Auguste Mangen	Spa 55	O	WIA	Spad XVI, ground fire.
Capt Landormy &	Br 238	P	WIA	
Lt Pierre Veunevet	Br 238	O	OK	Bréguet 14B2
Sgt Pierre Chanel	Sal 6	P	WIA	Salmson 2A2, combat with
S/Lt Marie Celerier	Sal 6	O	WIA	a Fokker Dr I.
Asp Gaston Briaumont	Br 129	P	WIA	
S/Lt Pacaud	Spa 12	P	KIAcc	Spad VII
Sgt Denis Auclair &	Br 207	P	Injured	
S/Lt Pierre Mandel	Br 207	O	Injured	Bréguet 14A2 N° 4809
Lt de Coutard	20?CA	O	Injured	Bréguet 14
Cpl Dumont &	Br 66	P	Injured	
S/Lt Laffaille	Br 66	O	Injured	Bréguet 14B2
Capt Desusclade	1er CAC	O	Injured	

10 October

Capt Poupon,	CO	Spa 37						8
Sgt Lecomte &		Spa 37						1
MdL Daniel		Spa 37	EA	X	Champagne			2
Lt Wertheim &	CO	Spa 84						5
Adj Delcuze		Spa 84	Balloon	XF	Brainville	1030	3
Lt Ambrogi	a.	Spa 90	Balloon	XF	Amelecourt	1407	12
Adj Pezon &		Spa 90						7

Adj Mace	b. Spa 90	Balloon	XF	Geline	1610	7
S/Lt Condemine	Spa 154	Balloon	XF	NE Orfeuil	1100	9
Capt Hay de Slade & CO	Spa 159					18
Sgt Fairchild	Spa 159	Balloon	XF	Champagne		1
Capt Hay de Slade CO	Spa 159	Balloon	XF	N Etain		19
Lt Henriot	Spa 161	EA	X	Flanders		1
Brig Piot	Spa 161	EA	X	Flanders		1
Lt Barny de Romanet CO	Spa 167	2 seater	X	S Bignicourt	0700	12
Sgt Dufour,	R 240					1
Brig Gagne &	R 240					2
Sol Delcroix	R 240	Scout	X	Champagne		2
Cpl Eubriet	Spa 98	Scout	P	Beaurepierre	1630	–
Adj Lachet	Spa 124	Balloon	P	Blaise	0715	–
Patrol	GC 12	Scout	P	N Sommepy	1535	–
???	GC	2 Balloons	P	Champagne		–
???	GC	6 EA	P	Champagne		–
???	GB	7 EA	P	Champagne		–

a.   Probably Bz 37, flamed at 14h07, AOK 19 Sector.
b.   Probably Bz 62, flamed at 16h10, AOK 19 Sector.

Casualties:

Cpl Vuille	Spa 77	P	MIA	Spad XIII
S/Lt Georges Leclerc	Spa 98	P	KIA	IV° Armée, Spad XIII.
Cpl Le Bescou	Spa 57	P	KIA	IV° Armée, Spad 7 N° 11281, probably by Ltn Hans von Freden, Jasta 50, (15).
MdL Cahen &	Spa 42	P	KIA	Flak
Lt Ourmade	Spa 42	O	KIA	Flak, IV° Armée, Spad XI.
Lt Desmolles	Br 281	O	KIA	
Cpl Gaston de Meirleir &	Br 282	P	KIA	Flak, III° Armée
Lt Jean Sicard	Br 282	O	KIA	Flak Bréguet 14A2
S/Lt Victor Fedoroff	Spa 89	P	WIA	Spad XIII, probably by Vfw Albert Haussmann, Jasta 13, unconf.
Lt Maurice Henriot	Spa 161	P	WIA	DOW 23 October 1918.
Lt Carlier	Sal 74	O	WIA	DOW, Salmson 2A2.
S/Lt Eve	Sal 56	O	WIA	Ground fire.
Sgt Maurice Finot &	Sal 273	P	OK	FTL during combat.
???	Sal 273	O	WIA	
Adj Pierre Meillant &	Br 134	P	KIAcc	
Sgt Noël Callois	Br 134	G	Injured	
Cpl Serre &	V 113	P	Injured	
Sgt Desmet	V 113	G	Injured	Voisin X
Lt Maisonnobe	R 46	O	Injured	Caudron R11
Sgt Bert	R 46	G	Injured	,,
Sgt Salignon	R 46	G	Injured	,,
Adj Roger André	25° Cie d'Aérostiers	XF		VI° Armée, probably by Obltn
		O	OK	Friedrich Röth, Jasta 16b, (25).
S/Lt Edmond Patry	91° Cie d'Aérostiers	XF		VI° Armée, probably by Obltn
		O	OK	Friedrich Röth, Jasta 16b, (26).
???	75° Cie d'Aérostiers	XF		X° Armée, probably by Uffz
		O	OK	Heinrich Haase, Jasta 21s, (6).
S/Lt Gaston Delmas	61° Cie d'Aérostiers	XF		II° Armée, probably by Ltn
		O	OK	Paul Schwirzke, Jasta 68, (2).
???	71° Cie d'Aérostiers	XF		Probably by Vfw Wilhelm
		O	OK	Stör, Jasta 68, (5).
Adj André	??? Cie d'Aérostiers	XF		Lorraine-Vosges Sector.
		O	OK	
S/Lt Pierre Richard	67° Cie d'Aérostiers			IV° Armée, attacked, not
		O	OK	flamed.
S/Lt Maurice Guigillon	51° Cie d'Aérostiers			IV° Armée, attacked, not
		O	OK	flamed.

Two other balloons were attacked, not flamed, in the Flanders Sector.

---

11 October

Sgt Daussin &	Spa 52				1
Lt Lucques	Spa 52	Pfalz	X	Altkirch	1

Casualties:

Lt Louis Hizaret &	Spa 286	P	KIAcc	
Sol Bonnafous	Spa 286	M	Injured	Spad XVI

Cpl Vedet &	Br 250	P	Injured			
Lt Guichard	Br 250	O	Injured	Bréguet 14A2		

12 October

S/Lt Fridberg &	Sal 251					1
S/Lt Madon	Sal 251	EA	X	Thugny		1
S/Lt Martenot de Cordoux a.	Spa 94	2 seater	P	E Tagnon		–
Lt Barny de Romanet CO	Spa 167	Gotha G	P	Courvrot		–

a.   Possibly Ltn Bernard Schînleben & Ltn Fritz Guillaume, KIAs.

Casualties:

Sgt Lucien Lacouture	Spa 95	P	Injured	DOW 2 November 1918. Spad		
S/Lt Millet	28° Cie d' Aérostiers			IV° Armée, probably by Ltn		
		O	OK	Hans v Freden, Jasta 60, (16).		
???	89° Cie d'Aérostiers			VIII° Armée, attacked, not		
		O	OK	flamed. 100+ bullet holes.		

13 October – No Claims

Casualties:

Cpl Lavanne &	VB 133	P	MIA	VI° Armée		
S/Lt Marchal	VB 133	O	MIA			
S/Lt Cytère	Sal 71	O	WIA	Salmson 2A2, ground fire.		
Cpl Tristan &	CIACB	P	Injured			
Sol Blondy	CIACB	B	Injured	Bréguet		

14 October

Lt de Durat,	Spa 37					1
S/Lt Guyou &	Spa 37					10
Sgt Lapierre	Spa 37	2 seater	X	Champagne		1
Lt Rondot	Spa 48	Balloon	XF	Champagne		1
Sgt Mercier	Spa 48	2 seater	X	Champagne		2
Lt Janel	Spa 82	Scout	X	Flanders		1
S/Lt Brun &	Spa 92					1
Sgt Copin	Spa 92	Balloon	XF	Montcornet	0800	1
Cpl Jeyseriat &	Spa 92					1
Adj Decatoire	Spa 92	Balloon	XF	Le Hardoye	0820	1
Adj Ondet,	Spa 94					2
Sgt Grimouille &	Spa 94					3
MdL Sainz	Spa 94	Rumpler C	X	Ecorday		2
Lt Barny de Romanet & CO	Spa 167					13
S/Lt F Dumas	Spa 167	Gotha G	X	Les Alleux	1310	2
Lt Arpheuil CO	Spa 170	EA	X			5
S/Lt Aggacio &	Br 230					–
S/Lt Mahieu	Br 230	Fokker D7	P	Bertoncourt		–
???	GC	Balloon	P	Laon		–
???	GC	2EA	P	Champagne		–
??? &	Spa 34					–
S/Lt Peigné	Spa 34	Scout	P	Flanders		–

Casualties:

MdL Georges Vercouter	Spa 82	P	MIA	Spad XIII, probably by Vfw		
				Otto Bieleit, Jasta 66, (3).		
Lt Lucien Jannel	Spa 82	P	WIA			
Asp Georges Bonneau	Spa 48	P	WIA			
S/Lt Gaudard	Br 260	O	WIA	V° Armée, ground fire.		
Lt Prevost	Sal 72	P	WIA	Ground fire.		
Capt Vachon & CO	Sal 39	P	WIA	DOW, S Bois Noyon.		
S/Lt Georges Gavoret	Sal 39	O	WIA	IV° Armée, Salmson 2A2,		
S/Lt Joublin	Sal 40	P	WIA	IV° Armée, Salmson 2A2, ground fire.		
Brig Roy	GDE	P	Injured			
Lt de Bernardy	??? Cie d'Aérostiers		XF	VI° Armée, probably by Ltn		
		O	OK	z S Reinhold Poss, MFJIV, (10).		

15 October

S/Lt Haegelen	Spa 100	Balloon	XF	Buzancy	1	515	20
Lt Dubois &	Br 55					–
Lt Marion	Br 55	Fokker D7	P	E Coucy		–

| MdL Denneulin | | Spa 3 | Scout | P | E Novy | 1345 | – |
| *Casualties:* None | | | | | | | |

---

16 October – No Claims
Casualties:

| MdL Tache | | RGAé | P | KIAcc | Spad | | |
| Lt Jean Arpheuil | CO | Spa 170 | P | Injured | | | |

---

17 October

S/Lt Mougeot		Spa 62	EA	X			2
Casualties:							
S/Lt Mathieu		Br 279	O	WIA	Flak		
Brig Audevard		CIACB	G	Injured	Bréguet 14B2		

---

18 October

S/Lt Guyou		Spa 37	EA	X	Champagne		11
S/Lt Gaudermen		Spa 68	Scout	X	NE Grand Pré		6
??? &		Spa 81					?
Adj Malfanti		Spa 81	Fokker D7	X			4
S/Lt Ambrogi &		Spa 90					13
Adj Mace	a.	Spa 90	Balloon	XF	Omeney	1415	8
S/Lt Ambrogi,		Spa 90					14
Adj Mace &		Spa 90					9
Sgt Auzuret	b.	Spa 90	Balloon	XF	Avricourt	1420	1
Adj Marinovitch &		Spa 94					18
Adj Ondet		Spa 94	2 seater	X	Champagne	1550	3
S/Lt Haegelen		Spa 100	EA	X	W Landres St Georges		21
Adj Drouilh &		Spa 103					4
Sgt Sansom		Spa 103	Fokker D7	XF	Arnicourt-Séry	1625	2
Adj Halberger &		Spa 153					5
S/Lt Bourgeois		Spa 153	LVG C	X	E Cernon		1
S/Lt Risacher		Spa 159	Fokker D7	X	Buzancy		5
Lt Barny de Romanet & CO		Spa 167					14
S/Lt F Dumas		Spa 167	Fokker D7	X	Givry-sur-Aisne	1430	3
Sgt Grillot		Spa 124	EA	P	N Falaise	1425	–
Sgt de Lombardon		Spa 167	2 seater	P	Charbogne	1430	–
Lt Barny de Romanet & CO		Spa 167					–
S/Lt F Dumas		Spa 167	Fokker D7	P	Givry-sur-Aisne	1430	–
Asp Bonneau		Spa 48	EA	FTL			–

a.   Probably Bz 211.
b.   Probably Bz 217.
Casualties:

Cpl Maufras		Spa 100	P	MIA		
Lt Henri Changine		Spa 82	P	MIA	Probably by Jasta 40s pilot.	
Cpl Paul Trepp		Spa 82	P	MIA	Probably by Jasta 40s pilot.	
Adj Georges Delcuze		Spa 84	P	WIA	Spad XIII	
MdL Charles Geronini		Spa 84	P	WIA	DOW 9 November 1918. Spad XIII	
Asp Georges Bonneau		Spa 84	P	WIA		

---

19 October – No Claims
Casualties:

Cpl Simon		Spa 157	P	KIA	IV° Armée, Spad VII, departed 09h15.
Lt Deicouin		Sal 51	O	WIA	Ground fire.
Lt Philippe Micoin			O	WIA	V° Armée, ground fire.

---

20 October

S/Lt Carretier &		Sal 39				–
Lt Boques &		Sal 39				–
MdL Stora &		Sal 39				–
1/Lt Cook (USAS)		Sal 39	Scout	P	Primat	–
Casualties: None						

---

21 October

S/Lt Bouyer,		Spa 49				12
S/Lt Brétillon,		Spa 49				8
Adj Arnoux &		Spa 49				5

Adj Hamot	a.	Spa 49	2 seater	XF	Mulhouse		5
S/Lt Bordes,		Spa 90					3
Adj Bizot &		Spa 90					10
Adj Pezon	b.	Spa 90	Balloon	XF	Avricourt	1015	8
MdL Chabrier		Spa 315	Scout	X	Vosges		4
MdL Uteau		Spa 315	Scout	X	Vosges		5
???		CA	EA	X	Vosges		–
???		???	EA	P	Vosges		–
???		GC	EA	P	Champagne		–

a.   Possibly Gefr Helmut Back, KIA Mühlhausen.
b.   Probably Bz 217, flamed at 11h19, AOK 19 Sector.

Casualties;

Sgt Lucien Kremer	Spa 154	P		MIA	V° Armée, Spad XIII N° 15460, probably by Ltn Werner Preuss, Jasta 66, (21).
Sgt Marcel Granger	Spa 159	P		MIA	Spad XIII, probably by Ltn Georg von Hantelmann, Jasta 15, (22).
Sgt Ludinard &	V 135	P		MIA	
Sgt Viennois	V 135	G		MIA	Voisin Renault
Brig Prevost	Spa 31	P		KIA	V° Armée, Spad VII #111
S/Lt Jean Bouyer	Spa 49	P		WIA	VII° Armée
Cpl Jean-Louis Tenten	Sal 52	P		WIA	VII° Armée
Lt Pierre du Cailar	Br 209	O		WIA	III° Armée, Bréguet
MdL Jacques Viriot	Spa 81	P		KIAcc	Spad VII
Sol Levesque	CIACB	M		KIAcc	
Sgt Auguste Leman	Spa 151	P		Injured	DOW 22 October 1918.
Lt Paul Brachet	Spa 84	P		Injured	Spad VII
???	82° Cie d'Aérostiers		O	OK	VIII° Armée, attacked, not flamed.
???	34° Cie d'Aérostiers		O	OK	VIII° Armée, attacked not flamed.

22 October

Lt Bonneton		Spa 69	Balloon	XF	Laon		9
Lt J Bordes &		Spa 90					4
Adj Mace	a.	Spa 90	Balloon	XF	Goin	0900	10
Adj Mace &		Spa 90					11
S/Lt Dencausse	b.	Spa 90	Balloon	XF	Geline	0905	3
Lt Bergé &	CO	Spa 124					3
Sgt Grillot		Spa 124	2 seater	X	Ballay	1620	3
Lt Bergé &	CO	Spa 124					4
Sgt Salinie		Spa 124	2 seater	X	Champagne		1
S/Lt Rigall,		R 242					1
Sgt Pipart &		R 242					2
Sol Roques		R 242	EA	X	Aspach		1
Sgt Boutin,		R 242					–
Sgt Gauthier &		R 242					–
Sol Thery &		R 242					–
Cpl Daulouet,		R 242					–
Sol Mandille &		R 242					–
Sol Piercon		R 242	EA	P	Forêt de la Hart		–
Lt Bonneton		Spa 69	Balloon	P	Laon		–
??? &		Br 211					–
Lt Larzat		Br 211	Scout	P			–

a.   Probably Bz 152.
b.   Probably Bz 36, flamed at 10h10, AOK 19 Sector.

Casualties:

Cpl Mille	Spa 31	P		MIA	
MdL Raynaud &	Br 234	P		MIA	Bréguet 14B2, probably by
S/Lt Stofft	Br 234	O		MIA	Ltn Karl Plauth, Jasta 51, (16).
Asp Tanays	CIACB	P		KIAcc	Spad VII
S/Lt Gilbert de Guingand	Spa 48	P		KIAcc	Spad XIII
Cpl Blanchard &	Spa 212	P		Injured	
Sol Lecam	Spa 212	M		Injured	Spad XVI
Cpl Rimblot	Spa 100	P		Injured	Spad VII
S/Lt Serot	F 110	O		Injured	Farman 50

23 October

S/Lt G Thomas	Spa 88	2 seater	X	Bois de Forges		6

Adj-Chef Delzenne		Spa 88	EA	X	St Georges		6
S/Lt Haegelen		Spa 100	EA	X	Aisne		22
Adj Bentejac &		Spa 124					4
Sgt Chadeau		Spa 124	2 seater	X	Peuville-et-Bay	1500	1
Adj Lachat		Spa 124	Fokker D7	X	Verpel	1510	3
S/Lt Robert		Spa 164	2 seater	XF	Bois de Vandy	1148	3
Lt Barny de Romanet & CO		Spa 167					15
S/Lt Lechevalier		Spa 167	2 seater	X	S La Chesne	1215	1
Lt Barny de Romanet CO		Spa 167	Fokker D7	X	Attigny	1625	16
S/Lt Nicodeau,		Spa 315					2
Adj Ferte &		Spa 315					2
Brig Catton	a.	Spa 315	Balloon	XF	Wasserbourg		3
Sgt Brière		Spa 3	2 seater	P	Novy	0825	–
Sgt Mingam		Spa 95	Rumpler C	P	N Nanteuil-sur-Aisne		–
Patrol		Spa 124	Balloon	P	Champagne		–
Lt Barny de Romanet CO		Spa 167	2 seater	P	La Chesne	1210	–
Cpl Daulouet,		R 242					–
Sol Mandille &		R 242					–
Sol Piercon		R 242	EA	P	SE Mulhouse		–

a.   Bz 128, flamed at Wasserbourg, at 13h50, AOK "B" Sector.

Casualties:

Cpl François Cottaz	Spa 93	P	KIA	Spad VII, 14h15, Château-Porcien.
Sgt Edwin B Fairchild	Spa 159	P	WIA	Spad XIII, possibly by Ltn Friedrich Noltenius, Jasta 11, (17).
S/Lt Pierre Carretier	Sal 39	P	WIA	IV° Armée, Salmson.
Adj Fleury &	???	P	WIA	
S/Lt Mathusière	???	O	OK	
Adj Velard,	F 25	P	KIAcc	
Lt Georges Manificat &	F 25	O	KIAcc	
Cpl Henry	F 25	G	KIAcc	Farman 13
Sgt Claudel &	V 116	P	KIAcc	
S/Lt Achard	V 116	O	KIAcc	Voisin Renault
Adj Roldes &	V 133	P	Injured	
Sgt Geutes	V 133	G	Injured	Voisin RX
Sgt Bosc	??? Cie d'Aérostiers			Attacked, not flamed,
		O	Injured	Laon Sector.

---

24 October

Capt de Sevin	CO	Spa 26	EA	X	NE Vouziers	1400	12
Adj Delmetz		Spa 80	Balloon	XF	Guise		3
Lt Barny de Romanet & CO		Spa 167					17
S/Lt Guiguet		Spa 167	2 seater	X	N Attigny	1500	5
VI° Armée		DCA	EA	X	Flanders		–
Lt Le Petit		Spa 67	2 seater	P	N Rethel	1150	–
Sgt Salze &		Sal 19					–
S/Lt Le Métayer		Sal 19	Fokker D7	P	V° Armée		–
S/Lt Guiguet &		Spa 167					–
Lt Barny de Romanet CO		Spa 167	Scout	P	N Attigny		–

Casualties:

Adj Maurice Champion &	Sal 6	P	POW	WIA, III° Armée,
S/Lt Jean-Paul Picot	Sal 6	O	POW	Flak, Salmson 2A2
Adj Adenis	Br 257	P	WIA	IV° Armée
S/Lt Léonce Brindejonc	Br 257	O	KIA	Bréguet 14A2 N° 3435.
Lt Max Berard &	Br 44	P	KIA	Bréguet 14A2, probably by
Lt Jacques Seyller	Br 44	O	KIA	Vfw Schneck, Jasta 9, (3).
Sgt Salze	Sal 19	P	OK	
S/Lt Yves Le Métayer	Sal 19	O	WIA	V° Armée
MdL Jacques Havard	Spa 89	P	KIAcc	Spad XIII
Adj Dorme	Sal 71	P	Injured	Salmson 2A2
MdL Sarazin &	Sal 230	P	Injured	
Sol Vacher	Sal 230	M	Injured	

---

25 October

Lt Barny de Romanet & CO	Spa 167				–
Sgt Bavol	Spa 167	EA	P	SW St Quentin-le-Petit	–

Casualties:

Adj Latapie &	Sal 262	P	MIA	

Lt Jouy	Sal 262	O	MIA	
S/Lt Albert Japy	Spa 140	O	WIA	V° Armée, Spad XVI, ground fire.
Cpl Canto	GDE	P	KIAcc	Salmson 2A2

26 October – No Claims
Casualties:

Lt Maurice Quenioux	*	CAM	P	KIA	Spad XIII N° 18816, at Gand. Probably by Ltn Carl Degelow, CO Jasta 40, (27).
Cpl Joachim Subercaze		Spa 81	P	KIAcc	Spad XIII
Cpl Henri Langevin		Spa 170	P	Injured	
S/Lt Bernardi &		85° Cie d'Aérostiers	XF		VI° Armée
S/Lt Ragué			O	OK	
Asp Martin		74° Cie d'Aérostiers	XF		VI° Armée
			O	OK	
S/Lt Bruyäre		??? Cie d'Aérostiers			VI° Armée, attacked, not flamed.
			O	OK	
Sgt Monteaux		??? Cie d'Aérostiers			VI° Armée, attacked, not flamed.

*   Dunkerque.

27 October

Adj Ruamps		Spa 87	2 seater	X	St Germaincourt	1345	9
S/Lt Lecomte		Spa 88	2 seater	XF	Champagne		3
S/Lt Marinovitch	a.	Spa 94	Fokker D7	XF	Lethour	1405	19
S/Lt Bourjade &		Spa 152					26
S/Lt Garin		Spa 152	Balloon	XF	Château-Porcien	1315	3
Lt Romatet,	CO	Spa 165					6
MdL Bonnet &		Spa 165					1
Sgt Gangloff		Spa 165	Fokker D7	X	St Quentin-le-Petit		1
Adj Thuiller &		Br 234					1
Lt Cappart		Br 234	EA	X	Ferme Jonqueuse		1
Capt Menj &	CO	GC 16					4
Patrol		GC 16	Fokker D7	X	Rethel		–
MdL Caltire &		Sal 39					–
Lt Boques &		Sal 39					–
MdL Leroy &		Sal 39					–
1/Lt Cook (USAS)		Sal 39	Fokker D7	P	Champagne		–
Adj Vincent		Spa 26	Fokker D7	P	NE Vouziers	1545	–
Lt Madon &	CO	Spa 38					–
S/Lt Casale		Spa 38	2 seater	P	La Selve	1145	–
S/Lt Bourjade,		Spa 152					–
S/Lt Garin &		Spa 152					–
Sgt Lac		Spa 152	Balloon	P	Ville-aux-Bois	1325	–

a.   Possibly Vfw Karl Schlegel, Jasta 45, KIA la Malmaison.

Casualties:

MdL Albert Noulet	Spa 161	P	MIA	Flanders Sector.
MdL Eugène Lengrand	Spa 112	P	MIA	V° Armée, Spad XIII, W Herpy, probably by a Jasta 73 pilot.
MdL Caudet &	Br 281	P	MIA	
S/Lt Peidenis	Br 281	O	MIA	
Cpl Francis Cottaz	Spa 93	P	KIA	Spad VII
MdL Léon Daniel	Spa 37	P	KIA	Spad XIII
S/Lt Jean Bordes	Spa 90	P	WIA	Spad, probably by Ltn Gustav Dörr, Jasta 45, u/c.
MdL Guillaume de Freslon de La Freslonière	Spa 112	P	WIA	V° Armée, Spad XIII, FTL in flames near Bergnicourt probably by a Jasta 73 pilot.
Capt Schlafer &	CO	Br 250	P	WIA	V° Armée, FTL 09h30.
Lt Guichard		Br 250	O	WIA	
Asp Jean-François Tilly		Br 127	O	WIA	Flak, Bréguet 14B2
Lt René Bordas		Sal 22	O	WIA	Salmson, ground fire.
Lt Edmond Delteil		???	P	KIAcc	
Sol Pachy		Br 111	G	Injured	
MdL Poupinot		CIACB	P	Injured	AR
Lt Desbrief		Spa ??	O	Injured	
Lt Linckenheyl		42° Cie d'Aérostiers		WIA	VII° Armée, probably by Uffz Christal Elfers, Jasta 69, (1), AOK "B".
S/Lt Dessarp			O	Injured	

28 October

S/Lt Artigau &		Spa 15				12
S/Lt G Thomas		Spa 88	Fokker D7	X	Fismes	7
Adj Usse		Spa 26	Scout	X	Arnicourt-Sorbon	1530	3
Lt Letourneau		Spa 26	Scout	X	Mery-Corgny	1545	2
Sgt Dard		Spa 26	Scout	X	Attigny-Vouziers	1545	1
S/Lt Cayol &		Spa 65				3
Sgt Périer		Spa 65	EA	X	Aisne	1
Adj Mace &		Spa 90				12
Adj Pezon	a.	Spa 90	Hannover CL	XF	N Champenoux	1000	9
MdL Sainz		Spa 94	Balloon	XF	Hauteville	3
Lt Coiffard	CO	Spa 154	Fokker D7	X	Rethel	1510	34
VII° Armée	b.	DCA	2 seater	XF	Bruyères	–
Patrol		Spa 38	EA	P	NW Château-Porcien	1530	–
Lt Laganne &		Spa 94		P		–
S/Lt Martenot de Cordoux		Spa 94	2 seater	P	St Clément	
S/Lt Bourjade		Spa 152	2 seater	P	Château-Porcien	1050	–
S/Lt Condemine		Spa 154	Fokker D7	P	NE Château-Porcien	1510	–
Lt Coiffard	CO	Spa 154	Fokker D7	P	Rethel	1510	–

a. Probably Uffz Bruno Weber & Vfw Otto Schütze, FlAbt 266 (A),KIAs Diedersdorf, AOK 19 Sector.
b. Possibly either Uffz Berk & Lt Sperka, FlA bt10, MIAs, or Gefr Gambs & Ltn Woller, FlAbt 43, MIAs, AOK "A" Sector.

Casualties:

Lt Michel Coiffard	CO	Spa 154	P	WIA	V° Armée, DOW 29 October 1918, Spad XIII, probably by a Jasta 72s pilot.
Sgt Gauthier		Spa ??	P	WIA	VII° Armée
Cpl Pezeyre		Sal 254	P	WIA	
Lt Blanc &		???	P	WIA	
Sgt Guillet		Br 221	G	OK	VII° Armée
Cpl Gillebaud		V 135	P	KIAcc	Voisin-Renault
Sgt Henri Dussord		Spa 94	P	KIAcc	Spad VII
MdL Hervé &		V 121	P	KIAcc	Voisin X
Sol Leprince		V 121	G	Injured	Voisin X
Sol Chastagne		RGAé	M	Injured	Spad VII
Sol Moreau		RGAé	M	Injured	Spad VII
Brig Fauché		V 121	P	Injured	
Sgt Sarazin &		???	P	Injured	
Cpl Roullier		???	B	Injured	
MdL Garnier &		???	P	Injured	
Sgt Lebarbier		???	B	Injured	
Adj-Chef Monginet &		???	P	Injured	
Adj Prévost		???	B	Injured	

29 October

Sgt Stanley		Spa 23	Fokker D7	X	Montzéville	1530	2
Capt Stoffels d'Hautefort &		Sal 33				1
S/Lt Rotival		Sal 33	Fokker D7	X	Aisne	1
S/Lt Casale		Spa 38	EA	X	N Rethel	1115	12
S/Lt Cayol		Spa 65	EA	X	Aisne	4
Adj Pautet &		Spa 65				1
MdL Launay		Spa 65	EA	X	Aisne	1
Lt Pendaries		Spa 67	2 seater	X	Amancourt-Lamtez	1317	7
S/Lt Battesti		Spa 73	EA	X	N Laon	7
MdL Tremeau		Spa 83	EA	X	Landifay	2
Adj-Chef Delzenne	a.	Spa 88	EA	X	Aisne	9
S/Lt Coadou	a.	Spa 88	EA	X	Aisne	8
Adj Pezon,		Spa 90				10
Adj Bizot &		Spa 90				11
Cpl Alliot	b.	Spa 90	Balloon	XF	Geline	1400	1
Adj Fremont &		Spa 102				1
Adj Péronne		Spa 102	2 seater	X	Marle	1
Capt Bonne,	CO	Spa 152				1
Adj Manson &		Spa 152				3
MdL Foulon		Spa 152	Balloon	XF	Laon	1055	1
S/Lt Bourjade,		Spa 152				27
S/Lt Garin &		Spa 152				4
Sgt Fos		Spa 152	Balloon	XF	Laon	1125	1

S/Lt Bourjade		Spa 152	Balloon	XF	Serancourt	1300	28
Lt Romatet &	CO	Spa 165					7
S/Lt Gerbault		Spa 165	Fokker D7	X	Château-Porcien		3
Asp Villard &		Spa 167					1
Sgt de Lombardon		Spa 167	2 seater	X	N Attigny	1030	3
Lt Barny de Romanet	CO	Spa 167	2 seater	X	S Bois des Loges	1500	18
MdL Clément &		Sal 217					1
Lt Schlesser		Sal 217	Scout	X			1
Sgt Lebroussard		Spa 26	2 seater	P	Longve	1330	–
S/Lt Casale &		Spa 38					–
Lt Volmerange		Spa 38	EA	P	Sissone	1200	–
Sgt Sansom &		Spa 103					–
Brig Ouvrard de Linière		Spa 103	2 seater	P	Le Chesné-Lametz	1355	–
S/Lt Bourjade		Spa 152	EA	P	Recouvrance	1540	–
V? Armée		???	EA	P	Banogne	1515	–
Escadre 1		GC	2 EA	P	Aisne		–
???		GC	EA	P	Aisne		–
???		GC	EA	P	Vosges		–
???		EdA	2 EA	P	Oise		–

a.   One of these claims was possibly Ltn Martin Fischer, Jasta 6.
b.   Probably Bz 62, attacked at 15h04 but not flamed, AOK 19 Sector.

Casualties:

S/Lt Henri Garin	Spa 152	P	KIA	V° Armée, Spad XIII, NE St Fergeux.
MdL Jean Antoine	Spa 163	P	MIA	Spad XIII
Cpl Deloye &	Br 243	P	MIA	
Lt Ledemy	Br 243	O	MIA	II° Armée, Bréguet 14B2.
Lt Charles Renard-Duverger &	Br 117	P	MIA	
Adj-Chef Guyot	Br 117	G	MIA	Bréguet 14B2
Sgt Paul Lefebvre	Spa 163	P	WIA	Spad XIII, IV° Armée
Lt de Villeneuve	???	P	WIA	Spad
Cpl Akar &	Br 206	P	WIA	
Lt Adrian	Br 206	O	WIA	Bréguet 14A2
S/Lt Max Rotival	Sal 33	O	WIA	
Lt Bardollet	Sal 234	O	WIA	
Lt Blanc &	Br 221	P	WIA	
Sgt Guillet	Br 221	G	OK	VII° Armée
Adj Fouchard	Spa 154	P	KIAcc	Spad XIII
Sgt Henri Dussourd	Spa 94	P	KIAcc	Spad VII
Adj Poittevin	CRA	P	KIAcc	Spad XIII
Sgt Battini &	RGAé	P	Injured	
Sol Morin	RGAé	M	Injured	Salmson
MdL Naud	Br 231	O	Injured	
???	86° Cie d'Aérostiers	XF		V° Armée, probably by Ltn
		O	OK	Wilhelm Schwartz, Jasta 73, (8).

30 October

Sgt Brière		Spa 3	2 seater	X	Chestres-Vouziers	1020	2
S/Lt de Tascher &		Spa 26					2
MdL Plessis		Spa 26	2 seater	X	E Vouziers	1145	1
Adj Ruamps		Spa 87	Scout	X	Rethel	1630	10
Lt Fonck		Spa 103	2 seater	XF	Falaise-Vouziers	1525	70
Lt Fonck		Spa 103	Scout	X	Semuy-Terron	1540	71
Lt Fonck		Spa 103	Scout	X	Semuy-Terron	1540	72
Patrol		Spa 103	Balloon	XF	Quatre-Champs	0810	–
Capt d'Argueeff	EM GC 21	2 seater	X	E Quatre-Champs	1540	15
Asp Nicodeau,		Spa 315					3
Sgt Gérard &		Spa 315					1
Sgt Boishardy	a.	Spa 315	Balloon	XF	St Croix-aux-Mines		3
Sgt Decatoire &		Spa 3					–
Sgt Clément		Spa 3	Scout	P	N Rethel	1105	–
Sgt Duval		Spa 23	2 seater	FTL	German lines		–
Sgt Stanley		Spa 23	2 seater	P			–
Sgt Stanley		Spa 23	Fokker DrI	P			–
Patrol		Spa 31	EA	P	NW St Fergeux	1025	–
Lt Madon &	CO	Spa 38					–
S/Lt Casale		Spa 38	EA	P	NE Château-Porcien	1215	–

Lt Larzillière dit Rocheron	Spa 87	Halb CL	P			–
Lt Freslon,	Spa 157					–
MdL Ferradat &	Spa 157					–
Sgt Gasperi	Spa 157	EA	P	Vouziers	1030	–
S/Lt Guiguet	Spa 167	2 seater	P	Dun-sur-Meuse	0815	–
Adj Baron	Spa 167	2 seater	P	N Rethel	1300	–
Lt Barny de Romanet CO	Spa 167	2 seater	P	NNW Rethel	1440	–
Sgt Becquerel	II° Armée	Fokker D7	P			–
???	EdA	2 EA	P	Vosges		–

a.   Probably BZug 114, flamed by three Spads, AOK "A" Sector.

Casualties:

Lt Charles Devèze de la Devèze &	Br 282	P	KIA	III° Armée	
S/Lt Robert Delange	Br 282	O	KIA	Bréguet 14A2	
Sgt Houroux &	Spa 264	P	WIA		
Lt Andral	Spa 264	O	KIA	Spad XVI	
Sgt Sicard	Sal 267	P	WIA	V° Armée, 12h00, Avancon.	
MdL Perrin &	Sal 267	G	KIA	Salmson 2A2	
Adj Bigot	Sal 22	G	KIA	Salmson	
Sgt Loriat &	Sal 41	P	WIA	VIII° Armée, probably by	
Sol Monjalat	Sal 41	G	WIA	Ltn Dumler, Jasta 76b,(1), AOK "B".	
Brig Henri Trouve	Spa 62	P	Injured	Spad VII	
Cpl Ollivier &	???	P	Injured		
Sgt Bellot	???	B	Injured		
Cpl Magloire &	???	P	Injured		
Sgt Sebesta	???	B	Injured		
Lt Robert Collas	47° Cie Aérostiers	XF		V° Armée, probably by Ltn	
	O	WIA		Karl Bohny, Jasta 17, (8).	

31 October

Lt Fonck	Spa 103	2 seater	X	N Vouziers	1120	73
Lt Fonck	Spa 103	Scout	X	E Vouziers	1135	74
Adj Ferte	Spa 315	EA	X	German lines		3
Patrol	Spa 26	2 seater	P	NW Vouziers	1405	–
Patrol	Spa 26	2 seater	P	Quatre-Champs	1420	–
V° Armée	???	EA	P	Banogne	1515	–
Patrol	Spa 67	2 seater	P	Allend-Huy	0945	–
Patrol	Spa 103	2 seater	P	Ballay	1130	–
Lt Bourjade	Spa 152	Fokker D7	P	N Château-Porcien	1055	–
Cpl Gérard	Spa 168	EA	P	St Fergeux	1140	–

Casualties

Brig Jean Catton	Spa 315	P	KIA	VII° Armée, Spad, probably by Ltn Sarnighausen, Jasta 69 (1), AOK "B" Sector.	
Cpl Lamy &	Br 269	P	KIA	VIII° Armée, Villacourt	
Sol Bousquet	Br 269	G	KIA	Bréguet 14A2	
Sgt Allizy &	Br 260	P	WIA		
Lt Besnard	Br 260	O	WIA	V° Armée, Bréguet.	
Cpl Marcel Mellet	Spa 68	P	Injured	Spad XIII	

During October 1918, French DCA units claimed 35 EA destroyed and 4 probables.

1 November

Sgt Lalanne &	Spa 31					1
Sgt Gautre	Spa 31	2 seater	X	N Novy	1215	1
Lt Casale &	Spa 38					13
Adj Fabre	Spa 38	2 seater	X	Sissone	1235	3
Sgt Lamouline	Spa 62	EA	X	VI° Armée		1
S/Lt Mougeot	Spa 62	EA	X	VI° Armée		3
Adj Dupont	Spa 62	EA	X	VI° Armée		3
MdL Sainz	Spa 94	Balloon	XF	Machemesnil	1055	4
Lt Fonck	Spa 103	Halb C	X	E Vouziers	1420	75
Sgt Schmitter &	Spa 103					3
MdL Gui	Spa 103	EA	X	Croix-aux-Mines		1
Cdt de Marancour & CO	GC 14					8
Adj Hudellet	Spa 75	EA	X	Marfontaine		4
??? &	Sal 264					?
S/Lt Bergougnan	Sal 264	Scout	X	German lines		1

Lt Sardier &	CO	Spa 48				–
Adj Quiles		Spa 48	Fokker	P		–
Patrol		Spa 103	2 seater	P	Croix-aux-Mines	1325	–
Lt Fonck		Spa 103	2 seater	P	Semuy	1435	–
Capt d'Argueeff	EM GC 21		2 seater	P	Quatre-Champs	1300	–
Capt d'Argueeff	EM GC 21		Scout	P	Morval		–
Sgt Robert		Spa 152	EA	P	St Quentin-le-Petit		–
Lt Beaudrin &		13° CA				–
Lt Bourguignon		13° CA	EA	P	V° Armée		–
S/Lt Bollinger		Spa 76	Scout	P	Dizy-le-Gros	1530	–
VI° Armée		EdA	EA	P	Flanders		–

Casualties:

Sgt Henri Fourcade	Spa 15	P	MIA	Probably by Ltn Herbert Mahn, Jasta 72s, (8).
Lt Boijoux &	???	P	MIA	
Lt Guillaume	???	O	MIA	
Lt Paul Antoni	Spa 92	P	KIA	V° Armée, 12h00.
Adj Etienne Manson	Spa 152	P	KIA	V° Armée, 11h38, S Château-Porcien, probably by Ltn Herbert Mahn, Jasta 72s, (9).
Sgt Alfred Huguet &	Spa 62	P	KIA	VI° Armée
Lt Lucien Balloux	Spa 62	P	KIA	
Adj Mathieu de Tonnac de Villeneuve	Spa 80	P	WIA	
Capt Pérouse &	34° CA	P	WIA	Ground fire.
S/Lt Henri Rabourdin	Br 227	O	WIA	
S/Lt Paul de Peyerimhoff	Br 123	P	WIA	
Lt Bonafié	Sal 18	O	WIA	Flak, VI° Armée
S/Lt de Billy &	Br 245	P	WIA	VII° Armée, Bréguet, probably by
Sol Galinat	Br 245	G	OK	Vfw Meinberg, Jasta 75, (2), AOK "B".

2 November

S/Lt Chartoire	Spa 31	Scout	P	S Montgon-Le Chesne	4

Casualties:

SM Angelo Rimoldi &	*	CAM	P	MIA	Borel-Odier BO.2 N° 05.
QM Marcel Robert	*	CAM	O	MIA	
EV1 Albert Joly	**	CAM	P	MIA	
Cpl Romanaise		Spa 12	P	KIA	Flak

*   Antibes.
**   St Raphaël.

3 November

Sgt Grimouille &	Spa 94					4
S/Lt Marinovitch	Spa 94	2 seater	X	Le Chesne	1536	20
S/Lt Marinovitch	Spa 94	2 seater	X	La Neuville		21
MdL Froussard &	Spa 94					2
S/Lt Guyou ??	Spa 93	EA	X			12
Sgt Dufour,	R 240					2
Adj Buisson &	R 240					4
Sol Raymond	R 240	Scout	XF	Aisne		3
Sgt Dufour,	R 240					3
Adj Buisson &	R 240					5
Sol Raymond	R 240	Scout	X	Aisne		4
Cpl Pileyre,	R 240					2
Sol Delcroix &	R 240					3
Sol Chabant	R 240	EA	X	Aisne		1
Sgt Zanna &	Br 272					1
S/Lt Ombredane	Br 272	Fokker D7	XF	Crepion		1
Patrol	Spa 3	2 seater	P	Doux	0915	–
Patrol	Spa 26	Fokker D7	P	Le Chesne	1240	–
Patrol	Spa 26	2 seater	P	Le Chesne	1420	–
MdL Froussard &	Spa 94					–
S/Lt Marinovitch	Spa 94	2 seater	P	S Le Chesne		–
Patrol	GC 17	EA	P	N Attigny	1400	–
Escadre 1	GC	2 seater	P	Faissault	1100	–
???	GB	EA	P	Aisne		–

Casualties:

MdL Louis Bilbault	Spa 88	P	MIA	Both of these probably downed		
MdL Léon Barré	Spa 88	P	WIA/FTL	by Ltn R Wenzl, Jasta 6, (10 & 11).		
Adj Eugène Legros	Spa 95	P	MIA	Probably by Ltn Werner Junck, Jasta 8, (5).		
Lt Labussière &	???	P	MIA			
Adj Duvigneux	???	O	MIA			
S/Lt Jauffret &	Br 214	P	OK			
S/Lt Maréchal	Br 214	O	WIA	II° Armée, Bréguet.		
Cpl Paul Simonet	Spa 86	P	KIAcc			
Lt Van Hache &	33° Cie d'Aérostiers		XF	VII° Armée, probably by Gefr Viktor,		
Adj Chevalier		O	OK	Jasta 71, (1), AOK "B" Sector.		

4 November

Lt Cayol	Spa 65	EA	X	Aisne		5
Sgt Connelly	Spa 163	Fokker D7	X	Suzanne	1215	7
S/Lt Morvan	Spa 163	Fokker D7	X	Ecordal	1215	2
MdL Gault,	R 240					4
Sgt Coolen &	R 240					4
Sol Pellon	R 240	EA	X	Aisne		1
Adj Vicaire,	R 240					3
Adj Pilleron &	R 240					3
Sgt Deviller	R 240	EA	X	Aisne		2
Patrol	Spa 26	EA	P	Bairon-La Chesne	1025	–
Patrol	Spa 26	EA	P	Bairon-La Chesne	1100	–
Sgt Battesti	Spa 93	EA	P			–
Sgt Aureille	Spa 102	2 seater	P			–
Sgt Pacod &	Spa 157					–
MdL Darnis	Spa 157	EA	P	SE La Chesne		–
S/Lt Cote &	Spa 95					–
Brig Poublanc	Spa 95	Fokker D7	P	Bois de Mont Dieu	1514	–
???	EdA	EA	P	Vosges		–

Casualties:

Sgt Albert Beroule	Spa 26	P	MIA	IV° Armée, Spad, departed 09h45.
MdL Marcel Cordier	Spa 84	P	MIA	Spad
Cpl Charles Houllier	Spa 88	P	MIA	Spad
Adj Robert Brière	Spa 88	P	MIA	Spad
MdL André Recoques	Spa 170	P	MIA	VI° Armée, probably Ltn Karl Ritscherle, Jasta 60, unconfirmed.
Cpl Clauzel &	???	P	MIA	
Cpl Herbault	???	M	MIA	
MdL Emile Picard	Spa 94	P	WIA	
Cpl Dupied &	???	P	KIAcc	
Sgt de la Mothe	???	O	Injured	
???	61° Cie d'Aérostiers		XF	II° Armée, probably by Ltn Paul
		O	OK	Schwirtzke, Jasta 68, (3).
S/Lt Schwartz &	96° Cie d'Aérostiers			VI° Armée, attacked, not
Asp Capital		O	OK	flamed, Flanders Sector.
Sgt Brezeiski	??? Cie d'Aérostiers			Bombarded in its bed, Oise
		O	WIA	Sector, also one ground crewman killed and one wounded.

5 November

Cpl Mano &		Sal 277				1
Sgt Raveneau	a.	Sal 277	Fokker D7	X	Marcheville	1
Cpl Mano &		Sal 277				–
Sgt Raveneau		Sal 277	Fokker D7	P	Vosges	–
???		GC	2EA	P	Aisne	–
???		GC	EA	P	Oise	–
???		CA	EA	P	Oise	–

a.   Probably Sgt Gustav Albrecht, Jasta 64w, KIA Marcheville.

Casualties:

Cpl Breton	Spa ??	P	MIA	
Capt Laère &	Br 7	P	MIA	Probably by Ltn Kurt
Sgt Fersey	Br 7	G	MIA	Seit, Jasta 80, (5), AOK 19 Sector.
Sgt Jean André	Spa 88	P	POW	Probably by a JG I pilot.
Sgt Charles Brousse	Br ??	G	WIA	

Cpl André Mano &	Sal 277	P	OK	
Sgt Pierre Raveneau	Sal 277	G	WIA	II° Armée, Salmson.

6 November – No Claims
Casualties:

MdL Darche	Br 8	P	WIA	Ground fire
Lt Voiron	Br 60	O	WIA	Ground fire
MdL Charles Fellot &	Br 232	P	WIA	IV° Armée, S Omiecourt,
MdL Groz	Br 232	O	OK	ground fire.

7 November – No Claims
Casualties:

QM Pierre Mounier *	CAM	O	KIAcc	Georges Levy 200 HP N° 136.
Sgt Fernand Halb &	Sal 13	P	OK	
Lt Gérard Gervais	Sal 13	O	Injured	Landing accident.

* Brest.

8 November – No Claims
Casualties:

MdL Emile Justrabot	Spa 153	P	POW	Spad XIII N° 15410.
			Escaped	9 November 1918.
Sgt Roger Cheyrolles &	Sal 264	P	POW	Ground fire, both
S/Lt Jacques Bergougnan	Sal 264	O	POW	escaped 10 November 1918.
Cpl René Journet &	Sal 56	P	MIA	II° Armée, Salmson, probably by
S/Lt Georges Huet	Sal 56	O	WIA	Uffz Alfred Böder, Jasta 65, (2).
Sgt Jean Devore &	Sal 264	P	KIA	
Lt Georges Bardollet	Sal 264	O	KIA	
Adj Georges Halberger	Spa 153	P	WIA	Spad, ground fire
Cpl Vacquié &	Br 9	P	WIA	VII° Armée, DOW, aircraft
Sgt Pardoux	Br 9	G	Injured	crash-landed by gunner.
Sgt Jacques de Peyerimhoff &	Br 123	P	OK	
Capt Albert Durand	Br 123	O	WIA	

9 November – No Claims
Casualties:

S/Lt Naty &	Sal 259	P	KIA	VI° Armée
Lt Seltier	Sal 259	O	KIA	Salmson 2A2
Capt Marie Augier				
de Moussac CO	Spa 166	P	WIA	Ground fire.
Lt Bonnigal	Sal 72	P	WIA	VI° Armée
S/Lt Mairey	Sal 18	O	WIA	VI° Armée, ground fire.
Lt Bourlet	???	O	WIA	
Lt Paul Desmaroux	Sal 19	O	WIA	
Sgt Berthelot	Spa 84	P	KIAcc	
Cpl Rouquier	???		Injured	

NOTE: Four aircraft failed to return from a mission over Laon Sector.

10 November

MdL Thiery	Spa 92	EA	P	Flanders –
Casualties:				
Cpl Allard	???	?	Injured	

11 November – No Claims – No Casualties
The November date for the following claim cannot be ascertained at this time:

| Adj Dupont | Spa 62 | EA | X | 3 |